WRISTWATCH ANNUAL

2006

THE CATALOG

of

PRODUCERS, MODELS,

and

SPECIFICATIONS

by

PETER BRAUN

ABBEVILLE PRESS PUBLISHERS

New York   London

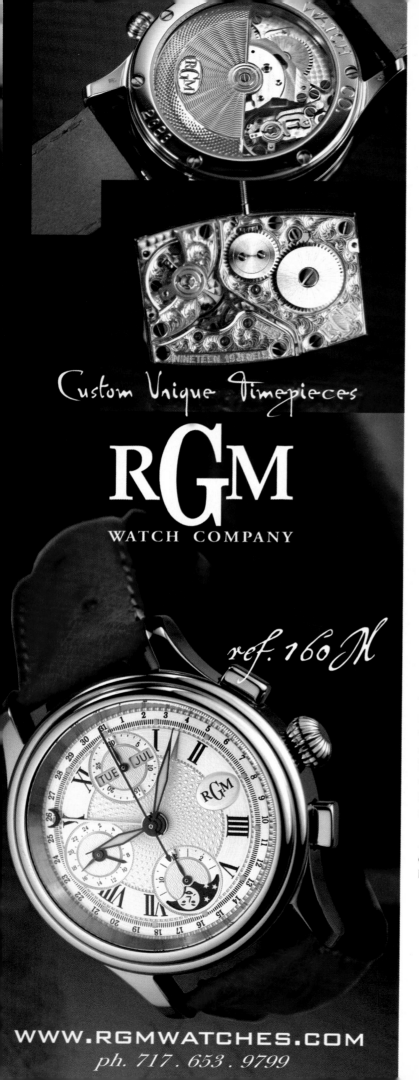
Dear Readers,

The new watch year is definitely under the seal of creativity. Large or small, each and every brand is doing everything humanly possible to bring the consumer the utmost in new ideas for his or her money. This applies to both the outside and the inside of the watch. Highly publicized statements of recent years released by the Swatch Group have really done their job in getting other manufacturers going on movement productions of their own. Where just a few short years ago, one could count the number of *manufactures* producing movements on two hands, today it is nearly impossible to keep up with the technological breakthroughs being achieved by creative companies situated at every level of the watch industry.

This also applies to the complication that is generally acknowledged as the industry's best and brightest: the tourbillon. Invented more than 200 years ago by Abraham-Louis Breguet to compensate for the effects of the earth's gravity on a pocket watch's rate, this traditional complication was kept alive by a handful of brands throughout the quartz years in wristwatches of uncommonly high quality and value. Perhaps it was Nicolas G. Hayek's purchase of the then-dusty Breguet brand with the promise of reviving this complication on a broader scale, but since the complication's highly publicized 200th anniversary in 2001, the number of brands incorporating the tourbillon into their own wristwatches has increased exponentially. While in 2001 there may have been fewer than fifteen companies to feature such a highlight in their collections, at last count in 2005 there were more than forty doing so. And some of the brands jumping on this "whirlwind bandwagon" are doing so without having first proved their horological competence or even built up to it by first presenting complications of less grandeur. An obvious question regarding the sheer number of tourbillon movements springing up remains: What type of place in the industry can this type of tourbillon occupy? And where can things go from here?

And that is the really interesting question. Where things go from here will, in our opinion, be in a totally different direction. Companies will begin to manufacture their own, more creative complications — different complications, creative technology that will not have Monsieur Breguet's signature on it. And that is good for everyone.

These complications don't have to be, and won't be, great or even important in the larger scheme of things. Companies won't reinvent the wheel, but they will show that Switzerland and Germany's watchmakers are staying on a mechanical roll. And this new phase has actually already begun. Just take a look at some of the new brands, watches, and complications cropping up: Carl F. Bucherer's TravelTec is a good example. So is the brand Hautlence. And look for a dynamite in-house progression made by Scalfaro in 2006. The list goes on . . .

. . . and most of this list will be found within these pages. So we hope you enjoy perusing the new collections and ideas produced by these creative heads and invite you to turn the page and begin!

Contents

JAEGER-LECOULTRE

REVERSO GRANDE GMT. Iconic Reverso watch, 8-day power-reserve, exclusive second time-zone with GMT differential. Mechanical movement 878, made in-house. Inside of the watch shown for illustration purposes only. **Manufacture Jaeger-LeCoultre, Vallée de Joux, Switzerland, since 1833.** www.jaeger-lecoultre.com

For your free copy of the Manufacture's book of Timepieces, please contact your local retailer or Jaeger-LeCoultre USA, 645 Fifth Avenue, 6th Floor, New York, NY 10022 tel (800) JLC Time.

In 1884, the Meridian Conference decided to introduce 24 time zones.

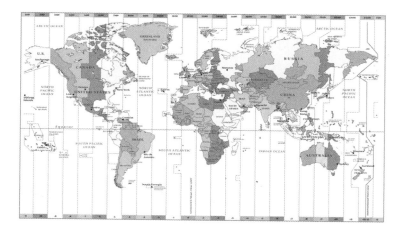

The world's 24 time zones.
When the world was divided into 24 time zones in 1884, the decision solved one of the era's most crucial problems: the plethora of local times. A year earlier, A. Lange & Söhne had already introduced pocket watches with two hand pairs. Their owners were able to set one pair to home time, the other to local time at their momentary location.

In the past 500 years, the art of mechanical timekeeping has been developed to stunning perfection. And some of the most important inventions were born in the mind of Adolph Lange. In 1845, he abandoned his privileged position as royal Saxon court horologist to establish the German precision watchmaking industry in the Ore Mountains. In Glashütte, he trained young men to become consummate craftspeople, developed totally new precision tools and invented pioneering mechanical devices and manufacturing methods. For the next 100 years, the watches of "A. Lange & Söhne" were among the most sought-after

Lange Uhren GmbH, D-01768 Glashütte, Germany. www.lange-soehne.com • For a complimentary catalogue and for your nearest authorized retailer,

Here's the synopsis.

The Lange 1 Time Zone.
Now, A. Lange & Söhne proudly introduces a time zone watch that addresses the challenges of the 21st century: the Lange 1 Time Zone. Apart from the main dial for home time, the patented outsize date, and the power-reserve indicator, it features a subsidiary dial that displays any of the world's 24 zone times with push button convenience.

A. LANGE & SÖHNE

GLASHÜTTE I/SA

in the world. But then, the division of Germany eradicated the proud company's name on timepiece dials. "A. Lange & Söhne" became a legend. Immediately after Germany was reunified, however, Adolph Lange's great-grandson Walter Lange returned to Glashütte to once again demonstrate Lange watchmaking artistry with the same love of innovation that had originally made the company famous around the globe. And as in the old days, Lange's unique watches are still meticulously crafted and assembled by hand. They will always be exclusive, as are the few jewellers in the world that stock "A. Lange & Söhne" masterpieces.

SWI
SWISS WATCH INTERNATIONAL

The **SWI** Group is a second generation family owned and operated business that has developed into an award winning innovator in the watch industry. **SWI** was created by virtue of the opportunities afforded to poor immigrants by the American dream. **SWI**'s founder and current chairman, Eli Ben-Shmuel, immigrated to the United States over a quarter century ago and with sheer determination, honesty and work ethic took the watch industry by storm.

Mr. Ben-Shmuel's legendary attributes include the development and distribution of the finest timepieces in the world. His dream continues with the successful transition of **SWI** into the reigns of his three sons. The transition has only strengthened **SWI**'s uncompromising mission: Providing everyone, regardless of their socio-economic status, luxury timepieces at affordable prices.

Among its growing list of achievements, **SWI** has been named in Inc. Magazine's prestigious Inc 500 list of America's 500 fastest growing, privately held companies for the past three consecutive years. The world's leaders in watch design create **SWI**'s innovative and sleek timepiece designs. True to our founder's doctrine, we include these high-grade complications in every watch we manufacture, but never in the price tag.

*Limited Edition of 500 pieces, this elegant **SWI** masterpiece is a mechanical automatic 25 jewel complete calendar and moon phase made of 316L surgical stainless steel case and deployant buckle. Available in various colors of Genuine Alligator and Ostrich straps. Day, date and month display. Black textured dial with silver hour markers and white hands or silver textured dial with black hour markers and blue hands. Sapphire crystal front and exhibition back.*
$4295

Limited Edition of 500 pieces, this mechanical automatic with 25 jewels has a full day display at 12 o'clock. 316L stainless steel case and deployant buckle. Available in Genuine Alligator or Ostrich strap. Silver textured dial with black hour markers and blue hands. Coin edge bezel. Sapphire crystal front and exhibition back.
$1995

Limited Edition of 100 pieces, 51 jewel mechanical automatic chronograph. Solid 18K rose gold case and buckle. Date function at 12 o'clock. Black textured dial with chronograph subdials located at 3, 6, and 9 o'clock. Available in Genuine Alligator or Ostrich strap. Rose gold Roman numerals and hour markers. Tachymetric scale. Sapphire crystal front and exhibition back.
$7995

Limited Edition of 100 pieces. Diamond Chronographs. Available in a 316L stainless steel or solid 18K rose gold case and buckle. Available in various exotic straps and silver or black textured dials. Large date display at 12 o'clock. **SWI** *51 jewel mechanical automatic chronograph movement. Tachymetric scale. Sapphire crystal front and exhibition back.*

Luxury has a name; Swiss Watch International. Each **SWI** timepiece merges over a quarter century of unmatched experience with elite opulence. The premier collections are all 100% Swiss made consisting of the finest raw materials including solid 18K rose gold, 18K white gold, solid 316L surgical grade stainless steel, the highest grade sapphire crystal and Top Wesselton diamonds. All leather straps are made of genuine Alligator or Ostrich leather and other exotic materials. The collections permeate elegance and sophistication for a lifetime of luxury.

Limited Edition of 500 pieces. 316L stainless steel case and deployant buckle. Available in Genuine Alligator or Ostrich strap. Full day display at 12 o'clock. Black textured dial with silver hour markers and white hands or silver textured dial with black hour markers and blue hands. **SWI** *25 jewel mechanical automatic movement. Coin edge bezel. Sapphire crystal front and exhibition back.*
$1995

Limited Edition of 500 pieces. 316L stainless steel sase and buckle. Available in Genuine Alligator or Ostrich strap. Large date display at 12 o'clock. Silver textured dial with black hour markers and blue hands. **SWI** *mechanical automatic chronograph movement. Tachymetric scale. Sapphire crystal front and exhibition back.*
$3995

Please visit our website at www.swiwatches.com or contact us at our toll free number for the U.S. at 1-866-746-7794 or 1-954-985-3827.

"le vrai bonheur est d'avoir sa passion pour métier"

LES COULEURS DU TEMPS

"100 fathoms below the surface
is no place for amateurs."

-Ingo Vollmer, deep sea diver
(pictured here with his Kobold SEAL
in aerospace-grade titanium)

KOBOLD

Embrace Adventure

for a free brochure, please phone 1-877-SOARWAY or visit www.koboldwatch.com

Glossary

Annual calendar

The automatic allowances for the different lengths of each month of a year in the calendar module of a watch. This type of watch also usually shows the month and date, and sometimes the day of the week (like this one by Patek Philippe) and the phases of the moon.

Antimagnetic

Mechanical movements are easily influenced by the magnetic fields often found in common everyday places. This problem is generally solved by the use of anti- or nonmagnetic components in the movement. Some companies, such as Sinn, IWC, and Bell & Ross, take things a step further and encase movements in antimagnetic cores such as the one shown here from Sinn's Model 756, the Duograph. Here the inner core is easily recognizable, as are the dial, movement holder ring, and second case back. These precautions make

the watch antimagnetic to 80,000 a/M – far exceeding the norms demanded by DIN and ISO.

Antireflection

A film created by steaming the crystal to eliminate light reflection and improve legibility. Antireflection functions best when applied to both sides of the crystal, but because it scratches, some manufacturers prefer to have it only on the interior of the crystal. It is mainly used on synthetic sapphire crystals. Dubey & Schaldenbrand applies antireflection on both sides for all of the company's wristwatches such as this Aquadyn model.

Automatic winding

A rotating weight, set into motion by moving the wrist, winds the spring barrel via the gear train of a mechanical watch movement. Automatic winding was invented during the pocket watch era in 1770 by Abraham-Louis Perrelet, who created a watch with a weight swinging back and forth (that of a pocket watch

IWC's automatic Caliber 50611

usually makes vertical movements contrary to a wristwatch). The first automatic-winding wristwatches, invented by John Harwood in the 1920s, utilized so-called hammer winding, whereby a weight swung in an arc between two banking pins. The breakthrough automatic winding movement via rotor began with the ball bearing Eterna-Matic in the late 1940s, and the technology hasn't changed fundamentally since. Today we speak of unidirectional winding and bidirectionally winding rotors, depending on the type of gear train used.

Balance

The beating heart of a mechanical watch movement is the balance. Fed by the energy of the mainspring, a tirelessly oscillating little wheel, just a few millimeters in diameter and possessing a spiral-shaped balance spring, sets the rhythm for the escape wheel and pallets with its vibration frequency. Today the balance is usually made of one piece of antimagnetic glucydur, an alloy that expands very little when exposed to heat.

Bar or cock

A metal plate fastened to the base plate at one point, leaving room for a gear wheel or pinion. The balance is usually attached to a bar called the balance cock. Glashütte tradition dictates that the balance cock be decoratively engraved by hand like this one by Glashütte Original.

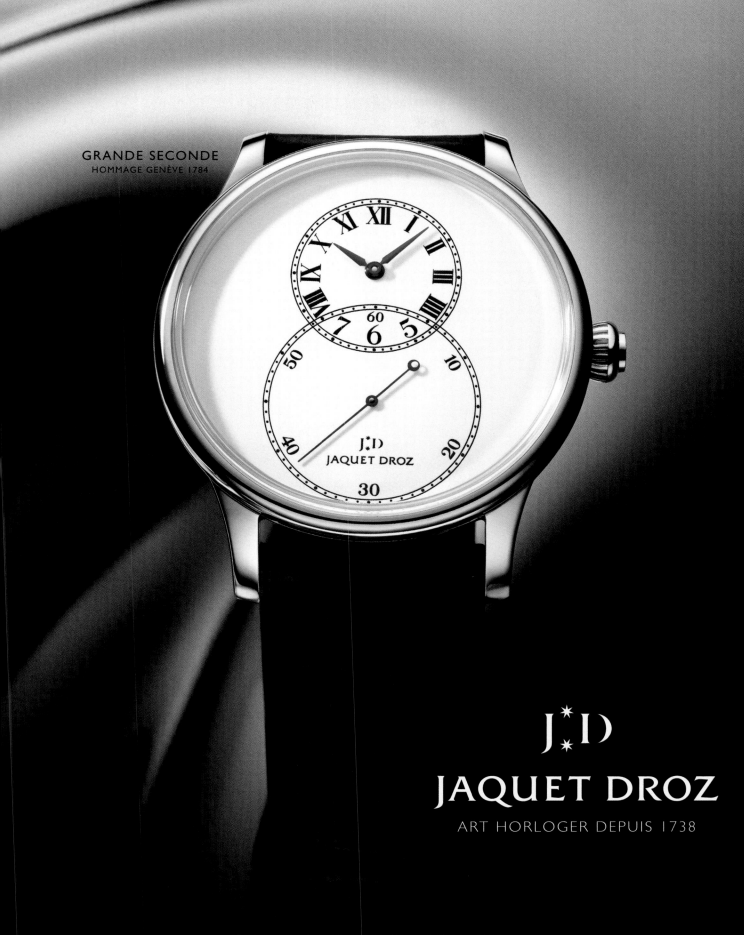

GRANDE SECONDE
HOMMAGE GENÈVE 1784

J*D

JAQUET DROZ

ART HORLOGER DEPUIS 1738

Beveling

To uniformly file down the sharp edges of a plate, bridge, or bar and give it a high polish. Edges are usually beveled at a 45° angle. As the picture shows, this is painstaking work that needs the skilled hands and eyes of an experienced watchmaker.

Blued screw

Traditional Swiss and Glashütte watchmaking dictates that a movement should contain blued screws for aesthetic reasons. Polished steel screws are heated (or tempered, as it is known in watch parlance) to 290°C. This process relaxes the steel, turning it a deep blue in color. Only a few *manufactures* still put the tempering process into effect with actual heat, others preferring the chemically induced version that assures an even color every time. Jaquet Droz and a few other brands even use blued screws as design elements on their dials.

Bridge

A metal plate fastened to the base plate at two points leaving room for a gear wheel or pinion. This vintage Favre-Leuba movement illustrates the point with three individual bridges.

Caliber

A term, similar to type or model, that refers to different watch movements. Pictured here is Heuer's Caliber 11, the legendary automatic chronograph caliber from 1969. This movement was a coproduction jointly researched and developed for four years by Heuer-Leonidas, Breitling, and Hamilton-Büren. Each company gave the movement a different name after serial production began.

Chronograph

From the Greek *chronos* (time) and *graphein* (to write). Originally a chronograph literally wrote, inscribing the time elapsed on a piece of paper with the help of a pencil attached to a type of hand. Today this term is used for watches that show not only the time of day, but also certain time intervals via independent hands that may be started or stopped at will. So-called stopwatches differ from chronographs because they do not show the time of day. This exploded illustration shows the complexity of a Breitling chronograph.

Chronometer

Literally, "measurer of time." As the term is used today, a chronometer denotes an especially accurate watch (one with a deviation of no more than 5 seconds a day for mechanical movements). Chronometers are usually supplied with an official certificate from an independent testing office such as the C.O.S.C. The largest producer of chronometers in 2004 was Rolex with 628,556 officially certified movements. Chopard came in fifth with more than 11,000 certified L.U.C. mechanisms like the 4.96 in the Pro One model shown here.

Column wheel

The component used to control chronograph functions within a true chronograph movement. The presence of a column wheel indicates that the chronograph is fully

GIVE YOUR WATCH WINDER A THRILL.

Dubey & Schaldenbrand

DS

1946 – SUISSE

integrated into the movement. In the modern era, modules are generally used that are attached to a base caliber movement. This particular column wheel is made of blued steel.

C.O.S.C.

The Contrôle Officiel Suisse de Chronométrage, the official Swiss testing office for chronometers. The C.O.S.C. is the world's largest issuer of so-called chronometer certificates, which are only otherwise given out individually by certain observatories (such as the one in Neuchâtel, Switzerland). For a fee, the C.O.S.C. tests the rate of movements that have been adjusted by watchmakers. These are usually mechanical movements, but the office also tests some high precision quartz movements. Those that meet the specifications for being a chronometer are awarded an official certificate as shown here.

Côtes de Genève

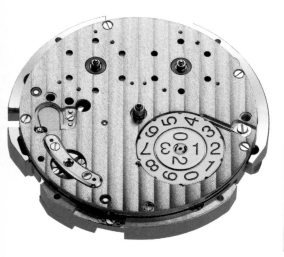

Also called *vagues de Genève* and Geneva stripes. This is a traditional Swiss surface decoration comprising an even pattern of parallel stripes, applied to flat movement components with a quickly rotating plastic or wooden peg. Glashütte watchmakers have devised their own version of *côtes de Genève* that is applied at a slightly different angle called Glashütte ribbing.

Crown

The crown is used to wind and set a watch. A few simple turns of the crown will get an automatic movement started, while a manually wound watch is completely wound by the crown. The crown is also used for the setting of various functions, almost always including at least the hours, minutes, seconds, and date. A screwed-down crown like the one on the TAG Heuer Aquagraph pictured here can be tightened to prevent water entering the case or any mishaps while performing extreme sports such as diving.

Equation of time

The mean time that we use to keep track of the passing of the day (24 hours evenly divided into minutes and seconds) is not equal to true solar time. The equation of time is a complication devised to show the difference between the mean time shown on one's wristwatch and the time the sun dictates. The Équation Marchante by Blancpain very legibly shows this difference via the golden sun-tipped hand that also rotates around the dial in a manner known to watch connoisseurs as *marchant*. Other wristwatch models such as the Eos Boreas by Martin Braun display the difference on an extra scale on the dial.

Escapement

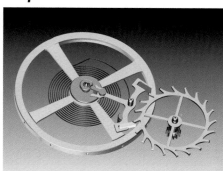

The combination of the balance, balance spring, pallets, and escape wheel, a subgroup which divides the impulses coming from the spring barrel into small, accurately portioned doses. It guarantees that the gear train runs smoothly and efficiently. The pictured escapement is one newly invented by Parmigiani Fleurier containing pallet stones of varying color, though they are generally red synthetic rubies. Here one of them is a colorless sapphire or corundum, the same geological material that ruby is made of.

Flyback chronograph

The new Patravi TravelTec GMT features a multiple time zone function unique in the history of watchmaking: the third time zone display can be set either eastward or westward using the new single push-button mechanism for which the patent is pending. The automatic CFB 1901 chronograph caliber also allows the wearer to quick-set local time in hourly increments and to set the date backwards as well. The new masterpiece from Carl F. Bucherer will thus delight both frequent flyers and those who appreciate complex watch movements.

CARL F. BUCHERER

FOR PEOPLE WHO DO NOT GO WITH THE TIMES.

www.carl-f-bucherer.com   info@cfbnorthamerica.com   800 395 4306

Gear train

A mechanical watch's gear train transmits energy from the mainspring to the escapement. The gear train comprises the minute wheel, the third wheel, the fourth wheel, and the escape wheel.

GMT

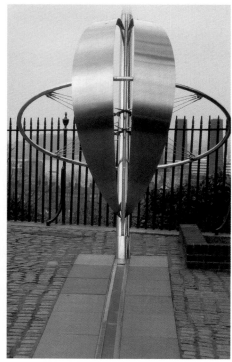

GMT, or Greenwich Mean Time, is based on the globe being divided into 24 time zones as established in the Meridian Conference of 1884. The zero meridian runs through the Royal Observatory in the London suburb of Greenwich (pictured). In contemporary watch terminology, GMT is often used to describe a wristwatch that displays a second time zone or a 24-hour indication.

A surface decoration usually applied to the dial and the rotor using a grooving tool with a sharp tip, such as a rose engine, to cut an even pattern onto a level surface. The exact adjustment of the tool for each new path is controlled by a device similar to a pantograph, and the movement of the tool can be controlled either manually or mechanically. Real *guillochis* (the correct term used by a master of guilloché) are very intricate and expensive to produce, which is why most dials decorated in this fashion are produced by stamping machines. Breguet is one of the very few companies to use real guilloché on every one of its dials.

Index

A regulating mechanism found on the balance cock and used by the watchmaker to adjust the movement's rate. The index changes the  effective length of the balance spring, thus making it move more quickly or slowly. This is the standard index found on an ETA Valjoux 7750.

Jewel

To minimize friction, the hardened steel tips of a movement's rotating gear wheels (called pinions) are lodged in synthetic rubies (fashioned as polished stones with a hole) and lubricated with a very thin

Luminous substance

Tritium is a slightly radioactive material used to coat hands, numerals, and hour markers on watch dials in order to make reading the time in the dark possible. Watches bearing tritium must be marked as such, with the letter T on the dial near 6 o'clock. It has now for the most part been replaced by nonradioactive materials such as SuperLumiNova and Traser technology (as seen on this Ball timepiece, a pioneer in the technology) due to medical misgivings and expected governmental regulation of its use.

Mainspring

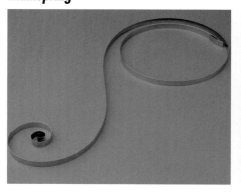

The mainspring, located in the spring barrel, stores energy when tensioned and passes it on to the escapement via the gear train as the tension relaxes. Today, mainsprings are generally made of Nivaflex, an alloy invented by Swiss engineer Max Straumann at the beginning of the 1950s. This alloy basically comprises iron, nickel, chrome, cobalt, and beryllium.

Manufacture

Modern definitions of this word are not clear-cut, but most experts agree that the term should be used for a company that manufactures at least one caliber, or extremely important parts of it such as the base plate, on premises. While ten years ago this constituted only a handful of companies in Switzerland and Germany, today's competitive market has forced a number of other creative souls to invest in developing their own movements. ETA, pictured, is without a doubt the largest *manufacture* in Switzerland. The word itself is derived from Latin (though horologists prefer to use the French variation) and means "made by hand."

Minute repeater

A striking mechanism with hammers and gongs for acoustically signaling the hours, quarter hours, and minutes elapsed since noon or midnight. The wearer pushes a slide, which winds the spring. Normally a repeater uses two different gongs to signal hours (low tone), quarter hours (high and low tones in succession), and minutes (high tone). Some watches have three gongs, called a carillon. The Chronoswiss Répétition à Quarts is a prominent repeating introduction of recent years.

Perlage

Surface decoration comprising an even pattern of partially overlapping dots, applied with a quickly rotating plastic or wooden peg. Also called circular graining, this embellishment had the original use of preventing dust and dirt from gathering on the movement's plates. Today it is mainly a traditional type of decoration. Here it is found on the plates of Frédérique Constant's *manufacture* Caliber FC 910-1.

Perpetual calendar

The calendar module for this type of timepiece automatically makes allowances for the different lengths of each month as well as leap years until the next secular year (in 2100). A perpetual calendar also usually shows the date, month, and four-year cycle, and may show the day of the week and moon phase as well, as does this one introduced by George J von Burg at Baselworld 2005.

Plate

A metal platform having several tiers for the gear train. The base plate of a movement usually incorporates the dial and carries the bearings for the primary pinions of the "first floor" of a gear train. The gear wheels are made complete by tightly fitting screwed-in bridges and bars on the back side of the plate. A specialty of the so-called Glashütte school, as opposed to the Swiss school, is the reverse completion of a movement not via different bridges and bars, but rather with a three-quarter plate. Glashütte Original's Caliber 65 (shown) displays a beautifully decorated three-quarter plate.

Power reserve display

A mechanical watch contains only a certain amount of power reserve. A fully wound modern automatic watch usually possesses between 36 and 42 hours of energy before it needs to be wound again. The power reserve display keeps the wearer informed about how much energy his or her watch still has in reserve, a function that is especially practical on manually wound watches with several days of possible reserve. The Nomos Tangente Power Reserve pictured here represents an especially creative way to illustrate the state of the mainspring's tension. On some German watches the power reserve is also displayed with the words "auf" and "ab."

Pulsometer

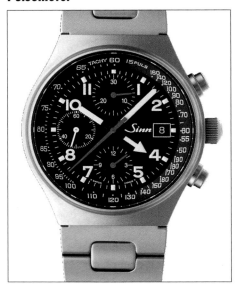

A scale on the dial, flange, or bezel that, in conjunction with the second hand, may be used to measure a pulse rate. A pulsometer is always marked with a reference number – if it is marked with *gradué pour 15 pulsations*, for example, then the wearer counts fifteen pulse beats. At the last beat, the second hand will show what the pulse rate is in beats per minute on the pulsometer scale. The scale on Sinn's World Time Chronograph (shown) is marked simply with the German world *Puls* (pulse), but the function remains the same.

Quartz

Timekeeping's technical revolution found its way to the world's wrists in the late 1960s. This was a principally Swiss invention – the first working quartz wristwatches were manufactured by Girard-Perregaux and Piaget as the result of an early joint venture within the Swiss watch industry, but Japanese firms, primarily Seiko, came to dominate the market with new technology. The quartz movement uses the famously stable

vibration frequency of a quartz crystal subjected to electronic tension (usually 32,868 Hz) as its norm. The fact that a quartz-controlled second hand jumps to the beat of each second is a concession to the use of outside energy.

Retrograde display

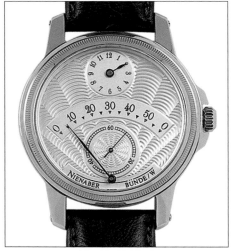

A retrograde display shows the time linearly instead of circularly. The hand continues along an arc until it reaches the end of its scale, at which precise moment it jumps back to the beginning instantaneously. This Nienaber model not only shows the minutes in retrograde form, it is also a regulator display.

Rotor

The rotor is the component that keeps an automatic watch wound. The kinetic motion of this part, which

contains a heavy metal weight around its outer edge, winds the mainspring. It can either wind unilaterally or bilaterally (to one or both sides) depending on the caliber. The rotor from this Temption timepiece belongs to an ETA Valjoux 7750.

Sapphire crystal

Synthetic sapphire crystal has become the material of choice to protect the dials of modern wristwatches. This material, known to gemologists as aluminum oxide (Al_2O_3) or corundum, can be colorless (corundum), red (ruby), blue (sapphire), or green (emerald). It is virtually scratchproof with a hardness of 10 on the Mohs scale; only a diamond is harder. Corundum is "grown" using a method invented by Auguste Victore Louis Verneuil in 1902 whereby a process that usually takes a hundred thousand years to complete is accelerated to just a few hours, hence the use of the term synthetic. The innovative Royal Blue Tourbillon by Ulysse Nardin pictured here not only features sapphire crystals on the front and back of the watch, but also actual plates made of both colorless and blue corundum within the movement.

Bobby Finder SP30:
stainless steel case with
patented rotating bezel designed
to protect the pushers,
with automatic mechanical
chronograph, on a polished
calf leather strap

711 fifth avenue, new york
www.dunhill.com. 800 776 4053
alfred dunhill, equipping gentlemen since 1893

A. DUNHILL LTD
LONDON

BR 01-94 INSTRUMENT

Bell **&** Ross

EDOX

Maître Horloger - Les Genevez
depuis 1884

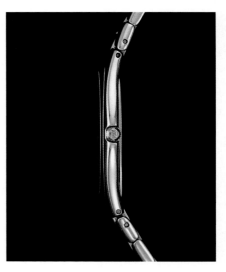

Master watchmakers since 1884

In 1884, master watchmaker Christian Ruefly-Flury decided to establish his own watch manufacturing business. He couldn't have chosen a better time: Swiss lever watches, thanks to their accuracy and reliability, were taking the world's market by storm. Through these, the Edox name was to become known in future in all four corners of the earth. The fast developing enterprise passed into the hands of Robert Kaufmann-Hugg in 1921, under whose management it became a joint-stock company.

Revolution with the Geoscope

This step accelerated Edox's expansion. In 1955, the company moved into larger premises to keep pace with increasing demand. In 1965, Robert Kaufmann-Hugg passed the management of the company to his nephew, Victor Flury-Liechti. New products were created, new customers won. For instance, the launch of the Delfin collection in the 1960's, an extremely watertight watch with a double back

and double gaskets, and then a few years later the revolutionary Geoscope, a universal-time watch giving both GMT and the position of the sun in the heavens.

Les Bémonts

Automatic Les Bémonts with visible heart

Edox is proud to present the automatic Les Bémonts collection with visible heart. The elegant stainless steel watch offers an insight through the scratchproof sapphire crystal into the complication precision inner workings. It is waterproof to a depth of 50 meters and comes with a worldwide Edox guarantee.

The art of understatement

Of all the possible ways of representing time, Edox has chosen what is probably the most subtle: the art of understatement, reduction to the essential. In our 120-year history, we have constantly delighted enthusiasts

The Les Bémonts collection with the EDOX quartz movement with calendar, of barely 1.4 mm thickness.

of ultra-slim, elegant watches with creations of discreet sophistication. The Les Bémonts collection is the expression of a perfect symbiosis of watchmaking expertise and aesthetic harmony. The classic circular models are joined by the geometry of the rectangle, brilliantly realized by the designer Christian Glauser, who needs no further introduction on the international scene.

Ultra-slim and elegant

The Les Bémonts collection is a tribute to that noble material, steel. Available in brush-finished, polished, in solid 18K gold or enhanced with sparkling diamonds, these watches are waterproof to 30 meters despite their ultra-slim profile. The heart of the timepiece ticks under the noble clockface which is protected by sapphire crystal: the exclusive Edox caliber 9" 26000 or 10 1⁄2 " 27000 of barely 1.4mm thickness, equipped with a calendar. The collection is rounded off by chronographs for both men and women which are described by experts as being the most elegant of their kind.

Automatic Les Bémonts with visible heart

Solid 18K Gold Automatic

EDOX Les Bémonts automatic 5-minute repetition

EDOX – EDOX, the traditional family-owned company based in the Swiss Jura, is one by one extending its portfolio with high-quality mechanical watches, manufactured in accordance with the best Swiss watchmaking tradition. This year with the EDOX Les Bémonts automatic with 5-minute repetition, which is probably the most complex and luxurious complication ever. The luxury version is skeletonized for purists and hand-made.

What is a complication?

A complication is essentially and simply nothing more than an additional piece of information on the time, which the automatic watch displays very elegantly. EDOX has decided to produce probably the most com-plex and luxurious complication: the 5-minute repetition. The existing, well-known and high-quality movement of the Les Bémonts model range was fitted with the necessary module for the 5-minute repetition. This is carried out by our watchmakers in the company's own studio at Les Genevez.

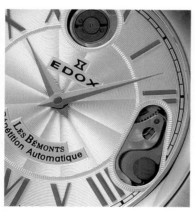

5-minute repetition

The movement is equipped with 2 tiny hammers: one strikes the hour, the other in a different tone every 5 minutes after the hour. The ringer mechanism can be activated by means of a small button at the bottom of the case at six o'clock.

Skeletonized for purists

For the purists among collectors of lavish complications and high-quality watches, EDOX has prepared an addition special feature: the EDOX Les Bémonts 5-minute repetition with skeletonized movement. Hand-made in accordance with the best watchmaking tradition, it achieves in its entirety the highest standards of the Swiss art of watchmaking.

Further details

The Les Bémonts Automatic-Bijoux is equipped with a transparent back that offers a fascinating view of the movement. The dial is partially skeletonized and allows you to observe the hammer motion. It has a scratch-resistant sapphire crystal and is waterproof down to 50 meters.

For information, please contact
The SWI Group
Toll Free: 1-866-746-7794 or
1-954-985-3827
Fax: 954-985-1828
Email: lior@swisswatchintl.com

Montres Edox & Vista SA
La Sagne au Droz
2714 Les Genevez
Switzerland
Tél: +41 32 484 90 91 Fax: +41 32 484 92 43
Email : info@edox.ch

Jacques Lemans

Jacques Lemans Rings in Good Value

by Elizabeth Doerr

The Jacques Lemans headquarters in St. Veit, Austria.

Good Swiss quality and moderate prices may not always be two things that go together, but in Jacques Lemans's case, they are in no way contradictory. This represents the philosophy of the company founded by Alfred Riedl three decades ago. Though the watches are manufactured in Wallbach, Switzerland, to ensure proper Swiss quality, this brand is headquartered in St. Veit, Austria. Well-known in Europe, the Middle East, and Asia, where it has done its main business until now, the brand is currently giving Americans the opportunity to get to know its watches and its version of good value.

Ensuring quality in every segment of its business, Jacques Lemans is now being distributed in the United States by Swiss Watch International, a company that can proudly look back on two generations and thirty years of experience in the distribution of European timepieces. SWI's involvement with the brand since introducing it stateside in 2003 has been extremely prosperous, certainly in part due to the great success of the company's show on

ShopNBC and the other occasions SWI is so adept at organizing for its brands. Jacques Lemans timepieces were, for example, part of celebrities' gift baskets at the 2004 Golden Globe Awards, an event that always grabs a fashion-conscious public's attention.

Jacques Lemans's timepieces are outfitted with Swiss ETA movements, either automatic or quartz depending on the style called for. Early in 2005, the brand presented a quartz-driven minute repeater, actually one of the highest complications known to mechanical watchmaking. Though it might seem unusual to offer a battery-powered timepiece of this caliber, the soothing, melodious ringing of the chimes remains a real highlight among watch enthusiasts — as does the price tag of an extremely affordable $499, thanks to that quartz movement.

The repeater's case is crafted in solid stainless steel since it is a known fact that this metal facilitates the sound of the gongs, though most luxury watchmakers are reluctant to use it as they fear giving a "cheap" aura to their high

Jacques Lemans Classic Series in rose gold retails for $3,295.

An annual calendar with moon phases also finds its home in the popular Geneve collection.

This minute repeater crafted in stainless steel retails for an eye-popping $499.

complication. Jacques Lemans's minute repeater is additionally outfitted with a scratchproof sapphire crystal and an American-made alligator skin strap. The user-friendly quartz movement can be set to ring anytime the wearer wishes. This repeater is being offered in a limited number of 1,000 for each different style.

All of Jacques Lemans's mechanical watches are outfitted with either ETA 2834-2 in the three-hand models or ETA 7750 or 7751 in the chronographs, such as those of the traditionally styled Jacques Lemans's Classic Series. These round 40 mm cases are designed with fluted bezels and case backs. The chronograph pushers and crown are vintage-styled for an extra touch of class. Their dials are embellished with an attractive guilloché pattern. The subdials located at 9 o'clock on some of the models contain GMT displays, which can either be used as 24-hour displays or second time zones. The scale shown on the flange (outside of the date ring) of the chronograph is a tachymeter scale used for measuring distances and speeds.

The cases and bracelets are made of surgical stainless steel, and some models have been given a coating of ten microns of 18-karat rose gold. This particular treatment makes the case and bracelet very durable and robust, and more scratch-resistant than solid gold wristwatches. The rose gold also gives the watch a classic, nostalgic feel to it while the tone remains warm. Continuing the quality vein, this brand's wristwatches have a full five-year guarantee in North America. In addition to being sold on ShopNBC, these timepieces can now also be found in North American retail jewelry stores for the same prices, which start at $350 and average up to about $1,400, though certain deluxe models set with gemstones can range up to $6,000.

The Geneve collection is also home to this mechanical moon phase model.

This interesting chronograph from the Geneve collection retails for $2,995.

One Hundred Years...

www.armandnicolet.com

ARMAND NICOLET
TRAMELAN

JL
JACQUES LEMANS

For over three decades, JACQUES LEMANS has stood for outstanding quality and competence in producing unique watch creations. JACQUES LEMANS offers the finest of Swiss-made watches at unmatched value and excellence. With the JACQUES LEMANS GENEVE Collection, made in Geneva and launched in 2005, JACQUES LEMANS combines the rich tradition of Swiss watch-making with timeless designs and functionality by using the highest grade automatic and quartz Swiss movements.

THE GRANDE CLASSIQUE
This very elegant round case design in 18K micron gold plating is a great addition to the beautiful Geneve Collection. The dial has a very rich texture design and the numerals and markers are hand applied. This slim timepiece equipped with a heavily decorated Swiss Automatic 25 jewel movement, displayed with a Sapphire crystal exhibition back. Date complication off-set at the 6 o'clock.

Jacques Lemans Distribution Center

Beautifully designed scratch-resistant Ceramic and stainless steel with a curved Sapphire crystal. Chronograph movement with an off-set date complication.

Swiss Automatic Chronograph highly decorated Caliber Valjoux 7750 with 25 jewels. Luminous hour and minute hands. Date display. Sapphire crystal front and exhibition back. Water resistant to 100 meters. Solid 316L Surgical grade stainless steel.

Unique Touneau case with 18K rosetone accents on the pushers and crown. Silver sun ray pattern dial with rosetone markers. Equipped with a highly decorated Valjoux 7750 Swiss Made 25 jewel automatic movement. Curved Sapphire crystal front and exhibition back. This beautiful watch is elegently displayed with a square grain genuine Alligator strap and dual deployant clasp.

THE DIVER'S COLLECTION
This 200 Meter Depth Meter is a diver's dream. It is capable of recording dive data which includes the current depth, dive elapsed time, the water temperature and has a built-in alarm chronograph feature. The enormous 45 mm case and uni-directional bezel will definitely grab anyone's attention. It comes packaged in a scuba tank design gift box.

Classic coin edge design layered in 10 microns of 18K gold. This complete calendar, moon phase and chronograph is equipped with a Swiss Made Automatic movement Caliber Valjoux 7751 with 25 jewels. Sapphire crystal front and exhibition back.

B.R.M.

Ticking at the Speed of Sound

by Elizabeth Doerr

The name of this company is fitting in more ways than one, and its owner Bernard Richards certainly meant for it to be that way. B.R.M. actually stands for Bernard Richards Manufacturing. However, any English speaker will probably end up pronouncing it "brrrm" in his or her mind, and even when these initials are said separately but quickly, the type of sound an automobile or motorcycle makes is usually what comes out.

And this is probably what Richards, an extreme motor sports enthusiast, was after. The timepieces he has created for his relatively new brand do indeed fit this name. Richards designs them himself, and his vision of luxury watchmaking is truly different from anything else around at the moment. Illustrating his enormous passion for the race car and motorcycle, he uses high-tech materials, such as carbon fiber and titanium. None of the components found in a B.R.M. watch are off-the-rack, either. These are all custom

B.R.M.'s V14-44 is powered by the Valjoux 7753 and measures 44 mm in diameter.

designed and – made, fitting perfectly into Richards's automotive ideal of the wristwatch. It has been a short four years since he abandoned his previous job of making accessories for other (and sometimes famous) luxury brands, which he had been doing since 1986. His work involved all kinds of objects, some not so very different from wristwatches, and he was also one of the first to use digital machines in that industry. In 2002 he set out on his own, completely dedicating his energies to wristwatches.

Richards is a self-taught designer who does not follow any certain school of thought or philosophy. The charming Frenchman sees things and is immediately inspired by them. "I never learned designing formally — in fact, I was a very bad boy in school. I just do what comes into my head. And it often comes quickly," he reveals. This, in fact, also extends to working with his hands, as Richards makes all his own prototypes as well.

Today, Richards's company employs fourteen people, and the amount of watches manufactured there has grown just as

This orange SCR model by B.R.M. is limited to 100 pieces worldwide and retails for $16,350.

ANONIMO
FIRENZE

Florentine Watchmaking Tradition

mod. 2014 Zulu Time

exponentially. "It took us about three years to really get going," he explains. "In the beginning I was just selling the watches I made to my friends, who loved them and often bought several." While B.R.M. produced only about fifty pieces in 2003, Richards forecasts about 2,400 pieces for the year 2006. With a factory located just outside of Paris, Richards's second goal is to bring quality watchmaking back to his home country, and in the near future he will be introducing products to underscore this desire. He has been extremely busy during this "start-up" period, creating his unusual pieces around the tried and trusted Valjoux 7750, the mechanical chronograph movement most often utilized in watch production — but not for much longer. Richards has set lofty goals for himself and his young venture, for it is fully his intention to set up a true *manufacture* in his French factory. As it stands, all the parts used in his

watches are either Swiss or French in origin, and the watches are completely assembled in France.

The collection comprises mainly chronographs in titanium, black PVD titanium, or stainless steel cases in sizes ranging from 38 to 44 mm. One massive exception to this is the new SCR Racing Skeleton, which measures in at 48 mm across. Collection prices range from $1,650 to $16,350 for this watch, limited worldwide to a total of 100 pieces in orange and 150 pieces in black and featuring a modified Valjoux 7753. Currently, timepieces by B.R.M. can be found in some of the best watch and jewelry stores all over the world. Aside from being available in France, Italy, Spain, Great Britain, Switzerland, Russia, Asia, and the UAE, in September of 2004 B.R.M. founded its own U.S. subsidiary in Dallas, Texas, and has since been very visible stateside. These stunningly unique, small-series

The titanium case of this GP 44 model is PVD blackened and reminiscent of a piston. It comes on a black rubber strap.

timepieces can be found at Neiman Marcus as well as exclusive independent jewelers such as Exquisite Timepieces in Naples, Florida, and Chatel in Carmel, California. "Despite these so-called successes, it has never been and never will be about money. It's a thrill for me to see my name and my products in the windows of the some of the best retail shops in the world," Richards says about his inspiration and the desire to remain small.

The V9 is attractively set with diamonds or colored stones (to match the strap color) around the flange inside the sapphire crystal. This model is 38 mm in diameter and can be worn well by both men and women.

The Five Time Zone Collection

JACOB & Co.

48 East 57th Street • New York, NY 10022 • 212 719 5887
For a store near you call 877 JACOB 01
or visit www.jacobandco.com

Giuliano Mazzuoli

The Emotions of Horological Design

by Elizabeth Doerr

The Manometro

Giuliano Mazzuoli is certain that his emotions have led him "to stumble into projects." This can certainly be said of his latest venture: designing wristwatches. Getting "inspiration from everyday objects" is a specialty of the Tuscan designer. Beginning his career close to home in the 1970s, he combined the graphic artistry of his father's business with the beauty of Florentine leather to create a line of agendas and organizers. Experiencing a desire to make something that lasts more than just one year, he then developed a line of pens inspired by some tools he spied in a mechanical workshop. This led to the creation of a range of writing instruments called Officina, Writing Instruments.

Mazzuoli's supreme strength as a designer is that ideas flow to him in a fairly automatic and emotional manner. He sees the world around him and instinctively channels the impressions gained into the concept subconsciously at work within him. And so it happened that one day Mazzuoli was talking on the phone while making some abstract sketches on paper laying about his desk. When he looked down, the doodles had automatically taken definite form: a ballpoint pen shaped like the famous Italian coffee pot designed by Alfonso Bialetti in the 1930s. Mazzuoli asserts, "Nothing is more difficult to design than true simplicity." And his Moka collection of writing instruments, appropriately named for their role model, was introduced to the world.

Mazzuoli then made the conscious decision to design a more complex object, one with many moving parts needed for precision. Combining this desire with the fact that his great-grandfather had been a clockmaker, Mazzuoli became all-encompassingly obsessed with the idea of making a watch. However, becoming inspired enough to create an innovative design was a little more difficult this time around. He did research in watch literature and magazines, which only ended up pointing out to him what had already been done. Deciding to start from scratch, he threw the books out and waited for his usual inspiration — which came in the form of a pressure gauge he spied one day, an everyday object once again.

The Italian word for pressure gauge is *manometro*, and that is precisely what Mazzuoli dubbed his new timepiece. The watch's stainless steel case is highly reminiscent of the everyday measuring instrument, but it also serves to represent timepiece housing not yet seen on the luxury watch market. It measures a decisive 45.2 mm in diameter and is 14.8 mm in height — an object that refuses to remain hidden under anyone's cuff. The stainless steel case back is secured with eight screws, guaranteeing water-resistance to 50 meters, or five atmospheres. Mazzuoli chose a trusty workhorse to power his new three-handed watch in the ETA 2824-2, outfitted with Incabloc shock protection and decorated with traditional *côtes de Genève*. Its dial, featuring luminous hands, is available in ivory, black, white, and blue, and the crown is positioned at either 2 or 10 o'clock.

Available on a handcrafted calfskin strap attached directly to the case, Giuliano Mazzuoli's Manometro is only sold in the United States through very select retailers in limited numbers and is priced at $3,500.

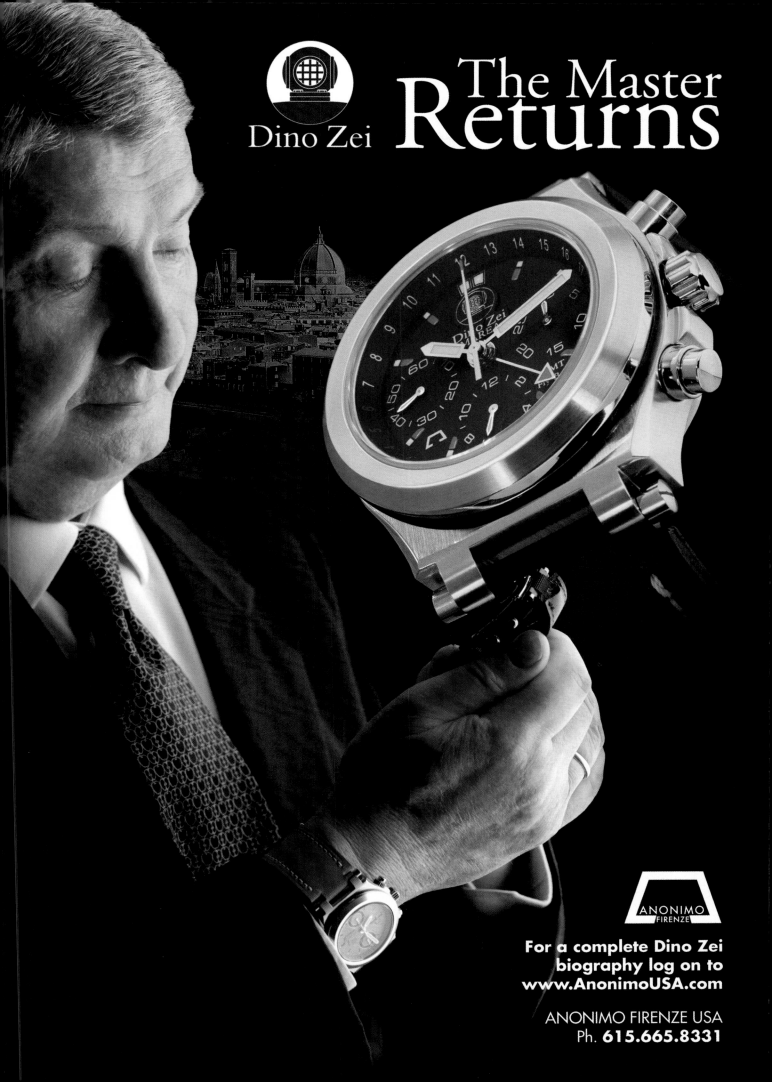

Officina del Tempo

An Italian Flair for Color

by Elizabeth Doerr

Italians have a true understanding of design. DOMUSHora and Officina del Tempo are part of the Italian fashion scene. They interact and meet regularly with Italy's leading fashion designers to discuss the newest styles, trends, and colors. DOMUSHora has experience in both the fashion and watch industries. This is why we are confident that the brands DOMUSHora is launching, already hot in Italy, will be enormously successful in the United States."

This statement given by Davide Murdocca, president of Officina del Tempo's U.S. distributor DOMUSHora, almost says it all. Released in Italy as a high-fashion watch brand, Officina del Tempo quickly made a huge name for itself. Finding the right partners in the U.S. with a good understanding of Italian fashion was key, and now that this has been achieved, success seems assured.

Murdocca's reference to styles, trends, and colors was no fluke, for this brand bases its watch designs on these principles, and the outcome is rather stunning — and rather popular at the moment. "The company's trendy, cutting-edge design and expansive use of color are possible because Officina del Tempo's

designers are Italian. In addition, Officina del Tempo meets regularly with Italy's leading fashion designers, and they are part of the inner circle where the newest trends are determined," adds Umberto Cipolla, vice president at DOMUSHora.

The brand's distinctive Italian design, vivid colors, striking cases, and use of gemstones make it instantly recognizable from any distance. Additionally, this company is dedicated to providing the most quality for the money. All cases are crafted in 316 L surgical steel or 18-karat gold on the limited models. Officina del Tempo chose to work with Italian leather company Morellato on their straps, a firm recognized throughout the industry as one of the best strap makers. Morellato supplies all the leather and stingray straps used on timepieces by Officina del Tempo. The lion's share of these watches is outfitted with quartz technology, some Swiss and some Japanese. All the mechanical models are outfitted with quality ETA movements.

The collection now comprises five main lines, which include models for both men and women. Marrakech has been perhaps the most well known until now, featuring a distinct case with a

The 18-karat rose gold Marrakech is limited to 100 pieces and retails for $4,200.

real edgy feel to it in every sense of the word. The dial design is truly unique and makes the timepiece an absolute eye-catcher. The rectangular-shaped case is offset by the roundness of the dial's main design; the numerals surround an oval area featuring a sunray pattern, and thus seem to be forced off the face of the dial. The 3 and the 9 actually already seem to have fallen off. All in all, it is a truly unique and distinctive look.

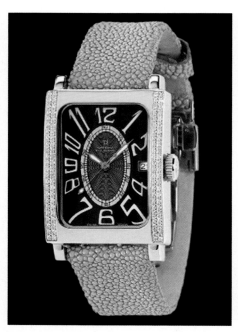

This Agadir model features a beautiful Morellato stingray strap.

This mechanical Marrakech in stainless steel is available for $920.

A Marrakech Chrono Gel in brilliant blue.

The limited gold Marrakech model is powered by a manually wound Unitas 6497.

Marrakech is home to several interesting quartz, manually wound, and automatic men's pieces and even chronograph versions featuring either 82 or 188 diamonds. The highlight of this collection, however, is the limited edition 18-karat rose gold model powered by an ETA Unitas 6497. There are only 100 of these in the world.

Agadir is just as varied, featuring a rectangular case that is less rounded than that of the Marrakech line. The Lady Galuchat features 23, 96, or 160 diamonds for a fresh bit of sparkle, and the men's timepieces also come in various colors and strap variations with 100, 108, or 180 diamonds, and even without them. This line also features a piece limited to 100: The men's 18-karat rose gold GMT Agadir, powered by an ETA 2893-2.

The third line is called Tonneau and actually contains two different tonneau cases, one with

The 18-karat rose gold Agadir, serially numbered, retails for $4,100.

conventional lugs and one with central strap and bracelet lugs. The Tonneau's top model is not limited, but this stainless steel model is serially numbered by hand on the case back and contains an ETA 2824-2 movement for absolute reliability. In a slight departure, the Tonneau Chronograph is also available on a steel mesh bracelet. Otherwise this line, like the other two, is available in a myriad of variations including diamonds and colors to suit every taste.

Officina del Tempo is also well known for its value pricing. The vividly styled timepieces found in this collection begin at just $335 for simple models without gems and continue up to

$6,000 for the premiere pieces covered with 357 diamonds. Michael Pucci, national sales manager and marketing director for DOMUSHora, reports that not only is Officina del Tempo the watch brand with the highest turnover at Neiman Marcus, but that many customers also buy several pieces from the collection at one time. Pucci credits this to "the vivid color palettes and reasonable cost." He continues to describe the U.S. presentation of the brand last year, "The response to Officina del Tempo has been immediate and intense. One of the world's hottest rock stars purchased seven Officina del Tempo watches while performing in Las Vegas. He was blown away by the color and style. And, of course, the price."

Officina del Tempo is available at fine jewelry stores such as Bailey, Banks and Biddle and department stores such as Neiman Marcus and Saks Fifth Avenue.

The Marrakech 2 Chrono Gel is set with 188 diamonds and retails for $3,250.

This model is from the striking new Safi line and retails for $495.

Regulator Retrograde Minutes
Model Reference: RRM
Movement: mechanical with automatic winding, ETA caliber 2836-2; in-house modification; Incabloc shock absorption system; superior timing
Functions: Regulator style with hours and retrograde minutes indicator
Case: 316L stainless steel, satin finished, 40mm diameter, transparent back case; water resistant to 5 ATM; blue steel hands
Dial: silver guilloche or black guilloche dial
Band: calf leather strap
Price: $1,050
Comments: limited production. Future production available in 42mm case

Bombardier I
Model reference: Azimuth Bombardier I
Movement: mechanical with manual winding, Fontainemelon caliber ST 96-4. Circa 1969
Functions: hours, minutes and seconds
Case: 316L stainless steel, Satin finished, 47mm diameter, solid back case with German military style markings; water resistant to 3 ATM; oversized onion crown; blackened hands with Super Luminova fillings
Dial: matt black dial with Super Luminova Arabic numerals
Band: brown calf strap with brass rivets, vintage style
Price: $950
Comments: limited edition of 200 examples based on this caliber

Base Mecha -1 BMF
Model reference: BM-1
Movement: mechanical with automatic winding, ETA caliber 2824; Incabloc shock absorption system; superior timing
Functions: hours, minutes, seconds and date modified to 6 o'clock position
Case: 316L stainless steel, sand blasted finish, tri-bloc case construction; 43mm maximum width; 47mm length; bezel secured by 8 Torx Drive tamper resistant screws; water resistant to 3 ATM; solid back case with transparent porthole exposing the balance wheel
Dial: carbon-fiber dial with applied "electronic" numerals
Band: black rubber strap
Price: $1,250
Comments: optional genuine horn back croco strap

Retrograde Minutes Day & Night
Model Reference: RMDN
Movement: mechanical with automatic winding, ETA caliber 2836-2, in-house modification; Incabloc shock absorption system; superior timing
Functions: regulator style with hours, 24-hours and retrograde minutes indicator
Case: 316L stainless steel, satin finished, 40mm diameter, transparent back case; water resistant to 5 ATM; blue steel hands
Dial: silver guilloche or black guilloche dial
Band: calf leather strap
Price: $1,150
Comments: limited production. Future production available in 42mm case

Jagdbomber
Model reference: Azimuth Jagdbomber
Movement: mechanical with manual winding, Unitas caliber 6497-1; Incabloc shock absorption system; Côtes de Genève finishing and blue screws
Functions: hours, minutes and subsidiary seconds
Case: 316L stainless steel, satin finished, 47mm diameter, transparent back case; water resistant to 3 ATM; oversized onion crown; blue steel hands with Super Luminova fillings
Dial: matt black dial with Super Luminova Arabic numerals
Band: brown buffalo strap on rivets with white stitching, or brown calf strap with brass rivets
Price: $1,450

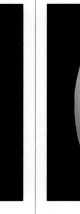

Gauge Mecha - 1 BMF - Concept Watch 2005
Model Reference: GM -1
Movement: mechanical with automatic winding, ETA caliber 2836-2, in-house modification; Incabloc shock absorption system; superior timing
Functions: Regulator style with hour disc indicator, 24-hour disc indicator and retrograde minutes indicator
Case: 316L stainless steel, satin finshed, tri-bloc case construction; 43mm maximum width; 47mm length; bezel secured by 8 Torx Drive tamper resistant screws; water resistant to 3 ATM; solid back case with transparent porthole exposing the balance wheel
Dial: carbon fiber dial or ivory colored dial
Band: black rubber strap
Price: $2,050
Comments: optional genuine horn back croco strap; comes standard with an automatic watch winder in oak wood casing; AC powered. Limited production

Exquisite Timepieces

A Collection of
The World's Finest
Timepieces

- ▶ ANONIMO
- ▶ ARMAND NICOLET
- ▶ ARNOLD & SON
- ▶ AUDEMARS PIGUET
- ▶ BAUME & MERCIER
- ▶ BEDAT & CO.
- ▶ BELL & ROSS
- ▶ BLANCPAIN
- ▶ BREGUET
- ▶ CÉDRIC JOHNER
- ▶ FORMEX
- ▶ FORTIS
- ▶ FRANCK MULLER
- ▶ GIRARD-PERREGAUX
- ▶ GLASHÜTTE ORIGINAL
- ▶ GRAHAM
- ▶ IWC
- ▶ JAEGER-LECOULTRE
- ▶ JAQUET DROZ
- ▶ OFFICINA DEL TEMPO
- ▶ OMEGA
- ▶ PANERAI
- ▶ ROGER DUBUIS
- ▶ SCATOLA DEL TEMPO
- ▶ TUTIMA
- ▶ UNDERWOOD

watchfinder.net
online watchmarket and more

watchfinder.net is an online watch market and watch resource that helps you find the watch you want and then find dealers from whom to purchase

- 100+ fine Swiss & German watch brands

- Modern, Vintage & Military watches

- Complete database of modern watches

- Trustworthy & established dealers from all over the world

www.watchfinder.net...   Online watchmarket and more

Alpina

Zentrale der
Alpina
Union Horlogère
A. G.
Unionsgasse 13
Biel / Schweiz

Siège central
Alpina
Union Horlogère
S. A.
13, rue de l'Union
Bienne / Suisse

Dugena (Deutsche Uhrmacher-Genossen-schaft Alpina) was created.

The brand Alpina was purchased several years ago by Aletta and Peter Stas, the active and very successful founders of Frédérique Constant, as a second brand, which provides a very sensible addition to the stable with respect to its models and design. The products of each of these brands are sold through differing distribution paths and also have varying target audiences. Thus, it is easy to see that they complement each other perfectly even from

a marketing and distribution aspect, not to mention their collections.

The Alpina line, the lion's share of which comprises stainless steel models, is still under construction and mostly targets a more experimenting type of consumer who enjoys watches with a sporty, almost streamlined design, possibly with a rubber strap and a clean dial. The prices of these watches allow even younger consumers an entry portal to mechanical watches, something which the brand obviously supports in the contemporary design and shape of its products.

Individuals with the same interests tend to achieve goals more effectively in a group. Watchmaker Gottlieb Hauser, hailing from Switzerland's Winterthur, discovered this fact for himself in 1883 and founded the Swiss Watchmaker Corporation (Schweizerische Uhrmacher-Corporation) in the same year. This group had the joint goal of purchasing watch components to get better prices and distributing finished products together as a group in order to be able to market them better. The concept quickly found recognition, and within just a short time numerous watchmakers had joined the cooperative. Together with qualified manufacturers, they began to develop their own calibers. Already in 1896 Alpina was registered as a trademark for movements and cases, and in 1901 it was introduced as a trade brand name.

From 1890, the group was headquartered in watch metropolis Biel. Right from the beginning, its products were outfitted only with high-quality components such as Breguet balance springs, balances fitted with gold screws, and heavy gold cases. In order to win over some German watchmakers, the successful cooperative, now called Alpina Union Horlogère, in 1909 founded the Präcisions-Uhrenfabrik Alpina in Glashütte and from then on sustained production workshops in Geneva, Biel, Besancon, and Glashütte. After World War II the name Alpina could no longer be used in Germany by order of the Allies, so

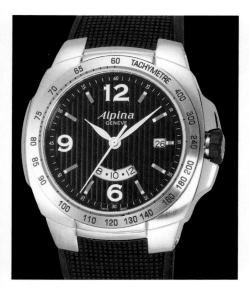

Avalanche GMT

Reference number: AL-300LBB4A6
Movement: quartz, AL Caliber 300 (base ETA 251.471)
Functions: hours, minutes, subsidiary seconds; date; 24-hour display (second time zone)
Case: stainless steel, ø 42 mm, bezel with tachymeter scale; sapphire crystal; water-resistant to 100 m
Band: rubber, buckle
Price: $495
Variations: with silver dial; with stainless steel bracelet

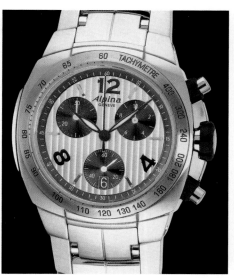

Avalanche Chronograph

Reference number: AL-350LSBB2A6B
Movement: quartz, AL Caliber 350 (base ETA 251.471)
Functions: hours, minutes, subsidiary seconds; chronograph; date
Case: stainless steel, ø 42 mm, bezel with tachymeter scale; sapphire crystal; water-resistant to 100 m
Band: stainless steel, folding clasp
Price: $990
Variations: with rubber strap; as women's model, ø 36 mm

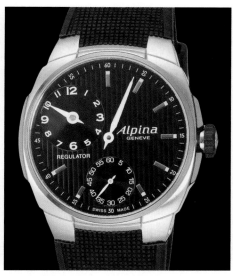

Avalanche Regulateur 1883

Reference number: AL-650LBBB4A6
Movement: manually wound, AL Caliber 650 (base ETA 6498-1 Unitas); ø 36.6 mm, height 4.5 mm; 17 jewels; 21,600 vph
Functions: hours (off-center), minutes, subsidiary seconds
Case: stainless steel, ø 42 mm; sapphire crystal; exhibition window case back; water-resistant to 100 m
Band: rubber, buckle
Price: $1,290
Variations: with silver dial; with stainless steel bracelet

Avalanche Automatic Chronograph

Reference number: AL-700LSS4A6B
Movement: automatic, AL Caliber 750 (base ETA 7750 Valjoux); ø 30 mm, height 7.9 mm; 25 jewels; 28,800 vph
Functions: hours, minutes, subsidiary seconds; chronograph; date
Case: stainless steel, ø 42 mm, bezel with tachymeter scale; sapphire crystal; water-resistant to 100 m
Band: stainless steel, folding clasp
Price: $1,690
Variations: with rubber strap

Startimer Automatic Chronograph

Reference number: AL-750LWW4R16
Movement: automatic, AL Caliber 750 (base ETA Valjoux 7750); ø 30 mm, height 7.9 mm; 25 jewels; 28,800 vph
Functions: hours, minutes, subsidiary seconds; chronograph; date; 24-hour display (second time zone)
Case: stainless steel, ø 42 mm, unidirectionally rotating bezel under crystal settable via crown and with 24-hour scale; sapphire crystal; exhibition window case back; water-resistant to 100 m
Band: leather, buckle
Price: $2,490
Variations: with rubber strap; with stainless steel bracelet

Heritage Chronograph

Reference number: AL-850Pb2S3H16
Movement: automatic, AL Caliber 850 (base ETA 2824-2 with module); ø 28 mm, height 6.1 mm; 37 jewels; 28,800 vph
Functions: hours, minutes, subsidiary seconds; chronograph; date
Case: stainless steel, 45 x 38 mm; sapphire crystal; exhibition window case back; water-resistant to 100 m
Band: leather, buckle
Price: $2,190
Variations: with rubber strap; with stainless steel bracelet

Svend Andersen

The international greats of the watchmaking scene seem to congregate in Geneva to find the horological rush they need to keep their creative juices flowing. One such creative opportunity was without a doubt the founding of the A.H.C.I. (Horological Academy of Independent Creators) in the middle of the 1980s in Geneva — by an Italian and a Dane living in the heart of Switzerland's watchmaking region: Vincent Calabrese and Svend Andersen.

Inventor and watchmaker Svend Andersen spent his formative years at the Danish School of Watchmaking, a school integrated into the Royal Technological Institute of Copenhagen. In 1963, at the age of twenty-one, he went to Switzerland to learn more about the world's finest timepieces. His first job was with Swiss luxury jeweler Gübelin in Lucerne where he worked in after-sales service. Recognizing Andersen's talent for languages, the company sent him to Geneva in 1965 to help out in the store, a gig that ended abruptly in 1969 when Andersen went on television to present a clock in a bottle that he had constructed after working hours. This project served its purpose, however, and Andersen was from then on known as the "watchmaker of the impossible," earning him a job on the Mount Olympus of watchmaking — in one of Patek Philippe's complication ateliers.

In the year 1979, Andersen founded his own workshop in Geneva, notably working on his perpetual flyback. In 1989 Andersen created his first world time watch and christened it Communication. This was followed by the subscription series Communication 24, of which Prince Consort Henrik of Denmark wears number one. Also in 1989 Andersen created the world's smallest calendar watch, a timepiece that was entered into the *Guinness Book of World Records* that year. Nineteen ninety-three saw the advent of Andersen's Perpetual 2000, as he puts it, "the only readable perpetual calendar on the market." The Mundus, a series of twenty-four numbered pieces from 1994, still counts as the thinnest automatic watch available (4.2 mm) and displays world time, various automata (some of them erotic), and some intricate designs based on vintage pocket and wristwatch movements incorporating every complication imaginable.

That time does not focus on just one moment is demonstrated by Andersen's Perpetual Secular Calendar, created in 1996, whose complicated gear train is crowned by a small pinion that turns once every 400 years in order to take into account the suppression of the leap year required to bring the Gregorian calendar in line with the solar year. Allowing precious moments to be documented discretely is the domain of a watch created in 1998 appropriately named Montre à Tact. Here the time is not indicated on the dial, but changes in increments shown in a window placed between the strap lugs. Just how difficult this apparently simple task turned out to be can only be appreciated by a glance inside the movement. The display drum surrounding the movement made winding by crown impossible, which is why Andersen decided to simply move the winding mechanism to the back of the case. He also used this same principle for his Montre avec Date Discrète where the drum features date divisions instead of hours. Due to the absence of a manual winding mechanism, this watch is supplied with a Scatola del Tempo watch winder. The case front, where the dial would normally be located, is available with individual hand engraving upon request.

Last year, the great Dane introduced a watch in homage to the standardized world time created by Sir Sandford Fleming in 1884. Appropriately, Andersen has named his new masterpiece 1884, dedicating the gold rotor to Fleming and including there his name, years of birth and death, bust, and the words "inventor of world time."

Grand Jour et Nuit

Reference number: KW1000SA
Movement: manually wound, Frédéric Piguet Caliber 15;
ø 35.64 mm, height 1.90 mm; 20 jewels; 21,600 vph;
ultra-flat jump hour module added to base movement
Functions: hours, minutes, subsidiary seconds;
day/night indication
Case: white gold, ø 42 mm, height 8 mm; sapphire crystal;
exhibition window case back; water-resistant to 30 m
Band: reptile skin, buckle
Remarks: silver dial with guilloché
Price: $29,000
Variations: in white and rose gold, with black or white dial

Orbita Lunae

Reference number: KW1010SA
Movement: automatic, AS Caliber 1147; ø 29.45 mm,
height 4.60 mm; 17 jewels; 21,600 vph
Functions: hours, minutes, sweep seconds; date, moon phase
Case: white gold, ø 38 mm, height 10 mm; sapphire crystal;
exhibition window case back; water-resistant to 30 m
Band: reptile skin, buckle
Remarks: dial made of blue gold
Price: $16,800
Variations: in rose gold and in two-tone (all $16,800)

Perpetual Secular Calendar

Movement: automatic, Andersen Caliber 423 (base
ETA 2892-3); ø 26.20 mm, height 4.85 mm; 21 jewels;
28,800 vph; power reserve 40 hours; côtes de Genève;
officially certified chronometer (COSC)
Functions: hours, minutes, sweep seconds; perpetual calendar
with date, month, leap year (on back) and secular indication
Case: white gold, ø 40 mm, height 11 mm; sapphire crystal;
exhibition window case back for displays
Band: reptile skin, buckle
Remarks: comes in a watch winder box
Price: $37,500
Variations: in yellow gold ($37,500)

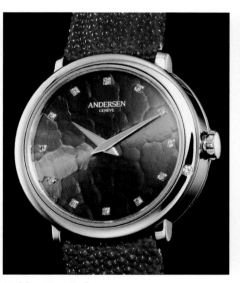

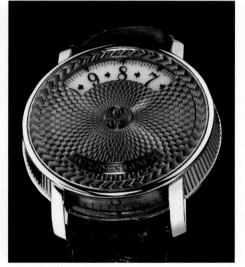

Eros Nature Classic

Reference number: KW1030 SA EROS
Movement: manually wound, Andersen Caliber; ø 28.55
mm, height 5.20 mm; 20 jewels; 18,000 vph; power reserve
46 hours; double gear train for erotic automaton on back
of watch
Functions: hours, minutes, sweep seconds; automaton on
back with erotic scene
Case: yellow gold, ø 38.5 mm, height 12 mm; sapphire
crystal; water-resistant to 30 m
Band: reptile skin, buckle
Remarks: shows automaton erotic scene on back
Price: $35,000

Golden Reminder

Reference number: KW1040SAWGLD
Movement: automatic, Andersen Caliber; ø 26 mm,
height 5.50 mm; 27 jewels; 28,800 vph
Functions: hours, minutes
Case: white gold, ø 36.6 mm, height 10.9 mm;
bidirectionally rotating white gold bezel with one diamond as
reminder; sapphire crystal; exhibition window case back;
water-resistant to 30 m
Band: stingray, buckle
Remarks: blue gold dial with 12 diamond markers
Price: $14,500
Variations: in yellow gold ($14,500)

Montre à Tact

Reference number: KW1020SA
Movement: automatic, AS Caliber 1147C; ø 25.80 mm,
height 4.10 mm; 17 jewels; 21,600 vph; time display also
found in window on side of case
Functions: hours, minutes
Case: white gold, ø 43 mm, height 9.8 mm; two correctors
for time-setting mechanism on case back; sapphire crystal;
water-resistant to 30 m
Band: reptile skin, buckle
Remarks: blue gold dial with guilloché
Price: $29,000
Variations: also available with rose gold guilloché dial

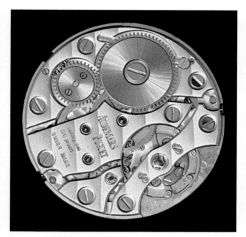

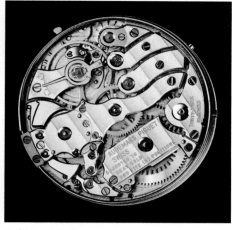

Caliber 3090-3900

Mechanical with manual winding, power reserve 48 hours
Functions: hours, minutes, subsidiary seconds; date; power reserve display
Diameter: 20.8 mm (9'''); **Height:** 4.1 mm; **Jewels:** 24
Balance: Cube (copper-beryllium) with adjustable eccentric weights; **Frequency:** 21,600 vph
Balance spring: flat hairspring with cemented balance spring stud; **Shock protection:** Kif Elastor
Number of individual parts: 177
Remarks: balance bridge; steel parts beveled and polished; base plate with perlage, bridges with *côtes de Genève*
Related calibers: 3090 (subsidiary seconds, height 2.8 mm, 21 jewels); 3091 (hours and minutes only); 3091 SQ (skeletonized)

Caliber 3120

Mechanical with automatic winding, rotor bilaterally winding; power reserve 60 hours
Functions: hours, minutes, sweep seconds; date
Diameter: 26.6 mm
Height: 4.25 mm
Jewels: 40
Balance: Cube (copper-beryllium) with adjustable eccentric weights
Frequency: 21,600 vph
Balance spring: flat hairspring
Shock protection: Kif Elastor
Remarks: balance bridge; rotor made of 22-karat gold; steel parts beveled and polished; base plate with perlage, bridges with *côtes de Genève*

Caliber 2873

Mechanical with manual winding, power reserve 48 hours
Functions: hours, minutes, subsidiary seconds; hour, quarter-hour, and minute repeater with carillon (three gongs)
Diameter: 22.3 mm (10''')
Height: 5 mm
Jewels: 34
Balance: glucydur with compensation screws
Frequency: 21,600 vph
Balance spring: flat hairspring
Shock protection: Kif Elastor
Number of individual parts: 337
Remarks: steel parts beveled and polished; base plate with perlage, bridges with *côtes de Genève*

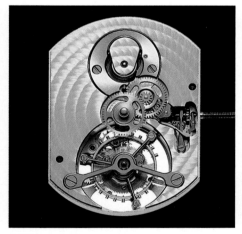

Caliber 2878

Mechanical with manual winding, one-minute tourbillon; power reserve 78 hours
Functions: hours, minutes; power reserve display
Diameter: 27 x 20.3 mm
Height: 6.1 mm
Jewels: 21
Balance: glucydur with four gold screws
Frequency: 21,600 vph
Balance spring: with Breguet terminal curve
Shock protection: Kif Elastor
Number of individual parts: 168
Remarks: steel parts beveled and polished; base plate with perlage, bridges with *côtes de Genève*

Caliber 2879-1

Mechanical with manual winding, one-minute tourbillon; power reserve 70 hours
Functions: hours, minutes, subsidiary seconds; chronograph
Diameter: 29.3mm (12 1/2''')
Height: 7.65 mm
Jewels: 25
Balance: glucydur with four gold screws
Frequency: 21,600 vph
Balance spring: with Breguet terminal curve
Shock protection: Kif Elastor
Number of individual parts: 234
Remarks: steel parts beveled and polished; base plate with perlage, bridges with *côtes de Genève*

Caliber 2885

Mechanical with automatic winding, power reserve 48 hours
Functions: hours, minutes, subsidiary seconds; perpetual calendar (date, day, month, moon phase, leap year indication); hour, quarter-hour, and minute repeater; split-seconds chronograph
Diameter: 31 mm (13 1/2''')
Height: 8.55 mm; **Jewels:** 52
Balance: glucydur with four gold screws
Frequency: 19,800 vph
Balance spring: with Breguet terminal curve
Shock protection: Kif Elastor
Number of individual parts: 648
Remarks: steel parts beveled and polished; base plate with perlage, bridges with *côtes de Genève*

Ball Watch Co.

The pocket watch and ensuing wristwatch industry that sprang up in America had a lot to do with the increasing popularity of trains and their need for precise timing. If an engineer's watch was off, people's lives could be in great danger. A need for great precision was recognized, and all of America's eastern railroad companies agreed upon a uniform time, including dividing the country into time zones, long before this was officially recognized or introduced by the government.

By 1893 many companies had adopted the General Railroad Timepiece Standards. Although these changed from year to year, the Standards included many characteristics found in high-quality Swiss watches: regulation in at least five positions, precision to within 30 seconds in a week, Breguet balance springs, and so on. And an American pocket watch industry emerged that was able to meet these qualifications. One of the chief players in developing these standards, and thus the industry, was Webster Clay Ball, or Webb C. Ball as he preferred to be known. Born in Fredericktown, Ohio, in 1847, Ball grew up on a farm. As a young man, he cast about for a career and became an apprentice to watchmaker George Lewin, the town's jeweler. From there he moved on to a sales position for John Dueber, a manufacturer of watch cases. After purchasing an interest in the firm of Whitcomb and Metten in 1879, he

was quick to buy out Metten, then founding the Whitcomb and Ball Jewelry Store with his new partner. Later the same year, he bought out Whitcomb and established the Webb C. Ball Company in Clevelend, Ohio. The enterprising Ball was the first jeweler to use the time signals of the Naval Observatory in Washington after Standard Time was adopted in 1883, thus bringing precise time to Cleveland. Legend has it that he also imported the first chronometer to Ohio, which he put on display in his store window.

On July 19, 1891, Ball was appointed chief inspector for Lake Shore Lines. He invented a watch inspection system and a set of timepiece guidelines that most American manufacturers set out to meet. Ball ended up being in charge of governing the precision of at least 175,000 miles of railroad, and he also extended his system into Mexico and Canada.

His inspection system was set up to keep records of a watch's performance using standard forms and uniform regulations, carefully supervising railroad time service with the aid of competent watchmakers. His system called for four standard watches to be present on every train, regardless of whether it was the passenger or freight variety. These timepieces were in the possession of the conductor, engineer, fireman, and rear brakeman. The watches were tested every two weeks and compared to standard Washington time. A variation of

more than 30 seconds caused a watch to be sent in and repaired or regulated as necessary.

Adventurous men such as Jim Whittaker, the first American to climb Mount Everest, and Richard Limeburner, a senior research specialist with the U.S. Global Ocean Ecosystems Dynamics, are helping to prove that Ball's tag line "since 1891, accuracy under adverse conditions" is not all marketing. But Ball hardly needs these testimonials. The company has been making quite a name for itself with simple, yet highly effective innovations in their watches: The micro gas tubes featured on Ball's dials, for example, ensure the best night-reading capability currently available, and 2005's TMT model is even outfitted with a mechanical thermometer!

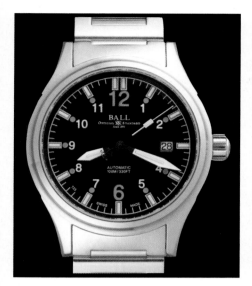

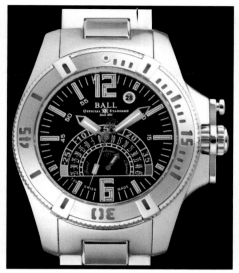

Fireman

Reference number: NM1088C-SJ-BKOR
Movement: automatic, ETA Caliber 2824-2; ø 25.6 mm, height 4.6 mm; 25 jewels; 28,800 vph, 38 hours power reserve
Functions: hours, minutes, sweep seconds; date
Case: stainless steel, ø 40 mm, height 11.1 mm; anti-reflective sapphire crystal; screwed-down case back; screwed-in crown; water-resistant to 100 m
Band: stainless steel, folding clasp
Remarks: 16 micro gas tubes on hands and dial for night-reading capability
Price: $799
Variations: on calf skin strap with buckle

Engineer Hydrocarbon TMT

Reference number: DT1016A-SJ-BK
Movement: automatic, Ball Caliber 9018 (base ETA 2892-A2); ø 25.6 mm, height 5.1 mm; 21 jewels; 28,800 vph, 42 hours power reserve, temperature endurance to -40°C
Functions: hours, minutes, sweep seconds; date; thermometer
Case: stainless steel, ø 40 mm, height 15.2 mm; unidirectionally rotating bezel with 60-minute scale; anti-reflective sapphire crystal; screwed-down case back; screwed-in crown; water-resistant to 300 m
Band: stainless steel, folding clasp
Remarks: 31 micro gas tubes on hands and dial
Price: $2,999

Engineer Master II Telemeter

Reference number: CM1020C-SJ-WH
Movement: automatic, ETA Valjoux Caliber 7750; ø 30 mm, height 7.9 mm; 25 jewels; 28,800 vph; 42 hours power reserve
Functions: hours, minutes, subsidiary seconds; chronograph; date, day
Case: stainless steel, ø 41 mm, height 16.2 mm; anti-reflective sapphire crystal; screwed-down case back; screwed-in crown; water-resistant to 100 m
Band: stainless steel, folding clasp
Remarks: 27 micro gas tubes on hands and dial
Price: $1,129
Variations: on calf skin strap with buckle

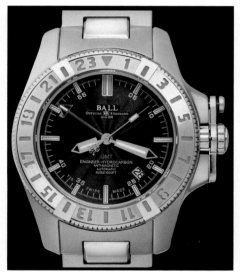

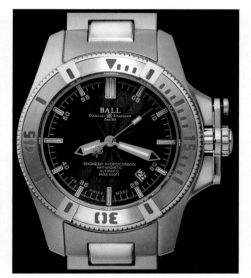

Engineer Hydrocarbon Chronograph

Reference number: DC1016A-SJ-WH
Movement: automatic, ETA Valjoux Caliber 7750; ø 30 mm, height 7.9 mm; 25 jewels; 28,800 vph; 42 hours power reserve; temperature endurance to -40°C
Functions: hours, minutes, subsidiary seconds; chronograph, date, day
Case: titanium, ø 42 mm, height 18.3 mm; unidirectionally rotating bezel with 60-minute scale; anti-reflective sapphire crystal; screwed-down case back; screwed-in crown;
Band: titanium/stainless steel, folding clasp
Remarks: 30 micro gas tubes on hands and dial; anti-magnetic to 12,000 A/m; shock-resistant to 7,500 Gs
Price: $2,399

Engineer Hydrocarbon GMT

Reference number: DG1016A-SJ-BK
Movement: automatic, ETA Caliber 2893-2; ø 25.6 mm, height 4.1 mm; 25 jewels; 28,800 vph, 42 hours power reserve; temperature endurance to -40°C
Functions: hours, minutes, sweep seconds; date, 2nd time zone
Case: stainless steel, ø 40 mm, height 14.1 mm; unidirectionally rotating bezel with 24-hour scale; anti-reflective sapphire crystal; screwed-down case back; screwed-in crown; water-resistant to 300 m
Band: stainless steel, folding clasp
Remarks: 17 micro gas tubes on hands and dial; anti-magnetic to 12,000 A/m; shock-resistant to 7,500 Gs
Price: $2,099

Engineer Hydrocarbon Classic

Reference number: DM1016A-SJ-BK
Movement: automatic, ETA Caliber 2892-A2; ø 25.6 mm, height 3.6 mm; 21 jewels; 28,800 vph, 42 hours power reserve; temperature endurance to -40°C
Functions: hours, minutes, sweep seconds; date
Case: stainless steel, ø 40 mm, height 14.1 mm; unidirectionally rotating bezel with 60-minute scale; anti-reflective sapphire crystal; screwed-down case back; screwed-in crown; water-resistant to 300 m
Band: stainless steel, folding clasp
Remarks: 16 micro gas tubes on hands and dial; anti-magnetic to 12,000 A/m; shock-resistant to 7,500 Gs
Price: $1,679

Trainmaster TMT

Reference number: NT1050D-SAJ-BK
Movement: automatic, Ball Caliber 9018 (base ETA 2892-A2); ø 25.6 mm, height 5.1 mm; 21 jewels; 28,800 vph, 42 hours power reserve;
Functions: hours, minutes, sweep seconds; date, thermometer
Case: stainless steel, ø 41 mm, height 12.6 mm; anti-reflective sapphire crystal; screwed-down exhibition case back; screwed-in crown; water-resistant to 50 m
Band: stainless steel, folding clasp
Remarks: 37 micro gas tubes on hands and dial for night reading capability; shock-resistant to 5000 Gs
Price: $2,799

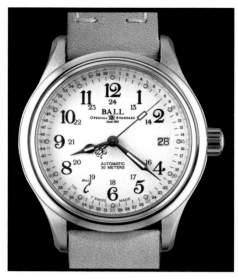

Trainmaster 60 Seconds

Reference number: NM1038D-LJ-WH
Movement: automatic, ETA Caliber 2892-A2; ø 25.6 mm, height 3.6 mm; 21 jewels; 28,800 vph, 42 hours power reserve
Functions: hours, minutes, sweep seconds; date
Case: stainless steel, ø 38,3 mm, height 10.6 mm; anti-reflective sapphire crystal; screwed-down exhibition case back; screwed-in crown; water-resistant to 100 m
Band: leather, buckle
Remarks: 15 micro gas tubes on hands and dial for night-reading capability
Price: $1,199
Variations: stainless steel bracelet with folding clasp

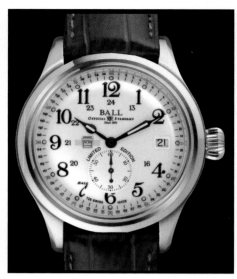

Trainmaster Louisville & Indiana RR Limited Edition

Reference number: NM1050D-L1J-WH
Movement: automatic, ETA Caliber 2895-2; ø 25.6 mm, height 4.35 mm; 30 jewels; 28,800 vph, 42 hours power reserve
Functions: hours, minutes, subsidiary seconds; date
Case: stainless steel, ø 41 mm, height 11.5 mm; anti-reflective sapphire crystal; exhibition case back; screwed-in crown; water-resistant to 50 m
Band: crocodile skin, buckle
Remarks: limited edition of 333 pieces; 14 micro gas tubes on hands and dial; shock-resistant to 5000 Gs
Price: $2,299

Trainmaster Pulsemaster

Reference number: CM10101D-LJ-WH
Movement: automatic, ETA Valjoux Caliber 7750; ø 30 mm, height 7.9 mm; 25 jewels; 28,800 vph, 42 hours power reserve
Functions: hours, minutes, sweep seconds; chronograph; date, day
Case: stainless steel, ø 41 mm, height 14.4 mm; anti-reflective sapphire crystal; exhibition case back; screwed-in crown; water-resistant to 50 m
Band: leather, buckle
Remarks: 18 micro gas tubes on hands and dial for night reading capability; shock-resistant to 5000 Gs
Price: $1,849
Variations: stainless steel bracelet with folding clasp

Trainmaster Voyager GMT

Reference number: GM1050D-L1AJ-BK
Movement: automatic, ETA Caliber 2893-2; ø 25.6 mm, height 4.1 mm; 25 jewels; 28,800 vph, 42 hours power reserve
Functions: hours, minutes, sweep seconds; date, second time zone
Case: stainless steel, ø 41 mm, height 12.5 mm; anti-reflective sapphire crystal; exhibition case back; screwed-in crown; water-resistant to 100 m
Band: leather, buckle
Remarks: 33 micro gas tubes on hands and dial for night-reading capability; shock-resistant to 5000 Gs
Price: $1,599
Variations: stainless steel bracelet with folding clasp

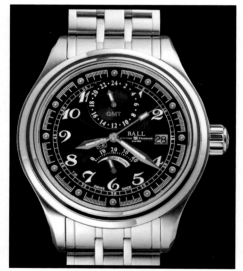

Trainmaster Voyager Power Reserve

Reference number: GM1050D-SJ-BK
Movement: automatic, Ball Caliber 9035 (base ETA 2892-A2); ø 25.6 mm, height 5.1 mm; 21 jewels; 28,800 vph, 42 hours power reserve
Functions: hours, minutes, sweep seconds; date, second time zone; power reserve display
Case: stainless steel, ø 41 mm, height 12.6 mm; anti-reflective sapphire crystal; exhibition case back; screwed-in crown; water-resistant to 50 m
Band: stainless steel, folding clasp
Remarks: 17 micro gas tubes on hands and dial for night-reading capability; shock-resistant to 5000 Gs
Price: $2,289

Trainmaster Voyager Dual Time
Reference number: GM1056D-LJ-BK
Movement: automatic, Ball Caliber 651 (base ETA 2892-A2); ø 25.6 mm, height 5.1 mm; 21 jewels; 28,800 vph, 42 hours power reserve
Functions: hours, minutes, sweep seconds; date, second time zone
Case: stainless steel, ø 41 mm, height 12.6 mm; anti-reflective sapphire crystal; exhbition case back; screwed-in crown
Band: leather, buckle
Remarks: 30 micro gas tubes on hands and dial for night-reading capability; shock-resistant to 5000 Gs
Price: $2,439

Engineer II Arabic
Reference number: NM1016C-S1AJ-BK
Movement: automatic, ETA Caliber 2836-2; ø 25.6 mm, height 5.05 mm; 25 jewels; 28,800 vph, 38 hours power reserve
Functions: hours, minutes, sweep seconds; date, day
Case: stainless steel, ø 38 mm, height 13 mm; anti-reflective sapphire crystal; screwed-down case back; screwed-in crown; water-resistant to 100 m
Band: stainless steel, folding clasp
Remarks: 27 micro gas tubes on hands and dial for night-reading capability; anti-magnetic to 4,800 A/m; shock-resistant to 5000 Gs
Price: $1,129

Engineer II Ohio
Reference number: NM1026C-LJ-BK
Movement: automatic, ETA Caliber 2824-2; ø 25.6 mm, height 4.6 mm; 25 jewels; 28,800 vph, 38 hours power reserve
Functions: hours, minutes, sweep seconds; date
Case: stainless steel, ø 38 mm, height 13.1 mm; anti-reflective sapphire crystal; screwed-down case back; screwed-in crown; water-resistant to 100 m
Band: crocodile skin, buckle
Remarks: 15 micro gas tubes on hands and dial for night-reading capability; anti-magnetic to 4,800 A/m; shock-resistant to 5000 Gs
Price: S899

Engineer Master II Chronometer
Reference number: NM1020C-LCAJ-SL
Movement: automatic, ETA Caliber 2824-2; ø 25.6 mm, height 4.6 mm; 25 jewels; 28,800 vph, 38 hours power reserve; officially certified chronometer (COSC)
Functions: hours, minutes, sweep seconds, date
Case: stainless steel, ø 40 mm, height 13 mm; anti-reflective sapphire crystal; screwed-down case back; screwed-in crown
Band: leather, buckle
Remarks: 27 micro gas tubes on hands and dial for night-reading capability; anti-magnetic to 4,800 A/m; shock-resistant to 5000 Gs
Price: $1,559
Variations: stainless steel bracelet with folding clasp

Conductor Chronograph Limited Edition
Reference number: CM1068D-LJ-BK
Movement: automatic, ETA Valjoux Caliber 7750; ø 30 mm, height 7.9 mm; 25 jewels; 28,800 vph, 42 hours power reserve
Functions: hours, minutes, sweep seconds; chronograph; date, day
Case: stainless steel, 38.5 x 51 mm, height 16.8 mm; anti-reflective sapphire crystal; exhibition case back; screwed-in crown; water-resistant to 50 m
Band: crocodile skin, buckle
Remarks: limited edition of 1,920 pieces; 18 micro gas tubes on hands and dial; shock-resistant to 5000 Gs
Price: $2,429
Variations: stainless steel bracelet with folding clasp

Conductor GMT Limited Edition
Reference number: GM1072D-SAJ-BK
Movement: automatic, ETA Caliber 2893-2; ø 25.6 mm, height 4.1 mm; 25 jewels; 28,800 vph, 42 hours power reserve
Functions: hours, minutes, sweep seconds; date, second time zone
Case: stainless steel, 35.5 x 47.5 mm, height 12.2 mm; anti-reflective sapphire crystal; exhibition case back; screwed-in crown; water-resistant to 50 m
Band: stainless steel, folding clasp
Remarks: limited edition of 1,920 pieces; 37 micro gas tubes on hands and dial for night-reading capability
Price: $2,299
Variations: crocodile skin strap with buckle

Baume & Mercier

The traditional brand Baume & Mercier, which celebrated its 175th anniversary in 2005, has experienced a remarkable amount of change in recent years. This Genevan brand has always belonged to the type of company to offer great diversity in their collection, from chronographs to diamond-studded timepieces. However, Baume & Mercier has often been judged by the consumer to be more of a producer of conservative watches — as connoisseurs of the brand can attest, an opinion that is quite wrong.

It is a fact that classic gold wristwatches have often left the workshops in Geneva and Switzerland's Jura region, for years belonging to the brand's most reliable and important bearers of turnover. Regardless, Baume & Mercier has always developed individual and imaginative products, especially where new case shapes are concerned.

The model family CapeLand, launched in 1997 and comprising round wristwatches, and the rectangular line Hampton, named after the Long Island bathing scene north of New York, have been successful for years and have as their target audience a fully different, younger set of consumers.

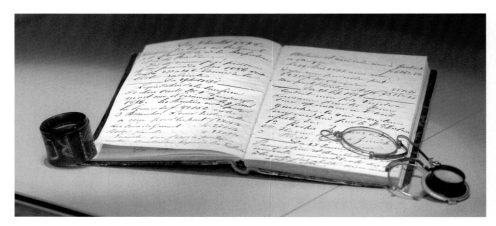

Additionally, the brand is constantly adding new variations to its two most important watch lines so that they remain highly recognizable.

The collection was enriched with the addition of a new model called the Hampton Chronograph, for example, a wristwatch combining both size and grace, two attributes that don't usually go together, in a completely attractive way. The CapeLand diver's watch, as another example, with its luminous yellow dial obviously appeals to consumers not interested in more simple automatic watches. Unusual combinations of case materials such as the ultra-light grey metal titanium and shiny, polished stainless steel tend to heighten acceptance for men under the age of forty, while young women are quite hip to Miss Protocole. This model is outfitted with an extra-long strap that is wrapped around the wrist several times and is easy to change.

Despite the somewhat prevalent sporty, masculine attitude, the elegance one has come to expect from Baume & Mercier has not been shortchanged and is achieved by a clever synthesis of shaped aesthetics and functionality — something that is very obviously the maxim when designing every new model.

The brand's youthful boss, Michel Nieto, has been careful to make sure that this old brand doesn't lose its ties to its roots. While other watch brands contain their grand treasure of historical models in well cared-for company museums, when making preparations for the anniversary year Nieto soon discovered to his dismay that Baume & Mercier has absolutely nothing along these lines. With a great deal of financial and organizational effort as well as worldwide searches, he was able to get an impressive collection of early products originally put on the market by Baume & Mercier together. This collection of timepieces through the ages, which feels quite like an old diary, provides a great deal of knowledge regarding the old days of the company and simultaneously represents a bridge between its 175-year-old history and the modern creativity of Baume & Mercier in the twenty-first century. And Michel Nieto is justifiably proud — of both.

Hampton Milleis

Reference number: MOA08245
Movement: automatic, BM Caliber 8395 (base ETA 2000-1);
ø 20 mm, height 3.6 mm; 20 jewels; 28,800 vph
Functions: hours, minutes; date
Case: yellow gold, 26 x 40 mm, height 9 mm;
sapphire crystal
Band: reptile skin, folding clasp
Price: $3,495
Variations: with quartz movement; small model (quartz)

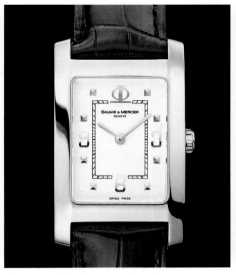

Hampton Classic

Reference number: MOA08435
Movement: quartz, BM Caliber 5001 (base ETA 901.001)
Functions: hours, minutes
Case: yellow gold, 24 x 40 mm, height 7 mm;
sapphire crystal
Band: reptile skin, buckle
Price: $2,695
Variations: small model

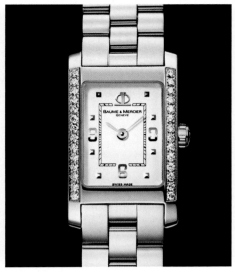

Hampton Classic

Reference number: MOA08407
Movement: quartz, BM Caliber 5001 (base ETA 901.001)
Functions: hours, minutes
Case: stainless steel, 22 x 34 mm, height 7 mm;
bezel set with 28 brilliant-cut diamonds; sapphire crystal
Band: stainless steel, folding clasp
Price: $2,995
Variations: without brilliant-cut diamonds

Hampton Milleis XL

Reference number: MOA08442
Movement: automatic, BM Caliber 11892-2 (base ETA
2892-2); ø 26.2 mm, height 3.6 mm; 21 jewels; 28,800 vph
Functions: hours, minutes, sweep seconds; date
Case: stainless steel, 30 x 46.5 mm, height 11 mm;
sapphire crystal; water-resistant to 50 m
Band: reptile skin, folding clasp
Price: $2,195
Variations: with stainless steel bracelet; with black dial and
brown leather strap

Hampton Classic Square Chronograph

Reference number: MOA08607
Movement: automatic, BM Caliber 122894 (base ETA
2894-2); ø 28 mm, height 6.1 mm; 37 jewels; 28,800 vph
Functions: hours, minutes, subsidiary seconds;
chronograph; date
Case: stainless steel, 34 x 45 mm, height 11.2 mm; sapphire
crystal; exhibition window case back; water-resistant to 50 m
Band: reptile skin, folding clasp
Price: $2,895
Variations: with black dial and brown leather strap

Hampton Classic Square

Reference number: MOA08605
Movement: automatic, BM Caliber 11824 (base ETA
2824-2); ø 25.6 mm, height 4.6 mm; 25 jewels; 28,800 vph
Functions: hours, minutes, sweep seconds; date
Case: stainless steel, 34 x 45 mm, height 10.6 mm;
sapphire crystal; water-resistant to 50 m
Band: reptile skin, folding clasp
Price: $1,795
Variations: with white dial and stainless steel bracelet

Riviera

Reference number: MOA08593
Movement: automatic, BM Caliber 11892-2 (base ETA 2892-2); ø 26.2 mm, height 3.6 mm; 21 jewels; 28,800 vph
Functions: hours, minutes, sweep seconds; date
Case: stainless steel, ø 38 mm, height 8.6 mm; sapphire crystal; water-resistant to 50m
Band: stainless steel, folding clasp
Price: $2,295
Variations: in steel/yellow gold; with quartz movement

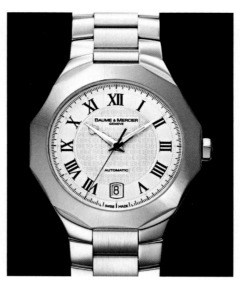

Classima Executives

Reference number: MOA08160
Movement: automatic, BM Caliber 11892-2 (base ETA 2892-2); ø 26.2 mm, height 3.6 mm; 21 jewels; 28,800 vph
Functions: hours, minutes, sweep seconds; date
Case: yellow gold, ø 33 mm, height 7 mm; sapphire crystal
Band: reptile skin, buckle
Price: $2,695
Variations: with quartz movement

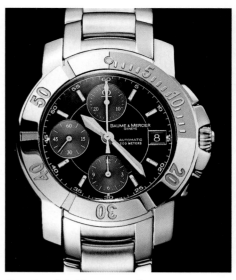

CapeLand S Chronograph

Reference number: MOA08502
Movement: automatic, BM Caliber 13750 (base ETA 7750); ø 30.4 mm, height 7.9 mm; 25 jewels; 28,800 vph
Functions: hours, minutes, subsidiary seconds; chronograph; date
Case: stainless steel, ø 41 mm, height 17 mm; unidirectionally rotating bezel; sapphire crystal; screwed-in crown; water-resistant to 200 m
Band: stainless steel, security folding clasp
Price: $2,995
Variations: with various dials; with rubber strap; in stainless steel/titanium

CapeLand S Ladies

Reference number: MOA08381
Movement: quartz, BM Caliber 10425 (base ETA 955.412)
Functions: hours, minutes, sweep seconds; date
Case: stainless steel, ø 36 mm, height 13.5 mm; bezel set with 36 brilliant-cut diamonds; sapphire crystal; screwed-in crown; water-resistant to 100 m
Band: reptile skin, folding clasp
Price: $4,995

Diamant

Reference number: MOA08568
Movement: quartz, BM Caliber 7425 (base ETA 956.112)
Functions: hours, minutes; date
Case: stainless steel, 22.6 x 34.3 mm, height 8.4 mm; sapphire crystal; oval crown set with one diamond
Band: stainless steel, folding clasp
Price: $1,395
Variations: set with 14 brilliant-cut diamonds; with lizard skin strap

Diamant

Reference number: MOA08600
Movement: quartz, BM Caliber 7425 (base ETA 956.112)
Functions: hours, minutes; date
Case: stainless steel/yellow gold, 22.6 x 34.3 mm, height 8.4 mm; sapphire crystal; oval crown set with one diamond
Band: stainless steel/yellow gold, folding clasp
Price: $1,995
Variations: set with 14 brilliant-cut diamonds

Riviera Chronograph XXL
Reference number: MOA08594
Movement: automatic, BM Caliber 13750 (base ETA 7750); ø 30.4 mm, height 7.9 mm; 25 jewels; 28,800 vph
Functions: hours, minutes, subsidiary seconds; chronograph; date
Case: stainless steel, ø 43 mm, height 14 mm; sapphire crystal; screwed-in crown; water-resistant to 100 m
Band: rubber, security folding clasp
Price: $2,895
Variations: with white dial

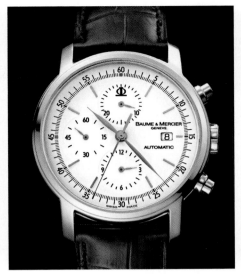

Classima Executives Chronograph XL
Reference number: MOA08620
Movement: automatic, BM Caliber 13753 (base ETA 7753); ø 30.4 mm, height 7.9 mm; 27 jewels; 28,800 vph
Functions: hours, minutes, subsidiary seconds; chronograph; date
Case: stainless steel, ø 39 mm, height 16.7 mm; sapphire crystal; screwed-in crown
Band: reptile skin, buckle
Price: $2,495
Variations: with black dial

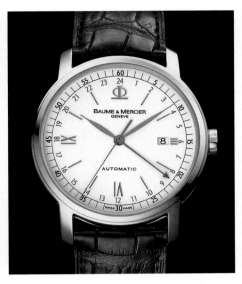

Classima Executives Chronograph XL
Reference number: MOA08591
Movement: automatic, BM Caliber 13750 (base ETA 7750); ø 30.4 mm, height 7.9 mm; 25 jewels; 28,800 vph
Functions: hours, minutes, subsidiary seconds; chronograph; date
Case: stainless steel, ø 42 mm, height 13.5 mm; sapphire crystal; screwed-in crown
Band: reptile skin, folding clasp
Price: $2,295
Variations: with black dial and brown leather strap

Classima Executives GMT XL
Reference number: MOA08462
Movement: automatic, BM Caliber 11893-2 (base ETA 2893-2); ø 26.2 mm, height 3.6 mm; 21 jewels; 28,800 vph
Functions: hours, minutes, sweep seconds; date; 24-hour display (second time zone)
Case: stainless steel, ø 42 mm, height 9.4 mm; sapphire crystal
Band: reptile skin, buckle
Price: $1,795

Classima Executives XL
Reference number: MOA08590
Movement: automatic, BM Caliber 11824 (base ETA 2824-2); ø 25.6 mm, height 4.6 mm; 25 jewels; 28,800 vph
Functions: hours, minutes, sweep seconds; date
Case: stainless steel, ø 42 mm, height 9.6 mm; sapphire crystal
Band: reptile skin, buckle
Price: $1,595
Variations: with black dial and black leather strap, quartz movement

Classima Executives XL
Reference number: MOA08461
Movement: manually wound, BM Caliber 16498 (base ETA 6498-2); ø 37.2 mm, height 4.2 mm; 17 jewels; 21,600 vph
Functions: hours, minutes, subsidiary seconds
Case: stainless steel, ø 42 mm, height 9.4 mm; sapphire crystal; sapphire crystal case back
Band: reptile skin, buckle
Price: $1,995

Bell & Ross

The tender beginnings of the French brand Bell & Ross lie several years in the past, and even though no one in the Parisian company headquarters plays with the thought of making the brand into an independent *manufacture*, the expertise now shown in the realization of new watch models is one born of experience and routine. And since the solvent perfume and fashion specialist Chanel has bought into the company, Bell & Ross also has its own production facilities in La Chaux-de-Fonds, a fact which has opened all pathways for designer Bruno Belamich and his team for somewhat more difficult or lavish designs. When founding his company, Carlos A. Rosillo was well aware of the risks of an entrepreneurial solo run, particularly since he had a clear idea of what "his" watch collection should be: The best materials, high-quality workmanship, and unconditional reliability and precision pretty much outlined Bell & Ross's fundamentals, and nothing less would do for the brand with the stylized ampersand (&) as its trademark. The short English-language name perfectly expressed the professional, instrument-like character of the watches

that had until then existed only in technical drawings. Right from the beginning Belamich showed a sure hand regarding technical features and aesthetic proportions, and what differentiates Bell & Ross from other manufacturers of so-called professional instruments is the absolutely attractive look of its watches, tactfully positioned between striking and martial while never being just functional, with all due respect to functionality, but also innovative in their visuals.

Instrument BRO1 is the name of the new product line by Bell & Ross, and in fact, it really is an impressive instrument — an airplane cockpit board instrument, to be more precise. The square case with its four visible screw heads is reminiscent of the frame of a cockpit instrument, and that is of course absolutely the goal — a goal that makes the watch seem even more massive on the wrist than it really is, even though 46 mm is still quite large.

Right from the beginning BRO1 has been available as a chronograph (ETA Caliber 2894) or as a simple three-hand watch, the latter also available with large date or power reserve display. The stainless steel

case is provided with a satin finish with polished edges or completely in matte black. The choice of dial colors is galvanic black or silver, each in combination with luminous hands and hour markers. With the advent of Instrument BRO1 the French brand is announcing its frontal attack on the wrists of professionals and scene followers alike, for the new watches are in fact as robust as they look after having undergone innumerable tests — something that certainly makes their attractiveness to watch fans outside of pilot's and nostalgic war circles even stronger. The watch also comes with its own tools to work on the strap lugs. In this way the watch can be set up on a desk or screwed onto a dashboard in addition to being worn as a wristwatch. Funny that no one else has come up with this idea yet ...

Vintage 123 Jump Hour

Movement: automatic, ETA Caliber 2892-A2, modified; ø 25.6 mm, height 3.6 mm; 30 jewels; 28,800 vph
Functions: hours (digital, jump), minutes; power reserve indicator
Case: rose gold, ø 37.5 mm, height 12 mm; sapphire crystal; exhibition window case back; screwed-in crown; water-resistant to 100 m
Band: reptile skin, double folding clasp
Remarks: limited to 99 pieces
Price: $11,900

Vintage 126 Large Annual Date

Movement: automatic, ETA Caliber 2894-2, modified; ø 28.6 mm, height 6.1 mm; 49 jewels; 28,800 vph
Functions: hours, minutes, subsidiary seconds; chronograph; annual calendar with large date and month
Case: rose gold, ø 39 mm, height 15 mm; sapphire crystal; exhibition window case back; screwed-in crown; water-resistant to 200 m
Band: reptile skin, double folding clasp
Remarks: limited to 99 pieces
Price: $12,900

BR01 Instrument

Reference number: BR01-94
Movement: automatic, ETA Caliber 2894-2; ø 28.6 mm, height 6.1 mm; 37 jewels; 28,800 vph
Functions: hours, minutes, subsidiary seconds; chronograph; date
Case: stainless steel, PVD-coated black, 46 x 46 mm, height 11.5 mm; bezel on monocoque case secured with 4 screws; sapphire crystal; screwed-in crown; water-resistant to 100 m
Band: textile, velcro clasp, also comes with leather strap
Price: $5,200
Variations: as three-hand watch, or with a choice of large date or power reserve display; without black PVD coating

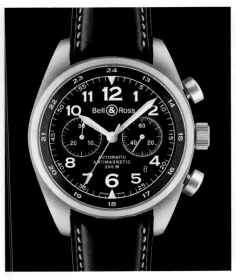

Vintage 126 XL

Movement: automatic, ETA Caliber 2894-2; ø 28.6 mm, height 6.1 mm; 37 jewels; 28,800 vph
Functions: hours, minutes, subsidiary seconds; chronograph
Case: stainless steel, ø 42.5 mm, height 16 mm; sapphire crystal; exhibition window case back; screwed-in crown; water-resistant to 200 m
Band: leather, double folding clasp
Price: $3,500

Military 126

Movement: automatic, ETA Caliber 2894-2; ø 28.6 mm, height 6.1 mm; 37 jewels; 28,800 vph
Functions: hours, minutes, subsidiary seconds; chronograph; date
Case: stainless steel, ø 39 mm, height 15 mm; sapphire crystal; exhibition window case back; screwed-in crown; water-resistant to 100 m
Band: leather, buckle
Remarks: limited to 999 pieces
Price: $3,250

Geneva 123

Movement: automatic, ETA Caliber 2895-1; ø 26.2 mm, height 4.35 mm; 30 jewels; 28,800 vph
Functions: hours, minutes, subsidiary seconds; date
Case: stainless steel, ø 37.5 mm, height 11.5 mm; sapphire crystal; case back with small exhibition window; screwed-in crown; water-resistant to 100 m
Band: alligator skin, double folding clasp
Remarks: limited to 500 pieces
Price: $2,100
Variations: with stainless steel bracelet ($2,600)

Classic Pilot 10th Anniversary

Movement: automatic, ETA Caliber 2894-2; ø 28.6 mm, height 6.1 mm; 37 jewels; 28,800 vph

Functions: hours, minutes, subsidiary seconds; chronograph; date

Case: stainless steel, ø 41 mm, height 14 mm; bidirectionally rotating bezel with 60-minute divisions; sapphire crystal; screwed-in crown; water-resistant to 100 m

Band: stainless steel, double folding clasp

Price: $4,500

Variations: with alligator skin strap ($4,000)

Classic Pilot Sapphire

Movement: automatic, ETA Caliber 2894-2; ø 28.6 mm, height 6.1 mm; 37 jewels; 28,800 vph

Functions: hours, minutes, subsidiary seconds; chronograph; date

Case: stainless steel, ø 41 mm, height 13.8 mm; bidirectionally rotating bezel with 60-minute divisions; sapphire crystal; screwed-in crown and buttons; water-resistant to 200 m

Band: calfskin, double folding clasp

Price: $3,350

Variations: with stainless steel bracelet ($3,950)

Function Index

Movement: quartz, ETA Caliber 988.431/988.432; multifunctional electronic module with LCD display integrated into the dial

Functions: hours, minutes; chronograph; perpetual calendar with date, day calendar week, month, leap year, second time zone; alarm and countdown

Case: stainless steel, ø 37.5 mm, height 11.5 mm; sapphire crystal; screwed-in crown; water-resistant to 100 m

Band: rubber, folding clasp

Price: $1,850

Variations: with calfskin strap ($1,950); with stainless steel bracelet ($2,450)

Grand Prix

Movement: automatic, ETA Caliber 7750 Valjoux; ø 30 mm, height 7.9 mm; 25 jewels; 28,800 vph

Functions: hours, minutes, subsidiary seconds; chronograph; date

Case: stainless steel, ø 41 mm, height 16 mm; sapphire crystal; recessed crown (T-Crown system), flat buttons; water-resistant to 200 m

Band: rubber, double folding clasp

Price: $2,500

Variations: with stainless steel bracelet ($2,600)

Mystery Diamond

Movement: automatic, ETA Caliber 2892-A2, modified; ø 25.6 mm, height 3.6 mm; 21 jewels; 28,800 vph; disk display with diamond set as hour marker

Functions: hours, minutes

Case: white gold, ø 34 mm, height 9.4 mm; bezel set with 40 brilliant-cut diamonds; sapphire crystal; exhibition window case back; water-resistant to 50 m

Band: alligator skin, folding clasp

Price: $14,900

Variations: in 18-karat yellow gold with row of diamonds ($13,600); in polished steel on alligator skin strap or stainless steel bracelet (from $2,900 to $9,000)

Medium 34 Automatic

Movement: automatic, ETA Caliber 2892-A2; ø 25.6 mm, height 3.6 mm; 21 jewels; 28,800 vph

Functions: hours, minutes; date

Case: stainless steel, ø 34 mm, height 9.4 mm; sapphire crystal; exhibition window case back; water-resistant to 100 m

Band: calfskin, folding clasp

Price: $2,000

Variations: on alligator skin strap ($2,100) or stainless steel bracelet ($2,600)

Golfing

On the World's
Most
Exceptional
Courses

MARK ROWLINSON

The latest volume in Abbeville's best-selling
Exceptional Destinations series

Golfing
on the World's Most Exceptional Courses
Illustrated with over one hundred inviting photographs, this is
the ultimate guide to twenty-five of the world's top golfing
vacations, selected for their awesome locations, venerable
traditions, notable course design, and first-rate
accommodations.

By Mark Rowlinson
100 full-color illustrations
160 pages · 8 1/4 × 9 1/2 in. · Cloth
ISBN 0-7892-0866-0 · $29.95

Ernst Benz

Swiss engineer and inventor Ernst Benz is also a pilot and gliding enthusiast. As such, he was always well aware of the necessity for accurate and instantly legible instruments while in the air. The Benz Micro aircraft chronograph he designed was in fact so successful that it is presently standard equipment in many single-engine planes, military trainers, jets, and sailplanes, with more than one thousand in daily use globally.

As the cockpit of a glider or sailplane is limited in space, but the need for accurate timekeeping remains critical, Benz decided to design a large-format, automatic-winding chronograph after receiving many inquiries from fellow pilots. Previously relying on ETA to supply him with the trustworthy movements to power his navigational instruments, he once again turned to the world's largest supplier of mechanical movements to furnish the energy for these instruments for the wrist. Being both Swiss and a pilot, he knows how important precision timing is. At the beginning, he produced some watches in very limited quantities, noticing that Swiss and German pilots, yachtsmen, and rally and race car drivers were utilizing them more than anyone else.

His signature 47 mm timepieces were originally introduced in two lines known as the Great Circle Chronograph and the Sports Watch. The response he had received from fellow aviators for the large-format timepiece was overwhelming, and his timepieces went into limited-quantity series.

After a short time, the Great Circle was rechristened the ChronoScope, and its success spawned a number of siblings including the ChronoSport and the Chrono-Lunar, a complete calendar chronograph including moon phase and 24-hour display. ChronoJewel was soon to follow, combining the sporty good looks of the large pilot's watch with bezels set with brilliant-cut diamonds ranging from a total of 1.25 to 5 full carats. The year 2005 saw the advent of the first traditionally sized line of Ernst Benz watches, a direct answer to the now more frequent request for medium-sized wristwatches. The 40 mm series certainly appeals to a more feminine wrist searching for the same oversized look as its masculine counterparts.

Now under new ownership, the quality Ernst Benz collections have been redivided into three obvious families: Traditional, Contemporary, and Diamond. Not only that, but the new ChronoFlite model, a GMT timepiece featuring a rotating bezel with a 24-hour scale, is currently being delivered to Ernst Benz dealers throughout North America. The ChronoDiver, also recently introduced, was going into production at the company's factory in Biel, Switzerland, in the fall of 2005.

Next up for this busy brand is a series of 36 mm timepieces in numerous variations including mother-of-pearl and diamond-set dials with optional diamond bezels for female watch fans. And the creativity certainly won't be stopping there: Now owned and managed by a third-generation watchmaker with an extreme amount of experience in vintage pieces, Ernst Benz will certainly be coming up with some real surprises in the near future — the horological connoisseur can rest assured of that.

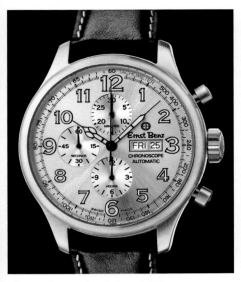

ChronoScope Traditional 47 mm

Reference number: GC 10113
Movement: automatic, ETA Valjoux Caliber 7750; ø 30 mm, height 7.9 mm; 25 jewels; 28,800 vph
Functions: hours, minutes, subsidiary seconds; date, day, chronograph
Case: stainless steel, ø 47 mm, height 16 mm; sapphire crystal; screwed-down exhibition case back; water-resistant to 50 m
Band: leather, buckle
Price: $2,295
Variations: black or white dial; on stainless steel bracelet ($2,495) or alligator skin strap; in 40 mm size

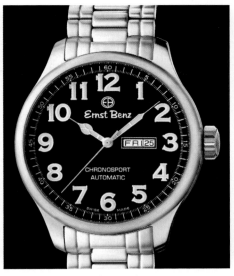

ChronoSport Traditional 47 mm

Reference number: GC 10211B
Movement: automatic, ETA Caliber 2836-2; ø 25.6 mm, height 4.6 mm; 25 jewels; 28,800 vph
Functions: hours, minutes, sweep seconds; date, day
Case: stainless steel, ø 47 mm, height 14 mm; sapphire crystal; screwed-down exhibition case back; water-resistant to 50 m
Band: stainless steel, folding clasp
Price: $1,495
Variations: white or copper-colored dial; on alligator skin strap; in 40 mm size ($1,395)

ChronoLunar 47 mm

Reference number: GC 10312
Movement: automatic, ETA Valjoux Caliber 7751; ø 30 mm, height 7.9 mm; 25 jewels; 28,800 vph
Functions: hours, minutes, subsidiary seconds; date, day, month, moon phase; chronograph; 24-hour display
Case: stainless steel, ø 47 mm, height 16.3 mm; sapphire crystal; screwed-down exhibition case back; water-resistant to 50 m
Band: alligator skin, buckle
Price: $3,695
Variations: black dial; on stainless steel bracelet; in 40 mm size ($3,595)

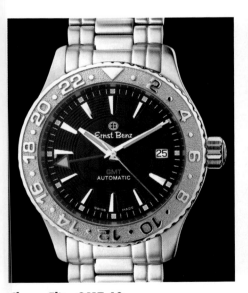

ChronoFlite GMT 40 mm

Reference number: GC 20521B
Movement: automatic, ETA Caliber 2893-2; ø 25.6 mm, height 4.1 mm; 21 jewels; 28,800 vph
Functions: hours, minutes, sweep seconds; date; second time zone
Case: stainless steel, ø 40 mm, height 11.2 mm; unidirectionally rotating bezel with 24-hour scale; sapphire crystal; screwed-down exhibition case back; water-resistant to 50 m
Band: stainless steel, folding clasp
Price: $1,995
Variations: silver dial; on a leather strap ($1,795)

ChronoSport Contemporary 40 mm

Reference number: GC 20222
Movement: automatic, ETA Caliber 2836-2; ø 25.6 mm, height 4.6 mm; 25 jewels; 28,800 vph
Functions: hours, minutes, sweep seconds; date, day
Case: stainless steel, ø 40 mm, height 13 mm; sapphire crystal; screwed-down exhibition case back; water-resistant to 50 m
Band: leather, buckle
Price: $1,295
Variations: black dial; on stainless steel bracelet or alligator skin strap; in 47 mm size ($1,395)

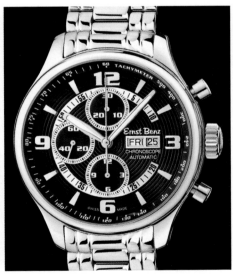

ChronoScope Contemporary 47 mm

Reference number: GC 10121 B
Movement: automatic, ETA Valjoux Caliber 7750; ø 30 mm, height 7.9 mm; 25 jewels; 28,800 vph
Functions: hours, minutes, subsidiary seconds; chronograph; date, day
Case: stainless steel, ø 47 mm, height 16 mm; sapphire crystal; screwed-down exhibition case back; water-resistant to 50 m
Band: stainless steel, folding clasp
Price: $2,695
Variations: white dial; on leather or alligator skin strap; in 40 mm size ($2,595)

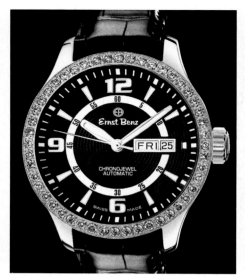

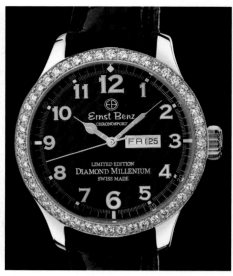

Diamond ChronoScope 40 mm

Reference number: GC 20113D

Movement: automatic, ETA Valjoux Caliber 7750; ø 30 mm, height 7.9 mm; 25 jewels; 28,800 vph

Functions: hours, minutes, subsidiary seconds; chronograph; date, day

Case: stainless steel, ø 40 mm, height 15.8 mm; bezel set with 48 brilliant-cut diamonds (1.25 ct); sapphire crystal; screwed-down exhibition case back; water-resistant to 50 m

Band: alligator skin, buckle

Price: $5,795

Variations: black or white dial; on stainless steel bracelet; in 47 mm size with 3.5 ct diamonds ($11,295)

ChronoJewel 40 mm

Reference number: GC 20221 D

Movement: automatic, ETA Caliber 2836-2; ø 25.6 mm, height 4.6 mm; 25 jewels; 28,800 vph

Functions: hours, minutes, sweep seconds; date, day

Case: stainless steel, ø 40 mm, height 13 mm; bezel set with 48 brilliant-cut diamonds (1.25 ct); sapphire crystal; screwed-down exhibition case back; water-resistant to 50 m

Band: alligator skin, buckle

Price: $4,895

Variations: white dial; on stainless steel bracelet; in 47 mm size with 3.5 ct diamonds ($10,395)

Diamond Millenium Limited Edition

Reference number: GC 5000

Movement: automatic, ETA Caliber 2836-2; ø 25.6 mm, height 4.6 mm; 25 jewels; 28,800 vph

Functions: hours, minutes, sweep seconds; date, day

Case: stainless steel/yellow gold, ø 47 mm, height 14 mm; 18-karat gold bezel set with 48 brilliant-cut diamonds (3.5 ct); sapphire crystal; screwed-down exhibition case back; water-resistant to 50 m

Band: crocodile skin, 18-karat yellow gold folding clasp

Remarks: limited edition of 100 numbered pieces

Price: $12,995

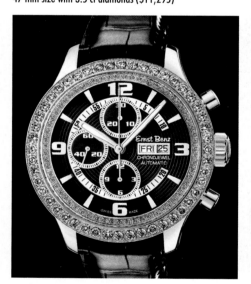

ChronoJewel 47 mm

Reference number: GC 10121 DD

Movement: automatic, ETA Valjoux Caliber 7750; ø 30 mm, height 7.9 mm; 25 jewels; 28,800 vph

Functions: hours, minutes, subsidiary seconds; chronograph; date, day

Case: stainless steel, ø 47 mm, height 16 mm; bezel set with 48 brilliant-cut diamonds, outer dial ring set with 64 brilliant-cut diamonds (5.0 ct total); sapphire crystal; screwed-down exhibition case back; water-resistant to 50 m

Band: alligator skin, buckle

Price: $14,695

Variations: on stainless steel bracelet; in 40 mm case size with 2 ct diamonds ($7,995)

Diamond ChronoLunar 40 mm

Reference number: GC 20312 D

Movement: automatic, ETA Valjoux Caliber 7751; ø 30 mm, height 7.9 mm; 25 jewels; 28,800 vph

Functions: hours, minutes, subsidiary seconds; chronograph; date, day, month, moon phase; 24-hour display

Case: stainless steel, ø 40 mm, height 15.8 mm; bezel set with 48 brilliant-cut diamonds (1.25 ct); sapphire crystal; screwed-down exhibition case back; water-resistant to 50 m

Band: alligator skin, buckle

Price: $6,995

Variations: black dial; on stainless steel bracelet; in 47 mm case size with 3.5 ct diamonds ($12,495)

ChronoJewel 47 mm

Reference number: GC 10122 DB

Movement: automatic, ETA Valjoux Caliber 7750; ø 30 mm, height 7.9 mm; 25 jewels; 28,800 vph

Functions: hours, minutes, subsidiary seconds; chronograph; date, day

Case: stainless steel, ø 47 mm, height 16 mm; bezel set with 48 brilliant-cut diamonds (3.5 ct); sapphire crystal; screwed-down exhibition case back; water-resistant to 50 m

Band: stainless steel, folding clasp

Price: $11,495

Variations: black dial; on alligator skin strap; in 40 mm case size wtih 1.25 ct diamonds ($5,995)

Blancpain

Blancpain celebrated its refounding in 1982 with a small collection of complicated watches in a classically round case, thereby making itself one of the forerunners of the renaissance of the mechanical watch. Now, less than twenty-five years later, there are so many other manufacturers in this niche market segment of the watch industry that hardly anyone remembers the shocked murmur going through the crowd of jewelers and watch dealers at the time.

Making its own brand of slowed-down time during that era, this brand was taking great risks. Today, however, it enjoys a comfortable advantage over others with regard to the tricky themes of classic and modern. Marc Hayek, grandson of Swatch Group founder Nicolas G. Hayek, experienced this change in paradigms in the world of luxury watches from a box seat. After all, in his family everything revolves around this topic, and the largest watch manufacturer in the world had to first take the step from "democratizing timekeeping," which had dictated its products and product qualities until then, to a new understanding of the wristwatch as a luxury item.

The base of Blancpain's model palette is built upon three collections — all different from one another and possessing distinctly individual characters. The Villeret collection is an homage to the roots of Blancpain and embodies the soul of the *manufacture*. It is based upon a new aesthetic: The lengths of the hands, the shape of the Roman numerals, the width of the bezel, and even the dimensions of the lugs exude elegance and harmony — despite a surprisingly moderate size. However, the dimensions and the simple dials of the models of the Villeret collection symbolize a certain reverence to classic pocket watches.

Watches of the Le Brassus collection originate in a know-how that has been passed down from generation to generation since 1735 and stands for the art of watchmaking. The majority of Blancpain's horological firsts introduced in the last century are to be found in this collection — even the quintessence of the legendary masterpieces, the model 1735, is at home here. This timepiece unites everything that is possible in the realm of micro-technology for the wrist in the smallest amount of space possible: This one single watch with an ultra-flat movement contains a tourbillon, a perpetual calendar, a rattrapante chronograph, a moon phase display, and a minute repeater.

The modern Léman collection combines the traditional art of watchmaking with practical characteristics that correspond to the active lifestyle of the wearer. Its name is a reference to Lac Léman, or Lake Geneva to English speakers, on whose shores the new technical and administrative facilities of the brand are located. The watches found in the Léman collection are suitable both for everyday as well as sports and travel.

In the years since Marc Hayek has been in charge, Blancpain has completed a careful strategic changeover with a clear course set for expansion in the firm's second location in Paudex near Lausanne where the administration and sales departments are located. Hayek, previously successful as an executive in the restaurant industry, also places a great deal of value on improving service in his watch business and has introduced a contemporary system for stocking watches and replacement parts.

Equation Marchante Le Brassus

Reference number: 4238-344255B
Movement: automatic, Blancpain Caliber 3863; ø 26.8 mm, height 5.25 mm; 39 jewels; 21,600 vph
Functions: hours, minutes, subsidiary seconds; perpetual calendar (date, day of the week, month, moon phase, leap year); both indirect and marchant displays of equation of time via additional minutes hand
Case: platinum, ø 42 mm, height 12.3 mm; sapphire crystal; exhibition window case back
Band: reptile skin, folding clasp
Remarks: limited to 50 pieces
Price: $127,700

Chrono Flyback Rattrapante Le Brassus

Reference number: 4246F-364255B
Movement: automatic, Blancpain Caliber 40F6; ø 26.2 mm, height 8 mm; 37 jewels; 21,600 vph
Functions: hours, minutes; split-seconds chronograph with flyback function; date; power reserve display
Case: red gold, ø 42 mm, height 15.1 mm; sapphire crystal; exhibition window case back
Band: reptile skin, folding clasp
Price: $38,300

Grande Complication Le Brassus

Reference number: 1735-342755
Movement: automatic, Blancpain Caliber 1735; ø 31.5 mm, height 11 mm; 44 jewels; 21,600 vph; one-minute tourbillon; power reserve 80 hours, 740 individual components
Functions: hours, minutes; hour, quarter hour, and minute repeater; split-seconds chronograph; perpetual calendar with date, day of the week, month, moon phase
Case: platinum, ø 42 mm, height 16.5 mm; sapphire crystal; exhibition window case back
Band: reptile skin, folding clasp
Remarks: limited to 30 pieces
Price: $783,100

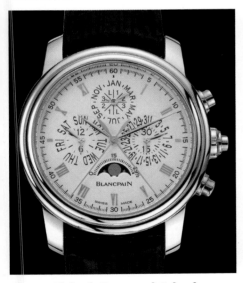

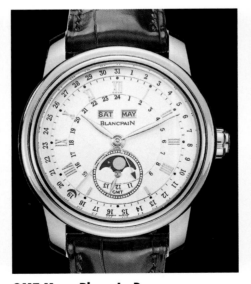

Chrono Flyback Perpetual Calendar Le Brassus

Reference number: 4286P-3442A55B
Movement: automatic, Blancpain Caliber 56F9A; ø 26.2 mm, height 8.1 mm; 38 jewels; 21,600 vph
Functions: hours, minutes; split-seconds chronograph with flyback function; perpetual calendar with date, day of the week, month, moon phase, leap year
Case: platinum, ø 42 mm, height 15 mm; sapphire crystal; exhibition window case back
Band: reptile skin, folding clasp
Remarks: limited to 100 pieces
Price: upon request

GMT Moon Phase Le Brassus

Reference number: 4276-3642A55B
Movement: automatic, Blancpain Caliber 67A6; ø 27 mm, height 6 mm; 30 jewels; 21,600 vph; twin spring barrels, power reserve 100 hours
Functions: hours, minutes, subsidiary seconds; date, day of the week, month, moon phase, 24-hour display (second time zone)
Case: red gold, ø 42 mm, height 13.3 mm; sapphire crystal; water-resistant to 50 m
Band: reptile skin, folding clasp
Price: $24,600
Variations: in platinum

Chrono Flyback Rattrapante Tourbillon Le Brassus

Reference number: 4289Q-3442A55B
Movement: automatic, Blancpain Caliber 56F9U; ø 27.6 mm, height 7.7 mm; 39 jewels; 21,600 vph; one-minute tourbillon
Functions: hours, minutes, subsidiary seconds; split-seconds chronograph with flyback function; perpetual calendar with date, day of the week, month, moon phase, leap year
Case: platinum, ø 42 mm, height 17.4 mm; sapphire crystal; exhibition window case back; water-resistant to 50 m
Band: reptile skin, folding clasp
Price: $207,700
Variations: with brilliant-cut diamonds

Ultra-Flat Villeret

Reference number: 6223-112755
Movement: automatic, Blancpain Caliber 1153; ø 26.2 mm,
height 3.25 mm; 28 jewels; 21,600 vph; twin spring barrels,
power reserve 100 hours
Functions: hours, minutes, sweep seconds; date
Case: stainless steel, ø 38 mm, height 9.2 mm;
sapphire crystal
Band: reptile skin, buckle
Price: $5,500
Variations: in white or red gold

Chrono Monopoussoir Villeret

Reference number: 6185-154655
Movement: automatic, Blancpain Caliber M185;
ø 31.8 mm, height 5.5 mm; 37 jewels; 21,600 vph; control
of chronograph functions via one single button
Functions: hours, minutes, subsidiary seconds;
chronograph; date
Case: white gold, ø 38 mm, height 11.4 mm; sapphire
crystal; exhibition window case back
Band: reptile skin, buckle
Price: $10,500

Ultra-Flat Women's Watch Villeret

Reference number: 6102-112795
Movement: automatic, Blancpain Caliber 953; ø 21 mm,
height 3.25 mm; 21 jewels; 21,600 vph
Functions: hours, minutes, sweep seconds
Case: stainless steel, ø 29 mm, height 8.7 mm;
sapphire crystal
Band: reptile skin, buckle
Remarks: comes with five bands in set
Price: $6,400
Variations: in red gold; with diamonds on the bezel

Complete Calendar with Moon Phase Villeret

Reference number: 6263-3642A55
Movement: automatic, Blancpain Caliber 6763; ø 27 mm,
height 4.9 mm; 30 jewels; 21,600 vph
Functions: hours, minutes, subsidiary seconds; date, day of
the week, month, moon phase
Case: red gold, ø 38 mm, height 10.7 mm; sapphire crystal;
exhibition window case back
Band: reptile skin, buckle
Price: $14,300
Variations: in white gold; in stainless steel

Tourbillon Power Reserve Villeret

Reference number: 6025-344255B
Movement: automatic, Blancpain Caliber 25; ø 23.9 mm,
height 4.85 mm; 29 jewels; 21,600 vph; one-minute
tourbillon; power reserve 168 hours
Functions: hours, minutes, subsidiary seconds (on tourbillon
cage); date; power reserve display
Case: platinum, ø 38 mm, height 10.3 mm; sapphire crystal;
exhibition window case back
Band: reptile skin, folding clasp
Price: $84,500
Variations: in red gold

Chrono Monopoussoir Rattrapante Villeret

Reference number: 6086-364253B
Movement: automatic, Blancpain Caliber M186;
ø 31.8 mm, height 5.8 mm; 37 jewels; 21,600 vph;
control of chronograph functions via one single button
Functions: hours, minutes, subsidiary seconds; split-seconds
chronograph; date
Case: red gold, ø 38 mm, height 13.1 mm; sapphire crystal;
exhibition window case back
Band: reptile skin, folding clasp
Remarks: limited to 99 pieces
Price: $33,900
Variations: in platinum

Réveil GMT Léman Anniversary Edition

Reference number: 2041B-363064B
Movement: automatic, Blancpain Caliber 1241; ø 31.7 mm, height 6.2 mm; 38 jewels; 21,600 vph
Functions: hours, minutes, subsidiary seconds; date; 24-hour display (second time zone); alarm display, power reserve display for alarm, alarm function indication
Case: red gold, ø 40 mm, height 13.3 mm; sapphire crystal; exhibition window case back
Band: reptile skin, folding clasp
Remarks: limited anniversary edition 270 pieces
Price: $24,800
Variations: in red gold

Aqualung Large Date Léman

Reference number: 2850B-113064B
Movement: automatic, Blancpain Caliber 6950; ø 32 mm, height 4.75 mm; 35 jewels; 21,600 vph; twin spring barrels, power reserve 70 hours
Functions: hours, minutes, sweep seconds; large date
Case: stainless steel, ø 40 mm, height 11.4 mm; sapphire crystal; exhibition window case back
Band: rubber, folding clasp
Remarks: limited to 2005 pieces
Price: $8,500

Chrono Flyback Perpetual Calendar Léman

Reference number: 2685F-363053B
Movement: automatic, Blancpain Caliber F585; ø 27 mm, height 7.1 mm; 35 jewels; 21,600 vph
Functions: hours, minutes; chronograph with flyback function; perpetual calendar with date, day of the week, month, moon phase, leap year
Case: red gold, ø 40 mm, height 14 mm; sapphire crystal; exhibition window case back
Band: reptile skin, folding clasp
Price: $34,200
Variations: in platinum with silver dial

Chrono Flyback Large Date Léman

Reference number: 2885-113053B
Movement: automatic, Blancpain Caliber 69F8; ø 32 mm, height 7 mm; 42 jewels; 21,600 vph
Functions: hours, minutes, subsidiary seconds; chronograph with flyback function; large date
Case: stainless steel, ø 40 mm, height 13.3 mm; sapphire crystal; exhibition window case back
Band: reptile skin, folding clasp
Price: $10,700

Tourbillon Large Date Léman

Reference number: 2825A-364253B
Movement: automatic, Blancpain Caliber 6925; ø 27.6 mm, height 6.35 mm; 35 jewels; 21,600 vph; one-minute tourbillon; power reserve 7 days
Functions: hours, minutes, subsidiary seconds (on tourbillon cage); large date; power reserve display
Case: red gold, ø 38 mm, height 12.4 mm; sapphire crystal; exhibition window case back
Band: reptile skin, folding clasp
Remarks: limited to 50 pieces
Price: upon request
Variations: in white gold

Tourbillon Large Date Léman

Reference number: 2825A-343053B
Movement: automatic, Blancpain Caliber 6925; ø 27.6 mm, height 6.35 mm; 35 jewels; 21,600 vph; one-minute tourbillon; power reserve 7 days
Functions: hours, minutes, subsidiary seconds (on tourbillon cage); large date; power reserve display
Case: platinum, ø 38 mm, height 12.4 mm; sapphire crystal; exhibition window case back
Band: reptile skin, folding clasp
Remarks: limited to 50 pieces
Price: $93,900
Variations: in white gold

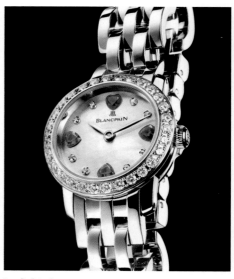

Minute Repeater

Reference number: 6036-344255
Movement: automatic, Blancpain Caliber 35; ø 23.9 mm, height 6.9 mm; 39 jewels; 21,600 vph
Functions: hours, minutes; hour, quarter hour, and minute repeater
Case: platinum, ø 38 mm, height 10.3 mm; sapphire crystal
Band: reptile skin, folding clasp
Price: $132,400

St. Valentin 2005

Reference number: 6102A-468895
Movement: automatic, Blancpain Caliber 953; ø 21 mm, height 3.25 mm; 21 jewels; 21,600 vph
Functions: hours, minutes, sweep seconds
Case: white gold, ø 29 mm, height 8.7 mm; bezel set with brilliant-cut diamonds; sapphire crystal
Band: reptile skin, buckle
Remarks: dial with heart-shaped diamond marker
Price: $10,200

Ladybird

Reference number: 0062-199735
Movement: automatic, Blancpain Caliber 615; ø 15.7 mm, height 3.9 mm; 29 jewels; 21,600 vph
Functions: hours, minutes
Case: white gold, ø 21.5 mm, height 9 mm; bezel set with brilliant-cut diamonds; sapphire crystal
Band: white gold, double folding clasp
Remarks: dial set with 4 heart-shaped rubies and 8 brilliant-cut diamonds
Price: $18,100

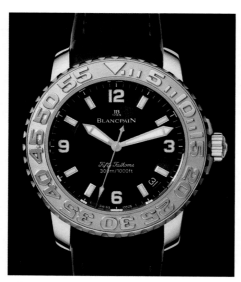

Fifty Fathoms

Reference number: 2200-113071
Movement: automatic, Blancpain Caliber 1151; ø 26.2 mm, height 3.25 mm; 28 jewels; 21,600 vph; twin spring barrels, power reserve 100 hours
Functions: hours, minutes, sweep seconds; date
Case: stainless steel, ø 40.5 mm, height 13 mm; unidirectionally rotating bezel with 60-minute divisions; sapphire crystal; water-resistant to 300 m
Band: stainless steel, double folding clasp
Price: $8,000

Air Command Concept

Reference number: 2285F-653066
Movement: automatic, Blancpain Caliber F185; ø 26.2 mm, height 5.5 mm; 37 jewels; 21,600 vph
Functions: hours, minutes, subsidiary seconds; chronograph with flyback function; date
Case: stainless steel/rubber, ø 40.5 mm, height 13.3 mm; unidirectionally rotating bezel with 60-minute divisions; sapphire crystal; water-resistant to 200 m
Band: stainless steel/rubber, double folding clasp
Price: $11,400

Chrono Monaco Yacht Show

Reference number: 2285A-113071
Movement: automatic, Blancpain Caliber F182; ø 26.2 mm, height 5.5 mm; 35 jewels; 21,600 vph
Functions: hours, minutes, subsidiary seconds; chronograph with flyback function; date
Case: stainless steel, ø 40 mm, height 13.3 mm; unidirectionally rotating bezel with 60-minute divisions; sapphire crystal; water-resistant to 200 m
Band: stainless steel, double folding clasp
Remarks: limited to 150 pieces
Price: $11,400

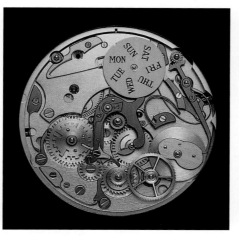

Caliber 502 QPLT

Mechanical with automatic winding, power reserve 45 hours
Functions: hours, minutes; perpetual calendar (date, day, month, leap year), linearly arranged displays with direct year change (Breguet patent 1997)
Diameter: 32.4 mm
Height: 5.07 mm
Jewels: 35
Balance: glucydur
Frequency: 18,000 vph
Balance spring: Nivarox flat hairspring
Shock protection: Kif
Remarks: escapement with straight pallets

Caliber 502 DPET

Mechanical with automatic winding, power reserve 45 hours
Functions: hours, minutes; perpetual calendar (date, day, month, leap year, moon phase), power reserve display; equation of time (combination of equation and perpetual calendar, patented in 1992)
Diameter: 32.4 mm
Height: 5.07 mm
Jewels: 35
Balance: glucydur
Frequency: 18,000 vph
Balance spring: Nivarox flat hairspring
Shock protection: Kif

Caliber 587

Mechanical with automatic winding, one-minute tourbillon; twin spring barrels; power reserve 120 hours
Functions: hours (off-center), minutes; subsidiary seconds (on tourbillon cage)
Diameter: 27.6 mm
Height: 5.5 mm
Jewels: 31
Balance: glucydur
Frequency: 21,600 vph
Remarks: movement partially skeletonized, engraved and finished completely by hand

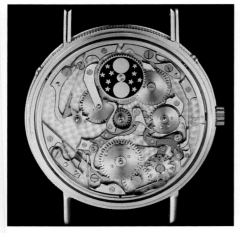

Caliber 502 QSE

Mechanical with automatic winding, power reserve 45 hours
Functions: hours, minutes (off-center); date, day, moon phase
Diameter: 32.4 mm
Height: 5.07 mm
Jewels: 35
Balance: glucydur
Frequency: 18,000 vph
Balance spring: Nivarox flat hairspring
Shock protection: Kif

Caliber 533 NT

Mechanical with manual winding, power reserve 47 hours
Functions: hours, minutes, subsidiary seconds; split-seconds chronograph
Diameter: 27.5 mm
Height: 7.1 mm
Jewels: 23
Balance: glucydur with weighted screws
Frequency: 18,000 vph
Balance spring: Breguet
Shock protection: Incabloc
Remarks: two column wheels to control the chronograph functions

Breitling

A street sign in Grenchen, a city located between Switzerland's Solothurn and Biel, upon which the buildings of Breitling's company headquarters are shown has a definite symbolic character: The word that accompanies them is "airfield."

The small airfield to which the sign points is one that Breitling president Théodore Schneider and vice president Jean-Paul Girardin, both men with a license to fly, lift off from several times a week using Breitling's company helicopter to go to La Chaux-de-Fonds. In so doing they are trading a 90-minute car ride on curvy mountainous roads for a short 15-minute helicopter flight.

In La Chaux-de-Fonds, one of the cities highest above sea level in Europe and, like Grenchen, a center of Swiss watchmaking, the Breitling Chronométrie was opened in January 2002. Here the watch movements used by the brand are all assembled.

The newest generation of machines is in use at the La Chaux-de-Fonds factory, where movements are lubricated by machine, pallets are adjusted to the thousandth of a millimeter, and balance springs are checked to see if they are sitting well in their balance spring buckles — enlarged, of course, to computer screen format.

Not far from the small train station Grenchen-Süd, directly next to the rails

connecting Zurich and Geneva, is where Breitling's traditional headquarters are located, a square functional building built in 1953 that has since attracted looks from the passengers of the passing trains with its obvious blue paint. It was given a compan-

ion at the end of the 1990s, a second Breitling building placed into a triangular piece of land across the train tracks. The buildings, offering a combined 4,000 square meters of production area, are joined by an underground tunnel.

The close relationship this watch company has to aeronautics, commercial aviation, and military air travel is ever-present in the Grenchen buildings. The large blinds, for example, that darken the windows like a shade should there be strong sun, display the cross section of aircraft carriers, the main entrance is decorated to resemble the ramp of a cargo freighter, and on top of the main building a genuine propeller airplane is "parked."

The (close to) triangular new building comprises inner galleries from which all rooms can be accessed. A special air-conditioning unit and a gigantic air cleaner located in the basement take care that the extremely clean rooms retain a consistent temperature of 22°C and a humidity of 40 to 60 percent and that they continue being as dust-free as possible. One room is much cooler than the others, with a constant temperature between 14 and 18°C. This is the room where the movements that have successfully passed the official C.O.S.C. chronometer test are kept while awaiting being housed in a Breitling case.

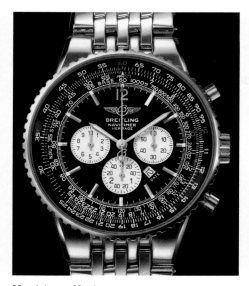

Navitimer Heritage

Reference number: J35350-017
Movement: automatic, Breitling Caliber 35 (base ETA 2892-A2); ø 25.6 mm, height 3.6 mm (base movement); 38 jewels; 28,800 vph; officially certified chronometer (COSC)
Functions: hours, minutes, subsidiary seconds; chronograph; date
Case: white gold, ø 43 mm, height 15.4 mm; bidirectionally rotating bezel with integrated slide rule and tachymeter scale; sapphire crystal
Band: white gold, folding clasp
Price: $25,000
Variations: in stainless steel or yellow gold with bracelet

Navitimer Montbrillant Datora

Reference number: A21330-045
Movement: automatic, Breitling Caliber 21 (base ETA 7751); ø 30 mm, height 7.9 mm; 25 jewels; 28,800 vph; officially certified chronometer (COSC)
Functions: hours, minutes, subsidiary seconds; chronograph; date, day of the week, month, 24-hour display
Case: stainless steel, ø 43 mm, height 14.1 mm; bidirectionally rotating bezel with integrated slide rule and tachymeter scale; sapphire crystal
Band: stainless steel, folding clasp
Price: $5,585
Variations: with leather strap

Navitimer World

Reference number: A24322-101
Movement: automatic, Breitling Caliber 24 (base ETA 7754); ø 30 mm, height 7.9 mm; 25 jewels; 28,800 vph; officially certified chronometer (COSC)
Functions: hours, minutes, subsidiary seconds; chronograph; date; 24-hour display (second time zone)
Case: stainless steel, ø 46 mm, height 15.6 mm; bidirectionally rotating bezel with integrated slide rule and 60-minute scale; sapphire crystal
Band: leather, buckle
Price: $4,560
Variations: in red gold; in white gold

Navitimer

Reference number: A23322-161
Movement: automatic, Breitling Caliber 23 (base ETA 7750); ø 30 mm, height 7.9 mm; 25 jewels; 28,800 vph; officially certified chronometer (COSC)
Functions: hours, minutes, subsidiary seconds; chronograph; date
Case: stainless steel, ø 41.8 mm, height 14.6 mm; bidirectionally rotating bezel with integrated slide rule and tachymeter scale; sapphire crystal
Band: leather, buckle
Price: $4,250
Variations: with steel bracelet; in yellow gold with strap

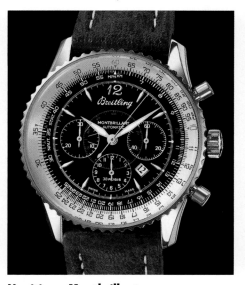

Navitimer Montbrillant

Reference number: A41330-101
Movement: automatic, Breitling Caliber 41 (base ETA 2892-2); ø 25.6 mm, height 3.6 mm (base movement); 38 jewels; 28,800 vph; officially certified chronometer (COSC)
Functions: hours, minutes, subsidiary seconds; chronograph; date
Case: stainless steel, ø 38 mm, height 13 mm; bidirectionally rotating bezel with tachymeter scale; mineral crystal
Band: leather, buckle
Price: $3,950
Variations: with stainless steel bracelet; in rose gold, with leather strap

Montbrillant Olympus

Reference number: A19350-3512
Movement: automatic, Breitling Caliber 19 (base ETA 2892-A2); ø 25.6 mm, height 3.6 mm (base movement); 38 jewels; 28,800 vph; officially certified chronometer (COSC)
Functions: hours, minutes, subsidiary seconds; chronograph; four-year calendar with date, day, month, moon phase
Case: stainless steel, ø 43 mm, height 15.3 mm; bidirectionally rotating bezel with integrated slide rule and tachymeter scale; sapphire crystal
Band: reptile skin, buckle
Price: $6,300
Variations: with steel bracelet; in rose gold with bracelet

Emergency Mission

Reference number: A73321-018
Movement: quartz, Breitling Caliber 73 (base ETA 251.262); officially certified chronometer (COSC)
Functions: hours, minutes, subsidiary seconds; chronograph; date; microantenna with aviation emergency frequency 121.5 MHz
Case: stainless steel, ø 45 mm, height 19.2 mm; bidirectionally rotating bezel with 60-minute divisions; sapphire crystal; screwed-in crown; water-resistant to 100 m
Band: stainless steel, folding clasp
Remarks: retractable emergency antenna
Price: $4,990

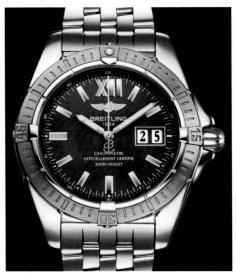

Cockpit

Reference number: A49350-105
Movement: automatic, Breitling Caliber 49 (base ETA 2892-A2); ø 25.6 mm, height 3.9 mm; 22 jewels; 28,800 vph; officially certified chronometer (COSC)
Functions: hours, minutes, sweep seconds; large date
Case: stainless steel, ø 41 mm, unidirectionally rotating bezel with 60-minute divisions; sapphire crystal; screwed-in crown; water-resistant to 300 m
Band: stainless steel, folding clasp
Price: $3,850
Variations: with leather strap; in stainless steel/yellow gold; in yellow gold

Chrono Cockpit

Reference number: A13358-095
Movement: automatic, Breitling Caliber 13 (base ETA 7750); ø 30 mm, height 7.9 mm; 25 jewels; 28,800 vph; officially certified chronometer (COSC)
Functions: hours, minutes, subsidiary seconds; chronograph; date
Case: stainless steel, ø 39 mm, unidirectionally rotating bezel with 60-minute divisions; sapphire crystal; screwed-in crown; water-resistant to 100 m
Band: stainless steel, folding clasp
Price: $4,300
Variations: in stainless steel/yellow gold; in yellow gold

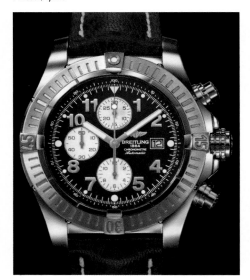

Super Avenger

Reference number: A13370-168
Movement: automatic, Breitling Caliber 13 (base ETA 7750); ø 30 mm, height 7.9 mm; 25 jewels; 28,800 vph; officially certified chronometer (COSC)
Functions: hours, minutes, subsidiary seconds; chronograph; date
Case: stainless steel, ø 48.4 mm, height 18.6 mm; undirectionally rotating bezel with 60-minute divisions; sapphire crystal; screwed-in crown; water-resistant to 300 m
Band: stainless steel, buckle
Price: $3,535
Variations: with leather strap; with reptile skin strap

Chronomat Evolution

Reference number: B13356-086
Movement: automatic, Breitling Caliber 13 (base ETA 7750); ø 30 mm, height 7.9 mm; 25 jewels; 28,800 vph; officially certified chronometer (COSC)
Functions: hours, minutes, subsidiary seconds; chronograph; date
Case: stainless steel, ø 40.5 mm, height 14.7 mm; unidirectionally rotating bezel with gold claws and 60-minute scale; sapphire crystal; screw-in crown and buttons in gold
Band: stainless steel/yellow gold, folding clasp
Price: $6,330
Variations: with leather strap; in white gold; in yellow gold

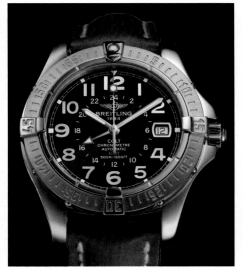

Colt GMT

Reference number: A32350-301
Movement: automatic, Breitling Caliber 32 (base ETA 2893-2); ø 25.6 mm, height 4.1 mm; 21 jewels; 28,800 vph; officially certified chronometer (COSC)
Functions: hours, minutes, subsidiary seconds; date; 24-hour display (second time zone)
Case: stainless steel, ø 40.5 mm, height 13.2 mm; unidirectionally rotating bezel with 60-minute divisions; sapphire crystal; screwed-in crown; water-resistant to 500 m
Band: leather, buckle
Price: $2,040
Variations: with stainless steel bracelet

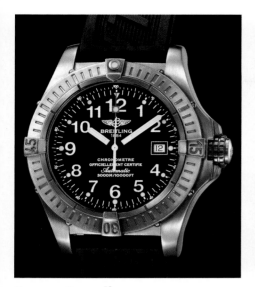

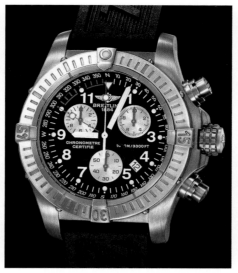

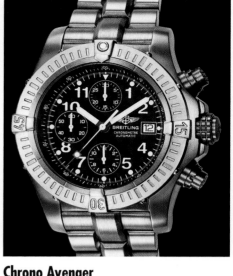

Avenger Seawolf

Reference number: E17370-1014
Movement: automatic, Breitling Caliber 44 (base ETA 2892-A2); ø 25.6 mm, height 3.6 mm; 21 jewels; 28,800 vph; officially certified chronometer (COSC)
Functions: hours, minutes, sweep seconds; date
Case: titanium, ø 44 mm, height 18.4 mm; unidirectionally rotating with bezel 60-minute divisions; sapphire crystal; screwed-in crown; water-resistant to 300 m
Band: rubber, buckle
Price: $2,445
Variations: with titanium bracelet

Chrono Avenger M1

Reference number: E73360-2014
Movement: quartz, Breitling Caliber 73 (base ETA 251.262); officially certified chronometer (COSC)
Functions: hours, minutes, subsidiary seconds; chronograph; regatta equipment (10-minute countdown); date
Case: titanium, ø 44 mm, height 17.2 mm; unidirectionally rotating bezel with 60-minute divisions; sapphire crystal; screwed-in crown; water-resistant to 1000 m
Band: rubber, buckle
Price: $2,825
Variations: with titanium link bracelet

Chrono Avenger

Reference number: E13360-308
Movement: automatic, Breitling Caliber 13 (base ETA 7750); ø 30 mm, height 7.9 mm; 25 jewels; 28,800 vph; officially certified chronometer (COSC)
Functions: hours, minutes, subsidiary seconds; chronograph; date
Case: titanium, ø 44 mm, height 17.6 mm; unidirectionally rotating bezel with 60-minute divisions; sapphire crystal; screwed-in crown; water-resistant to 300 m
Band: titanium, folding clasp
Price: $3,125
Variations: with diver's bracelet Diver Pro

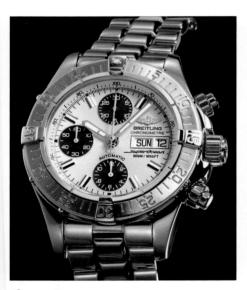

Chrono Superocean

Reference number: A13340-018
Movement: automatic, Breitling Caliber 13 (base ETA 7750); ø 30 mm, height 7.9 mm; 25 jewels; 28,800 vph; officially certified chronometer (COSC)
Functions: hours, minutes, subsidiary seconds; chronograph; date, day of the week
Case: stainless steel, ø 42 mm, height 15.1 mm; unidirectionally rotating bezel with 60-minute divisions; sapphire crystal; screwed-in crown and buttons; water-resistant to 500 m
Band: stainless steel, folding clasp
Price: $3,345
Variations: with leather strap; various dial colors

B - One

Reference number: A78362-101U
Movement: quartz, Breitling Caliber 78; COSC certified
Functions: hours, minutes, sweep seconds (analogue); chronograph with digital display für interval and addition timing as well as countdown, perpetual calendar with digital display for date, day, month, year, second time zone, world time; timer with alarm signal; additional 24-hour analogue time
Case: stainless steel, ø 43.2 mm, height 16.5 mm; bidirectionally rotating bezel with 60-minute divisions; sapphire crystal
Band: leather, buckle
Price: $3,950
Variations: in yellow gold/bracelet; in white gold/strap

B - Two

Reference number: A42362-118
Movement: automatic, Breitling Caliber 42 (base ETA 2892-A2); ø 25.6 mm, height 3.6 mm (base movement); 38 jewels; 28,800 vph; officially certified chronometer (COSC)
Functions: hours, minutes, subsidiary seconds; chronograph; date
Case: stainless steel, ø 44.8 mm, height 15.7 mm; bidirectionally rotating with 360-degree scale; sapphire crystal; water-resistant to 100 m
Band: stainless steel, folding clasp
Price: $3,345
Variations: in yellow gold with strap; in white gold with strap

Carl F. Bucherer

The Carl F. Bucherer watch brand represents a small empire in itself within the Bucherer group, totally individual and with a strong identity — there is certainly a reason that it bears the entire name of the company founder. Carl F. Bucherer can rely on competence gathered in the more than eighty years of its existence. During its long history, Carl F. Bucherer has been able to assert itself successfully, winning international fame and recognition for the technical and aesthetic quality of its products under difficult circumstances. In 1919, the visionary entrepreneur Bucherer introduced his first watch collection into which he poured not only his knowledge of watchmaking, but also his special feel for the needs of his demanding clientele.

Carl Friedrich Bucherer was an exceptional man, and he possessed the courage to veer off the beaten path. With creativity and wild enthusiasm, both he and the ensuing two generations of his family created a very successful company, displaying a special talent for uniting traditional values with new ideas.

In harmony with the values of its visionary company founder, the Carl F. Bucherer brand has consciously decided to avoid following short-lived trends, making its

dedication to authentic products the center of the brand philosophy.

However, continuity alone isn't what counts: The use of long years of experience and traditional talents as well as the very Swiss passion for the art of watchmaking is also the basis for utilizing the newest in technical developments.

Proof of this brand's technical competence is well represented by the Patravi Chronograph GMT model, whose hour hand can be quick-set simply by

manipulating the crown — independent of the minute hand — in increments of one hour, backward and forward. The date goes back and forth as necessary along with the hour hand.

And this year the company's designers went a step further with the Patravi TravelTec GMT, introduced at Baselworld 2005. This new jewel of the collection utilizes the exclusive Caliber CFB 1901, designed by Dubois-Dépraz, which makes the display of three time zones all at once possible: Local time (conventionally shown by the hour and minute hands), a reference time (on the flange, shown by a 24-hour scale), and a variable third time zone displayed on a 24-hour scale that can be moved forward and backward. The changing of the local time is done by moving the hour hand alone, which — uncoupled from the minute hand — can be adjusted via the crown. This can be done both forward and backward, and even the date travels in both directions along with it. The display of the third time zone is set by a new mono-button patent-pending mechanism. A highly complex gear construction housed within the left side of the case allows for the step-by-step rotation of the 24-hour disk in both directions. An opposite rotation is made possible by the rocking bar integrated into the button. In neutral position, the disk can be locked. After opening branches in Hong Kong and Munich, a Carl. F. Bucherer subsidiary was launched in the United States in May 2004. Carl F. Bucherer North America Inc. is headquartered in Dayton, Ohio, and is individually responsible for all activities in the U.S.

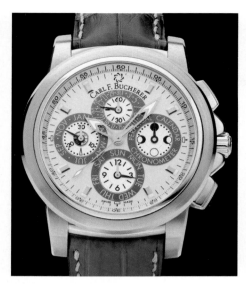

Patravi Tribute to Fritz Brun

Reference number: 00.10614.03.13.01
Movement: automatic, CFB Caliber 1959 (base ETA 2892-A2); ø 30 mm, height 7.7 mm; 38 jewels; 28,800 vph; officially certified chronometer (COSC); limited to 75 pieces
Functions: hours, minutes, subsidiary seconds; chronograph; perpetual calendar with date, day of the week, month, moon phase, leap year
Case: red gold, ø 42 mm, height 14.7 mm; sapphire crystal; screwed-down case back; exhibition window; screwed-in crown; water-resistant to 50 m
Band: reptile skin, folding clasp
Price: $36,900

Patravi TravelTec GMT

Reference number: 00.10620.08.33.01
Movement: automatic, CFB Caliber 1901; ø 28.6 mm, height 7.3 mm; 39 jewels; 28,800 vph
Functions: hours, minutes, subsidiary seconds; chronograph; 24-hour display (second time zone)
Case: stainless steel, ø 46.5 mm, height 15.5 mm; bidirectionally rotating bezel under crystal settable via crown and with 24-hour scale; sapphire crystal; screwed-down case back; exhibition window; screwed-in crown; water-resistant to 50 m
Band: leather, folding clasp
Price: $10,400
Variations: with stainless steel bracelet

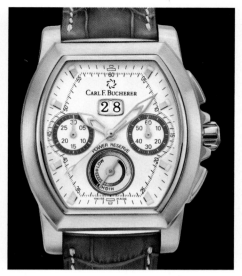

Patravi Tonneaugraph

Reference number: 00.10615.03.13.01
Movement: automatic, CFB Caliber 1960 (base ETA 2892-A2); ø 30 mm, height 7.3 mm; 47 jewels; 28,800 vph
Functions: hours, minutes, subsidiary seconds; chronograph; large date; power reserve display
Case: red gold, 39 x 52 mm, height 13.8 mm; sapphire crystal; screwed-down case back; screwed-in crown; water-resistant to 50 m
Band: reptile skin, folding clasp
Price: $6,900
Variations: in stainless steel; with diamond-set bezel

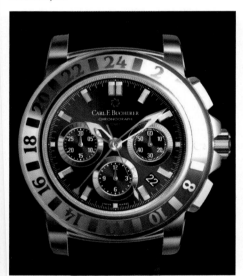

Patravi Chronograph GMT

Reference number: 00.10618.08.33.01
Movement: automatic, CFB Caliber 1901 (base ETA 2894-2); ø 28.6 mm, height 7.3 mm; 39 jewels; 28,800 vph
Functions: hours, minutes, subsidiary seconds; chronograph; date; 24-hour display (second time zone)
Case: stainless steel, ø 42 mm, height 14.1 mm; bidirectionally rotating bezel with 24-hour scale; sapphire crystal; screwed-down case back; exhibition window; screwed-in crown; water-resistant to 50 m
Band: reptile skin, folding clasp
Price: $5,100
Variations: with white dial; with stainless steel bracelet

Patravi Tonneau Power Reserve

Reference number: 00.10612.08.33.01
Movement: automatic, CFB Caliber 1953 (base ETA 2892-A2); ø 25.6 mm, height 5.1 mm; 28 jewels; 28,800 vph
Functions: hours, minutes, sweep seconds; date; 24-hour display (second time zone); power reserve display
Case: stainless steel, 48 x 36 mm, height 10.8 mm; sapphire crystal; screwed-down case back; screwed-in crown; water-resistant to 50 m
Band: reptile skin, folding clasp
Price: $4,500
Variations: with white dial; with stainless steel bracelet; with diamond-set bezel

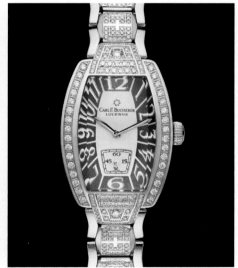

Tribute to Mimi

Reference number: 00.10801.02.12.32
Movement: manually wound, Ebauches SA Caliber 715; 26.4 x 19.9 mm, height 4 mm; 15 jewels; 18,000 vph ; original movement from the 1920s; limited to 70 pieces
Functions: hours, minutes, subsidiary seconds
Case: white gold; 108 brilliant-cut diamonds FC TW vvs (1.45 ct), 27.65 x 37.6 mm, height 11.5 mm; sapphire crystal (domed); screwed-down case back
Band: white gold, double folding clasp
Remarks: bracelet set with 420 brilliant-cut diamonds
Price: $53,000

Buti

This four-year-old company was founded by Italian Tommaso Buti, a well-known name in the Italian fashion industry. Buti's hot new concept includes designing these striking watches in Florence and having them manufactured in Switzerland using Swiss parts. This combination of Italian flair for design and Swiss love of detail and precision has produced a line of watches that looks like no other. "Time is an endless succession of moments in which events and the changing of things take place," says Buti, emphasizing that this visible concept of time is one that is all his own. Buti, a watch aficionado and collector, lives and works in Florence, a city that has been highly prized for its association with art, style, and design for centuries. Buti's own showroom is located in a historic palazzo in this city's center.

The movements utilized are of the finest quality: ETA bases with modifications made by a master, La Joux-Perret (formerly Jaquet), under the direction of an Italian watchmaker who cooperates with Buti and

who has been practicing the craft of watch-making since 1939. This watchmaker was also one of those whose skilled hands breathed life into the first Panerai collection, also created in Florence.

The highlight of Buti's collection is doubtlessly the Black Gold flyback chronograph, limited to fifty pieces worldwide. Buti has devised a process involving vacuum ionization that turns an ordinary 18-karat yellow gold case a dramatic black color. The exact process

naturally remains secret, but suffice it to say that the results are quite sensational. When such cases are paired with Buti's strikingly colored galvanized, marbled-relief dials, the outcome remains truly individual. This time-keeper features a Jaquet 8112 movement, which is based on the Valjoux 7750 and modified by the addition of a GMT display requiring an additional plate. Its elegant black dial prominently displays the number of limitation underneath the company's logo, and eight of the dial markers are represented by eight natural diamonds. The "Black" range also contains one other model featuring a split-seconds complication.

Only available in Europe and Asia until two years ago, Buti is currently being distributed in the United States by DOMUSHora, distribution specialists for Italian timepieces. DOMUSHora's vice president of marketing, Umberto Cipolla, describes Buti's collection as the ultimate in Italian sophistication and high-tech watchmaking, "We believe there is a niche market for these very special watches. Our plan is to limit distribution to selective (and selected) luxury retailers whose clientele includes collectors and those who appreciate very special timepieces."

DOMUSHora's president, Davide Murdocca, agrees, adding that his company is in a very good position to introduce this brand to North Americans. "Italians have a true understanding of design. DOMUSHora and Tommaso Buti are part of the Italian fashion scene. They interact and meet regularly with Italy's leading fashion designers to discuss newest styles, trends, and colors. DOMUSHora has experience in both the fashion and watch industries. This is why we are confident that this brand, already hot in Italy, will be enormously successful in the United States," he adds.

Deep Blue

Reference number: GTTTB
Movement: automatic, Jaquet Caliber 8147 (base ETA Valjoux 7750); 44 hours power reserve, soigné finish and rotor with TB logo
Functions: hours, minutes, subsidiary seconds; flyback chronograph, second time zone
Case: titanium, ø 44 mm; sapphire crystal, anti-reflective on both sides; screwed-in crown; water-resistant to 200 m
Band: reptile skin, buckle
Remarks: marbled dial; limited edition
Price: $8,900

Galileo

Reference number: GLA
Movement: automatic, Jaquet Caliber 8771 (base ETA Valjoux 7750); power reserve 40 hours, soigné finish and rotor with TB logo
Functions: hours, minutes, sweep seconds; second time zone
Case: stainless steel, ø 44 mm; sapphire crystal, anti-reflective on both sides; screwed-in crown; water-resistant to 200 m
Band: stainless steel, folding clasp
Price: $12,760
Variations: on reptile skin strap; in yellow gold, in white gold

Lulu

Reference number: LLA
Movement: automatic, Candino Caliber 28362-1 (base ETA)
Functions: hours, minutes, subsidiary seconds
Case: stainless steel, ø 38 mm, bezel satin-finished and secured with 16 screws; sapphire crystal, anti-reflective on both sides; screwed-in crown; water-resistant to 200 m
Band: reptile skin, folding clasp
Price: $5,280

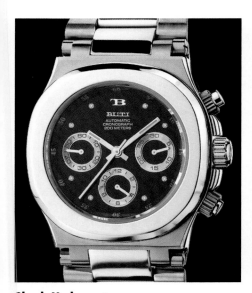

Shark Underwater

Reference number: SHA
Movement: automatic, Jaquet Caliber 8100 (base ETA Valjoux 7750); 28,000 vph, 44 hours power reserve
Functions: hours, minutes, subsidiary seconds; chronograph
Case: stainless steel, ø 44 mm; sapphire crystal; screwed-in crown and buttons; water-resistant to 200 m
Band: stainless steel, folding clasp
Price: $6,820
Variations: on leather strap

Black Gold

Reference number: GTTHEBLACK
Movement: automatic, Jaquet Caliber 8112 (base ETA); power reserve 40 hours, soigné finish and rotor with TB logo
Functions: hours, minutes, subsidiary seconds; flyback chronograph, second time zone
Case: blackened yellow gold, ø 44 mm; sapphire crystal, anti-reflective on both sides; screwed-in crown
Band: reptile skin, folding clasp
Remarks: blackened gold case; limited edition of 50 pieces
Price: $36,000

Yanik Sport

Reference number: YKOSPORT
Movement: automatic, Jaquet Caliber 8147 (base ETA Valjoux 7750); power reserve 40 hours; soigné finish and rotor with TB logo
Functions: hours, minutes, subsidiary seconds, date; chronograph
Case: rose gold, ø 44 mm; sapphire crystal, anti-reflective on both sides; water-resistant to 200 m
Band: rubber, folding clasp
Price: $13,900
Variations: in stainless steel; with diamond markers on dial

Bvlgari

Breathtaking jewelry pieces, scents to beguile the senses, elegant sunglasses, luxurious leather bags, and as the crowning jewel a hotel: Anyone with a penchant for exclusivity is well served by the Italian luxury brand Bvlgari's fine tradition. The brand's concept follows a distinct system within the family-owned company where president Paolo Bulgari and his brother Nicola firmly hold the reins. There is no idea going into production that the two brothers have not personally consented to. The Greek silversmith Sotirio Bulgari settled in Rome at the beginning of the last century and founded a shop called Old Curiosity Shop, named after the novel by Charles Dickens, in order to attract British and American tourists to the Eternal City. His selection of jewelry and accessories was impressive even then, and he soon opened another branch in St. Moritz. In order to continue developing and perfecting his art of jewelry and the production of silver wares, he made his shop on Via Condotti in Rome the flagship store, which it has remained until today.

In the 1990s Bvlgari extended its product portfolio to include perfumes and accessories, supporting its international expansion by going public and putting the holding company Bvlgari S.p.A. on the stock index.

Watches were already part of the program in the 1940s, but only in the '70s did a systematic collection become apparent. The most famous example is the Bvlgari-Bvlgari model: Created by designer Gérald Genta in 1977, it was not only a groundbreaking success for the company, but also the first watch produced in a large series under the company's own logo. Its double logo engraved into the bezel still continues to influence the company's watch design today.

Shortly thereafter the family founded Bvlgari Time S.A. in Switzerland's Neuchâtel. In 1993 Bvlgari embarked upon a new strategy and since then has distributed its watches worldwide through a network of exclusive dealers.

The next step in the evolution followed in mid-2000, when Bvlgari purchased Daniel Roth S.A. and Gérald Genta S.A., both established names in the production and manufacture of complicated and unusual watches.

Bvlgari then presented complicated models, thus securing its position within the established *haute horlogerie* community. In 2004 Bvlgari introduced the first grande complication completely developed and manufactured within the group. And this year a Bvlgari tourbillon as well as a limited-edition minute repeater were launched.

On the other hand, the Assioma model is a highlight of the typical unusual design of Bvlgari: Two rounded arcs characterize the shape and serve as a frame to the square case with the Bvlgari logo.

And with the newest version of the Bvlgari-Bvlgari, the Carbon Gold, the company is doing complete justice to its reputation for using unusual materials. The steel case of the quartz chronograph is coated with a robust carbon material.

The showstopper, however, is the method of distribution that Bvlgari has conceived for it: The Bvlgari Carbon Gold is available in twenty-seven variations in twenty-seven of the most important and exciting cities in the world including New York, London, Shanghai, Moscow, Kuala Lumpur, Tokyo, Aspen, Capri, and Cortina and limited to a total of 999 pieces. The final hurdle for fans of this wristwatch is certainly craftier than just giving it a high price would have been. At just over $1,000 the Carbon Gold is comparatively inexpensive, but in every Bvlgari shop there is a waiting list for the series. And the most loyal customers of each shop are given the privilege of being the first to decide if they would like to purchase the limited model. As you can see, a good relationship with your jeweler is really worth its weight in gold.

Bvlgari-Bvlgari Tourbillon

Reference number: BB 38 GLTB
Movement: manually wound, Daniel Roth Caliber R&G 052; ø 28 mm, height 4.4 mm; 20 jewels; 21,600 vph, power reserve 64 hours; one-minute tourbillon
Functions: hours, minutes; subsidiary seconds (on tourbillon cage); power reserve display (on the back)
Case: yellow gold, ø 38 mm, height 9.4 mm; engraved bezel; sapphire crystal; exhibition case back
Band: reptile skin, folding clasp
Remarks: limited to 25 pieces, numbered
Price: $78,000
Variations: in white gold

Bvlgari-Bvlgari Tourbillon

Reference number: BB 38 GLTB
Movement: Not only does the Bulgari Group profit from the purchase of the Daniel Roth Manufacture, the watch brand Bvlgari also finds many advantages in this family situation. The technology available in Daniel Roth's movement factory in Le Sentier makes the conception, design, and manufacture of the most complicated calibers possible — such as this impressive tourbillon.
Price: $78,000

Bvlgari-Bvlgari Chrono

Reference number: BB 38 SLD CH
Movement: automatic, Bvlgari Caliber MVA 080 (base ETA 2894-2); ø 28.6 mm, height 6.1 mm; 37 jewels; 28,800 vph, power reserve 42 h ; officially certified chronometer (COSC)
Functions: hours, minutes, subsidiary seconds; chronograph; date
Case: stainless steel, ø 38 mm, height 10.5 mm; engraved bezel; sapphire crystal; screwed-in crown
Band: reptile skin, buckle
Price: $4,600
Variations: with steel bracelet, in white gold with white dial

Bvlgari-Bvlgari Moon Phases

Reference number: BBW 38 GLMP/C3
Movement: automatic, LJP Caliber 3103 (base ETA 2892-A2); ø 27 mm, height 5.35 mm; 26 jewels; 28,800 vph, power reserve 42 h
Functions: hours, minutes, subsidiary seconds; date; moon phase
Case: white gold, ø 38 mm, height 9.2 mm; engraved bezel; sapphire crystal
Band: reptile skin, buckle
Remarks: limited to 99 pieces
Price: $16,700
Variations: in white or yellow gold (limited edition or non)

Bvlgari-Bvlgari Annual Calendar

Reference number: BB 38 GLAC 4/C1
Movement: automatic, Dubois-Dépraz Caliber 5733 (base ETA 2892-A2); ø 25.6 mm, height 5.2 mm; 21 jewels; 28,800 vph; power reserve 42 h
Functions: hours, minutes, sweep seconds; annual calendar with date, month
Case: yellow gold, ø 38 mm, height 9.8 mm; engraved bezel; sapphire crystal
Band: reptile skin, buckle
Remarks: limited to 99 pieces
Price: $16,700
Variations: in white or yellow gold (limited edition or non)

Bvlgari-Bvlgari Squelette

Reference number: BBW 33 GLSK/PA
Movement: automatic, ETA Caliber 2892-A2, modified and skeletonized by Parmigiani (base ETA 2892-A2); ø 25.6 mm, height 3.6 mm; 21 jewels; 28,800 vph, power reserve 42 h; movement completely skeletonized and hand-engraved
Functions: hours, minutes
Case: white gold, ø 33 mm, height 7.95 mm; engraved bezel; sapphire crystal; exhibition case back
Band: reptile skin, buckle
Price: $9,250
Variations: in yellow gold

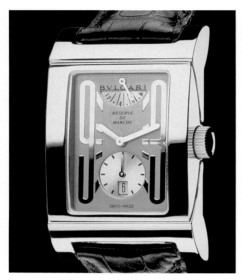

Rettangolo Réserve de Marche

Reference number: RT 49 PLD
Movement: manually wound, Parmigiani Caliber 115;
29.3 x 23.6 mm, height 6.55 mm; 28 jewels; 28,800 vph,
power reserve eight days
Functions: hours, minutes, subsidiary seconds; date; power
reserve display
Case: platinum, 47.65 x 29 mm, height 10.35 mm; sapphire
crystal; exhibition case back
Band: reptile skin, double folding clasp
Remarks: limited to 99 pieces
Price: upon request

Rettangolo Tourbillon

Reference number: RT 49 PLTB
Movement: manually wound, Claret Caliber 97;
37.5 x 27.3 mm, height 7.04 mm; 19 jewels; one-minute
tourbillon; power reserve 100 hours
Functions: hours, minutes
Case: platinum, 48.65 x 30.5 mm, height 11.5 mm;
sapphire crystal; exhibition case back
Band: reptile skin, folding clasp
Remarks: limited to 20 pieces, numbered
Price: $90,800

Anfiteatro Tourbillon

Reference number: AT 40 GLTB
Movement: manually wound, Bvlgari Caliber MVT 9902 TB
(base GP 9902); ø 28.8 mm, height 6.75 mm; 20 jewels;
21,600 vph, power reserve 75 h; one-minute tourbillon;
completely worked and engraved by hand
Functions: hours, minutes
Case: yellow gold, ø 40 mm, height 10.6 mm; engraved
flange; sapphire crystal
Band: reptile skin, buckle
Price: $77,600
Variations: in platinum

Anfiteatro Répétition Minutes

Reference number: AT 40 PLRM
Movement: manually wound, GP Caliber 9950; ø 28.8 mm,
height 6.75 mm; 45 jewels; 28,800 vph, power reserve 47 h;
completely worked and engraved by hand
Functions: hours, minutes, subsidiary seconds; hour, quarter
hour, and minute repeater
Case: platinum, ø 40 mm, height 11.25 mm; engraved
flange; sapphire crystal; exhibition case back
Band: reptile skin, buckle
Price: $124,000
Variations: in yellow gold

Diagono Professional Tachymeter Chronograph Rattrapante

Reference number: CHW 40 GLTARA
Movement: automatic, LJP Caliber 8601 (modified for
Bvlgari, base ETA 7750); ø 30.4 mm, height 8.4 mm; 31
jewels; 28,800 vph, power reserve 42 hours; COSC certified
Functions: hours, minutes, subsidiary seconds
split-seconds chronograph
Case: white gold, ø 40 mm, height 11.1 mm; engraved bezel
with tachymeter scale; sapphire crystal; exhibition case back;
screwed-in crown; water-resistant to 100 m
Band: reptile skin, folding clasp
Price: $29,700

Diagono Professional GMT Flyback

Reference number: GMT 40 SVD/FB
Movement: automatic, Dubois-Dépraz Caliber 21340
(exclusively developed for Bvlgari, base ETA 2892-A2);
ø 31.4 mm, height 6.8 mm; 53 jewels; 28,800 vph, power
reserve 42 hours; officially certified chronometer (COSC)
Functions: hours, minutes, subsidiary seconds; chronograph
with flyback function; date, 24-hour display; third time zone
Case: stainless steel, ø 40 mm, height 13.95 mm; bidirectionally rotating and with 24-hour scale; sapphire crystal;
screwed-in crown and buttons; water-resistant to 100 m
Band: rubber/stainless steel, double folding clasp
Price: $6,300

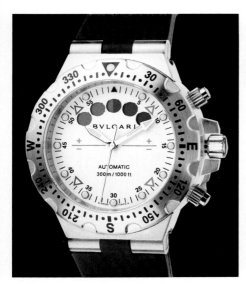

Diagono Professional Regatta

Reference number: SD 40 SV/RE
Movement: automatic, Dubois-Dépraz Caliber 42028 (modified for Bvlgari, base ETA 2892-A2); ø 30 mm, height 7.6 mm; 39 jewels; 28,800 vph, power reserve 42 h
Functions: hours, minutes, subsidiary seconds; chronograph with flyback function and countdown display
Case: stainless steel, ø 40 mm, height 15.6 mm; bidirectionally rotating bezel with 360-degree scale/directions; sapphire crystal; screwed-in crown and buttons; water-resistant to 100 m
Band: rubber/stainless steel, double folding clasp lines and arrows on dial as a course aid at a regatta
Price: $6,150

Diagono Professional GMT

Reference number: GMT 40 C5 SSD
Movement: automatic, Dubois-Dépraz Caliber 312 (base ETA 2892-A2); ø 26.2 mm, height 4.85 mm; 21 jewels, 28,800 vph, power reserve 42 h; officially certified chronometer (COSC); sweep chronograph minute counter
Functions: hours, minutes, subsidiary seconds; chronograph; 24-hour display (second time zone); date
Case: stainless steel, ø 40 mm, height 11.8 mm; bidirectionally rotating bezel with 24-hour scale; sapphire crystal; screwed-in crown and buttons; water-resistant to 100 m
Band: stainless steel, double folding clasp
Price: $5,800

Diagono Titaniumium

Reference number: TI38BTAVTD/SLN
Movement: automatic, ETA Caliber 2892-A2; ø 26.2 mm, height 3.6 mm; 21 jewels, 28,800 vph, power reserve 42 hours
Functions: hours, minutes, sweep seconds; date
Case: titanium/aluminum, ø 38 mm, height 9.25 mm; bezel in titanium; sapphire crystal; screwed-in crown; water-resistant to 100 m
Band: rubber/titanium, folding clasp
Price: $2,500
Variations: in women's size 32 mm

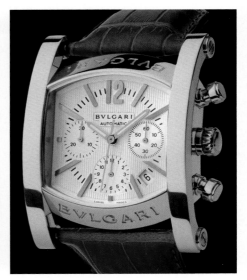

Ergon Chrono

Reference number: EGW 40 C5 GLD CH
Movement: automatic, ETA Caliber 2894-2; ø 28.6 mm, height 6.1 mm; 37 jewels; 28,800 vph, power reserve 42 h
Functions: hours, minutes, subsidiary seconds; chronograph; date
Case: white gold, 40.4 x 51 mm, height 12.3 mm; sapphire crystal
Band: reptile skin, folding clasp
Price: $13,050
Variations: as women's chronograph in stainless steel with mother-of-pearl dial and crocodile skin strap in pink, light blue, white and black, diamond markers and reptile skin strap

Assioma

Reference number: AA 44 C14 SSD
Movement: automatic, ETA Caliber 2892-A2; ø 26.2 mm, height 3.6 mm; 21 jewels, 28,800 vph, power reserve 42 h; personalized for Bvlgari with *côtes de Genève*, perlage and engraved logo
Functions: hours, minutes, sweep seconds; date
Case: stainless steel, ø 44 mm, height 11.1 mm; sapphire crystal
Band: stainless steel, folding clasp
Price: $3,750
Variations: with leather strap; in 39 mm; in 48 mm; in yellow gold with reptile skin strap

Assioma Chrono

Reference number: AA 48 C13 GLDCH
Movement: automatic, ETA Caliber 2094; ø 28.6 mm, height 6.1 mm; 33 jewels, 28,800 vph, power reserve 36 h; personalized for Bvlgari with *côtes de Genève*, perlage and engraved logo
Functions: hours, minutes, subsidiary seconds; chronograph; date
Case: yellow gold, ø 48 mm, height 13.35 mm; sapphire crystal
Band: reptile skin, folding clasp
Price: $10,900
Variations: in 44 mm; in stainless steel (with strap or bracelet)

Nouvelle Horlogerie Calabrese

The exceptional watchmaker Vincent Calabrese, born in Naples in 1944, is justifiably considered one of the most creative heads in the entire Swiss watch industry. The developments he has taken charge of for large and reputable Swiss watch companies are innumerable, and also something that the shy movement designer continues to be absolutely discreet about — uncharacteristic actually for a Neapolitan. Calabrese's special style is easily visible in each detail to the keen observer, though, and forms the basis for the international success of his own watch collection.

For a good year now Calabrese has been working with a circle of distribution professionals, changing the name of his company to Nouvelle Horlogerie Calabrese and moving its business headquarters to Biel. Under the direction of Herbert Gautschi, the new NHC team takes care of the marketing of Calabrese's unusual watches, allowing the master the freedom he needs to conceive newer and more daring instruments. His horological creations in the collection Spatiale are perhaps the best well known, as their bridges and pinions are arranged in just about any shape desired between two

sapphire crystals. They include such personal things as letters of the alphabet and outlines of a country on a map. The winding and setting crown is located on the back of the case, now termed a so-called backwinder. Calabrese has even packed a tourbillon, reduced to its most elementary components, in all its transparency between the two crystals, framed by a simple gold case with central strap lugs.

Calabrese is one of those rare creatures able to produce an entire watch by hand. While most of his movements are made of 18-karat gold, he is the only one today who has been able to achieve this in platinum as well. The playful way with shapes, colors, and functions that the cofounder of the A.H.C.I. (Academy of Independent Horologists) has displayed since founding his own brand in 1975 is underscored by his models featuring a jump hour complication in the cyclops eye which also functions as a minute hand revolving around the dial. The Ottica model attracts the eye of the beholder with its crystal ground for loupe effects, and the Analogica, an evolution of the concept, adds a wandering date window to the mix. Two models featuring power reserve displays are new this year: Central Power shows a wide smile as well as the remaining energy in the movement from a sweep power reserve display hand, and Beauty-Fuel utilizes a hand at the bottom edge of the dial to show the remaining power on a "sunshine" scale. Especially beautiful is the fact that a second time zone and day of the week are also included.

Ottica

Reference number: OTS.114
Movement: automatic, ETA Caliber 2892-A2, modified;
ø 25.6 mm, height 3.6 mm (base movement); 21 jewels;
28,800 vph; exclusive mechanism by Vincent Calabrese
Functions: hours (jump), in rotating window with minutes
marker, central seconds disk
Case: stainless steel, ø 40 mm, height 11.9 mm; sapphire
crystal with optical effect; exhibition window case back
Band: stainless steel, folding clasp
Price: $5,950
Variations: with leather strap; in rose gold; in 36 mm

Ottica Tesoro

Reference number: OTS.190
Movement: automatic, ETA Caliber 2892-A2, modified;
ø 25.6 mm, height 3.6 mm (base movement); 21 jewels;
28,800 vph; exclusive mechanism by Vincent Calabrese
Functions: hours (jump), in rotating window with minutes
marker, central seconds disk
Case: stainless steel, ø 40 mm, height 11.9 mm; bezel set
with 48 diamonds; sapphire crystal with optical effect;
exhibition window case back
Band: reptile skin, folding clasp
Price: $26,000
Variations: set with various colored gemstones

Analogica

Reference number: ANS.102
Movement: automatic, ETA Caliber 2892-A2, modified;
ø 25.6 mm, height 3.6 mm (base movement); 21 jewels;
28,800 vph; exclusive mechanism by Vincent Calabrese
Functions: hours (jump), in rotating window with minutes
marker, date (in rotating window)
Case: stainless steel, ø 40 mm, height 11.9 mm; sapphire
crystal; exhibition window case back
Band: stainless steel, folding clasp
Price: $6,900
Variations: with leather strap; in rose gold

Central-Power

Reference number: CPS.102
Movement: automatic, ETA Caliber 2892-A2, modified;
ø 25.6 mm, height 3.6 mm (base movement); 21 jewels;
28,800 vph; exclusive mechanism by Vincent Calabrese
Functions: hours, minutes, sweep seconds; date; day/night
indication; power reserve display
Case: stainless steel, 40.7 x 37.5 mm, height 10.8 mm;
sapphire crystal; exhibition window case back
Band: stainless steel, folding clasp
Price: $6,700
Variations: with leather strap; in round 40 mm case

Beauty-Fuel

Reference number: BFS.102
Movement: automatic, ETA Caliber 2892-A2, modified;
ø 25.6 mm, height 3.6 mm (base movement); 21 jewels;
28,800 vph; exclusive mechanism by Vincent Calabrese
Functions: hours, minutes, sweep seconds; date and day of
the week; additional 12-hour display (second time zone);
power reserve display
Case: stainless steel, 40.7 x 37.5 mm, height 10.8 mm;
sapphire crystal; exhibition window case back
Band: stainless steel, folding clasp
Price: $7,900
Variations: with leather strap; in round 40 mm case

FL'ORA

Reference number: FLS.229
Movement: automatic, ETA Caliber 2892-A2, modified;
ø 25.6 mm, height 3.6 mm (base movement); 21 jewels;
28,800 vph; exclusive mechanism by Vincent Calabrese
Functions: hours and minutes, additional hours (in window)
Case: stainless steel, ø 36 mm, height 11.9 mm; sapphire
crystal; exhibition window case back
Band: reptile skin, folding clasp
Remarks: mother-of-pearl dial with structure
Price: upon request
Variations: with diamond roses ($3,850) or diamond roses
and diamond bezel ($6,250); in rose gold with diamond roses

Cartier

There is hardly another watch brand that can look back over such a rich history filled with so many successful watch designs. Those of Cartier have reflected the zeitgeist so stylishly that the excitement of their shapes still thrills the watch-buying public even after decades. One hundred years after the introduction of its first wristwatch, Cartier is still able to reach into its pot of past creations with both hands and scoop out ideas. For behind the pot is a genius who understood like no other how to join aesthetics with comfort and practicality: The talented designer Louis Cartier.

The Santos 100, for example, is the modern version of the company's first wristwatch, which Cartier had developed for his friend Alberto Santos-Dumont, an inventor and visionary whose dream of flying led him to the limits of the possible. He needed to have a watch on his arm instead of in his pocket, for in his flying machines he literally had his hands full at all times.

Alberto Santos-Dumont did not wear a special flight suit in the cockpit, but always took to the skies in an elegant street suit with a stiff collar and a hat. The timekeeper on a strap must have appeared that much more obvious underneath the starched cuffs, which the Brazilian roué loved to push back for admirers. This unadorned watch was almost too sober and technical for the fashion that was en vogue a hundred years ago — form also had to follow function for Cartier. The fact that Louis Cartier went down such unusual paths speaks volumes for the creative strength of the designer.

The coolness and strength of the stainless steel case with the characteristic screws on the bezel lent the watch a very professional appearance.

The current Santos 100 concludes a century whose beginnings included the move of the watch from the vest pocket to the wrist — in all its various forms and shapes.

One such form is the Pasha, a round watch that Cartier created for the sovereign of Marrakech in the 1930s. It had to be water-resistant so that the ruler could enjoy his palace baths between appointments.

Today's new Pasha with its 42 mm diameter is similarly dimensioned to the Santos 100. Cartier even had Jaeger-LeCoultre develop a new automatic movement especially for it: Caliber 8000 MC with double spring barrels for 52 hours of power reserve at 11 lines in diameter and only 3.87 millimeters in height. The Collection Privée Cartier Paris took the Tortue into its fold this year, another of Louis Cartier's great designs. The Tortue XL Tourbillon Chronomonopoussoir houses a manually wound movement with a one-minute tourbillon and 72 hours of power reserve in a platinum case. Unique is the combination with a single-pusher chrono-graph whose functions are controlled by a button in the crown. Only forty pieces are to be made. The case measures 38 mm by 48 mm and thus expresses one thing very clearly: Cartier is definitely on the way to a new size.

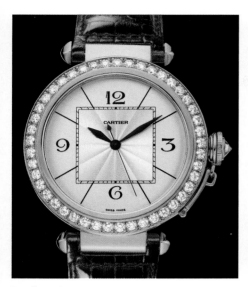

Pasha 42 mm

Reference number: WJ118751
Movement: automatic, Cartier Caliber 8000 (base Jaeger-LeCoultre); ø 25.6 mm, height 3.85 mm; 27 jewels; 28,800 vph
Functions: hours, minutes, sweep seconds
Case: white gold, ø 42 mm, height 8.95 mm; bezel set with diamonds; sapphire crystal; protective crown cap with diamond cabochon
Band: reptile skin, folding clasp
Price: $33,600
Variations: in yellow gold, in red gold

Tank Divan Two Time Zones

Reference number: WA302270
Movement: quartz, Cartier Caliber 056 and 059; two independent quartz movements
Functions: hours, minutes (double)
Case: white gold, 30.5 x 38.3 mm, height 6.2 mm; case set with diamonds; sapphire crystal; crown with diamond cabochon
Band: reptile skin, folding clasp
Remarks: two quartz movements
Price: $31,200
Variations: one time zone

Tankissime MM

Reference number: WE70039H
Movement: quartz, Cartier Caliber 57
Functions: hours, minutes
Case: white gold, 30.6 x 20.3 mm, height 3.9 mm; case sides set with diamonds; sapphire crystal; crown with diamond cabochon
Band: white gold, folding clasp
Price: $27,400
Variations: small model, in yellow gold, in red gold, also without diamonds

Tonneau GM

Reference number: WE400251
Movement: mechanichal, Cartier Caliber 8970MC (base Jaeger-LeCoultre 846); ø 15.3mm
Functions: hours, minutes
Case: white gold, 39.53 x 26.8 mm, height 8.9 mm; case set with diamonds; mineral crystal; crown with diamond cabochon
Band: reptile skin, folding clasp
Price: $22,500
Variations: small model, in red gold, with 2 time zones

Tortue PM

Reference number: WA505031
Movement: mechanichal, Cartier Caliber 430MC (base Piaget 430); ø 20.5 mm, height 2.1 mm; 18 jewels; 21,600 vph
Functions: hours, minutes
Case: red gold, 34 x 28 mm, height 7.6 mm; case set with diamonds; sapphire crystal; exhibition window case back; crown with diamond cabochon
Band: textile, folding clasp
Price: $19,200
Variations: large model, in yellow gold, in white gold

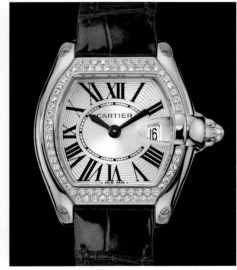

Roadster PM

Reference number: WE500160
Movement: quartz, Cartier Caliber 688
Functions: hours, minutes; date
Case: yellow gold, 37 x 32.8 mm, height 8.9 mm; bezel set with diamonds; sapphire crystal with magnifying lens; crown with diamond cabochon; water-resistant to 100 m
Band: reptile skin, folding clasp
Remarks: quick-change band system
Price: $14,000
Variations: on a metal bracelet, in white gold

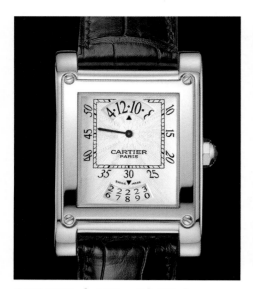

C.P.C.P.* Tank à Vis with Windows

Reference number: W1534551
Movement: manually wound, Cartier Caliber 9902MC ;
23.3 x 26 mm, height 3.5 mm; 24 jewels; 21,600 vph
Functions: hours (jump, disk display), minutes; date
(double-digit disk display)
Case: white gold, 40.6 x 28 mm, height 8.1 mm; sapphire
crystal; exhibition window case back; faceted sapphire crown
Band: reptile skin, folding clasp
Remarks: *= Collection Privée Cartier Paris; rectangular trans-
parent case back, rectangular movement, dial made of gold
Price: $24,600
Variations: in yellow gold, with two time zones

C.P.C.P.* Tortue XL

Reference number: W1546151
Movement: manually wound, Cartier Caliber 9601MC (base
Jaeger-LeCoultre); ø 25.6 mm, height 3.3 mm; 20 jewels;
28,800 vph
Functions: hours, minutes
Case: platinum, 48 x 38 mm, height 10.8 mm; mineral
crystal; exhibition window case back; faceted sapphire crown
Band: reptile skin, folding clasp
Remarks: *= Collection Privée Cartier Paris; dial made of gold
Price: $23,300
Variations: small model, in red gold

C.P.C.P.* Tortue XL Power Reserve

Reference number: W1545951
Movement: manually wound, Cartier Caliber 9910MC (base
Jaeger-LeCoultre); ø 32 mm, height 5.3 mm; 25 jewels;
28,800 vph
Functions: hours, minutes, subsidiary seconds; large date;
power reserve display
Case: white gold, 48 x 38 mm, height 11.6 mm; mineral
crystal; exhibition window case back; faceted sapphire crown
Band: reptile skin, folding clasp
Remarks: *= Collection Privée Cartier Paris; dial made of gold
Price: $22,800
Variations: in red gold

C.P.C.P.* Tonneau XL 2 Time Zones

Reference number: W1547951
Movement: manually wound, Cartier Caliber 9770MC (base
Jaeger-LeCoultre); 12.8 x 15.1 mm, height 2.9 mm; 18 jewels;
21,600 vph
Functions: hours, minutes (double), two time zones
Case: white gold, 51.4 x 29.4 mm, height 9.1 mm; mineral
crystal; two crowns with sapphire cabochons
Band: reptile skin, folding clasp
Remarks: *= Collection Privée Cartier Paris; two mechanical
movements, dial made of gold
Price: $19,900
Variations: in red gold

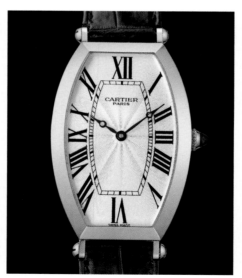

C.P.C.P.* Tonneau XL

Reference number: W1546251
Movement: manually wound, Cartier Caliber 9790MC
(base Jaeger-LeCoultre); 17.2 x 22.6 mm, height 2.9 mm;
21 jewels; 21,600 vph
Functions: hours, minutes
Case: red gold, 51.4 x 29.4 mm, height 8.9 mm; mineral
crystal; crown with sapphire cabochon
Band: reptile skin, folding clasp
Remarks: *= Collection Privée Cartier Paris; dial made of gold
Price: $13,500
Variations: in platinum

C.P.C.P.* Tank Chinoise GM

Reference number: W1542451
Movement: manually wound, Cartier Caliber 437MC (base
Piaget); ø 20.5 mm, height 2.1 mm; 18 jewels; 21,600 vph
Functions: hours, minutes
Case: red gold, 37.2 x 30.6 mm, height 7.7 mm; mineral
crystal; exhibition window case back; crown with
sapphire cabochon
Band: reptile skin, folding clasp
Remarks: *= Collection Privée Cartier Paris; dial made of gold
Price: $12,300
Variations: in platinum

Santos 100

Reference number: W20095Y1
Movement: automatic, Cartier Caliber 49 (base ETA 2892);
ø 25.6 mm, height 3.6 mm, 21 jewels, 28,800 vph
Functions: hours, minutes, sweep seconds
Case: red gold, 51 x 42 mm, height 10.3 mm; sapphire
crystal; crown with faceted sapphire; water-resistant to 100 m
Band: reptile skin, folding clasp
Price: $17,200
Variations: in yellow gold; in stainless steel/yellow gold;
in stainless steel

Santos Demoiselle GM

Reference number: W25062X9
Movement: quartz, Cartier Caliber 690
Functions: hours, minutes
Case: yellow gold, 36.5 x 26.7 mm, height 7 mm; sapphire
crystal; crown with faceted sapphire
Band: yellow gold, folding clasp
Price: $15,200
Variations: as small model; in stainless steel/yellow gold;
in stainless steel

Roadster Chronograph

Reference number: W62027Z1
Movement: automatic, Cartier Caliber 8510 (base ETA
2894); ø 12.5 mm, height 6.1 mm; 37 jewels; 28,800 vph
Functions: hours, minutes, subsidiary seconds;
chronograph; date
Case: stainless steel/yellow gold, 47.6 x 42.8 mm,
height 12.2 mm; sapphire crystal with magnifying lens;
water-resistant to 100 m
Band: stainless steel/yellow gold, calfskin and textile,
folding clasp
Remarks: quick-change band system
Price: $10,500

Mini Tonneau

Reference number: W15361X3
Movement: quartz, Cartier Caliber 28
Functions: hours, minutes
Case: yellow gold, 26 x 16 mm, height 6.4 mm;
sapphire crystal; crown with sapphire cabochon
Band: yellow gold, folding clasp
Price: $10,100
Variations: in white gold; in red gold

Santos Dumont

Reference number: W2007051
Movement: manually wound, Cartier Caliber 430MC
(base Piaget 430); ø 20.5 mm, height 2.1 mm; 18 jewels;
21,600 vph
Functions: hours, minutes
Case: white gold, 44.5 x 35.9 mm, height 7.8 mm; sapphire
crystal; crown with faceted sapphire
Band: reptile skin, folding clasp
Price: $10,700
Variations: in yellow gold; in red gold

Tank Américaine PM

Reference number: W2607456
Movement: quartz, Cartier Caliber 157
Functions: hours, minutes
Case: red gold, 34.8 x 19 mm, height 7.35 mm; mineral
crystal; crown with faceted sapphire
Band: reptile skin, buckle
Price: $5,800
Variations: in yellow gold

Roadster XL

Reference number: W62032X6
Movement: automatic, Cartier Caliber 8500 (base ETA 2893); ø 25.6 mm, height 4.1 mm; 21 jewels; 28,800 vph
Functions: hours, minutes, sweep seconds; date; 24-hour display (second time zone)
Case: stainless steel, 47.6 x 42.10 mm, height 11.4 mm; sapphire crystal with magnifying lens; water-resistant to 100 m
Band: stainless steel, calf skin, folding clasp
Remarks: quick-change band system
Price: $5,450

Tank Louis Cartier GM

Reference number: W1529756
Movement: quartz, Cartier Caliber 687
Functions: hours, minutes, date
Case: yellow gold, 33.7 x 25.5 mm, height 6.35 mm; mineral crystal; crown with sapphire cabochon
Band: reptile skin, buckle
Price: $5,550
Variations: as small model; in white gold

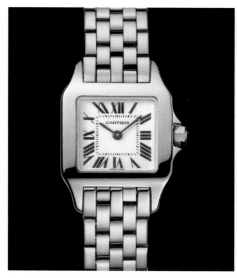

Santos Demoiselle PM

Reference number: W25066Z6
Movement: quartz, Cartier Caliber 157
Functions: hours, minutes
Case: stainless steel/yellow gold, 30.1 x 21.9 mm, height 5.9 mm; sapphire crystal; crown with spinel cabochon
Band: stainless steel/yellow gold, folding clasp
Price: $4,800
Variations: as large model; in yellow gold; in stainless steel

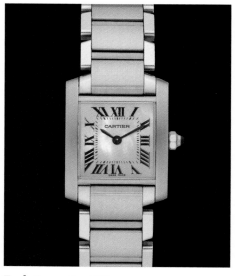

Tank Francaise PM

Reference number: W51027Q4
Movement: quartz, Cartier Caliber 57
Functions: hours, minutes
Case: stainless steel/red gold, 25.1 x 20.3 mm, height 5.8 mm; sapphire crystal; crown with spinel cabochon
Band: stainless steel/red gold, folding clasp
Remarks: pink mother-of-pearl dial
Price: $4,350
Variations: in yellow or white gold; in stainless steel/yellow gold; in stainless steel with white dial

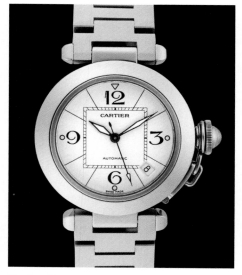

Pasha C

Reference number: W31074M7
Movement: automatic, Cartier Caliber 49 (base ETA 2892); ø 25.6 mm, height 3.6 mm; 21 jewels; 28,800 vph
Functions: hours, minutes, sweep seconds; date
Case: stainless steel, ø 35.3 mm, height 9.8 mm; sapphire crystal; crown with protective cap; water-resistant to 100 m
Band: stainless steel, folding clasp
Price: $3,900
Variations: with pink dial, with black dial, with two time zones, with chronograph

Must 21 Chronoscaph

Reference number: W10184U2
Movement: quartz, Cartier Caliber 272
Functions: hours, minutes, subsidiary seconds; chronograph; date
Case: stainless steel, ø 38.5 mm, height 12 mm; sapphire crystal; crown with cabochon; water-resistant to 100 m
Band: stainless steel, folding clasp
Price: $3,200
Variations: with black dial and rubber appliqués

Rum

This handsome volume, the first full-color guide to the history and appreciation of one of the world's favorite spirits, includes an island-by-island survey of the greatest pure rums.

Winner of the Drink Book prize at the 2004 Glenfiddich Food and Drink Awards

Text by Dave Broom
Photography by Jason Lowe
80 full-color illustrations
176 pages · 9½ × 11 in. · Cloth
ISBN 0-7892-0802-4 · $35.00

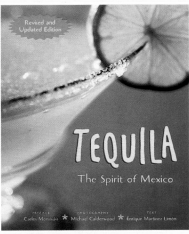

Tequila: The Spirit of Mexico
Revised and Updated Edition

A comprehensive guide to the culture and connoisseurship of tequila, this vibrantly illustrated volume features ratings of more than 100 brands.

"... captures the romance and spirit of Mexico."
—*Playboy*

By Enrique F. Martínez Limón
155 full-color illustrations
184 pages · 9½ × 11¼ in. · Cloth
ISBN 0-7892-0837-7 · $39.95

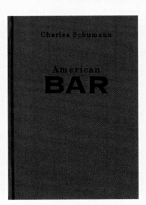

American Bar: The Artistry of Mixing Drinks

This "bar bible" provides recipes for mixing more than 500 drinks, classic and exotic, as well as tips for serving them correctly.

Over 200,000 copies sold!

"The drink mixer's bible." —*The New York Times*

By Charles Schumann
Over 100 two-color illustrations
392 pages · 5 × 6¾ in. · Hardcover
ISBN 1-55859-853-7 · $24.95

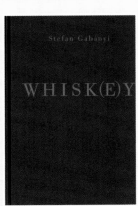

Whisk(e)y

Featuring more than 1,000 impressively detailed, alphabetized entries and hundreds of illustrations, this is the ultimate handbook for whisk(e)y lovers.

A selection of the Book-of-the-Month Club

Text by Stefan Gabányi
Illustrations by Günter Mattei
560 two-color illustrations
368 pages · 5 × 6¾ in. · Hardcover
ISBN 0-7892-0383-9 · $24.95

Chase-Durer

Chase-Durer was founded in 1992 by Marianne and Brandon Chase, who took the other half of the company name from their mentor and associate, watchmaker Stefan Durer. For the thirty years prior to entering the watch industry, the Chases were involved in the production and distribution of Hollywood films. Their interest in the watch industry was sparked by a desire to design, make, and distribute watches that are high in quality and reasonably priced. Delving deep into their material, the Chases began designing their first watches only after months of consultation with pilots. Then they went to the drawing board, followed by extensive prototype testing and, finally, production. This was more than a decade ago, and Chase-Durer is now known as a specialist in Swiss-made watches housed chiefly in solid stainless steel cases featuring scratchproof sapphire crystals and SuperLumiNova illumination for easy legibility day and night. The designs and production elements involved in each timepiece made by Chase-Durer are targeted to deliver to each customer the ultimate in dependability, performance, and legibility.

Despite offering all of these elements of a quality Swiss timepiece, Chase-Durer can be most admired for its honest and principled pricing strategy. This is a structure that raised a number of industry eyebrows at the beginning, but which has also obviously helped to raise awareness of what one is really paying for when buying a branded object.

"Prices for top-quality Swiss watches each contain thousands of dollars of profit for the manufacturer, and this is simply not necessary," states Brandon Chase. "There is no need to go beyond fair pricing for top quality to maintain our company's success and our customers' support."

This dedication to quality, performance, and reliability remains the Chases' number-one priority. Chase-Durer's designs are always pretested in the marketplace before they go

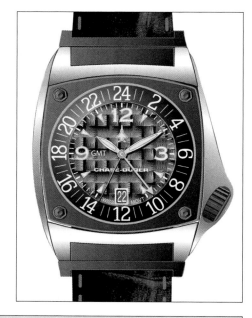

into full production. Currently, watches by Chase-Durer can be purchased in some of the finest watch and jewelry retail shops around the world. In the U.S. alone, hundreds of retailers have proudly joined the team, with this number increasing year by year. In addition, Chase-Durer's timepieces may also be ordered via the company's website, with the desired item easily and comfortably sent to the consumer from the nearest available retailer.

In fact, Chase-Durer is so sure of its quality that it automatically offers a two-year international guarantee on every one of its products, and a five-year incremental guarantee to boot. This is a rare occurrence in an industry that sells watches advertised to be passed on through the generations. Less publicized, but more than worth mentioning, are the aviation and other styled timepieces for women that are designed by Marianne Chase. Her complete and secure sense of style combined with the high-quality materials and production processes prevalent at the company make for incredibly attractive timepieces for women. And don't forget the price.

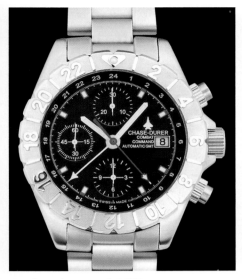

Combat Command GMT

Reference number: CD251.9BBS
Movement: automatic, ETA Caliber 7754; ø 30 mm, height 7.9 mm; 25 jewels; 28,800 vph
Functions: hours, minutes, subsidiary seconds; split-seconds chronograph, second and third time zones; date
Case: stainless steel, ø 40 mm, height 7.9 mm; unidirectionally rotating bezel; sapphire crystal, anti-reflective on both sides; exhibition case back; screwed-in crown and buttons; water-resistant to 100 m
Band: stainless steel, folding clasp
Price: $1,995

Apogee

Reference number: 499.8WG.LEA
Movement: automatic, CD Caliber 9055 (base ETA 2892-A2); ø 25.6 mm, height 5.10 mm; 30 jewels; 28,800 vph; 42 hours power reserve; 18-karat rose gold rotor with *côtes de Genève*, blued screws, movement rhodium-plated; lim. to 99
Functions: hours, minutes, sweep seconds; date, day, second time zone, power reserve display
Case: rose gold, ø 44 mm, height 11.05 mm; sapphire crystal; screwed-down exhibition case back; screwed-in crown; water-resistant to 50 m
Band: alligator skin, folding clasp in 18-karat rose gold
Price: $13,900

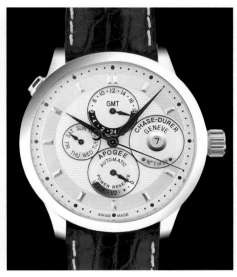

Apogee

Reference number: 499.1WS-LEA
Movement: automatic, CD Caliber 9055 (base ETA 2892-A2); ø 25.6 mm, height 5.10 mm; 30 jewels; 28,800 vph; 42 hours power reserve; 18-kt rose gold rotor with *côtes de Genève* and perlage, blued screws, movement rhodium-plated; lim. to 99
Functions: hours, minutes, sweep seconds; date, day, second time zone, power reserve display
Case: stainless steel, ø 44 mm, height 11.05 mm; sapphire crystal; screwed-down exhibition case back; water-resistant to 50 m
Band: alligator skin, folding clasp
Price: $6,900

Fighter Command Gold

Reference number: CD8WOX.ALLN
Movement: automatic, ETA Valjoux Caliber 7750; ø 30 mm, height 7.9 mm; 25 jewels; 28,800 vph
Functions: hours, minutes, subsidiary seconds; chronograph; date, day
Case: yellow gold, ø 40 mm, height 13 mm; sapphire crystal; screwed-down case back; screwed-in crown and buttons; water-resistant to 30 m
Band: reptile skin, folding clasp
Price: $5,995
Variations: with black enamel dial; 18-karat yellow gold bracelet ($9,995)

Abyss 1000 Professional Diving Automatic

Reference number: CD225.2LX1
Movement: automatic, ETA Caliber 2824-2; ø 25.6 mm, height 4.6 mm; 25 jewels; 28,800 vph
Functions: hours, minutes, sweep seconds; date
Case: stainless steel, ø 44 mm, height 11 mm; unidirectionally rotating bezel with 60-minute scale; sapphire crystal; screwed-down exhibition case back; screwed-in crown; water resistant to 300 m
Band: stainless steel, double folding clasp
Price: $1,295
Variations: with blue, black, silver, or rose gold dial

Tattico

Reference number: CD255.2BBX
Movement: automatic, ETA Caliber 2824-2; ø 25.6 mm, height 4.6 mm; 25 jewels; 28,800 vph
Functions: hours, minutes, sweep seconds; date
Case: stainless steel, 45 x 46 mm, height 12 mm; mineral crystal; screwed-down exhibition case back; water-resistant to 50 m
Band: stainless steel, folding clasp
Price: $995

Chopard

Chopard is one of the very few Swiss watch companies directed by a family. This family, originally hailing from Pforzheim, Germany, had already founded Eszeha in that city in 1904, a company which specialized in the production of watch bracelets and jeweled watches. During World War II the family lost everything, but by 1950 it had already begun a successful rebuilding stage. On the lookout for a "good Swiss name" in the watch industry, the Scheufeles became aware of Louis-Ulysse Chopard's life's work in 1963, a brand that was well on its way up the creek. The unusual resuscitation of this traditional brand, already proclaimed dead by some, has often been told. And still president Karl Scheufele has to laugh quietly to himself at the thought of all the shaking heads directed his way by his Pforzheim colleagues when he began putting together this new company in Geneva.

Far-sighted investments, modern marketing methods, and, last but not least, a rich treasure trove of unused ideas have pushed the development of the Chopard brand forward. While the company could only boast ten employees in 1963, today it proudly supports over 1,000 people in production workshops located in Geneva, Pforzheim,

and Fleurier, as well as in distribution positions all over the world.

This *manufacture* deserves a great deal of respect for the horological complication it presented at Baselworld 2005, introduced so quickly after the Quattro Tourbillon the previous year. No less a goal than an authentic perpetual calendar featuring a large date and a highly precise moon phase was envisioned, and it is quite easy to imagine the pride of the developmental team as they announced to their management that Caliber L.U.C. 96QP would be ready on time in the spring. This mechanism gets its energy from twin serially operating pairs of spring barrels, which lend it a power reserve of 70 hours. The rotating moon phase display located within the subsidiary seconds scale next to the double-digit large date showing the night sky over Geneva and turning once around its axis in one night is an especially yummy detail. Limited to 250 pieces, its production (mainly completed at the Geneva workshop due to the sought-after Seal of Geneva lent its movement) will most likely continue for a couple of years yet. In Fleurier, where the L.U.C. *manufacture* recently celebrated its tenth anniversary, the staff has meanwhile grown to just about one hundred employees, and room is slowly

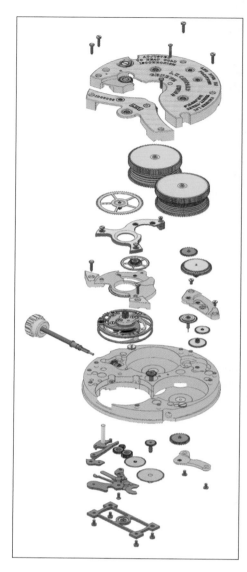

becoming scarce in the generous factory located next to the train station. The fine watch movements by in-house production, such as the perpetual calendar and the tourbillon mentioned above, have taken on a special position in the factory, a position that makes the need for more personnel in the design and assembly departments necessary. A further work-intensive engagement for the Chopard brand concerns its location in the traditional watchmaking town of Fleurier — or the development and establishment of the quality predicate "Qualité Fleurier" to be more exact. In cooperation with movement maker Vaucher Manufacture and various independent institutes, an extensive criteria catalogue was written that contains alongside the tests required of chronometers as set down by the C.O.S.C. and Chronofiable, further practical tests as well as additional aesthetic and technical prerequisites for the movements. Qualité Fleurier is a seal independent of any brand and can be applied for by any manufacturer of mechanical watch movements.

L.U.C. Lunar One 1.96

Reference number: 16/1894
Movement: automatic, L.U.C. Caliber QP; ø 33 mm, height 6 mm; 32 jewels; 28,800 vph; twin spring barrels; microrotor; officially certified chronometer (COSC); Seal of Geneva
Functions: hours, minutes, subsidiary seconds; perpetual calendar with large date, day of the week, month, orbital moon phase display, leap year; 24-hour display
Case: red gold, ø 40.5 mm, height 11.4 mm; sapphire crystal; exhibition window case back
Band: reptile skin, buckle
Remarks: limited to 250 pieces
Price: $46,770

L.U.C. Quattro

Reference number: 16/91863
Movement: manually wound, L.U.C. Caliber 1.98; ø 28.6 mm, height 3.7 mm; 39 jewels; 28,800 vph; four spring barrels, power reserve more than 200 hours; officially certified chronometer (COSC); Seal of Geneva
Functions: hours, minutes, subsidiary seconds; date, power reserve display
Case: platinum, ø 38 mm, height 10 mm; sapphire crystal; exhibition window case back
Band: reptile skin, buckle
Remarks: limited to 1,860 pieces
Price: $30,610

L.U.C. 4R Quattro Régulateur

Reference number: 16/1874
Movement: manually wound, L.U.C. Caliber 1.98-37089 (base L.U.C. 1.98 Quattro); ø 28 mm, height 4.9 mm; 39 jewels; 28,800 vph; four spring barrels, power reserve more than 200 hours; officially certified chronometer (COSC); Seal of Geneva; limited to 250 pieces
Functions: hours (off-center), minutes, subsidiary seconds; date; 24-hour display (second time zone); power reserve display
Case: yellow gold, ø 39.5 mm, height 11 mm; sapphire crystal; exhibition window case back
Band: reptile skin, folding clasp
Price: $32,330

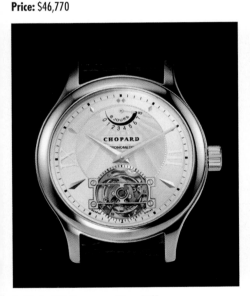

L.U.C. 4T Quattro Tourbillon

Reference number: 16/1869
Movement: manually wound, L.U.C. Caliber 1.02; ø 29.1 mm, height 6.5 mm; 33 jewels; 28,800 vph; one-minute tourbillon; Variner balance with weights, four spring barrels, power reserve more than 200 hours; COSC chronometer; Seal of Geneva
Functions: hours, minutes, subsidiary seconds (on tourbillon cage); power reserve display
Case: red gold, ø 36.4 mm, height 11 mm; sapphire crystal; exhibition window case back
Band: reptile skin, folding clasp
Remarks: limited to 100 pieces
Price: $95,030

L.U.C. Steel Wings Tourbillon

Reference number: 16/91901
Movement: manually wound, L.U.C. Caliber 4TB; ø 29.1 mm, height 6.5 mm; 33 jewels; 28,800 vph; one-minute tourbillon; Variner balance with weights four spring barrels, power reserve more than 216 hours; COSC chronometer; Seal of Geneva
Functions: hours, minutes, subsidiary seconds (on tourbillon cage); power reserve display
Case: platinum, ø 40.5 mm, height 11 mm; sapphire crystal; exhibition window case back
Band: reptile skin, folding clasp
Remarks: limited to 50 pieces
Price: $132,710

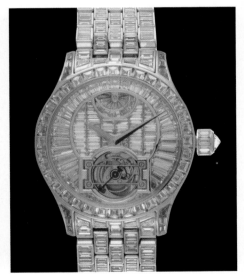

L.U.C. Tourbillon Baguette

Reference number: 14/1908-20
Movement: manually wound, L.U.C. Caliber 1.02; ø 29.1 mm, height 6.5 mm; 33 jewels; 28,800 vph; one-minute tourbillon; Variner balance with weights four spring barrels, power reserve more than 216 hours; COSC chronometer; Seal of Geneva
Functions: hours, minutes, subsidiary seconds; power reserve
Case: white gold, ø 40.5 mm, height 10.90 mm; completely paved with 197 baguette-cut diamonds; sapphire crystal; exhibition window case back
Band: white gold, with 300 baguette diamonds, folding clasp
Remarks: limited to 10 pieces
Price: $1,035,540

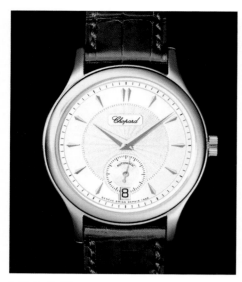

L.U.C. 1.96

Reference number: 16/1860/2
Movement: automatic, L.U.C. Caliber 1.96; ø 27.4 mm, height 3.3 mm; 32 jewels; 28,800 vph; twin spring barrels; microrotor; officially certified chronometer (COSC)
Functions: hours, minutes, subsidiary seconds; date
Case: yellow gold, ø 36,4 mm, height 7.75 mm; sapphire crystal; exhibition window case back
Band: reptile skin, buckle
Remarks: limited to 1,860 pieces; additional case back with honeycomb logo in set
Price: $13,300
Variations: in white or red gold; in platinum

L.U.C. 3.97 Tonneau

Reference number: 16/2267
Movement: automatic, L.U.C. Caliber 3.97; 27.4 x 23 mm, height 3.3 mm; 32 jewels; 28,800 vph; shaped movement; twin spring barrels; microrotor
Functions: hours, minutes, subsidiary seconds; date
Case: yellow gold, 37 x 41 mm, height 8.5 mm; sapphire crystal; exhibition window case back
Band: reptile skin, buckle
Remarks: limited to 1,860 pieces
Price: $17,570
Variations: in red gold; in white gold

L.U.C. GMT

Reference number: 16/1867
Movement: automatic, L.U.C. Caliber 4.96/1-H1 (base L.U.C. 4.96); ø 27.4 mm, height 4.15 mm; 34 jewels; 28,800 vph; twin spring barrels; microrotor; COSC chronometer
Functions: hours, minutes, sweep seconds; date; 24-hour display (second time zone)
Case: white gold, ø 38 mm, height 9.5 mm; sapphire crystal; exhibition window case back
Band: reptile skin, buckle
Remarks: limited to 1,860 pieces
Price: $11,830
Variations: in yellow gold; in red gold

L.U.C. Twin

Reference number: 16/1880
Movement: automatic, L.U.C. Caliber 4.96; ø 27.4 mm, height 3.3 mm; 31 jewels; 28,800 vph; twin spring barrels; microrotor; officially certified chronometer (COSC)
Functions: hours, minutes, sweep seconds; date
Case: white gold, ø 39 mm, height 9.2 mm; sapphire crystal; exhibition window case back
Band: reptile skin, buckle
Price: $9,210
Variations: in yellow gold

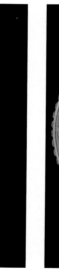

L.U.C. Twist

Reference number: 16/1888
Movement: automatic, L.U.C. Caliber 1.96; ø 27.4 mm, height 3.3 mm; 29 jewels; 28,800 vph; twin spring barrels; microrotor; officially certified chronometer (COSC); Seal of Geneva
Functions: hours, minutes, subsidiary seconds; date
Case: white gold, ø 39 mm, height 10 mm; sapphire crystal; exhibition window case back
Band: reptile skin, buckle
Price: $12,690

L.U.C. Pro One

Reference number: 16/8912/1
Movement: automatic, L.U.C. Caliber 4.96 Pro One; ø 27.4 mm, height 3.5 mm; 34 jewels; 28,800 vph; twin spring barrels; black microrotor; officially certified chronometer (COSC)
Functions: hours, minutes, sweep seconds; date
Case: stainless steel, ø 42 mm, height 13 mm; unidirectionally rotating bezel with 60-minute divisions; sapphire crystal; exhibition window case back; screwed-in crown; water-resistant to 300 m
Band: rubber, folding clasp
Price: $7,365

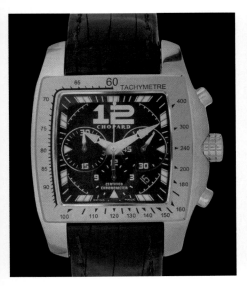

Tycoon

Reference number: 16/8961

Movement: automatic, ETA Caliber 2894-2; ø 28.6 mm, height 6.1 mm; 37 jewels; 28,800 vph; officially certified chronometer (COSC)

Functions: hours, minutes, subsidiary seconds; chronograph; date

Case: stainless steel, 39 x 46.5 mm, height 12.5 mm; bezel engraved with tachymeter scale; sapphire crystal; water-resistant to 50 m

Band: reptile skin, folding clasp

Price: $7,260

Dual Tec

Reference number: 16/2274

Movement: automatic, ETA Caliber 2671 and quartz ETA Caliber 952

Functions: hours, minutes (double); two time zones

Case: yellow gold, 36 x 49 mm, height 8.9 mm; sapphire crystal

Band: reptile skin, folding clasp

Price: $12,900

Variations: in white gold

Chronograph Jacky Ickx Edition 4

Reference number: 16/8998

Movement: automatic, Dubois-Dépraz Caliber 44560 (base ETA 2894); ø 29.3 mm, height 7.5 mm; 49 jewels; 28,800 vph; modified to accommodate 24-hour counter and large date; officially certified chronometer (COSC); ltd. to 1000 pcs

Functions: hours, minutes, subsidiary seconds; chronograph; large date

Case: stainless steel, ø 42.5 mm, height 15.3 mm; bezel engraved with tachymeter scale; sapphire crystal; screwed-in crown and buttons; water-resistant to 50 m

Band: reptile skin with holes, buckle

Price: $6,595

Chronograph Mille Miglia

Reference number: 16/8331

Movement: automatic, ETA Caliber 2894-2; ø 28.6 mm, height 6.1 mm; 37 jewels; 28,800 vph; officially certified chronometer (COSC)

Functions: hours, minutes, subsidiary seconds; flyback chronograph; date

Case: stainless steel, ø 40.5 mm, height 12.7 mm; sapphire crystal; water-resistant to 50 m

Band: rubber mit Dunlop tire profile, buckle

Price: $3,400

Variations: in yellow gold; in white gold

Chronograph Mille Miglia GMT 2005

Reference number: 16/8994

Movement: automatic, ETA Caliber 7754; ø 30.4 mm, height 7.9 mm; 25 jewels; 28,800 vph; officially certified chronometer (COSC)

Functions: hours, minutes, subsidiary seconds; chronograph; 24-hour display (second time zone); date

Case: stainless steel, ø 42.5 mm, height 14.8 mm; bezel engraved with 24-hour scale; sapphire crystal; water-resistant to 50 m

Band: rubber with Dunlop tire profile, buckle

Remarks: limited to 2005 pieces

Price: $4,380

Mille Miglia

Reference number: 15/8920

Movement: automatic, ETA Caliber 2894-2; ø 28.6 mm, height 6.1 mm; 37 jewels; 28,800 vph; officially certified chronometer (COSC)

Functions: hours, minutes, subsidiary seconds; chronograph; date

Case: stainless steel, ø 42.5 mm, height 13.9 mm; bezel engraved with tachymeter scale; sapphire crystal; water-resistant to 50 m

Band: stainless steel, folding clasp

Price: $5,300

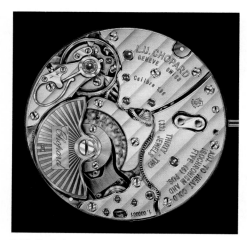

L.U.C. 1.96

Mechanical with automatic winding, power reserve 65 hours

Functions: hours, minutes, subsidiary seconds; date

Diameter: 27.4 mm

Height: 3.3 mm

Jewels: 32

Balance: glucydur

Frequency: 28,800 vph

Balance spring: Breguet

Index system: swan-neck fine adjustment

Remarks: two stacked, serially operating spring barrels, micro-rotor in 22-karat gold; base plate with perlage; beveled bridges with *côtes de Genève*, polished steel parts and screw heads; Seal of Geneva; official chronometer with C.O.S.C. certificate

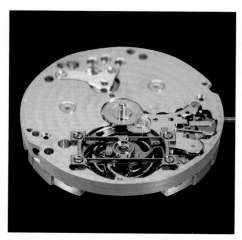

L.U.C. 1.02

Mechanical with manual winding, one-minute tourbillon; power reserve appx. 200 hours

Functions: hours, minutes, subsidiary seconds; power reserve display

Diameter: 29.1 mm

Height: 6.1 mm

Jewels: 33

Balance: Variner with adjustable eccentric weights

Frequency: 28,800 vph

Individual components: 224

Remarks: two stacked, serially operating spring barrels; base plate with perlage; beveled bridges with *côtes de Genève*, polished steel parts and screw heads; Seal of Geneva; official chronometer with C.O.S.C. certificate

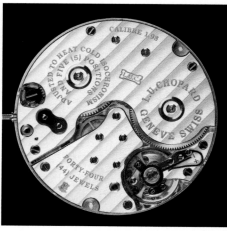

L.U.C. 1.98

Mechanical with manual winding, power reserve appx. 200 hours

Functions: hours, minutes, subsidiary seconds; date; power reserve display

Diameter: 28.6 mm; **Height:** 3.7 mm; **Jewels:** 39

Balance: Glucydur

Frequency: 28,800 vph

Balance spring: Breguet

Index system: swan-neck fine adjustment

Remarks: two stacked, serially operating spring barrels, micro-rotor in 22-karat gold; base plate with perlage; beveled bridges with *côtes de Genève*, polished steel parts and screw heads; Seal of Geneva; official chronometer with C.O.S.C. certificate

L.U.C. 4.96

Mechanical with automatic winding, power reserve 65 hours

Functions: hours, minutes, sweep seconds; date

Diameter: 27.4 mm

Height: 3.3 mm

Jewels: 34

Balance: glucydur

Frequency: 28,800 vph

Balance spring: flat hairspring, Nivarox I

Index system: micrometer screw

Remarks: two stacked, serially operating spring barrels, micro-rotor in 18-karat gold; base plate with perlage; beveled bridges with *côtes de Genève*, polished steel parts and screw heads; official chronometer with C.O.S.C. certificate

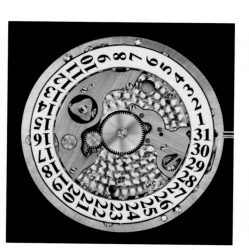

L.U.C. 4.96

The dial side of Caliber 4.96 from the Chopard L.U.C. 2000 Sport model.

L.U.C. 3.96

Mechanical with automatic winding, power reserve 65 hours

Functions: hours, minutes, subsidiary seconds; date

Diameter: 27.4 mm

Height: 3.3 mm

Jewels: 32

Balance: glucydur

Frequency: 28,800 vph

Balance spring: flat hairspring, Nivarox I

Index system: micrometer screw

Remarks: two stacked, serially operating spring barrels, micro-rotor in 18-karat gold; base plate with perlage; beveled bridges with *côtes de Genève*, polished steel parts and screw heads; official chronometer with C.O.S.C. certificate

Chronoswiss

For many, we are a brand that is already very old," ponders Gerd-Rüdiger Lang, founder and boss at Chronoswiss. Amazed, but also proud, he points out that his brand is also mentioned in the same breath as centuries-old traditional Swiss watch companies.

Actually, Chronoswiss has only been in existence for the past twenty-two years. At the time the company was founded, the future looked dismal for mechanical watches and for Lang's beloved profession of watchmaking. Quartz watches were in, and mechanical watches and movements were literally dumped by the ton into the garbage.

Back then, Lang, who was running a special workshop for the repair of chronographs, was already feeling the "Fascination of Mechanics" that would coin his future, making this a slogan that has become his brand's motto. The logo and corporate identity, also unmistakable hallmarks of the brand, were created at this early stage.

"I have been lucky, and I have often done the right thing, without knowing exactly at that moment that it was the right thing to do," says the modest chronograph expert in a quiet manner that radiates a great deal of composure. It is also the inner attitude of the company's boss, who still confirms the authenticity of each Chronoswiss watch with a hand-signed certificate, which differentiates Chronoswiss from other companies within the watch industry.

And after twenty-two years a new era has dawned over Chronoswiss: Lang is building his very own new factory on the outskirts of Munich — thus proving once again that he is an open-minded thinker during a time when many companies are moving their factories to Asia for financial reasons. He, however, plans on moving all forty of his employees to the new building in Karlsfeld by the end of 2006. Not only will the production and administration departments be at home there, but also Lang's planned educational facility and a watch museum. What a jump in development: Just twenty years ago the design of Chronoswiss's watches was grinned at by the competition. The unmistakable look of the typical voluminous Chronoswiss case is of large crystals, an onion-shaped crown, fluted edges, and strong, curved strap lugs. The beginning of the 1990s brought with it a number of imitators, however, and today Chronoswiss watches are absolutely in

fashion. Chronoswiss acted as a bridge builder between horological traditions of the past and modern watch creations, consequently introducing the sapphire crystal case back for all of its models, which has become standard in the industry today.

In the future, a woman will also help in determining the destiny of Chronoswiss: Natalie Lang, daughter of the company head, has completed her watchmaking education in Switzerland as well as ensuing training in management, optimally preparing her for the position of "junior boss." Her signature is visible in the current Timemaster automatic line with its trendy, colorful leather straps and dials. The collection comprises a total of seven colors, from old rose and peppermint green to sunny yellow.

The end of 2005 will also see the serial introduction of the perpetual calendar first shown in April as a study — yet another complicated model for the collection.

The newest addition to the collection is however the unusual Digiteur. This rec-

tangular watch limited to 999 pieces breaks all of the design conventions Lang set down for his company with its jump hours and digital minutes and seconds. Inside the case there ticks a vintage, shaped movement from the 1940s. Its appearance allows it only to be recognized at second glance as the child of its father — by the signature screwed-in strap lugs and sapphire crystal case back.

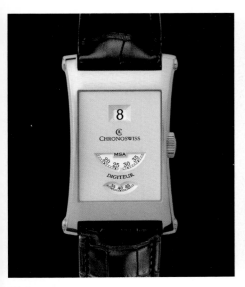

Digiteur

Reference number: CH 1371 R si
Movement: manually wound, FEF Caliber 130; ø 17.5 mm, height 25.6 mm; 15 jewels; 18,000 vph; remnant stock of an FEF Caliber with disk displays
Functions: hours (digital, jump), minutes and seconds (both disk displays in window)
Case: red gold, 27.7 x 45.5 mm, height 11 mm; sapphire crystal; exhibition window case back
Band: crocodile skin, buckle
Remarks: limited edition 999 pieces
Price: $12,400
Variations: in yellow or white gold; in platinum

Chronograph Rattrapante

Reference number: CH 7321
Movement: automatic, Chronoswiss Caliber C.732 (base ETA 7750); ø 30 mm, height 5.4 mm; 23 jewels; 28,800 vph; patented split-seconds mechanism; movement finished with *côtes de Genève*; individually numbered
Functions: hours, minutes (off-center), subsidiary seconds; chronograph with split-seconds
Case: yellow gold, ø 38 mm, height 15.25 mm; sapphire crystal; exhibition window case back
Band: crocodile skin, buckle
Price: $16,900
Variations: gold/stainless steel; yellow or white gold; platinum

Répétition à Quarts

Reference number: CH 1643 co
Movement: automatic, Chronoswiss Caliber C.126 (base Enicar 165 with strike module E 94 by Dubois-Dépraz); ø 28 mm, height 8.35 mm; 38 jewels; 21,600 vph
Functions: hours, minutes, subsidiary seconds; quarter repeater
Case: stainless steel, ø 40 mm, height 14 mm; sapphire crystal; exhibition window case back
Band: crocodile skin, buckle
Price: $24,950
Variations: in yellow, red or white gold, in yellow gold/steel or red gold/steel, in platinum; dial painted silver or white

Chronoscope

Reference number: CH 1523 rc
Movement: automatic, Chronoswiss Caliber C.125 (base Enicar 165); ø 26.8 mm, height 6.8 mm; 30 jewels; 21,600 vph; chronograph with column wheel control integrated into base movement; operation via one single button
Functions: hours (off-center), minutes, subsidiary seconds; chronograph
Case: stainless steel, ø 38 mm, height 13 mm; sapphire crystal; exhibition window case back; crown with integrated chronograph button
Band: crocodile skin, buckle
Price: $8,150

Delphis

Reference number: CH 1423
Movement: automatic, Chronoswiss Caliber C.124 (base Enicar 165); ø 28.6 mm, height 6.9 mm; 32 jewels; 21,600 vph; *côtes de Genève*
Functions: hours (digital, jump), minutes (retrograde), subsidiary seconds (analogue)
Case: stainless steel, ø 38 mm, height 11 mm; sapphire crystal; exhibition window case back
Band: crocodile skin, buckle
Price: $7,150
Variations: in yellow, red or white gold, in yellow gold/steel or red gold/steel, in platinum (limited edition)

Kairos Medium Diamonds

Reference number: CH 1421 R ku
Movement: automatic, ETA Caliber 2892-A2; ø 25.6 mm, height 5.75 mm; 21 jewels; 28,800 vph; *côtes de Genève*
Functions: hours, minutes, sweep seconds; date
Case: stainless steel, ø 34 mm, height 8.3 mm; bezel set with 60 brilliant-cut diamonds; sapphire crystal; exhibition window case back
Band: crocodile skin, buckle
Price: $13,500
Variations: without diamonds; with black dial; various bands, also with deployant clasp

Klassik Chronograph

Reference number: CH 7403
Movement: automatic, Chronoswiss Caliber C.741 (base ETA 7750); ø 30 mm, height 5.4 mm; 23 jewels; 28,800 vph
Functions: hours, minutes, subsidiary seconds; chronograph; date
Case: stainless steel, ø 37 mm, height 13.9 mm; sapphire crystal; exhibition window case back
Band: crocodile skin, buckle
Price: $7,150
Variations: with tachymeter or pulsometer scale

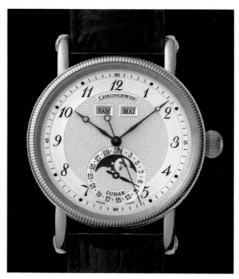

Lunar Complete Calendar

Reference number: CH 9321
Movement: automatic, Chronoswiss Caliber C.931 (base ETA 2892-A2); ø 25.6 mm, height 5.75 mm; 21 jewels; 28,800 vph; calendar dial train by Dubois-Dépraz
Functions: hours, minutes, sweep seconds; date, day of the week, month, moon phase
Case: rose gold, ø 38 mm, height 10.65 mm; sapphire crystal; exhibition window case back
Band: crocodile skin, buckle
Price: $12,700
Variations: in stainless steel ($6,450) yellow gold/stainless steel ($8,300); with matching metal bracelets

Lunar Chronograph

Reference number: CH 7523 L
Movement: automatic, Chronoswiss Caliber C.755 (base ETA 7750); ø 30 mm, height 5.4 mm; 23 jewels; 28,800 vph
Functions: hours, minutes, subsidiary seconds; chronograph; date; moon phase
Case: stainless steel, ø 38 mm, height 15 mm; sapphire crystal; exhibition window case back
Band: crocodile skin, buckle
Price: $6,500
Variations: in yellow, red or white gold, in yellow gold/stainless steel or red gold/stainless steel, in platinum (limited edition), various dials, various bands

Opus

Reference number: CH 7522 S
Movement: automatic, Chronoswiss Caliber C.741 S (base ETA 7750); ø 30 mm, height 5.4 mm; 23 jewels; 28,800 vph; movement completely skeletonized and decorated; dials individually numbered
Functions: hours (off-center), minutes, subsidiary seconds; chronograph
Case: yellow gold/stainless steel, ø 38 mm, height 15 mm; sapphire crystal; exhibition window case back
Band: crocodile skin, buckle
Price: $12,500
Variations: in yellow gold, stainless steel or platinum

Orea Lady

Reference number: CH 7161 R
Movement: automatic, ETA Caliber 7001; ø 23.30 mm, height 2.5 mm; 17 jewels, 21,600 vph
Functions: hours, minutes, subsidiary seconds
Case: red gold, ø 29 mm, height 7.9 mm; sapphire crystal; exhibition window case back
Band: crocodile skin, buckle
Remarks: genuine enameled dial
Price: $6,400
Variations: in yellow gold, yellow gold/stainless steel or stainless steel; various bands, also with deployant clasp; also as Orea Automatic and Orea Manual Wind

Pathos Platinum

Reference number: CH 7320 S
Movement: automatic, Chronoswiss Caliber C.732 S (base ETA 7750); ø 30 mm, height 5.4 mm; 23 jewels; 28,800 vph; movement completely skeletonized and decorated; dials individually numbered
Functions: hours, minutes; (off-center), subsidiary seconds; chronograph with split-seconds
Case: platinum, ø 38 mm, height 15.25 mm; sapphire crystal; exhibition window case back
Band: crocodile skin, buckle
Price: $45,500
Variations: in yellow gold, yellow gold/steel or steel

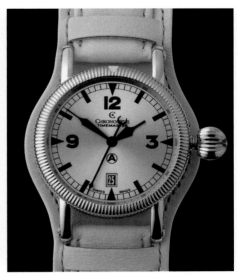

Régulateur Gold

Reference number: CH 1221
Movement: automatic, Chronoswiss Caliber C.122 (base Enicar 165); ø 26.8 mm, height 5.3 mm; 30 jewels; 21,600 vph
Functions: hours (off-center), minutes, subsidiary seconds
Case: rose gold, ø 38 mm, height 10.5 mm; sapphire crystal; exhibition window case back
Band: crocodile skin, buckle
Price: $10,200
Variations: in yellow gold, yellow gold/stainless steel or stainless steel; various dials, various bands, also with deployant clasp

Timemaster 24 Hours Day/Night

Reference number: CH 6433 D N
Movement: manually wound, Chronoswiss Caliber C.672 (base ETA Unitas 6497-1); ø 36.6 mm, height 5.4 mm; 18 jewels; 18,000 vph; two-tone dial for day and night times
Functions: hours, minutes, sweep seconds
Case: stainless steel, ø 44 mm, height 12.3 mm; bidirectionally rotating bezel with reference marker; sapphire crystal; exhibition window case back; extra-large crown, screwed-down; water-resistant to 100 m
Band: crocodile skin and extendable leather strap, buckle
Price: $6,750
Variations: with black dial

Timemaster Automatic

Reference number: CH 2833 ro
Movement: automatic, ETA Caliber 2892-A2; ø 25.6 mm, height 3.6 mm; 21 jewels; 28,800 vph
Functions: hours, minutes, sweep seconds; date
Case: stainless steel, ø 40 mm, height 13 mm; bidirectionally rotating bezel with reference marker; sapphire crystal; exhibition window case back; extra-large crown, screwed-down; water-resistant to 100 m
Band: leather, buckle
Price: $3,800
Variations: with yellow, green, red, light blue, blue or mint green dial, with matching straps

Timemaster Flyback

Reference number: CH 7633 LE lu SBL
Movement: automatic, Chronoswiss Caliber C.763 (base ETA 7750); ø 30 mm, height 7.9 mm; 29 jewels; 28,800 vph
Functions: hours, minutes, subsidiary seconds; chronograph with flyback function
Case: stainless steel, ø 40 mm, height 13 mm; bidirectionally rotating bezel with reference marker; sapphire crystal; exhibition window case back; extra-large crown (left), screwed-down; water-resistant to 100 m
Band: stainless steel, double folding clasp
Remarks: available for right- or left-handers; luminous dial
Price: $8,150

Tora Chronograph

Reference number: CH 7323
Movement: automatic, Chronoswiss Caliber C.743 (base ETA 7750); ø 30 mm, height 5.4 mm; 23 jewels; 28,800 vph
Functions: hours, minutes, subsidiary seconds, chronograph; date; 24-hour display (second time zone)
Case: stainless steel, ø 38 mm, height 15.1 mm; sapphire crystal; exhibition window case back
Band: crocodile skin, buckle
Price: $7,600
Variations: in yellow, red or white gold, in yellow gold/stainless steel or red gold/stainless steel, in platinum (limited edition); also with black dial; various bands

Régulateur à Tourbillon Squelette

Reference number: CH 3121 S W
Movement: manually wound, Chronoswiss Caliber C.361 (base STT); ø 30 mm, height 5.4 mm; 23 jewels; power reserve appx. 72 hours; flying one-minute tourbillon; twin spring barrels
Functions: hours (off-center), minutes
Case: white gold, ø 38 mm, height 10.5 mm; sapphire crystal; exhibition window case back
Band: crocodile skin, buckle
Price: $67,500
Variations: in yellow gold, red gold or platinum (limited edition); various bands, also with deployant clasp

Caliber C.126 (dial side)

Base caliber: C.122 (Enicar 165) with strike train module E 94 by Dubois-Dépraz
Mechanical with automatic winding, power reserve 35 hours; ball-bearing rotor in platinum, skeletonized and gold-plated
Functions: hours, minutes, subsidiary seconds; quarter-hour repeater
Diameter: 28 mm; **Height:** 8.35 mm; **Jewels:** 38
Balance: glucydur, three-legged
Frequency: 21,600 vph; **Shock protection:** Incabloc
Balance spring: Nivarox I flat hairspring, with fine adjustment via eccentric screw
Remarks: all-or-nothing strike train; two gongs; base plate with perlage; beveled bridges with perlage; *côtes de Genève*; rotor with *côtes de Genève*

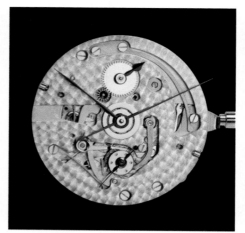

Caliber C.125 (dial side)

Base caliber: C.122 (Enicar 165)
Mechanical with automatic winding, power reserve 35 hours; ball-bearing rotor in platinum, skeletonized and gold-plated
Functions: hours (off-center), minutes, subsidiary seconds; chronograph
Diameter: 26.8 mm (11 "'); **Height:** 7.85 mm
Jewels: 30; **Balance:** glucydur, three-legged
Frequency: 21,600 vph; **Shock protection:** Incabloc
Balance spring: Nivarox I flat hairspring, with fine adjustment via eccentric screw
Remarks: column wheel chrono mechanism integrated into base movement; crown button for start-stop-reset; ball-bearing chronograph center wheel; base plate with perlage; beveled bridges with perlage; *côtes de Genève*

Caliber C.111

Base caliber: Marvin 700
Mechanical with manual winding, power reserve 46 hours
Functions: hours, minutes, subsidiary seconds
Diameter: 29.4 mm (13 "')
Height: 3.3 mm
Jewels: 17
Balance: glucydur, three-legged
Frequency: 21,600 vph
Shock protection: Incabloc
Balance spring: Nivarox I flat hairspring
Remarks: bridges with perlage; polished pallet fork, escape wheel, and screws

Caliber C.122

Base caliber: Enicar 165
Mechanical with automatic winding, power reserve 40 hours; ball-bearing rotor, skeletonized and gold-plated
Functions: hours, minutes, subsidiary seconds
Diameter: 26.8 mm (11 "')
Height: 5.3 mm
Jewels: 30
Balance: glucydur, three-legged
Frequency: 21,600 vph
Shock protection: Incabloc
Balance spring: Nivarox I flat hairspring
Remarks: base plate with perlage; beveled bridges with perlage and *côtes de Genève*; rotor with *côtes de Genève*; polished pallet fork, escape wheel, and screws

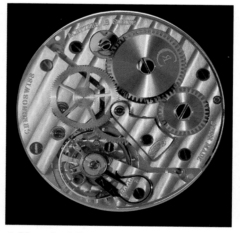

Caliber C.672

Base caliber: ETA 6497-1
Mechanical with manual winding, power reserve appx. 50 hours; stop-seconds (balance stop)
Functions: hours, minutes, sweep seconds
Diameter: 36.6 mm (16 1/2 "')
Height: 5.4 mm; **Jewels:** 18
Balance: glucydur, three-legged
Frequency: 18,000 vph
Shock protection: Incabloc
Balance spring: Nivarox I flat hairspring, swan-neck fine adjustment
Remarks: beveled bridges with *côtes de Genève*; polished pallet fork, escape wheel, and screws; escape bridge with perlage

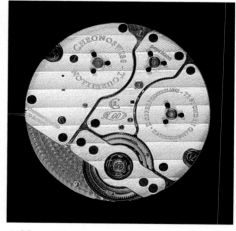

Caliber C.361

Base caliber: STT 6361
Mechanical with manual winding, power reserve 72 hours; twin spring barrels; one-minute tourbillon, ruby ball bearing
Functions: hours (off-center), minutes
Diameter: 30 mm (13 "')
Height: 5.4 mm
Jewels: 23, three of which are embedded in gold chatons
Balance: glucydur, with weighted screws
Frequency: 28,800 vph
Shock protection: Incabloc
Balance spring: Nivarox I flat hairspring
Remarks: bridges with *côtes de Genève*

Exceptional Destinations books from Abbeville Press:
A perfect combination of beautiful photography and useful travel information

Bicycling
Along the World's Most Exceptional Routes

An outstanding guide to twenty-five scenic bicycling vacations around the world for riders of all abilities.

"Bicycling is an international inspiration for dedicated cyclists and ideal for armchair travelers . . ."
—*Midwest Book Review*

By Rob Penn
100 full-color illustrations
160 pages · 8¼ × 9½ in. ·
Cloth
ISBN 0-7892-0846-6 · $29.95

Cooking School Holidays
in the World's Most Exceptional
Places

An appetizing guide to learning vacations for food lovers at the world's most prestigious and scenically situated cooking schools.

"Just the cover of *Cooking School Holidays* makes you want to run to the computer and book a flight to one of the cooking schools featured in this beautifully illustrated guide."
—*Trump World*
Magazine

By Jenni Muir
150 full-color illustrations
160 pages · 8¼ × 9½ in. ·
Cloth ISBN 0-7892-0836-9 ·
$29.95

Golfing
on the World's Most Exceptional Courses

A magnificent guide to twenty-five of the world's top golfing vacations, selected for their breathtaking locations, venerable traditions, notable course design, and first-rate accommodations.

By Mark Rowlinson
100 full-color illustrations
160 pages · 8¼ × 9½ in. ·
Cloth
ISBN 0-7892-0866-0 · $29.95

Spas:
Exceptional Destinations
Around the World

A dream book of places to be pampered and unwind that unveils the world's twenty-five best vacation spas.

"From its cool blue cover to the inside photos of sand-dune joggers and massage recipients, this is a volume that fuels daydreams."
—Christopher Reynolds, *Los Angeles Times*

By Eloise Napier
240 full-color illustrations
160 pages · 8¼ × 9½ in. ·
Cloth
ISBN 0-7892-0798-2 · $29.95

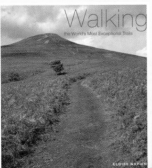

Walking
the World's Most Exceptional Trails

The ultimate guide to the world's top walking vacations, selected for their unusual locations, spectacular scenery, and awesome wildlife.

Selected as one of independent booksellers' top gift recommendations in *USA Today*!

By Eloise Napier
240 full-color illustrations
160 pages · 8¼ × 9½ in. ·
Cloth ISBN 0-7892-0801-6 ·
$29.95

Frédérique Constant

A letta and Peter Stas decided to found their own watch production at the end of the 1980s. Named after Aletta's great-grandmother (Frédérique Schreiner) and Peter's great-grandfather (Constant Stas), this new company was created to compete in a segment of the watch market that in no way lacks brands.

Financed with some of their own capital and a private loan from a good friend, the young couple designed their timepiece in Holland and had 350 of them made in Switzerland, immediately reinvesting the profits into the second collection. And the latter still characterizes the way the pair operates today, with continually increasing success.

The 350 pieces once sold at the beginning of the '90s have turned into a good 50,000 watches per year. The company's entry level piece currently retails for about $400, with the brand positioned in the middle segment of the Swiss watch industry's conceptual prestige pyramid.

Since it is no longer enough today to just encase a purchased automatic movement to be really successful in the mechanical watch industry, several years ago Frédérique Constant decided to elevate itself from the masses by implementing a simple, though exciting idea: The base plate and dial were opened up in the region of the movement's balance and escapement so that one would be able to observe the balance's excited swinging on the front of the watch. The obvious association with a quickly beating heart was also reflected in the name of the collection, Heart Beat.

Then in October 2001, the Stases finally decided to develop their own movement, which led to the presentation of the Caliber FC 910 Heart Beat about two years ago. This manually wound movement was completely designed to position the large balance and the escapement feeding it with energy as the visual center of the entire

piece. In order to reach this goal, the balance and other components of the movement were "turned around." To do this, the balance cock was moved to the dial side, making the balance and the busily pulsating balance spring visible from the front of the watch. At the same time, a component secured with two screws determines the action on the dial side, multitasking to hold the skeletonized balance cock and index, determining the height of the dial train gears, and adding to the attractive visuals of the dial.

Dominated by models outfitted with the new *manufacture* Caliber FC 910 Heart Beat, the brand's mechanical watches now comprise 40 percent of the approximately 100 different models in the collection (not to mention the sixty variations) — with increasing tendencies.

There also remains good reason for utilizing quartz movements at this brand. "We always use quartz movements for certain special characteristics or functions," Peter

Stas explains. "All of our thin watches, for example, are outfitted with a quartz movement only 1.9 mm high. We also have quartz watches with small complications such as a moon phase display or a date hand. We mainly use quartz movements for two reasons: First of all, we can make flatter watches with them than with mechanical movements. And second of all, we can sell a watch for 500 euros that has a very interesting outward appearance. This is also Frédérique Constant's philosophy: To make classic, handsome watches at a reasonable price."

After moving several times within Geneva — unavoidable due to the consistent growth of the company — Aletta and Peter Stas finally decided to build a modern building with approximately 3,000 square meters of factory space in Geneva's industrial suburb Plan-les-Ouates. The building is scheduled for completion in the fall of 2005.

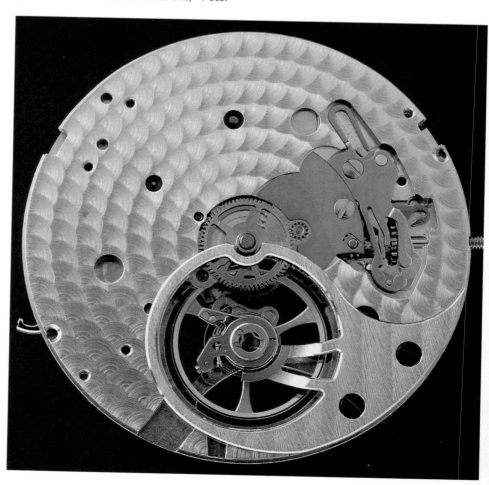

Classics Heart Beat Manufacture Moon

Reference number: FC-915MC4H6
Movement: manually wound, Frédérique Constant Manufacture Caliber FC 915; ø 30.5 mm, height 3.5 mm; 19 jewels; 28,800 vph; *manufacture* caliber with "upside-down" positioning of the balance and escapement on the dial side
Functions: hours, minutes; date; moon phase
Case: stainless steel, ø 41 mm, height 10 mm; sapphire crystal; exhibition window case back
Band: leather, buckle
Price: $5,999
Variations: in rose gold

Highlife Heart Beat Manufacture

Reference number: FC-910MC3H9
Movement: manually wound, Frédérique Constant Manufacture Caliber FC 910; ø 30.5 mm, height 3.3 mm; 17 jewels; 28,800 vph; *manufacture* caliber with "upside-down" positioning of the balance and escapement on the dial side
Functions: hours, minutes
Case: rose gold, ø 39.5 mm, height 8.5 mm; sapphire crystal; exhibition window case back
Band: reptile skin, buckle
Price: $9,399
Variations: in stainless steel

Highlife Heart Beat Retrograde

Reference number: FC-680AS3H6
Movement: automatic, Frédérique Constant Caliber FC 680 (base ETA 2892-A2); ø 25.6 mm, height 3.6 mm; 21 jewels; 28,800 vph; modified with partial skeletonizing
Functions: hours, minutes, subsidiary seconds (retrograde)
Case: stainless steel, ø 38 mm, height 10.5 mm; sapphire crystal; exhibition window case back
Band: ostrich leather, buckle
Price: $5,649
Variations: with black dial; various bands; in rose gold; in platinum

Classics Automatic Chronometer

Reference number: FC-303CA3P5
Movement: automatic, Frédérique Constant Caliber FC 303 (base ETA 2824); ø 25.6 mm, height 4.6 mm; 25 jewels; 28,800 vph; officially certified chronometer (COSC)
Functions: hours, minutes, sweep seconds; date
Case: stainless steel (PVD-gold plated), ø 38 mm, height 10 mm; sapphire crystal
Band: leather, buckle
Price: $1,299
Variations: in stainless steel

Classics Big Date Dual Time

Reference number: FC-325MC3P6
Movement: automatic, Frédérique Constant Caliber FC 325 (base ETA 2892); ø 25.6 mm, height 3.6 mm; 21 jewels; 28,800 vph
Functions: hours, minutes, sweep seconds; large date; second time zone
Case: stainless steel, ø 38 mm, height 10.9 mm; sapphire crystal; exhibition window case back
Band: leather, buckle
Price: $2,199
Variations: in PVD-gold plated

Classics Index Chronograph

Reference number: FC-392S5B6B
Movement: automatic, Frédérique Constant Caliber FC 392 (base ETA 7750); ø 30 mm, height 7.9 mm; 25 jewels; 28,800 vph
Functions: hours, minutes, subsidiary seconds; chronograph; date
Case: stainless steel, ø 42 mm, height 14.1 mm; sapphire crystal; exhibition window case back
Band: stainless steel, folding clasp
Price: $2,199
Variations: PVD-rose gold plated; leather strap; black dial

Classics Tonneau Automatic

Reference number: FC-303M4T6
Movement: automatic, Frédérique Constant Caliber FC 303 (base ETA 2824); ø 25.6 mm, height 4.6 mm; 25 jewels; 28,800 vph
Functions: hours, minutes, sweep seconds; date
Case: stainless steel, 47 x 36 mm, height 11.2 mm; sapphire crystal
Band: leather, buckle
Price: $1,049
Variations: in PVD-gold plated

Classics Tonneau Automatic

Reference number: FC-310M4T5
Movement: automatic, Frédérique Constant Caliber FC 310-3 (base ETA 2824); ø 25.6 mm, height 4.6 mm; 25 jewels; 28,800 vph; modified with partial skeletonizing
Functions: hours, minutes, sweep seconds
Case: stainless steel (PVD-gold plated), 47 x 36 mm, height 11.2 mm; sapphire crystal; exhibition window case back
Band: leather, buckle
Price: $1,299
Variations: in stainless steel

Classics Carree

Reference number: FC-303MC4C25
Movement: automatic, Frédérique Constant Caliber FC 303 (base ETA 2824); ø 25.6 mm, height 4.6 mm; 25 jewels; 28,800 vph
Functions: hours, minutes, sweep seconds; date
Case: stainless steel (PVD-gold plated), 30.6 x 39.1 mm, height 10.5 mm; sapphire crystal; exhibition window case back
Band: leather, buckle
Price: $1,149
Variations: in stainless steel

Classics Automatic

Reference number: FC-303MC3P5
Movement: automatic, Frédérique Constant Caliber FC 303 (base ETA 2824); ø 25.6 mm, height 4.6 mm; 25 jewels; 28,800 vph
Functions: hours, minutes, sweep seconds; date
Case: stainless steel (PVD-gold plated), ø 38 mm, height 10 mm; sapphire crystal
Band: leather, buckle
Price: $949
Variations: in stainless steel

Classics Automatic

Reference number: FC-303V4B4
Movement: automatic, Frédérique Constant Caliber FC 303 (base ETA 2824); ø 25.6 mm, height 4.6 mm; 25 jewels; 28,800 vph
Functions: hours, minutes, sweep seconds; date
Case: stainless steel (PVD-gold plated), ø 38 mm, height 10 mm; sapphire crystal
Band: leather, buckle
Price: $1,099
Variations: in stainless steel

Classics Ladies

Reference number: FC-303MPWD2P5
Movement: automatic, Frédérique Constant Caliber FC 303 (base ETA 2824); ø 25.6 mm, height 4.6 mm; 25 jewels; 28,800 vph
Functions: hours, minutes, sweep seconds; date
Case: stainless steel (PVD-gold plated), ø 35 mm, height 10 mm; sapphire crystal; exhibition window case back
Band: reptile skin, buckle
Price: $1,449
Variations: in stainless steel; with stainless steel link bracelet

Classics Heart Beat

Reference number: FC-310MC4C26
Movement: automatic, Frédérique Constant Caliber FC 310-3 (base ETA 2824); ø 25.6 mm, height 4.6 mm; 25 jewels; 28,800 vph; modified with partial skeletonizing
Functions: hours, minutes, sweep seconds
Case: stainless steel, 30.6 x 39.1 mm, height 10.5 mm; sapphire crystal; exhibition window case back
Band: leather, buckle
Price: $1,249
Variations: in PVD-gold plated

Persuasion Automatic Moonphase

Reference number: FC-360M4P6
Movement: automatic, Frédérique Constant Caliber FC 360 (base ETA 2892); ø 25.6 mm, height 3.6 mm; 21 jewels; 28,800 vph
Functions: hours, minutes, sweep seconds; date, day of the week, month, moon phase
Case: stainless steel, ø 40 mm, height 11 mm; sapphire crystal; exhibition window case back
Band: leather, buckle
Price: $1,949
Variations: with silver plated dial; in PVD-gold plated

Persuasion Moonphase Carree

Reference number: FC-365B4C6
Movement: automatic, Frédérique Constant Caliber FC 365 (base ETA 2892); ø 25.6 mm, height 3.6 mm; 21 jewels; 28,800 vph
Functions: hours, minutes, sweep seconds; date, day of the week, month, moon phase
Case: stainless steel, 39.5 x 36.5 mm, height 11.3 mm; sapphire crystal; exhibition window case back
Band: leather, buckle
Price: $2,149
Variations: with silver plated dial; in PVD-gold plated

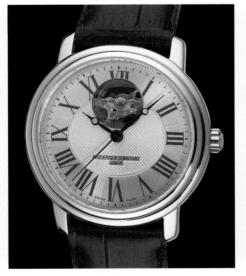

Persuasion Automatic

Reference number: FC-303M3P6B
Movement: automatic, Frédérique Constant Caliber FC 303 (base ETA 2824); ø 25.6 mm, height 4.6 mm; 25 jewels; 28,800 vph
Functions: hours, minutes, sweep seconds; date
Case: stainless steel, ø 38 mm, height 10 mm; sapphire crystal
Band: stainless steel, folding clasp
Price: $999
Variations: with leather strap; in PVD-gold plated

Persuasion Automatic

Reference number: FC-310M3P6
Movement: automatic, Frédérique Constant Caliber FC 310 (base ETA 2824); ø 25.6 mm, height 4.6 mm; 25 jewels; 28,800 vph; modified with partial skeletonizing
Functions: hours, minutes, sweep seconds
Case: stainless steel, ø 38 mm, height 10 mm; sapphire crystal; exhibition window case back
Band: leather, buckle
Price: $1,149
Variations: with stainless steel bracelet; with gold plated case; with black dial

Persuasion Ladies

Reference number: FC-303M2P6
Movement: automatic, Frédérique Constant Caliber FC 303 (base ETA 2824); ø 25.6 mm, height 4.6 mm; 25 jewels; 28,800 vph
Functions: hours, minutes, sweep seconds; date
Case: stainless steel, ø 35 mm, height 10 mm; sapphire crystal; exhibition window case back
Band: reptile skin, buckle
Price: $899
Variations: with stainless steel bracelet

Corum

Corum, the bird of paradise among Swiss watch brands, turned fifty in 2005. A brand with a varied history to look back on, the individual design of its products always remains recognizable. The Corum watch seems above all to represent the opportunity of living a certain type of creativity that includes pleasure in design experimentation. The brand's founders René Bannwart and his son Jean-René, as well as Severin Wunderman, Corum's current owner, all seem to get a real kick out of managing their watch company along these lines.

The fact that these watches also tell the time was a characteristic of a timepiece that the Bannwarts didn't feel needed to be pointed out in any extra way. Even the ideological discussion of whether a watch should have a quartz or a mechanical movement was definitely secondary. These timepieces needed to be unusual and creative in their design, utilizing remarkable materials to achieve this end.

These are also the criteria that current owner Wunderman laid down at the beginning of his reign over Corum. That which the Bannwarts had built up with their brand finds a continuation under Wunderman's

aegis. And original design ideas are being resuscitated by the expressiveness and experimenting nature of a man who can look back on such grand economic successes and who has gone through such personal lows that the thought of a model not being a runner in terms of sales doesn't really discomfit him all that much. This freedom from immediate economic constraints takes root in a new independence, in the creativity of product designers who may unfold their entire repertoire, bearing some truly very exotic fruits.

The first watches presented under the new owner's wing were certainly daring interpretations of the Corum credo. Not only the Baselworld 2000 exhibition booth, whose outer glass cases contained originals from Wunderman's extensive collection of art instead of watches, caused a great deal of excitement that year. The Corum boss's Bubble model inspired just as much horror

as enthusiasm. These extra-large watches with their colossal, highly domed sapphire crystals and colorful dials were, however, economically successful right from the start. Today's collection comprises just as many fashion-conscious models, manufactured in large numbers to carry turnover, as successful models from the brand's past, summarized in the Heritage collection. Here one finds models such as the classic Coin Watch made of a genuine gold twenty-dollar coin, and the fully reworked reissue of the Golden Bridge with its legendary baton movement completely encased in sapphire crystal.

Exquisite timepieces such as a tourbillon model, whose transparent movement is made of sapphire plates only 0.3 mm thick, have just as much room in the collection as the artfully painted miniatures on the dials of some unique pieces and the successful evergreen Admiral's Cup.

Coin Watch

Reference number: 82.355.56MU51
Movement: automatic, Corum Caliber CO 082 (base ETA 2892-A2); ø 25.6 mm, height 3.6 mm; 21 jewels; 28,800 vph
Functions: hours, minutes
Case: yellow gold, ø 36 mm, height 7.5 mm; sapphire crystal; crown with diamond
Band: reptile skin, buckle
Remarks: dial and case back made of an original $20 coin
Price: $12,000

Golden Bridge

Reference number: 113.550.56 M600 00007
Movement: manually wound, Corum Caliber CO GB 001; 33 x 4.9 mm, height 3 mm; 19 jewels; 28,800 vph; baton movement with crown at 6 o'clock; hand-engraved bridges and plates
Functions: hours, minutes
Case: yellow gold, 37 x 32 mm, height 10 mm; case made of sapphire crystal on all sides; exhibition window case back
Band: yellow gold, double folding clasp
Price: $25,000

Golden Bridge

Reference number: 113.550.55/0001 0000R
Movement: manually wound, Corum Caliber CO GB 001; 34 x 4.9 mm, height 3 mm; 15 jewels; 28,800 vph; baton movement with crown at 6 o'clock; hand-engraved bridges and plates
Functions: hours, minutes
Case: red gold, 37 x 32 mm, height 10 mm; case made of sapphire crystal on all sides; exhibition window case back
Band: reptile skin, buckle
Price: $18,000
Variations: in yellow or white gold, in platinum

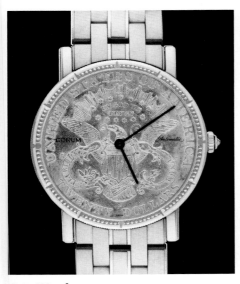

Coin Watch

Reference number: 82.355.56 M500 MU 51
Movement: automatic, Corum Caliber CO 082 (base ETA 2892-A2); ø 25.6 mm, height 3.6 mm; 21 jewels; 28,800 vph
Functions: hours, minutes
Case: yellow gold, ø 36 mm, height 7.5 mm; sapphire crystal; crown with diamond
Band: yellow gold, double folding clasp
Remarks: dial and case back made of an original $20 coin
Price: $18,000

Admiral's Cup Chrono 44

Reference number: 985.630.56 0F02 AA32
Movement: automatic, Corum Caliber SW 002/CO 985 COSC (base ETA 2892-A2 with chronograph module by Dubois-Dépraz); ø 30 mm, height 6.9 mm; 57 jewels; 28,800 vph; officially certified chronometer (COSC)
Functions: hours, minutes, subsidiary seconds; chronograph; date
Case: yellow gold, ø 44 mm, height 12 mm; bidirectionally rotating bezel with nautical flag numerals and 360° scale; sapphire crystal; screwed-in crown; water-resistant to 50 m
Band: reptile skin, double folding clasp
Price: upon request

Admiral's Cup Regatta Marées

Reference number: 977.631.55 V771 AN42
Movement: automatic, Corum Caliber CO 977 COSC (base ETA 2892-A2 with exclusive tide module by Dubois-Dépraz); ø 26.2 mm, height 5.2 mm; 21 jewels; 28,800 vph; officially certified chronometer (COSC); limited to 500 pieces
Functions: hours, minutes, sweep seconds; date; moon phase; tides and strength of tides
Case: rose gold, ø 44 mm, height 12 mm; bezel with nautical flag numerals; sapphire crystal; exhibition window case back; water-resistant to 30 m
Band: rose gold/carbon fiber, folding clasp
Price: $26,000

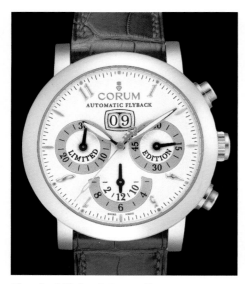

Classical Flyback Large Date

Reference number: 996.201.20 0F02 BA 06
Movement: automatic, Corum Caliber CO 996 COSC (base ETA 2892-A2 with chronograph module by Dubois-Dépraz); ø 30 mm, height 7.3 mm; 49 jewels; 28,800 vph; officially certified chronometer (COSC); limited edition
Functions: hours, minutes, subsidiary seconds; flyback chronograph; large date
Case: stainless steel, ø 43 mm, height 14 mm; sapphire crystal; exhibition window case back; water-resistant to 30 m
Band: reptile skin, folding clasp
Price: $5,495
Variations: with stainless steel bracelet

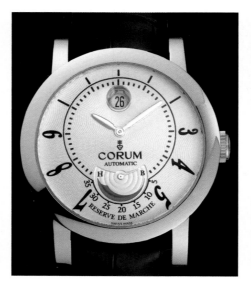

Classical Power Reserve

Reference number: 973.201.20 0F02 BA 12
Movement: automatic, Corum Caliber CO 973 PW (base ETA 2892-A2 with module by Jaquet); ø 26.2 mm, height 4.3 mm; 22 jewels; 28,800 vph; officially certified chronometer (COSC)
Functions: hours, minutes; date; power reserve display
Case: stainless steel, ø 42 mm, height 11 mm; sapphire crystal; exhibition window case back; water-resistant to 30 m
Band: reptile skin, folding clasp
Price: $3,000
Variations: with stainless steel bracelet

Classical GMT

Reference number: 983.201.20 0F03 FB24
Movement: automatic, Corum Caliber CO 983 GMT (base ETA 2892-A2 with module 313 by Dubois-Dépraz); ø 26.2 mm, height 4.65 mm; 21 jewels; 28,800 vph; officially certified chronometer (COSC); GMT hour hand activated via button
Functions: hours, minutes, sweep seconds; date; 24-hour display (second time zone)
Case: stainless steel, ø 42 mm, height 11 mm; bidirectionally rotating bezel with names of time zone reference cities; sapphire crystal; exhibition window case back; water-resist. to 30 m
Band: reptile skin, folding clasp
Price: $3,995

Bubble Skeleton

Reference number: 082.150.20 0F01
Movement: automatic, ETA Caliber 2892-A2; ø 25.6 mm, height 3.6 mm; 21 jewels; 28,800 vph; completely skeletonized and PVD-coated black
Functions: hours, minutes, sweep seconds
Case: stainless steel, ø 45 mm, height 19 mm; solid domed sapphire crystal; exhibition window case back; screwed-in crown; water-resistant to 200 m
Band: reptile skin, double folding clasp
Price: $4,695

Bubble Bats

Reference number: 082.150.20 0F01 BATS
Movement: automatic, Corum Caliber CO 082 (base ETA 2892-A2); ø 25.6 mm, height 3.6 mm; 21 jewels; 28,800 vph
Functions: hours, minutes, sweep seconds; date
Case: stainless steel, ø 45 mm, height 19 mm; solid domed sapphire crystal; exhibition window case back; screwed-in crown; water-resistant to 200 m
Band: reptile skin, double folding clasp
Remarks: Bubble of the Year 2005, this model was only produced in the year 2005
Price: $3,295

Bubble Privateer

Reference number: 082.150.20 F701 PIRA
Movement: automatic, Corum Caliber CO 082 (base ETA 2892-A2); ø 25.6 mm, height 3.6 mm; 21 jewels; 28,800 vph
Functions: hours, minutes, sweep seconds; date
Case: stainless steel, ø 45 mm, height 19 mm; solid domed sapphire crystal; exhibition window case back; screwed-in crown; water-resistant to 200 m
Band: stainless steel, double folding clasp
Remarks: Collectors Series, limited to 1,955 pieces
Price: $3,295

Admiral's Cup Trophy 41

Reference number: 082.833.20 F373 AB52
Movement: automatic, Corum Caliber CO 082 (base ETA 2892-A2); ø 25.6 mm, height 3.6 mm; 21 jewels; 28,800 vph
Functions: hours, minutes, sweep seconds; date
Case: stainless steel, ø 41 mm, height 10 mm; sapphire crystal; screw-in crown with security bow; water-resistant to 100 m
Band: rubber, double folding clasp
Price: $2,395
Variations: with stainless steel bracelet

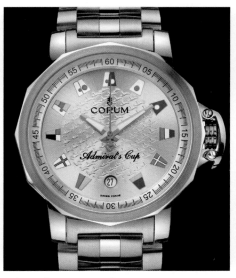

Admiral's Cup Trophy 41

Reference number: 082.830.20 V780 A52
Movement: automatic, Corum Caliber CO 082 (base ETA 2892-A2); ø 25.6 mm, height 3.6 mm; 21 jewels; 28,800 vph
Functions: hours, minutes, sweep seconds; date
Case: stainless steel, ø 41 mm, height 10 mm; sapphire crystal; screw-in crown with security bow; water-resistant to 100 m
Band: stainless steel, folding clasp
Price: $2,695
Variations: with rubber strap

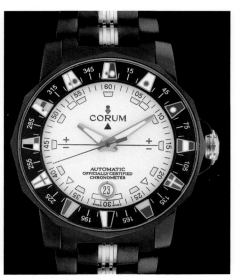

Admiral's Cup 44

Reference number: 982.633.30 V785 AA32
Movement: automatic, Corum Caliber CO 982 COSC (base ETA 2892-A2); ø 25.6 mm, height 3.6 mm; 21 jewels; 28,800 vph; officially certified chronometer (COSC)
Functions: hours, minutes, sweep seconds; date
Case: stainless steel, ionized, ø 44 mm, height 12 mm; bidirectionally rotating with nautical flag numerals and 360° scale; sapphire crystal; exhibition window case back; screwed-in crown; water-resistant to 50 m
Band: stainless steel, ionized, double folding clasp
Price: $3,995

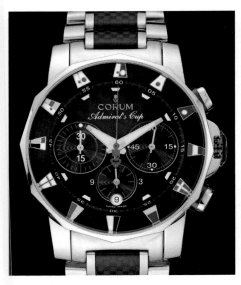

Admiral's Cup Regatta Chrono

Reference number: 985.631.20 V771 AN42
Movement: automatic, Corum Caliber CO 985 (base ETA 2892-A2 with chronograph module by Dubois-Dépraz); ø 30 mm, height 6.9 mm; 57 jewels; 28,800 vph; officially certified chronometer (COSC); limited to 2,000 pieces
Functions: hours, minutes, subsidiary seconds; chronograph; date
Case: stainless steel, ø 44 mm, height 12 mm; bezel with nautical flag numerals; sapphire crystal; exhibition window case back; screwed-in PVD-coated crown; water-resistant to 100 m
Band: stainless steel/carbon fiber, folding clasp
Price: $5,895

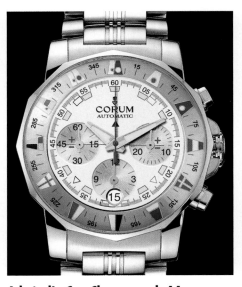

Admiral's Cup Chronograph 44

Reference number: 985.630.20 V785 AA32
Movement: automatic, Corum Caliber SW 002/CO 285 COSC (base ETA 2892-A2 with chronograph module by Dubois-Dépraz); ø 30 mm, height 6.9 mm; 57 jewels; 28,800 vph; officially certified chronometer (COSC)
Functions: hours, minutes, subsidiary seconds; chronograph; date
Case: stainless steel, ø 44 mm, height 12 mm; bidirectionally rotating bezel with nautical flag numerals and 360° scale; sapphire crystal; exhibition window case back; screw-in crown
Band: stainless steel, folding clasp
Price: $5,195

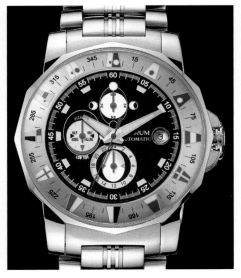

Admiral's Cup Marées 44

Reference number: 977.630.20 V785 AB32
Movement: automatic, Corum Caliber CO 277 (base ETA 2892-A2 with exclusive tide module by Dubois-Dépraz); ø 26.2 mm, height 5.2 mm; 21 jewels; 28,800 vph; officially certified chronometer (COSC)
Functions: hours, minutes, sweep seconds; date; moon phase; tides and strength of tides
Case: stainless steel, ø 44 mm, height 12 mm; bidirectionally rotating bezel with nautical flag numerals and 360° scale; sapphire crystal; exhibition window case back; screw-in crown
Band: stainless steel, folding clasp
Price: $5,995

Cuervo y Sobrinos

Havana — the name has a magic sound of Caribbean joie de vivre to it, of tropical temperatures and music that doesn't really jibe with today's reality in every way. Despite this, the romantic picture of La Habana, as the Cuban capital city is known by its residents, seems to effortlessly survive all times, even the hardest of them. Against a background of fading affluence and the peeling facades of a societal model, the epoch of rich tobacco plantations and sugar barons seems more like a fairy tale than anything else. Ramón Rio y Cuervo and his sister's sons kept a watchmaking workshop and an elegant shop on Quinto Avenida where they sold fine Swiss pocket watches (and, of course, less fine American models as well). Along with the advent of tourism from the nearby coast of Florida at the beginning of the twentieth century, the business developed with wristwatches, whose dials Don Ramón soon had printed with his own name,

as did other jewelers in New York, Paris, and even Lucerne. And Cuervo y Sobrinos — Cuervo and Nephews — was born.

Under the initiative of a Spanish businessman and watch connoisseur, the traditional brand was resuscitated a few years ago. In cooperation with various Swiss workshops, Don Ramón's heirs have developed a new wristwatch collection, striking in its unusual case shapes and dial details and definitely awakening nostalgic memories of the 1940s. Tobacco and cigars, the two typical products of the island, play an important role in the new watches' identity. For one, all the watches are delivered in a prestigious and, of course, fully functional humidor made of precious woods. For another, the individual model families are all named after famous cigar formats.

For example, there is the Espléndido, whose case reminds one with its strongly tailored shaped of the immense popularity of the "hour glass" models of the '40s, which

almost all big Genevan brands carried in their programs. With a length of 47 mm including lugs and a width of 32.5 mm at the narrowest spot of the "hour glass," this watch is anything but delicate even though its long lugs make the leather strap comfortably hug even the smallest of wrists. Prominente's case shape is reminiscent of 1930s style. It's slightly domed, making it comfortable to wear despite its respectable length of 52 mm. Cuervo y Sobrinos's watch model Torpedo doesn't display pointed ends like the cigar of the same name, rather it illustrates a cultivated, round case with very striking lugs whose shape is recognizable as that of the previously mentioned Espléndido. While the world continues to wait for the end of the Cuban revolution, this new yet old watch brand looks back over the past, at the same time most likely giving a little taste of the future.

Prominente S.T.

Reference number: 1011.1C

Movement: automatic, ETA Caliber 2671; ø 17.2 mm, height 4.8 mm; 25 jewels; 28,800 vph

Functions: hours, minutes, sweep seconds

Case: stainless steel, domed, 30.5 x 52 mm, height 10 mm; sapphire crystal

Band: reptile skin, double folding clasp

Price: $3,300

Variations: in 18-karat rose gold ($7,700); various dial variations

Prominente D.T.

Reference number: 1112.1N

Movement: automatic, ETA Caliber 2671; ø 17.2 mm, height 4.8 mm; 25 jewels; 28,800 vph; 2 separate automatic movements

Functions: hours, minutes (double), two time zones

Case: stainless steel, domed, 30.5 x 52 mm, height 10 mm; sapphire crystal

Band: reptile skin, double folding clasp

Price: $4,150

Variations: in 18-karat rose gold ($9,250); various dial variations

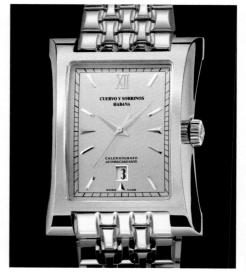

Esplendidos

Reference number: 2412B.1RD

Movement: automatic, ETA Caliber 2824-2; ø 25.6 mm, height 4.6 mm; 25 jewels; 28,800 vph

Functions: hours, minutes, sweep seconds; date

Case: stainless steel, domed, 37 x 47 mm, height 12.2 mm; sapphire crystal

Band: stainless steel, double folding clasp

Price: $3,900

Variations: with leather strap; in 18-karat rose gold ($8,950); various dial variations

Cyclos

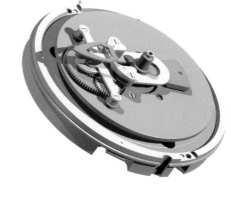

A rchitect and designer John C. Ermel was searching for a way of showing the time on a conventional and intuitively legible 12-hour dial where the hours of the day and night would be unmistakably distinguishable from each other. During his search he happened upon a long-forgotten technology that was never developed far enough to become functional.

The DualPhase display by Cyclos (realized by master watchmakers Robert Greubel and Stephen Forsey of CompliTech) is made possible by two spiral-shaped, overlapping 12-hour numeral circles of varying diameters and an hour hand that can grow and shrink as necessary. Its double-looped spring creates this effect by an overlapping rotation as well as a movement in a radial direction. In mathematics, this is called a Pascal Snail, and since it follows a strict law, it was possible to construct a mechanism that moves hands in the same way.

The effect of this interesting technology is surprising: when the date changes, the outer tip of the hour hand begins its path around the inner numeral circle, changing again at six o'clock in the morning to the outer scale. By the time noon has come along, the hand has "grown" almost two millimeters and runs along the outer scale. At 6 o'clock in the evening it has once again "shrunk" to its minimum length and from then until midnight displays the time on the inner ring.

Sometimes you just have to look at things twice to get them.

day&night Transparent

Reference number: TRL-YG
Movement: automatic, Cyclos Caliber CW 1 (base ETA 2892-A2); ø 33 mm, height 6.6 mm; 21 jewels; 28,800 vph; patented Dual Phase 24-hour display with hour hand that changes in length; officially certified chronometer (COSC)
Functions: hours (24-hour display), minutes, sweep seconds; date
Case: yellow gold, ø 39 mm, height 12.8 mm; sapphire crystal; exhibition window case back; water-resistant to 50 m
Band: reptile skin, folding clasp
Remarks: skeletonized dial reveals mechanics of the hands
Price: $19,350

day&night Parity

Reference number: PAR-WG
Movement: automatic, Cyclos Caliber CW 1 (base ETA 2892-A2); ø 33 mm, height 6.6 mm; 21 jewels; 28,800 vph; patented Dual Phase 24-hour display with hour hand that changes in length; officially certified chronometer (COSC)
Functions: hours (24-hour display), minutes, sweep seconds; date
Case: white gold, ø 39 mm, height 12.8 mm; sapphire crystal; exhibition window case back; water-resistant to 50 m
Band: reptile skin, folding clasp
Price: $19,350
Variations: in steel ($8,500) and steel with diamond bezel

a.m./p.m.

Reference number: APD-SS
Movement: automatic, Cyclos Caliber CW 1 (base ETA 2892-A2); ø 33 mm, height 6.6 mm; 21 jewels; 28,800 vph; patented Dual Phase 24-hour display with hour hand that changes in length; officially certified chronometer (COSC)
Functions: hours (24-hour display), minutes, sweep seconds; date
Case: stainless steel, ø 39 mm, height 12.8 mm; sapphire crystal; exhibition window case back; water-resistant to 50 m
Band: reptile skin, folding clasp
Price: $7,900
Variations: with silver-colored dial

d.freemont

David Freemont McCready was first introduced to watchmaking about fifty years ago. Raised in Altoona, Pennsylvania, an area that houses more clock- and watchmaking than any other in the United States, McCready came in contact with the micromechanical art form at the tender age of fifteen as the result of an agreement between his father, a man also fascinated by mechanics and electronics, and a local watchmaker. After a number of months occupied with this learning experience, the teenaged McCready's technical mind turned to more pressing matters: motorcycles and automobiles, a love of which would also accompany him throughout his life. Twenty-five years later, the early activity became a hobby, and the previous experience in watchmaking manifested itself in the restoration and repair of wristwatches.

In the early 1990s, this rekindled interest coupled with the maturity necessary to own a business led to the establishment of d.freemont, Inc. Having spent the greater part of three decades as a technical sales engineer, McCready's instincts and unspent creativity guided him in creating his own wristwatches. His company philosophy stresses the importance of customer satisfaction and the development of consumer loyalty. d.freemont watches are offered exclusively via McCready's own Internet website both to assure the consumer of the timepieces' source and as a way to cut the retail cost by forgoing the middleman. Functionality and attention to detail are the typical characteristics of d.freemont watches. When designing his watches, it is not McCready's intent to latch on to a current trend, but rather to make his timepieces classic and collectible. His goal is to keep the concentration on the real purpose of the watch — telling time — all the while at-tempting to incorporate an enduring presence binding the timepiece to the owner.

d.freemont's original mechanical collection was inspired by well-known locations in North America and Europe, with McCready striving to capture their essence and flavor in the design. Famous names such as Barcelona, Rockefeller Center, Miami, Niagara, 90212 Rodeo Drive, and even Basel adorn the watches ranging in price from $280 to $1,850.

McCready considers his best work to be the Acugraph line, the leading model of which, Acugraph 7750, is a chronograph whose honest intent is to tell the time clearly without forcing the wearer to first wade through many other visual displays before finally getting to the meat. The Acugraph's features are much simpler than those of other chronographs. There is, for example, only one chapter ring for the combined functions of tachymeter, telemeter, and pulsometer. This eliminates the superfluous ranges of these timing parameters in favor of the ranges most commonly used. Proving that McCready's creative mind isn't only technical, 2002 saw the release the Ancyent Marinere model. This piece was inspired by the 1798 poem *The Rime of the Ancient Mariner* by Samuel Taylor Coleridge. McCready endeavored to capture the ballad's message in the watch's design, subtly reminding man that it is his duty to be kind.

McCready's main interest lies in supplying his customers with the best quality he can. Each of the watches, even those that sell for under $300, is timed in two positions just before shipping and delivered with a computer-aided certificate bearing the owner's name and the watch's precise rate.

The New Yorker
Reference number: 10101
Movement: automatic, d.freemont Caliber df.24 (base ETA 2824-A2); ø 27 mm, height 7 mm; 25 jewels; 28,800 vph
Functions: hours, minutes, sweep seconds; date
Case: stainless steel, ø 36 mm, height 9 mm; sapphire crystal; exhibition window case back
Band: leather, folding clasp
Price: $415

Sapphire Power Reserve
Reference number: DSCF00 43
Movement: automatic, Caliber GMT92 (base ETA 2892-A2); ø 26 mm, height 7 mm; 21 jewels; 28,800 vph
Functions: hours, minutes, sweep seconds; date; power reserve display, second time zone
Case: stainless steel, ø 33.5 mm, height 9 mm; sapphire crystal; exhibition window case back
Band: stainless steel, folding clasp
Price: S750

Precision Automatic
Reference number: DSCF00 39
Movement: automatic, Caliber PA 28 (base ETA 2824); ø 26 mm, height 5 mm; 25 jewels; 28,800 vph
Functions: hours, minutes, sweep seconds; date
Case: stainless steel, ø 36 mm, height 9.5 mm; sapphire crystal; exhibition window case back
Band: leather, buckle
Price: $350

Basel
Reference number: DSCF00 40
Movement: automatic, Caliber B750 (base ETA Valjoux 7750); ø 30 mm, height 7 mm; 25 jewels; 28,800 vph
Functions: hours, minutes, subsidiary seconds; date; chronograph
Case: stainless steel, ø 38 mm, height 13 mm; sapphire crystal; screwed-down case back; screwed-in crown and buttons
Band: polymer, double folding clasp
Price: $1,250

Acugraph 14K
Reference number: DSCF00 41
Movement: automatic, Caliber A750 (base ETA Valjoux 7750); ø 30 mm, height 7 mm; 25 jewels; 28,800 vph
Functions: hours, minutes, subsidiary seconds; date; chronograph
Case: white gold, ø 40 mm, height 12.5 mm; sapphire crystal; exhibition window case back
Band: leather, folding clasp
Price: S2,850

Rodeo Drive
Reference number: DSCF00 42
Movement: quartz, Caliber 980 (base ETA); ø 18 mm, 15 jewels
Functions: hours, minutes, subsidiary seconds
Case: stainless steel, 31 x 35 mm, height 7 mm; mineral crystal
Band: stainless steel, folding clasp
Price: S175

De Bethune

Only a scant few years ago, in 2002 to be exact, the watch brand De Bethune was called to life. And this little brand had a big load of plans on its roster.

The name De Bethune is derived from a French knight, Le Chevalier de Bethune, who lived in the eighteenth century. He is mentioned in *Watch and Clockmakers of the World* as the inventor of one escapement each for a grandfather clock and a pocket watch.

Nothing less than "the best watches in the world" is what David Zanetta, president of the new brand, and Denis Flageollet, cofounder and technical director, were after. The first products to emerge prove that this rather grandiose statement is something that the industry should really sit up and take notice of. Neither costs nor effort have been spared in manufacturing timepieces already ready to take on the greats of the Swiss watch *manufactures* in regard to technology and quality. Just a short time after being called to life, this brand features extremely complicated pieces in its collection, the design and construction of which would normally take several years to complete.

In the remote mountain village of La Chaux l'Auberson, the company manufactures about 300 timepieces per year, all housed in a case uniquely and instantly recognizable as that of De Bethune. These cases are made solely of 18-karat gold or platinum, and their gold dials feature hands made of gold or blued steel. Every one of the components — largely made in-house — is carefully finished by hand and finely polished. The autonomous manually wound caliber, the shape of which is more than vaguely reminiscent of a medieval shield, is outfitted with gold wheels and would easily

fulfill the requirements necessary for a Seal of Geneva. This, however, is not one of the company's goals. "We would rather have the Poincon de Bethune," Zanetta jokes. The young brand's lightning-quick development is easily explained: Before striking out on their own, Zanetta and Flageollet were both employed by THA (Techniques Horlogères Appliquées SA), one of the few very highly qualified companies active behind the scenes for the great brands, making the successes of the Swiss watch industry possible. Flageollet, today directing the technical aspects of De Bethune, took several of his former colleagues with him when he bought the village's previous pub and turned it into a factory for *haute horlogerie*. Because of this, today the young

brand practically only employs experienced specialists in design and manufacture of fine watches.

In the last couple of years, these specialists have not only built complicated timepieces of the finest quality, including minute repeaters, perpetual calendars, and watches containing an equation of time, but also an autonomous movement, a spherical moon phase display, and a patented balance. This balance, made of extremely light titanium and a four-legged oscillating component instead of a wheel, bears four platinum weights and swings with a flat balance spring also developed by De Bethune, which, according to the company's movement designers, possesses the same behavior as a Breguet balance spring.

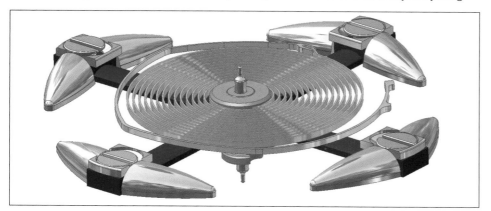

Perpetual Calendar with Moon Phase

Reference number: DB 15
Movement: manually wound, De Bethune Caliber DB 2004; ø 30 mm, height 5.9 mm; 24 jewels; 28,800 vph; twin spring barrels, power reserve appx. 100 hours; balance made of titanium and platinum weights; completely finished by hand
Functions: hours, minutes; perpetual calendar with date, day of the week, month, moon phase (three-dimensional model of moon), leap year
Case: white gold, ø 43 mm, height 13 mm; sapphire crystal; exhibition window case back
Band: reptile skin, buckle
Price: $69,900

Perpetual Calendar with Moon Phase

Reference number: DB 17
Movement: manually wound, De Bethune Caliber DB 2004; ø 30 mm, height 5.9 mm; 24 jewels; 28,800 vph; twin spring barrels, power reserve appx. 100 hours; balance made of titanium and platinum weights; completely finished by hand
Functions: hours, minutes; perpetual calendar with date, day of the week, month, moon phase (three-dimensional model of moon), leap year
Case: white gold, ø 43 mm, height 13 mm; sapphire crystal; exhibition window case back
Band: reptile skin, buckle
Price: $79,000

8 Day Power Reserve

Reference number: DB S
Movement: manually wound, De Bethune Caliber DB 2014; ø 30 mm, height 6 mm; 29 jewels; 21,600 vph; twin spring barrels, power reserve 192 hours; balance made of titanium and platinum weights; completely finished by hand
Functions: hours, minutes; moon phase (three-dimensional model of moon)
Case: platinum, ø 42.5 mm, height 11 mm; sapphire crystal; exhibition window case back
Band: reptile skin, buckle
Remarks: skeletonized dial allows view into the movement
Price: $45,500

Monopoussoir Chronograph

Reference number: DB 8
Movement: manually wound, De Bethune Caliber DB 5008 (base LJP 5000); ø 24 mm, height 5.5 mm; 21 jewels; 21,600 vph; short timekeeper to 45 minutes; column wheel control and crown button for start-stop-reset functions
Functions: hours, minutes, sweep seconds; chronograph (45-minute counter)
Case: white gold, ø 42 mm, height 8 mm; sapphire crystal; exhibition window case back
Band: reptile skin, buckle
Price: $31,500
Variations: in red gold; in platinum; various dial variations

Automatic

Reference number: DB 5
Movement: automatic, De Bethune Caliber DB 7002 (base AS 2072); ø 25.5 mm, height 7.2 mm; 20 jewels; 21,600 vph
Functions: hours, minutes, sweep seconds
Case: yellow gold, ø 42 mm, height 8 mm; sapphire crystal; exhibition window case back
Band: reptile skin, buckle
Price: $13,900
Variations: in white gold; in platinum

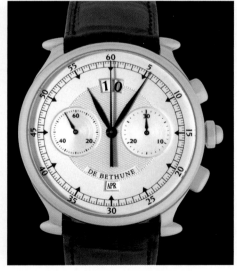

Chronograph with Large Date

Reference number: DB 12
Movement: manually wound, De Bethune Caliber DB 4040 (base Venus 175); ø 31.5 mm, height 7.8 mm; 25 jewels; 18,000 vph; contemporary form of classic column wheel chronograph movement with large date display
Functions: hours, minutes, subsidiary seconds; chronograph; large date, month
Case: red gold, ø 42 mm, height 13 mm; sapphire crystal; exhibition window case back
Band: reptile skin, folding clasp
Price: $39,900
Variations: in white gold

De Grisogono

In the eyes of dyed-in-the-wool watch fans, it is often a handicap for a jewelry producer to move over to the discipline of watches, especially if that jeweler has often stood in the limelight with his shimmering creations and extravagant productions. This was also the case with the brand De Grisogono and its founder Fawaz Gruosi at their debut in the watch industry. And it was for this reason that Instrumento No. Uno was received with half-hearted applause in 2000, regardless of the fact that the watch disposed of a complete second time zone display, separately settable via the single crown, a slightly domed case with movable lugs, and a mechanical automatic movement that left quite a good impression.

In the meantime skeptics must certainly have also recognized that De Grisogono not only displays a remarkable creativity in the development of its new models, but also

perfectly handcrafted manufacturing qualities.

This series of remarkable watches was continued with the unveiling of Instrumento Doppio in the spring of 2002. The "double instrument" truly earns its name as it not only offers the functions of a chronograph with large date on one side, but also a second time zone on the other. In order to put hands on the "back" of the watch, the automatic movement needed to be completely reworked (extending the dial train to include separately settable hands on the back and the front) and several modules added. Instrumento Doppio Tre then followed as a logical development on the theme: Instead of a chronograph, this timepiece offers the dial visuals of the Instrumento No. Uno with two full sets of hands to display dual time zones. Together with the set of hands on the back of the watch, Instrumento Doppio Tre offers three

perfectly legible and cleanly separated displays of time, making it more than just a watch — Instrumento Doppio Tre is actually three watches in one.

And this is also obvious in its dimensions: With a length of 60 mm, a width of 36 mm, and a height of 18 mm, Instrumento Doppio Tre is really almost as big as three watches put together. In comparison, the Instrumento Grande, introduced in 2005, appears almost small with its dimensions of 39.7 x 48.3 mm and height of 12.8 mm. Truly *grande*, however, is the date display located on the lowest part of the dial, which offers optimal clarity and excellent legibility with its phenomenal size.

The second introduction of 2005 is the Occhio model. Like the "eye" of a camera's lens, a rosette-shaped, movable diaphragm assembly allows the observer a glance at the timepiece's real attraction after a slide has been activated: a minute repeater strike train, whose little hammers intone the current hour, the number of quarter-hours that have passed since the last full hour, and the number of minutes gone by since the last full quarter-hour. Not only is this an acoustic pleasure, it is also a visual one, revealed in the 414 finely decorated individual components comprising, among other things, black plates and bridges. With the final gong of a tiny hammer, the ceramic blades once again close the diaphragm, and the Occhio Ripetizione Minuti once again becomes an — almost — normal wristwatch.

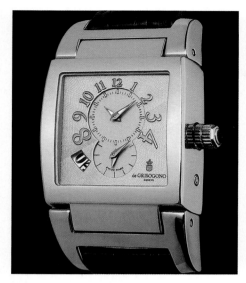

Instrumento No. Uno

Reference number: UNO DF/N1
Movement: automatic, ETA Caliber 2892-A2 with module for second time zone and large date; ø 25.6 mm, height 5.75 mm; 21 jewels; 28,800 vph; black movement finish with blued screws
Functions: hours, minutes; large date; second time zone
Case: stainless steel, 53 x 33 mm, height 10.8 mm; sapphire crystal; exhibition window case back
Band: reptile skin, double folding clasp
Price: $10,900
Variations: in various dial versions, case materials and bands

Instrumento Grande

Reference number: N06
Movement: automatic, ETA Caliber 2892-A2 with module for large date; ø 25.6 mm, height 3.6 mm (base caliber); 21 jewels; 28,800 vph; black movement finish with blued screws
Functions: hours, minutes; large date
Case: rose gold, 39.7 x 48.3 mm, height 12.8 mm; case with transparent sides; sapphire crystal; exhibition window case back
Band: reptile skin, double folding clasp
Price: $11,700
Variations: in stainless steel

Power Breaker

Reference number: N02
Movement: automatic, ETA Caliber 2892-A2 with chronograph module by Dubois-Dépraz; ø 30 mm, height 7.3 mm; 49 jewels; 28,800 vph
Functions: hours, minutes; chronograph
Case: stainless steel, polished and PVD-coated, 54.2 x 43.3 mm, height 15.2 mm; sapphire crystal
Band: rubber, double folding clasp
Remarks: the first 500 pieces bear the signature of Renault F1 team manager Flavio Briatore engraved on the case back
Price: $12,400
Variations: in bronzed gold with brown rubber strap

Instrumento Tondo

Reference number: TONDO RM N01
Movement: automatic, RM Caliber 14-899 (base ETA 2892-A2 with module for second time zone and power reserve display); ø 25.6 mm, height 5.75 mm; 21 jewels; 28,800 vph; black movement finish with blued screws
Functions: hours, minutes; date; 24-hour display (second time zone); power reserve display
Case: stainless steel, ø 38.5 mm, height 10.5 mm; sapphire crystal; exhibition window case back
Band: reptile skin, double folding clasp
Price: $10,050
Variations: in red or white gold

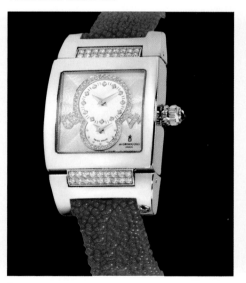

Instrumentino

Reference number: TINO S2
Movement: automatic, ETA Caliber 2892-A2 with module for second time zone; ø 25.6 mm, height 5.75 mm; 21 jewels; 28,800 vph
Functions: hours, minutes; second time zone
Case: white gold, 49 x 29 mm, height 10 mm; lugs set with brilliant-cut diamonds; sapphire crystal; exhibition window case back; crown with black diamond cabochon
Band: stingray, double folding clasp
Remarks: dial with set with brilliant-cut diamonds
Price: $16,850

Instrumento Doppio Tre

Movement: automatic, ETA Caliber 2892-A2, modified with dial train on back, large date and module for two additional time zones; 30 x 30 mm, height 8.8 mm; 28,800 vph; black movement finish with blued screws
Functions: hours, minutes; second time zone; large date (front); hours, minutes (back)
Case: stainless steel, 60 x 36 mm, height 18 mm; case can be turned and rotated 180°, lockable by screw; frame with movable strap lugs; two sapphire crystals
Band: reptile skin, double folding clasp
Price: $21,050

DeWitt

In fewer than four years, the team has managed to conjure up a starting collection comprising a minute repeater, a tourbillon, a split-seconds chronograph with isolator, and a perpetual calendar featuring two retrograde displays — all based on the finest *ébauches* there are, for example, from the house of Chopard. But it was only with the introduction of the striking Académia case that the brand received its own individualized look. This complex creation with screwed-on elements makes visible the complex technology that it houses — such as the Tourbillon Différentiel, which disposes of a self-developed, three-dimensional differential to communicate between the twin spring barrels and the power reserve in addition to the exclusive tourbillon com-plication. The very masculine collection Académia is perfectly suited as a platform for technical elements and highly refined display complications such as these.

The Alma Utopia model proves that the team is also capable of putting technically clever complications into women's watches without relying solely on the sumptuous setting of jewels on cases and dials. This

particular model is outfitted with a mechanical movement containing a calendar display featuring two retrograde hands, one for the first digit and the other for the second digit of the date. It was completely conceived and produced in Vandoeuvres. Alongside the great complications, this little *manufacture* located on Lake Geneva also masters the finer arts of watchmaking; that these disciplines are not necessarily mutually exclusive is plain to see on these pages.

E ven if this exclusive watch brand only debuted two years ago, it would not be correct to call the watchmakers found working in the old manor house high above Lake Geneva "newcomers." In fact, this team of watchmakers is an experienced one that has been together for years, inventing the most complicated mechanisms that the Swiss watch industry has ever spewed forth. But, of course, they didn't do this under the name DeWitt.

Brand founder Jerôme De Witt is also not a newcomer to the watch industry, and his family's history is even longer than that of many established Swiss *manufactures*. He is a descendent of Napoleon Bonaparte, or to be more precise of his brother Jerôme (Hieronymus), once King of Westphalia. Without a doubt, this illustrious heritage helped along his passion for technical miracles, and his talent as a manager and coordinator of business projects was also no accident.

These engineers, watchmakers, case makers, and gem setters are blessed with ideal working conditions in the renovated manor house located in Geneva's noble villa suburb Vandoeuvres, including a quiet location, large rooms, and an unchangeable view of Lake Geneva. The De Witts' domicile is only a stone's throw away, and thus Jerôme is always accessible when there are important things to decide in the little *manufacture*.

Académia Répétition Minutes

Reference number: AC.8801.53.M750
Movement: manually wound, DeWitt Caliber DW 8801 (base Claret 88); ø 27.6 mm, height 5.7 mm; 31 jewels; 21,600 vph; finely finished, *côtes de Genève*
Functions: hours, minutes, subsidiary seconds; hour, quarter hour, and minute repeater
Case: red gold, ø 43 mm, height 11.9 mm; sapphire crystal
Band: reptile skin, folding clasp
Remarks: partially skeletonized dial allows a view into the repeater mechanics
Price: $253,000
Variations: in white gold

Académia Tourbillon Différentiel

Reference number: AC.8002.28.M954
Movement: manually wound, DeWitt Caliber DW 8002; ø 30 mm, height 8.9 mm; 24 jewels; 21,600 vph; flying one-minute tourbillon; patented differential gear in the winding mechanism; power reserve 110 hours; finely finished, *côtes de Genève*
Functions: hours, minutes; power reserve display
Case: titanium/red gold, ø 43 mm, height 12 mm; bezel in titanium with rubber inlays; sapphire crystal
Band: rubber, double folding clasp in red gold
Price: $177,900

Académia Double Fuseau

Reference number: AC.2001.53.M650
Movement: automatic, DeWitt Caliber DW 2001 (base ETA 2892-A2 with module for second time zone and 24-hour display); ø 26.2 mm, height 4.95 mm; 21 jewels; 28,800 vph
Functions: hours, minutes, sweep seconds; date; two 24-hour displays (second time zone)
Case: red gold, ø 43 mm, height 14 mm; sapphire crystal
Band: reptile skin, buckle
Price: $21,900
Variations: in white gold; four various dial variations

Académia Seconde Rétrograde

Reference number: AC.1101.48.M601
Movement: automatic, DeWitt Caliber DW 1101 (base ETA 2892-A2 with module for retrograde seconds); ø 29.2 mm, height 5.45 mm; 21 jewels; 28,800 vph
Functions: hours, minutes, subsidiary seconds (retrograde)
Case: white gold, ø 43 mm, height 14 mm; sapphire crystal
Band: reptile skin, buckle
Price: $21,900
Variations: in white gold; four various dial variations

Alma Utopia

Reference: AL.1301.51.M657
Movement: automatic, DeWitt Caliber DW 1301 (base ETA 2000); ø 19.4 mm, height 3.6 mm; 20 jewels; 28,800 vph; patented date display with one hand for each digit
Functions: hours, minutes; date (with two hands)
Case: rose gold, 31.2 x 21.4 mm, height 11.2 mm; sapphire crystal
Band: satin, buckle
Price: $14,900
Variations: in white gold; various dial variations; with gemstones

Alma Tempia

Reference: AL.0401.48/02.M03/01
Movement: quartz, DeWitt Caliber DW 0401 (base ETA Autoquartz)
Functions: hours, minutes
Case: white gold, 31.2 x 21.4 mm, height 11.2 mm; bezel set with 195 round diamonds ; sapphire crystal
Band: satin, buckle
Remarks: center of dial with paved with diamonds
Price: $38,900

Doxa

In 1889, Georges Ducommun, at barely the age of twenty, founded his own reassembly atelier in Le Locle. It was the stepping-stone to a career which might be termed typically American by a European in this day and age. Within just a few years, Ducommun's backyard workshop had been turned into a veritable factory, over whose door the proud brand name Doxa was emblazoned.

The industrious craftsman obviously knew how to enjoy the finer things in life as well, for he made his home in the idyllic Château des Monts castle high above Le Locle, where today the world-famous watch museum is

housed. He managed the steep path to the factory in the mornings and evenings by horse-drawn buggy — so it's no wonder that the talented designer showed a very early interest in automobiles. Ducommun was one of the first in the entire canton of Neuchâtel to possess an "iron carriage." It was his car that led him to one of his most successful business ideas: Doxa was soon manufacturing large numbers of clocks for automobile dashboards, outfitted with eight-day movements that Ducommun patented in 1908. Very clever.

These historical anecdotes were very important for the new launch of the traditional

Doxa brand; thus there exists once again a pocket watch with an eight-day movement at Doxa. And there is also a sporty chronograph named for the legendary automobile race: The Coppa Milano-San Remo, which was attended by Europe's racing elite in the years between the two world wars.

A further highlight of the company's history, also commemorated by the contemporary owners, was the success of the diver's watch Sub 300T. When this watch was issued in 1967, it was clearly very different from most of the other so-called professional diver's watches. The U.S. Diving Association turned out to be a valuable consultant, and the American frogmen obviously knew exactly what they needed: a light-colored dial for mid-range diving depths, where it is not yet dark enough for luminous numerals, and a wide case base that lays securely on the arm.

The special feature of this watch, however, is the two rows of numerals found on the unidirectionally rotating bezel: The inner ring of numbers is a conventional *minuterie*, but the outer set constitutes a display of depth in meters. When used with the min-ute display found on the inner half of the bezel, it is a functional decompression table: When, at the beginning of the dive, both markers are set to the top of the minute display, it is possible to read from the bezel that at a diving depth of 30 meters it is about time to think about slowly getting back to the surface after about 25 minutes; at 40 meters, after 15 minutes; and, correspondingly, at 20 meters, only after 50 minutes. Very, very clever.

The contemporary Doxa product developers who pulled the striking '60s design of the Sub 300T out of the drawer and are now offering it to watch collectors and traditionally minded divers in various limited editions were also very clever. The limited edition Sub 300T is delivered with a certificate signed by Clive Cussler, author of the Dirk Pitt series, whose hero of the same name wears a Doxa diving watch during his fictitious paperback adventures. Cinematic fans were able to experience both Dirk Pitt and his Doxa live when Cussler's *Sahara* opened on the big screen in 2005. This film starred Matthew McConnaughey as the legendary NUMA agent and featured the unmistakable "orange-faced Doxa" on his arm alongside costar Penelope Cruz.

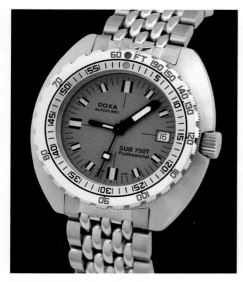

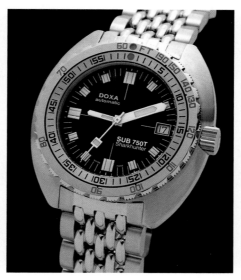

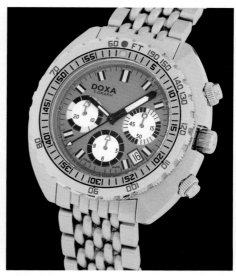

SUB 750T Professional

Reference number: 7500330003
Movement: automatic, ETA Caliber 2824-2; ø 25.6 mm, height 4.6 mm; 25 jewels; 28,800 vph
Functions: hours, minutes, sweep seconds; date
Case: stainless steel, ø 45 mm, height 14 mm; unidirectionally rotating bezel with engraved decompression table (patented); sapphire crystal; screwed-in crown; water-resistant to 750 m
Band: stainless steel, folding clasp
Remarks: re-edition of the original from 1969 with its characteristic "dwarf" hour hand, limited to 5,000 pieces
Price: $1,890

SUB 750T Sharkhunter

Reference number: 7500330002
Movement: automatic, ETA Caliber 2824-2; ø 25.6 mm, height 4.6 mm; 25 jewels; 28,800 vph
Functions: hours, minutes, sweep seconds; date
Case: stainless steel, ø 45 mm, height 14 mm; unidirectionally rotating bezel with engraved decompression table (patented); sapphire crystal; screwed-in crown; water-resistant to 750 m
Band: stainless steel, folding clasp
Remarks: re-edition of the original from 1969 with its characteristic "dwarf" hour hand, limited to 5,000 pieces
Price: $1,890

SUB 600 T-Graph

Reference number: 6000330001
Movement: automatic, ETA Caliber 2894-2; ø 28.6 mm, height 6.1 mm; 37 jewels; 28,800 vph
Functions: hours, minutes, subsidiary seconds; chronograph; date
Case: stainless steel, ø 45 mm, height 18 mm; unidirectionally rotating with engraved decompression table (patented); sapphire crystal; screwed-in crown and buttons; water-resistant to 600 m
Band: stainless steel, folding clasp
Remarks: limited edition of 250 pieces for the year 2005
Price: $3,990

Flieger II

Reference number: 600.10.101.01
Movement: manually wound, ETA Caliber 2804; ø 25.6 mm, height 3.35 mm; 17 jewels; 28,800 vph
Functions: hours, minutes, sweep seconds; date
Case: stainless steel, ø 34 mm, height 7 mm; hesalite crystal
Band: leather, buckle
Remarks: re-edition of the Doxa pilot's watch from 1948
Price: $790

Deco

Reference number: 251.10.012.02
Movement: automatic, ETA Caliber 2824-2; ø 25.6 mm, height 4.6 mm; 25 jewels; 28,800 vph
Functions: hours, minutes, sweep seconds; date
Case: stainless steel, 42 x 36 mm, height 8 mm; sapphire crystal; exhibition window case back
Band: leather, folding clasp
Remarks: re-edition of the Doxa Grafic from 1956
Price: $1,290

8 Days

Reference number: 1889.15
Movement: manually wound, Doxa Caliber 11.B; ø 50.6 mm, height 9 mm; 15 jewels; 18,000 vph; skeletonized and decorated, eight days power reserve
Functions: hours, minutes, subsidiary seconds
Case: stainless steel, palladium-coated, ø 66 mm, height 18.5 mm; sapphire crystal; exhibition window case back
Remarks: re-edition of an original from 1910
Price: $3,990
Variations: with gold-plated case

Dubey & Schaldenbrand

It's just a simple little spring really. That's all that watchmakers Georges Dubey and René Schaldenbrand found worthy of patenting on March 12, 1946, when they registered their invention. The story behind it? The development of a simple mechanism to enhance the split-seconds function of a stopwatch.

Dubey, an instructor at the reputable school of watchmaking in La Chaux-de-Fonds, and watchmaker Schaldenbrand had wound the spirally shaped spring around the stem of the sweep second hand of a Landeron chronograph caliber. This little spring was the inge-nious main ingredient of the reset system for the large second hand of the rattrapante. This less expensive to manufacture "people's rattrapante" took the hearts of watch fans by storm, and its official name, Index Mobile, became synonymous with that of the Dubey & Schaldenbrand brand, which the two watchmakers founded upon their invention. Today the Dubey & Schaldenbrand phil-osophy is not only cemented in the ingenious invention of its founding fathers, but rests also in the anachronistic, affectionate care for production founded on the principles of the classic art of making beautiful watches. The

owner of the company, Cinette Robert, a daughter of the watchmaker dynasty Meylan-LeCoultre and an absolute expert on early watch masterpieces, has an impressive talent for combining the technology of mod-ern mechanical movements with timeless and classic lines.

The Index Mobile once again plays an important role in the new collection's leading models — even if it is only an aesthetic and no longer a technical one. The models Spiral Cap, Spiral VIP, and Spiral Venus contain visible Isoval balance springs from Dubey & Schaldenbrand's original stock. Mounted at the base of the second hand — without function — they lend the dial a very special and technical appearance.

Dubey & Schaldenbrand movements also receive special attention from the skilled hand of an engraver. Every watch thus decorated becomes in effect an individual work of art since the prescribed patterns are always slightly different, determined as they are by the imagination of the artist, and as a result contribute to the exclusive quality of each piece. The Venus calibers 220 and 277 used in the Spiral Venus model — which are already rarities as they are literally few and far between forty years after their production ended — become true treasures after they have been engraved and decorated.

Aerodyn Duo

Reference number: ADUO/ST/BKG
Movement: automatic, ETA Caliber 2892-A2, modified; ø 25.6 mm, height 4.9 mm; 26 jewels; 28,800 vph
Functions: hours, minutes, sweep seconds; date; second time zone; additional 24-hour display
Case: stainless steel, domed, 33 x 44 mm, height 11.7 mm; sapphire crystal
Band: reptile skin, buckle
Price: $4,750
Variations: in rose gold

Aerodyn Date

Reference number: ADAT/RG/SIG
Movement: automatic, ETA Caliber 2892-A2, modified; ø 25.6 mm, height 4.9 mm; 26 jewels; 28,800 vph
Functions: hours, minutes, subsidiary seconds; large date
Case: rose gold, domed, 33 x 44 mm, height 11.8 mm; sapphire crystal
Band: reptile skin, buckle
Price: $10,950
Variations: in stainless steel

Aerochrono

Reference number: AERO/RG/SIG
Movement: automatic, ETA Caliber 2094; ø 23.9 mm, height 5.5 mm; 33 jewels; 28,800 vph
Functions: hours, minutes, subsidiary seconds; chronograph; date
Case: rose gold, domed, 33 x 44 mm, height 12.2 mm; sapphire crystal; exhibition window case back
Band: reptile skin, buckle
Price: $13,950
Variations: in stainless steel

Sonnerie GMT

Reference number: GMTA/ST/WHG
Movement: automatic, LJP Caliber 5900 (base AS 5008); ø 30 mm, height 7.75 mm; 31 jewels; 28,800 vph; twin spring barrels for movement and alarm
Functions: hours, minutes, sweep seconds; date; 24-hour display (second time zone); alarm
Case: stainless steel, domed, 38 x 50 mm, height 15.5 mm; sapphire crystal; exhibition window case back
Band: reptile skin, buckle
Price: $6,950

Aquadyn

Reference number: AQUA/ST/BKS
Movement: automatic, ETA Caliber 2892-A2, modified; ø 25.6 mm, height 4.9 mm; 26 jewels; 28,800 vph
Functions: hours, minutes, subsidiary seconds; large date
Case: stainless steel, domed, 37 x 47 mm, height 14.1 mm; sapphire crystal; screwed-in crown; water-resistant to 100 m
Band: rubber/stainless steel, folding clasp
Price: $5,950
Variations: in rose gold with buckle

Aerodyn Trophee

Reference number: ATRO/RG/SIG
Movement: manually wound, Aurore Caliber 19; 18 x 25 mm, height 4.0 mm; 18,000 A /h; bridges hand-engraved, limited series of 175 pieces
Functions: hours, minutes, sweep seconds
Case: rose gold, domed, 33 x 44 mm, height 11.5 mm; sapphire crystal; exhibition window case back
Band: reptile skin, buckle
Price: $13,950

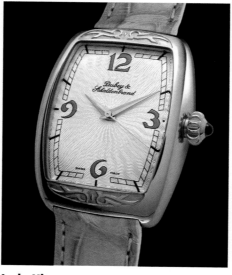

Gran' Chrono Astro

Reference number: AGCA/RG/SIB
Movement: automatic, ETA Caliber 7751; ø 30 mm, height 7.9 mm; 25 jewels; 28,800 vph; bridges hand-engraved, rotor skeletonized with company logo
Functions: hours, minutes; chronograph; date, day of the week, month, moon phase
Case: rose gold, domed, 38 x 50 mm, height 15.5 mm; sapphire crystal; exhibition window case back
Band: reptile skin, buckle
Price: $17,500
Variations: in stainless steel

Lady Ultra

Reference number: ALUL/RG/SIG
Movement: automatic, ETA Caliber 2671; ø 17.2 mm, height 4.8 mm; 25 jewels; 28,800 vph
Functions: hours, minutes, sweep seconds
Case: rose gold, domed, 27 x 37 mm, height 10.1 mm; sapphire crystal
Band: reptile skin, buckle
Price: $7,950
Variations: in stainless steel

Spiral VIP

Movement: The Spiral VIP's movement is based on a very modified ETA Valjoux chronograph Caliber 7751, with which the watchmakers, skeletonizers, and engravers at Dubey & Schaldenbrand's workshops were able to show their stuff. Not only did the movement's aesthetics profit from this special treatment, so did the technology: The movement is officially certified according to the C.O.S.C. chronometer norm.

Spiral VIP

Reference number: SVIP/RG/SIG
Movement: automatic, ETA Caliber 7751, modified; ø 30 mm, height 7.9 mm; 25 jewels; 28,800 vph; hand-engraved; chronograph second hand with a visible, though functionless, spring from the legendary Index Mobile split-seconds chronograph
Functions: hours, minutes, subsidiary seconds; chronograph; date, day of the week, month, moon phase; 24-hour display
Case: rose gold, with movable strap lugs, ø 40 mm, height 14.3 mm; sapphire crystal; exhibition window case back; crown with sapphire cabochon
Band: reptile skin, buckle
Price: $17,500

Spiral Rattrapante

Reference number: SPIR/ST/SIB
Movement: automatic, ETA Caliber 7750, modified; ø 30 mm, height 8 mm; 30 jewels; 28,800 vph; hand-engraved; chronograph second hand with a visible, though functionless, spring from the legendary Index Mobile split-seconds chronograph
Functions: hours, minutes, subsidiary seconds; split-seconds chronograph; date
Case: stainless steel, with movable strap lugs, ø 40 mm, height 14.7 mm; sapphire crystal; exhibition window case back; crown with sapphire cabochon
Band: reptile skin, buckle
Price: $9,950

Spiral One

Reference number: SPI1/ST/SIB
Movement: automatic, ETA Caliber 7750, modified; ø 30 mm, height 7.9 mm; 25 jewels; 28,800 vph; hand-engraved; chronograph second hand with a visible, though functionless, spring from the legendary Index Mobile split-seconds chronograph
Functions: hours, minutes, subsidiary seconds; chronograph; date
Case: stainless steel, with movable strap lugs, ø 40 mm, height 14.3 mm; sapphire crystal; exhibition window case back; crown with sapphire cabochon
Band: reptile skin, buckle
Price: $6,450

Roger Dubuis

Roger Dubuis

Carlos Dias

Roger Dubuis's skill as a watchmaker has been undisputed for decades. However, translating that into the successful watch brand Roger Dubuis, a marque that has fans of *haute horlogerie* swooning, has taken until recently — just shortly before the talented master watchmaker himself retired.

In 1980 he ventured out on his own by opening a small repair and restoration workshop and immediately received his first contracts for construction and detail development at the same time. Soon, Dubuis was known as a specialist in unusual problem solving, and designers for all the great Genevan brands, whenever they happened to be at a loss for a good solution, came knocking at his door. Dubuis would probably still be doing this today for comparatively modest fees if destiny hadn't led Carlos Dias to walk through the door of his workshop before the end of that first year. Dias, a passionate lover of fine watches, actually only wanted Dubuis to repair one of his timepieces, but this first visit turned into regular meetings and, later, a business partnership.

In the eight years since it was founded, the *manufacture* has designed and constructed eight base movements and a total of fourteen variations that tick their way through six watch lines. And now Dias has created a completely new watch genre — following the idea of the motorized all-terrain sport utility vehicle (SUV), his creation is called the Sports Activity Watch (SAW). With three lines — the round Easy Diver, the square Sea More, and the rectangular AquaMare — the project includes sporty yet precious tickers, powered of course by *manufacture* movements created on-premises.

From the very beginning, Dubuis's own contribution to the movements' production was large enough to allow him to put the desirable Seal of Geneva on them. The strict rules applying to the use of the seal secured him not only the admiration of his colleagues but also the support of the customers who had gotten to know the young brand, so demanding of itself. As a member of the Groupement Genevois de Cabinotiers, a loose organization of quality- and status-conscious Genevan watchmakers and engineers, Dubuis today feels even more obliged to work according to Geneva's "watch purity law."

The wondrous, airy construction housing the *manufacture* in the industrial quarter of Meyrin-Satigny became too small after only two years of use and has been expanded by yet another building. The great amount of energy put into this expansion serves the goal of achieving the greatest amount of production freedom possible: Except for just a small amount of parts supplied, almost all of the components that make up Roger Dubuis watches are made on machines located here. Even if the number of pieces in each series is not that large, the technical energy put into constructing the filigreed components is immense.

To judge by the impressive set of machines, Dias still has quite a few plans for the Roger Dubuis brand.

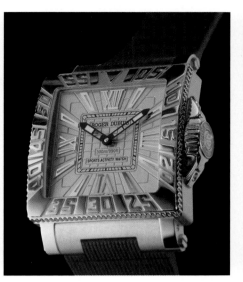

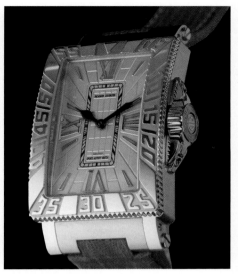

S.A.W. EasyDiver
Reference number: SE46 56 9/0
Movement: manually wound, RD Caliber 56; ø 25.6 mm, height 5.05 mm; 25 jewels; 21,600 vph; Seal of Geneva
Functions: hours, minutes, subsidiary seconds; chronograph
Case: stainless steel, ø 46 mm, height 17 mm; unidirectionally rotating bezel in white gold with 60-minute divisions; sapphire crystal; screwed-in crown and buttons; water-resistant to 300 m
Band: reptile skin, buckle
Remarks: limited to 280 pieces
Price: $21,400
Variations: in stainless steel, limited to 888 pieces; in yellow, red or white gold, limited to 28 pieces each

S.A.W. AcquaMare
Reference number: G4157 9/0
Movement: automatic, RD Caliber 14; ø 25.6 mm, height 3.43 mm; 31 jewels; 28,800 vph; Seal of Geneva
Functions: hours, minutes
Case: stainless steel, domed, 43 x 43 mm, height 15 mm; bezel in white gold with 60-minute scale; sapphire crystal; screwed-in crown; water-resistant to 300 m
Band: reptile skin, buckle
Remarks: limited to 280 pieces
Price: $14,950
Variations: in stainless steel, limited to 888 pieces

S.A.W. SeaMore
Reference number: MS 34 21 9 2.53
Movement: automatic, RD Caliber 14; ø 25.6 mm, height 3.43 mm; 31 jewels; 28,800 vph; Seal of Geneva
Functions: hours, minutes
Case: stainless steel, domed, 56 x 34 mm, height 15 mm; bezel in white gold with 60-minute scale; sapphire crystal; screwed-in crown; water-resistant to 300 m
Band: reptile skin, buckle
Remarks: limited to 280 pieces
Price: $13,5000
Variations: in stainless steel, limited to 888 pieces

Much More Minute Repeater
Reference number: M34 26 0/9.63
Movement: manually wound, RD Caliber 26; 30 jewels; 21,600 vph; Seal of Geneva
Functions: hours, minutes, subsidiary seconds; hour, quarter hour, and minute repeater
Case: white gold, domed, 34 x 45 mm, height 13 mm; sapphire crystal; exhibition window case back
Band: reptile skin, buckle
Remarks: limited to 28 pieces
Price: upon request

Golden Square Flying Tourbillon
Reference number: G40 035/N1.52
Movement: manually wound, RD Caliber 03; 33.8 x 33.8 mm; 27 jewels; 21,600 vph; flying one-minute tourbillon; crown button for date correction
Functions: hours, minutes (off-center), subsidiary seconds (on tourbillon cage); large date; power reserve display
Case: rose gold, domed, 40 x 40 mm, height 12 mm; sapphire crystal; exhibition window case back
Band: reptile skin, buckle
Remarks: limited to 28 pieces
Price: $124,000

Golden Square Dual Time
Reference number: G43 5747 5N 37.56DT
Movement: manually wound, RD Caliber 5747; ø 25.6 mm, height 4.8 mm; 25 jewels; 21,600 vph; module for two time zones with jump hour display
Functions: hours (double, jump), minutes
Case: rose gold, domed, 43 x 43 mm, height 11.8 mm; sapphire crystal; exhibition window case back
Band: reptile skin, buckle
Remarks: limited to 28 pieces
Price: $36,900
Variations: in white gold

Golden Square Perpetual Calendar

Reference number: G43 5729 5/5.7
Movement: automatic, RD Caliber 57; ø 25.6 mm, height 5.95 mm; 25 jewels; 21,600 vph; 5 jump window displays; Seal of Geneva
Functions: hours, minutes; perpetual calendar with date, day of the week, month, moon phase, leap year, 24-hour display (second time zone)
Case: rose gold, domed, 43 x 43 mm, height 12 mm; sapphire crystal; exhibition window case back
Band: reptile skin, buckle
Remarks: limited to 28 pieces
Price: upon request

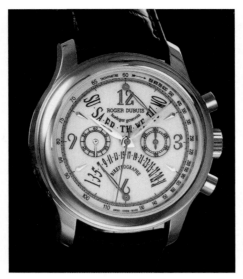

Hommage Bi-Retrograde Chronograph

Reference number: H40 5630 0/5.6
Movement: manually wound, RD Caliber 5630; ø 27.5 mm, height 7.42 mm; 25 jewels; 21,600 vph; column wheel control of chronograph functions; Seal of Geneva
Functions: hours, minutes, subsidiary seconds; chronograph; date and day of the week (retrograde)
Case: white gold, ø 40 mm, height 11 mm; sapphire crystal; exhibition window case back
Band: reptile skin, buckle
Remarks: limited to 28 pieces
Price: $39,000
Variations: in rose gold; in various dial variations

Sympathie Tourbillon

Reference number: S40 1102 0/N96.5
Movement: manually wound, RD Caliber 1102; ø 28 mm, height 5.96 mm; 9 jewels; 21,600 vph; one-minute tourbillon; Seal of Geneva
Functions: hours, minutes, subsidiary seconds; perpetual calendar with date and day of the week (both retrograde), month, moon phase, leap year
Case: white gold, 40 x 40 mm, height 14 mm; sapphire crystal; exhibition window case back
Band: reptile skin, buckle in white gold
Remarks: limited to 28 pieces
Price: $154,000

Sympathie Bi-Retrograde Perp. Cal.

Reference number: S37 5772 5/6.3
Movement: automatic, RD Caliber 5772; ø 25.6 mm, height 4.8 mm; 29 jewels; 21,600 vph; patented double retrograde mechanism; Seal of Geneva
Functions: hours, minutes, sweep seconds; perpetual calendar with date and day of the week (retrograde), month, moon phase, leap year
Case: rose gold, 37 x 37 mm, height 11 mm; sapphire crystal; exhibition window case back
Band: reptile skin, buckle
Remarks: limited to 28 pieces
Price: $34,000

Sympathie Chronographe QP Bi-Retrograde par le Centre

Reference number: S43 5610 0/5.0
Movement: manually wound, RD Caliber 5610; ø 27.5 mm, height 8,07 mm; 21 jewels; 21,600 vph; column wheel control of chronograph functions; Seal of Geneva
Functions: hours, minutes, subsidiary seconds; chronograph; perpetual calendar with date and day of the week (retrograde), calendar weeks, month, moon phase, leap year
Case: white gold, 43 x 43 mm, height 12 mm; sapphire crystal; exhibition window case back
Band: reptile skin, folding clasp in white gold
Price: $76,700

Follow Me

Reference number: F17 540/FBD F2.7A
Movement: manually wound, RD Caliber 54; ø 18 mm, height 2.5 mm; 19 jewels; 21,600 vph
Functions: hours, minutes
Case: white gold, cross-shaped, 40 x 40 mm, height 10 mm; bezel and lugs set with 48 baguette-cut diamonds and 115 brilliant-cut diamonds; sapphire crystal
Band: double reptile skin, double buckle
Remarks: limited to 28 pieces
Price: $71,500
Variations: various dial variations

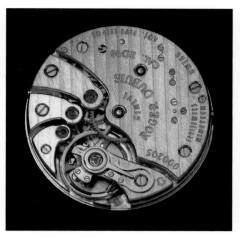

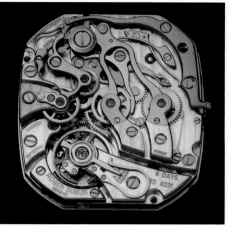

Caliber RD 28

Mechanical with manual winding, column-wheel control of chronograph functions, manipulated by one single button on crown

Functions: hours, minutes, subsidiary seconds; chronograph
Diameter: 25.6 mm (10 ''')
Height: 5.05 mm
Jewels: 25
Balance: glucydur, three-legged
Frequency: 21,600 vph
Balance spring: Breguet, swan-neck fine adjustment
Remarks: 224 individual components; rhodium-plated plates; *côtes de Genève*; Seal of Geneva

Caliber RD 98

Mechanical with manual winding
Functions: hours, minutes, subsidiary seconds
Diameter: 25.6 mm (10 ''')
Height: 3.8 mm
Jewels: 19
Balance: glucydur, three-legged
Frequency: 21,600 vph
Balance spring: flat hairspring, swan-neck fine adjustment
Remarks: 134 individual components; rhodium-plated plates; *côtes de Genève*; Seal of Geneva

Caliber RD 8230

Mechanical with manual winding, column-wheel control of chronograph functions, manipulated by one single button on crown; twin spring barrels, power reserve appx. eight days
Functions: hours, minutes, subsidiary seconds; chronograph; power reserve display
Dimensions: 31 x 28 mm (13 1/2''')
Height: 7.6 mm; **Jewels:** 25
Balance: glucydur, three-legged
Frequency: 21,600 vph
Balance spring: flat hairspring, swan-neck fine adjustment
Remarks: 315 individual components; rhodium-plated plates; *côtes de Genève*; Seal of Geneva
Related calibers: RD 8231 (without power reserve display); RD 82 (without chronograph, 21 jewels, 4.1 mm high)

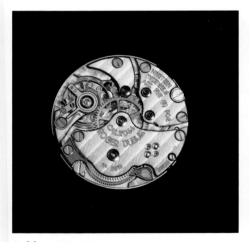

Caliber RD 54

Mechanical with manual winding
Functions: hours, minutes
Diameter: 18 mm (8''')
Height: 2.5 mm
Jewels: 19
Balance: glucydur, three-legged
Frequency: 21,600 vph
Balance spring: flat hairspring, swan-neck fine adjustment
Remarks: 105 individual components; rhodium-plated plates; *côtes de Genève*; Seal of Geneva

Caliber RD 03

Mechanical with manual winding; one-minute tourbillon
Functions: hours, minutes; large date; power reserve display
Dimensions: 33.8 x 33.8 mm (15''')
Height: 5.7 mm
Jewels: 27
Frequency: 21,600 vph
Balance spring: flat hairspring
Remarks: flying one-minute tourbillon; precisely jumping large date; 270 individual components; rhodium-plated plates; *côtes de Genève*; Seal of Geneva

Caliber RD 03

The dial side of the shaped tourbillon movement from the Roger Dubuis *manufacture*.

... continued from page 183

IWC *pronounced as in English*
Stands for International Watch Company, founded in Switzerland by American Florentine Ariosto Jones.

Jacob & Co. jākəb
Russian-born American Jacob Arabo's first name, company founder and owner.

Jacques Lemans jäk ləmän
French-sounding name chosen by Austrian owner and founder Alfred Riedl.

Jaeger-LeCoultre yāgər ləkūltr
Taken from the last names of Swiss founders Pierre Jaeger and Charles-Antoine LeCoultre.

Jaquet Droz jäkā drō
Taken from Swiss Pierre Jaquet Droz's last name.

Jean-Mairet & Gillman jän mārā ā gilmän
Swiss founder and owner César Jean-Mairet's last name coupled with the last name of his maternal grandparents, also famous watchmakers.

JeanRichard jänrichär
Taken from Swiss watchmaker Daniel JeanRichard's name.

Cédric Johner jōnər
Swiss goldsmith/watchmaker Cédric Johner's name.

F.P. Journe jurn
French master watchmaker François-Paul Journe's name.

Urban Jürgensen jūrgənsən
Danish watchmaker Urban Jürgensen's name.

Kobold kōbolt
Taken from American founder and president Michael Kobold's last name, a man of German descent.

Maurice Lacroix morēs läkwä
Fictional francophone name chosen for brand by Swiss parent company Desco von Schulthess.

A. Lange & Söhne ä längə ūnt sönə
Taken from German founding watchmaker Ferdinand Adolph Lange's name.

Limes lēməs
Brand name fabricated by the German Ickler family.

Longines lonjēn
Swiss founder Ernest Francillon bought a property by the name of Longines, built a factory there, and named his brand after it.

Giuliano Mazzuoli mätzūōlē
Italian designer Giuliano Mazzuoli's name.

Meistersinger mīstərzingər
Name chosen by German founder Manfred Brassler.

Richard Mille rēschär mēl
French owner and founder Richard Mille's name.

Milus mēlūs
Name chosen by Swiss founder Paul William Junod.

H. Moser & Cie. mōzər
Name of Swiss founder Heinrich Moser.

Louis Moinet lūē moinā
Name of Breguet's French contemporary Louis Moinet.

Montblanc mōnblänk
Name of the German-based famed writing instrument company derived from the Swiss/French mountain Mont Blanc.

Movado mōvädō
A name originating in the synthetic world language Esperanto and meaning "constantly in motion."

Mühle mülə
Last name of German founder Robert Mühle.

Franck Muller fränk mülər
Name of Swiss-born watchmaker Franck Muller.

Ulysse Nardin ūlis närdən
French-language name of Swiss founder Ulysse Nardin.

NBY *pronounced as in English*
No Barriers Yäeger, a name constructed by German master watchmaker Martin Braun, loosely inspired by pilot Chuck Yeager's name.

Armand Nicolet ärmänd nēkōlā
Name of Swiss-born watchmaker Armand Nicolet.

Nivrel nēvrel
A registered Swiss name acquired by German Gerd Hofer for his company.

Nomos nōmōs
The name of an historical Glashütte watch company. German owner and founder of the modern Nomos company, Roland Schwertner, acquired the name after the fall of the Berlin Wall.

Omega ōmägä
Name chosen for the company by Swiss founder Louis Brandt's sons, Louis Paul and César.

Oris oris
Named by Swiss founders Paul Cattin and Georges Christian for the small stream that runs near the factory.

Panerai pänərī
The Italian word *officine* (previously included in the brand's name) means workshops, and Panerai is taken from the name of the Italian founder, Guido Panerai.

Parmigiani pärmijänē
Last name of Swiss founder watchmaker Michel Parmigiani.

Patek Philippe pätek filēp
Last names of founding Polish immigrant to Switzerland, entrepreneur Antoine Norbert de Patek, and French watchmaker Adrien Philippe.

Piaget pēäjā
French-language last name of Swiss founder Georges Piaget.

Paul Picot pōl pēkō
Name chosen by Italian entrepreneur Mario Boiocchi for his company.

Porsche Design porshə dəsin
Taken from German owner, and founder of the original licensing automobile brand, Ferdinand A. Porsche's last name.

Rado rädō
Later director Paul Lüthi christened the Swiss company Schlup & Co. Rado in the mid 1950s.

Auguste Reymond augüst rämōn
Taken from Swiss founder Auguste Reymond's name.

RGM *pronounced as in English*
Taken from American founder and owner Roland G. Murphy's initials.

Rolex rōlex
German-born founder Hans Wildorf took the name from a combination of the Spanish words *relojes excelentes* (excellent watches) and modified it.

Daniel Roth dänyel rōt
Taken from Swiss founding watchmaker Daniel Roth's name.

Scalfaro skälfärō
Name invented by German founding brothers Kuhnle.

Jörg Schauer yörg shauər
Taken from German-born goldsmith, founder, and owner Jörg Schauer's name.

Alain Silberstein älən silbərstīn
Taken from French-born architect, founder, and owner Alain Silberstein's name.

Sinn zin
Taken from German-born founder Helmut Sinn's last name.

Sothis zōtis
German-born founder and owner Wolfgang Steinkrüger chose this name from Egyptian mythology for his brand.

Stowa shtōvä
Derived from the name of German founder Walter Storz.

SWI *pronounced as in English*
Brand name invented by the Ben-Schmuel family, standing for Swiss Watch International.

Swiss Army *pronounced as in English*
Brand name used by Karl Elsener and his ensuing family members for the U.S. version of the Swiss brand Victorinox.

TAG Heuer täg hoiər
Taken from Swiss founding watchmaker Edouard Heuer's last name and the TAG group, who bought the brand in 1985.

Temption temptsēōn
Name chosen by German founder and owner Klaus Ulbrich combining *temp*us and func*tion*.

Tissot tisō
French-language last name of Swiss founders Charles-Félicien and Charles-Emile Tissot (father and son respectively).

Tutima tūtēmä
Brand name derived from Latin word *tutus*, meaning certain or protected, by German-born founder Dr. Ernst Kurtz.

Vacheron Constantin väshərōn cōnstäntən
French-language last names of Swiss founders Jean-Marc Vacheron and Francois Constantin.

Ventura *pronounced as in English*
Swiss-born founder and owner Pierre Nobs named his company after Ventura, California.

Vollmer fōlmər
Last name of German founding family.

Harry Winston *pronounced as in English*
The name of prominent New Yorker jeweler Harry Winston, born in 1896.

Xemex zəməx
Name invented by Swiss founders and owners, designer Ruedi Külling and businessman Hans-Peter Hanschick.

Zenith *pronounced as in English*
Swiss-born founder Georges Favre-Jacot gave this name to his company.

Zeno *pronounced as in English*
André-Charles Eigeldinger, son of the second owner of the parent company, introduced the Zeno brand, the name of which is derived from the Greek word *zenodopolus*, meaning "gift of Zeus" or "divine offering."

Epos

Epos, at home in Switzerland's bilingual city of Biel, was founded in 1983 by Peter Hofer. This is a company that was one of the most active manufacturers of private label watches for many years which has until now sold very little under its own brand name — a state of affairs that greatly changed during 2003. Bought in that year by Tomdi Chonge, a Swiss national of Tibetan origin, the concentration has shifted to the company's own production and marketing thereof.

Though Chonge, who previously managed another Swiss watchmaking firm, is concentrating on the widespread branding of Epos, the original concept of creating pieces using seasoned artisans from the Swiss watchmaking industry to combine classic designs — and some classic movements —

with modern materials and reliability has not changed.

These are watches that have proven their quality and honorable pricing policy a thousand times over — under foreign names, of course. Epos's leading models are in a somewhat higher market segment, both in quality and price. The brand sets itself apart from continuous comparisons with famous faces made by other brands with its unique cases, dials, and hands as well as perfect quality to the smallest detail. Small complications such as jump hours, power reserve displays, regulator dial trains, calendars, and flyback chronographs are created in cooperation with reputable specialists such as Dubois-Dépraz and La Joux-Perret. The legendary Eight Day watch — only currently available in the Epos line

and manifested in the Edition Antiquité model — is based on a vintage manually wound Hebdomas pocket watch caliber, and represents just one of the highlights in the collection.

More conservative manually wound and automatic models in pleasing round and rectangular cases as well as convincing chronograph classics in a 1940s style represent the bread and butter of the company, in which Chonge's entire family is now involved. And though this might be the case, it hasn't stopped Chonge from creating more upscale pieces in 2005, such as a tourbillon and a five-minute repeater in limited editions, which are extremely pleasing to the eye as well as the ear due to the obvious amount of hand craftsmanship that has gone into their movements.

Edition Antiquité

Reference number: 3340
Movement: manually wound, Hebdomas Caliber 15'''; movement according to historical model from the 19th century; 8 days power reserve, decorated visible balance cock
Functions: hours, minutes
Case: stainless steel, ø 42 mm, height 14 mm; sapphire crystal
Band: leather, buckle
Remarks: enameled dial
Price: $3,750
Variations: with gold-plated case; with white or black dial

Edition Antiquité Duograph

Reference number: 3364
Movement: automatic, ETA Caliber 7750; ø 30 mm, height 7.9 mm; 25 jewels; 28,800 vph; côtes de Genève and blued screws
Functions: hours, minutes, subsidiary seconds; chronograph; date
Case: stainless steel, ø 42 mm, height 14 mm; sapphire crystal; exhibition window case back
Band: leather, buckle
Price: $2,150
Variations: various dials

Tonneau

Reference number: 3363
Movement: manually wound, Peseux Caliber P7046 Epos; ø 25.6 mm, height 4.6 mm; 25 jewels; 28,800 vph; autonomous, patented movement module for regulator; movement finely finished
Functions: hours (off-center), minutes, subsidiary seconds; date, moon phase
Case: stainless steel, 30 x 40 mm, height 8.9 mm; sapphire crystal; exhibition window case back
Band: leather, buckle
Price: $2,150
Variations: with black or grey dial

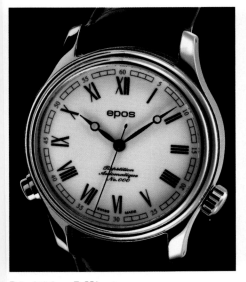

Répétition 5 Minutes

Reference number: 3373
Movement: automatic, Dubois-Dépraz Caliber D 88 (base ETA 2892-A2); ø 36.2 mm, height 7.35 mm; 21 jewels; 28,800 vph; repeater module and rotor finely finished
Functions: hours, minutes, sweep seconds; five-minute repeater
Case: stainless steel, ø 42 mm, height 12.9 mm; sapphire crystal; exhibition window case back
Band: leather, buckle
Remarks: limited to 200 pieces
Price: $13,000
Variations: in gold-plated stainless steel, limited to 100 pieces

Action Team Springende Stunde

Reference number: 3370
Movement: manually wound, AS Caliber 1727; finely finished with côtes de Genève and blued screws
Functions: hours (jump); minutes (off-center), subsidiary seconds
Case: stainless steel, ø 42 mm, height 9 mm; sapphire crystal; exhibition window case back
Band: leather, buckle
Price: $2,150
Variations: with silver dial

Free Soul

Reference number: 3369
Movement: automatic, ETA Caliber 6497-2 Unitas; ø 36.6 mm, height 4.5 mm; 17 jewels; 21,600 vph; partially skeletonized, finely finished
Functions: hours, minutes, subsidiary seconds
Case: stainless steel, ø 42 mm, height 10 mm; sapphire crystal; exhibition window case back
Band: leather, buckle
Price: $1,350
Variations: various dials

Louis Erard

A Swiss watchmaking firm with a long tradition, Louis Erard is named after the founder of the company, a man who started up a small movement reassembly business of his own in 1937, just after the world economic crisis of that era. Erard, the son of a well-known watchmaking family, remained behind the scenes for his entire working life as a supplier to a number of distinguished watch manufacturers. However, he encouraged his sons René and Jean-Louis to distance themselves from movement reassembly and concentrate on the design and manufacture of watch movements. Thus, modern technology was continually being introduced into the small factory, the name of which only few insiders had ever heard.

It was Louis Erard's grandson Paul who thought of employing lucrative marketing for the company's high-quality products in the late 1970s, putting together a complete line of his own watches as an independent brand.

Good things come to those who wait in the Swiss world of watches, and it was indeed a number of years before Paul was able to present his own completed collection under the slogan "l'espirit du temps." In 1978 the company changed its name from Louis Erard et Fils to plain Louis Erard, and almost fifty years after the original founding, an independent brand with a complete watch line was presented to the general public.

In the 1980s the company was quickly moving upward, establishing a larger factory in La Chaux-de-Fonds, and even entering world markets of the Middle East and Asia. After the founding family left the company in 1992, it was sold to Concept Deux, but changed hands yet again in 1993. With the support of an international investor consortium, Alain Spinedi bought the rights to the brand and moved production to Le Noirmont, a small town outside of La Chaux-de-Fonds. There, industrious hands once again reassemble watches for reputable outside brands, but they also take intense care of the house's own collection. The brand includes watches with elegantly designed cases and dials, meticulously conceived down to the finest detail, and beautifully executed. The watches also frequently house interesting "little complications" such as a power reserve indicator, a regulator dial train, or an unusually placed subsidiary-second dial. And despite keenly calculated prices, Louis Erard has continually received appropriate attention from watch enthusiasts in the middle-income bracket.

In this modern era, the motto "l'esprit du temps" has been changed into the more fluent English phrase "The Spirit of Time," and the brand's beginnings on the U.S. market look more than promising.

Heritage Cadran Paris

Reference number: 69 250 AA06
Movement: automatic, ETA Caliber 2824-2; ø 25.6 mm, height 4.6 mm; 25 jewels; 28,800 vph
Functions: hours, minutes, sweep seconds; date
Case: stainless steel, ø 40.3 mm, height 11 mm; sapphire crystal
Band: leather, folding clasp
Price: $750
Variations: with black dial; with stainless steel bracelet

Heritage Cadran Paris Chronograph

Reference number: 73 255 AA09
Movement: automatic, ETA Caliber 7750 Bicompax; ø 30 mm, height 7.9 mm; 25 jewels; 28,800 vph
Functions: hours, minutes; chronograph; date
Case: stainless steel, ø 40.3 mm, height 14 mm; sapphire crystal
Band: leather, folding clasp
Price: $1,875
Variations: with white dial; with stainless steel bracelet

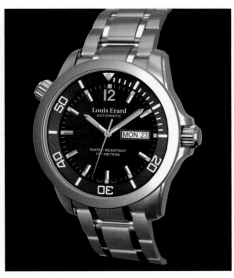

Move

Reference number: 72 400 AA02M
Movement: automatic, ETA Caliber 2836-2; ø 25.6 mm, height 5.05 mm; 25 jewels; 28,800 vph
Functions: hours, minutes, sweep seconds; date and day of the week
Case: stainless steel, ø 40.3 mm, height 11 mm; bidirectionally rotating bezel under crystal with 60-minute divisions; sapphire crystal
Band: stainless steel, folding clasp
Price: $2,175
Variations: on leather strap ($1,995); with white dial

Carrée

Reference number: 69 500 AA02
Movement: automatic, ETA Caliber 2824-2; ø 25.6 mm, height 4.6 mm; 25 jewels; 28,800 vph
Functions: hours, minutes, sweep seconds; date
Case: stainless steel, 35 x 35 mm, height 11 mm; sapphire crystal
Band: leather, folding clasp
Price: $1,200
Variations: with white or bronze-colored dial; PVD-gold plated case ($1,275 on strap)

1931 Large Date

Reference number: 42 202 AA02
Movement: automatic, ETA Caliber 2824-2 with large date by Dubois-Dépraz; ø 25.6 mm, height 4.6 mm (base caliber); 25 jewels; 28,800 vph
Functions: hours, minutes, subsidiary seconds; large date
Case: stainless steel, ø 40.3 mm, height 10 mm; sapphire crystal
Band: leather, folding clasp
Price: $2,325
Variations: with white dial; PVD-gold plated case ($2,400)

1931 Moon Phase

Reference number: 43 203 AA01
Movement: automatic, ETA Caliber 2824-2 with calendar module by Dubois-Dépraz; ø 25.6 mm, height 4.6 mm (base caliber); 25 jewels; 28,800 vph
Functions: hours, minutes, sweep seconds; date, day of the week, month, moon phase
Case: stainless steel, ø 40.3 mm, height 10 mm; sapphire crystal
Band: leather, folding clasp
Price: $2,445
Variations: with black dial; PVD-gold plated case ($2,535)

Eterna

A look back can also be a look ahead — as evidenced by watch manufacturer Eterna. This company is currently reminiscing about the legendary expedition of Thor Heyerdahl from Peru to Polynesia on his balsa raft *KonTiki*. This Heyerdahl did while wearing a timepiece by the traditional brand hailing from Grenchen on his wrist, and for this reason Eterna has named a complete line of models for the *KonTiki*.

The line received a couple of impressive siblings this year. For one the KonTiki Diver, a rather special diver's watch for which the terms "secure on the wrist" and "protection of the movement" have separate but equal meanings. The movement is housed in a spectacular type of container that is water-resistant to 1,000 meters and secured to a "bridge."

The second introduction will make fans of the brand extremely joyful as it is an ex-pedition watch called KonTiki GMT and features a 24-hour hand with an inner rotating ring upon which the reference cities of twenty-four time zones are printed. The cities included were those that played a role in the *KonTiki* expedition, thus honoring Heyerdahl's historical achievement.

Eterna can proudly look back on a long history as one of the leading Swiss watch brands. In the year 1876 the first watch bearing this name appeared on the market: Eterna was the new brand name for the watches coming from a factory that had been founded in 1856. Since then, the brand has proved its technical competence again and again.

Eterna's logo illustrates the brand's importance: five dots in the shape of a pentagon. This symbol represents the five tiny steel balls in the ball bearing that Eterna's engineers invented in 1948 — the one that rocketed the brand to worldwide fame in one fell swoop. This trailblazing invention in micromechanics still represents a worldwide watchmaking standard today and is utilized by countless watch companies.

The positioning of the watch families 1948 and the evergreen KonTiki are proof positive that Eterna is careful to keep its great past positioned in the conscious memory of the watch fan. This is not to say that the company would like to be regarded as old-fashioned, but the return to old values does fit into the horological world's contemporary frame of mind.

For Eterna this is all part of the corporate objective for the future — a very promising future as the year 1995 proved, when Eterna went into the hands of no less than Professor Ferdinand Alexander Porsche. Since the takeover by F. A. P. Beteiligung GmbH, not only has Eterna produced Porsche Design's watches, but a positive side effect has emerged in the form of the developmental support, innovative talent, and creativity emanating in Eterna's direction from F. A. Porsche's design office. Company president Ernst F. Seyr has lots of plans racing around in his head. After the spectacular developments recently introduced in the name of sister brand Porsche Design, it's not hard to believe that he can make Eterna into what it once was: a watch brand with its own movement production, a genuine *manufacture*.

And this traditional Swiss brand is working very hard at once again becoming precisely this. Even though its R&D capacity has been at least partially zapped in the past few years for Porsche Design's ambitious Indicator project, now the technicians at Eterna can fully concentrate on their own complete watch movement. It needs to be done at the latest by 2006, for during that year the brand will be celebrating its 150th anniversary. Perhaps by then Eterna's grand past will already have become part of its future.

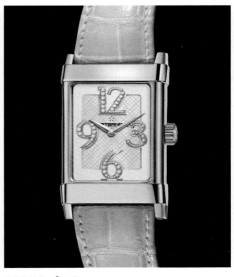

KonTiki GMT

Reference number: 1593.41
Movement: automatic, ETA Caliber 2893-2; ø 25.6 mm, height 4.1 mm; 21 jewels; 28,800 vph; Eterna rotor
Functions: hours, minutes, sweep seconds; date; 24-hour display (second time zone or world time)
Case: stainless steel , ø 42.4 mm, height 13.5 mm; bezel under crystal with world time scale, rotatable from the outside via the bezel (patented); sapphire crystal; screwed-in crown; water-resistant to 200 m
Band: stainless steel, folding clasp with wetsuit extension
Price: Sfr 3,050
Variations: with rubber strap

KonTiki Four-Hand Watch

Reference number: 1592.41
Movement: automatic, ETA Caliber Eterna 636 (base 2836-2 H6); ø 25.6 mm, height 5.05 mm; 25 jewels; 28,800 vph; date hand by Eterna
Functions: hours, minutes, sweep seconds; date
Case: stainless steel, ø 40 mm, height 11.7 mm; sapphire crystal; screwed-in crown; water-resistant to 120 m
Band: leather, buckle
Price: Sfr 1,950
Variations: with stainless steel bracelet; with rubber strap; dial in beige

1935 Lady Quartz

Reference number: 8790
Movement: quartz, ETA Caliber 956112,0
Functions: hours, minutes
Case: stainless steel, 37.1 x 23.3 mm, height 8.7 mm; sapphire crystal; screwed-in crown
Band: reptile skin, folding clasp
Price: Sfr 1,900
Variations: various crocodile skin straps and dials; with stainless steel bracelet

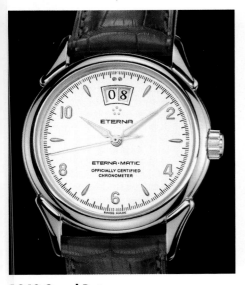

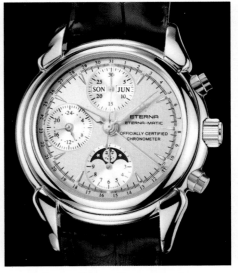

1948 Grand Date

Reference number: 8425.69.10
Movement: automatic, ETA Caliber Eterna 608 (base 2892 A2); Eterna-Matic original ball bearing rotor
Functions: hours, minutes, sweep seconds, large date
Case: rose gold, ø 40 mm, height 11 mm; sapphire crystal; exhibition window case back; screwed-in crown
Band: reptile skin , folding clasp
Price: Sfr 7,250
Variations: in stainless steel; with black reptile skin strap, black dial and diamond bezel

1948 Alarm

Reference number: 8510.69.41
Movement: automatic, AS Caliber 5008; ø 30 mm, height 7.6 mm; 31 jewels; 28,800 vph; case designed exactly according to plans of the first Eterna-Matic from 1948
Functions: hours, minutes, sweep seconds; alarm; date, day of the week
Case: rose gold, ø 39 mm, height 14.2 mm; sapphire crystal; exhibition window case back
Band: reptile skin, folding clasp
Remarks: numbered edition
Price: Sfr 8,300
Variations: in stainless steel

1948 Moon Phase Chronograph

Reference number: 8515.41.10
Movement: automatic, ETA Caliber 7751; ø 30 mm, height 7.9 mm; 25 jewels; 28,800 vph; officially certified chronometer (COSC); case designed exactly according to plans of the first Eterna-Matic from 1948
Functions: hours, minutes, subsidiary seconds; chronograph; date, day of the week, month, moon phase
Case: stainless steel, ø 39 mm, height 14 mm; sapphire crystal; exhibition window case back
Band: reptile skin, folding clasp
Remarks: numbered edition
Price: Sfr 3,700

Jacques Etoile

The year 2005 was one under the sign of the moon for Jacques Etoile, but also one containing an important anniversary for the brand. Master watch-makers Horst and Klaus Jakob (father and son) celebrated the fiftieth year of their watch and jewelry store in Lörrach, Germany, the business from which Jacques Etoile Uhren GmbH was created. And as befits this circumstance, it was of course celebrated with the creation of a fine little series of timepieces: Klaus Jakob had found some of the vintage caliber AS 1123 during his sojourns in Switzerland and later even the matching Universo hands to go with them. These hands are factory-new even though they were made in the founding year of the Jakobs' company, 1955. From these ingredients he created fifty steel and twenty rose gold watches, which are all personally assembled by the Jakobs themselves.

This is also true of the two new series Lune & Etoile and Lunamatic. The dials, which Klaus had made by his neighbor Schätzle in Weil am Rhein, are quite lavish in their production. The customer can even have his or her own zodiac sign printed on the dial of the Lune & Etoile. For the Lunamatic the status of the moon is displayed twice — once for the Northern and once for the Southern Hemisphere.

Owner Klaus Jakob is also a passionate diver. For this reason he now also has a diver's watch in his collection which does justice to the demands of professionals both in equipment and quality (water-resistant to 500 meters).

However, master watchmaker Klaus Jakob's heart beats above all for old traditions — and vintage movements that are no longer in production. This tireless collector somehow always manages to unearth old hand-assembled calibers or perhaps only

parts of them on remote dusty shelves or in some forgotten box on his extensive travels through the Swiss watchmaking country-side. Then he lovingly reworks and places them in attractive, classic cases. Thanks to a respectable pricing policy, these limited editions of exceptional watches are snapped up immediately by interested buyers.

In the last few years Klaus Jakob has estab-lished himself as one of the leading spe-cialists in the working and finishing of the legendary column-wheel chronograph movement caliber Venus 175, causing a loyal following to flock to his company. The technical beauty and spectacular finish of his Venus movements hold a special place of honor in collectors' circles.

Jakob also has somewhat of a monopoly on the use of the Unitas caliber 6300, no longer in production. Outside of Jacques Etoile, there is no company with watches utilizing this movement in its program, although the 6300 has proved its qualities a thousand times over. After Jakob's finishing touches, the movement appears in a splen-dor that the original watchmakers of the Unitas movement *manufacture* could probably only have dreamed of.

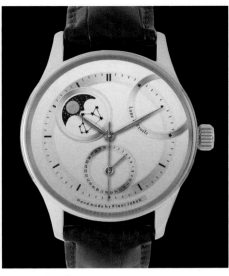

Indianapolis

Movement: automatic, ETA Caliber 2824-2; ø 25.6 mm, height 4.6 mm; 25 jewels; 28,800 vph; super soigné finish
Functions: hours, minutes, sweep seconds; date
Case: stainless steel, ø 38 mm, height 9.7 mm; sapphire crystal; exhibition window case back
Band: leather, buckle
Price: $995
Variations: with silver dial

Atlantis

Movement: automatic, ETA Caliber 2824-2; ø 25.6 mm, height 4.6 mm; 25 jewels; 28,800 vph; protected against magnetic fields
Functions: hours, minutes, sweep seconds; date
Case: stainless steel, ø 43 mm, height 13.3 mm; unidirectionally rotating bezel with 60-minute divisions; sapphire crystal; screwed-in crown; water-resistant to 500 m
Band: reptile skin, buckle
Price: $1,795
Variations: with stainless steel bracelet ($2,095); with black dial

Lune & Etoile

Movement: automatic, ETA Caliber 2824-2, modified; ø 25.6 mm, height 4.6 mm; 25 jewels; 28,800 vph; super soigné finish
Functions: hours, minutes, sweep seconds; date, moon phase
Case: stainless steel, ø 38 mm, height 9.7 mm; sapphire crystal; exhibition window case back
Band: leather, buckle
Remarks: upon request with individual sign of the Zodiac
Price: $1,850
Variations: with black dial

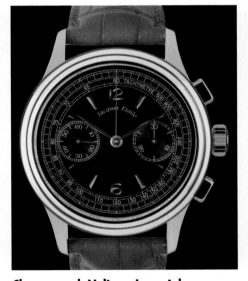

Lunamatic

Movement: automatic, ETA Caliber 2824-2, modified; ø 25.6 mm, height 4.6 mm; 25 jewels; 28,800 vph; super soigné finish
Functions: hours, minutes, sweep seconds; date, double moon phase
Case: stainless steel, ø 38 mm, height 9.7 mm; sapphire crystal; exhibition window case back
Band: leather, buckle
Price: $1,850
Variations: with silver dial

Chronograph Valjoux Imperial

Reference number:
Movement: automatic, ETA Caliber 7750; ø 30 mm, height 7.9 mm; 25 jewels; 28,800 vph; super soigné finish
Functions: hours, minutes, subsidiary seconds; chronograph
Case: stainless steel, ø 42 mm, height 13 mm; sapphire crystal; exhibition window case back
Band: leather, buckle
Price: $3,250
Variations: with silver dial

Metropolis

Reference number:
Movement: manually wound, Unitas Caliber 6300; ø 29.4 mm, height 4.62 mm; 19 jewels; 18,000 vph; rare vintage *manufacture* movement, lavishly reworked
Functions: hours, minutes, sweep seconds
Case: stainless steel, ø 38 mm, height 10 mm; sapphire crystal; exhibition window case back
Band: leather, buckle
Price: $1,950
Variations: various dials

Fabergé

At Baselworld 2005 Fabergé, after an absence from the watch market of almost ninety years, made its comeback. Fabergé became famous for its jeweled eggs of the same brand name that were originally manufactured solely for the family of the Russian czars. After the Russian October Revolution of 1917, production was halted and only in the recent past taken up again. Now the revival of the brand as a manufacturer of wristwatches is also a reality thanks to craftsman Victor Mayer. This current licensee of the name is located in Pforzheim, Germany, and enjoys an excellent reputation in the industry for enamel work. The enameling and guilloché are so important because they are authentic Fabergé techniques. And they can also be found in the current watch collection for women and men oriented upon historic models.

The name of the men's collection, Agathon, is an homage to Peter Carl Fabergé's younger brother, who with his brilliant creative ideas contributed conclusively to the first great successes of the brand at the end of the nineteenth century. Another line from the men's collection is the Carrée — timepieces that fascinate with their fine, square cases. They are crafted in gold, inspired stylistically from art deco, and also available if so desired with a square enameled dial. The women's collection Anastasia, a word that is actually Greek for "the risen," is, for one thing, dedicated to the youngest daughter of the last czar and, for another, symbolic of the revival of the traditional watchmaking art practiced by Fabergé.

The design of the watch collection was inspired by early sketches for Fabergé watches. While creating details such as the crown, buckle, and rotor, design elements typical of the brand such as the Romanov eagle, the sign of the last czar's court jeweler, and above all the characteristic egg shape were utilized. The outline of the buckle is derived from the oval shape as is the signet featuring the blue-enameled Cyrillic letter F.

Each individual piece achieves uniqueness through the microscopic irregularities of the enamel, which bear witness to the authenticity of the handwork done on it. High-quality materials, traditional crafts, and a timelessly elegant design are what characterize Fabergé's precious watches.

Agathon

Reference number: M 1105
Movement: automatic, ETA Caliber 2892-A2; ø 25.6 mm, height 3.6 mm; 21 jewels; 28,800 vph; finely finished with sunburst decoration and engraved rotor
Functions: hours, minutes, sweep seconds
Case: white gold, ø 40 mm, height 10 mm; sapphire crystal; exhibition window case back
Band: reptile skin, buckle in white gold with enameled logo
Remarks: genuine enameled dial, manufactured according to vintage techniques
Price: 8,800 euros
Variations: in yellow or rose gold

Anastasia

Reference number: M 1001
Movement: quartz, ETA Caliber 976.001
Functions: hours, minutes
Case: white gold, 29 x 24.5 mm, height 7.8 mm; bezel set with 48 brilliant-cut diamonds; sapphire crystal
Band: reptile skin, buckle in white gold with enameled emblem
Remarks: genuine enameled dial, manufactured according to vintage techniques
Price: 8,400 euros
Variations: in yellow gold

Carré

Reference number: M 1112
Movement: manually wound, Fabergé Caliber F 1933 (base Piguet 810); ø 18.8 mm, height 2 mm; 20 jewels; 21,600 vph; finely finished with côtes de Genève and blued screws
Functions: hours, minutes
Case: rose gold, 36 x 28.5 mm, height 8 mm; sapphire crystal; exhibition window case back; crown with sapphire cabochon
Band: reptile skin, buckle in rose gold with enameled emblem
Remarks: genuine enameled dial, manufactured according to vintage techniques
Price: 12,000 euros

Formex

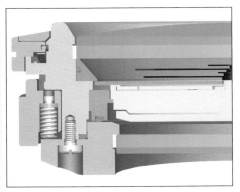

Shock protection — this horological term can be understood in a variety of ways and therefore correspondingly interpreted in varying manners. The shock protection that movement manufacturers put in place to guarantee that sensitive bearings and other components of the balance remain undamaged when hit was

not developed enough for the designers at Formex. They felt the need to devise a watch case with built-in shock absorbers, practically forming a separate chassis for the beautiful bodywork of the timepiece. The fact that these watches are somewhat larger than general, due to the lavish construction of their cases, is something the company's watchmakers in Switzerland's Lengnau have taken into consideration. In fact, they make a virtue of this necessity and invest a great deal of care in the martial look of their generously proportioned chronographs. These stopwatch timekeepers play

an important role in Formex's collection, and in the association of the robust timepieces with sporty transportation on land, in the air, and on the water. The palette of practical features extends from the prominent tachymeter scale to the optimally positioned chronograph buttons impossible to activate by accident. And should conditions in the cockpit become somewhat rowdy, such as behind the wheel of a Cigarette class offshore racing boat, these timepieces' shock protection will be certain to protect their mechanical innards from damaging on-the-spot acceleration.

Chrono Tacho

Reference number: 3751.8032
Movement: automatic, ETA Caliber 7750 Valjoux; ø 30 mm, height 7.9 mm; 25 jewels; 28,800 vph
Functions: hours, minutes, subsidiary seconds; chronograph; date
Case: stainless steel/titanium, ø 46 mm, height 22 mm; case with shock protection; sapphire crystal; exhibition window case back; screwed-in crown; water-resistant to 100 m
Band: stainless steel/titanium, folding clasp
Remarks: comes with rubber and leather straps in set
Price: $2,300
Variations: various dial colors

Chrono Slide Rule

Reference number: 65001.9022
Movement: automatic, ETA Caliber 7754; ø 30 mm, height 7.9 mm; 27 jewels; 28,800 vph; finely finished, *côtes de Genève*
Functions: hours, minutes, subsidiary seconds; chronograph; 24-hour display (second time zone); date
Case: stainless steel/titanium, 44 x 43 mm, height 20 mm; case with shock protection; bezel under crystal with slide rule scale; sapphire crystal; exhibition window case back; screwed-in crown and buttons; water-resistant to 100 m
Band: rubber, buckle
Remarks: comes with steel/titanium bracelet, strap in set
Price: $3,400

Diver GMT

Reference number: 20001.6020
Movement: automatic, ETA Caliber 2892-A2; ø 25.6 mm, height 3.6 mm; 21 jewels; 28,800 vph; finely finished, *côtes de Genève*
Functions: hours, minutes, sweep seconds; 24-hour display (second time zone); date
Case: stainless steel/titanium, ø 46 mm, height 23 mm; case with shock protection; bezel with 60-minute scale; sapphire crystal; exhibition window case back; water-resistant to 300 m
Band: rubber, buckle
Remarks: comes with steel/titanium bracelet, strap in set
Price: $1,950

Fortis

After more than ten years of continuous commitment to wrist-watches for use in space, the name of Fortis is now almost automatically associated with air and space travel. Insiders know, however, that the Swiss manufacturer can look back upon almost one hundred years of history, already producing the world's first serial wristwatches with automatic winding in the 1920s. Today the heart of the brand continues to beat in the place of its founding, Grenchen, located just a few miles north of Biel.

The combination of great functionality and contemporary design has brought the brand growing amounts of attention and recognition in the last two decades. Specialists of the most important space travel agencies were already counting on Fortis watches at the beginning of the 1990s. It was not marketing strategy that brought these partnerships together. It was more the fact that managing director Peter Peter was following the call of Russian generals to Star City, the educational center where the cosmonauts were stationed. He came back with the order to develop a watch to be used in space and received for his commitment the Star of the Blue Planet award. The timekeepers without compromise of the Fortis Official Cosmonaut Chronograph series bear the testing seal of the cosmonauts' educational facility, officially acknowledged since the 1960s, as well as the exclusive national emblem of the Russian space agency. At the International Space Station ISS, the space-tested chronographs have shown the time since 1994. Currently, Fortis chronographs are accompanying the work done on the ISS, the largest community building project of humans in space, as an official piece of equipment.

The company's archives reveal several trendsetting innovations and technically demanding developments. Following this tradition, Fortis introduced a unique generation of watches with the Automatic Chronograph Alarm. In patented Caliber F2001 there revolves a special rotor to drive two spring barrels guaranteeing power reserve in both the movement and the alarm. It is a complex mechanism for displaying the date and time, measuring time intervals, and giving a reminder at a certain time, powered by an automatic movement that gets its energy from the wearer's wrist and is not dependent upon a battery.

The pilot's watches, also outfitted with automatic watch movements, meanwhile enjoy a normed status and belong to the official equipment of international flying squadrons. Having received several international awards, the Flieger Chronograph model was crowned number one in Europe at the first European Aviation Watch Award, for it convinced an expert international jury with its functional clarity. The name Fortis comes from Latin and means "strong." In the future this brand will certainly continue to stand as a guarantee for continuity, reliability, and durability — virtues that the company's founders had already obligated themselves to when they named their brand.

B-42 Marine Master

Reference number: 647.10.41 K
Movement: automatic, ETA Caliber 2836-2; ø 25.6 mm, height 5.05 mm; 25 jewels; 28,800 vph
Functions: hours, minutes, sweep seconds; date and day of the week
Case: stainless steel, brushed, ø 42 mm, height 13 mm; unidirectionally rotating bezel with 60-minute divisions; sapphire crystal; screwed-in crown; water-resistant to 200 m
Band: rubber, folding clasp
Price: $1,325
Variations: steel bracelet ($1,400), leather strap ($1,100), deployant clasp

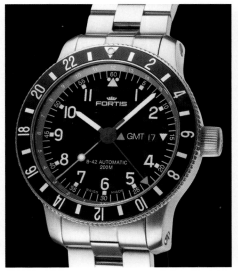

B-42 Official Cosmonaut GMT

Reference number: 649.10.11 M
Movement: automatic, ETA Caliber 2893-2; ø 25.6 mm, height 4.1 mm; 21 jewels; 28,800 vph
Functions: hours, minutes, sweep seconds; 24-hour display (second time zone); date
Case: stainless steel, brushed, ø 42 mm, height 12.5 mm; unidirectionally rotating bezel with 24-hour scale; sapphire crystal; screwed-in crown; water-resistant to 200 m
Band: stainless steel, folding clasp with overall extension
Price: $1,700
Variations: dial in silver opaline, leather strap ($1,400), deployant clasp, rubber strap ($1,400)

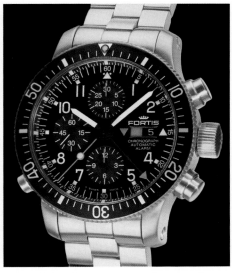

B-42 Official Cosmonaut Chrono Alarm

Reference number: 639.22.11 M
Movement: automatic, Fortis Caliber F2001 (base ETA 7750); ø 30 mm, height 7.9 mm; 32 jewels; 28,800 vph; integrated alarm movement with automatic winding
Functions: hours, minutes, subsidiary seconds; chronograph; date; alarm
Case: stainless steel, brushed, ø 42 mm, height 17 mm; unidirectionally rotating bezel with 60-minute divisions; sapphire crystal; screwed-in crown; water-resistant to 200 m
Band: stainless steel, buckle
Price: $6,300
Variations: dial in silver opaline, leather strap ($6,000)

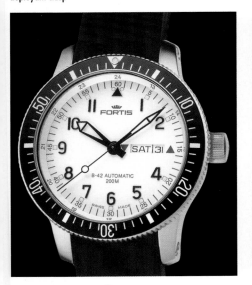

B-42 Diver Day/Date

Reference number: 648.10.12 K
Movement: automatic, ETA Caliber 2836-2; ø 25.6 mm, height 5.05 mm; 25 jewels; 28,800 vph
Functions: hours, minutes, sweep seconds; date and day of the week
Case: stainless steel, brushed, ø 42 mm, height 15 mm; unidirectionally rotating bezel with 60-minute divisions; sapphire crystal; exhibition window case back; screwed-in crown; water-resistant to 200 m
Band: rubber, buckle
Price: $1,200
Variations: black dial, stainless steel bracelet ($1,500)

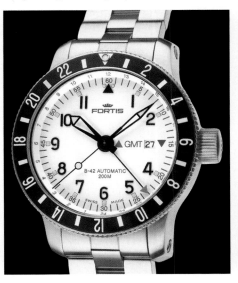

B-42 Diver GMT

Reference number: 650.10.12 M
Movement: automatic, ETA Caliber 2893-2; ø 25.6 mm, height 4.1 mm; 21 jewels; 28,800 vph
Functions: hours, minutes, subsidiary seconds; chronograph, GMT (second time zone); date
Case: stainless steel, brushed, ø 42 mm, height 15 mm; unidirectionally rotating bezel with 24-hour scale; sapphire crystal; exhibition window case back; screwed-in crown; water-resistant to 200 m
Band: stainless steel, folding clasp with overall extension
Price: $1,800
Variations: black dial, leather or rubber strap ($1,500)

B-42 Diver Chronograph Alarm

Reference number: 641.10.12 C
Movement: automatic, Fortis Caliber F2001 (base ETA 7750); ø 30 mm, height 7.9 mm; 32 jewels; 28,800 vph; integrated alarm movement with automatic winding
Functions: hours, minutes, subsidiary seconds; chronograph; date; alarm
Case: stainless steel, brushed, ø 42 mm, height 17 mm; unidirectionally rotating bezel with 60-minute divisions; sapphire crystal; exhibition window case back; screwed-in crown; water-resistant to 200 m
Band: crocodile skin, buckle
Price: $6,500

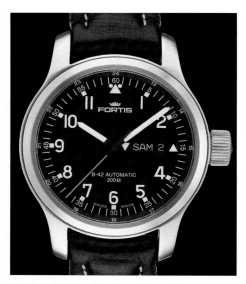

B-42 Pilot Professional Day/Date

Reference number: 645.10.11
Movement: automatic, ETA Caliber 2836-2; ø 25.6 mm, height 5.05 mm; 25 jewels; 28,800 vph
Functions: hours, minutes, sweep seconds; date and day of the week
Case: stainless steel, brushed, ø 42 mm, height 15 mm; sapphire crystal; exhibition window case back; screwed-in crown; water-resistant to 200 m
Band: leather, buckle
Price: $1,000
Variations: with steel bracelet or rubber strap ($1,000)

B-42 Pilot Professional Chronograph

Reference number: 635.22.11
Movement: automatic, ETA Caliber 7750; ø 30 mm, height 7.9 mm; 25 jewels; 28,800 vph
Functions: hours, minutes, subsidiary seconds; chronograph; date, day of the week
Case: stainless steel, sandblasted, ø 42 mm, height 15 mm; sapphire crystal; exhibition window case back; screwed-in crown; water-resistant to 200 m
Band: leather, buckle
Price: $2,100
Variations: with steel bracelet ($2,400) or rubber strap ($2,100); as GMT model with second time zone

B-42 Pilot Professional Chrono Alarm

Reference number: 636.22.11
Movement: automatic, Fortis Caliber F2001 (base ETA 7750); ø 30 mm, height 7.9 mm; 32 jewels; 28,800 vph; integrated alarm movement with automatic winding
Functions: hours, minutes, subsidiary seconds; chronograph; date; alarm
Case: stainless steel, sandblasted, ø 42 mm, height 15 mm; sapphire crystal; screwed-in crown; water-resistant to 200 m
Band: leather, buckle
Price: $5,650
Variations: deployant clasp, steel bracelet ($5,950) or rubber strap ($5,650)

B-42 Flieger Day/Date

Reference number: 645.10.12
Movement: automatic, ETA Caliber 2836-2; ø 25.6 mm, height 5.05 mm; 25 jewels; 28,800 vph
Functions: hours, minutes, sweep seconds; date and day of the week
Case: stainless steel, brushed, ø 42 mm, height 15 mm; sapphire crystal; exhibition window case back; screwed-in crown; water-resistant to 200 m
Band: leather, buckle
Price: $1,100
Variations: black dial, deployant clasp, steel bracelet ($1,400) or rubber strap ($1,100)

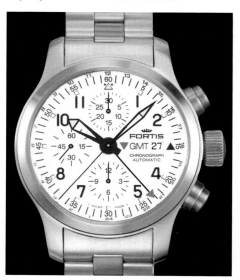

B-42 Flieger Chronograph GMT

Reference number: 637.10.12 M
Movement: automatic, ETA Caliber 7750; ø 30 mm, height 7.9 mm; 25 jewels; 28,800 vph
Functions: hours, minutes, subsidiary seconds; chronograph; date; 24-hour display (second time zone)
Case: stainless steel, sandblasted, ø 42 mm, height 15 mm; sapphire crystal; exhibition window case back; screwed-in crown; water-resistant to 200 m
Band: stainless steel, folding clasp with overall extension
Price: $3,400
Variations: leather strap ($3,100), deployant clasp, rubber strap ($3,100)

B-42 Flieger Chronograph Alarm

Reference number: 636.10.12 C
Movement: automatic, Fortis Caliber F2001 (base ETA 7750); ø 30 mm, height 7.9 mm; 32 jewels; 28,800 vph; integrated alarm movement with automatic winding, star decoration on movement parts and rotor
Functions: hours, minutes, subsidiary seconds; chronograph; date; alarm
Case: stainless steel, brushed, ø 42 mm, height 15 mm; sapphire crystal; exhibition window case back; screwed-in crown; water-resistant to 200 m
Band: crocodile skin , buckle
Price: $6,150

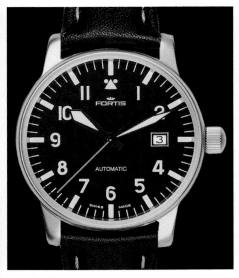

Flieger Automatic

Reference number: 595.10.41
Movement: automatic, ETA Caliber 2824-2; ø 25.6 mm, height 4.6 mm; 25 jewels; 28,800 vph
Functions: hours, minutes, sweep seconds; date
Case: stainless steel, sandblasted, ø 40 mm, height 11 mm; mineral crystal; screwed-down case back; screwed-in crown; water-resistant to 200 m
Band: leather, buckle
Price: $625
Variations: deployant clasp, steel bracelet ($775) or rubber strap ($625), exhibition case back, anti-reflective sapphire crystal, also in 34 mm diameter

Flieger GMT

Reference number: 596.11.11 M
Movement: automatic, ETA Caliber 2893-2; ø 25.6 mm, height 4.1 mm; 21 jewels; 28,800 vph
Functions: hours, minutes, sweep seconds; 24-hour display (second time zone); date
Case: stainless steel, brushed, ø 40 mm, height 11 mm; mineral crystal; screwed-down case back; screwed-in crown; water-resistant to 200 m
Band: stainless steel, folding clasp with overall extension
Price: $1,040
Variations: leather strap ($890), deployant clasp, rubber strap ($890), exhibition case back, in 34 mm diameter

Flieger Chronograph

Reference number: 597.11.11
Movement: automatic, ETA Caliber 7750; ø 30 mm, height 7.9 mm; 25 jewels; 28,800 vph
Functions: hours, minutes, subsidiary seconds; chronograph; date, day of the week
Case: stainless steel, brushed, ø 40 mm, height 15 mm; mineral crystal; screwed-down case back; screwed-in crown; water-resistant to 100 m
Band: leather, buckle
Remarks: awarded the European Aviation Watch Award in 2005
Price: $1,600

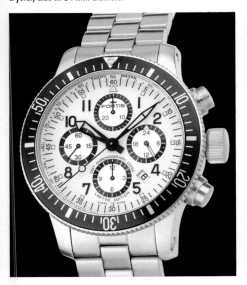

B-42 Chronograph GMT Chronometer

Reference number: 651.10.12 M
Movement: automatic, ETA Caliber 7750, modified; ø 30 mm, height 7.9 mm; 28 jewels; 28,800 vph; COSC chronometer
Functions: hours, minutes, subsidiary seconds; chronograph; 24-hour display; date
Case: stainless steel, brushed, ø 42 mm, height 15 mm; unidirectionally rotating bezel with 60-minute divisions; sapphire crystal; exhibition window case back; screwed-in crown
Band: stainless steel, folding clasp with overall extension
Remarks: limited to 100 pieces
Price: $4,600
Variations: leather or rubber strap ($4,300), crocodile strap

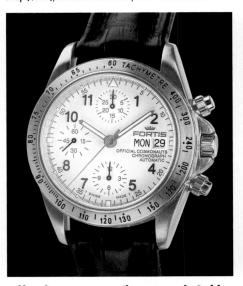

Official Cosmonaut Chronograph Gold

Reference number: 630.50.12
Movement: automatic, ETA Caliber 7750; ø 30 mm, height 7.9 mm; 25 jewels; 28,800 vph
Functions: hours, minutes, subsidiary seconds; chronograph; date, day of the week
Case: yellow gold, ø 38 mm, height 15 mm; bezel engraved with tachymeter scale; sapphire crystal; case back with the official logo of the Russian space authorities; screwed-in crown and buttons; water-resistant to 200 m
Band: crocodile skin, buckle
Price: $9,250
Variations: edition package

Flieger Chronograph Gold Edition

Reference number: 597.50.12
Movement: automatic, ETA Caliber 7750; ø 30 mm, height 7.9 mm; 25 jewels; 28,800 vph
Functions: hours, minutes, subsidiary seconds; chronograph; date, day of the week
Case: yellow gold, ø 40 mm, height 15 mm; sapphire crystal; exhibition window case back; water-resistant to 100 m
Band: crocodile skin, buckle
Price: $9,850
Variations: edition package

Gérald Genta

The Grande Sonnerie's wondrous case back.

Retrograde displays, windows with jumping numerals, dials made of unusual materials and structures and beset with holes, daring colors, printed crystals, abstract case shapes — among the ranks of noble watch brands, Gérald Genta sticks out like an exotic bird of paradise. Some models are even outfitted with several retrograde displays or a skeletonized dial revealing the jump hour display's disks, or that of the date or even the weekday. With half-circle scale segments, psychedelic "dancing" numerals, and a window display for the hours, all similarities with a normal wristwatch end after the fact that one binds it to the wrist.

After the departure of its founder and namesake, the Gérald Genta brand has excelled in developing its own dynamic, one that is rather comparable to that of the famous designer's own creative genius. The brand's motto: consistently modern, reliably unusual, and, above all, unique.

The brand's new owners certainly have inherited a difficult act to follow. For a number of decades Genta, a descendant of Italian ancestors born in Geneva, was the designer to set the tone in noble Swiss watchmaking with his creativity — even if it wasn't always under his own name. Genta only founded his own brand at the beginning of the 1990s. Before that, he worked as a stylist for such famous houses as Audemars Piguet, Patek Philippe, Bvlgari, and Omega, influencing an entire epoch of Swiss watchmaking with his *lignes douces* style.

Even if the *grandseigneur* no longer personally directs the business of the brand named for him (after a short intermezzo under the wings of the Singaporean Hour Glass company, it has now been incorporated into the expanding Bulgari group), his successors at the drawing board still feel obligated to express his special feeling for style.

Gérald Genta's watches today still display the characteristic soft curves, but the playful details have given way to a more modern and striking use of shapes and functional elements. Unusual horological solutions are however still the brand's trademark. For example, in the octagonal case of the new Octo Tourbillon Incontro, a lavishly finished tourbillon shares its space with a quartz movement whose displays are visible on the case back. And the Arena Chrono Quattro Retro basically overflows with retrograde displays for minutes, date, and stop functions — crowned by the characteristic jump hour display at 12 o'clock.

Gérald Genta shares its development and manufacture of complicated watch movements with the individualist brand Daniel Roth, also a member of the Bulgari group — just as they share company headquarters in the Genevan quarter Pâquis and production factories in the Vallée de Joux's Le Sentier.

Both of these brands have no problem existing alongside Bvlgari, as each has its own market segment to cover. Bvlgari embodies the modern, sporty style; Daniel Roth stands for more classical watches with complications; and Gérald Genta chiefly represents the avant-garde in design and function. This is the way it has always been, by the way.

Arena Chrono Quattro Retro

Reference number: ABC.Y.80.290.CN.BD
Movement: automatic, Gérald Genta Caliber GG 7800; ø 36 mm, height 8.5 mm; 37 jewels; 21,600 vph; first movement with four retrograde functions (two chronograph counters, minute hand, date hand)
Functions: hours (digital, jump); minutes (retrograde); date (retrograde); chronograph (two retrograde counters)
Case: titanium, ø 45 mm, height 15.4 mm; sapphire crystal; exhibition window case back; screwed-in crown, flat buttons integrated into case side; water-resistant to 100 m
Band: reptile skin, folding clasp
Price: $26,500

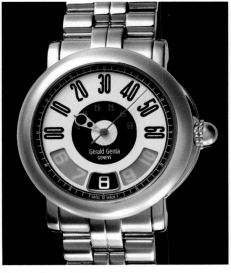

Arena Sport Retro

Reference number: RSP.L.10.261.B1.BD
Movement: automatic, Gérald Genta Caliber GG 7510; ø 26.2 mm, height 5.9 mm; 21 jewels; 28,800 vph
Functions: hours (digital, jump); minutes (retrograde), sweep seconds
Case: stainless steel, ø 38 mm, height 11 mm; sapphire crystal; screwed-in crown
Band: stainless steel, folding clasp
Price: $9,350
Variations: in 41 mm case; dial in yellow/black; with rubber strap ($8,000); with rubber bezel ($8,300); with diamonds (from $10,650); ltd. version with fiberglass dial

Octo Tourbillon Incontro

Reference number: OTL.Y.76.940.CN.BD
Movement: automatic + quartz, Gérald Genta + ETA Caliber GG 9051 and ETA 988.332 (LCD); ø 29 mm, height 5.90 mm; 54 jewels; 21,600 vph; power reserve 64 h; flying minute tourbillon; additional quartz movement with LCD on back
Functions: hours (retrograde), minutes; digital hours, minutes, seconds, date, day, timer, alarm, chrono on the back
Case: platinum, ø 42.5 mm, height 16.65 mm; tantalum bezel; sapphire crystal; crowns with hawk's eye cabochons
Band: reptile skin, folding clasp
Remarks: dial made of cloisonné ceramic; ltd. to 15 pieces
Price: $185,400

Octo Tourbillon Incontro (back)

In the new Tourbillon Incontro, the designers at Gérald Genta have combined the classic horological specialty of a flying one-minute tourbillon featuring an innovative retrograde hour display with a modern "soulless" high-tech quartz movement, whose LCD displays were banned to the decoratively chased case back.

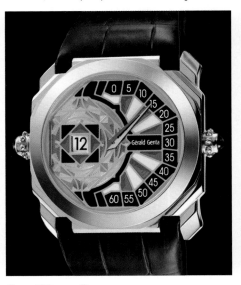

Octo Minute Repeater

Reference number: ORM.Y.50.771.CN.BD
Movement: automatic, Gérald Genta Caliber GG 8561; ø 28.5 mm, height 7.38 mm; 37 jewels; 21,600 vph
Functions: hours (digital, jump); minutes (retrograde); hour, quarter hour, and minute repeater
Case: red gold, ø 42.5 mm, height 11.98 mm; sapphire crystal; exhibition window case back; crowns with hawk's eye cabochons
Band: reptile skin, folding clasp
Remarks: limited to 8 pieces
Price: $243,650
Variations: four watches each in red and white gold

Fantasy Racing

Reference number: RSF.X.10.123.CA.BD.RUB
Movement: automatic, Gérald Genta Caliber GG 7510; ø 26.2 mm, height 5.9 mm; 21 jewels; 28,800 vph
Functions: hours (digital, jump); minutes (retrograde)
Case: stainless steel, ø 41 mm, height 11 mm; bezel in rubber; sapphire crystal; screwed-in crown
Band: rubber, folding clasp
Price: $8,600
Variations: with polished bezel made of stainless steel ($8,350)

Gevril

The idyllically forested and equally peaceful highs and lows of the Swiss Jura mountains have traditionally been a mecca of watchmaking creativity. It was here that many world-famous names cultivated their talents and lay down the foundations for companies and legacies that would survive both the ravages of time and the quartz boom of the 1970s. Jacques Gévril certainly numbered as one of the gifted watchmakers of the eighteenth century to make a name for himself here.

Born in 1722 in La Chaux-de-Fonds, Gévril began his career as a restorer of timepieces, creating his first chronometer in 1743. He invented many watch and clock movements, and in the year 1744 he made horological history by creating a repetition dial. In 1758 he became the first Swiss watchmaker to ever export a timepiece, together with Pierre Jaquet Droz, and the recipient of this original work was the king of Spain. He was sub-sequently named watchmaker to the Spanish crown, remaining behind when Jaquet Droz returned to Switzerland. Gévril's family continued in the watchmaking tradition for a few generations, creating many fine and unique timepieces along the way that may still be found in the world's best watch museums. Eventually, however, the company closed, becoming another historic name lying dormant for a modern entrepreneur to reawaken like Sleeping Beauty.

This happened in the early 1990s when Switzerland's UTime, an international distribution conglomerate handling some of the most prestigious names in the business, purchased the rights to the Gevril name and created a high-end line with some interesting characteristics — such as the unlocked crown indicator and the exchangeable bezel system. In the late '90s, UTime disbanded and sold the rights to all of the brands it owned. After a brief stint with an American jeweler, in 2001 Gevril was bought by First SBF Holding, spearheaded and masterminded by Samuel Friedmann.

Friedmann, born in 1970 in Lugano, Switzerland, is a man with a long history in the watch business. His lifelong dream was to own his own watch brand, and he patiently waited for many years until the right brand name came along. Although he possessed the know-how and connections to have created his own brand at any time, he was painfully aware of the advantages of a name with a certain history, and when the Gevril name once again became available, he lost no time in fulfilling his destiny. His was a passion that was awakened for the first time at age seventeen. The youth, wanting to buy a watch for his brother, noticed that the particular Swiss city he was in contained a myriad of watch stores. He became fascinated by the ticking timepieces and their fine blend of art and science and

immediately decided to enter the watch business, bucking a career in his family's upscale clothing boutiques. After graduating from college, Friedmann opened a sales office in Lugano that sold complicated pieces to collectors and also dealt in liquidation of overstocked watches. His later move to the United States had more to do with the love for his American wife than for watches, and today Friedmann is headquartered in New York, although he is more often than not to be found at the workshop in Tramelan, Switzerland, rather than the 6,000-square-foot villa that he has made into Gevril's head office.

Well equipped to lead his company into the new century, Friedmann has set his sights on quality and building the brand. In just four years, the collection has grown to encompass seven watch families and more than seventy models. The most recent standout timepiece is the Serenade: Housed in a characteristically large rectangular Avenue of Americas case, the Serenade is run by a movement designed by Gevril in cooperation with Swiss movement specialists. This movement powers the unique displays that illustrate two separate time zones and their accompanying day/night indicators. The Serenade is available only in a very limited edition of fifty pieces each of 18-karat rose gold, 18-karat white gold, and platinum.

Avenue of Americas Chronograph

Reference number: 5111
Movement: automatic, Caliber GV AOAWZ1 (base Dubois-Dépraz 2020/ETA 2824); ø 30 mm, height 7.5 mm; 51 jewels; 28,800 vph
Functions: hours, minutes, subsidiary seconds; chronograph
Case: rose gold, 44 x 34 mm, height 12.25 mm; sapphire crystal; exhibition window case back; water-resistant to 50 m
Band: crocodile skin, buckle
Remarks: limited edition of 100 pieces
Price: $10,995

Avenue of Americas GMT Power Reserve

Reference number: 5025
Movement: automatic, Caliber GV AOAX32 (base ETA 2892-A2); ø 26 mm, height 5.2 mm; 25 jewels; 28,800 vph
Functions: hours, minutes, sweep seconds; date; power reserve display; second time zone
Case: stainless steel, 44 x 34 mm, height 12.25 mm; sapphire crystal; exhibition window case back; water-resistant to 50 m
Band: crocodile skin, buckle
Remarks: limited edition of 500 pieces
Price: $7,995

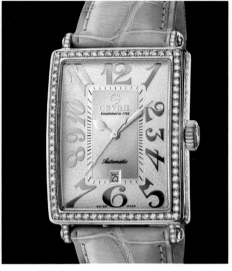

Avenue of Americas Glamour Collection

Reference number: 6207NV
Movement: automatic, Caliber GV AOA3J1 (base ETA 2892-A2); ø 26 mm, height 4.6 mm; 25 jewels; 28,800 vph
Functions: hours, minutes, sweep seconds; date
Case: stainless steel, 44 x 34 mm, height 12.25mm; bezel and lugs set with a row of diamonds; sapphire crystal; exhibition window case back; water-resistant to 50 m
Band: crocodile skin, buckle
Remarks: limited edition of 100 pieces
Price: $14,995
Variations: available with various combinations of diamonds

Lafayette

Reference number: 2912
Movement: automatic, Caliber GV 993 (base Dubois-Dépraz 2020/ETA 2824); ø 30 mm, height 7.5 mm; 51 jewels; 28,800 vph
Functions: hours, minutes, subsidiary seconds; chronograph
Case: stainless steel, ø 37 mm, height 14.25 mm; bezel set with a row of diamonds (one carat); Hesalite crystal; water-resistant to 100 m
Band: crocodile skin, buckle
Remarks: limited edition of 500 pieces
Price: $8,495
Variations: available without diamond bezel ($5,295)

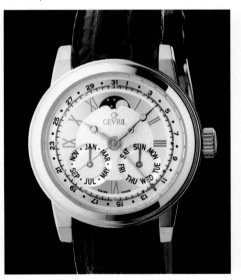

Soho Deluxe

Reference number: 2605L
Movement: automatic, Caliber GV 6113 (base Dubois-Dépraz 9200/ETA 2824); ø 25.98 mm, height 6.2 mm; 25 jewels; 28,800 vph
Functions: hours, minutes, sweep seconds; date, day, month; moon phase
Case: yellow gold, ø 39 mm, height 12.4 mm; sapphire crystal; exhibition window case back; water-resistant to 50 m
Band: crocodile skin, buckle
Remarks: limited edition of 100 pieces
Price: $17,495

Sea Cloud

Reference number: 3107
Movement: automatic, Caliber GV 7B89 (base Dubois-Dépraz 2020/ETA 2824); ø 30 mm, height 7.5 mm; 51 jewels; 28,800 vph
Functions: hours, minutes, subsidiary seconds; chronograph
Case: stainless steel, ø 40 mm, height 14.1 mm; unidirectionally rotating bezel in 18-karat gold embossed with minute scale; sapphire crystal, anti-reflective; screwed-down case back; screwed-in crown and buttons; water-resistant to 200 m
Band: stainless steel, folding clasp
Remarks: limited edition of 500 pieces
Price: $5,995

Girard-Perregaux

A more than 200-year-old history rich in records and spectacular designs: The prerequisites were excellent when Luigi Macaluso purchased the somewhat dusty *manufacture* Girard-Perregaux in La Chaux-de-Fonds. And as fast as you can say "tourbillon," he made it into one of the leading watch *manufactures* for complicated timepieces.

Moving in and opening the new *manufacture* building in upper La Chaux-de-Fonds fulfilled a longtime dream for the president of the SoWind Group and director of GP Macaluso. But only through the systematic acquisition of property and empty buildings around the main factory located on Place Girardet did it become possible to cleanly separate production workshops, representation space, and management offices for the two watch brands Girard-Perregaux and JeanRichard from each other while keeping them connected by short pathways. Villa JeanRichard and its museum for tools and tooling machines is located just a few steps away from the Girard-Perregaux Museum within Villa Marguerite, and in between them the main factory and manufacturing buildings pretty much take up the rest of the block.

And the result? New editions of the legendary tourbillon models with three gold bridges, enchanting minute repeaters, world time watches, and chronograph specialties. They all ensure that this company will retain its prominent position among the genuine Swiss *manufactures*.

Last year, the relaunch of the Laureato was on center stage. In the 1970s, this noble sports watch took its place in history when the case, which features a striking screwed-down hexagonal bezel, housed a highly

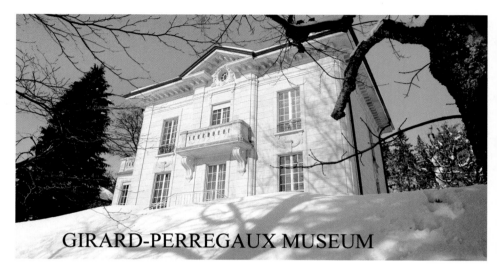

GIRARD-PERREGAUX MUSEUM

precise quartz caliber of the company's own production. Girard-Perregaux was in fact a pioneer in this technology, establishing today's normed oscillation frequency of 32,768 Hz.

In the '80s, the model disappeared from the collection, but was dusted off once again in 1995, stylistically reworked, and outfitted with *manufacture* caliber GP 3100. A chronograph version was even introduced, as well as a variation containing the legendary Tourbillon under Three Gold Bridges, causing quite an uproar in the industry. Now another revamped model has been introduced: The third generation is called Laureato EVO 3, and this year the chronograph line was added to in the form of a perpetual calendar featuring date, day, month, and moon phase displays.

After ten years of close cooperation with the Italian race car and sports car manufacturer Ferrari, Girard-Perregaux is now

concentrating on sponsoring activities in sailing, and that at the highest level possible: the America's Cup.

As a partner of the BMW Oracle Team, the Swiss brand supports the top challenger, and Macaluso could hardly resist outfitting each of the members of both sailing teams — a total of thirty-four men — with a

special edition of the Sea Hawk featuring a BMW-Oracle logo and the engraved name of the team member on the case back. The Sea Hawk Tourbillon pictured here, manufactured in extremely limited numbers, remains reserved for the captains — in every sense.

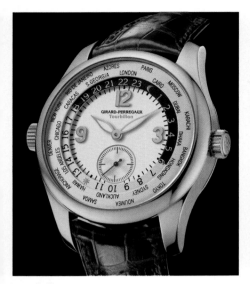

Tourbillon ww.tc

Reference number: 99350-52-8M-BAEA
Movement: manually wound, GP Caliber 098GO; ø 29 mm,
20 jewels; 21,600 vph; one-minute tourbillon on the back of
the movement
Functions: hours, minutes, subsidiary seconds; 24-hour
display (world time)
Case: rose gold, ø 43 mm, height 13.15 mm; bidirectionally
rotating bezel with 24-hour scale under crystal; sapphire
crystal; exhibition window case back
Band: reptile skin, folding clasp
Price: $165,000
Variations: in white gold

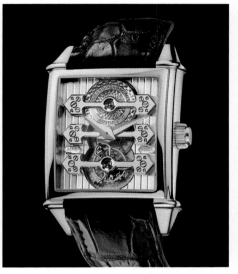

Vintage Tourbillon with 3 Gold Bridges

Reference number: 99870.0.52.000
Movement: automatic, GP Caliber 9600C; 32 jewels;
21,600 vph; one-minute tourbillon; microrotor
Functions: hours, minutes
Case: red gold, 32 x 32 mm, height 11.95 mm;
sapphire crystal
Band: reptile skin, folding clasp
Price: $129,500
Variations: in yellow, white, or red gold; in platinum

Vintage 1945 Tourbillon with One Gold Bridge

Reference number: 99850.0.52.815
Movement: automatic, GP Caliber 9610C; 32 jewels;
21,600 vph; one-minute tourbillon; microrotor
Functions: hours, minutes
Case: red gold, 32 x 32 mm, height 11.95 mm;
sapphire crystal
Band: reptile skin, folding clasp
Price: $115,000
Variations: in yellow, rose or white gold; in platinum

Sea Hawk II Pro

Reference number: 49940.T.21.6117
Movement: automatic, GP Caliber 033RO (base GP 3300);
ø 25.6 mm, height 4.55 mm; 27 jewels; 28,800 vph
Functions: hours, minutes, sweep seconds; date;
power reserve display
Case: titanium, ø 44 mm, height 20.11 mm; unidirectionally
rotating bezel with 60-minute divisions; sapphire crystal;
screwed-in crown; water-resistant to 3000 m
Band: titanium, folding clasp
Remarks: case with two valves
Price: $7,950
Variations: with rubber strap

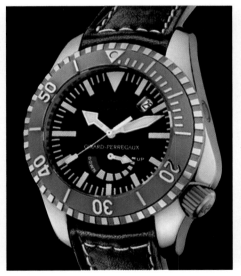

Sea Hawk II Pro

Reference number: 49941-21-631-HDBA
Movement: automatic, GP Caliber 033RO (base GP 3300);
ø 25.6 mm, height 4.55 mm; 27 jewels; 28,800 vph
Functions: hours, minutes, sweep seconds; date;
power reserve display
Case: polished titanium, ø 44 mm, height 20.11 mm;
unidirectionally rotating bezel with 60-minute divisions;
sapphire crystal; screwed-in crown; water-resistant to 3000 m
Band: leather, double folding clasp
Remarks: case with two valves
Price: $7,950

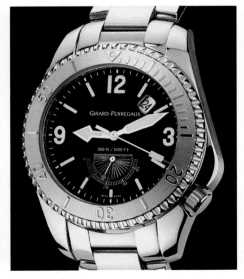

Sea Hawk II

Reference number: 49900.1.11.6146
Movement: automatic, GP Caliber 033RO (base GP 3300);
ø 25.6 mm, height 4.55 mm; 27 jewels; 28,800 vph
Functions: hours, minutes, sweep seconds; date; power
reserve display
Case: stainless steel, ø 42 mm; unidirectionally rotating
bezel with 60-minute divisions; sapphire crystal; screwed-in
crown; water-resistant to 300 m
Band: stainless steel, folding clasp
Price: $7,500
Variations: with rubber strap/deployant clasp; in titanium
with rubber strap or with titanium bracelet

Vintage XXL Perpetual Calendar

Reference number: 90270.0.52.6175
Movement: automatic, GP Caliber 3170; ø 30 mm; 44 jewels; 28,800 vph
Functions: hours, minutes, subsidiary seconds; chronograph; perpetual calendar with date, day of the week, month, moon phase, leap year
Case: rose gold, 36 x 37 mm, height 14.9 mm; sapphire crystal; exhibition window case back
Band: reptile skin, folding clasp
Price: $47,500
Variations: in white gold

Vintage King Size Chrono GMT

Reference number: 25975.0.52.1051
Movement: automatic, GP Caliber 033CO; 61 jewels; 28,800 vph
Functions: hours, minutes, subsidiary seconds; chronograph; 24-hour display (second time zone); date
Case: rose gold, 31.95 x 32 mm, height 12.4 mm; sapphire crystal; exhibition window case back
Band: reptile skin, folding clasp
Price: $21,500
Variations: in white gold ($25,000)

Vintage Large Date Moon Phase

Reference number: 25800.0.52.815
Movement: automatic, GP Caliber 3330 (base GP 3300); ø 28.6 mm, height 4.9 mm; 32 jewels; 28,800 vph
Functions: hours, minutes, subsidiary seconds; large date; moon phase
Case: red gold, 32 x 32 mm, height 11.2 mm; sapphire crystal; exhibition window case back
Band: reptile skin, folding clasp
Price: $15,000
Variations: in yellow gold; in white gold

Vintage Power Reserve

Reference number: 25850.0.52.6456
Movement: automatic, GP Caliber 033RO (base GP 3300); ø 25.6 mm, height 4.55 mm; 27 jewels; 28,800 vph
Functions: hours, minutes, subsidiary seconds; date; power reserve display
Case: red gold, 32 x 32 mm, height 11.2 mm; sapphire crystal; exhibition window case back
Band: reptile skin, folding clasp
Price: $14,500
Variations: in yellow gold; in white gold

Vintage King Size

Reference number: 25830.1.11.1151
Movement: automatic, GP Caliber 03390-00N10; ø 25.6 mm, height 3.28 mm; 28 jewels; 28,800 vph
Functions: hours, minutes, subsidiary seconds; date
Case: stainless steel, 32 x 32 mm, height 11 mm; sapphire crystal; exhibition window case back
Band: reptile skin, buckle
Price: upon request
Variations: with stainless steel bracelet

Vintage Foudroyante XXL

Reference number: 90210.0.53.6046
Movement: automatic, GP Caliber E04C0 (base ETA Valjoux 7750); ø 30 mm; height 8.75 mm; 40 jewels; 28,800 vph; mechanism for *foudroyante* 1/8 second with its own spring barrel; two column wheels
Functions: hours, minutes, subsidiary seconds; split-seconds chronograph with *foudroyant* seconds (1/8-second counter)
Case: white gold, 37 x 37 mm, height 15.3 mm; sapphire crystal
Band: reptile skin, folding clasp
Price: $34,500
Variations: in yellow or rose gold

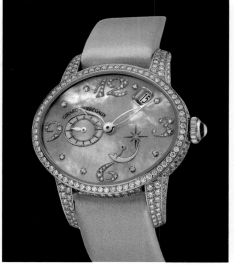

Cat's Eye Moon Phase

Reference number: 08049D0A51.72L7
Movement: automatic, GP Caliber 033LO (base GP 3300); ø 25.6 mm, height 4.55 mm; 32 jewels; 28,800 vph
Functions: hours, minutes, subsidiary seconds; moon phase
Case: yellow gold, 30.24 x 35.24 mm, height 10.45 mm; bezel set with 68 diamonds; sapphire crystal; exhibition window case back
Band: satin, folding clasp
Remarks: genuine mother-of-pearl-dial with eight diamond markers
Price: $17,500
Variations: in rose or white gold

Cat's Eye Power Reserve Pavée

Reference number: 80480D53P962-KK9D
Movement: automatic, GP Caliber 033RO (base GP 3300); ø 25.6 mm, height 4.55 mm; 27 jewels; 28,800 vph
Functions: hours, minutes, subsidiary seconds; power reserve display
Case: white gold, 35.24 x 30.24 mm, height 10.45 mm; bezel, case sides and lugs set with 315 diamonds; sapphire crystal; exhibition window case back
Band: satin, folding clasp
Remarks: genuine mother-of-pearl-dial with diamond markers and paved numerals
Price: $19,500

Cat's Eye Tourbillon

Reference number: 9949D53P961-KK9D
Movement: manually wound, GP Caliber 9702-A; 20 jewels; 21,600 vph; one-minute tourbillon under one gold bridge
Functions: hours, minutes
Case: rose gold, 30.6 x 35.6 mm, height 10.8 mm; bezel set with 68 diamonds; sapphire crystal; exhibition window case back
Band: satin, folding clasp set with 14 diamonds
Remarks: genuine mother-of-pearl-dial with four diamond markers
Price: $125,000
Variations: in white gold; case set with 303 diamonds

Richeville Lady

Reference number: 02656D0Q11.143
Movement: quartz, GP Caliber 13100; 7 jewels
Functions: hours, minutes
Case: stainless steel, 30 x 30 mm, height 8 mm; bezel, case sides and lugs set with 152 diamonds; sapphire crystal
Band: satin, buckle
Price: upon request

Richeville Large Date Moon Phase

Reference number: 27600.0.52.6151
Movement: automatic, GP Caliber 3330 (base GP 3300); ø 28.6 mm, height 4.9 mm; 32 jewels; 28,800 vph
Functions: hours, minutes, subsidiary seconds; large date; moon phase
Case: rose gold, 37 x 37 mm, height 10.5 mm; sapphire crystal; exhibition window case back
Band: reptile skin, folding clasp
Price: $16,500
Variations: in yellow gold; in white gold

Richeville Chronograph

Reference number: 27650.0.52.6151
Movement: automatic, GP Caliber 3370 (base GP 3300 with Dubois-Dépraz 2021 module); ø 25.6/30 mm, height 6.5 mm; 63 jewels; 28,800 vph
Functions: hours, minutes, subsidiary seconds; chronograph; date
Case: red gold, 37 x 37 mm, height 12.5 mm; sapphire crystal; exhibition window case back
Band: reptile skin, folding clasp
Price: $17,500
Variations: in yellow gold, in white gold, in stainless steel

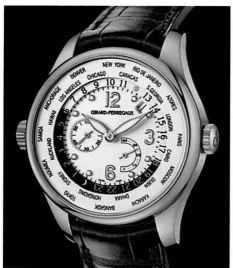

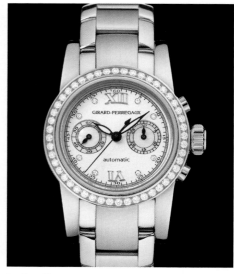

ww.tc Power Reserve

Reference number: 49850-52-815-BA6D
Movement: automatic, GP Caliber 033GO; 27 jewels; 28,800 vph
Functions: hours, minutes, subsidiary seconds; 24-hour display (world time); power reserve display
Case: rose gold, ø 41 mm, height 10.95 mm; bidirectionally rotating bezel under crystal with 24-hour scale; sapphire crystal; exhibition window case back
Band: reptile skin, folding clasp
Price: $21,000
Variations: in white gold ($24,000)

ww.tc Chronograph

Reference number: 49800.0.53.6146A
Movement: automatic, GP Caliber 3387 (base GP 3300 with chronograph module by Dubois-Dépraz and 24-hour module by GP); ø 30 mm, height 8 mm; 63 jewels; 28,800 vph
Functions: hours, minutes, subsidiary seconds; chronograph; date; 24-hour display (world time)
Case: white gold, ø 43 mm, height 13.4 mm; bidirectionally rotating bezel under crystal and with 24-hour scale; sapphire crystal; exhibition window case back; screwed-in crown
Band: reptile skin, buckle
Price: $31,500
Variations: in titanium; in yellow or rose gold; in platinum

Lady Chrono

Reference number: 08046D1A11.11M7
Movement: automatic, GP Caliber 030CO-00LSS; ø 23.3 mm, height 6.28 mm; 38 jewels; 28,800 vph; column wheel control of chronograph functions
Functions: hours, minutes, subsidiary seconds; chronograph
Case: stainless steel, ø 32 mm, height 11.7 mm; bezel set with 48 diamonds; sapphire crystal; exhibition window case back
Band: stainless steel, folding clasp
Price: upon request

Laureato EVO3

Reference number: 80180.1.11.6516
Movement: automatic, GP Caliber 33CO-A0VAA; ø 26.2 mm; 52 jewels; 28,800 vph; sweep chronograph minute counter
Functions: hours, minutes, subsidiary seconds; chronograph; date; 24-hour display (second time zone)
Case: stainless steel, ø 44 mm, height 15.1 mm; sapphire crystal; exhibition window case back; screwed-in crown and buttons; water-resistant to 50 m
Band: stainless steel, folding clasp
Price: $11,250
Variations: with light dial; in titanium with rubber strap

Laureato EVO3 Perpetual Calendar

Reference number: 90190-52-231-BBED
Movement: automatic, GP Caliber Q 031CO; 44 jewels; 28,800 vph
Functions: hours, minutes, subsidiary seconds; chronograph; perpetual calendar with date, day of the week, month, moon phase, leap year; day/night indication
Case: rose gold, ø 44 mm, height 15.1 mm; sapphire crystal; exhibition window case back; screwed-in crown and buttons; water-resistant to 50 m
Band: reptile skin, folding clasp
Price: upon request
Variations: in white gold

Vintage 1945 Lady Souveraine

Reference number: 25730.0.51.11M
Movement: automatic, GP Caliber 3200T (base GP 3200); 22 x 23.1 mm, height 3.28 mm; 27 jewels; 28,800 vph
Functions: hours, minutes, sweep seconds
Case: yellow gold, 26.2 x 26.2 mm; sapphire crystal
Band: reptile skin, buckle
Price: $11,500
Variations: in yellow or red gold with leather strap; in white gold with leather strap

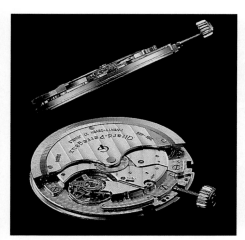

Caliber 3100

Mechanical with automatic winding, power reserve 42 hours
Functions: hours, minutes, sweep seconds; date
Diameter: 11″ (26 mm)
Height: 2.98 mm
Jewels: 27
Balance: glucydur
Frequency: 28,800 vph
Balance spring: Nivarox 1 flat hairspring, fine adjustment via micrometer screw
Shock protection: Kif
Related caliber: 3000 (diameter 23.9 mm)

Caliber 3100

Mechanical with automatic winding, power reserve 42 hours
Functions: hours, minutes, sweep seconds; date
Diameter: 11″ (26 mm)
Height: 2.98 mm
Jewels: 27
Balance: glucydur
Frequency: 28,800 vph
Balance spring: Nivarox 1 flat hairspring, fine adjustment via micrometer screw
Shock protection: Kif
Related caliber: 3000 (diameter 23.9 mm)

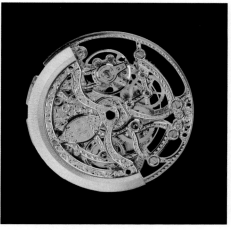

Caliber 3100 skeletonized

Mechanical with automatic winding, power reserve 42 hours
Functions: hours, minutes, sweep seconds
Diameter: 11 ″ (26 mm)
Height: 2.98 mm
Jewels: 27
Balance: glucydur
Frequency: 28,800 vph
Balance spring: Nivarox
Shock protection: Kif
Remarks: movement completely skeletonized and engraved by hand

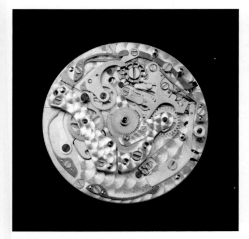

Caliber 3080 (dial side)

Mechanical with automatic winding, power reserve 42 hours
Functions: hours, minutes, subsidiary seconds; chronograph; date
Diameter: 10 ′″ (23.9 mm)
Height: 6.28 mm
Jewels: 38
Balance: glucydur
Frequency: 28,800 vph
Balance spring: Nivarox
Shock protection: Kif
Remarks: column-wheel control of chronograph functions

Caliber 9600

Mechanical with automatic winding; one-minute tourbillon; power reserve 48 hours
Functions: hours, minutes, subsidiary seconds (on tourbillon cage)
Diameter: 28.6 mm
Height: 6.22 mm
Jewels: 30
Frequency: 21,600 vph
Remarks: patented design of the tourbillon under three gold bridges; automatic winding with micro-rotor made of platinum

Glashütte Original

Glashütte Original occupies quite a special place in the exclusive circle of manufacturers of fine mechanical watches. There is hardly another company that can offer such spectacular production depth, and hardly another model range fascinates dyed-in-the-wool watch connoisseurs as this one does. It is the rich experience and the great knowledge of the designers, technicians, and watchmakers that lend these watches a certain authenticity, making them so sought-after by collectors. The new factory allows an extraordinarily transparent view into all of the production areas of watchmaking, from the manufacture and finishing of the most miniscule parts to the assembly of complete watches. This flagship building stands for the virtues that have determined the actions of Glashütte's master watchmakers since 1845: precision, reliability, functionality, and aesthetics.

Each and every watch movement is designed by a team of experienced engineers at home at Glashütte's Altenberger Str. 1. All the components such as plates, screws, pinions, wheels, levers, spring barrels, balance wheels, and tourbillon cages are created, with only few exceptions, in this most modern of production facilities. In the workshops, these parts are finished lavishly by hand and then assembled by talented watchmakers, some of whom were educated in the company's own Alfred Helwig School of Watchmaking. At the end of a long and difficult process, little precision treasures in watchmaking will have been created, forming the platform for Glashütte Original's excellent and exclusive reputation.

After the highly regarded PanoMaticChrono with its exclusively developed Caliber 95 (including an "intelligent" winding mechanism with a bilaterally winding rotor via a stepped gear), this *manufacture* introduced a new mechanical movement in 2005: Caliber 100. This innovative masterpiece featuring a resetting mechanism, twin spring barrels, and a power reserve of 55 hours will beat in the models of the redesigned Senator collection from now on. The Sport Evolution Panorama Date and the Sport Evolution Chronograph were con-

ceived for the sporty watch connoisseur. Alongside expert know-how, an old *manufacture* also needs to display its ties to the region it is located in as well as its past. Glashütte Original can proudly look back on a history of 160 years of continuous production of mechanical watches — in good as well as bad times, this company has held fast to its location in Glashütte and today proudly declares itself an ambassador of "handmade in Germany." The *manufacture* feels a definite obligation to the spreading of German watch culture and involves itself in a myriad of activities. With guided tours on a learning path open to the public, every interested visitor is introduced to the world of watchmaking and witnesses the complex manufacturing of Glashütte Original's noble timekeepers. The *manufacture* has also meanwhile developed a meeting place for art and culture. Regular concerts, book readings, and exhibitions take care that new ways of experiencing time are introduced in the company's architecturally interesting atrium.

PanoMaticTourbillon

Reference number: 93-01-01- 01-04
Movement: automatic, Glashütte Original Caliber 93;
ø 32.2 mm, height 7.65 mm; 40 jewels plus two diamond
endstones; 21,600 vph; flying one-minute tourbillon
Functions: hours, minutes (off-center), subsidiary seconds
(on tourbillon cage); panorama date
Case: rose gold, ø 39.4 mm, height 12.3 mm; sapphire
crystal; exhibition window case back
Band: reptile skin, double folding clasp
Remarks: limited to 100 pieces
Price: $90,000
Variations: in platinum, limited to 50 pieces

PanoMaticChrono

Reference number: 95-01-03-03-04
Movement: automatic, Glashütte Original Caliber 95-01;
ø 32.2 mm, height 7.3 mm; 41 jewels; 28,800 vph; centered
bilaterally winding rotor via stepped gear
Functions: hours, minutes, subsidiary seconds; chronograph
with flyback function; panorama date
Case: platinum, ø 39.4 mm, height 12.3 mm; sapphire
crystal; exhibition window case back
Band: reptile skin, buckle
Remarks: limited to 200 pieces
Price: $44,500

PanoMaticChrono

Reference number: 95-01-01-01-04
Movement: automatic, Glashütte Original Caliber 95-01;
ø 32.2 mm, height 7.3 mm; 41 jewels; 28,800 vph; centered
bilaterally winding rotor via stepped gear
Functions: hours, minutes, subsidiary seconds; chronograph
with flyback function; panorama date
Case: rose gold, ø 39.4 mm, height 12.3 mm; sapphire
crystal; exhibition window case back
Band: reptile skin, double folding clasp
Price: $37,250

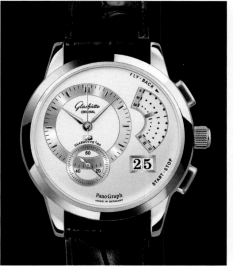

PanoRetroGraph

Reference number: 60-01-04-03-04
Movement: manually wound, Glashütte Original Caliber 60;
ø 32.2 mm, height 7.2 mm; 54 jewels; 28,800 vph
Functions: hours, minutes, subsidiary seconds; chronograph
with flyback and countdown with acoustic tone;
panorama date
Case: rose gold, ø 39.4 mm, height 13.3 mm; sapphire
crystal; exhibition window case back
Band: reptile skin, double folding clasp
Price: $49,000
Variations: in platinum, limited to 50 pieces; in white gold,
limited to 150 pieces

PanoGraph

Reference number: 61-01-02-02-04
Movement: manually wound, Glashütte Original Caliber 61;
ø 32.2 mm, height 7.2 mm; 41 jewels; 28,800 vph
Functions: hours, minutes, subsidiary seconds; chronograph
with flyback function; panorama date
Case: stainless steel, ø 39.4 mm, height 13.3 mm; sapphire
crystal; exhibition window case back
Band: reptile skin, double folding clasp
Price: $12,400
Variations: in rose gold; in platinum, limited to 200 pieces

PanoReserve

Reference number: 65-01-01-01-04
Movement: manually wound, Glashütte Original Caliber
65-01; ø 32.2 mm, height 6.1 mm; 48 jewels; 28,800 vph
Functions: hours, minutes, subsidiary seconds; panorama
date; power reserve display
Case: rose gold, ø 39.4 mm, height 11 mm; sapphire crystal;
exhibition window case back
Band: reptile skin, double folding clasp
Price: $15,100
Variations: in stainless steel; in platinum, limited
to 200 pieces

PanoMaticReserve

Reference number: 90-03-03-03-04
Movement: automatic, Glashütte Original Caliber 90-03; ø 32.6 mm, height 7 mm; 61 jewels; 28,800 vph; off-center rotor; duplex swan-neck fine adjustment
Functions: hours, minutes, subsidiary seconds; power reserve display
Case: platinum, ø 39.3 mm, height 12.6 mm; sapphire crystal; exhibition window case back
Band: reptile skin, buckle
Price: $21,750
Variations: in rose gold; in stainless steel

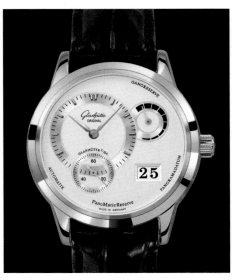

PanoMaticReserve

Reference number: 90-03-01-01-04
Movement: automatic, Glashütte Original Caliber 90-03; ø 32.6 mm, height 7 mm; 61 jewels; 28,800 vph; off-center rotor; duplex swan-neck fine adjustment
Functions: hours, minutes, subsidiary seconds; power reserve display
Case: rose gold, ø 39.3 mm, height 12.6 mm; sapphire crystal; exhibition window case back
Band: reptile skin, double folding clasp
Price: $14,850
Variations: in platinum; in stainless steel

Senator Perpetual Calendar

Reference number: 100-02-05-03-04
Movement: automatic, Glashütte Original Caliber 100-02; ø 31.15 mm, height 7.1 mm; 59 jewels; 28,800 vph; reset mechanism
Functions: hours, minutes, sweep seconds; perpetual calendar with panorama date, day of the week, month, moon phase, leap year
Case: platinum, ø 40 mm, height 12.4 mm; sapphire crystal; exhibition window case back
Band: reptile skin, buckle
Price: $29,800
Variations: in rose gold; in stainless steel

PanoMaticDate

Reference number: 90-01-01-01-04
Movement: automatic, Glashütte Original Caliber 90-01; ø 32.6 mm, height 7 mm; 47 jewels; 28,800 vph; off-center rotor; duplex swan-neck fine adjustment
Functions: hours, minutes, subsidiary seconds; panorama date
Case: rose gold, ø 39.4 mm, height 11.9 mm; sapphire crystal; exhibition window case back
Band: reptile skin, buckle
Price: $13,600
Variations: in stainless steel; in platinum, limited to 200 pieces

PanoMaticLunar

Reference number: 90-02-02-02-04
Movement: automatic, Glashütte Original Caliber 90-02; ø 32.6 mm, height 7 mm; 47 jewels; 28,800 vph; off-center rotor; duplex swan-neck fine adjustment
Functions: hours, minutes, subsidiary seconds; panorama date; moon phase
Case: stainless steel, ø 39.4 mm, height 11.9 mm; sapphire crystal; exhibition window case back
Band: reptile skin, double folding clasp
Price: $8,800
Variations: in rose gold; in platinum, limited to 200 pieces

Senator Perpetual Calendar

Reference number: 100-02-01-01-04
Movement: automatic, Glashütte Original Caliber 100-02; ø 31.15 mm, height 7.1 mm; 59 jewels; 28,800 vph; reset mechanism
Functions: hours, minutes, sweep seconds; perpetual calendar with panorama date, day of the week, month, moon phase, leap year
Case: rose gold, ø 40 mm, height 12.4 mm; sapphire crystal; exhibition window case back
Band: reptile skin, double folding clasp
Price: $22,900
Variations: in platinum; in stainless steel

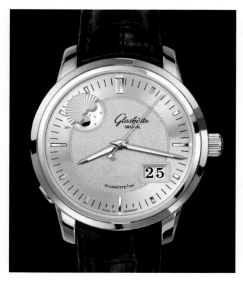

Senator Panorama Date with Moon Phase

Reference number: 100-04-03-02-14
Movement: automatic, Glashütte Original Caliber 100-04; ø 31.15 mm, height 5.8 mm; 55 jewels; 28,800 vph; reset mechanism
Functions: hours, minutes, sweep seconds; panorama date; moon phase
Case: stainless steel, ø 40 mm, height 11.3 mm; sapphire crystal; exhibition window case back
Band: stainless steel, double folding clasp
Price: $10,500
Variations: in rose gold

Senator Up and Down

Reference number: 100-01-02-01-04
Movement: automatic, Glashütte Original Caliber 100-01; ø 31.15 mm, height 5.8 mm; 63 jewels; 28,800 vph; reset mechanism
Functions: hours, minutes, sweep seconds; date; moon phase; power reserve display
Case: rose gold, ø 40 mm, height 11.3 mm; sapphire crystal; exhibition window case back
Band: reptile skin, double folding clasp
Price: $15,700
Variations: in stainless steel

Sport Evolution Panorama Date

Reference number: 39-42-44-04-14
Movement: automatic, Glashütte Original Caliber 39-42; ø 30.95 mm, height 5.9 mm; 44 jewels; 28,800 vph
Functions: hours, minutes, sweep seconds; panorama date
Case: stainless steel, ø 42 mm, height 13.8 mm; unidirectionally rotating bezel with 60-minute divisions; sapphire crystal; exhibition window case back; water-resistant to 200 m
Band: stainless steel, double folding clasp
Price: $8,000

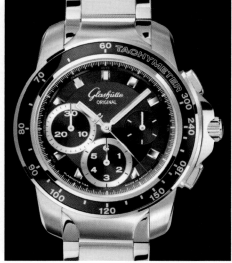

Senator Panorama Date

Reference number: 100-03-02-01-04
Movement: automatic, Glashütte Original Caliber 100-03; ø 31.15 mm, height 5.8 mm; 51 jewels; 28,800 vph; reset mechanism
Functions: hours, minutes, sweep seconds; panorama date
Case: stainless steel, ø 40 mm, height 11.3 mm; sapphire crystal; exhibition window case back
Band: reptile skin, double folding clasp
Price: $14,200
Variations: in rose gold

Senator Chronograph

Reference number: 39-31-31-41-04
Movement: automatic, Glashütte Original Caliber 39-31; ø 31.15 mm, height 7.2 mm; 51 jewels; 28,800 vph; reset mechanism
Functions: hours, minutes, subsidiary seconds; chronograph
Case: rose gold, ø 40 mm, height 13,15 mm; sapphire crystal; exhibition window case back
Band: reptile skin, double folding clasp
Price: $11,600
Variations: in stainless steel

Sport Evolution Chronograph

Reference number: 39-31-43-03-14
Movement: automatic, Glashütte Original Caliber 39-31; ø 31.15 mm, height 7.2 mm; 51 jewels; 28,800 vph
Functions: hours, minutes, subsidiary seconds; chronograph
Case: stainless steel, ø 42 mm, height 14.5 mm; bezel with tachymeter scale; sapphire crystal; exhibition window case back; water-resistant to 100 m
Band: stainless steel, double folding clasp
Price: $6,950

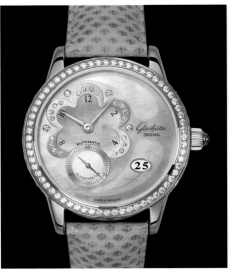

Lady Karree Manual Wind

Reference number: 21-01-03-98-04
Movement: manually wound, Glashütte Original Caliber 21; 17.5 x 13.8 mm, height 3.7 mm; 17 jewels; 28,800 vph
Functions: hours, minutes
Case: stainless steel, 23.5 x 24.5 mm, height 8 mm; elongated case flanks in white gold set with 88 brilliant-cut diamonds; sapphire crystal; exhibition window case back
Band: stainless steel, double folding clasp
Price: $9,300
Variations: in rose gold, without diamond-covered flanks

BlackSecret

Reference number: 90-03-54-54-04
Movement: automatic, Glashütte Original Caliber 90-03; ø 32.6 mm, height 7 mm; 61 jewels; 28,800 vph; off-center rotor; duplex swan-neck fine adjustment
Functions: hours, minutes, subsidiary seconds, panorama date, power reserve display
Case: white gold, ø 39.3 mm, height 12.6 mm; case, bezel and lugs set with 274 black brilliant-cut diamonds; sapphire crystal; exhibition window case back; crown with diamond
Band: lizard skin, buckle set with 22 brilliant-cut diamonds
Remarks: gold dial set 53 white and 161 black diamonds
Price: $46,200

PinkPassion

Reference number: 90-01-52-52-04
Movement: automatic, Glashütte Original Caliber 90-01; ø 32.6 mm, height 7 mm; 41 jewels; 28,800 vph; off-center rotor; duplex swan-neck fine adjustment
Functions: hours, minutes, subsidiary seconds; panorama date
Case: white gold, ø 39.3 mm, height 12.6 mm; bezel set with 64 brilliant-cut diamonds; sapphire crystal; exhibition window case back; crown with pink sapphire cabochon
Band: Aqualino, buckle set with 22 brilliant-cut diamonds
Remarks: dial made of mother-of-pearl and set with 24 brilliant-cut diamonds
Price: $27,700

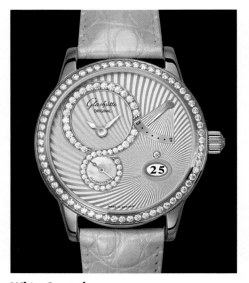

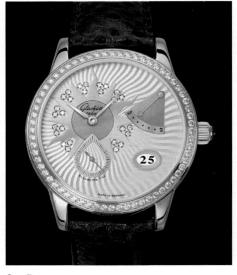

Lady Sport Automatic

Reference number: 39-11-15-41-16
Movement: automatic, Glashütte Original Caliber 39-11; ø 26.2 mm, height 4.3 mm; 25 jewels; 28,800 vph
Functions: hours, minutes, sweep seconds; date
Case: stainless steel, ø 31 mm, height 10.5 mm; sapphire crystal with magnifying lens, anti-reflective; exhibition window case back; screwed-in crown; water-resistant to 100 m
Band: stainless steel, double folding clasp
Price: $4,850
Variations: in rose gold

WhiteCrystal

Reference number: 65-01-50-50-04
Movement: manually wound, Glashütte Original Caliber 65-01; ø 32.2 mm, height 6.1 mm; 48 jewels, 5 in chatons; 28,800 vph; off-center rotor; duplex swan-neck fine adjustment
Functions: hours, minutes, subsidiary seconds; panorama date; power reserve display
Case: white gold, ø 39.3 mm, height 11.8 mm; bezel set with 64 brilliant-cut diamonds; sapphire crystal; exhibition window case back; crown with brilliant-cut diamond
Band: reptile skin, buckle set with 22 brilliant-cut diamonds
Remarks: hand-guilloché dial, mother-of-pearl and diamond
Price: $28,900

SunRay

Reference number: 65-01-51-51-04
Movement: manually wound, Glashütte Original Caliber 65-01; ø 32.2 mm, height 6.1 mm; 48 jewels, 5 in chatons; 28,800 vph; off-center rotor; duplex swan-neck fine adjustment
Functions: hours, minutes, subsidiary seconds; panorama date; power reserve display
Case: rose gold, ø 39.3 mm, height 11.8 mm; bezel set with 64 brilliant-cut diamonds; sapphire crystal; exhibition window case back; crown with violet sapphire cabochon
Band: Aqualino, buckle set with 22 brilliant-cut diamonds
Remarks: guilloché dial with 27 diamonds
Price: $26,000

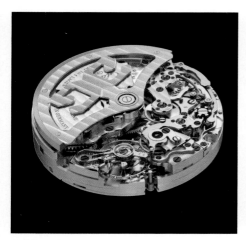

Caliber 95

Mechanical with automatic winding, twin spring barrels with step gear, bilateral winding in two speeds
Functions: hours, minutes (off-center), subsidiary seconds; chronograph with flyback function; panorama date
Diameter: 32.2 mm; **Height:** 7.3 mm ; **Jewels:** 41
Balance: screw balance with 18 gold balance screws
Frequency: 28,800 vph
Balance spring: Breguet, swan-neck fine adjustment
Remarks: separate wheel bridges for winding and chronograph; immaculately finished movement, beveled edges, polished steel parts, screw-mounted gold chatons, blued screws, winding wheels with double sunburst decoration, bridges and cocks with Glashütte ribbing, hand-engraved balance cock

Caliber 93

Mechanical with automatic winding, flying one-minute tourbillon; off-center rotor; power reserve 48 hours
Functions: hours, minutes (off-center), subsidiary seconds (on tourbillon cage); panorama date
Diameter: 32.2 mm; **Height:** 7.65 mm (without tourbillon cage); **Jewels:** 46 plus two diamond endstones
Balance: screw balance with 18 gold balance screws in tourbillon carriage, one revolution per minute
Frequency: 21,600 vph; **Balance spring:** Breguet
Remarks: flying one-minute tourbillon on dial side, immaculately finished movement; beveled edges, polished steel parts, screw-mounted gold chatons, blued screws, winding wheels with double sunburst decoration, bridges and cocks with Glashütte ribbing; hand-engraved balance cock

Caliber 90

Mechanical with automatic winding; power reserve 42 hours
Functions: hours, minutes (off-center), sweep seconds; panorama date, moon phase
Diameter: 32.6 mm; **Height:** 7 mm;
Jewels: 41
Balance: screw balance with 18 gold balance screws
Frequency: 28,800 vph
Balance spring: flat hairspring, duplex swan-neck fine adjustment (for rate and beat)
Shock protection: Incabloc
Remarks: immaculately finished movement; beveled edges, polished steel parts ; hand-engraved balance cock; three-quarter plate with Glashütte ribbing; off-center skeletonized rotor with 21-karat gold oscillating weight

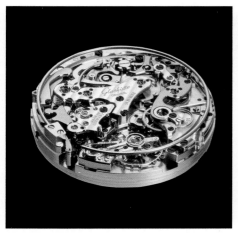

Caliber 60

Mechanical with manual winding, power reserve 42 hours
Functions: hours, minutes, subsidiary seconds; panorama date; chronograph with flyback and countdown functions (30 minutes, acoustic signal via gong)
Diameter: 32.2 mm; **Height:** 7.2 mm
Jewels: 54
Balance: screw balance with 18 gold balance screws
Frequency: 28,800 vph
Balance spring: flat hairspring, swan-neck fine adjustment
Remarks: immaculately finished movement, beveled edges, polished steel parts, screw-mounted gold chatons, blued screws, winding wheels with double sunburst pattern, bridges and cocks decorated with Glashütte ribbing, balance cock engraved by hand

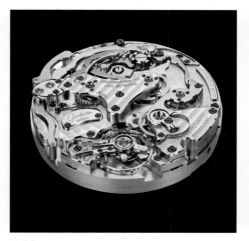

Caliber 61

Mechanical with manual winding, power reserve 42 hours
Functions: hours, minutes, subsidiary seconds; chronograph with flyback function
Diameter: 32.2 mm
Height: 7.2 mm
Jewels: 41
Balance: screw balance with 18 gold balance screws
Frequency: 28,800 vph
Balance spring: flat hairspring, swan-neck fine adjustment
Remarks: immaculately finished movement, beveled edges, polished steel parts, blued screws, screw-mounted gold chatons, winding wheels with double sunburst pattern, bridges and cocks with Glashütte ribbing; balance cock engraved by hand

Caliber 65

Mechanical with manual winding, power reserve 42 hours
Functions: hours, minutes, subsidiary seconds; power reserve display
Diameter: 32.2 mm; **Height:** 6.1 mm
Jewels: 48
Balance: screw balance with 18 gold balance screws
Frequency: 28,800 vph
Balance spring: flat hairspring, duplex swan-neck fine adjustment (for rate and beat)
Remarks: immaculately finished movement, beveled edges, polished steel parts, blued screws, screw-mounted gold chatons, three-quarter plate decorated with Glashütte ribbing; winding wheels with double sunburst pattern; balance cock engraved by hand

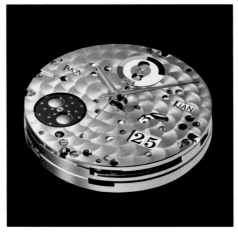

Caliber 65

Mechanical with manual winding, power reserve 42 hours
Functions: hours, minutes, subsidiary seconds; power reserve display
Diameter: 32.2 mm; **Height:** 6.1 mm
Jewels: 48
Balance: screw balance with 18 gold balance screws
Frequency: 28,800 vph
Balance spring: flat hairspring, duplex swan-neck fine adjustment (for rate and beat)
Remarks: immaculately finished movement, beveled edges, polished steel parts, blued screws, screw-mounted gold chatons, three-quarter plate decorated with Glashütte ribbing; winding wheels with double sunburst pattern; balance cock engraved by hand

Caliber 39-50 (dial side)

Mechanical with automatic winding, power reserve 40 hours, stop-seconds
Functions: hours, minutes, sweep seconds; perpetual calendar with panorama date, day, month, moon phase, leap year indication
Diameter: 31.15 mm; **Height:** 7.2 mm
Jewels: 48
Frequency: 28,800 vph
Balance spring: flat hairspring, swan-neck fine adjustment
Shock protection: Incabloc
Remarks: immaculately finished movement, beveled edges, polished steel parts, winding wheels with sunburst decoration, three-quarter plate with Glashütte ribbing, skeletonized rotor with 21-karat gold oscillating weight

Caliber 21

Mechanical with manual winding, power reserve 38 hours
Functions: hours, minutes
Dimensions: 17.5 x 13.8 mm
Height: 3.7 mm
Jewels: 17
Frequency: 28,800 vph
Balance spring: flat hairspring
Remarks: immaculately finished movement, beveled edges, polished steel parts, blued screws, three-quarter plate decorated with Glashütte ribbing, winding wheels with sunburst decoration

Caliber 42

Mechanical with manual winding, power reserve 40 hours
Functions: hours, minutes
Dimensions: 26 x 20.5 mm
Height: 4.3 mm
Balance: screw balance with 18 gold balance screws
Frequency: 28,800 vph
Balance spring: flat hairspring, swan-neck fine adjustment
Remarks: immaculately finished movement, beveled edges, polished steel parts, blued screws, screwed-mounted gold chatons, three-quarter plate decorated with Glashütte ribbing, winding wheels with double sunburst decoration

Glycine

Glycine is getting precise: With its new diver's watch Lagunare this brand hailing from Biel has presented its first chronometer since the 1950s.
In 1952 Glycine introduced the famed vacuum chronometer, so well known because of its incredible resistance to water and shocks. The new Lagunare chronometer is a legitimate successor to the historical model, as it not only includes a movement officially certified by the C.O.S.C., but also a double case back to

protect the mechanism. Diving time is shown by a rotating ring inside the crystal, which is adjusted by a screwed-in crown located at 2 o'clock.
Glycine Watch SA is however more of a specialist known for making pilot's watches. This is underscored by the brand, which celebrated its ninetieth anniversary last year with a noble, large timepiece for the wrist: Airman 7 in rose gold. This model is outfitted with three independent automatic movements and therefore measures a

remarkable 53 millimeters in diameter. Large watches have always been one of the specialties of this watch brand. Founded in the year 1914, the brand at first produced voluminous watches with gold and platinum cases for solvent men. The production of watches containing mechanical movements was continued into the 1970s, even though the consumer was by then demanding quartz watches almost exclusively.
At the same time, Glycine has always been one of the front-runners of new trends in mechanical watches. For example, in 1938 Glycine was one of the twenty-nine exhibitors at the first Basel Fair after the Great Depression and ensuing world economic crisis in the early 1930s. Since then, Glycine hasn't missed a single Basel Fair. After the war, Glycine was one of the first Swiss brands to put its money on the automatic movement. In 1948 the company was already able to show an entire range of automatic watches. In the year 1996 the company once again took up designing large-formatted watches, something that represented one of the traditional firm's most important production arms in the '50s and '60s. On the American and, especially, the Italian markets, Glycine has been strongly represented since the middle of the 1990s with oversized chronographs and sports watches.
One of the first extra-large Glycine watches was the KMU model, a remake of the company's well-known military watches. Now following the KMU 48 model is a limited edition of 250 pieces of the KMU Big Second, with a large display of subsidiary seconds at 9 o'clock and a dial that is almost completely covered with luminous substance.

Airman 7

Reference number: 3829.151-D9
Movement: automatic, ETA Caliber 1 x 2893-2, 2 x 2671-2; 3 independent ETA automatic movements, one with an additional 24-hour display
Functions: hours, minutes, sweep seconds; date; three time zones; additional 24-hour display (fourth time zone)
Case: stainless steel, ø 53 mm, height 12.3 mm; sapphire crystal; exhibition window case back; crowns at 3, 8 and 10
Band: rubber, buckle
Price: $3,625
Variations: in various dial versions

Airman MLV

Reference number: 3830.15SL-D69
Movement: automatic, ETA Caliber 2893-2; ø 25.6 mm, height 4.1 mm; 21 jewels; 28,800 vph
Functions: hours (24-hour display), minutes, sweep seconds; date; additional 24-hour display (second time zone)
Case: stainless steel, ø 42 mm, height 11.5 mm; bidirectionally rotating bezel with 24-hour scale; sapphire crystal; exhibition window case back; water-resistant to 200 m
Band: rubber, buckle
Remarks: dial with luminous substance; ltd. ed. of 500 pieces
Price: $1,650
Variations: with stainless steel bracelet

Airman 9

Reference number: 3840.191-LB9
Movement: automatic, ETA Caliber 7754; ø 30 mm, height 7.9 mm; 25 jewels; 28,800 vph; rose gold-plated rotor with *côtes de Genève* and engraving
Functions: hours, minutes; chronograph; date; 24-hour display (second time zone)
Case: stainless steel, ø 44 mm, height 15 mm; bidirectionally rotating bezel with 24-hour scale; sapphire crystal; exhibition window case back; screwed-in crown; water-resistant to 50 m
Band: leather, double folding clasp
Price: $3,875
Variations: with stainless steel bracelet

Lagunare LCC 1000

Reference number: 3844.19-D9
Movement: automatic, ETA Caliber 2824-2; ø 25.6 mm, height 4.6 mm; 25 jewels; 28,800 vph; officially certified chronometer (COSC)
Functions: hours, minutes, sweep seconds; date
Case: stainless steel, ø 46 mm, height 13 mm; unidirectionally rotating bezel under crystal with 60-minute divisions; sapphire crystal; screwed-in crowns; water-resistant to 300 m
Band: rubber, buckle
Price: $2,350
Variations: with blue or orange dial

KMU Big Second

Reference number: 3847.15SL-LB3
Movement: manually wound, ETA Caliber 6497-1 Unitas; ø 36.6 mm, height 4.5 mm; 17 jewels; 18,000 vph; bridges with chess board decoration, blued screws
Functions: hours, minutes, subsidiary seconds
Case: stainless steel, ø 48 mm, height 12.5 mm; sapphire crystal; exhibition window case back; water-resistant to 50 m
Band: leather, buckle
Remarks: limited to 250 pieces
Price: $1,450

Stratoforte

Reference number: 3803.14T-D69
Movement: automatic, ETA Caliber 7750; ø 30 mm, height 7.9 mm; 25 jewels; 28,800 vph
Functions: hours, minutes, subsidiary seconds; chronograph; date
Case: stainless steel, ø 46 mm, height 15 mm; bezel engraved with tachymeter scale; sapphire crystal; exhibition window case back; water-resistant to 50 m
Band: rubber, buckle
Price: $1,800
Variations: with stainless steel bracelet; dial in yellow, black or blue

Graham

Drive left" is the slogan of the martially designed Graham Chronofighter. This could be interpreted either as driving on the left side of the road or as something being powered from the left. At any rate, the slogan, the name of the brand, and the watch all leave an unmistakably British taste on the tongue. The Swiss group The British Masters has breathed new life into the old name Graham with such unusual watch creations as this one. The moniker is derived from one of the most important figures in the history of watchmaking: The great George Graham is not only the namesake of the cylinder escapement from the eighteenth century, but is also said to be the inventor of the chronograph.

Graham began working for the famous Thomas Tompion in 1695, but soon started his own business — with the ambition of outdoing his master. Most of the watches that were built at this time deviated in rate precision by up to ten minutes per day. Graham was one of the first whose watches didn't deviate more than one second per day. Graham

even received the contract from the Greenwich Royal Observatory to build its master clock. He was also inducted into the Royal Society, an organization that was originally reserved for scientists and astronomers only.

His inventions made Graham famous throughout Europe, even if he had none of them patented — his moral ideals did not allow him to! He preferred to share his knowledge with his colleagues. Because of his great deeds performed in the name of his homeland, the English Parliament agreed on interring his earthly remains in Westminster Abbey's nave, where they still reside today.

Regardless of the merits of his development of precision timekeeping, it was one of the short-time-interval keeping mechanisms Graham invented that was to coin this new and modern wristwatch brand. Until the present day nothing has changed about the basic principle of the chronograph, in which a second dial train can be coupled or un-coupled from the watch's flow of energy as desired. Thus, chronographs of all types have played the main

role in the Graham's model policies, from the simple chrono all the way to flyback and split-seconds versions featuring a *seconde foudroyante*, a lightning-fast display of an eighth of a second.

The brand's most important flagship piece is the Chronofighter model, whose unusual thumb lever mechanism embodies the entire fascination of the most popular of boy toys in watches. Similar buttons were built for British bomber pilots sixty years ago, who couldn't reliably press the comparatively small crown button of their pilot's chrono-graphs with their big gloves on.

The new leading model of the Graham collection is the Swordfish chronograph, also available for lefties and outfitted with a very special visual: In this case it's the ap-plied magnifying lenses over the two chro-nograph counters, whereby it is worth mentioning that the little crystals are each surrounded by a lavishly constructed bezel. For friends of characteristically British peculiarities, "drive left" is a clear pro-fession of driving on the wrong side of the street, of open roadsters, and plaid flat caps. And no other watch embodies these cute eccentricities as graphically as Chronofighter, Swordfish, and company.

Chronofighter Classic

Reference number: 2CFAS.B01A.L31B
Movement: automatic, Graham Caliber 1722 (base ETA 7750); ø 30.5 mm, height 8.75 mm; 30 jewels; 28,800 vph; chronograph controls (start/stop) via crown button; officially certified chronometer (COSC); movement finished with *côtes de Genève*
Functions: hours, minutes, subsidiary seconds; chronograph
Case: stainless steel, ø 43 mm, height 16 mm; sapphire crystal; crown buttons with security device; water-resistant to 50 m
Band: leather, buckle
Price: $7,900

Chronofighter

Reference number: 2CFAX.S08A.C54B
Movement: automatic, Graham Caliber 1722 (base ETA 7750); ø 30.5 mm, height 8.75 mm; 30 jewels; 28,800 vph; chronograph controls (start/stop) via crown button; officially certified chronometer (COSC); movement finished with *côtes de Genève*
Functions: hours, minutes, subsidiary seconds; chronograph
Case: platinum, ø 43 mm, height 16 mm; sapphire crystal; crown buttons with security device; water-resistant to 50 m
Band: reptile skin, buckle
Price: $55,000

Swordfish

Reference number: 2SWAS.B01A.K06B
Movement: automatic, Graham Caliber 1726 (base ETA 7750); ø 30.5 mm, height 8.75 mm; 30 jewels; 28,800 vph; movement finished with *côtes de Genève*
Functions: hours, minutes, subsidiary seconds; chronograph
Case: stainless steel, ø 46.2 mm, height 16 mm; sapphire crystal with magnifying lens above the counters; screwed-in crown; water-resistant to 50 m
Band: rubber, buckle
Price: $7,500
Variations: also for right-handers (crown and buttons on the left side of the case); in red gold

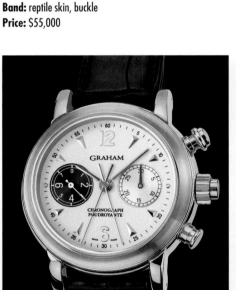

Grand Silverstone

Reference number: 2GSIAS.B01A.K07B
Movement: automatic, Graham Caliber 1721 (base ETA 7750); ø 30.5 mm, height 8.75 mm; 30 jewels; 28,800 vph; movement finished with *côtes de Genève*
Functions: hours, minutes, subsidiary seconds; chronograph with flyback function; large date; 24-hour display (second time zone)
Case: stainless steel, ø 44 mm, height 15 mm; sapphire crystal; screwed-in crown; water-resistant to 50 m
Band: rubber, buckle
Price: $7,900

Foudroyante

Reference number: 2LIAP.S04A.C01B
Movement: automatic, Graham Caliber 1695 (base ETA 7750); ø 30.5 mm, height 8.75 mm; 30 jewels; 28,800 vph; mechanism for *foudroyante* 1/8 second with its own spring barrel; two column wheels
Functions: hours, minutes; split-seconds chronograph with *foudroyante* seconds (1/8-second counter)
Case: rose gold, ø 42 mm, height 16 mm; sapphire crystal; screwed-in crown; water-resistant to 50 m
Band: reptile skin, buckle
Price: $29,150
Variations: in stainless steel

Mastersplit

Reference number: 2MSBR.S01A.C80B
Movement: manually wound, Graham Caliber 4445 (base Venus 175); ø 31.3 mm, height 6.8 mm; 17 jewels; 18.800 vph; column wheel control of chronograph functions; movement finished with *côtes de Genève*
Functions: hours, minutes, subsidiary seconds; split-seconds chronograph
Case: red gold, ø 43.5 mm, height 16.5 mm; sapphire crystal; exhibition window case back; water-resistant to 50 m
Band: reptile skin, buckle
Price: $33,500
Variations: with black dial

Hanhart

Hand-held stopwatches and pilot's chronographs made the watch brand Hanhart well known in watch circles. Already in the early 1920s this watch manufacturer from the Black Forest was building its first mechanical stopwatches, and in 1926 high-quality pocket and wristwatches were added. In 1938 this company hailing from the village of Gütenbach developed the legendary one-button chronograph Caliber 40, which was reissued in 2003 under the name Primus. For this watch, a manually wound ETA Valjoux 7760 was so modified by Hanhart that all three chronograph functions (start-stop-reset in succession) could be activated by just one button.

The automatic chronograph introduced in 2005 called Red X is oriented on the design of the classic pilot's chronographs from 1939. The Red X, limited to 1,939 pieces, features a red chronograph button, and this color also plays an important role in other functions, as the name clearly states. Both stop hands and the hand for the permanent subsidiary seconds are painted in this color. Red markers and a red seam in the classic calfskin leather strap underscore the model's striking design.

Connoisseurs of the logo and characteristic "Hanhart stud" on the leather strap have easily identified these symbols for quality and reliability for more than sixty years, even though the wristwatch section of this small company had been sorely neglected for a long time. But a good name will survive, and the widespread trend toward retro design has favored the return of a manufacturer with a proven and "evolved" tradition.

On the initiative of two enterprising product developers at Hanhart, wristwatches were once again added to the mechanical and electronic stopwatches and timers from Gütenbach, and with much care and attention to detail, the collection was gradually expanded. In 1997 two replicas of military pilot's chronographs from World War II represented the starting point for the new Hanhart collection. Dial details, hands, and the fluted bezel featuring a reference mark are identical in every respect with the look of the original watch produced in 1939. Although Hanhart generally utilizes ETA movements, the case specialists succeeded in duplicating the characteristic asymmetrical offset positioning of the buttons with respect to the crown by integrating a number of linkages. Decades of experience in making manually wound stopwatches, the mechanisms of which are still made in-house, was most likely a great help in this endeavor.

The Minos and Sirius models have been removed a bit from the characteristic design originally stipulated in the "Description, Operation, and Maintenance Regulation for Air Force Watches" and break with the tradition of black dials, fluorescent hands, and fluorescent Arabic numerals. That certainly would have been in keeping with "stopwatch king" Willy Hanhart's philosophy as he developed a special enthusiasm for sports timing after the war. The Admiral and Gold chronographs are dedicated to the founder and captain of the brand, both available with a choice of manually wound or automatic movements and — to offset the pilot's look — a matte white dial.

The current chronograph, Dornier by Hanhart, extends this line of "civilian" timepieces in a consistent manner. The initiator of this watch was Irén Dornier, grandson of the legendary airplane builder Claude Dornier and a fan of classic mechanics. He had a chronograph manufactured at the factory in Gütenbach that is dedicated to the legendary flying boat Do-X, a vessel that accompanied him on a journey of a special type: In 2004, with the Hanhart chronograph strapped to his wrist, Irén Dornier flew once around the globe in the historical water aircraft Do 24 ATT.

Fliegerchronograph Tachy-Tele Replica

Reference number: 702.1101-00
Movement: manually wound, ETA Caliber 7760; ø 30 mm, height 6.2 mm; 21 jewels; 28,800 vph; modified button positions
Functions: hours, minutes, subsidiary seconds; chronograph
Case: stainless steel, ø 40 mm, height 13.7 mm; bidirectionally rotating bezel with reference marker; sapphire crystal; water-resistant to 100 m
Band: leather, buckle
Price: $3,000
Variations: with brown leather strap

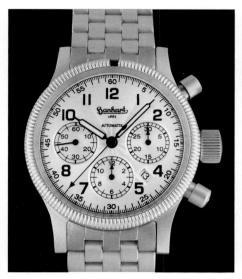

Sirius Chronograph

Reference number: 710.020A-00
Movement: automatic, ETA Caliber 7750; ø 30 mm, height 7.9 mm; 25 jewels; 28,800 vph; modified button positions
Functions: hours, minutes, subsidiary seconds; chronograph; date
Case: stainless steel, ø 40 mm, height 15.4 mm; bidirectionally rotating bezel with reference marker; sapphire crystal; exhibition window case back; screwed-in crown; water-resistant to 100 m
Band: stainless steel, folding clasp
Price: $4,000
Variations: with black dial; with leather strap

Admiral Chronograph

Reference number: 715.0001-00
Movement: automatic, ETA Caliber 7750; ø 30 mm, height 7.9 mm; 25 jewels; 28,800 vph; modified button positions
Functions: hours, minutes, subsidiary seconds; chronograph
Case: stainless steel, ø 40 mm, height 15 mm; bidirectionally rotating bezel with reference marker; sapphire crystal; exhibition window case back; water-resistant to 100 m
Band: leather, buckle
Price: $3,400
Variations: with black dial

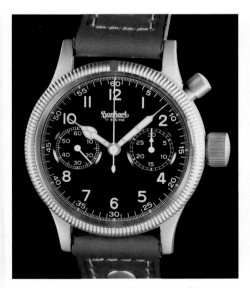

Primus One-Button Chronograph

Reference number: 704.0100-00
Movement: manually wound, Hanhart Caliber 704 (base ETA 7760); ø 30 mm, height 6.2 mm; 21 jewels; 28,800 vph; movement modified to one single button (start-stop-reset)
Functions: hours, minutes, subsidiary seconds; chronograph
Case: stainless steel, ø 40 mm, height 13.7 mm; bidirectionally rotating bezel with reference marker; sapphire crystal
Band: leather, buckle
Price: $3,200
Variations: as an automatic, with leather strap or stainless steel bracelet

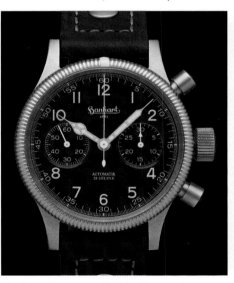

Hanhart Pioneer Caliber II

Reference number: 716.0100-00
Movement: automatic, Hanhart Caliber 716 (base ETA 7750); ø 30 mm, height 7.9 mm; 28 jewels; 28,800 vph; modified button positions
Functions: hours, minutes, subsidiary seconds; chronograph
Case: stainless steel, ø 40 mm, height 15 mm; bidirectionally rotating bezel with reference marker; sapphire crystal; exhibition window case back
Band: leather, buckle
Price: $3,400
Variations: various leather straps; with stainless steel bracelet

Dornier by Hanhart

Reference number: 790.0708-00
Movement: automatic, Hanhart Caliber 790 (base ETA 7750); ø 30 mm, height 7.9 mm; 28 jewels; 28,800 vph; gold-plated rotor
Functions: hours, minutes, subsidiary seconds; chronograph; date
Case: stainless steel, ø 42 mm, height 16.5 mm; sapphire crystal; exhibition window case back; crown with onyx cabochon
Band: reptile skin, buckle
Remarks: specially shaped chronograph buttons
Price: $6,300
Variations: with beige or copper-colored dial

Harwood

England's King Alfred the Great used a candle with hour markings to measure the time; in the Middle Ages the hourglass was the only mobile way of measuring the passage of the hours; and Anne Boleyn received a wall clock at her wedding to Henry VIII. Every French king had to pass a watchmaker's test, for as highest regent of his country he had the divine obligation of mastering time.

There were a good thousand years between the beginnings of timekeeping with the simplest of measures all the way to the invention of the wristwatch. While at the turn of the century, a gentlemen's pocket watch (sometimes decorated with erotic themes under the hinged lid) was a solid fixture on the landscape, it was women who helped the wristwatch to wide acceptance, for they needed watches to organize the day. Watchmakers of this era eyed these developments with horror, for they feared the repairs the sensitive mechanisms placed on such an open area as the wrist, exposed as they were to shocks and the wrath of all weather, would need. However, contrary to the vest pocket, the wrist is really the optimal place for a watch. It is a place where the automatic variation can get energy, for it is only at this place on the body that a rotor can sensibly wind the mainspring enough.

The history of the wristwatch began only at the start of the twentieth century, thus comparatively recently, as it fell at a time when other new technological developments such as air travel and television were changing the world from the inside out. In researching the annals of automatic winding, one runs into three outstanding personalities who have become this story's main figures. One of them is the English watchmaker and inventor John Harwood. After Abraham Louis Perrelet had constructed the first pocket watch with an automatic movement between 1770 and 1776, Harwood received patent number 10 65 83 for the development of a *montre bracelet perpetuel* at the Federal Office of the Swiss Confederation for Intellectual Property in Bern on September 1, 1924. We have him to thank for the first automatic wristwatches, which caused quite an uproar at their premiere, after being produced in a small series in Switzerland. A special trademark of the Harwood until today is its classic appearance: The watch without a crown. By eliminating an opening in the case for the winding stem, John Harwood created a water- and dust-resistant timepiece. The otherwise usual functions of the crown were taken over by a coin-edged rotating bezel, with whose help the watch can be wound and set.

Despite all the prophecies of doom, Harwood automatic watches proved to be surprisingly precise during their time, as rare collector's pieces at auction will confirm today. As an homage to their inventor, a limited edition watch in steel and noble platinum was created, whose enameled dial features a subject by the talented Swiss miniature painter Louis Reguin (1872–1948). Another collector's piece housed in an elegant, flat case of only 35 mm diameter in sterling silver is also a commemoration to John Harwood.

Automatic

Reference number: 516.10.15
Movement: automatic, ETA Caliber 2892-2, modified;
ø 25.6 mm, height 3.6 mm; 21 jewels; 28,800 vph; setting
of hands and winding via rotating bezel
Functions: hours, minutes, sweep seconds
Case: stainless steel, ø 39 mm, height 9.5 mm; bidirection-
ally rotating bezel for winding and setting hands; sapphire
crystal; exhibition window case back
Band: leather, buckle
Price: $3,150
Variations: with stainless steel bracelet; with reptile skin
strap; as women's model (ø 35 mm)

Automatic

Reference number: 516.10.11
Movement: automatic, ETA Caliber 2892-2, modified;
ø 25.6 mm, height 3.6 mm; 21 jewels; 28,800 vph; setting
of hands and winding via rotating bezel
Functions: hours, minutes, sweep seconds
Case: stainless steel, ø 39 mm, height 9.5 mm; bidirection-
ally rotating bezel for winding and setting hands; sapphire
crystal; exhibition window case back
Band: stainless steel, folding clasp
Price: $3,150
Variations: with leather or reptile skin strap; as women's
model (ø 35 mm)

Automatic

Reference number: 501.41.12 C
Movement: automatic, ETA Caliber 2892-2, modified;
ø 25.6 mm, height 3.6 mm; 21 jewels; 28,800 vph; setting
of hands and winding via rotating bezel
Functions: hours, minutes, sweep seconds
Case: stainless steel, ø 35 mm, height 9.5 mm; bidirection-
ally rotating bezel for winding and setting hands; sapphire
crystal; exhibition window case back
Band: reptile skin, buckle
Price: $3,450
Variations: with reptile skin strap; in yellow gold;
as women's model (ø 35 mm)

Automatic

Reference number: 516.10.15 D M
Movement: automatic, ETA Caliber 2892-2, modified;
ø 25.6 mm, height 3.6 mm; 21 jewels; 28,800 vph; setting
of hands and winding via rotating bezel
Functions: hours, minutes, sweep seconds
Case: stainless steel, ø 39 mm, height 9.5 mm; bidirection-
ally rotating bezel with diamonds for winding and setting
hands; sapphire crystal; exhibition window case back
Band: stainless steel, folding clasp
Price: $7,300

Automatic

Reference number: 500.10.15 D M
Movement: automatic, ETA Caliber 2892-2, modified;
ø 25.6 mm, height 3.6 mm; 21 jewels; 28,800 vph; setting
of hands and winding via rotating bezel
Functions: hours, minutes, sweep seconds
Case: stainless steel, ø 35 mm, height 9.5 mm; bidirection-
ally rotating bezel with diamonds for winding and setting
hands; sapphire crystal; exhibition window case back
Band: stainless steel, folding clasp
Price: $6,000

Automatic Louis Reguin

Reference number: 517.10 LRC
Movement: automatic, ETA Caliber 2892-2, modified;
ø 25.6 mm, height 3.6 mm; 21 jewels; 28,800 vph; setting
of hands and winding via rotating bezel
Functions: hours, minutes, sweep seconds
Case: stainless steel, ø 39 mm, height 9.5 mm; bidirection-
ally rotating bezel for winding and setting hands; sapphire
crystal; exhibition window case back
Band: reptile skin, buckle
Remarks: enameled dial in honor of the artist Louis Réguin
Price: $4,600
Variations: in platinum

Hermès

Between Hermès and the horses found on its coat of arms, there has always been a concrete, yet tender and smooth relationship: leather. Horses, riding, and travel are themes that have dominated the history of the house since its founding in 1837 when Thierry Hermès (who was born in Germany's Krefeld) opened a little saddlery in Paris's Quartier de la Madeleine. In 1928 Emile-Maurice Hermès began selling watches in his shop on the French metropolis's Faubourg Saint-Honoré. These were watches that he had had made by reputable Swiss manufactories according to his designs. To celebrate the seventy-fifth anniversary of the Hermès watch, the company — which is still independent today — has taken a remarkable initiative.

The new Dressage model (French for the training of animals, a term often used in equestrian sports) follows not only in the tradition of famous wristwatch creations by the company such as Kelly (1975), Arceau

(1978), Harnais (1996), and Hour H (1997), but also continues in its old tradition of co-operating directly with exclusive movement manufacturers. The building in Biel housing La Montre Hermès is home to several assembly and toolmaking workshops as well as production machines for various watch

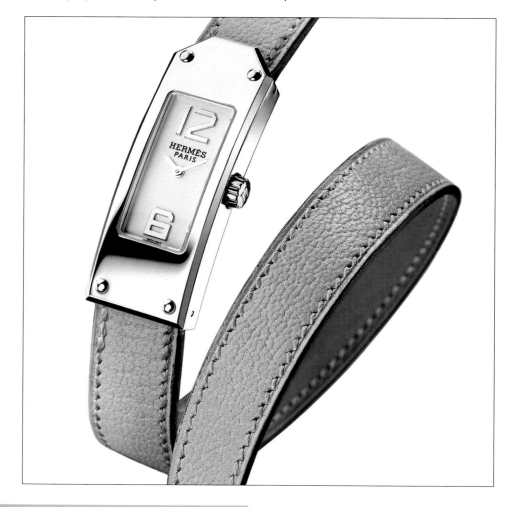

components on more than 3,800 square meters of floor. However, with only eighty-five employees it is just impossible to make one's own true watch movement production — and even putting them in 140,000 watches per year would not be economical.

Searching for an exclusive and qualitatively remarkable movement manufacturer, Hermès found what it was looking for in the sleepy little town of Fleurier — a town that used to be a flourishing bastion of the Swiss watchmaking industry. Not quite two years ago, the movement *manufacture* Vaucher, a subsidiary company of the watch manufacturer Parmigiani in charge of the development and production of the exquisite automatic and manually wound movements for the small noble brand, opened its doors there.

Vaucher Caliber P1928, made exclusively for Hermès and used in the Dressage model, is based on Parmigiani's Caliber 331 with automatic winding. At 25.6 mm in diameter and 3.5 mm in height, it is one of the flattest movements around, although it offers a good 55 hours of power reserve thanks to its twin spring barrels. The shape and decoration of the bridges and cocks are personalized for Hermès, engraved with the characteristic H.

Along with the platinum version featuring a genuine mother-of-pearl dial limited to seventy-five pieces that comes with a C.O.S.C. chronometer certificate, there are unlimited versions in red, white, and yellow gold, with the dial either in mother-of-pearl or silver. The simple case shape is common to all of the versions as is the unmistakable dial design featuring twelve medallions as hour markers.

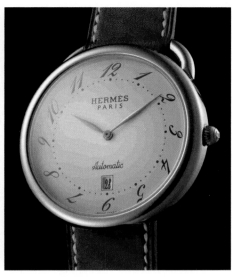

Dressage

Reference number: DR 1.770.213 M
Movement: automatic, Vaucher Caliber P 1928; ø 25.6 mm, height 3.5 mm; 32 jewels; 28,800 vph; rotor's oscillating weight in red gold
Functions: hours, minutes, sweep seconds; date
Case: red gold, 40 x 46 mm, height 9.72 mm; sapphire crystal; exhibition window case back; screwed-in crown; water-resistant to 50 m
Band: reptile skin, folding clasp
Price: $15,100
Variations: in yellow gold; in white gold; with mother-of-pearl dial

Dressage Moon Phases

Reference number: DR 2.765.712 M
Movement: automatic, Vaucher Caliber P 1929; ø 25.6 mm, height 3.5 mm; 32 jewels; 28,800 vph; rotor's oscillating weight in red gold
Functions: hours, minutes, sweep seconds; date (retrograde); moon phase
Case: platinum, 40 x 46 mm, height 9.72 mm; sapphire crystal; exhibition window case back; screwed-in crown; water-resistant to 50 m
Band: reptile skin, folding clasp
Price: $34,500
Variations: in rose gold; with mother-of-pearl dial

Arceau Automatic

Reference number: 4.810.130
Movement: automatic, ETA Caliber 2892-A2; ø 25.6 mm, height 3.6 mm; 21 jewels; 28,800 vph
Functions: hours, minutes, sweep seconds; date
Case: stainless steel, ø 41 mm, height 11 mm; sapphire crystal; water-resistant to 50 m
Band: leather, buckle
Price: $1,700
Variations: with dark grey dial; various leather straps

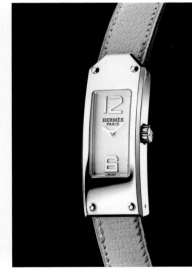

Nomade Compass

Reference number: NO 2.910
Movement: automatic, ETA Caliber autoquartz; protected against magnetic fields
Functions: hours, minutes, sweep seconds; date; compass
Case: stainless steel, ø 39 mm, height 14 mm; bipartite case opened and closed by hinge, with compass in the lower half of the case; sapphire crystal; water-resistant to 50 m
Band: calf skin, buckle
Price: $1,900
Variations: with black or silver-colored dial

Heure "H" Double Tour

Reference number: HH1.510
Movement: quartz, ETA Caliber 901.001
Functions: hours, minutes
Case: stainless steel, 21 x 21 mm, height 7 mm; sapphire crystal
Band: double calf skin strap, buckle
Price: appx. $1,250
Variations: various leather straps and dials

Kelly II

Reference number: KT1.210
Movement: quartz, ETA Caliber 956.412
Functions: hours, minutes
Case: stainless steel, 15 x 42 mm, height 7 mm; sapphire crystal
Band: double calf skin strap, buckle
Price: upon request
Variations: various leather straps and dials (white, black, jeans blue)

Hublot

Jean-Claude Biver was already speaking of a "Big Bang" when initially asked about his recipe for freshening up Hublot's collection, the prestigious brand that had turned down a bit of a dead-end street. Hublot's owner, Carlo Crocco, had outfitted the charismatic watch executive who had so successfully repositioned Blancpain with extensive authority and entrusted him with his life's work. When Crocco realized his vision of a watch as a "porthole" (French: *hublot*) in matte brushed metal on a rubber strap that smelled lightly of vanilla twenty-five years ago, he called it "la montre des montres" — the "watch of all watches." This is also what the company was named until just recently. Simplicity was trump among the avant-garde, and thanks to the demonstrative nonconformism of the Hublot watch, the company was able to utilize the luxury theme in a carefree manner. But times have changed, and for this reason Biver has let off his "Big Bang," as promised.

The new "Hublot of all Hublots" has retained the technical attitude of its predecessors, but pulls way ahead of them in the choice of design materials. The case of the Big Bang is built in several layers of different high-tech materials and precious metals, expressed both in the fissured case shape as well as in the daring color composition, including black PVD coatings, Kevlar, carbon fiber, and aluminum contrast against red gold, platinum, and white ceramic. Even the rubber strap, which until now was only available in black, has finally taken on all the

colors of the rainbow, and then some. The *manufacture* La Joux-Perret is in charge of the technology found in the new chronograph module and an oscillating weight made from the heavy metal tungsten. The topics of water and seafaring remain the same at Hublot — *nomen est omen* — with the brand retaining a close relationship to them. Alongside the unchanged commitment to extreme regattas and record chases on and under the water, the brand now acts as a partner to the prestigious Yacht Club de Monaco and functions as the official timekeeper for all regattas taking place under the patronage of the club and the royal house. A special edition of the Big Bang bears, along with the YCM logo, a reproduction of the *Tuiga*, a teakwood racing yacht from 1909 that is now owned by the Yacht Club de Monaco. Another partnership associates Hublot with Wally, the manufacturer of the sportiest luxury sailing yachts, including the elite circle of Wally Class sailors with boats over 24 meters in length. Here Hublot is also in

charge of the official timekeeping and supports the introduction of the Performance Data Acquisition System, which keeps the participants (and audience) informed of the current distances and positions of the boats participating in the regatta.

Big Bang

Reference number: 301.PB.131.PB
Movement: automatic, ETA Caliber HUB44, developed by La Joux-Perret (base ETA 7750); ø 30 mm, height 7.9 mm; 25 jewels; 28,800 vph
Functions: hours, minutes, subsidiary seconds; chronograph; date
Case: red gold, ø 44.5 mm, height 16 mm; bezel in black ceramic; sapphire crystal; exhibition window case back; screwed-in crown; water-resistant to 100 m
Band: red gold/ceramic, double folding clasp
Remarks: dial made of carbon fiber
Price: $19,900

Big Bang

Reference number: 301.PB.131.RX
Movement: automatic, ETA Caliber HUB44, developed by La Joux-Perret (base ETA 7750); ø 30 mm, height 7.9 mm; 25 jewels; 28,800 vph
Functions: hours, minutes, subsidiary seconds; chronograph; date
Case: red gold, ø 44.5 mm, height 16 mm; bezel in black ceramic; sapphire crystal; exhibition window case back; water-resistant to 100 m
Band: rubber, folding clasp
Remarks: dial made of carbon fiber
Price: $16,100

Big Bang

Reference number: 301.SB.131.SB
Movement: automatic, ETA Caliber HUB44, developed by La Joux-Perret (base ETA 7750); ø 30 mm, height 7.9 mm; 25 jewels; 28,800 vph
Functions: hours, minutes, subsidiary seconds; chronograph; date
Case: stainless steel, ø 44.5 mm, height 16 mm; bezel in black ceramic; sapphire crystal; exhibition window case back; water-resistant to 100 m
Band: stainless steel/ceramic, double folding clasp
Remarks: dial made of carbon fiber
Price: $12,300

Big Bang

Reference number: 301.SH.131.RW
Movement: automatic, ETA Caliber HUB44, developed by La Joux-Perret (base ETA 7750); ø 30 mm, height 7.9 mm; 25 jewels; 28,800 vph
Functions: hours, minutes, subsidiary seconds; chronograph; date
Case: stainless steel, ø 44.5 mm, height 16 mm; bezel in white ceramic; sapphire crystal; exhibition window case back; water-resistant to 100 m
Band: rubber, folding clasp
Remarks: dial made of carbon fiber
Price: $11,400

Big Bang

Reference number: 301.SX.130.RX
Movement: automatic, ETA Caliber HUB44, developed by La Joux-Perret (base ETA 7750); ø 30 mm, height 7.9 mm; 25 jewels; 28,800 vph
Functions: hours, minutes, subsidiary seconds; chronograph; date
Case: stainless steel, ø 44.5 mm, height 16 mm; bezel in stainless steel; sapphire crystal; exhibition window case back; water-resistant to 100 m
Band: rubber, folding clasp
Price: $8,500

Big Bang

Reference number: 301.SX.130.SX
Movement: automatic, ETA Caliber HUB44, developed by La Joux-Perret (base ETA 7750); ø 30 mm, height 7.9 mm; 25 jewels; 28,800 vph
Functions: hours, minutes, subsidiary seconds; chronograph; date
Case: stainless steel, ø 44.5 mm, height 16 mm; bezel in stainless steel; sapphire crystal; exhibition window case back; water-resistant to 100 m
Band: white gold/ceramic, folding clasp
Price: $9,500

IWC

The history of IWC began when Switz-erland was still a land of low labor costs. In the year 1868 American Florentine Ariosto Jones, until then director of the watch factory F. Howard & Cie in Boston, founded the International Watch Company in Schaffhausen. Far away from the master watchmakers in Geneva, who feared com-petition from the New World, Jones not only found the schooled personnel he was looking for in the German-speaking part of Switz-erland, but also Heinrich Moser, a pioneer in the industry who used the power of the Rhine water that flowed through the city to create the much-needed electric energy. Jones was not only a successful entrepreneur, but also a talented watch designer. He created a fine mechanical movement with

some remarkable characteristics for his IWC pocket watches: a temperature-compensating bimetallic balance, a Breguet balance spring bent by hand, a three-quarter plate, and the long index he used for fine adjust-ments of the movement. It is exactly these characteristics that the new F.A. Jones model features, a wristwatch with a pocket watch movement in a Portuguese case that was introduced at the S.I.H.H. in Geneva in 2005. The Jones is supposed to reach the market by the end of 2005 in a limited edition: 500 in platinum, 1000 in rose gold, and 2000 in stainless steel.

Since this brand has been owned by the prestigious Richemont group, along with sister brands Jaeger-LeCoultre and A. Lange & Söhne, its collection has been restruc-

tured. At the top of the product pyramid are specialties such as the Grande Complication and the legendary Da Vinci, for example. Underneath these one finds the Portuguese family, covering the elegant watch segment. The basis for this "technical men's brand" — as IWC loves to call itself — is however its sports watches. These are divided into three product families, one each for water, land, and air, respectively. Naturally the timepieces made for water are diver's watches. Last year IWC introduced a new generation of them in the Aquatimer, a name that is a tradition at the company. In 1967, IWC launched its first diver's watch called Aquatimer, a simple, round time-keeper with two crowns. One of the crowns, located at 2 o'clock, was in charge of winding and setting; the second at 4 o'clock was used to move the rotating ring located underneath the sapphire crystal in a counterclockwise manner. An unusual solution: Normally the diver's ring is de-signed as a rotating bezel on the outside. This new family of diver's watches com-prises four models, and all of them feature their rings underneath the crystal.

The models of the earthy Ingenieur family introduced in 2005 illustrate that IWC is helping itself to its own traditions again. In 1955 the watchmakers from Schaffhausen presented the first wristwatch by this name, and the Ingenieur created by Gérald Genta in 1976 became a true design icon. Like every other Ingenieur before them, the current models are also protected against the negative influence of magnetic fields by an inner core made of soft iron. And even more important for watch connoisseurs and IWC's legacy is the *manufacture* movement inside the Ingenieur Automatic, which is outfitted with the patented Pellaton wind-ing system and special shock protection. The element air naturally has as its ticking symbols pilot's watches, which also possess a long tradition at IWC. The current leading model in this family is the Large Pilot's Watch with its seven-day automatic move-ment. Above and beyond that, there are four different timepieces in this line that all answer to the name Spitfire.

Ingenieur Automatic
Reference number: 322701
Movement: automatic, IWC Caliber 80110; ø 30 mm, height 7.25 mm; 28 jewels; 28,800 vph; Pellaton winding, shock-protected rotor; protected against magnetic fields via soft iron core
Functions: hours, minutes, sweep seconds; date
Case: stainless steel, ø 42.5 mm, height 14.5 mm; sapphire crystal; screwed-in crown; water-resistant to 120 m
Band: stainless steel, folding clasp
Price: $7,200

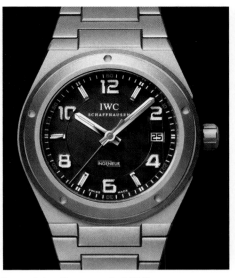

Ingenieur Automatic AMG
Reference number: 322702
Movement: automatic, IWC Caliber 80110; ø 30 mm, height 7.25 mm; 28 jewels; 28,800 vph; Pellaton winding, shock-protected rotor; protected against magnetic fields via soft iron core
Functions: hours, minutes, sweep seconds; date
Case: titanium, ø 42.5 mm, height 14.5 mm; sapphire crystal; screwed-in crown; water-resistant to 120 m
Band: titanium, folding clasp
Price: $7,200
Variations: with textile strap

Ingenieur Chronograph
Reference number: 372501
Movement: automatic, IWC Caliber 79350 (base ETA 7750); ø 30 mm, height 7.9 mm; 25 jewels; 28,800 vph
Functions: hours, minutes, subsidiary seconds; chronograph
Case: stainless steel, ø 42.5 mm, height 13.5 mm; sapphire crystal; screwed-in crown; water-resistant to 120 m
Band: stainless steel, folding clasp
Price: $7,700

Ingenieur Chronograph AMG
Reference number: 372504
Movement: automatic, IWC Caliber 79350 (base ETA 7750); ø 30 mm, height 7.9 mm; 25 jewels; 28,800 vph
Functions: hours, minutes, subsidiary seconds; chronograph
Case: titanium, ø 42.5 mm, height 13.5 mm; sapphire crystal; screwed-in crown; water-resistant to 120 m
Band: textile, buckle
Price: $6,700
Variations: with titanium link bracelet

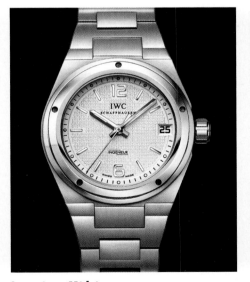

Ingenieur Midsize
Reference number: 451501
Movement: automatic, IWC Caliber 30110 (base ETA 2892-A2); ø 25.6 mm, height 3.6 mm; 23 jewels; 28,800 vph
Functions: hours, minutes, sweep seconds; date
Case: stainless steel, ø 34 mm, height 10 mm; sapphire crystal; screwed-in crown; water-resistant to 120 m
Band: stainless steel, folding clasp
Price: $4,400

Ingenieur Midsize
Reference number: 451501
Movement: automatic, IWC Caliber 30110 (base ETA 2892-A2); ø 25.6 mm, height 3.6 mm; 23 jewels; 28,800 vph
Functions: hours, minutes, sweep seconds; date
Case: stainless steel, ø 34 mm, height 10 mm; sapphire crystal; screwed-in crown; water-resistant to 120 m
Band: textile, buckle
Price: $3,800

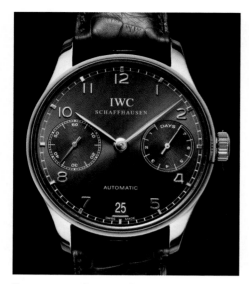

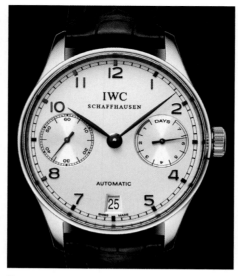

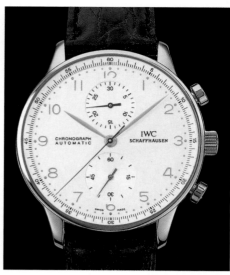

Portuguese Automatic

Reference number: 500106
Movement: manually wound, IWC Caliber 50010;
ø 38.2 mm, height 7.44 mm; 44 jewels; 18,000 vph; Pellaton
winding (patented), shock-protected rotor; protected against
magnetic fields via soft iron core
Functions: hours, minutes, subsidiary seconds; date; power
reserve display
Case: white gold, ø 42.3 mm, height 13.9 mm; sapphire
crystal; exhibition window case back
Band: reptile skin, folding clasp
Price: $19,400
Variations: in red gold; in platinum

Portuguese Automatic

Reference number: 500107
Movement: manually wound, IWC Caliber 50010;
ø 38.2 mm, height 7.44 mm; 44 jewels; 18,000 vph; Pellaton
winding (patented), shock-protected rotor; protected against
magnetic fields via soft iron core
Functions: hours, minutes, subsidiary seconds; date; power
reserve display
Case: stainless steel, ø 42.3 mm, height 13.9 mm;
sapphire crystal
Band: reptile skin, buckle
Price: $10,400
Variations: in red gold; in platinum

Portuguese Chrono Automatic

Reference number: 371401
Movement: automatic, IWC Caliber 79240 (base ETA 7750);
ø 30 mm, height 7.9 mm; 25 jewels; 28,800 vph
Functions: hours, minutes, subsidiary seconds; chronograph
Case: stainless steel, ø 40.9 mm, height 12.3 mm;
sapphire crystal
Band: reptile skin, buckle
Price: $6,700
Variations: various dial versions; in red or yellow gold;
in white gold

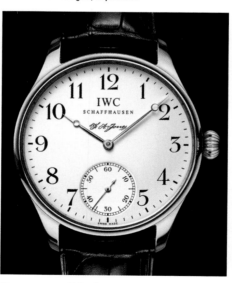

Portuguese Perpetual Calendar

Reference number: 502101
Movement: automatic, IWC Caliber 50611; ø 38.2 mm;
66 jewels; 18,000 vph; Pellaton winding (patented), shock-
protected rotor; protected against magnetic fields via soft
iron core
Functions: hours, minutes, subsidiary seconds; perpetual
calendar with date, day, month, four-digit year display,
double moon phase (for southern and northern hemispheres)
Case: red gold, ø 44.2 mm, height 15.5 mm; sapphire
crystal; exhibition window case back
Band: reptile skin, folding clasp
Price: $30,000

Portuguese F.A. Jones

Reference number: 544202
Movement: manually wound, IWC Caliber 98290;
ø 38.2 mm, 18 jewels; 18,000 vph; according to an historical
model, containing extra-long index and special decoration
Functions: hours, minutes, subsidiary seconds
Case: platinum, ø 43 mm, height 11.7 mm; sapphire crystal;
exhibition window case back
Band: reptile skin, buckle
Remarks: homage to IWC founder Florence Ariosto Jones;
limited to 500 pieces
Price: $31,500
Variations: in red gold, limited to 1,000 pieces

Portuguese F.A. Jones

Reference number: 544203
Movement: manually wound, IWC Caliber 98290;
ø 38.2 mm, 18 jewels; 18,000 vph; according to an historical
model, containing extra-long index and special decoration
Functions: hours, minutes, subsidiary seconds
Case: stainless steel, ø 43 mm, height 11.7 mm; sapphire
crystal; exhibition window case back
Band: reptile skin, buckle
Remarks: homage to IWC founder Florence Ariosto Jones;
limited to 3,000 pieces
Price: $9,900
Variations: in red gold, limited to 1,000 pieces

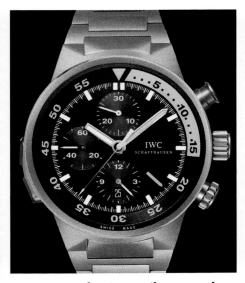

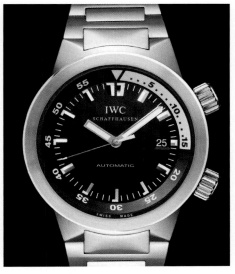

Aquatimer Split Minute Chronograph

Reference number: 372301
Movement: automatic, IWC Caliber 79470 (base ETA 7750); ø 30 mm, height 8.2 mm; 30 jewels; 28,800 vph
Functions: hours, minutes, subsidiary seconds; chronograph with additional separately stoppable minute hand (flyback)
Case: titanium, ø 44 mm, height 16.3 mm; unidirectionally rotating bezel under crystal with 60-minute divisions; sapphire crystal; screwed-in crown; water-resistant to 120 m
Band: titanium, folding clasp with security button clasp
Price: $10,300

Variations: with rubber strap

Aquatimer Automatic 2000

Reference number: 353804
Movement: automatic, IWC Caliber 30110 (base ETA 2892-A2); ø 25.6 mm, height 3.6 mm; 21 jewels; 28,800 vph
Functions: hours, minutes, sweep seconds; date
Case: titanium, ø 42 mm, height 14.8 mm; unidirectionally rotating bezel under crystal with 60-minute divisions; sapphire crystal; screwed-in crown; water-resistant to 2000 m
Band: rubber, folding clasp with security button clasp
Price: $4,000

Variations: with titanium link bracelet

Aquatimer Automatic

Reference number: 354801
Movement: automatic, IWC Caliber 30110 (base ETA 2892-A2); ø 25.6 mm, height 3.6 mm; 21 jewels; 28,800 vph
Functions: hours, minutes, sweep seconds; date
Case: stainless steel, ø 42 mm, height 12.8 mm; unidirectionally rotating bezel under crystal with 60-minute divisions; sapphire crystal; screwed-in crown; water-resistant to 1000 m
Band: stainless steel, folding clasp with security button clasp
Price: $5,000

Variations: with rubber strap

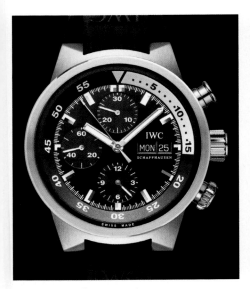

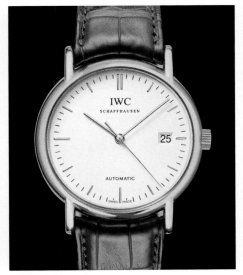

Aquatimer Chrono Automatic

Reference number: 371923
Movement: automatic, IWC Caliber 79320 (base ETA 7750); ø 30 mm, height 7.9 mm; 25 jewels; 28,800 vph
Functions: hours, minutes, subsidiary seconds; chronograph; date, day of the week
Case: stainless steel, ø 42 mm, height 13.4 mm; unidirectionally rotating bezel under crystal with 60-minute divisions; sapphire crystal; screwed-in crown; water-resistant to 120 m
Band: rubber, folding clasp with security button
Price: $4,500

Variations: with stainless steel bracelet; in titanium with rubber or titanium bracelet

Portofino Automatic

Reference number: 353318
Movement: automatic, IWC Caliber 30110 (base ETA 2892-A2); ø 25.6 mm, height 3.6 mm; 23 jewels; 28,800 vph
Functions: hours, minutes, sweep seconds; date
Case: red gold, ø 38 mm, height 8.6 mm; sapphire crystal
Band: reptile skin, buckle
Price: $6,600

Variations: with red gold bracelet; in stainless steel (with reptile skin strap or link bracelet)

Portofino Automatic

Reference number: 353314
Movement: automatic, IWC Caliber 30110 (base ETA 2892-A2); ø 25.6 mm, height 3.6 mm; 23 jewels; 28,800 vph
Functions: hours, minutes, sweep seconds; date
Case: yellow gold, ø 38 mm, height 8.6 mm; sapphire crystal
Band: reptile skin, buckle
Price: $6,600

Variations: with yellow gold bracelet; in stainless steel (with reptile skin strap or link bracelet)

Da Vinci

Reference number: 375811
Movement: automatic, IWC Caliber 79261 (base ETA 7750 with module for perpetual calendar)
Functions: hours, minutes, subsidiary seconds; chronograph; perpetual calendar with date, day of the week, month, four-digit year display, moon phase
Case: red gold, ø 41.5 mm, height 16.4 mm; sapphire crystal; screwed-in crown
Band: reptile skin, buckle
Price: $24,300
Variations: in stainless steel

Small Da Vinci

Reference number: 373605
Movement: quartz, IWC Caliber 630; mechanical chronograph module
Functions: hours, minutes, subsidiary seconds; chronograph; date; moon phase
Case: stainless steel, ø 29 mm, height 8.3 mm; sapphire crystal; screwed-in crown
Band: reptile skin, buckle
Price: $3,400
Variations: in yellow gold

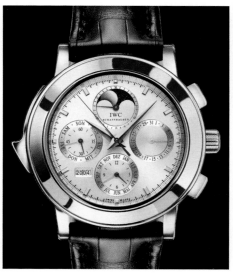

Grande Complication

Reference number: 377019
Movement: automatic, IWC Caliber 79091
Functions: hours, minutes, subsidiary seconds; chronograph; perpetual calendar with date, day of the week, month, year, moon phase; hour, quarter hour, and minute repeater
Case: yellow gold, ø 42.2 mm, height 16.3 mm; sapphire crystal; screwed-in crown
Band: reptile skin, buckle
Price: $195,000
Variations: in platinum

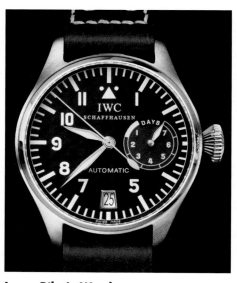

Large Pilot's Watch

Reference number: 500201
Movement: automatic, IWC Caliber 5011; ø 38.2 mm, height 7.44 mm; 44 jewels; 18,000 vph; Pellaton automatic winding (patented); theoretical power reserve 8 1/2 days, mechanically limited to 7 days; soft iron core for protection against magnetic fields
Functions: hours, minutes, sweep seconds; date; power reserve display
Case: stainless steel, ø 46.2 mm, height 15.8 mm; sapphire crystal; screwed-in crown; water-resistant to 60 m
Band: buffalo leather, folding clasp
Price: $12,900

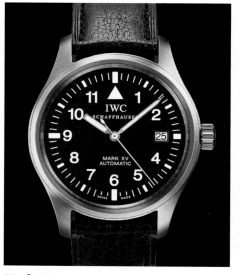

Mark XV

Reference number: 325301
Movement: automatic, IWC Caliber 37524 (base ETA 2892-A2); ø 25.6 mm, height 3.6 mm; 21 jewels; 28,800 vph; soft iron core for protection against magnetic fields
Functions: hours, minutes, sweep seconds; date
Case: stainless steel, ø 38 mm, height 10.5 mm; sapphire crystal; screwed-in crown; water-resistant to 60 m
Band: buffalo leather, folding clasp
Price: $3,400
Variations: with stainless steel bracelet

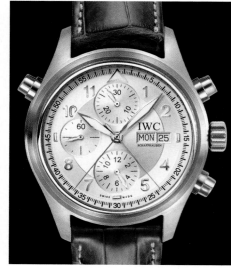

Pilot's Double Chrono Spitfire

Reference number: 371341
Movement: automatic, IWC Caliber 79230 (base ETA 7750); ø 30 mm, height 7.9 mm; 25 jewels; 28,800 vph; soft iron core for protection against magnetic fields
Functions: hours, minutes, subsidiary seconds; split-seconds chronograph; date, day of the week
Case: stainless steel, ø 42 mm, height 16.2 mm; sapphire crystal; screwed-in crown; water-resistant to 60 m
Band: reptile skin, buckle
Price: $9,200
Variations: with stainless steel bracelet

india:

journey

through the

heart of a

Roland and Sabrina Michaud   ·   Olivier Germain-Thomas

continent

This beautifully produced volume is a groundbreaking photographic journey, illustrated with 155 captivating images and illuminating the variety of cultural traditions that constitute life in modern India, one of the world's top five travel destinations.

Text by Olivier Germain-Thomas
Photographs by
Roland and Sabrina Michaud
155 full-color illustrations
324 pages · $10\frac{1}{4} \times 11\frac{3}{4}$ in. · Cloth
ISBN 0-7892-0869-5 · $75.00

Jacob & Co.

American pop culture would currently be unthinkable without Jacob & Co. From hip-hop to mainstream, and from sportscaster to movie diva, anyone who's anyone is wearing a watch by "Jacob the Jeweler" these days.

This type of attention positively smacks of the short-lived and cheap. And even though Jacob's masterfully designed, overly large timepieces kicked off a trend all their own — even calling to life a great deal of "icy" copycats, certainly the purest form of flattery — they are anything but cheap and trendy. Jacob Arabo grew up in Russia, where his passion for creating jewelry developed during his formative years. After immigrating to the United States as a teenager, Arabo enrolled in a jewelry design course with the intent of developing his natural talents. Showing exceptional aptitude, he was urged to begin his career in earnest and thus immediately began designing for a number of jewelry labels and private clients. In 1986, a short five years after that, Arabo opened his current company, Diamond Quasar, and from then on designed exclusively for his own label, Jacob & Co.

Despite the way the current collection might appear to conservative watch fans, these timepieces are not cheap throwaways. The bezels are interchangeable and screwed-down, and they even come in a set including straps of varying color (and a changing tool!) and bezels to match the dial. The non-jeweled 40-mm collection begins at $8,800 and continues on up to about $62,000 in the 47-mm case. The Diamond Collection can burn a hole of up to $155,000 in one's wallet for full pavé and a jeweled map of the world on the dial.

Arabo's signature timepiece, aptly dubbed the 5 Time Zone Watch, was inspired both by his jewelry creations and the jet-set lifestyle of so many of the celebrity clients that he had meanwhile amassed. This timepiece is certainly unique. The colorful dial is separated into four fields, each representing the glamour-puss time zones L.A., New York, Paris, and Tokyo. The main sweep hands are used for the wearer's local time. Jacob & Co. has extended this theme almost as far as it can go and offers a veritable myriad of dial colors and materials (bling!) in precious metal cases. Although celebrities prefer to wear the in-your-face, 47-mm version, which is certainly visible at any distance and detectable by any TV camera, 40 mm versions do exist in all variations.

New in 2005, Jacob & Co. is currently in the process of releasing a mechanical version of the 5 Time Zone Watch. This timepiece's movement is based on the new ETA *ébauche* A07.111, which itself is based on ETA's own Valjoux 7750 without the chronograph functions, but has been duly modified by industry specialists to accommodate the large number of extra time zones. This watch is certainly the first of its kind, and deserving of any watch connoisseur's respect. Accordingly, it is limited to 1,800 pieces in stainless steel, 190 pieces in 18-karat gold, and 99 pieces in platinum.

Seriously contemplating a front attack on the *haute horlogerie* market, Jacob & Co. has even taken their mechanical complications a step further: Tourbillons sure to please all of the senses were likewise introduced in 2005. The Rainbow Tourbillon even features a total of twelve time zones divided amongst four subdials. Though they are fairly difficult to read, they are certainly pretty to look at and easy to appreciate.

Rainbow Tourbillon

Reference number: Rainbow 1
Movement: manually wound, Jacob Caliber JC100018
jewels; 21,600 vph, power reserve 120 hours; Jacob & Co.
engraving and colored bridges
Functions: hours, minutes, 12 time zones
Case: platinum, ø 47.5 mm, height 15.95 mm; sapphire
crystal; exhibition window case back; water-resistant to 30 m
Band: reptile skin, folding clasp
Remarks: limited edition of 18 pieces each in rose, yellow
and white gold as well as 18 pieces in platinum
Price: $305,000
Variations: rose, yellow, or white gold ($240,000)

Five Time Zone Automatic

Reference number: H-24
Movement: automatic, Jacob Caliber JC25 (base ETA
A07.111); ø 37.20 mm; 24 jewels; 28,800 vph, power
reserve 46 hours; Jacob & Co. engraving as well as two-tone
galvanization on automatic bridge and rotor
Functions: hours, minutes, sweep seconds; five time zones
Case: stainless steel, ø 48.5 mm, height 15.95 mm; sapphire
crystal; exhibition window case back; water-resistant to 30 m
Band: reptile skin, folding clasp
Remarks: limited edition of 1,800 pieces in steel, 190 pieces
in gold, and 99 pieces in platinum
Price: $12,800

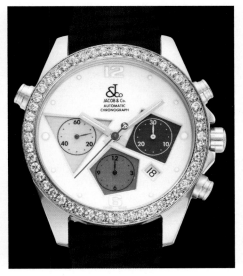

Automatic Chronograph

Reference number: AC-M4
Movement: automatic, ETA Caliber 7753; ø 30.40 mm,
height 7.90 mm; 27 jewels; 28,800 vph, power reserve
46 hours; top-quality finishing
Functions: hours, minutes, subsidiary seconds;
chronograph; date
Case: stainless steel, ø 40 mm, height 14.95 mm; interchangeable plain and diamond bezels, bezel with diamonds (2 ct);
mineral crystal; exhibition case back; water-resistant to 30 m
Band: reptile skin, delivered with additional four colored
polyurethane straps, folding clasp
Price: $10,200

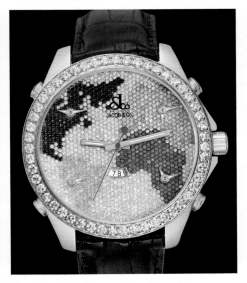

The World is Yours Five Time Zone

Reference number: JC-47
Movement: quartz, ø 17.50 mm, height 3.50 mm; 7 jewels:
ETA 956.112 for main display and 4 x ETA 280.002 for subdials
Functions: hours, minutes, sweep seconds; date; five time
zones total
Case: stainless steel, ø 47 mm, height 13.25 mm; interchange-
able plain and diamond bezels, 7.75 ct diamonds (3.25 on bezel
and 4.5 on dial); mineral crystal; water-resistant to 100 m
Band: reptile skin, delivered with additional four colored
polyurethane straps, folding clasp
Remarks: dial with natural pink, yellow and black diamonds
Price: $32,500

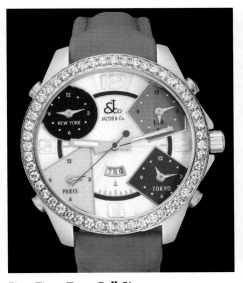

Five Time Zone Full Size

Reference number: JC-1
Movement: quartz; ø 17.50 mm, height 3.50 mm; 7 jewels;
five independent quartz movements: ETA 956.112 for main
display and 4 x ETA 280.002 to power subdial time zones
Functions: hours, minutes, sweep seconds; date; five time
zones total
Case: stainless steel, ø 47 mm, height 13.25 mm;
interchangeable plain and diamond bezels, with diamonds
(3.25 ct); mineral crystal; water-resistant to 100 m
Band: polyurethane, delivered with additional four colored
polyurethane straps, folding clasp
Price: $12,700

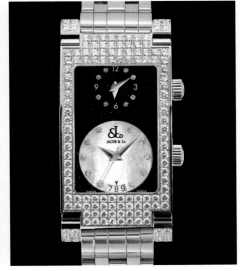

Angel Collection Two Time Zone

Reference number: JC-A18
Movement: quartz, ETA Calibers 956.112 and E01.001;
ø 11 mm, height 2.50 mm; 5 jewels; two independent quartz
movements, one for main dial with date and one for subdial
with second time zone
Functions: hours, minutes, sweep seconds; date,
second time zone
Case: stainless steel, 44.20 x 24.80 mm, height 8.90 mm;
case paved with 3.30 ct diamonds; mineral crystal; screwed-
down case back; water-resistant to 30 m
Band: stainless steel, folding clasp
Price: $16,900

Jaeger-LeCoultre

After the Gyrotourbillon I that was so proudly presented last year — a timepiece that wrote a chapter in watch history all its own due to its unique technology — the bar was set high for the Jaeger-LeCoultre *manufacture*. How do you top such a masterpiece? By giving yourself the ultimate challenge, of course, and developing a new chronograph movement. Some probably would have wished for a more classic housing for the first chronograph movement with automatic winding to issue from the quite traditionally minded *manufacture* Jaeger-LeCoultre. Perhaps some might not have thought so much dynamic self-assurance possible from the quiet watchmakers in their distant Jura valley. But just possibly people thinking thoughts like these must have slept through the developments of the last couple years entirely; otherwise it

would have been clear to them that the Compressor family would be the only possible home for a new technical development of this scope.

The specifications of the new chronograph movement had been determined long before work had begun on it. It was to be a modern watch movement in line with today's technology and leaving no room for mundane column wheel nostalgia — even if Caliber 751/752 naturally contains just such a column wheel. This mechanism remains, of course, the most reliable and technically elegant solution for chronograph functions. Though progress is entirely admirable, it just can't hurt to look back on the work of the old masters now and then. This is something Jaeger-LeCoultre's watchmakers recognized when searching for a precision clutch system for their chronograph mechanism. They

decided upon an axial coupling connecting two gear wheels creating a frictional connection without delay without having to wait for the first available space as would two wheels that connect from the side. In its elementary proportions the Compressor case almost seems like an old friend, but now it bears three compressors on its right side, a crown and two buttons. All three are outfitted with the patented compression key, which guarantees absolute water resistance when rotated even just halfway. The buttons are also blocked by this rotation so that they can't be activated by accident.

The Master Compressor Extreme World Chronograph is a whole size bigger than the "normal" chronograph, for it is actually outfitted with an additional case. The movement is hermetically sealed in a container made of titanium, which is surrounded by the outer case. A little room to breathe remains, however, about 0.5 mm between the bezel and the case back, and thanks to a clever shock-protection system, this extra room can keep strong impacts from affecting the sensitive workings of the watch movement. Tests have proven that it is especially shocks coming from an axial direction that do the most damage to a watch.

The generously dimensioned case also possesses a spring mechanism on its back so that straps can be easily changed by its owner. Switching between leather, rubber, and metal bands is child's play on this watch and does not require the use of any type of tools. Jaeger-LeCoultre has belonged to the Richemont group for five years now, and brand developments with more and more new movement designs of the most modern kind have made the company a real topic of discussion in recent years. These are not only used in the brand's own model palette, but also in those of the large concern's sibling brands. Supplying watch movements to competitor brands outside of the group is thus being reduced more and more.

Master Minute Repeater Antoine LeCoultre

Reference number: 164 64 20
Movement: manually wound, JLC Caliber 947; ø 34.7 mm, height 8.95 mm; 41 jewels; 21,600 vph; twin spring barrels, 15 days power reserve
Functions: hours, minutes; minute repeater; power reserve display, torque display
Case: platinum, ø 44 mm, height 15 mm; sapphire crystal; exhibition window case back; water-resistant to 50 m
Band: reptile skin, folding clasp
Remarks: limited to 200 pieces
Price: $175,000

Master Grand Réveil

Reference number: 163 64 4A
Movement: automatic, JLC Caliber 909/1; ø 30 mm, height 8.3 mm; 36 jewels; 28,800 vph
Functions: hours, minutes, sweep seconds; perpetual calendar (date, day of the week, month, double moon phase, year); alarm; display of alarm function (choice of gong or vibration)
Case: platinum, ø 43 mm, height 16 mm; sapphire crystal; water-resistant to 50 m
Band: reptile skin, folding clasp
Price: $54,000
Variations: in red gold; in stainless steel

Master Calendar

Reference number: 151 24 2D
Movement: automatic, JLC Caliber 924; ø 26 mm, height 4.9 mm; 32 jewels; 28,800 vph
Functions: hours, minutes, subsidiary seconds; date, day of the week, month, moon phase; power reserve display
Case: red gold, ø 40 mm, height 13 mm; sapphire crystal; exhibition window case back; water-resistant to 50 m
Band: reptile skin, folding clasp
Price: $15,000
Variations: in stainless steel (with leather strap or link bracelet)

Master Control

Reference number: 139 24 20
Movement: automatic, JLC Caliber 899; ø 26 mm, height 3.3 mm; 32 jewels; 28,800 vph
Functions: hours, minutes, sweep seconds; date
Case: red gold, ø 40 mm, height 9 mm; sapphire crystal; exhibition window case back; water-resistant to 50 m
Band: reptile skin, folding clasp
Price: $11,000
Variations: in stainless steel (with leather strap or link bracelet)

Master Gyrotourbillon

Reference number: 600 64 20
Movement: manually wound, JLC Caliber 177; ø 36.3 mm, height 10.85 mm; 77 jewels; 21,600 vph; spherical tourbillon with two rotating axes, power reserve 150 hours; ltd. to 75
Functions: hours, minutes, subsidiary seconds (on tourbillon cage); direct display of equation of time; perpetual calendar with date (two retrograde hands), month (retrograde) and leap year (on back); power reserve display
Case: platinum, ø 43 mm, height 14.9 mm; sapphire crystal; case back with small exhibition window
Band: reptile skin, folding clasp
Price: $325,000

Master Eight Days Perpetual

Reference number: 161 24 2D
Movement: manually wound, JLC Caliber 876; height 6.6 mm; 37 jewels; 28,800 vph; twin spring barrels, power reserve 8 days
Functions: hours, minutes; perpetual calendar with date, day of the week, month, year (four-digit); day/night indication; power reserve display
Case: red gold, ø 41.5 mm, height 11 mm; sapphire crystal; exhibition window case back; water-resistant to 50 m
Band: reptile skin, folding clasp
Price: $38,500
Variations: in platinum with reptile skin strap

Master Eight Days

Reference number: 160 24 20
Movement: manually wound, JLC Caliber 877; ø 32 mm, height 5.3 mm; 25 jewels; 28,800 vph; twin spring barrels, power reserve 8 days; movement with decorated with *côtes Soleillées*
Functions: hours, minutes, subsidiary seconds; large date; day/night indication; power reserve display
Case: red gold, ø 41.5 mm, height 10.9 mm; sapphire crystal; exhibition window case back; water-resistant to 50 m
Band: reptile skin, folding clasp
Price: $16,750

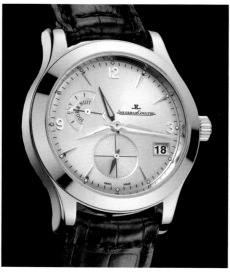

Master Hometime

Reference number: 162 84 20
Movement: automatic, JLC Caliber 975; ø 30 mm, height 5.7 mm; 29 jewels; 28,800 vph; ceramic bearing rotor
Functions: hours, minutes, subsidiary seconds; separately adjustable hour hand (second time zone); day/night indication (coupled to main time); date
Case: stainless steel, ø 40 mm, height 10 mm; sapphire crystal; exhibition window case back; water-resistant to 50 m
Band: reptile skin, folding clasp
Price: $6,150
Variations: with stainless steel bracelet; in red gold with leather strap

Master Compressor Extreme World Chronograph

Reference number: 176 84 70
Movement: automatic, JLC Caliber 752; ø 25.6 mm, height 5.6 mm; 41 jewels; 28,800 vph; ceramic bearing rotor
Functions: hours, minutes, subsidiary seconds (red/white disk display); chronograph; date; display of 24 time zones
Case: titanium/stainless steel, ø 46.3 mm, height 17 mm; double case with anti-shock system; sapphire crystal; compression key system on crown and buttons (patented)
Band: reptile skin, folding clasp
Price: $12,750
Variations: in titanium/platinum limited to 200 pieces

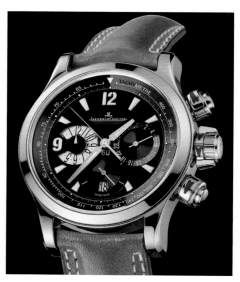

Master Compressor Chronograph

Reference number: 175 84 70
Movement: automatic, JLC Caliber 751; ø 25.6 mm, height 5.6 mm; 41 jewels; 28,800 vph; ceramic bearing rotor
Functions: hours, minutes, subsidiary seconds; chronograph; date
Case: stainless steel, ø 41.5 mm, height 14 mm; sapphire crystal; compression key system on crown and buttons (patented); water-resistant to 100 m
Band: reptile skin, folding clasp
Price: $8,450
Variations: in red gold (with leather strap or red gold bracelet); in stainless steel with link bracelet

Master Compressor Chronograph Lady

Reference number: 174 84 70
Movement: quartz, JLC Caliber 631 Mecaquartz; ø 23.3 mm, height 3.7 mm; 25 jewels; 32,768 Hz; quartz-based movement with mechanical chronograph dial train
Functions: hours, minutes, subsidiary seconds; chronograph; date
Case: stainless steel, ø 36.8 mm, height 11 mm; sapphire crystal; compression key system on crown and buttons (patented); water-resistant to 100 m
Band: calf skin, folding clasp
Price: $4,500
Variations: in red gold; in stainless steel

Master Compressor Dualmatic

Reference number: 173 84 70
Movement: automatic, JLC Caliber 972; ø 30 mm, height 6.14 mm; 29 jewels; 28,800 vph
Functions: hours, minutes, subsidiary seconds; separately adjustable hour hand (second time zone); 24-hour display (coupled with second time zone), date
Case: stainless steel, ø 41.5 mm, height 11 mm; bidirectionally rotating bezel under crystal; sapphire crystal; compression key system on crown and buttons (patented); water-resistant to 100 m
Band: leather, folding clasp
Price: $6,400

JeanRichard

According to legend, Daniel JeanRichard was fourteen years old when he held his first watch in his hand in 1679. And it didn't even work. A horse dealer on his way through town had noticed the filigreed iron wares and silver jewelry that young Daniel had put together. The dealer had an English pocket watch in his baggage that had stopped working somewhere between London and Basel. The young JeanRichard with his obvious talent appeared trustworthy to him, and he gave Daniel the valuable timepiece to repair. He wanted to pick it up again a few weeks later on his way home from Geneva.

And Daniel JeanRichard actually did repair the watch with his primitive tools. During the repair process he also memorized all of the details, allowing him to build an exact replica of the watch during the following winter. In the middle of nowhere, somewhere between Geneva and the French border in the Jura region of Switzerland, where the snow piled so high in the winter that the farms were covered and their residents sometimes didn't see their neighbors for weeks at a time, in the village of La Sagne, nestled in a valley between La Chaux-de-Fonds and Le Locle, is exactly where a boy achieved that

which no one in the entire canton of Neuchâtel had accomplished until then: He made an entire pocket watch from nothing, just his memory.

Today, Massimo Macaluso directs Jean-Richard's business. He was just a few years older than the brand's namesake when his father first introduced him to the world of watches. Despite this, the Italian has still been able to retain his wonderful youthful enthusiasm. After working for many years in an import business for Swiss watches, his father, Luigi Macaluso, bought his own Swiss watch brand. Using the Girard-Perregaux *manufacture* as a springboard, he created JeanRichard as a second brand and systematically extended the collection, heading it toward the more upscale — so that it now even includes a tourbillon.

The next big step was already taken under the aegis of Massimo: The introduction of an autonomous movement by the caliber name of JR 1000, produced exclusively for JeanRichard by GP Manufacture. We are not talking about a redecorated Girard-Perregaux caliber, which would have been far too expensive for what it was intended. No, Caliber JR 1000 displays a number of unique characteristics, such as subsidiary

seconds which are driven outside of the flow of energy by a micromodule gear wheel with a special tooth shape that can also double as the driving source for additional complications if necessary. Additionally, the use of a double third wheel makes it possible to arrange a direct sweep seconds display under its own power, making room for a larger spring barrel if necessary.

With Girard-Perregaux's know-how in the background, JeanRichard introduced a minute repeater with an imposing cathedral gong as this year's highlight, the movement of which is finished by hand and also features a little turning fine adjustment that is regulated by hand. The company has even had a wooden tone amplifier built for its treasure. The movement is housed in the company's characteristic square TV screen case. But because technologies of the future are created by understanding traditions, Jean-Richard has moved into the main building of Schwob Frères in La Chaux-de-Fonds, the founding place of the Cyma watch brand, and opened an interesting museum for tools and tooling machines in the building now known as Villa JeanRichard, just a short walking distance from Girard-Perregaux's headquarters.

Paramount JR 1000

Reference number: 61108-11-60A-AA6
Movement: automatic, JR Caliber 1000; ø 25.6 mm, height 5.1 mm; 32 jewels; 28,800 vph; twin spring barrels; 22-karat white gold oscillating weight
Functions: hours, minutes, subsidiary seconds; date
Case: stainless steel, 34.3 x 36.5 mm, height 11.15 mm; sapphire crystal
Band: reptile skin, buckle
Remarks: limited to 1,000 pieces
Price: $4,250
Variations: in rose gold, limited to 25 pieces

Caliber JR 100

Movement: Girard-Perregaux's sibling brand proudly presents its first autonomous movement, JR 1000. This movement features a modern design with an incredibly low amount of elements borrowed from other calibers made by GP Manufacture, Girard-Perregaux's movement department — and now JeanRichard's as well.

Paramount Square

Reference number: 62118-11-61A-AAE
Movement: automatic, JR Caliber 10RJ (base JR 1000); ø 25.6 mm; height 4.9 mm; 25 jewels; 28,800 vph; linear display of power reserve indication
Functions: hours, minutes, sweep seconds; date; power reserve display
Case: stainless steel, 36.3 x 36.9 mm, height 12.1 mm; sapphire crystal
Band: reptile skin, buckle
Price: $7,250
Variations: with white dial

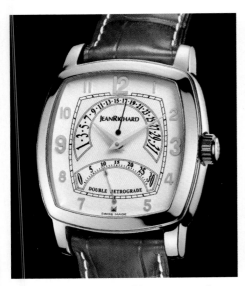

Grand TV Screen Double Rétrograde

Reference number: 23116-49-10A-AAE
Movement: automatic, JR Caliber 23 (base ETA 2892-A2); ø 25.6 mm, height 4.35 mm; 30 jewels; 28,800 vph
Functions: hours, minutes, subsidiary seconds (retrograde); date (retrograde)
Case: rose gold, 39 x 41 mm, height 11 mm; sapphire crystal
Band: reptile skin, buckle
Price: $17,500

TV Screen Minute Repeater

Reference number: 86016-53-10A-AAED
Movement: manually wound, JR Caliber 88 (base Christophe Claret); ø 30 mm; height 6.8 mm; 32 jewels; 28,800 vph; finely finished movement, decorated by hand
Functions: hours, minutes, subsidiary seconds; hour, quarter hour, and minute repeater
Case: white gold, 43 x 45 mm, height 13.85 mm; sapphire crystal; exhibition window case back
Band: reptile skin, folding clasp
Remarks: limited to six pieces
Price: $260,000

TV Screen Perpetual Calendar

Reference number: 80116-53-10A-AA4D
Movement: automatic, JR Caliber 80 33 QJ (base 25.6 mm, height 7.55 mm; 27 jewels; 28,800 vph
Functions: hours, minutes, sweep seconds; perpetual calendar (date, day of the week, month, moon phase, leap year)
Case: white gold, 39 x 41 mm, height 11 mm; sapphire crystal
Band: reptile skin, folding clasp
Price: $42,000
Variations: in rose gold

TV Screen Milady Joaillerie

Reference number: 26113 E 11B-A6A
Movement: automatic, JR Caliber 25 (base ETA 2671);
ø 17.2 mm, height 4.8 mm; 25 jewels; 28,800 vph
Functions: hours, minutes, sweep seconds; date
Case: stainless steel, 31.7 x 28.7 mm, height 9.7 mm;
bezel set with emeralds; sapphire crystal
Band: stingray, folding clasp
Price: $18,500
Variations: in various color variations

TV Screen Milady

Reference number: 26113-49-11A-AF2
Movement: automatic, JR Caliber 26 (base ETA 2671);
ø 17.2 mm, height 4.8 mm; 25 jewels; 28,800 vph
Functions: hours, minutes, sweep seconds; date
Case: rose gold, 31.7 x 28.7 mm, height 9.7 mm;
sapphire crystal
Band: satin, buckle
Remarks: genuine mother-of-pearl-dial
Price: upon request
Variations: in various dial and strap variations; in stainless
steel on strap ($2,500) or bracelet ($2,950)

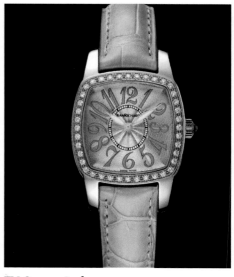

TV Screen Lady

Reference number: 26006-D11A91A-AA9D
Movement: automatic, JR Caliber 26 (base ETA 2671);
ø 17.2 mm; height 4.8 mm; 25 jewels; 28,800 vph
Functions: hours, minutes, sweep seconds
Case: stainless steel, 28 x 29 mm, height 9.48 mm;
bezel set with 44 brilliant-cut diamonds; sapphire crystal
Band: reptile skin, folding clasp
Price: upon request
Variations: without diamonds ($2,000 on bracelet or
$1,500 on strap); with completely paved case

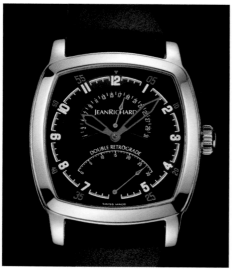

TV Screen Double Rétrograde

Reference number: 23116-11-61A-AC6
Movement: automatic, JR Caliber 23 (base ETA 2892-A2
with module 2315 by Agenhor); ø 25.6 mm, height 4.35 mm;
30 jewels; 28,800 vph
Functions: hours, minutes, subsidiary seconds (retrograde);
date (retrograde)
Case: stainless steel, 39 x 41 mm, height 11 mm;
sapphire crystal
Band: rubber, folding clasp
Price: $8,500
Variations: with leather strap; in rose gold ($17,500);
diverse dial variations

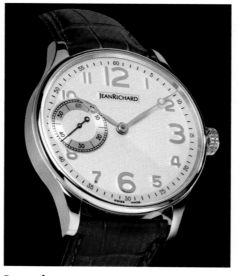

Bressel

Reference number: 16012-11-10B-AAED
Movement: manually wound, JR Caliber 16 (base ETA
6497-2 Unitas); ø 36.6 mm, height 4.5 mm; 17 jewels;
21,600 vph
Functions: hours, minutes, subsidiary seconds
Case: stainless steel, ø 43 mm, height 10.75 mm;
mineral crystal
Band: reptile skin, folding clasp
Price: $2,350
Variations: various dials; in rose gold ($17,500)

TV Screen Chronoscope

Reference number: 25030-11-EOA-AAED
Movement: automatic, JR Caliber 25 (base ETA 2824-2
with module 2020 by Dubois-Dépraz); ø 28.8 mm,
height 6.9 mm; 51 jewels; 28,800 vph
Functions: hours, minutes, subsidiary seconds; chronograph
Case: stainless steel, 43.2 x 43.2 mm, height 14.5 mm;
bidirectionally rotating bezel under crystal with 60-minute
divisions; sapphire crystal
Band: reptile skin, buckle
Price: $3,950
Variations: various dials

21ST CENTURY
HOTEL

Newly built hotels are being admired throughout the world by travelers and architects, and this strikingly illustrated survey features the best new designs, from the lavishly appointed Ritz-Carlton Miami to a Quebec hotel constructed entirely of snow and ice.

By Graham Vickers
230 illustrations, 210 in full color
240 pages · 9¼ × 11¼ in. · Cloth
ISBN 0-7892-0859-8 · $65.00

Published by **ABBEVILLE PRESS**
137 Varick Street, New York, N.Y. 10013
1-800-ARTBOOK (in U.S. only)
Also available wherever fine books are sold
Visit us at www.abbeville.com

F. P. Journe

Born in 1957 in Marseille, France, a career as a watchmaker and movement designer was not necessarily the profession François-Paul Journe would have prophesied for himself at the time. If he had been a better student, he may have done something completely different with his life: He only embarked upon an apprenticeship as a watchmaker because he had been booted from school — and because his uncle had already gone down the same path. So perhaps it was something like genetic talent that got passed to him after all? He ended his education in Paris at the above-mentioned uncle's workshop, but soon thereafter he discovered that repairing watches as a simple watchmaker was no longer enough for him. He began to build his own movements, all the while dreaming of a tourbillon and then actually achieving it. He was barely twenty years old at the time. In order to realize his dream of making his own watches — an entire collection of them, as a matter of fact — Journe opened his first workshop in the Paris suburb of Saint-Germain-des-Prés, where he completed highly specialized instruments with numerous technical and aesthetic refinements for a very special type of collector clientele, with all work on the pieces lavishly done by hand. Additionally, he continued to work as a restorer of watches and clocks and for quite a while was in charge of caring for the timekeepers found in the museum Arts et Métiers.

In 1986 he joined the Academy of Independent Horologists, the world-renowned A.H.C.I., which provided a springboard to greater international fame. He moved from Paris to Geneva, where he founded his own brand, establishing it with a consistently developed collection and a logical, aesthetic language of the highest degree. Characteristic of Journe's design is the off-center arrangement of the dials, held by screwed-on, polished frames. While it is possible that these elements are also being reproduced by other reputable brands, this should be viewed as a form of flattery and not a reason for retreating from this unmistakable design. The most remarkable thing

Geneva's old city center considering the extravagant amount of attention and handwork that they receive in Journe's little *manufacture*.

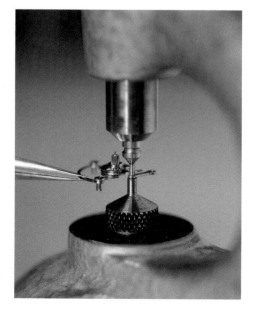

— and for a watchmaker the most unusual — is that Journe designs his watches from the outside in. This means that he first creates the "face" of the watch and arranges the displays purely from an aesthetic standpoint. Only at the end does he slip on the shoes of movement designer in order to arrange the functions found inside the watch correspondingly.

Horological specialties such as the Chronomètre à Resonance, the movement of which contains two independent balances swinging in a contrarotating manner to influence each other in a stabilizing way, secure Journe the undivided attention of watch collectors who are literally lined up to be the next one lucky enough to own one of his famous pieces. At least one entire annual production is always sold out in advance. But more than 700 to 1,000 watches per year are hardly to be expected from the building located in

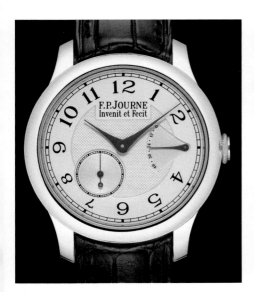

Chronomètre Souverain

Movement: automatic, FP Journe Caliber 1304; ø 30 mm, height 3.7 mm; 21 jewels; 21,600 vph; plates and bridges made of 18-karat rose gold; balance with "invisible" gear train connection; twin spring barrels

Functions: hours, minutes, subsidiary seconds; power reserve display

Case: platinum, ø 40 mm, height 6.5 mm; sapphire crystal; exhibition window case back

Band: crocodile skin, buckle in platinum

Price: $22,200

Variations: in rose gold ($18,900)

Chronomètre à Resonance

Movement: manually wound, FP Journe Caliber 1499-2; ø 32 mm, height 4.8 mm; 36 jewels; 21,600 vph; unique movement concept with two escapements that influence and stabilize each other; plates and bridges made of 18-karat gold

Functions: hours, minutes (double for two time zones); power reserve display

Case: platinum, ø 40 mm, height 9 mm; sapphire crystal; exhibition window case back

Band: crocodile skin, buckle in platinum

Price: $49,000

Variations: in rose gold ($45,000)

Tourbillon Souverain à seconde morte

Movement: manually wound, FP Journe Caliber 1403; ø 32 mm, height 6.35 mm; 26 jewels; 21,600 vph; one-minute tourbillon; escapement with "seconde morte"; patented remontoir; plates and bridges made of 18-karat gold

Functions: hours, minutes (off-center), subsidiary seconds; power reserve display

Case: platinum, ø 40 mm, height 10 mm; sapphire crystal; exhibition window case back

Band: platinum, folding clasp

Price: $121,500

Variations: in rose gold with crocodile skin strap ($96,200)

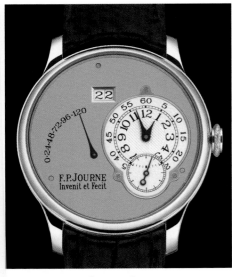

Octa Réserve de Marche

Movement: automatic, FP Journe Caliber 1300-2; ø 30 mm, height 5.7 mm; 30 jewels; 21,600 vph; twin spring barrels, power reserve 120 hours; plates and bridges made of 18-karat rose gold

Functions: hours, minutes (off-center), subsidiary seconds; large date; power reserve display

Case: platinum, ø 38 mm, height 10 mm; sapphire crystal; exhibition window case back

Band: crocodile skin, buckle in platinum

Price: $25,700

Variations: in red gold ($23,100)

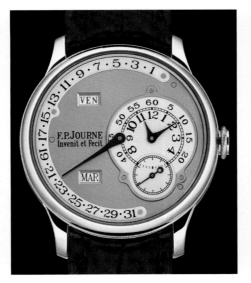

Octa Calendrier

Movement: automatic, FP Journe Caliber 1300-2; ø 30 mm, height 5.7 mm; 32 jewels; 21,600 vph; twin spring barrels, power reserve 120 hours; plates and bridges made of 18-karat rose gold

Functions: hours, minutes (off-center), subsidiary seconds; annual calendar with date (retrograde), day of the week and month; power reserve display

Case: platinum, ø 38 mm, height 10 mm; sapphire crystal; exhibition window case back

Band: crocodile skin, buckle in platinum

Price: $37,600

Variations: in red gold ($34,600)

Octa Divine

Movement: automatic, FP Journe Caliber 1300-2; ø 30 mm, height 5.7 mm; 32 jewels; 21,600 vph; twin spring barrels, power reserve 120 hours; plates and bridges made of 18-karat rose gold

Functions: hours, minutes (off-center), subsidiary seconds; large date, moon phase; power reserve display

Case: platinum, ø 38 mm, height 10.5 mm; sapphire crystal; exhibition window case back

Band: crocodile skin, buckle in platinum

Price: $30,500

Variations: in red gold ($27,900)

Urban Jürgensen & Sønner

Watches by Urban Jürgensen & Sønner are backed by more than two hundred years of watchmaking tradition. Since the company was founded in 1773, knowledge and experience have been passed on from generation to generation, and the construction of mechanical watch movements has developed into an art form.

In the eighteenth century, Urban Jürgensen manufactured precision timekeepers for seafarers and astronomers. The beauty and precision of his watches were the foundation on which his reputation as an outstanding expert in his field was built. King Frederik VI of Denmark appointed him official supplier to the Danish court, and the Danish Admiralty appointed him marine watchmaker to the Royal Navy.

Today, a small group of highly qualified watchmakers in Switzerland are preserving the image and tradition of what was once the greatest name in precision watchmaking. The new brand, Urban Jürgensen & Sønner, produces very small editions or individual complicated watches in a classical style of eternal beauty and unsurpassed quality. Three different workshops exclu-sively produce mechanical timekeepers, starting from the complete design of the movement, the solid precious-metal cases, and hand-guilloché dials and ending with the hands manufactured by hand in a truly anachronistic way from gold bars. Urban Jürgensen & Sønner products certainly live up to the name and the tradition of the company.

The small range of models encompasses wristwatches of which most have perpetual calendars (a specialty of the company) and can be equipped with either normal or split-seconds chronographs as well as particularly melodious and sophisticated minute re-peaters. A further specialty of Urban Jürgensen & Sønner is the one-minute tourbillon, which has been developed to perfection under the expert hands of the master watchmakers.

Upon special customer request, Urban Jürgensen & Sønner also manufactures high-quality, customized wristwatches and, in particular, pocket watches. Tourbillons, minute repeaters, perpetual calendars, jump hours — the client can have virtually anything he desires, if his wallet allows.

Reference 1

Movement: automatic, Caliber; ø 30 mm, height 11 mm; 31 jewels; 36,000 vph; very finely finished movement
Functions: hours, minutes, subsidiary seconds; chronograph; date, day of the week, month, moon phase
Case: platinum, ø 40 mm, height 14 mm; sapphire crystal
Band: reptile skin, buckle in platinum
Price: $71,000

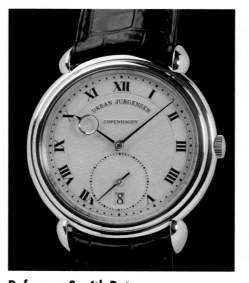

Reference 8 with Date

Movement: automatic, Caliber; ø 25.6 mm, height 3.25 mm; 31 jewels; 28,800 vph; twin spring barrels; very finely finished movement
Functions: hours, minutes, subsidiary seconds; with/without date
Case: platinum, ø 38 mm, height 8 mm; sapphire crystal; exhibition window case back
Band: reptile skin, buckle in platinum
Price: $27,400
Variations: in yellow or rose gold

Minute Repeater

Movement: manually wound, Caliber; very finely finished movement
Functions: hours, minutes, subsidiary seconds; hour, quarter hour, and minute repeater
Case: platinum, ø 40 mm, height 11 mm; sapphire crystal
Band: reptile skin, buckle in platinum
Price: $272,800

Kurth

Just about twelve miles north of Cologne lies the small town of Kerpen, nowadays world renowned as the hometown of multiple Formula 1 world champion Michael Schumacher and his brother Ralf. Motors roar in Kerpen, of course, but extraordinary watches were also produced here until recently. Now Franz Kurth has retired to the absolute tranquility of the picturesque Eifel town Dorsel.

At an age when most men are beginning to speculate on retirement, Kurth still goes to his workshop every day as usual for work. His atelier excels because it encompasses one of the most comprehensive "spare parts stores" for vintage Swiss precision watches. For some time now Kurth has been reworking parts of his enormous stock of old movements and has been putting them into solid, handmade cases of outstanding quality that have "it" in them — literally.

Each and every part of the manually wound movements is the result of time-consuming, meticulous craftsmanship. They are taken apart, skeletonized, engraved, gilded, polished, ground, beveled, refined, and fine-tuned or improved with a new fine adjustment.

Kurth's collection cannot be categorized in terms of style, but rather orients itself colossally on the availability of the vintage *manufacture* movements used. Despite this, Kurth does manage to produce small series utilizing common movements by the *manufactures* Valjoux, Peseux, Unitas, and ETA.

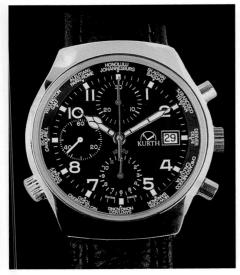

Anniversary World Time Chrono No. 2
Reference number: 2000-4St.Jubl.2
Movement: automatic, ETA Caliber 7750 Valjoux; ø 30 mm, height 7.9 mm; 25 jewels; 28,800 vph
Functions: hours, minutes, subsidiary seconds; chronograph; date
Case: stainless steel, ø 40 mm, height 14.75 mm; bidirectionally rotating bezel under crystal with world time zone divisions; mineral crystal; exhibition window case back
Band: leather, buckle
Price: 680 euros
Variations: without exhibition case back

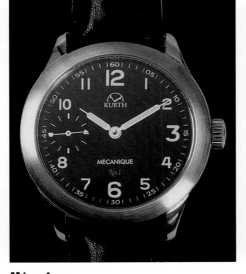

Mécanique
Reference number: 6497-4/St.
Movement: manually wound, ETA Caliber 6497 Unitas; ø 36.6 mm, height 4.5 mm; 17 jewels; 18,000 vph; finely finished movement
Functions: hours, minutes, subsidiary seconds
Case: stainless steel, ø 42 mm, height 9.8 mm; sapphire crystal; exhibition window case back
Band: leather, buckle
Price: 746 euros

Paris Chronograph
Reference number: 2009-1/G.
Movement: automatic, ETA Caliber 7750 Valjoux; ø 30 mm, height 7.9 mm; 25 jewels; 28,800 vph; finely finished movement
Functions: hours, minutes, subsidiary seconds; chronograph; date and day of the week
Case: yellow gold, ø 37.5 mm, height 13.3 mm; sapphire crystal; exhibition window case back
Band: leather, buckle in yellow gold
Price: 5,550 euros
Variations: in stainless steel

Kobold

Kobold is a watch company renowned for precise wrist instruments especially made for explorers and adventurers. Over the years, this small, family-owned company has been able to position itself among the crème de la crème of instrument watch manufacturers by concentrating on making watches for polar explorers, a small but elite segment of the market. "In recent years, the company's flagship watch, the Polar Surveyor Chronograph, was worn by more polar explorers and on more polar expeditions than any other watch," explains company founder Michael Kobold. There is a good reason for this: Kobold has recognized the fact that every timepiece is a potential lifeline. Therefore, the company's production department takes special care in ensuring the accuracy and uncompromising reliability of each Kobold the company delivers. Indeed, at temperatures as low as minus 90 degrees Celsius and weather conditions that include complete whiteouts and fierce winds, a polar explorer's equipment can mean the difference between life and death. "My life depends on accurate timing and navigation," confirms legendary explorer Ben Saunders, a longtime Kobold wearer.

The Polar Surveyor Chronograph was introduced in 2002 after more than two years of continuous research and design. It is the world's first automatic wristwatch to feature displays for local time, a second time zone (24-hour display), the date, a chronograph, and an AM/PM indicator for local time. The latter is a most crucial function, allowing polar explorers to determine whether it is night or day during months of perpetual daylight. The Polar Surveyor Chronograph, which was developed in cooperation with legendary polar explorer Sir Ranulph Fiennes, is housed in the company's Soarway case, which consists of thirty-two individual parts. Its core is milled from a solid block of surgical stainless steel and features screw-locked strap bars, push pieces, case back, and crown for extra security and water resistance.
In 2005, Kobold launched the Soarway Diver SEAL, a wristwatch manufactured especially for deep-sea divers. The SEAL is of generous proportions, measuring 44 mm in diameter and a whopping 17.75 mm in height. This wristwatch's size was determined by actor and *Soprano*-star James Gandolfini, one of Kobold's friends and a man of generous proportions himself. "Jim told me that my watches were too small for

him, so we set out to design a watch for big people like him," explains the company's twenty-six-year-old founder. The watch was later named after this particular sea creature because it most resembled "what Jim would look like in a diver's suit," Kobold adds with hearty enthusiasm. Gandolfini later appeared in a controversial print ad campaign for the company in which he wears his SEAL prototype, indicating with his middle finger that he thinks "Kobold is No. 1."
The SEAL, boasting a water resistance of 1,000 meters, was well received among professional and amateur divers, collectors, and a host of celebrities. Former U.S. president Bill Clinton was seen wearing his SEAL shortly after the watch made its debut, and actor Kiefer Sutherland wears one in the popular prime-time TV series *24*. In 2006, Kobold plans to introduce titanium and PVD-coated versions of the SEAL as well as a limited edition of five rose gold models.
While the Kobold brand is continuing to gain in popularity among connoisseurs, its energetic founder maintains that "Kobold will never produce more than 2,500 watches per year," thus ensuring that the brand remains "a boutique watch company with a unique character."

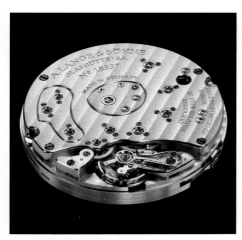

Caliber L 901.0 (Lange 1)

Mechanical with manual winding; twin serially operating spring barrels, power reserve 72 hours, stop-seconds

Functions: hours, minutes, subsidiary seconds; large date; power reserve indicator

Diameter: 30.4 mm; **Height:** 5.9 mm

Jewels: 53, including 9 screw-mounted gold chatons

Balance: glucydur with weighted screws

Frequency: 21,600 vph

Balance spring: Nivarox 1 with special terminal curve and swan-neck fine adjustment; beat adjustment via regulating screw

Shock protection: Incabloc

Remarks: chiefly manufactured, assembled, and decorated by hand according to highest quality criteria

Caliber L 901.5 (dial side)

Mechanical with manual winding; twin serially operating spring barrels, power reserve 72 hours, stop-seconds

Functions: hours, minutes, subsidiary seconds; large date; moon phase

Diameter: 30.4 mm; **Height:** 5.9 mm

Jewels: 54, including 9 screw-mounted gold chatons

Balance: glucydur with weighted screws

Frequency: 21,600 vph

Balance spring: Nivarox 1 with special terminal curve and swan-neck fine adjustment; beat adjustment via regulating screw

Remarks: chiefly manufactured, assembled, and decorated by hand according to highest quality criteria; moon phase driven by hour wheel, thus continuously in motion; precise dial train with deviation of only one day in 122.6 years

Caliber L 031.1 (Lange Time Zone)

Mechanical with manual winding; twin serially operating spring barrels, power reserve 72 hours, stop-seconds

Functions: hours, minutes, subsidiary seconds, second time zone with reference city ring; large date; power reserve display; day/night indication for both time zones

Diameter: 34.1 mm; **Height:** 6.65 mm

Jewels: 54, 9 of which are in screw-mounted chatons

Balance: glucydur with weighted screws

Frequency: 21,600 vph; Balance spring: Nivarox 1 with special terminal curve and swan-neck fine adjustment; beat adjustment with regulating screw;

Shock protection: Incabloc

Remarks: chiefly manufactured, assembled, and decorated by hand according to the highest quality criteria

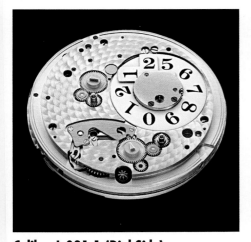

Caliber L 031.1 (Dial Side)

The new movement found in the Lange 1 Time Zone shown here from the dial side. The mechanism for synchronizing the reference city and the second time zone can well be seen from this angle, as can the hand chucks for the two day/night indications for both the local and home times.

Caliber L 921.4 (Langematik)

Mechanical with automatic winding, bidirectionally winding three-quarter rotor in 21-karat gold and platinum, winding mechanism with four micro-ball bearings; power reserve 46 hours, stop-seconds with automatic return to zero ("zero reset")

Functions: hours, minutes, subsidiary seconds; large date

Diameter: 30.4 mm; **Height:** 5.55 mm; **Jewels:** 45

Balance: glucydur with weighted screws

Frequency: 21,600 vph

Balance spring: Nivarox 1 with swan-neck fine adjustment; beat adjustment via regulating screw

Shock protection: Incabloc

Remarks: chiefly manufactured, assembled, and decorated by hand according to highest quality criteria

Related calibers: L 921.2 (SAX-O-MAT without date, 36 jewels)

Caliber L 922.1 (Langematik Perpetual)

Mechanical with automatic winding, bidirectionally winding three-quarter rotor in 21-karat gold and platinum; power reserve 46 hours, stop-seconds with automatic return to zero ("zero reset")

Functions: hours, minutes, subsidiary seconds; perpetual calendar (large date, day, month, moon phase, leap year); 24-hour display with day/night indication

Diameter: 30.4 mm; **Height:** 5.4 mm; **Jewels:** 43

Balance: glucydur with weighted screws

Frequency: 21,600 vph

Balance spring: Nivarox 1 with swan-neck fine adjustment; beat adjustment via regulating screw

Shock protection: Incabloc

Remarks: synchronized/ind. setting of calendar functions

Caliber L 001.1 (Lange Double Split)

Mechanical with manual winding; power reserve 36 hours, stop-seconds; isolator mechanis; two column wheels for chrono

Functions: hours, minutes, subsidiary seconds; large date; chronograph with flyback function and double rattrapante for seconds and minutes

Diameter: 30.6 mm; **Height:** 9.54 mm

Jewels: 40 including 4 screw-mounted gold chatons

Balance: glucydur with eccentric regulating screws

Frequency: 21,600 vph

Balance spring: on-premises manufacture with collet (patent pending), swan-neck fine adjustment

Shock protection: Incabloc

Remarks: chiefly manufactured, assembled, and decorated by hand according to highest quality criteria

Caliber L 951.1 (Datograph)

Mechanical with manual winding; power reserve 36 hours, stop-seconds; column wheel for chronograph functions

Functions: hours, minutes, subsidiary seconds; large date; chronograph with flyback mechanism and exactly jumping minute counter

Diameter: 30.6 mm; **Height:** 7.5 mm

Jewels: 40, including 4 screw-mounted gold chatons

Balance: glucydur with weighted screws

Frequency: 18,000 vph

Balance spring: Nivarox 1 with special terminal curve and swan-neck fine adjustment; beat adjustment via regulating screw

Remarks: chiefly manufactured, assembled, and decorated by hand according to highest quality criteria

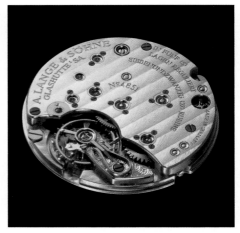

Caliber L 942.1 (1815 Up and Down)

Mechanical with manual winding, power reserve 45 hours, stop-seconds

Functions: hours, minutes, subsidiary seconds; power reserve display

Diameter: 25.6 mm

Height: 3.7 mm

Jewels: 27, including 6 screw-mounted gold chatons

Balance: glucydur with weighted screws

Frequency: 21,600 vph

Balance spring: Nivarox 1 with swan-neck fine adjustment; beat adjustment via regulating screw

Shock protection: Incabloc

Remarks: chiefly manufactured, assembled, and decorated by hand according to highest quality criteria

Caliber L 931.3 (Cabaret)

Mechanical with manual winding, power reserve 42 hours, stop-seconds

Functions: hours, minutes, subsidiary seconds; large date

Dimensions: 25.6 x 17.6 mm

Height: 4.95 mm

Jewels: 30, including 3 screw-mounted gold chatons

Balance: glucydur with weighted screws

Frequency: 21,600 vph

Balance spring: Nivarox 1 with swan-neck fine adjustment; beat adjustment via regulating screw

Shock protection: Incabloc

Remarks: chiefly manufactured, assembled, and decorated by hand according to highest quality criteria

Caliber L 931.3 (Cabaret Moon Phase)

Mechanical with manual winding, power reserve 42 hours, stop-seconds

Functions: hours, minutes, subsidiary seconds; large date; moon phase

Dimensions: 25.6 x 17.6 mm

Height: 5.05 mm

Jewels: 31, including 3 screw-mounted gold chatons

Balance: glucydur with weighted screws

Frequency: 21,600 vph

Balance spring: Nivarox 1 with swan-neck fine adjustment; beat adjustment via regulating screw

Shock protection: Incabloc

Remarks: chiefly manufactured, assembled, and decorated by hand according to highest quality criteria

Caliber L 941.3 (Saxonia)

Mechanical with manual winding, power reserve 42 hours, stop-seconds

Functions: hours, minutes, subsidiary seconds; large date

Diameter: 25.6 mm

Height: 4.95 mm

Jewels: 30, including 3 screw-mounted gold chatons

Balance: glucydur with weighted screws

Frequency: 21,600 vph

Balance spring: Nivarox 1 with swan-neck fine adjustment; beat adjustment via regulating screw

Shock protection: Incabloc

Remarks: chiefly manufactured, assembled, and decorated by hand according to highest quality criteria

This stunning celebration of the fifty most sought-after cars of all time, from the Rolls Royce Silver Ghost to the Ferrari F40, is now available in a newly revised and updated edition.

By Andrew Frankel
280 full-color illustrations
256 pages · 9 × 11⅜ in. · Cloth
ISBN 0-7892-0843-1 · $39.95

Limes

If the term *manufacture case* existed, it would hardly apply better to another watch manufacturer than to Limes. This company was originally purely a case maker, and for this reason Limes's watches shine in their wonderfully produced, classically designed cases.

The Ickler case manufacturer produces above all high-quality watch cases for internationally renowned customers using strict quality codes and "made in Germany." The different case parts are manufactured by highly qualified employees who work on the most modern of CNC machines. Both the treatment of the case surfaces and the assembly of the watches require a large amount of talent and training.

Ickler GmbH was founded in 1924 by Karl Ickler, a trained chain maker who worked as a production foreman in foreign companies at the beginning of his career. He founded the watch case manufacturing company upon returning to Pforzheim. After World War II, the company was rebuilt by the founder's sons, Heinz and Kurt. Today the

company is managed by a third-generation Ickler, Thomas, an industrial engineer who at the end of the 1990s decided not only to manufacture high-quality cases, but also complete watches.

In 1990 the company began producing private label watches. Decades-long experience in the watch industry, a high level of quality, an already established production capability, and above all the desire to create something of his own led Thomas Ickler to the planning of the watch brand Limes a few years later. The concept was clear: high-quality Swiss movements in lavish *manufacture* cases by Ickler.

The lion's share of the Limes collection, in stainless steel and titanium, can be purchased for between $500 and $2,500. Watches in 18-karat rose or white gold can cost up to the $5,500 mark. For this amount of money, the customer gets high-quality, well-outfitted, and stylistically attractive watches, which cultivate their own aesthetic apart from short-lived fashion trends and need not fear any

comparison to products from the established competition.

The new Pharo full calendar chronograph with moon phase is certainly a highlight of the Limes collection and combines technology and sophistication at an elevated level. The flat and very elegant watch has a larger case than its predecessor as well as a newly designed dial. The decorated chronograph movement Valjoux 7751 can be seen through the sapphire crystal covering the screwed-down case back.

Limes watches are so popular with watch fans because they are able to transmit the fascination of mechanics at a remarkable price-performance ratio. This is not only true of the aptly named model family Principio, whose Principio Polis was newly interpreted for 2005 in a rather simple incarnation and outfitted with reliable an ETA movement.

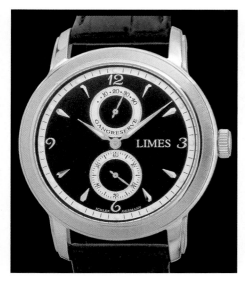

Pharo Power Reserve

Reference number: U6258-LHR1.3E
Movement: manually wound, ETA Caliber 7001 with module for power reserve display; ø 23.3 mm, height 2.5 mm (base caliber); 17 jewels; 21,600 vph
Functions: hours, minutes, subsidiary seconds; power reserve display
Case: stainless steel, ø 40 mm, height 9.4 mm; domed sapphire crystal, doubly anti-reflective; exhibition window case back; water-resistant to 50 m
Band: leather, buckle
Price: $1,595
Variations: in steel/gold; steel link or milanaise bracelet

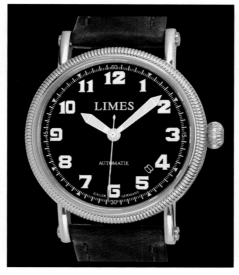

Classic Vintage 1924

Reference number: U7624R-LA4.2
Movement: automatic, ETA Caliber 2824; ø 25.6 mm, height 4.6 mm; 25 jewels; 28,800 vph
Functions: hours, minutes, sweep seconds; date
Case: stainless steel, ø 38 mm, height 9.6 mm; sapphire crystal; exhibition window case back; water-resistant to 50 m
Band: leather, buckle
Price: $595
Variations: dial in silver, black leather strap, stainless steel bracelet

112 Bauhaus

Reference number: U9427.1-LA3.1E
Movement: automatic, ETA Caliber 2892; ø 25.6 mm, height 3.75 mm; 21 jewels; 28,800 vph
Functions: hours, minutes
Case: stainless steel, ø 36.7 mm, height 7.2 mm; sapphire crystal; exhibition window case back; water-resistant to 50 m
Band: leather, buckle
Price: $895
Variations: various dial versions; with stainless steel bracelet

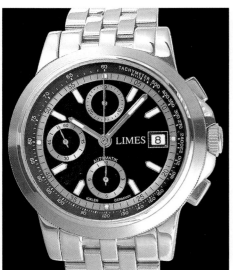

Endurance Polis

Reference number: U8715RB-LC2.1
Movement: automatic, ETA Caliber 7750; ø 30 mm, height 7.9 mm; 25 jewels; 28,800 vph
Functions: hours, minutes, subsidiary seconds; chronograph; date
Case: stainless steel, ø 41 mm, height 13.5 mm; sapphire crystal; exhibition window case back; water-resistant to 100 m
Band: stainless steel, double folding clasp
Price: $1,895
Variations: with silver dial; with stainless steel bracelet; as 3-hand watch with date (ETA 2824)

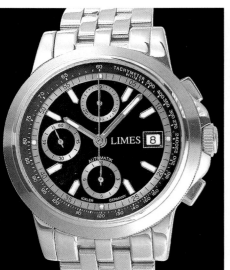

Endurance 1000

Reference number: U8787-LA2.2
Movement: automatic, ETA Caliber 2824; ø 25.6 mm, height 4.6 mm; 25 jewels; 28,800 vph
Functions: hours, minutes, sweep seconds; date
Case: stainless steel, ø 41.2 mm, height 12.2 mm; unidirectionally rotating bezel with 60-minute divisions; sapphire crystal; screwed-in crown; water-resistant to 1000 m
Band: rubber, folding security clasp
Price: $995
Variations: with leather strap with rubber coating; with stainless steel bracelet; as chronogaph (ETA 7750)

Integral Chrono

Reference number: U8484-LC4.1
Movement: automatic, ETA Caliber 7750; ø 30 mm, height 7.9 mm; 25 jewels; 28,800 vph
Functions: hours, minutes, subsidiary seconds, chronograph, date
Case: stainless steel, 38.5 x 41.3 mm, height 13.3 mm; sapphire crystal; exhibition window case back; water-resistant to 50 m
Band: leather, buckle
Price: $1,995
Variations: with black dial; with stainless steel bracelet; as 3-hand watch with date (ETA 2824)

Longines

Shortly after the beginning of the new century, Longines celebrated the manufacture of a total of 30 million watches since its founding in 1832. However, this is a company history that can be proud of a lot more than just high production numbers hiding behind a gigantic number of timepieces. Above all, what comes to light is that this old brand could occupy a much more prominent place within the brand hierarchy of the Swatch Group due to its immense history. Longines has outfitted polar researchers such as Amundsen and pioneers in aviation such as Lindbergh and von Weems with its products, later reaping an excellent reputation for board watches for airplanes and continuing to keep a hand in sports timing.

Longines is one of the few brands in recent years that has truly understood how to retain traditional values and classic watch design in its product palette while balancing them with a model policy dominated by the newest in watch technology and contemporary shapes.

The classic line is well represented by the Master Collection: Beautiful chronographs, one even containing only two subsidiary dials in a classically symmetric division, and men's watches with large date or power reserve displays mirror the glorious '40s of the Longines *manufacture*. In such successful remakes the pride of the brand is manifested time and again by highlighting its own achievements. Longines especially understands how to fulfill its position within

the larger group at the upper end of the middle segment without compulsively feeling the need to cling to its tradition with nostalgic flashbacks.

Seeing how modern, youthful, and full of élan the traditional brand's models such as DolceVita, Conquest, opposition, and Evidenza are today, it is certainly hard to believe that this is a company with a more than 170-year history. A visit to the company's own museum, however, quickly makes clear what a grand history this brand has enjoyed and with how much imagination and spirit of invention the company's employees have worked in the immense production building located on the outskirts of the small Jura town St. Imier. Here, in the museum located on the uppermost floor of the old factory building, it becomes apparent that Longines has been involved in just about every area of watch technology, often playing the role of pioneer and trendsetter in the industry.

This is, in fact, the case with the original Evidenza model family, styled after a Longines watch from the year 1925, which bull's-eyed consumers' taste during a time that was dominated by social upheaval and multilayered reorientation. Capturing such currents and turning them into product ideas is one of the most elementary demands on a designer, and those employed by Longines have always mastered this perfectly.

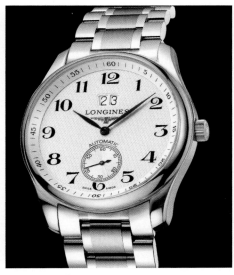

Master Collection Automatic

Reference number: L2.628.4.78.3
Movement: automatic, Longines Caliber L619 (base ETA 2892-A2); ø 25.6 mm, height 3.6 mm; 21 jewels; 28,800 vph
Functions: hours, minutes, sweep seconds; date
Case: stainless steel, ø 38.5 mm, height 9.1 mm; sapphire crystal; exhibition window case back
Band: reptile skin, double folding clasp
Price: $1,500
Variations: with metal bracelet

Master Collection Chronograph

Reference number: L2.629.4.78.3
Movement: automatic, Longines Caliber L651 (base ETA 2894-2); ø 28.6 mm, height 6.1 mm; 37 jewels; 28,800 vph
Functions: hours, minutes, subsidiary seconds; chronograph; date
Case: stainless steel, ø 40 mm, height 11.6 mm; sapphire crystal; exhibition window case back
Band: reptile skin, double folding clasp
Price: $2,100
Variations: with metal bracelet

Master Collection Large Date

Reference number: L2.676.4.78.6
Movement: automatic, Longines Caliber L601 (base ETA 2892-A2, modified); ø 30 mm, height 5.35 mm; 30 jewels; 28,800 vph
Functions: hours, minutes, subsidiary seconds; large date
Case: stainless steel, ø 40 mm, height 11.66 mm; sapphire crystal; exhibition window case back
Band: metal bracelet, double folding clasp
Price: upon request
Variations: with reptile skin strap ($2,000)

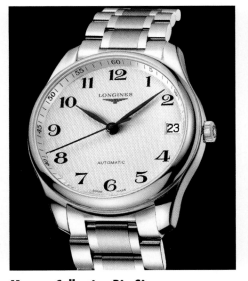

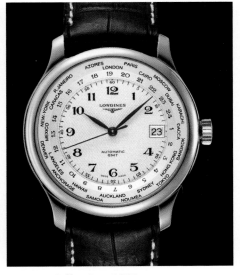

Master Collection Maxi

Reference number: L2.640.4.78.3
Movement: manually wound, Longines Caliber L512 (base ETA 6498-2 Unitas); ø 36.6 mm, height 4.5 mm; 17 jewels; 21,600 vph
Functions: hours, minutes, subsidiary seconds
Case: stainless steel, ø 47.5 mm, height 13.95 mm; sapphire crystal; exhibition window case back
Band: reptile skin, double folding clasp
Price: $2,300

Master Collection Big Size

Reference number: L2.665.4.78.6
Movement: automatic, Longines Caliber L691 (base ETA A07 111); ø 36.6 mm, height 7.9 mm; 24 jewels; 28,800 vph
Functions: hours, minutes, sweep seconds; date
Case: stainless steel, ø 42 mm, height 14.21 mm; sapphire crystal; exhibition window case back
Band: metal bracelet, double folding clasp
Price: $1,700
Variations: with reptile skin strap

Master Collection GMT

Reference number: L2.631.4.78.3
Movement: automatic, Longines Caliber L635 (base ETA 2824-2); ø 25.6 mm, height 4.6 mm; 25 jewels; 28,800 vph
Functions: hours, minutes, sweep seconds; date; 24-hour display disk with world time city (second time zone)
Case: stainless steel, ø 38.5 mm, height 10.95 mm; sapphire crystal; exhibition window case back
Band: reptile skin, double folding clasp
Price: $2,200
Variations: with metal bracelet

Master Collection Big Date

Reference number: L2.648.4.78.3
Movement: automatic, Longines Caliber L607 (base ETA 2896); ø 25.6 mm, height 4.85 mm; 21 jewels; 28,800 vph
Functions: hours, minutes, sweep seconds; large date
Case: stainless steel, ø 40 mm, height 11.06 mm; sapphire crystal; exhibition window case back
Band: reptile skin, double folding clasp
Price: $1,900
Variations: with metal bracelet

Master Collection Power Reserve

Reference number: L2.666.4.78.3
Movement: automatic, Longines Caliber L693 (base ETA A07 161); ø 36.6 mm, height 7.9 mm; 24 jewels; 28,800 vph
Functions: hours, minutes, sweep seconds; date; power reserve display
Case: stainless steel, ø 42 mm, height 14.21 mm; sapphire crystal; exhibition window case back
Band: reptile skin, double folding clasp
Price: $2,000
Variations: with metal bracelet

Master Collection Moon Phase

Reference number: L2.673.4.79.3
Movement: automatic, Longines Caliber L678 (base ETA 7751); ø 30 mm, height 7.9 mm; 25 jewels; 28,800 vph
Functions: hours, minutes, subsidiary seconds; chronograph; date, day of the week, month, moon phase; 24-hour display
Case: stainless steel, ø 40 mm, height 14.24 mm; sapphire crystal; exhibition window case back
Band: reptile skin, double folding clasp
Price: $2,600
Variations: with metal bracelet

Conquest 1958

Reference number: L1.611.6.78.2
Movement: automatic, Longines Caliber L633 (base ETA 2824-2); ø 25.6 mm, height 4.6 mm; 25 jewels; 28,800 vph
Functions: hours, minutes, sweep seconds; date
Case: rose gold, ø 35 mm, height 9.75 mm; Hesalite crystal
Band: reptile skin, buckle
Price: $2,800
Variations: in yellow gold

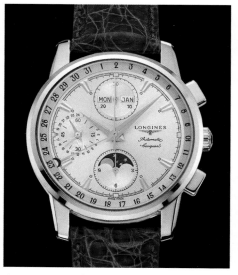

Conquest Replica Chronograph Moon Phase

Reference number: L1.642.4.76.3
Movement: automatic, Longines Caliber L678.2 (base ETA 7751); ø 30 mm, height 7.9 mm; 25 jewels; 28,800 vph
Functions: hours, minutes, subsidiary seconds; chronograph; date, day of the week, month, moon phase; 24-hour display
Case: stainless steel, ø 38.5 mm, height 13.8 mm; Hesalite crystal
Band: reptile skin, buckle
Price: upon request

Flagship Replica

Reference number: L4.746.8.72.0
Movement: automatic, Longines Caliber L609 (base ETA 2895-1); ø 25.6 mm, height 4.35 mm; 30 jewels; 28,800 vph
Functions: hours, minutes, subsidiary seconds
Case: rose gold, ø 35 mm, height 10.3 mm; Hesalite crystal
Band: reptile skin, buckle
Price: $2,800
Variations: in yellow gold

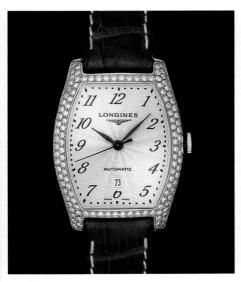

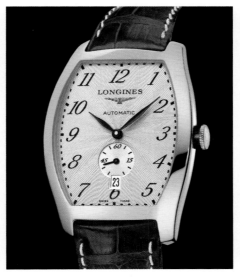

Evidenza

Reference number: L2.142.0.73.4
Movement: automatic, Longines Caliber L595 (base ETA 2000/1); ø 19.4 mm, height 3.6 mm; 20 jewels; 28,800 vph
Functions: hours, minutes, sweep seconds; date
Case: stainless steel, 26 x 30.6 mm, height 8.1 mm; case set with 156 diamonds; sapphire crystal
Band: reptile skin, double folding clasp
Price: $5,850
Variations: with black dial

Evidenza

Reference number: L2.642.6.73.2
Movement: automatic, Longines Caliber L615 (base ETA 2895/1); ø 25.6 mm, height 4.35 mm; 30 jewels; 28,800 vph
Functions: hours, minutes, subsidiary seconds; date
Case: yellow gold, 33.1 x 38.75 mm, height 10.45 mm; sapphire crystal
Band: reptile skin, buckle
Price: $3,825
Variations: in red gold

Evidenza Chronograph

Reference number: L2.643.8.73.2
Movement: automatic, Longines Caliber L650 (base ETA 2894-2); ø 28.6 mm, height 6.1 mm; 37 jewels; 28,800 vph
Functions: hours, minutes, subsidiary seconds; chronograph; date
Case: rose gold, 34.9 x 40 mm, height 12.45 mm; sapphire crystal
Band: reptile skin, buckle
Price: $5,925
Variations: in yellow gold

Evidenza Large Date

Reference number: L2.670.4.73.4
Movement: automatic, Longines Caliber L599 (base ETA 2892-A2, modified); ø 25.6 mm, height 5.35 mm; 30 jewels; 28,800 vph
Functions: hours, minutes, subsidiary seconds; large date
Case: stainless steel, 33.1 x 38.75 mm, height 10.45 mm; sapphire crystal
Band: reptile skin, double folding clasp
Price: $1,900
Variations: with black dial

Evidenza Power Reserve

Reference number: L2.672.4.73.4
Movement: automatic, Longines Caliber L602 (base ETA 2897-5); ø 25.6 mm, height 4.95 mm; 21 jewels; 28,800 vph
Functions: hours, minutes, sweep seconds; date; power reserve display
Case: stainless steel, 33.1 x 38.75 mm, height 10.45 mm; sapphire crystal
Band: reptile skin, double folding clasp
Price: $2,150
Variations: with black dial

Evidenza Moon Phase

Reference number: L2.671.4.79.4
Movement: automatic, Longines Caliber L600 (base ETA 2892-A2); ø 25.6 mm, height 5.35 mm; 21 jewels; 28,800 vph
Functions: hours, minutes, sweep seconds; date, day of the week, month, moon phase
Case: stainless steel, 33.1 x 38.75 mm, height 10.45 mm; sapphire crystal
Band: reptile skin, double folding clasp
Price: $2,800
Variations: with black dial

MeisterSinger

At first glance it would seem that something is not quite right with these watches. With their purposeful sobriety, the dials seem somehow a bit, well, empty. Of course, watches don't always have to be chronographs or perpetual calendars, literally filled with scales and hands. But is one hand all by itself enough?

A good two hundred years after the introduction of the historical *montre à souscription* by Breguet — a type of "people's" pocket watch that was paid for in installments and which only possessed a simple movement without minute hand — Manfred Brassler has come up with the idea to once again manufacture a mechanical watch possessing only a single hand. The designer chose a large case, 43 mm in diameter, with a relatively large dial area and made clear markings on the minute scale for the half and quarter hour as well as the five minute intervals. The very pointy

(hour) hand is long enough to clearly move along the markings at the edge of the dial, and it actually becomes possible to rather accurately read the one-handed watch to within two or three minutes without trouble. No layperson alive needs a watch that is more precise than that.

Brassler had previously produced very successful watches (with Watch People), including extraordinarily modern and design-oriented timekeepers. The Scrypto models, which have, by the way, also been available right from the beginning as conventional two-handed watches, play with emotions located in the grey area situated between the Renaissance and the Space Age. In front, a purposefully sober dial whose numerals from 1 to 9 even carry an extra 0 (as if the human brain arranges the hours using a decimal program), while behind it a movement oscillating at the frequency of 18,000 or 28,800 vph ticks audibly.

Contrary to its more mundane siblings, the Scrypto Edition 1Z, introduced about two years ago, is powered by an Unitas manually wound movement, today produced by ETA and known under the caliber name of 6497, decorated to the nines. The fact that the 6497 is a rather largely dimensioned pocket watch movement with a diameter of 37 mm does not represent a problem for the large case of the Scrypto — to the contrary: Underneath the large sapphire crystal case back, the black-tie mechanism is visible without obstruction. The trouble the watchmakers went to becomes obvious: A screw balance, a beautifully finished swan-neck fine adjustment, *côtes de Genève* across all bridges, blued screws, gold-flushed engravings — there is hardly anything left to add to this simple, robust serial movement. And the dial does not languish in its shadow: Characteristic for the style of the house that plays with the contradictions between old and new, conservative and progressive, and traditional and avant-garde, the Scrypto Edition 1Z is outfitted with a genuine enamel dial. There are only a few workshops left in Switzerland's Jura region that understand this delicate craft of turning a small brass plate into a work of art needing up to thirty steps per piece. Today, the same tools and kilns are used that were used a hundred years ago — even though the typography of the dial is 100-percent MeisterSinger.

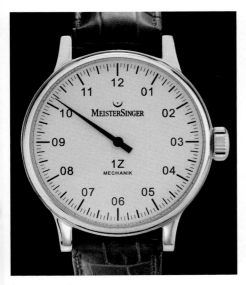

Scrypto 1Z

Reference number: AM3.03
Movement: manually wound, ETA Caliber 2801-2; ø 25.6 mm, height 3.35 mm; 17 jewels; 28,800 vph
Functions: hours (every marker stands for five minutes)
Case: stainless steel, ø 43 mm, height 11.5 mm; mineral crystal; exhibition window case back
Band: leather, buckle
Price: $895
Variations: with silver, white or black dial; in 38 mm case diameter

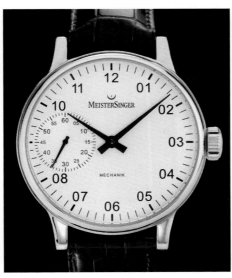

Scrypto Unitas

Reference number: AM5.01
Movement: manually wound, ETA Unitas Caliber 6497-1; ø 36.6 mm, height 4.5 mm; 17 jewels; 21,600 vph; finely finished with blued screws and *côtes de Genève*
Functions: hours, minutes, subsidiary seconds
Case: stainless steel, ø 43 mm, height 12.5 mm; mineral crystal; exhibition window case back
Band: leather, buckle
Price: $1,195
Variations: with beige or black dial

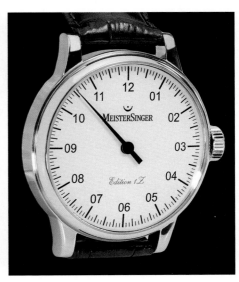

Edition Scrypto 1Z

Reference number: ED.1.01
Movement: manually wound, ETA Unitas Caliber 6497-1; ø 36.6 mm, height 4.5 mm; 17 jewels; 21,600 vph; finely finished with blued screws and *côtes de Genève*
Functions: hours (every marker stands for five minutes)
Case: stainless steel, ø 43 mm, height 12.7 mm; mineral crystal; exhibition window case back
Band: reptile skin, double folding clasp
Remarks: genuine enameled dial; limited to 222 pieces
Price: $4,350

JAARO

Reference number: AM6.04
Movement: manually wound, ETA Unitas Caliber 6497-1; ø 36.6 mm, height 4.5 mm; 17 jewels; 21,600 vph; finely finished with blued screws and *côtes de Genève*
Functions: hours (every marker stands for five minutes)
Case: stainless steel, ø 43 mm, height 12.5 mm; mineral crystal; exhibition window case back
Band: leather, buckle
Price: $1,295
Variations: with red gold dial

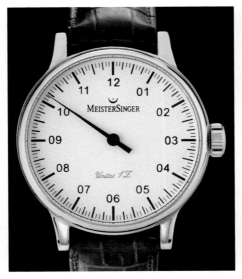

Scrypto Unitas 1Z

Reference number: AM6.03
Movement: manually wound, ETA Unitas Caliber 6497-1; ø 36.6 mm, height 4.5 mm; 17 jewels; 21,600 vph; finely finished with blued screws and *côtes de Genève*
Functions: hours (every marker stands for five minutes)
Case: stainless steel, ø 43 mm, height 12.5 mm; mineral crystal; exhibition window case back
Band: leather, buckle
Price: $1,295
Variations: with black or silver-white dial

Scrypto 3Z Automatic

Reference number: AM7.03
Movement: automatic, ETA Caliber 2824-2; ø 25.6 mm, height 4.6 mm; 25 jewels; 28,800 vph
Functions: hours, minutes, sweep seconds; date
Case: stainless steel, ø 43 mm, height 12.5 mm; mineral crystal; exhibition window case back
Band: leather, buckle
Price: $1,050
Variations: with black or silver-white dial

Richard Mille

I have absolutely no historical relationship to watchmaking," says Richard Mille, "and therefore no obligations either. The mechanics of my watches orient themselves on that which is technically possible, and at best on that which Formula 1 automobiles and space travel technology have to offer." He did not say this out of any desire to provoke, and that is never what might bring the fifty-four-year-old Frenchman to say something inflammatory about his watches. Richard Mille does indeed have a relationship with traditional watchmaking, even if his current product appearance and company philosophy may not feature anything recognizable from it.

Mille is not an engineer by profession, but rather a marketing expert who earned his first paychecks in the watch segment of the French arms, automobile, and space travel concern Matra in the early 1980s. This was a time of departure, of fundamental changes in technology, and the European watch industry was confronted with gigantic challenges. Mille was responsible for traditional French watch brands such as Yema and Yaz, for which he created completely new product palettes in the lowest price segment. When Matra dissolved its watch division and sold it to Seiko, Mille went to Paris to work for the reputable jeweler Mauboussin, for whom he developed an original watch collection. The highlight of that series was a tourbillon with plates and bridges made of rock crystal, which Mille had designed and made at the specialty workshop of Renaud & Papi, already a subsidiary of Audemars Piguet at the time.

Since then, Mille has enjoyed a very hearty friendship with Audemars Piguet's managing director, Georges-Henri Meylan, and when the Frenchman founded a small watch factory in Les Breuleux together with Dominique Guenat, he could be certain of the support of the talented designers employed by Renaud & Papi.

Mille is as little a watchmaker as Enzo Ferrari was an automobile designer. Like the famous sports car manufacturer and racing team owner, however, he had a clear idea of what he wanted, and his goals are certainly comparable to those of the technological excellence of Formula 1. Mille, the passionate automobile fan, transposed the technical aesthetics of racing cars and airplanes to the world of watches and has created in his short career as a watch manufacturer numerous "conversation pieces" that are not only exciting because of their breathtaking technical specialties, but also because of their exclusive price tags. Movement plates made of highly resilient carbon nanofibers; ultra-light aluminum silicon carbide (called Alusic); springs, bars, levers, and chronograph column wheels made of titanium; and new tooth shapes with reduced pressure angles are just some of the things that Mille has thought up and demanded to test watchmakers and take them to their limits. But in Renaud & Papi he has found the right collaborators, for these inventive technicians had already developed functions and features of their own which have been utilized in so-called project watches by Audemars Piguet. Features such as a spring-suspended tourbillon bridge, a selector switch for crown functions, and a torque indicator for the mainspring are serially built into Richard Mille's watches — if you can really speak of "serial production" when describing the few hundred watches that Mille manufactures per year.

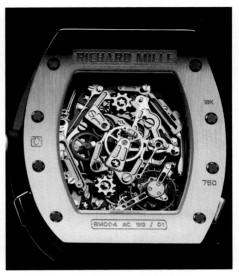

Tourbillon

Reference number: RM 002 V2
Movement: manually wound, Richard Mille Caliber RM 002-V2; 30.2 x 28.6 mm, height 6.35 mm; 23 jewels; 21,600 vph; one-minute tourbillon with ceramic endstone; carbon nanofiber base plate, Arcap gear train bridge; jewels in white gold chatons; function button for winding (W), reset (N) and hand setting (H)
Functions: hours, minutes; power reserve and torque displays; display for function selection switch (W-N-H)
Case: rose gold, 45 x 38.3 mm, height 11.85 mm; sapphire crystal; exhibition window case back
Band: rubber, folding clasp
Price: $195,000

Chronograph Rattrapante

Reference number: RM 004 V2
Movement: manually wound, Richard Mille Caliber RM 004-V2; 30.2 x 28.6 mm, height 8.9 mm; 37 jewels; 21,600 vph; carbon nanofiber base plate, titanium gear train bridge and column wheels; function button for winding (W), reset (N) and setting (H)
Functions: hours, minutes, subsidiary seconds; split-seconds chronograph, power reserve/torque displays; function selection
Case: rose gold, 48 x 39 mm, height 15.05 mm; sapphire crystal; exhibition window case back
Band: rubber, folding clasp
Price: $135,000

Chronograph Rattrapante (back)

Movement: Despite the movement finish's appearance smacking of very modern machines, in the design of Richard Mille's Rattrapante Chronograph traditional construction elements from fine watchmaking such as twin column wheels and a screw balance are in evidence.

Tourbillon Dual Time

Reference number: RM 003 V2
Movement: manually wound, Richard Mille Caliber RM 003-V2; 30.2 x 28.6 mm, height 6.35 mm; 23 jewels; 21,600 vph; one-minute tourbillon with ceramic endstone; carbon nanofiber base plate, Arcap gear train bridge; jewels in white gold chatons; function button for winding (W), reset (N) and setting (H)
Functions: hours, minutes; 12-hour display (second zone); power reserve/torque displays; function selection (W-N-H)
Case: white gold, 48 x 39.3 mm, height 13.85 mm; sapphire crystal; exhibition window case back
Band: rubber, folding clasp
Price: $229,000

Tourbillon Felipe Massa

Reference number: RM 009-1
Movement: manually wound, Richard Mille Caliber RM 009 FM; 30.2 x 28.6 mm, height 6.35 mm; 19 jewels; 21,600 vph; one-minute tourbillon; aluminum-lithium base plate, titanium and aluminum-copper-magnesium alloy bridges and tourbillon cage; jewels in titanium chatons
Functions: hours, minutes
Case: Alusic (aluminum and silicon carbide), 45 x 37.8 mm, height 12.65 mm; sapphire crystal; exhibition case back
Band: rubber, folding clasp
Remarks: limited to 25 pieces; special series for Felipe Massa
Price: $349,000

Tourbillon Felipe Massa (back)

Movement: With this special edition tourbillon model honoring Brazilian Formula 1 race driver Felipe Massa, the designers at Richard Mille ventured into using exotic high-tech materials utilized in space travel and automobile racing. The case made of Alusic is lighter and more robust than any material used on watches until now. Nitrile gaskets guarantee water-resistance, and the direct encasing of the movement in rubber bearings without a movement holder ring ensures shock protection. A total weight of less than 30 grams (case and movement together) makes Tourbillon RM 009 the lightest mechanical complicated watch ever made.

Milus

At the beginning of Milus's history stands Paul William Junod (1896–1951). He founded the company in 1919 in Biel, and it remained in his family's possession until 2002. With the inauguration of the new enterprise Milus International SA, financially supported by the Peace Mark Group from Hong Kong, the brand has entered a new era. After a successful relaunch at Baselworld 2003, the new collections are in full production swing.

Milus has dedicated itself to the elegant luxury watch, and more than three-quarters of its collection is devoted to women. Although gentlemen have a smaller selection to choose from at Milus, they will certainly enjoy their choices: Xephios, Herios, Agenios, and Aurigos are the mysterious names of Greek origin adorning these personally designed timepieces outfitted to a great extent with the manually wound Peseux 7001. Their slim cases hug the wrist and exude a fine charm. While the shape of the case can seem a bit extravagant, these watches' movements are extremely reliable.

Xephios

Reference number: XEP 002

Movement: automatic, ETA Caliber 2836-2; ø 25.6 mm, height 5.05 mm; 25 jewels; 28,800 vph

Functions: hours, minutes, sweep seconds; date and day of the week

Case: stainless steel, ø 36 mm, height 11,17 mm; sapphire crystal

Band: reptile skin, folding clasp

Price: $2,600 Sfr

Variations: various dial variations; in rose gold

Herios

Reference number: HER 202

Movement: manually wound, ETA Caliber 7001 Peseux; ø 23.3 mm, height 2.5 mm; 17 jewels; 21,600 vph

Functions: hours, minutes, subsidiary seconds

Case: rose gold, 36.5 x 39 mm, height 10 mm; sapphire crystal; exhibition window case back

Band: reptile skin, folding clasp

Price: $8,900 Sfr

Variations: various dial variations; in stainless steel

Agenios Haute Joaillerie

Reference number: AGE 327

Movement: manually wound, ETA Caliber 7001 Peseux; ø 23.3 mm, height 2.5 mm; 17 jewels; 21,600 vph

Functions: hours, minutes, subsidiary seconds

Case: white gold, 37 x 46 mm, height 10 mm; bezel and case sides set with brilliant-cut and baguette-cut diamonds; sapphire crystal; exhibition window case back

Band: white gold set with diamonds, folding clasp

Price: $155,700 Sfr

Variations: various dial variations; in rose gold and stainless steel; also without gemstones

H. Moser & Cie.

From 1820 until 1824, Heinrich Moser learned the art of watchmaking in Schaffhausen from his father, a man who — like Heinrich's grandfather — fulfilled the role of "city watchmaker." Moser struck out on his own in 1825 at the age of twenty-one, and the following year moved to St. Petersburg, Russia, a city that offered competent watchmakers a good basis for business in that era. In 1828, upon founding H. Moser & Cie, the birth of his own watch brand was finally achieved. Today's Moser Schaffhausen AG watch factory abstains from entering the general *manufacture* discussion and continues to work within the concept of classic Swiss division of labor: Individual components of the watches developed in Schaffhausen are purchased from the best supplier companies in the Swiss watch industry.

It's obvious that this does not detract from the timepieces' quality in any way. The finely decorated plates and bridges of the watches, regulated in six positions, are outfitted with a double-pull crown mechanism in order to place the different positions of the crown most precisely. These timekeepers are also outfitted with a "flash calendar" display, which sees to it that the date jumps directly to the beginning of the following month when the end of one month has been reached — for example, at the end of February, when from the 28th or 29th the next number is a one.

The new movements contain a new type of escapement comprising a removable plate that bears the pallets, escape wheel, and balance. This complete subgroup is simply secured to the movement with two screws, very easy to remove and replace. When the watch goes in for revisions, this escapement is easily taken out and replaced with a new one from Schaffhausen.

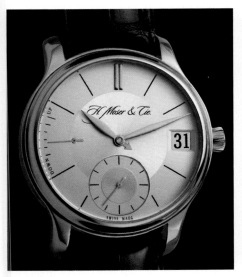

Moser Perpetual 1

Reference number: 341.501-004

Movement: manually wound, Moser Caliber HMC 341.501; ø 34 mm, height 5.8 mm; 30 jewels; exchangeable escapement with gold pallets and gold escape wheel; twin spring barrels, 7 days power reserve; double pull crown mechanism

Functions: hours, minutes, subsidiary seconds; perpetual calendar with large date and small sweep month hand, leap year on back; power reserve display

Case: red gold, ø 40.8 mm, height 11.05 mm; sapphire crystal; exhibition window case back

Band: reptile skin, folding clasp

Price: $29,500

Monard Date Limited Edition

Reference number: 342.502-L01

Movement: manually wound, Moser Caliber HMC 342.502; ø 34 mm, height 5.8 mm; 28 jewels; exchangeable escapement with gold pallets and gold escape wheel; twin spring barrels, 7 days power reserve; double pull crown mechanism

Functions: hours, minutes, sweep seconds; large date

Case: red gold, ø 41 mm, height 1085 mm; sapphire crystal; exhibition window case back

Band: reptile skin, buckle

Remarks: limited to 200 pieces

Price: $21,800

Variations: in white gold ($17,500); in platinum ($22,500)

Mayu

Reference number: 321.503-003

Movement: manually wound, Moser Caliber HMC 321.503; ø 34 mm, height 5.8 mm; 27 jewels; exchangeable escapement with gold pallets and gold escape wheel; double pull crown mechanism

Functions: hours, minutes, subsidiary seconds

Case: platinum, ø 38.8 mm, height 9.3 mm; sapphire crystal; exhibition window case back

Band: reptile skin, buckle

Price: $15,000

Variations: in yellow gold ($9,900); in white gold with enameled dial, limited to 50 pieces ($14,500)

Montblanc

Montblanc, a company named for Europe's highest mountain and found at the summit of luxury writing instruments, has been aiming to take on a protruding position among watch manufacturers for years — with increasing success. When the first watches by Montblanc were introduced in 1997, this brand so rich in another tradition garnered a lot of head-shaking at first. The "sidestep" into a foreign industry was naturally accompanied by some commentary.

But the success of the new watch brand issuing from a reputable, almost one-hundred-year-old company soon quieted even the skeptics, and the first collection launched nine years ago has been followed by models of an obviously much better quality.

Today, Montblanc's watches don't need to fear comparison to other brands' models in this price class. The development of the design, originally thought to be too dainty, and its evolution to include modern and sporty style elements find more recognition from year to year on the occasion of the S.I.H.H.

Writing instrument manufacturer Montblanc, like many watch brands, has its roots in craft and technology. Like the components of a movement, the most important parts of the brand's costly fountain pens are created in half-automated precision. In the modern production halls of the company headquarters near Hamburg's famous soccer stadium, automatic CNC machines stamp and form parts. Gold writing nibs are finely finished and polished by hand, after which they receive a narrow cut for ink flow with the aid of a paper-thin diamond disk. Nibs, ink tanks, and cartridge mechanics are strictly examined by quality control and must pass a great deal of testing very similar to the usual controls in watch production.

It's not surprising that the brand is also currently following the trend toward larger wristwatches. The Star XXXL Chronograph GMT Automatic presented in 2005 is a great example of this. It unites classic chronograph displays with the 24-hour indication already hinted at in the model's name. GMT (Greenwich Mean Time) is the term used for the zero meridian that goes

through the London suburb of Greenwich. All time displays in the world come back to this one imaginary line in one form or another. These three letters have become the modern term for watches that show two or more time zones on their dials, though one of these can either be a day/night indicator or a 24-hour indicator.

The Star XXXL model comprises a wide flange underneath the crystal that slants away in a 45° angle from the silver-plated dial decorated with a guilloché pattern up to the edge of the case and features a wide, skeletonized hand. This hand clearly differs from the thin, almost antique-looking leaf shape of the hour and minute hands, and it wonderfully fulfills the task set out for it in the clean and clear way that has become characteristic of Montblanc's watches.

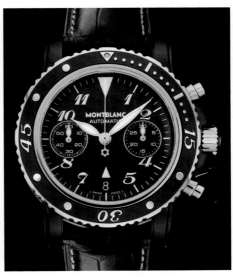

Time Walker GMT Automatic

Reference number: 36064
Movement: automatic, Montblanc Caliber 4810/405
(base ETA 2893-2); ø 25.6 mm, height 4.1 mm; 21 jewels;
28,800 vph
Functions: hours, minutes, sweep seconds; date;
24-hour display (second time zone)
Case: stainless steel, ø 42 mm, height 12 mm; sapphire
crystal; exhibition window case back
Band: stainless steel, double folding clasp
Price: $2,650
Variations: with leather strap

Time Walker Chrono Automatic

Reference number: 36063
Movement: automatic, Montblanc Caliber 4810/502 (base
ETA 7753); ø 30 mm, height 7.9 mm; 25 jewels; 28,800 vph
Functions: hours, minutes, subsidiary seconds;
chronograph; date
Case: stainless steel, ø 43 mm, height 15.2 mm;
sapphire crystal
Band: leather, buckle
Price: $3,100
Variations: with stainless steel bracelet

Sport Chronograph Automatic

Reference number: 35777
Movement: automatic, Montblanc Caliber 4810/50 (base
ETA 7750); ø 30 mm, height 7.9 mm; 25 jewels; 28,800 vph
Functions: hours, minutes, subsidiary seconds;
chronograph; date
Case: stainless steel, ø 43 mm, height 15 mm;
unidirectionally rotating bezel with 60-minute divisions;
sapphire crystal; screwed-in crown
Band: reptile skin, double folding clasp
Price: $2,450
Variations: with stainless steel bracelet

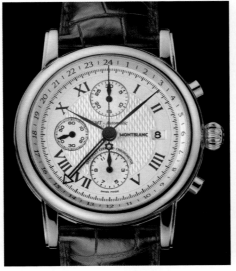

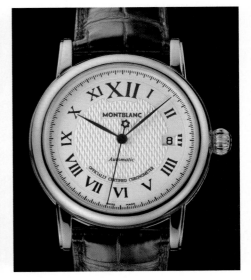

Sport Pilot Automatic

Reference number: 36042
Movement: automatic, Montblanc Caliber 4810/504 (base
ETA 7750); ø 30 mm, height 7.9 mm; 25 jewels; 28,800 vph
Functions: hours, minutes, subsidiary seconds;
chronograph; date
Case: stainless steel, PVD-coated black, ø 41 mm,
height 15 mm; unidirectionally rotating bezel with 60-minute
divisions; sapphire crystal; screwed-in crown
Band: reptile skin, double folding clasp
Price: $2,550
Variations: with stainless steel bracelet

Star XXXL Chronograph GMT

Reference number: 36038
Movement: automatic, Montblanc Caliber 4810/503 (base
ETA 7754); ø 30 mm, height 7.9 mm; 25 jewels; 28,800 vph;
officially certified chronometer (C.O.S.C.)
Functions: hours, minutes, subsidiary seconds; chronograph;
date; 24-hour display (second time zone)
Case: red gold, ø 42 mm, height 14.8 mm; sapphire crystal
Band: reptile skin, double folding clasp
Price: upon request
Variations: in stainless steel ($2,750)

Star XXL Automatic

Reference number: 36040
Movement: automatic, ETA Caliber 2892-A2; ø 25.6 mm,
height 3.6 mm; 21 jewels; 28,800 vph; officially certified
chronometer (C.O.S.C.)
Functions: hours, minutes, sweep seconds; date
Case: red gold, ø 41.5 mm, height 12.2 mm;
sapphire crystal
Band: reptile skin, double folding clasp
Price: upon request
Variations: in stainless steel ($1,550)

Movado

This company's name originates in the synthetic world language Esperanto and means "constantly in motion." It's an aphorism that not only fits the internal workings of a watch, but also stands for the Diteshein family's restless spirit of invention when founding the brand in 1881 in Switzerland's La Chaux-de-Fonds. In the first one hundred years of its existence, this company registered close to one hundred patents.

Since 1984, Movado has belonged to the North American Watch Corporation, which was long ago rechristened Movado Group, Inc. This brand resides there alongside sister brand Concord and, for the last two years, Ebel.

The destinies of Movado and Ebel have crossed more than once in the last hundred years, and Zenith also shares some of its past with these two brands. In 1970 and 1971 Movado was already entrenched in the holding group Mondia-Zenith-Movado and shortly thereafter was sold together with Zenith to the American Zenith Radio Corporation. Movado's factory was moved to Le Locle; the Diteshein family lost all influence. In 1978 the Zenith group was bought back by Swiss industrial magnate Paul Castella, and the Movado brand was purchased by the North American Watch Corp. in 1984, owned by the Cuban-born Grinberg family.

The LVMH Group (Louis Vuitton, Moet & Hennessy) went shopping in the winter of 1999, buying TAG Heuer, Ebel, and Zenith one after the other — for a considerable sum. At Christmas 2003 the luxury and luxury foods concern separated itself again from the misunderstood Ebel brand, which from then on was destined to perk up the top segment of Grinberg's group of brands at the side of evergreen Movado.

Movado enjoys a comfortable advantage: Everyone knows the legendary Museum Watch whose nearly blank dial without numerals or markers was created by the American artist Nathan George Horwitt in 1947. The Museum Watch, whose dot at 12 o'clock symbolizes the midday sun, owes its name to the fact that it was quickly accepted into the permanent collections of reputable museums all over the world, such as the Museum of Modern Art in New York. Today, the Museum Watch is offered in innumerable variations that are all characterized by Horwitt's clear, timeless design. Thus, it's not hard to imagine the conflict of interest that the designers and watchmakers of the small workshop must have felt when confronted with the task of making the Museum Watch into a tourbillon. Naturally, every watchmaker would like to present his or her tourbillon at the most prominent spot on the dial, but Horwitt's creation allows this special position to be filled by the dot alone.

Wisely, the design and watchmaking departments were cleanly separated, with the result that the Museum Tourbillon looks just like a normal Museum Watch at first glance — except that it is 42 mm in diameter and more than 13 mm in height, making it larger and far more stately than in its usual presentation. When the heavy platinum case is turned over, it becomes clear that this is something unique in every sense of the word: For the Museum Tourbillon is truly a proof of skill illustrating the ambitions that the Movado Group harbors in the watch industry.

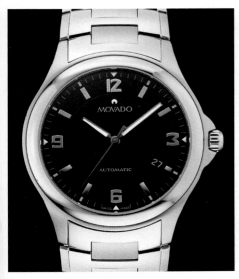

Museum Automatic Sport

Reference number: 0605700
Movement: automatic, ETA Caliber 2824-2; ø 25.6 mm, height 4.6 mm; 25 jewels; 28,800 vph
Functions: hours, minutes, sweep seconds; date
Case: stainless steel, ø 40 mm, height 11 mm; sapphire crystal; exhibition window case back
Band: stainless steel, folding clasp
Price: $1,195

Eliro Chrono

Reference number: 0605571
Movement: quartz, ETA Caliber 251.471
Functions: hours, minutes, subsidiary seconds; chronograph; date
Case: stainless steel, 32 x 44 mm, height 12 mm; sapphire crystal
Band: stainless steel, folding clasp
Price: $1,795

Gentry Sport Chronograph

Reference number: 0605531
Movement: quartz, ETA Caliber G15.21/21A
Functions: hours, minutes, subsidiary seconds; chronograph; date
Case: stainless steel, partially PVD-coated, ø 38 mm, height 11 mm; bezel partially PVD-coated; sapphire crystal
Band: stainless steel, partially PVD-coated, folding clasp
Price: $895
Variations: as three-hand watch in men's and women's sizes

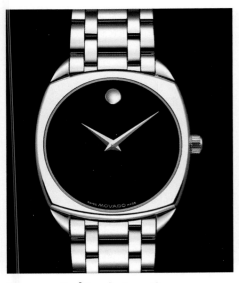

Museum Cushion Automatic

Reference number: 0605568
Movement: automatic, ETA Caliber 2892-A2; ø 25.6 mm, height 3.6 mm; 21 jewels; 28,800 vph
Functions: hours, minutes
Case: stainless steel, ø 36 mm, height 11 mm; sapphire crystal
Band: stainless steel, folding clasp
Remarks: Nathan Horwitts famous design trait; sun dot at 12 o'clock
Price: $1,395

Museum Automatic

Reference number: 0605276
Movement: automatic, ETA Caliber 2892-A2; ø 25.6 mm, height 3.6 mm; 21 jewels; 28,800 vph
Functions: hours, minutes
Case: stainless steel, ø 42 mm, height 11 mm; sapphire crystal; exhibition window case back
Band: stainless steel, folding clasp
Remarks: Nathan Horwitts famous design trait; sun dot at 12 o'clock
Price: $1,195

SE Automatic

Reference number: 0605322
Movement: automatic, ETA Caliber 2892-A2; ø 25.6 mm, height 3.6 mm; 21 jewels; 28,800 vph
Functions: hours, minutes
Case: stainless steel, ø 42 mm, height 11 mm; sapphire crystal
Band: stainless steel, folding clasp
Remarks: Nathan Horwitts famous design trait; sun dot at 12 o'clock
Price: $1,495

Mühle

The brand Nautische Instrumente Mühle Glashütte is advertised with the cryptic slogan "a young company with a long tradition."
This company, today making electronic ship's clocks as well as high-quality wristwatches, has only been back in the possession of its founding family for the past eleven years, with the nucleus of it now more than 135 years old. When Robert Mühle founded the first company answering to the name Mühle, it specialized in gauges for watchmakers, among other things, and later also included clocks and tachometers for automobiles in its repertoire. After the end of World War II, Hans Mühle became managing director of the company then renamed Messtechnik Glashütte. The founder's grandson continued in the family tradition and, as one of the few independent entrepreneurs of the GDR, manufactured complicated parts for the photography and cinema industries as well as dial trains for pressure and temperature measuring instruments.
His son Hans-Jürgen Mühle, who studied precision mechanics and optics in Jena, took over the company in 1970 and managed it for another two years until it was expropriated and turned into a "people's

company." During the time leading up to the great political upheavals, Hans-Jürgen Mühle worked for VEB Glashütter Uhrenbetriebe (the forerunner of today's Glashütte Original) and was one of its directors until 1992. A scant two years later he founded Nautische Instrumente Mühle-Glashütte. As the generations before him, Hans-Jürgen Mühle and later his son Thilo at first took matters into their own hands and began with the production of ship's chronometers and electronic timekeeping systems for boats. In 1996 the entrepreneurs started making wristwatches — and today 15,000 watches per year are sold all over the world bearing their name.
New models are important, but they aren't everything. And in the continuous development and improvement of products, one needs to remain involved. Hans-Jürgen Mühle proves this in the recent development of a special fine adjustment device for the complicated models in his collection shaped like a woodpecker's neck. The individual components of this subgroup, including the spring, index, and balance cock, are manufactured in the company's own mechanical workshop.
During developmental and test phases for new products, the company often works

with select partners. For example, for the S.A.R. Rescue Timer, the Glashütte-based company entered into a partnership with the DGzRS (Deutsche Gesellschaft zur Rettung Schiffbrüchiger or the German Sea Rescue Service). This especially robust automatic watch featuring a 4 mm thick sapphire crystal and exceptional legibility at night can be said to be the official timer on fifty-six rescue cruisers of the DGzRS. The experience of these seamen flows into the development of the watches. After all, the words "nautische Instrumente" in the company's official name also refer to watches that are able to fulfill professional demands. And this is true of the current diver's watch Rasmus, which Thilo Mühle has developed in cooperation with the German national free diving team.

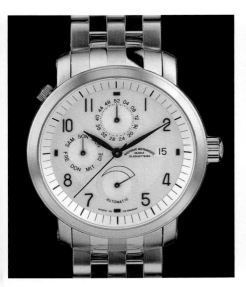

Business-Timer

Reference number: M1-30-65-MB
Movement: automatic, ETA Caliber 2892-A2 with module; ø 25.6 mm, height 3.6 mm; 21 jewels; 28,800 vph; Mühle special finish; with autonomous woodpecker neck fine adjustment, module plate and gold-platinum rotor
Functions: hours, minutes, sweep seconds; date, day of the week, calendar week; power reserve display
Case: stainless steel, ø 40.3 mm, height 10 mm; sapphire crystal; exhibition window case back; screwed-in crown; water-resistant to 50 m
Band: stainless steel, double folding clasp
Price: $3,050

Mercurius

Reference number: M1-24-25-LB
Movement: automatic, ETA Caliber 2824-2; ø 25.6 mm, height 4.6 mm; 25 jewels; 28,800 vph; Mühle special finish
Functions: hours, minutes, sweep seconds; date
Case: stainless steel, ø 38.5 mm, height 10.4 mm; sapphire crystal; exhibition window case back; screwed-in crown; water-resistant to 100 m
Band: reptile skin, double folding clasp
Price: $1,050
Variations: with stainless steel bracelet; with blue or black dial

Lufthansa Tachymeter

Reference number: M1-35-03-LB
Movement: automatic, ETA Caliber 7750 Valjoux; ø 30 mm, height 7.9 mm; 25 jewels; 28,800 vph; Mühle special finish
Functions: hours, minutes, subsidiary seconds; chronograph; date and day of the week
Case: stainless steel, ø 42 mm, height 13.5 mm; bidirectionally rotating bezel under crystal with 60-minute divisions; sapphire crystal; exhibition window case back; water-resistant to 100 m
Band: leather, double buckle
Price: $3,300

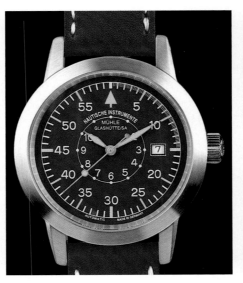

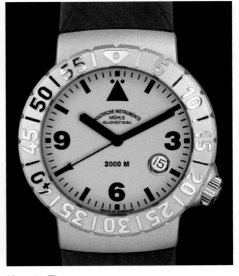

Teutonia II Chronograph

Reference number: M1-30-95-LB
Movement: automatic, ETA Caliber 7750 Valjoux; ø 30 mm, height 7.9 mm; 25 jewels; 28,800 vph; Mühle special finish
Functions: hours, minutes, subsidiary seconds; chronograph; date, day of the week
Case: stainless steel, ø 42 mm, height 15.5 mm; sapphire crystal; exhibition window case back; water-resistant to 100 m
Band: reptile skin, double folding clasp
Price: $2,850

Big Sports M 12

Reference number: M1-26-33/4-LB
Movement: automatic, ETA Caliber 2824-2; ø 25.6 mm, height 4.6 mm; 25 jewels; 28,800 vph; Mühle special finish
Functions: hours, minutes, sweep seconds; date
Case: stainless steel, ø 42 mm, height 12.9 mm; sapphire crystal; screwed-in crown; water-resistant to 100 m
Band: leather, buckle
Price: $890
Variations: with stainless steel bracelet; with white or blue dial

Nautic-Timer

Reference number: M1-41-27-KB
Movement: automatic, ETA Caliber 2824-2; ø 25.6 mm, height 4.6 mm; 25 jewels; 28,800 vph; Mühle special finish
Functions: hours, minutes, sweep seconds; date
Case: stainless steel, ø 42 mm, height 13.7 mm; unidirectionally rotating bezel with 60-minute divisions; extra thick sapphire crystal (4 mm); screwed-in crown; water-resistant to 2000 m
Band: rubber, folding clasp with security and wetsuit extension
Price: $1,900
Variations: with stainless steel bracelet; with black dial

Franck Muller

The meteoric rise of the watch brand Franck Muller, founded little more than ten years ago, is without equal in the world of Swiss watches. The brand's success is the result of a clever model policy paired with a feel for shapes, colors, and surfaces. The double-curved case shape of the Cintrée Curvex is incomparable in its characteristic 1920s gracefulness and has brought Franck Muller its commercial breakthrough. The models of this collection wonderfully document the creative conflict between "young" and "old" that has characterized the life and work of the eponymous Genevan watchmaker since his debut. While the brand's namesake has retired more and more from daily activities during the last two years, the person who made it possible for the young watchmaker Franck Muller to find his way into big business has

stepped into the foreground: Vartan Sirmakes, the owner originally of a case factory and a man brave enough to take on the Franck Muller adventure.

Other things that have not been widely communicated until now are that the Franck Muller Group, founded in 1997, employs more than 500 people and owns outright or the majority of five companies.

Technocase is Sirmakes's former main company and produces watch cases and crystals in Geneva's industrial suburb Plan-les-Ouates with 130 employees. Geco in Meyrin manufactures crowns, small parts, and metal link bracelets with fifty employees and is now building a department for hand production. Dials come from Linder in Les Bois (more than fifty employees), and wheels, pinions, balances, and plates are supplied by Pignon Juracie SA in Lajoux with something like twenty employees.

And then there's Watchland: a second manufacturing building has now been placed on the castle grounds surrounding the main building in Genthod, in which 300 employees finish parts, assemble movements, and mount complete watches — from the simple three-hand timepieces outfitted with supplied movements all the way to the breathtakingly complicated watches containing tourbillons. Additionally, the development and design departments are housed here, as well as the management and international distribution center that coordinates 545 points of sale worldwide, including sixteen of its own boutiques. But not only is the production of finished watches running at capacity: Plans for the production of two autonomous movement calibers — an automatic base movement by the name of Liberty and a column-wheel chronograph dubbed Freedom (both supposedly on their feet without the help of supplied Swatch Group parts) are nearing perfection. The automatic movement is already past the prototype stage, and the lavishly manufactured chronograph has already undergone a first baptism of fire.

Naturally the collection is extended every year with the addition of new, technically interesting and aesthetically daring watches in order to remain the leader in the international jet-set scene and in newly conquered markets — as well as to continue its venerable presence in the markets of the "old" world.

Long Island

Reference number: 1000 SC
Movement: automatic, FM Caliber 2800; ø 26.2 mm, height 3.75 mm; 21 jewels; 28,800 vph; with platinum rotor
Functions: hours, minutes
Case: white gold, 43 x 30.5 mm, height 8.15 mm; sapphire crystal
Band: reptile skin, buckle in white gold
Price: $13,400
Variations: in rose, red or yellow gold; in platinum ($21,400)

Long Island Color Dreams

Reference number: 1200 SC
Movement: automatic, FM Caliber 2800 ; ø 26.2 mm, height 3.75 mm; 21 jewels; 28,800 vph; with platinum rotor
Functions: hours, minutes
Case: stainless steel, 45 x 32.4 mm, height 11.23 mm; sapphire crystal
Band: reptile skin, buckle
Price: $8,400
Variations: in white, rose, red or yellow gold ($14,200); in platinum ($22,200)

Long Island Chronograph Monopulsant

Reference number: 1100 MP
Movement: automatic, FM Caliber 5000; ø 24.6 mm, height 4.2 mm; 25 jewels; 28,800 vph; one button for start-stop-reset
Functions: hours, minutes, subsidiary seconds; chronograph
Case: white gold, 45 x 32.4 mm, height 10.30 mm; sapphire crystal
Band: reptile skin, buckle in white gold
Price: $30,400
Variations: in yellow gold or platinum ($39,200)

Long Island Master Calendar

Reference number: 1200 MCL
Movement: automatic, FM Caliber 2800; ø 26.2 mm, height 5.35 mm; 21 jewels (base movement); 28,800 vph; module for complete calendar and moon phases
Functions: hours, minutes; date, day of the week, month, moon phase
Case: white gold, 45 x 32.4 mm, height 11.23 mm; sapphire crystal
Band: reptile skin, buckle in white gold
Price: $23,000
Variations: in yellow, rose or red gold; in platinum ($32,600)

Long Island Chronograph

Reference number: 1200 CC AT
Movement: automatic, FM Caliber 2094; ø 23.9 mm, height 5.5 mm; 25 jewels; 28,800 vph; with platinum rotor
Functions: hours, minutes, subsidiary seconds; chronograph; date
Case: white gold, 45 x 32.4 mm, height 11.23 mm; sapphire crystal
Band: reptile skin, buckle in white gold
Price: $24,000
Variations: in yellow, rose or red gold

Long Island Tourbillon

Reference number: 1200 T
Movement: manually wound, FM Caliber 2001; 22.90 x 30.60 mm, height 5.3 mm; one-minute tourbillon
Functions: hours, minutes, subsidiary seconds (on tourbillon cage)
Case: white gold, 45 x 32.4 mm, height 11.23 mm; sapphire crystal
Band: reptile skin, buckle in white gold
Price: $96,000
Variations: in yellow, rose or red gold; in platinum ($104,000)

Cintrée Curvex Casablanca

Reference number: 8880 CDT
Movement: automatic, FM Caliber 7753; ø 25.6 mm,
height 3.6 mm; 21 jewels; 28,800 vph; with platinum rotor
Functions: hours, minutes, sweep seconds; date
Case: stainless steel, 55.40 x 39.60 mm, height 15 mm;
sapphire crystal
Band: leather, buckle
Price: $7,000

Cintrée Curvex Grand Guichet

Reference number: 6850 S6 GG
Movement: automatic, FM Caliber 2800 DD; ø 26.20 mm,
height 5.35 mm; 28,800 vph; module for large date
Functions: hours, minutes, subsidiary seconds; large date
Case: stainless steel, 47 x 34 mm, height 11.40 mm;
sapphire crystal
Band: reptile skin, buckle in yellow gold
Price: $11,800
Variations: in rose or red gold; in white gold; in yellow gold
($18,200); in platinum ($26,200)

Cintrée Curvex Casablanca Chronograph

Reference number: 8885 CCDT
Movement: automatic, FM Caliber 7002 CD (base ETA);
ø 30 mm, height 7.9 mm; 25 jewels; 28,800 vph
Functions: hours, minutes, subsidiary seconds;
chronograph; date
Case: stainless steel, 55.40 x 39.60 mm, height 17.15 mm;
sapphire crystal
Band: reptile skin, buckle
Price: $11,000

Cintrée Curvex Chrono Birétrograde

Reference number: 7850 CC B
Movement: automatic, FM Caliber 7000 B; ø 30 mm,
height 7.9 mm; 25 jewels (base movement); 28,800 vph;
module for retrograde seconds display and retrograde
30-minute counter
Functions: hours, minutes, seconds (retrograde); chronograph
Case: white gold, 48.7 x 35.3 mm, height 13.50 mm;
sapphire crystal
Band: leather, buckle in white gold
Price: $28,800
Variations: in yellow, rose or red gold; in stainless steel
($20,800); in platinum ($36,800)

Cintrée Curvex Chrono QP Biretrograde

Reference number: 6850 CC QP B
Movement: automatic, FM Caliber 5888 BR; ø 30 mm,
height 7.9 mm; 25 jewels (base movement); 28,800 vph;
module for perpetual calendar with retrograde displays
Functions: hours, minutes; chronograph; perpetual calendar
with date and day of the week (retrograde), month, moon
phase, leap year
Case: yellow gold, 47 x 34 mm, height 13 mm;
sapphire crystal
Band: reptile skin, buckle in yellow gold
Price: $64,100
Variations: in white, rose or red gold; in platinum ($72,100)

Cintrée Curvex Quantième Perpétuel

Reference number: 7851 QPE
Movement: automatic, FM Caliber 2800; module for
perpetual calendar with retrograde displays
Functions: hours, minutes, sweep seconds; perpetual
calendar with date, day of the week, month (retrograde),
moon phase, leap year; 24-hour display
Case: white gold, 48.7 x 35.3 mm, height 14 mm;
sapphire crystal
Band: reptile skin, buckle in white gold
Price: $57,400
Variations: in white, rose or red gold; in platinum
($65,400)

Long Island Lady
Reference number: 902 QZ D 1P
Movement: quartz, ETA Caliber 956032
Functions: hours, minutes
Case: white gold, 32.25 x 22.9 mm, height 8 mm; case and inner section of dial set with diamonds; sapphire crystal
Band: reptile skin, buckle in white gold
Price: $21,600
Variations: in yellow, rose or red gold; in platinum ($30,400)

Long Island Color Dreams
Reference number: 1200 SC COL DR
Movement: automatic, FM Caliber 1200 SC; ø 25.6 mm, height 3.6 mm; 21 jewels; 28,800 vph
Functions: hours, minutes
Case: stainless steel, 45 x 32.40 mm, height 11.23 mm; sapphire crystal
Band: reptile skin, buckle in white gold
Price: $8,400
Variations: in rose, red or yellow gold ($14,200); in platinum ($22,200)

Conquistador Cortez Chronograph
Reference number: 10000 CC KING
Movement: automatic, FM Caliber ; ø 30 mm, height 7.9 mm; 25 jewels; 28,800 vph
Functions: hours, minutes, subsidiary seconds; chronograph, date
Case: stainless steel, 45 x 45 mm, height 14.95 mm; sapphire crystal
Band: stainless steel, double folding clasp
Price: $19,800
Variations: in white, rose or red gold ($31,800); in platinum ($43,000)

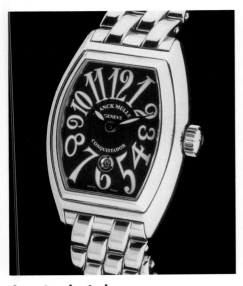

Conquistador Lady
Reference number: 8005 LSC 0
Movement: automatic, FM Caliber 2600 (base ETA 2000/1); ø 19.4 mm, height 3.6 mm; 20 jewels; 28,800 vph; with platinum rotor
Functions: hours, minutes, sweep seconds; date
Case: stainless steel, 39 x 28 mm, height 11 mm; sapphire crystal
Band: stainless steel, folding clasp
Price: $6,400
Variations: in rose, red, white or yellow gold with leather strap ($12,000); in platinum ($19,200)

Conquistador King Chronograph
Reference number: 8005 CC KING
Movement: automatic, FM Caliber 7002; ø 30 mm, height 8.4 mm; 25 jewels; 28,800 vph
Functions: hours, minutes, subsidiary seconds; chronograph
Case: stainless steel, 56.45 x 40.35 mm, height 15.45 mm; sapphire crystal
Band: stainless steel, folding clasp
Price: $19,800
Variations: in yellow gold ($31,800); in platinum ($43,000)

Cintrée Curvex Crazy Hours
Reference number: 7851 CH DIA
Movement: automatic, FM Caliber 2003; ø 26.2 mm, height 5.35 mm; 21 jewels; 28,800 vph; special dial train module for seemingly arbitrary jump hour display
Functions: hours (jump), minutes
Case: white gold, 35.3 x 48.7 mm, height 11.40 mm; case set with diamonds; sapphire crystal
Band: reptile skin, folding clasp
Price: $41,200
Variations: in rose, red or yellow gold

NBY

No Barriers Yäeger

No barriers — this is a motto that is leading Black Forest-based master watchmaker Martin Braun down some brand-new paths. He has impressively proved his ability to innovate for many years with his classically designed watches.

Since 2004, Braun has also manufactured sports watches in pilot's dress, which, however, fit neither with the philosophy nor the price policies of his established Martin Braun brand. For this reason, he spontaneously created a new label: NBY.

It stands for No Barriers Yäeger. This proper name reminds one vaguely of Chuck Yeager, the pilot who was the first to break the sound barrier. However, Braun didn't want to name his brand for any one person. He just wanted a simple, catchy moniker, though the association with piloting is not undesirable.

The goal of Braun's new brand is to offer pilot's watches at an acceptable price without cutting corners on quality and finally putting an end to "the yawning chasm of unimaginativeness that exists most decidedly in the entry-level price class for mechanical watches." The individualist watchmaker has certainly been successful in that — he didn't just more or less copy his design from old pilot's watches, preferring to give his collection its very own face. Characteristic are the double-digit hour numerals of boxy design which are generously inlaid with fluorescent SuperLumiNova, as are the markers and hands. The "12" is always depicted by a double zero at NBY.

The collection comprises ten different models divided into four model families. Especially attractive is the relatively simple three-hand watch by the name of Delta, powered by an ETA 2824-2 and available in many dial designs. The same movement runs the second model family as well, which includes Tendence, Turbulence, and ILS, whose dials mimic various airplane instruments.

Braun used a lot of imagination when he put the chronograph family Charlie together. Here one finds hands in the subsidiary dials that look like propellers, one half painted blue and one half white. The scale markers on the totalizers are actually only semicircles broken up by white and blue numerals. A little difficult to read, but very original. The variation Charlie Short Flight, however, is excellently legible for, as the name hints, it only features a minute counter. Tango is an only child so far, outfitted with an additional 24-hour display that can also be used as a second time zone.

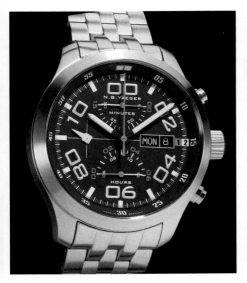

Charlie

Reference number:
Movement: automatic, ETA Caliber 7750; ø 30 mm,
height 7.9 mm; 25 jewels; 28,800 vph
Functions: hours, minutes, subsidiary seconds; chronograph;
date, day of the week
Case: stainless steel, ø 42 mm, height 14 mm; sapphire
crystal; screwed-in crown; water-resistant to 100 m
Band: leather, additional rubber strap, buckle
Price: $2,195
Variations: with stainless steel bracelet

Delta

Reference number:
Movement: automatic, ETA Caliber 2824-2; ø 25.6 mm,
height 4.6 mm; 25 jewels; 28,800 vph
Functions: hours, minutes, sweep seconds; date
Case: stainless steel, ø 40 mm, height 11 mm; sapphire
crystal; screwed-in crown; water-resistant to 100 m
Band: leather, additional rubber strap, buckle
Price: $925
Variations: with stainless steel bracelet

Tango

Reference number:
Movement: automatic, ETA Caliber 2893-2; ø 25.6 mm,
height 4.1 mm; 21 jewels; 28,800 vph
Functions: hours, minutes, sweep seconds; date;
24-hour display (second time zone)
Case: stainless steel, ø 40 mm, height 11 mm; sapphire
crystal; screwed-in crown; water-resistant to 100 m
Band: leather, additional rubber strap, buckle
Price: $1,675
Variations: with stainless steel bracelet

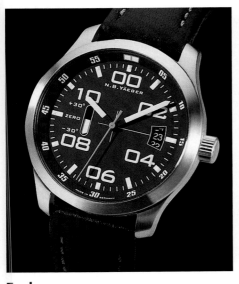

Tendence

Reference number:
Movement: automatic, ETA Caliber 2824-2; ø 25.6 mm,
height 4.6 mm; 25 jewels; 28,800 vph
Functions: hours, minutes, sweep seconds; date; symbolic
display of angle of inclination
Case: stainless steel, ø 40 mm, height 11 mm; sapphire
crystal; screwed-in crown; water-resistant to 100 m
Band: leather, additional rubber strap, buckle
Price: $1,075
Variations: with stainless steel bracelet

Long Flight

Reference number:
Movement: automatic, ETA Caliber 7750; ø 30 mm,
height 7.9 mm; 25 jewels; 28,800 vph
Functions: hours, minutes, subsidiary seconds; chronograph;
date and day of the week
Case: stainless steel, ø 42 mm, height 14 mm; sapphire
crystal; screwed-in crown; water-resistant to 100 m
Band: leather, additional rubber strap, buckle
Price: $2,195
Variations: with stainless steel bracelet

Delta Sector

Reference number:
Movement: automatic, ETA Caliber 2824-2; ø 25.6 mm,
height 4.6 mm; 25 jewels; 28,800 vph
Functions: hours, minutes, sweep seconds; date
Case: stainless steel, ø 40 mm, height 11 mm; sapphire
crystal; screwed-in crown; water-resistant to 100 m
Band: leather, additional rubber strap, buckle
Price: $925
Variations: with stainless steel bracelet

Ulysse Nardin

When Rolf Schnyder purchased Ulysse Nardin in 1983, the tide had taken most everything with it except a sonorous name. Schnyder himself knew little about watchmaking. Despite this, the man with the unconventional ideas led the washed-up company to new heights and found in the multitalented Dr. Ludwig Oechslin, watchmaker, astronomer, and scientist, the ideal collaborator to aid in fishing the company out of the water. Oechslin's specialty is the astronomic timepiece, as he is learned not only in the complicated mechanics of celestial models, but in the actual cosmos in which we exist as well. He began his cooperation with Ulysse Nardin by creating the memorable Trilogy of Time: Tellurium Johannes Kepler, Astrolabium Galileo Galilei, and Planetarium Copernicus, three extraordinary wristwatches that display the positions of the heavenly bodies in the firmament according to the conception of the world of each of the timepieces' namesakes.

Before Oechslin took on his new job as curator of the watch museum in La Chaux-de-Fonds, he created a few more specialty timepieces for Ulysse Nardin. The Freak was one of these, presented at the Basel Watch Fair 2002. This is a most unusual name for a most unusual watch, with certainly the most unusual tourbillon ever created, and for which Oechslin invented a brand-new escapement. The year 2003 presented the watch-buying public with another example of Oechslin's power of invention and the power of Ulysse Nardin's technicians to turn his ideas into reality: The Sonata. "Nothing shows more impressively than the Sonata itself where Ulysse Nardin stands today," explains the company president, not without a little pride. Schnyder is not only talking about the high technical level upon which the brand does its work, but also its economic success and resulting expansion. Because space was getting tight in "downtown" Le Locle and didn't allow for another annex to the factory, Schnyder went ahead and bought a modern factory building in the industrial area of neighboring La Chaux-de-Fonds. Management, distribution headquarters, assembly, and high watchmaking remain at home in Le Locle, but all machine-driven departments moved to the adjacent town.

Two stories comprising 2,250 square meters of space provide a home not only to production machines for every possible type of stamping, turning, and milling work, but also the development and design departments for *manufacture* movements and special complications. Under the direction of Pierre Gygax and Lucas Humair, the ideas which have spewed from Dr. Oechslin are put into watches.

Terms such as "selective photolithography process," "electrofoaming," and "silicon and diamond etching" show what's going on inside the *manufacture*'s four walls: Intense work with cooperation partners for the research and development of new materials for watch movements is on-going — everything that will serve to improve reliability, make maintenance a thing of the past, and better use energy. At the turn of the millennium the company was already testing its patented Dual Direct escapement made of silicon, and two short years later technicians were experimenting with balance springs and escape wheels made of diamond.

The newest research result and the momentary highlight of this developmental work is the Freak Diamond Heart, outfitted with the Dual Ulysse Escapement, an escapement system made of synthetic diamond.

And Ulysse Nardin can surely say of this watch that it represents an important milestone in the history of the art of watchmaking.

Perpetual Calendar GMT+/-

Reference number: 329-60
Movement: automatic, Ulysse Nardin Caliber UN 32; ø 31 mm, height 6.95 mm; 34 jewels; 28,800 vph; perpetual calendar mechanism (adjustable forward/backward), large date, and patented mechanism for quick-setting the hour hand, COSC certified chronometer; limited to 500 pieces
Functions: hours, minutes, subsidiary seconds; perpetual calendar with large date, day, month, year; second time zone
Case: platinum, ø 42 mm, height 12.7 mm; sapphire crystal; exhibition window case back
Band: reptile skin, folding clasp
Price: $49,800

Perpetual Calendar GMT+/-

Reference number: 320-82
Movement: automatic, Ulysse Nardin Caliber UN 32; ø 31 mm, height 6.95 mm; 34 jewels; 28,800 vph; perpetual calendar mechanism (adjustable forward/backward), large date, and patented mechanism for quick-setting the hour hand
Functions: hours, minutes, subsidiary seconds; perpetual calendar with large date, day, month, year; second time zone
Case: white gold, ø 40 mm, height 12.7 mm; sapphire crystal; exhibition window case back
Band: reptile skin, folding clasp
Price: $39,800

Sonata

Reference number: 660-88
Movement: automatic, Ulysse Nardin Caliber UN 66; ø 34 mm, height 7.2 mm; 109 jewels; 28,800 vph; alarm with gong, 24 hour mechanism that makes mistaking 7:35 for 19:35 impossible; countdown display (rest of alarm time); settable exactly to the minute; large date adjustable forward and backward via the crown
Functions: hours, minutes, subsidiary seconds; alarm with gong, second time zone, large date, countdown/alarm time
Case: red gold, ø 42 mm, height 13 mm; sapphire crystal
Band: reptile skin, folding clasp
Price: upon request

Sonata

Reference number: 666-88
Movement: automatic, Ulysse Nardin Caliber UN 66; ø 34 mm, height 7.2 mm; 109 jewels; 28,800 vph; alarm with gong, 24 hour mechanism that makes mistaking 7:35 for 19:35 impossible; countdown display (rest of alarm time); settable exactly to the minute; large date adjustable forward and backward via the crown
Functions: hours, minutes, subsidiary seconds; alarm with gong, second time zone, large date, countdown/alarm time
Case: white gold, ø 42 mm, height 13 mm; sapphire crystal
Band: reptile skin, folding clasp
Price: upon request

Freak 28,800

Reference number: 020-88
Movement: manually wound, Ulysse Nardin Caliber UN 01; ø 31 mm, height 7.2 mm; 28 jewels; 28,800 vph; karussell tourbillon with patented Dual Ulysse escapement made of nickel phosphor, movement components function as hands; power reserve 7 days
Functions: hours, minutes
Case: white gold, ø 42.5 mm, height 12.65 mm; sapphire crystal; exhibition window case back
Band: reptile skin, folding clasp
Price: upon request
Variations: in red gold

Royal Blue Tourbillon

Reference number: 799-80
Movement: manually wound, Ulysse Nardin Caliber UN 74; ø 31 mm, height 7.2 mm; 28 jewels; 28'800 vph 4Hz; flying tourbillon with large sapphire endstone, circular toothed winding, 130 hours power reserve, sapphire plates
Functions: hour and minute hands
Case: platinum, ø 41 mm, height 13.5 mm; sapphire crystal; exhibition window case back
Band: reptile skin, folding clasp
Remarks: limited to 30 pieces
Price: upon request
Variations: in red gold, also limited to 30 pieces

Ulysse I Chronometer

Reference number: 276-88
Movement: automatic, Ulysse Nardin Caliber UN 27 (base ETA 2892); ø 25.6 mm, height 5.1 mm; 28 jewels; 28,800 vph; officially certified chronometer (C.O.S.C.)
Functions: hours, minutes, subsidiary seconds; date; power reserve display
Case: red gold, ø 40 mm, height 12 mm; sapphire crystal; screwed-in crown and buttons; water-resistant to 100 m
Band: reptile skin, buckle
Remarks: power reserve display designed from a 1912 UN pocket watch
Price: $11,900

Michelangelo Gigante Chronometer

Reference number: 276-68/412
Movement: automatic, Ulysse Nardin Caliber UN 27 (base ETA 2892); ø 25.6 mm, height 5.1 mm; 28 jewels; 28,800 vph; officially certified chronometer (C.O.S.C.)
Functions: hours, minutes, subsidiary seconds; date; power reserve display
Case: stainless steel, 38 x 43 mm, height 15.36 mm; sapphire crystal; screwed-in crown; water-resistant to 100 m
Band: reptile skin, double folding clasp
Remarks: power reserve display designed from a 1912 UN pocket watch
Price: $14,800

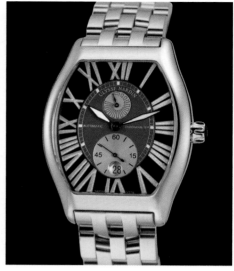

Michelangelo Gigante Chronometer

Reference number: 273-68-7/412
Movement: automatic, Ulysse Nardin Caliber UN 27 (base ETA 2892); ø 25.6 mm, height 5.1 mm; 28 jewels; 28,800 vph; officially certified chronometer (C.O.S.C.)
Functions: hours, minutes, subsidiary seconds; date; power reserve display
Case: stainless steel, 38 x 43 mm, height 15.36 mm; sapphire crystal; screwed-in crown; water-resistant to 100 m
Band: stainless steel, double folding clasp
Remarks: power reserve display designed from a 1912 UN pocket watch
Price: $6,650

Maxi Marine Chronograph

Reference number: 356-66-3/354
Movement: automatic, Ulysse Nardin Caliber UN 26 (base ETA 2892 /Dubois-Dépraz); ø 25.6 mm, height 5.1 mm; 28 jewels; 28,800 vph
Functions: hours, minutes, subsidiary seconds; date; chronograph, power reserve display
Case: red gold, ø 41 mm, height 11.8 mm; sapphire crystal; screwed-in crown and buttons; water-resistant to 200 m
Band: rubber/red gold , folding clasp
Remarks: exclusive 45-minute counter
Price: $19,600
Variations: also in stainless steel as limited edition

Maxi Marine Chronograph

Reference number: 353-66-3/323
Movement: automatic, Ulysse Nardin Caliber UN 26 (base ETA 2892 / Dubois-Dépraz); ø 25.6 mm, height 5.1 mm; 28 jewels; 28,800 vph
Functions: hours, minutes, subsidiary seconds; date; chronograph, power reserve display
Case: stainless steel, ø 41 mm, height 11.8 mm; sapphire crystal; screwed-in crown and buttons; water-resistant to 200 m
Band: rubber/titanium, folding clasp
Remarks: exclusive 45-minute counter
Price: $6,200
Variations: also in red gold as limited edition

Maxi Marine Chronometer

Reference number: 266-66/62
Movement: automatic, Ulysse Nardin Caliber UN 26 (base ETA 2892); ø 25.6 mm, height 5.1 mm; 28 jewels; 28,800 vph; officially certified chronometer (C.O.S.C.)
Functions: hours, minutes, subsidiary seconds; date; power reserve display
Case: red gold, ø 41 mm, height 11.8 mm; sapphire crystal; screwed-in crown; water-resistant to 200 m
Band: reptile skin, folding clasp
Price: $15,900
Variations: with rubber strap

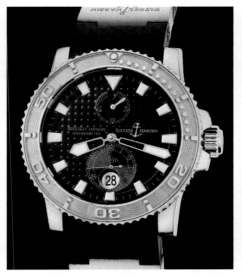

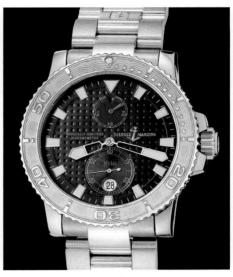

Maxi Marine Chronometer

Reference number: 266-66
Movement: automatic, Ulysse Nardin Caliber UN 26 (base ETA 2892); ø 25.6 mm, height 5.1 mm; 28 jewels; 28,800 vph; officially certified chronometer (C.O.S.C.)
Functions: hours, minutes, subsidiary seconds; date; power reserve display
Case: red gold, ø 41 mm, height 11.8 mm; sapphire crystal; screwed-in crown; water-resistant to 200 m
Band: reptile skin, folding clasp
Price: $15,900
Variations: with rubber strap

Maxi Marine Diver Chronometer

Reference number: 266-33-3A/92
Movement: automatic, Ulysse Nardin Caliber UN 26 (base ETA 2892); ø 25.6 mm, height 5.1 mm; 28 jewels; 28,800 vph; officially certified chronometer (C.O.S.C.)
Functions: hours, minutes, subsidiary seconds; date; power reserve display
Case: red gold, ø 42.7 mm, height 12 mm; sapphire crystal; screwed-in crown; water-resistant to 300 m
Band: rubber/titanium, folding clasp
Price: $23,800
Variations: also in 40 mm case diameter

Maxi Marine Diver Chronometer

Reference number: 263-33-7/92
Movement: automatic, Ulysse Nardin Caliber UN 26 (base ETA 2892); ø 25.6 mm, height 5.1 mm; 28 jewels; 28,800 vph; officially certified chronometer (C.O.S.C.)
Functions: hours, minutes, subsidiary seconds; date; power reserve display
Case: stainless steel, ø 42.7 mm, height 12 mm; sapphire crystal; screwed-in crown; water-resistant to 300 m
Band: stainless steel, double folding clasp
Price: $6,550
Variations: also in 40 mm case diameter

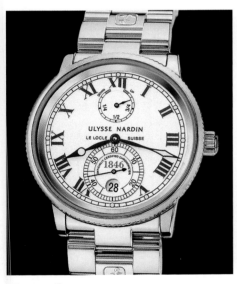

Marine Chronometer

Reference number: 263-22-7/30GR
Movement: automatic, Ulysse Nardin Caliber UN 26 (base ETA 2892); ø 25.6 mm, height 5.1 mm; 28 jewels; 28,800 vph; officially certified chronometer (C.O.S.C.)
Functions: hours, minutes, subsidiary seconds; date; power reserve display
Case: stainless steel, ø 38.5 mm, height 11 mm; sapphire crystal; screwed-in crown; water-resistant to 200 m
Band: stainless steel, double folding clasp
Price: $5,550
Variations: with leather strap; in various dial versions

GMT +/- Big Date Dual Time

Reference number: 226-87/61
Movement: automatic, Ulysse Nardin Caliber UN 22 (base ETA 2892); ø 25.6 mm, height 5.35 mm; 23 jewels; 28,800 vph; patented mechanism for quick-setting the hour hand, adjustable forward and backward via the crown
Functions: hours, minutes, sweep seconds; large date; second time zone
Case: red gold, ø 40 mm, height 11.8 mm; sapphire crystal; exhibition window case back; screwed-in crown; water-resistant to 100 m
Band: reptile skin, buckle
Price: $13,800

GMT +/- Big Date Dual Time

Reference number: 223-88/60
Movement: automatic, Ulysse Nardin Caliber UN 22 (base ETA 2892); ø 25.6 mm, height 5.35 mm; 23 jewels; 28,800 vph; patented mechanism for quick-setting the hour hand, adjustable forward and backward via the crown
Functions: hours, minutes, sweep seconds; large date; second time zone
Case: stainless steel, ø 40 mm, height 11.8 mm; sapphire crystal; exhibition window case back; screwed-in crown; water-resistant to 100 m
Band: reptile skin, buckle
Price: $4,950

Armand Nicolet

Armand Nicolet was born in Tramelan, Switzerland, in 1884 as a member of a watchmaking dynasty. Tramelan was at the time an important horological city, and many members of his family were well known for doing business there. It has been handed down that Armand opened his own workshop at the beginning of the twentieth century, but the first written records were registered when Nicolet Watch showed its wares at the World's Fair in 1939. Armand Nicolet passed away in 1939, but he lives on as the namesake for a company of horological excellence that is still at home in the Jura region's Tramelan. Relaunched in 2001, modern-day Armand Nicolet timepieces utilize the best in contemporary technical reliability and traditional horological finesse.

The current Nicolet collection comprises five main lines. The first four to be issued were based on a small set of models with purist cases and lots of juicy complications sure to please watch fans. M02 and Sloop Royal each comprise three classically designed models, with Sloop Royal appealing to the sportier, yet elegant crowd. M02 is aimed at the individualist.

The Hunter collection is at home in classically proportioned, 38 mm, 18-karat yellow gold cases. This line includes most of the complications known to watchmaking at the current time, including a classic regulator, but not yet including a tourbillon. Sales manager Alessandro Braga explains that he thinks it is still too early for this newly refounded brand to introduce such a complication.

Arc Royal features classically designed silvered dials that mark the passing of time with blued steel hands on Roman numerals. The 39 mm gold case with movable lugs is classic, yet fresh as the new dawn. The complications include everything from subsidiary seconds to a chronograph with a complete calendar.

A recent addition to the collection, and without a doubt the most stunning yet, is a limited edition that has had collectors licking their lips. Based upon a remnant movement of the original Nicolet stock from 1948, Caliber UT 176 experienced some modifications in 2003 to bring it up to today's speed. The revisions performed include the addition of an Incabloc shock protection device, the enhancement of the swan-neck fine adjustment, and the noble decoration of the surfaces with a beautiful *côtes de Genève* pattern to create a model of great simplicity and elegance. As there were only 135 pieces of this movement remaining intact, this timepiece is obviously automatically limited. The dial comprises the underside of the base plate, naturally decorated with the above-mentioned Geneva stripes, and a marker scale that features a striking guilloché subsidiary seconds dial following the shape of the stepped bezel. This masterpiece's transparent case back illustrates the complete beauty of the movement and its modifications, rendering the blued screws, decorated surfaces, and swan-neck fine adjustment especially visible. The edition comprises both white and rose gold models on either a black or brown strap with a gold buckle and retails for $10,800.

MO2 Complete Calendar
Reference number: 7142B NR P914NR2
Movement: automatic, Caliber AN 9200/2824-2 TND/TNK (base ETA 2824-2); ø 25.6 mm; 25 jewels; 28,800 vph; 40 hours power reserve; *côtes de Genève* on rotor, bridges finished with *addouci* pattern
Functions: hours, minutes, sweep seconds; date, day, month, moon phase
Case: rose gold, ø 43 mm, height 12 mm; anti-reflective sapphire crystal; exhibition window case back; water-resistant to 50 m
Band: alligator skin, buckle
Price: $9,900

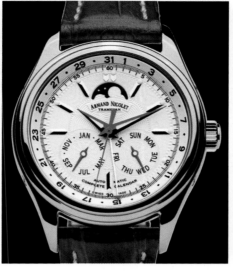

MO2 Complete Calendar
Reference number: 9142B AG P914MR2
Movement: automatic, Caliber AN 9200/2824-2 TND/TNK (base ETA 2824-2); ø 25.6 mm; 25 jewels; 28,800 vph; 40 hours power reserve; *côtes de Genève* on rotor, bridges finished with *addouci* pattern
Functions: hours, minutes, sweep seconds; date, day, month, moon phase
Case: stainless steel, ø 43 mm, height 12 mm; anti-reflective sapphire crystal; exhibition window case back; water-resistant to 100 m
Band: alligator skin, folding clasp
Price: $3,990

MO2 Chronograph
Reference number: 7144A AG P914MR2
Movement: automatic, Caliber AN 2045/2824-2 (base ETA 2824-2); ø 25.6 mm; 49 jewels; 28,800 vph; 40 hours power reserve; *côtes de Genève* on rotor, bridges finished with *addouci* pattern
Functions: hours, minutes, subsidiary seconds; chronograph
Case: rose gold, ø 43 mm, height 12 mm; anti-reflective sapphire crystal; exhibition window case back; water-resistant to 50 m
Band: alligator skin, buckle
Price: $9,600
Variations: on rose gold bracelet ($18,100); with black dial

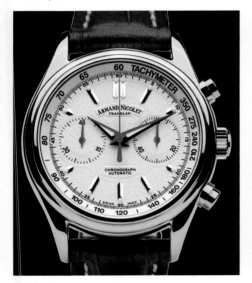

MO2 Chronograph
Reference number: 9144A AG P914MR2
Movement: automatic, Caliber AN 2045/2824-2 (base ETA 2824-2); ø 25.6 mm; 49 jewels; 28,800 vph; 40 hours power reserve; *côtes de Genève* on rotor, bridges finished with *addouci* pattern
Functions: hours, minutes, subsidiary seconds; chronograph
Case: stainless steel, ø 43 mm, height 12 mm; anti-reflective sapphire crystal; exhibition window case back; water-resistant to 100 m
Band: alligator skin, folding clasp
Price: $3,590
Variations: on stainless steel bracelet ($4,090); with black dial

MO2 Big Date and Small Seconds
Reference number: 7146A NR P914NR2
Movement: automatic, Caliber AN 14000/2824-2 (base ETA 2824-2); ø 25.6 mm; 30 jewels; 28,800 vph; 40 hours power reserve; *côtes de Genève* on rotor, bridges finished with *addouci* pattern
Functions: hours, minutes, subsidiary seconds; large date
Case: rose gold, ø 43 mm, height 12 mm; anti-reflective sapphire crystal; exhibition window case back; water-resistant to 50 m
Band: alligator skin, buckle
Price: $9,300
Variations: on rose gold bracelet ($17,800); with silver dial

MO2 Big Date and Small Seconds
Reference number: 9146A AG P914MR2
Movement: automatic, Caliber AN 14000/2824-2 (base ETA 2824-2); ø 25.6 mm; 30 jewels; 28,800 vph; 40 hours power reserve; *côtes de Genève* on rotor, bridges finished with *addouci* pattern
Functions: hours, minutes, subsidiary seconds; large date
Case: stainless steel, ø 43 mm, height 12 mm; anti-reflective sapphire crystal; exhibition window case back; water-resistant to 100 m
Band: alligator skin, folding clasp
Price: $3,590
Variations: on steel bracelet ($4,090); with black dial

Rainer Nienaber

I don't have any chronographs in my collection," says Rainer Nienaber, leaving this statement open at the end and also leaving the listener unsure as to whether this is an elementary concept or not. That he doesn't need them might be the part left out, for even without chronographs this man hailing from Germany's Westphalia region can proudly display a remarkable collection of wristwatches and wall clocks.

Nienaber, born in 1955, learned the trade of toolmaker in a company that specialized in making cameras and precision measuring technology. Since electronics had not yet become popular in all areas of this fine technology at that time, Nienaber experienced the world of precision production as a craftsman, and his favorite measurement was to become the thousandth of a millimeter. After his time in the army (Germany has a mandatory draft), he began to learn a new trade, discovering at the same time that he had found a career in which he could use

both his creativity and his dexterity. Beginning with the repair of watches, he quickly developed into a designer of timepieces, thoroughly enjoying the construction and finishing of his ticking friends. From there, it was just a small step to becoming a producer himself, and it was only a question of time before Nienaber began to design wristwatches.

The handcrafted precision regulators he builds are known far beyond the borders of Germany and are very well received by collectors. Nienaber has designed his King Size Regulator for the wrist to follow in the footsteps of his clocks, using dial designs that are extremely loyal to those of the larger timepieces. Since there is no wristwatch movement in existence that features subsidiary seconds at 12 o'clock, however, he correspondingly rebuilt an old manually wound AS movement and can now proudly present the world's first and only wrist regulator with the "correct" dial divisions.

Despite his love of traditional watch complications, Nienaber also experiments with uncommon displays. The RetroLator combines the unusual regulator display with a retrograde minute indicator, and this mix makes for a real eye-catcher.

King Size Retrograde Hours

Movement: manually wound, AS Caliber 1130; ø 29 mm, height 4 mm; 17 jewels; 21,600 vph; dial train modified for retrograde hour hand; movement finely finished with *côtes de Genève*

Functions: hours (retrograde), minutes; subsidiary seconds

Case: stainless steel, ø 41 mm, height 10 mm; bezel in rose gold; sapphire crystal; exhibition window case back

Band: ostrich leather, double folding clasp

Price: $4,395

Variations: on stainless steel bracelet ($4,645) with stainless steel bezel ($3,795); in medium 36 mm size

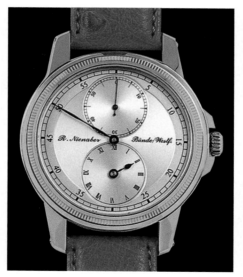

King Size Regulator

Movement: manually wound, RN Caliber 92R; ø 30 mm, height 4.5 mm; 17 jewels; 21,600 vph; dial train with traditional regulator arrangement of the subsidiary seconds at 12 o'clock

Functions: hours (off-center), minutes, subsidiary seconds

Case: stainless steel, ø 41 mm, height 10 mm; bezel in rose gold; sapphire crystal; exhibition window case back

Band: ostrich leather, double folding clasp

Price: $8,950

Variations: on stainless steel bracelet ($9,200); in stainless steel with ETA module movement

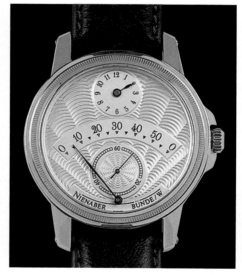

King Size RetroLator

Movement: manually wound, AS Caliber 1130; ø 29.5 mm, height 4 mm; 17 jewels; 21,600 vph; dial train modified for retrograde minute and and precisely jumping hour hand; movement finely finished with *côtes de Genève*

Functions: hours (jump), minutes (retrograde), subsidiary seconds

Case: stainless steel, ø 41 mm, height 10 mm; sapphire crystal; exhibition window case back

Band: ostrich leather, double folding clasp

Price: $4,795

Variations: on stainless steel bracelet ($5,045); in stainless steel with rose gold bezel ($5,395)

Nivrel

N ivrel's owner, Gerd Hofer, who has added the tag line "since 1936" to his label, explains quite frankly how he called the Fédération de l'Industrie Horlogère Suisse ten years ago during his search for a "good" brand name for his newly founded watch business, Time Art GmbH. Stored there "temporarily" are countless names of Swiss watchmakers that have disappeared from the market until an interested party acquires and reactivates them. Hofer resurrected the name Nivrel, plain and simple, without any history, without any sort of background information on the firm — without even a logo. And his level of openness and honesty about all this is rather uncommon in the industry. Nivrel's watches themselves are also crafted with openness and honesty: Everything that looks like gold actually is gold, usually 18 karat. The crystals are always made of synthetic sapphire, and if the hour indica-

tors are raised, then they are most certainly applied to the dial — never just stamped. The watch movements are beautifully finished, and the rings that secure them to the cases, as one would expect, are made of metal instead of plastic. Hofer's credo: "Attention to quality in the details shouldn't drive up the costs so high that one could justify poorer craftsmanship." This is quite a remarkable statement, as there are simpler mechanical watches by Nivrel that can be easily acquired for a small amount of money. And extras, such as large date, moon phase, and various other calendar features, can be had for a very moderate price. This is made possible, on the one hand, by a modular system, in which a relatively modest number of movements and case types are varied to

produce a wide range of very attractive models. On the other hand, Hofer consistently works with first-class suppliers as opposed to maintaining expensive internal development and production departments.

The ideas for his watches, however, come only from Hofer himself. "The idea is what counts," he says. And after looking over his current collection it becomes clear that he is not only a good businessman.

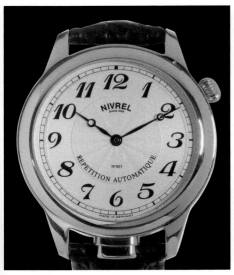

Five-Minute Erotic Repeater

Reference number: N 950.001-6
Movement: automatic, Dubois-Dépraz Caliber 87 (base ETA 2892-A2); ø 36.2 mm, height 7.35 mm; 21 jewels; 28,800 vph; repeater module and rotor hand-skeletonized and engraved
Functions: hours, minutes, sweep seconds; five-minute repeater
Case: stainless steel, ø 42 mm, height 13 mm; sapphire crystal; exhibition window case back
Band: reptile skin, buckle
Price: $17,500
Variations: in rose gold

Caesar Chrono

Reference number: N 520.002
Movement: automatic, ETA Caliber 7751; ø 30 mm, height 7.9 mm; 25 jewels; 28,800 vph
Functions: hours, minutes, subsidiary seconds; chronograph; date, day of the week, month, moon phase; 24-hour display
Case: stainless steel, ø 39.7 mm, height 15 mm; sapphire crystal; exhibition window case back
Band: leather, buckle
Price: $2,500

Caesar

Reference number: N 110.002
Movement: automatic, ETA Caliber 2892-2; ø 25.6 mm, height 4.6 mm; 25 jewels; 28,800 vph
Functions: hours, minutes, sweep seconds; date
Case: stainless steel, ø 39.7 mm, height 12 mm; sapphire crystal; exhibition window case back
Band: leather, buckle
Price: $1,150

Nomos

There sure was something going on in Glashütte on March 17, 2005. This was the day that the Saxon brand's production department moved into its new home in the small town's former train station — located directly across the street from Glashütte Original and A. Lange & Söhne's headquarters.

On this day it also became clear that Nomos is now manufacturing important components of the company's own new automatic movement as well as the manually wound "adoptive" caliber that it has been continually upgrading during the last few years with the company's own developments, such as date and power reserve displays. This means that Nomos has deservedly achieved the status of a true *manufacture*, as managing director Uwe Ahrendt notes, not without a little pride. The Tangomat (this name is a combination of Tangente and automatic) is the work of designer Mirko Heyne, who very intelligently juggled components already available in-house and a flat winding mechanism with a sliding-gear assembly and a duplex wheel integrated underneath the three-quarter plate.

The lion's share of the movement is concentrated on a surface of just about 23 mm, but the option of adding the (encircling) date ring led Heyne to make the base plate 34.65 mm in diameter right from the beginning. Any standard case would have more than enough room for that anyway.

The rotor utilizes almost all of the movement's large diameter, which without a doubt makes it work much more dynamically.

As was already done at the introduction of the date and power reserve models, the first 250 watches of the automatic pre-series have been given to voluntary testers who must wear the watches and record their findings in extensive detail over a three-month period. These experimental movements are housed in modified Tangente cases, even though the Tangomat will eventually receive its own, more sporty

case. Serial production will most likely not begin before the end of 2005, as founder Roland Schwertner still has plenty of plans for his brand.

Since April 1, 2005, only the updated calibers Alpha, Beta, and Delta are being housed in the manually wound models, which contain numerous components that are produced in the new train station premises. These movements are easily recognized by their three-quarter plates and their newly designed balance cocks as well as the shiny rhodium-plated finish with Glashütte ribbing, as most of Nomos's watches will be outfitted with sapphire crystal case backs in the future.

Tangente

Movement: manually wound, Nomos Caliber Alpha; ø 23.3 mm, height 2.6 mm; 17 jewels; 21,600 vph; three-quarter plate, movement surfaces rhodium-plated, Glashütte ribbing and Langeleist perlage; ratchet and crown wheels decorated with Glashütte sunburst pattern

Functions: hours, minutes, subsidiary seconds

Case: stainless steel, ø 35 mm, height 6.6 mm; sapphire crystal; exhibition window case back

Band: Shell Cordovan leather, buckle

Price: $1,650

Variations: with closed case back ($1,500)

Ludwig

Movement: manually wound, Nomos Caliber Alpha; ø 23.3 mm, height 2.6 mm; 17 jewels; 21,600 vph; three-quarter plate, movement surfaces rhodium-plated, Glashütte ribbing and Langeleist perlage; ratchet and crown wheels decorated with Glashütte sunburst pattern

Functions: hours, minutes, subsidiary seconds

Case: stainless steel, ø 35 mm, height 6.25 mm; sapphire crystal

Band: Shell Cordovan leather, buckle

Price: $1,450

Variations: with sapphire crystal exhibition case back ($1,600)

Orion

Movement: manually wound, Nomos Caliber Alpha; ø 23.3 mm, height 2.6 mm; 17 jewels; 21,600 vph; three-quarter plate, movement surfaces rhodium-plated, Glashütte ribbing and Langeleist perlage; ratchet and crown wheels decorated with Glashütte sunburst pattern

Functions: hours, minutes, subsidiary seconds

Case: stainless steel, ø 35 mm, height 8.4 mm; sapphire crystal, domed; exhibition window case back

Band: Shell Cordovan leather, buckle

Price: $1,600

Variations: with white dial and sapphire crystal exhibition case back ($1,900); with closed case back, anthracite or white dial

Tetra

Movement: manually wound, Nomos Caliber Alpha; ø 23.3 mm, height 2.6 mm; 17 jewels; 21,600 vph; three-quarter plate, movement surfaces rhodium-plated, Glashütte ribbing and Langeleist perlage; ratchet and crown wheels decorated with Glashütte sunburst pattern

Functions: hours, minutes, subsidiary seconds

Case: stainless steel, 27.5 x 27.5 mm, height 6.05 mm; sapphire crystal

Band: Shell Cordovan leather, buckle

Price: $1,600

Variations: Tetra large 29.5 x 29.5 mm ($1,700); Tetra large with exhibition case back ($1,850)

Tangente Sport Date

Movement: manually wound, Nomos Caliber Beta; ø 32.15 mm, height 2.8 mm; 23 jewels; 21,600 vph; three-quarter plate, movement surfaces rhodium-plated, Glashütte ribbing and Langeleist perlage; ratchet and crown wheels decorated with Glashütte sunburst pattern

Functions: hours, minutes, subsidiary seconds; date

Case: stainless steel, ø 36.5 mm, height 7.5 mm; sapphire crystal; water-resistant to 100 m

Band: strengthened Shell Cordovan leather, buckle

Price: $2,200

Variations: without date display ($1,650)

Tangente Date Power Reserve

Movement: manually wound, Nomos Caliber Delta; ø 32.15 mm, height 2.8 mm; 23 jewels; 21,600 vph; three-quarter plate, movement surfaces rhodium-plated, Glashütte ribbing and Langeleist perlage; ratchet and crown wheels decorated with Glashütte sunburst pattern

Functions: hours, minutes, subsidiary seconds; date, power reserve display

Case: stainless steel, ø 35 mm, height 6.6 mm; sapphire crystal; exhibition window case back

Band: Shell Cordovan leather, buckle

Price: $3,000

Omega

When Omega introduced its new escapement system five years ago, everyone seemed to have misgivings. The company had indeed developed the coaxial escapement together with "watch pope" George Daniels according to his concept, but whether this mechanism — which ran wonderfully in Daniels's handmade instruments — could function in the long run in serially manufactured watches was not yet clear. Just as unclear was if it would be able to achieve the precision and freedom from maintenance for which Omega strived.

Five years later the company is showing a strapping array of coaxial watches in its program, both in the elegant Constellation and De Ville lines as well as in the diver's collection Seamaster. All of these models are tested by the independent Swiss testing organization C.O.S.C. and have received an official chronometer certificate for their especially precise rates.

The industrial production of the coaxial escapement invented by Daniels, which practically runs without lubrication, was a great challenge for Omega's watchmakers. Now once again Omega finally possesses movements in its program that underscore the brand's *manufacture* status, which has been an arguable one due to the fact that the Swatch Group is strict in its division of labor. The company offers two case sizes for its Seamaster Planet Ocean: Alongside a variation in 42 mm diameter, one can also buy a version that measures a proud 45.5 mm across. Inside both of them tick the — meanwhile reliable — Omega Caliber 2500 featuring a coaxial escapement with 48 hours of power reserve. The design of the stainless steel watch is based on that of the first Seamaster model dating from 1957. Obvious additions to it are the manual helium valve at 10 o'clock and the arrow-shaped hand (Broad Arrow). In addition, the new model is water-resistant to a whopping 600 meters.

A technically demanding new product is the Omega De Ville Chronographe Rattrapante. This split-seconds chronograph makes it possible to measure two events at once via two coupled stop-seconds hands that start at the same time, but end at different times — like during a foot race with two contestants.

Conspicuous is the innovative dial design with its unusually large subdials, so large that they just about run right into each other. Its designers play with two levels: The totalizers are milled out of the dial, and the stop displays lie deeper in the dial than the normal time display. For the subsidiary seconds display at 9 o'clock, Omega utilized something very artful in order to keep the dial's information completely legible. Instead of the usual, full circle displaying the seconds, there are two concentric semicircles here. The inner has a scale of 0 to 30, while the outer scale is for 31 to 60 seconds. A second hand with two arms of varying lengths makes its rounds around this scale, thus showing the time. Just as unusual is the wide date window that shows both the current date as well as the previous and following days.

The De Ville Rattrapante is powered by Omega Caliber 3612 with 52 hours of power reserve, coaxial escapement, and a balance spring without index. The split-seconds functions are controlled by two column wheels. They make sure that starting, stopping, and resetting are precise and without a hitch. Its vertical pivoting ensures that the stop-seconds hand doesn't jump or hesitate when the chronograph is started.

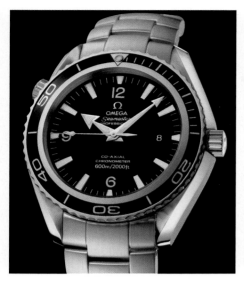

Seamaster Planet Ocean Co-Axial

Reference number: 2200.50.00
Movement: automatic, Omega Caliber 2500C (base Omega 1120); ø 25.6 mm, height 4.1 mm; 27 jewels; 25 200 vph; co-axial escapement; officially certified chronometer (C.O.S.C.)
Functions: hours, minutes, sweep seconds
Case: stainless steel, ø 45.5 mm, height 15.05 mm; unidirectionally rotating bezel with 60-minute divisions; sapphire crystal; screwed-in crown; water-resistant to 600 m
Band: stainless steel, folding clasp
Remarks: case with helium valve
Price: $3,295
Variations: in 42 mm case diameter; leather or rubber strap

Seamaster Planet Ocean Co-Axial

Reference number: 2909.50.38 f.c.
Movement: automatic, Omega Caliber 2500C (base Omega 1120); ø 25.6 mm, height 4.1 mm; 27 jewels; 25.200 vph; co-axial escapement; officially certified chronometer (C.O.S.C.)
Functions: hours, minutes, sweep seconds
Case: stainless steel, ø 42 mm, height 14.2 mm; unidirectionally rotating bezel with 60-minute divisions; sapphire crystal; screwed-in crown; water-resistant to 600 m
Band: reptile skin, folding clasp
Remarks: case with helium valve
Price: $3,095
Variations: 45.5 mm diameter; steel bracelet, rubber strap

Seamaster Apnea 300 m

Reference number: 2595.30.00
Movement: automatic, Omega Caliber 3601 (base Omega 1120); ø 30 mm, height 7.9 mm; 39 jewels; 28,800 vph
Functions: hours, minutes, sweep seconds; short-term timer (regatta timer) with different colors
Case: stainless steel, ø 41.5 mm, height 14 mm; unidirectionally rotating bezel with 60-minute divisions; sapphire crystal; case back with a dedication from Jacques Magniol; screwed-in crown and buttons; water-resistant to 300 m
Band: stainless steel, folding clasp
Price: $3,295
Variations: with black dial; with rubber strap

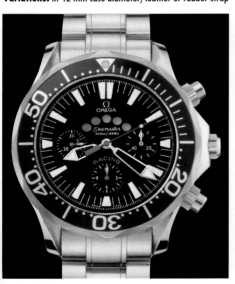

Seamaster Racing 300 m

Reference number: 2569.52.00
Movement: automatic, Omega Caliber 3602 (base Omega 1120); ø 30 mm, height 7.9 mm; 39 jewels; 28,800 vph; officially certified chronometer (C.O.S.C.)
Functions: hours, minutes, subsidiary seconds; chronograph; regatta countdown display
Case: stainless steel, ø 44 mm, height 15 mm; unidirectionally rotating bezel with 60-minute divisions; sapphire crystal; screwed-in crown and buttons; water-resistant to 300 m
Band: stainless steel, folding clasp
Price: $4,595
Variations: with leather strap; in titanium

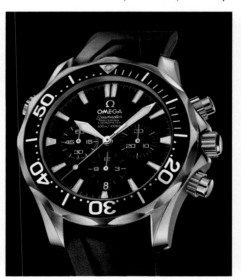

Seamaster Chrono Diver 300 m

Reference number: 2894.52.91
Movement: automatic, Omega Caliber 3301; ø 27 mm, height 6.85 mm; 33 jewels; 28,800 vph; column wheel control of chronograph functions; official COSC chronometer
Functions: hours, minutes, subsidiary seconds; chronograph; date
Case: stainless steel, ø 41.5 mm, height 15 mm; unidirectionally rotating bezel with 60-minute divisions; sapphire crystal; screwed-in crown and buttons; water-resistant to 300 m
Band: rubber, buckle
Remarks: case with helium valve
Price: $3,595

Seamaster 300 M Chrono Olympic

Reference number: 2894.51.91
Movement: automatic, Omega Caliber 3303; ø 27 mm, height 6.85 mm; 33 jewels; 28,800 vph; column wheel control of chronograph functions; official COSC chronometer
Functions: hours, minutes, subsidiary seconds; chronograph; date
Case: stainless steel, ø 41.5 mm, height 15 mm; unidirectionally rotating bezel with 60-minute divisions; sapphire crystal; screwed-in crown and buttons; water-resistant to 300 m
Band: rubber, buckle
Remarks: Olympic Collection (total 4 watches); helium valve
Price: $3,695

Seamaster Railmaster XXL Chronometer

Reference number: 2806.52.37
Movement: manually wound, Omega Caliber 2201 (base ETA Unitas 6498-2); ø 36.6 mm, height 4.5 mm; 17 jewels; 21,600 vph; officially certified chronometer (C.O.S.C.)
Functions: hours, minutes, subsidiary seconds
Case: stainless steel, ø 49.2 mm, height 11 mm; sapphire crystal; exhibition window case back; water-resistant to 150 m
Band: reptile skin, folding clasp
Price: $3,095

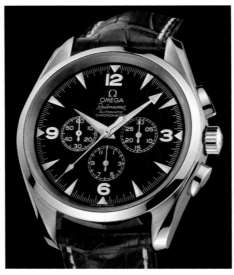

Seamaster Aqua Terra Railmaster Big Size Chronograph

Reference number: 2812.52.37
Movement: automatic, Omega Caliber 3205 (base Omega 3300); ø 27 mm, height 6.85 mm; 33 jewels; 28,800 vph; column wheel control of chronograph functions; officially certified chronometer (C.O.S.C.)
Functions: hours, minutes, subsidiary seconds; chronograph
Case: stainless steel, ø 42.2 mm, height 15 mm; sapphire crystal; screwed-in crown; water-resistant to 150 m
Band: reptile skin, folding clasp
Price: $3,795
Variations: with stainless steel bracelet

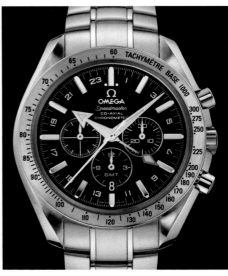

Speedmaster Broad Arrow XL Co-Axial GMT

Reference number: 3581.50.00
Movement: automatic, Omega Caliber 3603 (base Piguet 1285); co-axial escapement; official COSC chronometer
Functions: hours, minutes, subsidiary seconds; chronograph; date; 24-hour display (second time zone)
Case: stainless steel, ø 44.25 mm, height 15.2 mm; bezel engraved with tachymeter scale; sapphire crystal; exhibition window case back; water-resistant to 100 m
Band: stainless steel, folding clasp
Price: $6,295
Variations: with calfskin leather strap; with white dial

Speedmaster Michael Schumacher The Legend Collection

Reference number: 3507.51.00
Movement: automatic, Omega Caliber 3301 (base Omega 3300); ø 27 mm, height 6.85 mm; 33 jewels; 28,800 vph; column wheel for chronograph functions; COSC chronometer
Functions: hours, minutes, subsidiary seconds; chronograph; date
Case: stainless steel, ø 42 mm, height 14.2 mm; bezel in black aluminum with tachymeter scale; sapphire crystal; water-resistant to 100 m
Band: stainless steel, folding clasp
Price: $4,095

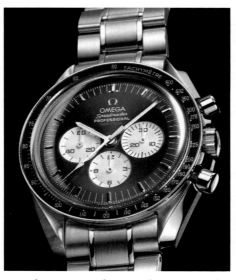

Speedmaster Professional Moonwatch "First Space Walk"

Reference number: 3565.80.00
Movement: manually wound, Omega Caliber 1861 (base Lémania 1873); ø 27 mm, height 6.87 mm; 18 jewels; 21,600 vph
Functions: hours, minutes, subsidiary seconds; chronograph
Case: stainless steel, ø 42 mm, height 14.3 mm; bezel in blue aluminum with tachymeter scale; Plexiglas; exhibition window case back; water-resistant to 50 m
Band: stainless steel, folding clasp
Remarks: anniversary "edition First Space Walk"; ltd. to 2005 pcs.
Price: $3,195

Speedmaster Broad Arrow

Reference number: 3551.20.00
Movement: automatic, Omega Caliber 3303; ø 27 mm, height 6.85 mm; 33 jewels; 28,800 vph; column wheel control of chronograph functions; official COSC chronometer
Functions: hours, minutes, subsidiary seconds; chronograph; date
Case: stainless steel, ø 42 mm, height 13.8 mm; bezel engraved with tachymeter scale; sapphire crystal; water-resistant to 100 m
Band: stainless steel, folding clasp
Price: $4,695
Variations: with leather strap

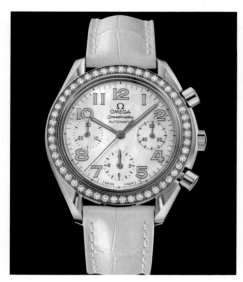

Speedmaster Ladies

Reference number: 3835.74.34 f.c.
Movement: automatic, Omega Caliber 3220; ø 30 mm, height 6.5 mm; 47 jewels; 28,800 vph
Functions: hours, minutes, subsidiary seconds; chronograph
Case: stainless steel, ø 35.5 mm, height 12.55 mm; bezel set with 49 diamonds; sapphire crystal; water-resistant to 100 m
Band: reptile skin, folding clasp
Price: $7,395
Variations: leather strap and dial variations; with stainless steel bracelet

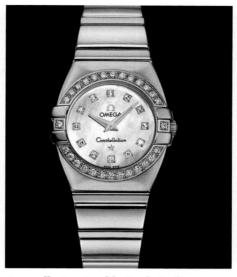

Constellation Double Eagle Ladies

Reference number: 1389.75.00
Movement: quartz, Omega Caliber 1376
Functions: hours, minutes
Case: stainless steel/yellow gold, ø 24 mm, height 9 mm; bezel in yellow gold set with 28 diamonds; sapphire crystal; water-resistant to 100 m
Band: stainless steel/yellow gold, folding clasp
Remarks: mother-of-pearl dial set with 12 diamonds
Price: $5,095
Variations: in yellow gold, with and without brilliant-cut diamonds

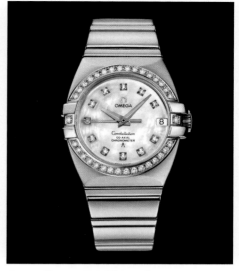

Constellation Double Eagle Co-Axial Ladies

Reference number: 1599.75.00
Movement: automatic, Omega Caliber 2500C (base Omega 1120); ø 25.6 mm, height 4.1 mm; 27 jewels; 28,800 vph; co-axial escapement; officially certified chronometer (C.O.S.C.)
Functions: hours, minutes, sweep seconds; date
Case: stainless steel, ø 31 mm, height 9 mm; bezel set with 36 diamonds; sapphire crystal; exhibition window case back; water-resistant to 100 m
Band: stainless steel, folding clasp
Remarks: mother-of-pearl dial set with 12 diamonds
Price: $6,295

Constellation Double Eagle Co-Axial Chronograph

Reference number: 1819.51.91 f.c.
Movement: automatic, Omega Caliber 3313 (base Omega 3303); ø 27 mm, height 6.85 mm; 37 jewels; 28,800 vph; co-axial escapement; COSC chronometer; column wheel
Functions: hours, minutes, subsidiary seconds; chronograph; date
Case: stainless steel, ø 41 mm, height 11 mm; bezel in black aluminum with Roman hour markers; sapphire crystal; exhibition window case back; water-resistant to 100 m
Band: rubber, folding clasp
Price: $4,995

De Ville X2 Co-Axial Big Date

Reference number: 7711.30.39 f.c.
Movement: automatic, Omega Caliber 2610 (base Omega 2500C); ø 25.6 mm, height 5.35 mm; 28 jewels; 25.200 vph; co-axial escapement; officially certified chronometer (C.O.S.C.)
Functions: hours, minutes, sweep seconds; large date
Case: white gold, 35 x 35 mm, height 12.8 mm; sapphire crystal; water-resistant to 50 m
Band: reptile skin, folding clasp
Price: $11,895

De Ville Co-Axial Chronograph Rattrapante

Reference number: 4847.50.31 f.c.
Movement: automatic, Omega Caliber 3612 (base Omega 3303); ø 27 mm, height 6.85 mm; 33 jewels; 28,800 vph; co-axial escapement; column wheel; COSC chronometer
Functions: hours, minutes, subsidiary seconds; split-seconds chronograph; date
Case: stainless steel, ø 41 mm, height 14.8 mm; sapphire crystal; exhibition window case back; screwed-in crown; water-resistant to 100 m
Band: reptile skin, folding clasp
Price: $9,795

De Ville Ladies Co-Axial Chronograph

Reference number: 4877.60.37 f.c.
Movement: automatic, Omega Caliber 3313 (base Omega Piguet 3303); ø 27 mm, height 6.85 mm; 37 jewels; 28,800 vph; co-axial escapement; column wheel; COSC chronometer
Functions: hours, minutes, subsidiary seconds; chronograph; date
Case: stainless steel, ø 35 mm, height 12.46 mm; bezel set with 42 diamonds; sapphire crystal; exhibition window case back; crown set with brilliant-cut diamond; water-resistant to 100 m
Band: leather, folding clasp
Price: $10,795

De Ville Prestige Co-Axial Small Seconds

Reference number: 4813.40.01
Movement: automatic, Omega Caliber 2202 (base Omega 2500C); ø 25.6 mm, height 4.85 mm; 33 jewels; 25.200 vph; co-axial escapement; officially certified chronometer (C.O.S.C.)
Functions: hours, minutes, subsidiary seconds
Case: stainless steel, ø 39 mm, height 10.05 mm; sapphire crystal; water-resistant to 30 m
Band: reptile skin, buckle
Price: $2,895
Variations: availabe with a silver dial

Exclusive Collection Aquarella

Reference number: 5778.71.56
Movement: automatic, Omega Caliber 2200 (base Omega 1120); ø 25.6 mm, height 4.75 mm; 29 jewels; 28,800 vph; officially certified chronometer (C.O.S.C.)
Functions: hours, minutes, subsidiary seconds
Case: stainless steel, ø 40.2 mm, bezel and lugs set with 80 diamonds, flange set with 48 pink sapphires; sapphire crystal; water-resistant to 50 m
Band: reptile skin, buckle
Price: $12,295
Variations: dial flange available with diamonds and colored gemstones in various colors

Omegamania

Reference number: 5886.70.56
Movement: quartz, Omega Caliber 4000
Functions: hours, minutes
Case: white gold, 27 x 27.7 mm, height 8 mm; bezel in Omega shape set with 41 diamonds; sapphire crystal; water-resistant to 30 m
Band: leather, buckle
Price: $8,795
Variations: diverse dial colors; in rose gold

Museum Collection Centenary 1948

Reference number: 5704.60.02
Movement: automatic, Omega Caliber 2202 (base Omega 2500C); ø 25.6 mm, height 4.85 mm; 33 jewels; 25.200 vph; co-axial escapement; officially certified chronometer (C.O.S.C.)
Functions: hours, minutes, subsidiary seconds
Case: rose gold, ø 36 mm, height 11 mm; sapphire crystal; water-resistant to 30 m
Band: reptile skin, buckle
Remarks: limited to 1,948 pieces
Price: $7,595

Museum Collection Tonneau Renversé

Reference number: 5705.30.01
Movement: automatic, Omega Caliber 2202 (base Omega 2500C); ø 25.6 mm, height 4.85 mm; 33 jewels; 25.200 vph; co-axial escapement; officially certified chronometer (C.O.S.C.)
Functions: hours, minutes, subsidiary seconds
Case: white gold/rose gold, 35.8 x 46.2 mm, height 13.2 mm; sapphire crystal; water-resistant to 30 m
Band: reptile skin, buckle
Remarks: limited to 1952 pieces
Price: $12,195

Caliber 2201

Base caliber: ETA 6498
Mechanical with manual winding, power reserve 60 hours
Functions: hours, minutes, subsidiary seconds
Diameter: 36.6 mm (16 3/4''')
Height: 4.5 mm
Jewels: 17
Balance: glucydur, three-legged
Frequency: 21,600 vph
Balance spring: Nivarox I flat hairspring
Shock protection: Incabloc
Remarks: base plate with perlage, bridges and cocks with *côtes de Genève*; officially certified C.O.S.C. chronometer

Caliber 3602

Base caliber: 1120
Mechanical with automatic winding, power reserve 40 hours
Functions: hours, minutes, subsidiary seconds; short time interval counter (regatta countdown display)
Diameter: 30 mm
Height: 7.9 mm
Jewels: 49
Balance: glucydur
Frequency: 28,800 vph

Caliber 2500C

Mechanical with automatic winding, co-axial escapement; power reserve 44 hours
Functions: hours, minutes, sweep seconds; date
Diameter: 25.6 mm (11 1/2''')
Height: 3.9 mm
Jewels: 27
Balance: glucydur, with gold regulating screws
Frequency: 28,800 vph
Balance spring: freely swinging
Remarks: base plate with perlage, bridges and rotor with *côtes de Genève*, rhodium-plated; officially certified C.O.S.C. chronometer

Caliber 2610

Base caliber: 2500C
Mechanical with automatic winding, co-axial escapement; power reserve 48 hours
Functions: hours, minutes, sweep seconds; large date
Diameter: 25.6 mm
Height: 5.35 mm
Jewels: 28
Balance: glucydur, with gold regulating screws
Frequency: 25,200 vph
Balance spring: freely swinging
Remarks: base plate with perlage, bridges and rotor with *côtes de Genève*, rhodium-plated; officially certified C.O.S.C. chronometer, rate optimized by new oscillating frequency

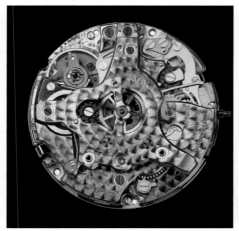

Caliber 3612

Base caliber: 3313
Mechanical with automatic winding; co-axial escapement; power reserve 52 hours
Functions: hours, minutes, subsidiary seconds; date; split-seconds chronograph
Diameter: 27 mm (12''')
Height: 8.45 mm
Jewels: 38
Balance: glucydur
Frequency: 28,800 vph
Balance spring: freely swinging
Remarks: control of chronograph functions via two intermediate wheels; officially certified C.O.S.C. chronometer

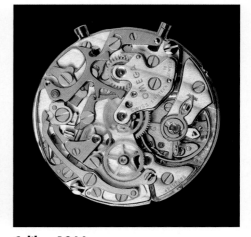

Caliber 1866

Base caliber: Nouvelle Lémania 1874
Mechanical with manual winding, power reserve 45 hours
Functions: hours, minutes, subsidiary seconds; date; moon phase; chronograph
Diameter: 27 mm (12''')
Height: 6.87 mm
Jewels: 18
Balance: glucydur, four-legged
Frequency: 21,600 vph
Balance spring: Nivarox I flat hairspring with fine adjustment
Remarks: base plate with perlage, beveled bridges with *côtes de Genève*; rhodium-plated; polished levers with beveled and polished edges

Oris

Watch fans all over the world think of Oris first and foremost as a line of mechanical watches at a reasonable price. This little brand, which celebrated its hundredth anniversary last year, sees the demand of its followers as a challenge, proving that it is possible to have a clever model policy and consistent passion for mechanical watches even in a hotly contested price segment and do well there — as long as the consumer continues to avoid confusing reasonable with cheap and the brand continues develop its individual concepts.

One of these individual concepts is quoting one's own past in these times of retro culture. That is something Oris does well, as evidenced by its current replica of the Chronoris model from 1970. The cushion-shaped case, the calfskin leather strap with holes, and the color combination black and orange breathe new life into the '70s remake without having an old-fashioned effect. The unconventionally modified ETA 7750 replaces the *manufacture* movement that ran the original.

After all, from 1910 until 1982 Oris was a genuine *manufacture* with a large degree of autonomy. All of the company's movements, their parts, and their finishing were

produced in Oris's own ateliers, with the exception of mainsprings, balance springs, and jewels. In the 1950s Oris employed around 600 people and produced one to two million wristwatches and more than 100,000 alarm clocks per year.

Since its founding year of 1904, Oris has striven to bring high-quality mechanical watches of the company's own design outfitted with interesting movements to the market. Today there is hardly another company that can offer mechanical watches in comparative quality at these very competitive prices.

Fortunately, Oris has been able to call upon a rich fund of historical models that all seem to have that *je ne sais quoi* about them. One need only think about the hand-winding alarm watch outfitted with the AS Caliber 1730 and its carefully modernized 1950s design, which was obviously so much to the taste of an entire generation of mechanical watch consumers with its moderate price that, for a while, the demand for it seemed almost hysterical.

That sparked, in a manner of speaking, the beginning of Oris's second career. Strongly fueled by the catchy slogan "it's high mech" and with just the right feel for consumer tastes, the brand has presented models full of character such as the Pointer, outfitted with an unusual sweep calendar hand, and the Complication, featuring a calendar and a moon phase. And there is one model line that has become something of a trademark for Oris with its largely dimensioned crown, therefore appropriately named Big Crown.

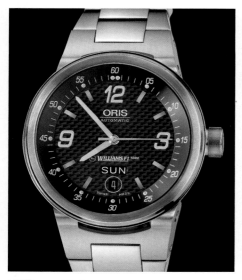

Williams F1 Team Day Date

Reference number: 635 7560 41 65
Movement: automatic, Oris Caliber 635 (base ETA 2836-2);
ø 25.6 mm, height 5.05 mm; 25 jewels; 28,800 vph
Functions: hours, minutes, sweep seconds; date
Case: stainless steel, ø 40.5 mm, height 10.5 mm; sapphire
crystal; exhibition window case back; water-resistant to 50 m
Band: stainless steel, folding clasp
Price: $975

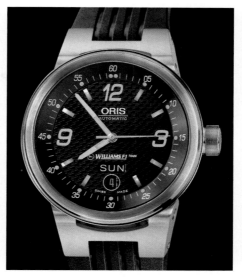

Williams F1 Team Day Date

Reference number: 635 7560 41 64
Movement: automatic, Oris Caliber 635 (base ETA 2836-2);
ø 25.6 mm, height 5.05 mm; 25 jewels; 28,800 vph
Functions: hours, minutes, sweep seconds; date
Case: stainless steel, ø 40.5 mm, height 10.5 mm; sapphire
crystal; exhibition window case back; water-resistant to 50 m
Band: rubber, folding clasp
Price: $895

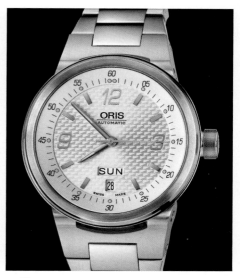

Williams F1 Team Day Date

Reference number: 635 7560 41 61
Movement: automatic, Oris Caliber 635 (base ETA 2836-2);
ø 25.6 mm, height 5.05 mm; 25 jewels; 28,800 vph
Functions: hours, minutes, sweep seconds; date
Case: stainless steel, ø 40.5 mm, height 10.5 mm; sapphire
crystal; exhibition window case back; water-resistant to 50 m
Band: stainless steel, folding clasp
Price: $975

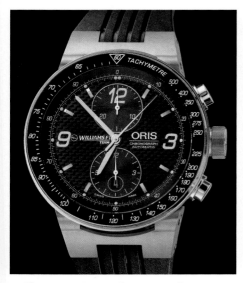

Williams F1 Team Chronograph

Reference number: 673 7563 41 84
Movement: automatic, Oris Caliber 673 (base ETA 7750);
ø 30 mm, height 7.9 mm; 25 jewels; 28,800 vph
Functions: hours, minutes; chronograph; date
Case: stainless steel, ø 45 mm, height 14 mm; bezel with
tachymeter scale; sapphire crystal; exhibition window case
back; water-resistant to 50 m
Band: rubber, folding clasp
Remarks: carbon fiber dial
Price: $2,250
Variations: with stainless steel bracelet ($2,325)

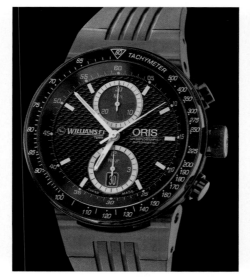

Williams F1 Chronograph

Reference number: 673 7563 47 54
Movement: automatic, Oris Caliber 673 (base ETA 7750);
ø 30 mm, height 7.9 mm; 25 jewels; 28,800 vph
Functions: hours, minutes; chronograph; date
Case: stainless steel, PVD-coated black, ø 45 mm,
height 14 mm; bezel with tachymeter scale; sapphire crystal;
exhibition window case back; water-resistant to 50 m
Band: rubber, folding clasp
Remarks: carbon fiber dial
Price: $2,325

Big Crown Chronograph

Reference number: 581 7567 40 61
Movement: automatic, Oris Caliber 673 (base ETA 7750);
ø 30 mm, height 7.9 mm; 25 jewels; 28,800 vph
Functions: hours, minutes; chronograph; date
Case: stainless steel, ø 42 mm, height 14.7 mm; Plexiglas;
exhibition window case back
Band: leather, buckle
Price: $1,850
Variations: with stainless steel bracelet ($1,995); with rose
gold bezel on strap ($1,895) or stainless steel bracelet
($2,095)

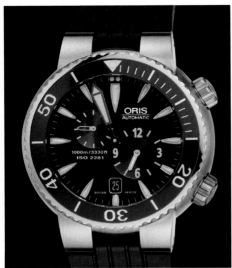

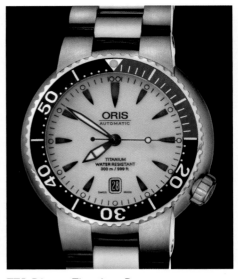

TT1 Master Diver

Reference number: 649 7541 70 54
Movement: automatic, Oris Caliber 649 (base ETA 2836-2); ø 25.6 mm, height 5.05 mm; 27 jewels; 28,800 vph
Functions: hours (off-center), minutes, subsidiary seconds; date
Case: titanium, ø 44 mm, height 15.2 mm; unidirectionally rotating bezel with 60-minute divisions under crystal; sapphire crystal; screwed-in crown; water-resistant to 1000 m
Band: rubber, folding clasp with wetsuit extension
Remarks: helium valve; additional titanium bracelet in set
Price: $1,995

TT1 Divers Titanium

Reference number: 633 7541 70 54
Movement: automatic, Oris Caliber 633 (base ETA 2824-2); ø 25.6 mm, height 4.6 mm; 25 jewels; 28,800 vph
Functions: hours, minutes, sweep seconds; date
Case: titanium, ø 44 mm, height 15.2 mm; unidirectionally rotating bezel with 60-minute divisions under crystal; sapphire crystal; exhibition window case back; screwed-in crown; water-resistant to 1000 m
Band: titanium, folding clasp
Remarks: helium valve
Price: $1,525
Variations: on a rubber strap ($1,395)

TT1 Divers Titanium Date

Reference number: 633 7562 70 59
Movement: automatic, Oris Caliber 633 (base ETA 2824-2); ø 25.6 mm, height 4.6 mm; 25 jewels; 28,800 vph
Functions: hours, minutes, sweep seconds; date
Case: titanium, ø 44 mm, height 12.7 mm; unidirectionally rotating bezel with 60-minute divisions; sapphire crystal; exhibition window case back; screwed-in crown; water-resistant to 300 m
Band: titanium, folding clasp
Price: $1,525
Variations: on a rubber strap ($1,395)

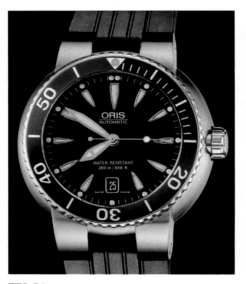

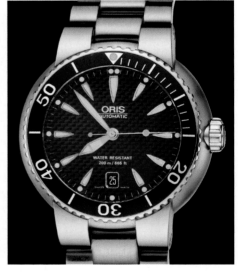

TT1 Divers Titanium Chronograph

Reference number: 674 7542 70 54
Movement: automatic, Oris Caliber 674 (base ETA 7750); ø 30 mm, height 7.9 mm; 25 jewels; 28,800 vph
Functions: hours, minutes, seconds; chronograph; date
Case: titanium, ø 44 mm, height 14.75 mm; unidirectionally rotating bezel with 60-minute divisions under crystal; sapphire crystal; exhibition window case back; screwed-in crown; water-resistant to 300 m
Band: rubber, folding clasp with wetsuit extension
Remarks: helium valve
Price: $2,350
Variations: with titanium bracelet ($2,495)

TT1 Divers

Reference number: 633 7533 94 54
Movement: automatic, Oris Caliber 633 (base ETA 2824-2); ø 25.6 mm, height 4.6 mm; 25 jewels; 28,800 vph
Functions: hours, minutes, sweep seconds; date
Case: stainless steel, ø 44 mm, height 12.5 mm; unidirectionally rotating bezel with 60-minute divisions; sapphire crystal; exhibition window case back; water-resistant to 200 m
Band: rubber, folding clasp
Price: $1,050

TT1 Divers

Reference number: 633 7533 95 55
Movement: automatic, Oris Caliber 633 (base ETA 2824-2); ø 25.6 mm, height 4.6 mm; 25 jewels; 28,800 vph
Functions: hours, minutes, sweep seconds; date
Case: stainless steel, ø 44 mm, height 12.5 mm; unidirectionally rotating bezel with 60-minute divisions; sapphire crystal; exhibition window case back; water-resistant to 200 m
Band: stainless steel, folding clasp
Price: $1,195

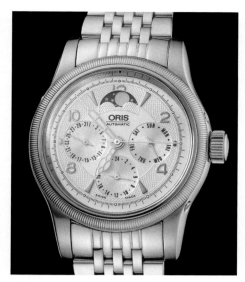

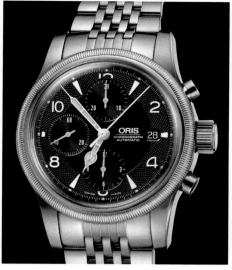

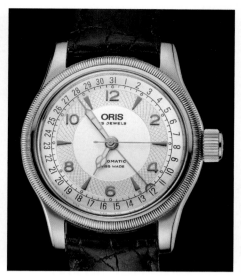

Big Crown Complication

Reference number: 581 7566 43 61
Movement: automatic, Oris Caliber 581 (base ETA 2688/2671); ø 23.6 mm, height 5.6 mm; 17 jewels; 28,800 vph; movement diameter modified
Functions: hours, minutes, sweep seconds; date, day of the week, moon phase; 24-hour display (second time zone)
Case: stainless steel, ø 38 mm, height 12 mm; rose gold-plated bezel; Plexiglas; exhibition window case back; water-resistant to 50 m
Band: stainless steel, gold-plated links, folding clasp
Price: $1,425
Variations: with leather strap ($1,250) or steel bracelet

Big Crown Chronograph

Reference number: 674 7567 40 64
Movement: automatic, Oris Caliber 674/675 (base ETA 7750); ø 30 mm, height 7.9 mm; 25 jewels; 28,800 vph
Functions: hours, minutes, subsidiary seconds; chronograph; date
Case: stainless steel, ø 42 mm, height 14.7 mm; Plexiglas; exhibition window case back; water-resistant to 50 m
Band: stainless steel, folding clasp
Price: upon request
Variations: with leather strap

Big Crown Pointer Date

Reference number: 654 7543 40 61
Movement: automatic, Oris Caliber 654 (base ETA 2824-2); ø 25.6 mm, height 4.6 mm; 25 jewels; 28,800 vph
Functions: hours, minutes, sweep seconds; date
Case: stainless steel, ø 40 mm, height 11 mm; Plexiglas; exhibition window case back; water-resistant to 50 m
Band: leather, buckle
Price: $850
Variations: with stainless steel bracelet ($1,025)

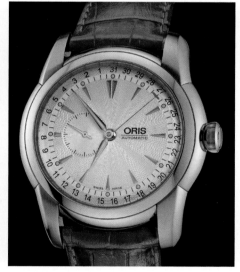

Artelier Complication

Reference number: 581 7564 40 51
Movement: automatic, Oris Caliber 581 (base ETA 2688/2671); ø 23.6 mm, height 5.6 mm; 17 jewels; 28,800 vph; movement diameter modified
Functions: hours, minutes, sweep seconds; date, day of the week, moon phase; 24-hour display (second time zone)
Case: stainless steel, ø 40.5 mm, height 11.8 mm; sapphire crystal; exhibition window case back
Band: leather, folding clasp
Price: $1,425
Variations: with stainless steel bracelet ($1,595)

Artelier Chronograph

Reference number: 676 7547 40 51
Movement: automatic, Oris Caliber 676 (base ETA 7754); ø 30 mm, height 7.9 mm; 25 jewels; 28,800 vph
Functions: hours, minutes, subsidiary seconds; chronograph; date
Case: stainless steel, ø 44.5 mm, height 14.6 mm; sapphire crystal; exhibition window case back
Band: leather, folding clasp
Price: $2,495
Variations: with stainless steel bracelet ($2,650)

Artelier Pointer Date

Reference number: 644 7545 40 51
Movement: automatic, Oris Caliber 644 (base ETA 2836-2); ø 25.6 mm, height 5.05 mm; 27 jewels; 28,800 vph
Functions: hours, minutes, subsidiary seconds; date
Case: stainless steel, ø 42.5 mm, height 11.1 mm; sapphire crystal; exhibition window case back
Band: leather, folding clasp
Price: $1,195
Variations: with stainless steel bracelet ($1,325)

Panerai

Guido Panerai & Figlio, founded in 1860 in Florence, originally specialized in precision mechanics and quickly advanced to become the official supplier of the Italian navy. Panerai provided this government organization with especially progressive and precise instruments such as compasses, depth measuring devices, and torpedo fuses. The company, which had in the meantime become Officine Panerai, manufactured its first timekeeper in 1936 — a diver's watch for combat swimmers called the Radiomir. Throughout the decades, the company's highly specialized product palette made the name Panerai synonymous with measuring maritime space and time, surely forming the base of Officine Panerai's unique reputation among international watch collectors.

This Italian cult brand has managed to garner quite a following stateside. Panerai's business has been brilliant since it was taken over by the Richemont group eight years ago, and the constant investment is now certainly paying off. The directors of this company, which today numbers around 120 employees, as well as the departments for advertising and marketing are quartered in offices on Via Ludovico di Breme in Milan. The design and development departments are also situated in the Northern Italian metropolis.

Sixty-five employees are occupied with the assembly of the watches, however, which takes place completely in Switzerland's Neuchâtel. Just a few steps away from the banks of Lake Neuchâtel there is a spacious building that previously served as the city's police station before it was used for a number of years by another watch company and then purchased by Panerai two years ago. Before the production of the company's own watch caliber containing a large power reserve and a large, linear power reserve display starts in earnest, Manufacture Panerai continues to lavishly rework ETA *ébauches* (Valjoux and Unitas calibers). This is also true of the rest of the stock of the vintage Angelus eight-day movement with which the first Luminors became famous, and which are now being prepared for a limited special edition at the factory in Neuchâtel.

Although the company has moved its main residence to Switzerland, it has not forgotten its roots. The Bottega d'Arte Panerai in the heart of Florence was one of the best addresses for fine Swiss watches in the year 1900. Today the little shop can still be found ensconced in Palazzo Arcivescovile, the archbishop's palace in Florence and a building classified as a historical monument. A sign in the narrow glass window self-confidently proclaims the shop a *laboratorio di idee*, or idea laboratory. Until the 1990s it was Maria Teresa Abetti Panerai, Giuseppe Panerai's widow, who was to be found behind the counter of the old watch shop. After the death of her husband in 1972, she took over its direction.

Now eighty-two years old, Signora Panerai has followed the development of her previous company with interest and goodwill. "I am very impressed, especially because I have the impression that the work that my family began in the past is now being continued," says the *grande dame*. "It's very nice to observe how many projects Panerai has going, and I am proud of it."

Radiomir Base

Reference number: PAM00210
Movement: manually wound, Panerai Caliber OP X; ø 36.6 mm, height 4.5 mm; 17 jewels; 21,600 vph; officially certified chronometer (C.O.S.C.)
Functions: hours, minutes
Case: polished stainless steel, ø 45 mm; sapphire crystal; exhibition window case back; water-resistant to 100 m
Band: leather, buckle
Price: $4,050

Radiomir 8 Days

Reference number: PAM00197
Movement: manually wound, Panerai Caliber OP XIV; ø 32 mm, height 5.3 mm; 33 jewels; 28,800 vph; power reserve 8 days; officially certified chronometer (C.O.S.C.)
Functions: hours, minutes, subsidiary seconds
Case: rose gold, ø 45 mm; sapphire crystal; exhibition window case back; water-resistant to 100 m
Band: reptile skin, buckle
Price: $19,700
Variations: in polished stainless steel with black dial

Radiomir Rattrapante

Reference number: PAM00214
Movement: automatic, Panerai Caliber OP XVIII; ø 30 mm, height 8.3 mm; 27 jewels; 28,800 vph; officially certified chronometer (C.O.S.C.)
Functions: hours, minutes, subsidiary seconds; split-seconds chronograph
Case: polished stainless steel, ø 45 mm; sapphire crystal; exhibition window case back; water-resistant to 100 m
Band: reptile skin, buckle
Price: $10,400

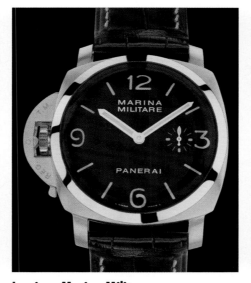

Luminor Marina Logo

Reference number: PAM00005
Movement: manually wound, Panerai Caliber OP II; ø 36.6 mm, height 4.5 mm; 17 jewels; 21,600 vph; officially certified chronometer (C.O.S.C.)
Functions: hours, minutes, subsidiary seconds
Case: polished stainless steel, ø 44 mm; sapphire crystal; crown with security brake lever lock; water-resistant to 300 m
Band: leather, buckle
Price: $5,300

Luminor Marina Militare

Reference number: PAM00217
Movement: manually wound, Panerai Caliber OP XI; ø 36.6 mm, height 4.5 mm; 17 jewels; 21,600 vph; officially certified chronometer (C.O.S.C.)
Functions: hours, minutes, subsidiary seconds
Case: satin-finished stainless steel, ø 47 mm; sapphire crystal; exhibition window case back; crown with security brake lever lock; water-resistant to 100 m
Band: reptile skin, buckle
Remarks: limited to 1,000 pieces
Price: $9,500

Luminor Base Left-Handed

Reference number: PAM00219
Movement: manually wound, Panerai Caliber OP X; ø 36.6 mm, height 4.5 mm; 17 jewels; 21,600 vph; officially certified chronometer (C.O.S.C.)
Functions: hours, minutes
Case: polished stainless steel, ø 44 mm; sapphire crystal; exhibition window case back; crown with security brake lever lock; water-resistant to 300 m
Band: leather, buckle
Price: $4,200

Luminor 1950 Flyback

Reference number: PAM00212
Movement: automatic, Panerai Caliber OP XIX; ø 30 mm, height 8.1 mm; 27 jewels; 28,800 vph; officially certified chronometer (C.O.S.C.)
Functions: hours, minutes, subsidiary seconds; flyback chronograph
Case: satin-finished stainless steel, ø 44 mm; sapphire crystal; exhibition window case back; crown with security brake lever lock; water-resistant to 100 m
Band: nylon, buckle
Price: $8,700

Luminor 1950 Rattrapante

Reference number: PAM00213
Movement: automatic, Panerai Caliber OP XVIII; ø 30 mm, height 8.3 mm; 27 jewels; 28,800 vph; officially certified chronometer (C.O.S.C.)
Functions: hours, minutes, subsidiary seconds; split-seconds chronograph
Case: satin-finished stainless steel, ø 44 mm; sapphire crystal; exhibition window case back; crown with security brake lever lock; water-resistant to 100 m
Band: nylon, buckle
Price: $10,750

Luminor Chrono Daylight

Reference number: PAM00188
Movement: automatic, Panerai Caliber OP XII; ø 30 mm, height 7.9 mm; 27 jewels; 28,800 vph; officially certified chronometer (C.O.S.C.)
Functions: hours, minutes, subsidiary seconds; chronograph; date
Case: satin-finished stainless steel, ø 44 mm, bezel engraved with tachymeter scale; sapphire crystal; crown with security brake lever lock; water-resistant to 100 m
Band: reptile skin, buckle
Price: $6,150
Variations: with black dial

Luminor Marina Automatic

Reference number: PAM00120
Movement: automatic, Panerai Caliber OP III; ø 30 mm, height 7.9 mm; 21 jewels; 28,800 vph; officially certified chronometer (C.O.S.C.)
Functions: hours, minutes, subsidiary seconds; date
Case: satin-finished stainless steel, ø 40 mm; sapphire crystal; crown with security brake lever lock; water-resistant to 300 m
Band: stainless steel, folding clasp
Price: $5,300

Luminor Power Reserve

Reference number: PAM00090
Movement: automatic, Panerai Caliber OP IX; ø 30 mm, height 7.9 mm; 21 jewels; 28,800 vph; officially certified chronometer (C.O.S.C.)
Functions: hours, minutes, subsidiary seconds; date; power reserve display
Case: polished stainless steel, ø 44 mm; sapphire crystal; crown with security brake lever lock; water-resistant to 300 m
Band: reptile skin, buckle
Price: $5,100

Luminor Submersible 2500

Reference number: PAM 00194
Movement: automatic, Panerai Caliber OP III; ø 30 mm, height 7.9 mm; 21 jewels; 28,800 vph; officially certified chronometer (C.O.S.C.)
Functions: hours, minutes, subsidiary seconds; date
Case: titanium, ø 47 mm; unidirectionally rotating bezel with white gold appliqués; sapphire crystal; crown with security brake lever lock; water-resistant to 2500 m
Band: rubber, buckle
Remarks: limited to 1000 pieces
Price: $8,650

IWC.
Engineered for men.

IWC
SCHAFFHAUSEN
SINCE 1868

He'll have to wait.

Ingenieur Automatic. Ref. 3227: In 1868, watchmaker F. A. Jones founded the International Watch Company in Schaffhausen. Since then, our engineers have developed many of today's legendary timepieces – the Portuguese family, the Pilot's Watches, the Da Vinci and the Aquatimer series. It's good to know that our watches aren't just packed with technical advances. But also with the passion of our engineers.

Mechanical IWC manufactory movement I Automatic Pellaton winding system (figure) I Shock-absorbing system I Date I Soft-iron inner case for protection against magnetic fields up to 80,000 A/ml IWC bracelet system I Antireflective sapphire glass I Water-resistant to 400 feet I Stainless steel

Exquisite Timepieces
A Collection of the World's Finest Timepieces

The Village on Venetian Bay
4380 Gulf Shore Blvd. N., Suite 800 Naples, Fl 34103

(239) 262-4545 • (800) 595-5330
website: www.exquisitetimepieces.com

Parmigiani

Michel Parmigiani, a trained watch restorer of Italian descent, was for a long time unknown in the watch business. His skills, on the other hand, were very well known to famous European museums, where he achieved prominence for his talented reparation work on watches that had been judged beyond help by other experts in the field. With the complete refurbishment of the famous Montre Sympathique by Abraham-Louis Breguet, a task that no one else had even dared to attempt, Parmigiani's name became recognized in the rest of the horological world overnight. Soon after this, Parmigiani began developing and producing his own calibers, although he stayed with the sizes familiar to him from his clock and pocket watch "patients." When, in May 1996, on the initiative of the Sandoz Foundation, which subsequently acquired a 51 percent stake in his company, he launched his own collection of wristwatches, it didn't take long before he created his first "small" watch movement. Similar to other top brands of the Swiss watchmaking industry, Parmigiani Fleurier has meanwhile developed a certain company structure, within which the brand with its quality demands, it model design, development, and design of watch movements as well as the departments for PR, marketing, distribution, and sales makes up only half of the picture. For the other half, the brand is supported by sister companies occupied with the industrial production of movements and components, companies that are mainly active in the background, but which are also independent firms taking part in industry happenings. In other words, a graphic illustration of the current company structure housed underneath the roof of the Sandoz Foundation would have Parmigiani Fleurier SA on one side and Vaucher Manufacture Fleurier SA and several of its subsidiaries right across from it on the other side. Since 2000, these subsidiaries have included AtoKalpa SA, located about an hour and a half northeast of Fleurier's position in the Val de Travers. This company's name is derived from *atom*, the Greek word for "the smallest" and the Sanskrit term *kalpa* for "the biggest." About sixty men and women work here, divided into several workshops for the development, manufacture, and finishing of mainly round parts such as stems and pinions.

Of late, balance springs and the components needed for a new pallet escapement

are also made here by Vaucher and Ato-Kalpa's engineers, optimized according to information given them by Parmigiani Fleurier. Thus the impulse angle (which is of decisive importance for the gear train's energy transmission to the pallets) was recalculated, the surface quality of the escape wheel teeth improved, and the "contact zones" of the impulse pin and the pallet fork (where energy from the pallets' movements is transmitted to the balance) freshly determined. Pallets have different shapes ground into them in varying high-quality watch movements, and thus different working angles. Parmigiani and Vaucher are most likely the first in the industry to use one red ruby for the engaging pallet stone and one white (colorless) sapphire for the exit pallet stone.

Kalpa Grande Automatique

Reference number: PF009963
Movement: automatic, Parmigiani Caliber 331; 32 jewels; 28,800 vph; twin spring barrels
Functions: hours, minutes, sweep seconds; date
Case: stainless steel, 46.6 x 34 mm, height 9.25 mm; sapphire crystal; exhibition window case back
Band: Hermès alligator, folding clasp
Price: $8,100

Kalpa Grande Automatique

Reference number: PF009228
Movement: automatic, Parmigiani Caliber 331; 32 jewels; 28,800 vph; twin spring barrels
Functions: hours, minutes, sweep seconds; date
Case: rose gold, 46.6 x 34 mm, height 9.25 mm; sapphire crystal; exhibition window case back
Band: Hermès alligator, buckle
Price: $14,700
Variations: in white gold ($16,600) or yellow gold ($13,300)

Kalpa XL Automatique

Reference number: PF009236
Movement: automatic, Parmigiani Caliber 331; 32 jewels; 28,800 vph; twin spring barrels
Functions: hours, minutes, sweep seconds; date
Case: stainless steel, 53 x 37.2 mm, height 10.7 mm; sapphire crystal; exhibition window case back
Band: stainless steel, folding clasp
Price: $9,100
Variations: various colored dials

Kalpa XL Hebdomadaire

Reference number: PF003333
Movement: manually wound, Parmigiani Caliber 110; 28 jewels; 21,600 vph; twin spring barrels, 8 days power reserve
Functions: hours, minutes, subsidiary seconds; date; power reserve display
Case: stainless steel, 53 x 37.2 mm, height 11.2 mm; sapphire crystal; exhibition window case back
Band: Hermès alligator, folding clasp
Price: $17,000
Variations: various colored dials

Kalpa XL Tourbillon

Reference number: PF008643
Movement: manually wound, Parmigiani Caliber 500; 28 jewels; 21,600 vph; 30-second tourbillon; twin spring barrels, 8 days power reserve
Functions: hours, minutes, sweep seconds; power reserve display
Case: rose gold, 53 x 37.2 mm, height 11.5 mm; sapphire crystal; exhibition window case back
Band: Hermès alligator, folding clasp
Price: $193,000
Variations: in platinum ($210,000)

Kalpa XL Répétition Minutes

Reference number: PF008621
Movement: manually wound, Parmigiani Caliber 350; 33 jewels; 21,600 vph
Functions: hours, minutes, subsidiary seconds; hour, quarter hour, and minute repeater
Case: platinum, 53 x 37.2 mm, height 11 mm; sapphire crystal; exhibition window case back
Band: Hermès alligator, folding clasp
Price: $267,000
Variations: in rose gold ($230,000)

Toric Chronographe

Reference number: PF002646
Movement: automatic, Parmigiani Caliber 190; 31 jewels; 36,000 vph; column wheel control of chronograph functions; officially certified chronometer (C.O.S.C.)
Functions: hours, minutes, subsidiary seconds; chronograph; date
Case: rose gold, ø 40 mm, height 12.3 mm; sapphire crystal; exhibition window case back; crown with sapphire cabochon
Band: Hermès alligator, buckle
Price: $21,600
Variations: in white gold ($23,100), yellow gold ($19,800) and platinum ($31,100)

Toric Quantième Perpetuel Rétrograde

Reference number: PF002614
Movement: automatic, Parmigiani Caliber 333; 32 jewels; 28,800 vph; autonomous module for retrograde perpetual calendar; twin spring barrels
Functions: hours, minutes, sweep seconds; perpetual calendar (day, retrograde date, month, year, leap year, precision moon phase)
Case: white gold, ø 40.5 mm, height 11.3 mm; sapphire crystal; exhibition window case back; sapphire cabochon crown
Band: Hermès alligator, buckle
Price: $55,000
Variations: in rose gold ($55,000); with gemstones

Toric Répétition Minutes GMT

Reference number: PF000462
Movement: manually wound, Parmigiani Caliber 251; 33 jewels; 18,000 vph
Functions: hours, minutes subsidiary seconds; 24-hour display (second time zone); date; hour, quarter hour, and minute repeater
Case: rose gold, ø 42 mm, height 13.2 mm; sapphire crystal; exhibition window case back; crown with sapphire cabochon
Band: Hermès alligator, buckle
Price: $276,000
Variations: in platinum ($328,000); with gemstones

Toric Corrector

Reference number: PF010172
Movement: manually wound, Parmigiani Caliber 252; 33 jewels; 18,000 vph; autonomous module for retrograde perpetual calendar; twin spring barrels; corrector button for immediate setting of calendar and moon phase functions
Functions: hours, minutes; perpetual calendar (day, retrograde date, month, leap year, precision moon phase), minute repeater
Case: platinum, ø 42 mm, height 14.2 mm; sapphire crystal; exhibition window case back; crown with sapphire cabochon
Band: Hermès alligator, folding clasp
Price: $393,000

Toric Westminter

Reference number: PF004184
Movement: manually wound, Parmigiani Caliber 255; 42 jewels; 21,600 vph; one-minute tourbillon
Functions: hours, minutes; 24-hour display (second time zone); hour, quarter hour, and minute repeater with four gongs (Westminster gong)
Case: rose gold, ø 42 mm, height 14.25 mm; sapphire crystal; exhibition window case back; crown with sapphire cabochon
Band: Hermès alligator, buckle
Price: $480,000
Variations: in white gold ($480,000)

Bugatti 370 Type Limited Edition

Reference number: PF008221
Movement: manually wound, Parmigiani Caliber 370; 37 jewels; 21,600 vph; movement with several plates and levels; twin serially operating spring barrels, 10 days power reserve
Functions: hours, minutes; power reserve display
Case: white gold, 32.4 x 52.5 mm, height 18.6 mm; sapphire crystal
Band: Hermès leather, custom-made, folding clasp
Remarks: starter instrument with electric motor to wind the movement
Price: $234,000
Variations: three dial variations: red, grey, or black

Patek Philippe

Patek Philippe Advanced Research: These are words that just don't seem to fit in with the image of one of the most important watch *manufactures* in the world. Advanced Research stands for the fundamental research that the company has now been doing for more than fifteen years. Patek Philippe is constantly on the lookout for new materials and technology to make the mechanical watch a progressive timekeeper even in this new millennium. While Patek Philippe is always keyed into grand history and classically shaped timepieces, the *manufacture* has always fought in the very front research ranks in its more than 160-year-old history. Since 1893, this company has registered more than seventy patents, among them such groundbreaking

developments as the first winding and setting mechanism without a separate key and the Gyromax balance for fine adjustment without an index.

In the current age, however, more than 500 years after the history of timekeeping began, developmental possibilities for normal mechanical watches are most likely exhausted. For this reason, Patek Philippe took a logical step in a new direction in the mid-1990s: Research on high-tech materials. More than fifty people work in Patek Philippe's R&D department. This team is always looking for solutions to the last of watchmaking's big worries: even better rate precision, better use of energy, and the avoidance of maintenance. In the department called Nouvelles Technologies em-

ployees concern themselves solely with material composition and production techniques. The researchers employed there cooperate with a few reputable Swiss universities and research institutes, such as the Technical University in Lausanne and the Institute for Microtechnology at the University of Neuchâtel.

The first big result of these cooperative enterprises is something that Patek Philippe introduced at this year's Baselworld: An escape wheel made of silicon and serially installed into the annual calendar bearing the reference number 5020.

What exactly is the usefulness of this new material, generally known for the part it plays in the computer industry? Even Abraham-Louis Breguet complained of unsatisfactory rate stability due to lubrication: "Give me a perfect oil, and I will give you a perfect watch movement," he was recorded as saying. Two hundred years of development later, Patek Philippe has decided to go a different direction — admitting that the best oil is actually no oil at all. For this reason, the escape wheel made of silicon runs completely lubrication-free. And there are other characteristics that make silicon attractive for watchmaking: Its great hardness combined with a certain flexibility, freedom from rust, low weight, anti-magnetism, and an absolutely smooth surface.

Additionally, the manufacture of a silicon escape wheel is actually simpler than that of a traditional metal wheel. A machine cuts a perfectly smoothed surface precise to one-thousandth of a millimeter in one simple step. For the manufacture of a traditional wheel more than thirty steps are usually necessary.

The silicon escape wheel is being introduced this year in an annual calendar (ref. 5020) bearing the predicate Advanced Research and limited to 250 pieces.

Outside of this hidden innovation, there are other new things to see at the *manufacture* this year: The Nautilus is coming up on its thirtieth birthday. As a little preview of the expected anniversary editions it has received a new look alongside some attractive little complications such as power reserve and moon phase displays. For sporty and fashion-conscious women, this watch is also available in different dial and strap colors that range from white and pink to green.

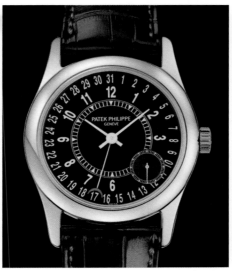

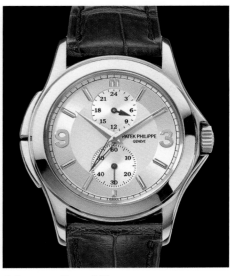

Calatrava

Reference number: 5296
Movement: automatic, Patek Philippe Caliber 324 SC;
ø 27 mm, height 3.3 mm; 29 jewels; 21,600 vph;
Seal of Geneva
Functions: hours, minutes, sweep seconds; date
Case: white gold, ø 38 mm, height 8.5 mm; sapphire crystal;
exhibition window case back
Band: reptile skin, buckle
Price: $17,400

Calatrava

Reference number: 6000
Movement: automatic, Patek Philippe Caliber 240 PS C;
ø 27.5 mm, height 2.53 mm; 27 jewels; 21,600 vph;
microrotor; Seal of Geneva
Functions: hours, minutes, subsidiary seconds; date
Case: white gold, ø 37 mm, height 10.15 mm; sapphire
crystal; exhibition window case back
Band: reptile skin, folding clasp
Price: $17,950

Calatrava Travel Time

Reference number: 5134
Movement: manually wound, Patek Philippe Caliber 215 PS
FUS 24 H; ø 21.9 mm, height 3.35 mm; 18 jewels; 28,800 vph;
Seal of Geneva; hour hand adjustable forward and backward
Functions: hours, minutes, subsidiary seconds; second time
zone; 24-hour display
Case: yellow gold, ø 37 mm, height 9.8 mm; sapphire
crystal; exhibition window case back
Band: reptile skin, folding clasp
Price: $19,900
Variations: in rose or white gold ($21,500), in platinum
($34,150)

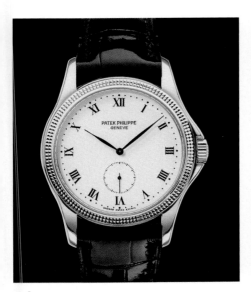

Calatrava

Reference number: 5115
Movement: manually wound, Patek Philippe Caliber
215 PS; ø 21.9 mm, height 2.55 mm; 18 jewels; 28,800 vph;
Seal of Geneva
Functions: hours, minutes, subsidiary seconds
Case: rose gold, ø 35 mm, height 8.1 mm; bezel decorated
with *clous de Paris*; sapphire crystal
Band: reptile skin, buckle
Price: $17,900
Variations: in yellow gold ($16,500); in white gold
($17,900)

Calatrava Grande Taille

Reference number: 5127
Movement: automatic, Patek Philippe Caliber 315 SC;
ø 27 mm, height 3.22 mm; 30 jewels; 21,600 vph;
Seal of Geneva
Functions: hours, minutes, sweep seconds; date
Case: yellow gold, ø 37 mm, height 8.5 mm; sapphire
crystal; exhibition window case back; screwed-in crown
Band: reptile skin, buckle
Price: $16,100
Variations: in rose or white gold ($17,400)

Calatrava

Reference number: 5196
Movement: manually wound, Patek Philippe Caliber 215
PS; ø 21.9 mm, height 2.55 mm; 18 jewels; 28,800 vph;
Seal of Geneva
Functions: hours, minutes, subsidiary seconds
Case: rose gold, ø 37 mm, height 6.8 mm; sapphire crystal
Band: reptile skin, buckle
Price: $14,850
Variations: in white gold ($14,850); in yellow gold
($13,600); in platinum ($24,100)

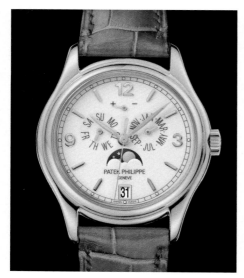

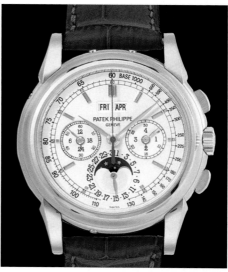

Annual Calendar

Reference number: 5146
Movement: automatic, Patek Philippe Caliber 315 S IRM QA LU; ø 30 mm, height 5.22 mm; 36 jewels; 21,600 vph; Seal of Geneva
Functions: hours, minutes, sweep seconds; date, day of the week, month (programmed for one year); power reserve display
Case: yellow gold, ø 39 mm, height 11.2 mm; sapphire crystal; exhibition window case back
Band: reptile skin, folding clasp
Price: $25,500
Variations: in white gold ($26,800)

Gondolo Calendario

Reference number: 5135
Movement: automatic, Patek Philippe Caliber 324 S QA LU 24 H; ø 31.4 mm, height 5.78 mm; 34 jewels; 28,800 vph; Seal of Geneva; new Gyromax balance with four legs
Functions: hours, minutes, sweep seconds; annual calendar with date, day of the week, month, moon phase; 24-hour display
Case: white gold, 51 x 40.33 mm, height 11.7 mm; sapphire crystal
Band: reptile skin, buckle
Price: $31,100
Variations: in yellow gold ($29,650)

Chronograph Perpetual Calendar

Reference number: 5970 R
Movement: manually wound, Patek Philippe Caliber CH 27-70 Q; ø 30 mm, height 7.2 mm; 24 jewels; 18,000 vph; Seal of Geneva
Functions: hours, minutes, subsidiary seconds; AM/PM display; chronograph; perpetual calendar with date, day of the week, month, moon phase, leap year
Case: rose gold, ø 40 mm; sapphire crystal; exhibition window case back
Band: reptile skin, folding clasp
Price: $96,350
Variations: in white gold ($96,350)

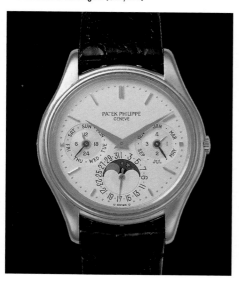

Perpetual Calendar

Reference number: 3940
Movement: automatic, Patek Philippe Caliber 240 Q; ø 27.5 mm, height 3.88 mm; 27 jewels; 21,600 vph; Seal of Geneva; microrotor in gold
Functions: hours, minutes; perpetual calendar with date, day of the week, month, moon phase, leap year; 24-hour display
Case: yellow gold, ø 35.95 mm, height 9 mm; sapphire crystal
Band: reptile skin, buckle
Price: $51,650
Variations: in white or rose gold ($53,950), in platinum ($63,500)

10 Jours Tourbillon

Reference number: 5101 P
Movement: manually wound, Patek Philippe Caliber 28-20 REC10 PS IRM; 28 x 20 mm, height 6.3 mm; 29 jewels; 21,600 vph; Seal of Geneva; one-minute tourbillon; 10 days power reserve; officially certified chronometer (C.O.S.C.)
Functions: hours, minutes, subsidiary seconds; power reserve display
Case: platinum, 51.7 x 29.6 mm, height 12.2 mm; sapphire crystal; exhibition window case back
Band: platinum, buckle
Remarks: dial with black oxidized gold numerals
Price: upon request

Sky Moon

Reference number: 5102
Movement: automatic, Patek Philippe Caliber 240 LU CL; ø 38 mm, height 6.26 mm; 45 jewels; 21,600 vph; Seal of Geneva
Functions: hours, minutes; moon phase and age of moon; celestial chart
Case: white gold, ø 43.1 mm, height 9.78 mm; sapphire crystal; exhibition window case back
Band: reptile skin, buckle
Price: upon request

Net2Watches

Exhibit   Buy   Sell   Trade

Pre-owned and collectible
wristwatches, pocket watches,
art and sculpture clocks

ONE MARKET, MANY EXHIBITORS

We put the world of watches in the palm of your hand!

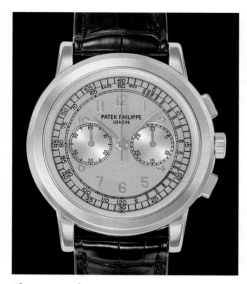

Chronograph

Reference number: 5070
Movement: manually wound, Patek Philippe Caliber CH 27-70 Q; ø 27.5 mm, height 5.57 mm; 24 jewels; 18,000 vph; Seal of Geneva; column wheel control of chronograph functions
Functions: hours, minutes, subsidiary seconds; chronograph
Case: rose gold, ø 42 mm, height 13 mm; sapphire crystal; exhibition window case back
Band: reptile skin, folding clasp
Price: $42,750
Variations: in white gold ($42,750)

Nautilus

Reference number: 3712/1
Movement: automatic, Patek Philippe Caliber 240 PS IRM C LU; ø 31 mm, height 3.98 mm; 29 jewels; 21,600 vph; microrotor; Seal of Geneva
Functions: hours, minutes, subsidiary seconds; date, moon phase; power reserve display
Case: stainless steel, 42 x 38 mm, height 8.37 mm; sapphire crystal; exhibition window case back; screwed-in crown; water-resistant to 60 m
Band: stainless steel, folding clasp
Price: $20,750

Ellipse d'Or

Reference number: 3738/100
Movement: automatic, Patek Philippe Caliber 240; ø 27.5 mm, height 2.53 mm; 27 jewels; 21,600 vph; Seal of Geneva
Functions: hours, minutes
Case: rose gold, 33.7 x 35.6 mm, height 5.65 mm; sapphire crystal
Band: reptile skin, buckle
Price: $17,000
Variations: in white gold ($17,000); in yellow gold ($15,800)

Gondolo

Reference number: 5111
Movement: manually wound, Patek Philippe Caliber 215 PS; ø 21.9 mm, height 2.55 mm; 18 jewels; 28,800 vph
Functions: hours, minutes, subsidiary seconds
Case: white gold, 47.8 x 32.9 mm, height 9.45 mm; sapphire crystal
Band: reptile skin, buckle
Price: $17,000
Variations: in yellow gold ($15,800); in rose gold ($17,000); in platinum/rose gold ($27,250)

Gondolo

Reference number: 5109
Movement: manually wound, Patek Philippe Caliber 215 PS; ø 21.9 mm, height 2.55 mm; 18 jewels; 28,800 vph; Seal of Geneva
Functions: hours, minutes, subsidiary seconds
Case: white gold, 43 x 30 mm, height 7.22 mm; sapphire crystal
Band: reptile skin, buckle
Remarks: gold-plated dials in the colors of the case
Price: $16,950
Variations: in yellow gold ($15,700), in rose gold ($16,950), in platinum ($27,150)

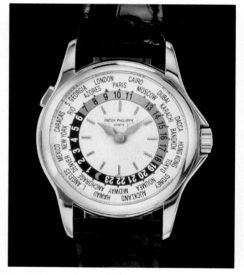

World Time Watch

Reference number: 5110
Movement: automatic, Patek Philippe Caliber 240 HU; ø 27.5 mm, height 3.88 mm; 33 jewels; 21,600 vph; Seal of Geneva; contrarotating dial disks with 24-hour display and world reference cities, synchronized via button; gold microrotor
Functions: hours, minutes; world time (24 hours/second time zone)
Case: rose gold, ø 37 mm, height 9.4 mm; sapphire crystal; exhibition window case back
Band: reptile skin, buckle
Price: $28,400
Variations: yellow gold, white gold, platinum ($40,000)

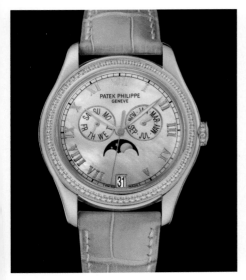

Annual Calendar

Reference number: 4936
Movement: automatic, Patek Philippe Caliber 315 S QA LU;
ø 30 mm, height 5.22 mm; 34 jewels; 21,600 vph; Seal
of Geneva
Functions: hours, minutes, sweep seconds; date, day of the
week, month, moon phase (programmed for one year)
Case: yellow gold, ø 37 mm, height 11.3 mm; bezel set with
78 brilliant-cut diamonds; sapphire crystal; exhibition case back
Band: reptile skin, buckle
Remarks: mother-of-pearl dial
Price: $28,700
Variations: in white gold ($29,950)

Calatrava

Reference number: 4906
Movement: quartz, Patek Philippe Caliber E 19C
Functions: hours, minutes; date
Case: yellow gold, ø 28 mm, height 7 mm; bezel set with
96 diamonds; sapphire crystal
Band: satin, buckle
Remarks: mother-of-pearl dial with diamond markers
Price: $15,200
Variations: in rose or white gold ($16,200)

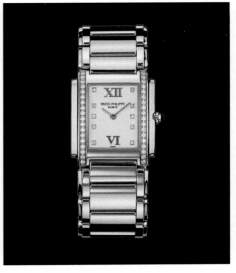

Twenty-4

Reference number: 4910/10A
Movement: quartz, Patek Philippe Caliber E 15
Functions: hours, minutes
Case: stainless steel, 25.1 x 30 mm, height 6.8 mm;
case sides set with diamonds; sapphire crystal
Band: stainless steel, folding clasp
Price: $8,600

Twenty-4

Reference number: 4920
Movement: quartz, Patek Philippe Caliber E 15
Functions: hours, minutes
Case: rose gold, 25 x 30 mm, height 6.83 mm; case sides set
with diamonds; sapphire crystal; crown with brilliant-cut
solitaire diamond
Band: satin, buckle
Remarks: dial with eight diamond markers
Price: $14,350
Variations: in white gold with grey or opal-white dial and
rose gold with opal-white dial ($14,350)

Gondolo

Reference number: 4868
Movement: quartz, Patek Philippe Caliber E 15
Functions: hours, minutes
Case: white gold, 28 x 28 mm, height 6.9 mm; bezel set
with 80 diamonds; sapphire crystal; crown with
diamond cabochon
Band: textile, buckle
Price: $29,560
Variations: with pearl bracelet in rose or white gold
($29,650)

Aquanaut Luce

Reference number: 5067A
Movement: quartz, Patek Philippe Caliber E 23 SC
Functions: hours, minutes, sweep seconds; date
Case: stainless steel, 35 x 34 mm, height 7.9 mm; bezel set
with 46 brilliant-cut diamonds; sapphire crystal; screwed-in
crown; water-resistant to 60 m
Band: Tropical, folding clasp
Price: $10,950
Variations: in Mysterious Black, Pure White, Ocean Blue,
Adventurous Khaki, Luscious Plum or Midnight Blue; in small
size ($9,600)

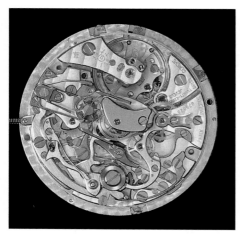

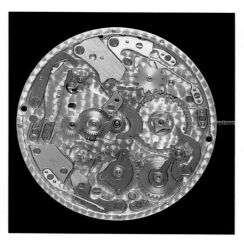

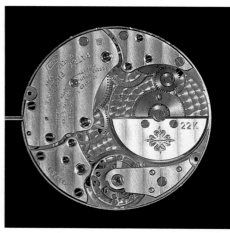

Caliber 27-70/150

Mechanical with manual winding, power reserve 58 hours
Functions: hours, minutes, subsidiary seconds, perpetual calendar (date, day, month, leap year, moon phase); 24-hour display; chronograph (minutes, seconds, split-seconds)
Diameter: 30 mm (13 1/2''')
Height: 8.86 mm
Jewels: 28 (escape wheel with endstone)
Balance: Gyromax, with eight masselotte regulating weights
Frequency: 18,000 vph
Balance spring: Breguet
Shock protection: Kif
Remarks: base plate with perlage, Seal of Geneva, 404 individual parts

Caliber 27-70/150

Caliber 27-70/150 from the dial side.

Caliber 240 PS

Base caliber: 240
Mechanical with automatic winding, power reserve 46 hours, off-center ball bearing micro-rotor in 22-karat gold, unidirectionally winding and integrated into the movement
Functions: hours, minutes, subsidiary seconds at 4 o'clock
Diameter: 27.5 mm (12 1/4''')
Height: ultra flat, 2.4 mm
Jewels: 27 (escape wheel with endstone)
Balance: Gyromax, with eight masselotte regulating weights
Frequency: 21,600 vph
Balance spring: flat hairspring
Shock protection: Kif
Remarks: base plate with perlage, beveled bridges and micro-rotor with *côtes de Genève*, 161 individual parts

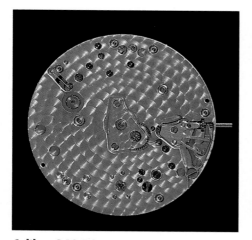

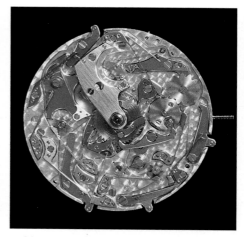

Caliber 240 PS

Caliber 240 from the dial side. The large surface of the micro-rotor recessed in the movement, which reduces the height of the construction greatly, can be clearly seen.
Related calibers: Base caliber 240 differs from Caliber 240 PS in the absence of a second hand; 240 Q (240 with perpetual calendar and 24-hour indication); 240/154 (240 PS with power reserve indicator and moon phase, diameter 31 mm, height 3.85 mm)

Caliber 315/136

Mechanical with automatic winding, power reserve 46 hours, central ball-bearing rotor in 21-karat gold, unidirectionally winding
Functions: hours, minutes, sweep seconds, perpetual calendar (retrograde date, day, month, leap year, moon phase)
Diameter: 28 mm (12 1/2''')
Height: 5.25 mm
Jewels: 31 (escape wheel with endstone)
Balance: Gyromax, with eight masselotte regulating weights
Frequency: 21,600 vph
Balance spring: flat hairspring
Shock protection: Kif

Caliber 315/136

Caliber 315/136 from the dial side.
Remarks: base plate with perlage, beveled bridges with *côtes de Genève*, rotor with *côtes circulaires* and an engraved cross of the Order of Calatrava, 368 individual parts
Related calibers: 330 SC (315 SC with date disk positioned closer to the center, height 3.5 mm)

Caliber 315/198

Mechanical with automatic winding, power reserve 46 hours, central ball-bearing rotor in 21-karat gold, unidirectionally winding
Functions: hours, minutes, sweep seconds, annual calendar (date, day, month); 24-hour indication
Diameter: 30 mm (13 1/4'''); **Height:** 5.22 mm
Jewels: 35 (escape wheel with endstone)
Balance: Gyromax, with eight masselotte regulating weights
Frequency: 21,600 vph
Balance spring: flat hairspring
Shock protection: Kif
Remarks: base plate with perlage, beveled bridges with *côtes de Genève*, rotor with *côtes circulaires* and an engraved cross of the Order of Calatrava, 316 individual parts

Caliber 324

Mechanical with automatic winding, power reserve 46 hours, central ball-bearing rotor in 21-karat gold, unidirectionally winding
Functions: hours, minutes, sweep seconds, annual calendar with three window displays (date, day, month) and moon phase; 24-hour indication
Diameter: 31.4 mm; **Height:** 5.78 mm; **Jewels:** 34
Balance: Gyromax, with four masselotte regulating weights
Frequency: 28,800 vph
Balance spring: flat hairspring
Shock protection: Kif
Remarks: Seal of Geneva; base plate with perlage, beveled bridges with *côtes de Genève*, rotor with *côtes circulaires* and an engraved cross of the Order of Calatrava

Caliber 16-250

Mechanical with manual winding, power reserve 36 hours
Functions: hours, minutes
Diameter: 16.3 mm (7''')
Height: 2.5 mm
Jewels: 18 (escape wheel with endstone)
Balance: ring, monometallic
Frequency: 28,800 vph
Balance spring: flat hairspring, with Triovis regulation and fine adjustment via micrometer screw
Shock protection: Incabloc
Remarks: base plate with perlage, beveled bridges with *côtes de Genève*, 99 individual parts

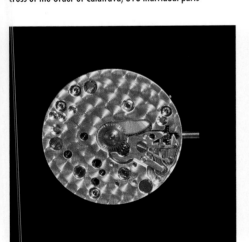

Caliber 16-250

Caliber 16-250 from the dial side.

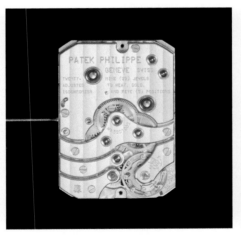

Caliber 28-20/220

Mechanical with manual winding, twin serially operating spring barrels, power reserve 10 days (240 hours)
Functions: hours, minutes, subsidiary seconds; power reserve display
Dimensions: 28 x 20 mm
Height: 5.05 mm
Jewels: 29 (escape wheel with endstone)
Balance: Gyromax in beryllium bronze with eight masselotte regulating weights
Frequency: 21,600 vph
Balance spring: flat hairspring
Shock protection: Kif
Remarks: base plate with perlage, beveled bridges with *côtes de Genève*, Seal of Geneva

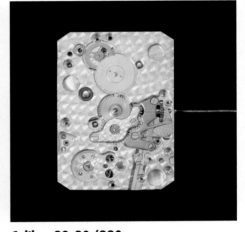

Caliber 28-20/220

Caliber 28-20/220 as seen from the dial side. All steel parts such as springs, levers, and bars are beveled and polished according to the regulations for the Seal of Geneva, and their surfaces are brushed by hand. The holes for the screws in the steel parts are also polished. In addition, each and every tooth on the toothed wheels and pinions are polished by hand with a hard-wood disk. This is, by the way, the case for all Patek Philippe movements that bear the Seal of Geneva.

Piaget

A lot has happened over the last few years at this exclusive watchmaker in remote La Côte-aux-Fées. Piaget is known to a wider audience as a brand that manufactures jeweled timepieces. One of the lesser known facts in today's industry, however, is that Piaget has been one of the most important Swiss producers of *ébauches* and movement parts for more than one hundred years, supplying some of the industry's most renowned companies and creating numerous movement classics.

In comparison to other genuine watch *manufactures*, this company has communicated less of its illustrious history to a broad audience, something that may be based in the fact that Piaget has only concentrated on producing watches under its own name since the 1950s.

The challenge of being responsible for designing and supplying movements for the Richemont watch group and its leading brand, Cartier, has awakened the old spirit of mechanical tradition at this company. The 400/500P caliber family created as a result is, of course, also now being used in

diverse models of Piaget's own continually growing collection, which meanwhile even includes a tourbillon.

The elegant rectangular Emperador Tourbillon is powered by *manufacture* Caliber 600, a shaped, manually wound movement containing a flying one-minute tourbillon at 12 o'clock. The real showstopper is the incredibly flat construction height of only 3.5 mm, made possible by a tourbillon cage that juts out from the surface of the dial a bit. This cage is an exceptionally complex structure comprising forty-two individual components and weighing only 0.2 grams thanks to its conservative dimensions (the balance's diameter is only 7.5 mm). The three main components making up the tourbillon cage are constructed of feather-light titanium, connected to one another by miniscule screws and taps.

By decorating the circle around the center of the tourbillon cage with *côtes de Genève*, Piaget is going down an unusual path in terms of the finishing of the movement's back. This is also evident in the numerous retracted corners (*angles

rentrants), making the use of machine tools impossible on them, and speaks for the remarkably lavish amount of detail work: A master beveler (*maître angleur*) needs an entire week before the individual parts of Piaget Caliber 600P live up to the expectations of its constructor.

As an homage to its eminent *manufacture* tradition, and almost seeming to form a counterpoint to the opulent jeweled pieces it is now famous for, Piaget presented the round Altiplano XL to complement the successful square model already featured in the collection. The company's Genevan designers have created a minimalized watch that even goes along well with the Bauhaus motto "form follows function." This timepiece's elegant overall appearance is additionally underscored by its case, as its height comprises a svelte 4.3 mm. This ultra-flat construction was made possible by the company's own manually wound Caliber 430 P, which itself is only 2.1 mm high.

Piaget rightfully presents itself today as a *manufacture* of the finest quality, dedicated to traditional watchmaking skills and technical innovation. This is also documented by the completely modern factory building in Plan-les-Ouates, a Genevan industrial area jokingly referred to as the "watch suburb" by locals due to the growing settlement of watch companies there. The manufacture of cases and bracelets and the accompanying tasks of polishing, rhodium-plating, and jewel-setting are performed on the just about 4,000 m^2 of contemporary premises. The movement *manufacture* will, however, remain in the peace and tranquility of the mountainous Jura town La Côte-aux-Fées.

Emperador Tourbillon

Reference number: GOA 28073
Movement: manually wound, Piaget Caliber 600P;
22.4 x 28.7 mm, height 3.5 mm (without tourbillon cage);
24 jewels; 21,600 vph; flying one-minute tourbillon
Functions: hours, minutes, subsidiary seconds (on tourbillon
cage); power reserve display
Case: rose gold, 32 x 41 mm, height 10 mm; sapphire
crystal; exhibition window case back
Band: reptile skin, buckle
Price: $97,500

Emperador Retrograde Seconds

Reference number: GOA 28072
Movement: automatic, Piaget Caliber 560P; ø 20.5 mm
(base movement); 21,600 vph
Functions: hours, minutes, subsidiary seconds
(retrograde); date
Case: white gold, 32 x 41 mm, height 10 mm; sapphire
crystal; exhibition window case back
Band: reptile skin, buckle
Price: $14,800

Rectangle XL Retrograde Seconds

Reference number: GOA 28061
Movement: automatic, Piaget Caliber 561P; ø 20.5 mm
(base movement); 21,600 vph
Functions: hours, minutes, subsidiary seconds (retrograde);
date; power reserve display
Case: rose gold, 31 x 46 mm, height 9.5 mm;
sapphire crystal
Band: reptile skin, buckle
Price: $14,700

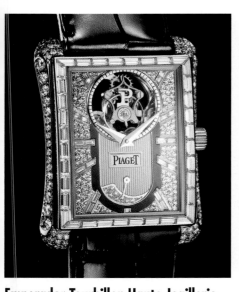

Emperador Tourbillon Haute Joaillerie

Reference number: GOA 30018
Movement: manually wound, Piaget Caliber 600P;
22.4 x 28.7 mm, height 3.5 mm (without tourbillon cage);
24 jewels; 21,600 vph; flying one-minute tourbillon
Functions: hours, minutes, subsidiary seconds (on tourbillon
cage); power reserve display
Case: white gold, 32 x 41 mm, height 10 mm; bezel with
baguette-cut diamonds, case sides set with diamonds;
sapphire crystal; exhibition window case back
Band: reptile skin, buckle
Remarks: diamond and lapis lazuli dial; 11 baguette markers
Price: $150,000

Altiplano Fingerprint

Reference number: GOA 30022
Movement: manually wound, Piaget Caliber 430P;
ø 20.5 mm, height 2.1 mm; 18 jewels; 21,600 vph
Functions: hours, minutes
Case: white gold, ø 36 mm, height 9 mm; bezel set with
78 diamonds; sapphire crystal
Band: satin, folding clasp
Remarks: dial with fingerprint made of 286 diamonds
Price: $25,500

Altiplano Ultra-Thin

Reference number: GOA 29112
Movement: manually wound, Piaget Caliber 430P;
ø 20.5 mm, height 2.1 mm; 18 jewels; 21,600 vph
Functions: hours, minutes
Case: white gold, ø 38 mm, height 8 mm; sapphire crystal
Band: reptile skin, buckle
Price: $9,300
Variations: in yellow gold

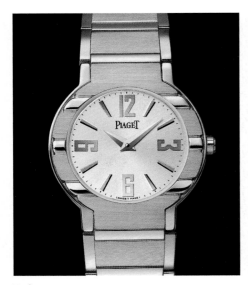

Polo

Reference number: GOA 26029
Movement: quartz, Piaget Caliber 690P
Functions: hours, minutes
Case: yellow gold, ø 28 mm, height 9 mm; sapphire crystal
Band: yellow gold, folding clasp
Price: $14,200
Variations: in various case sizes; also in white gold

Polo

Reference number: GOA 29049
Movement: quartz, Piaget Caliber 690P
Functions: hours, minutes
Case: white gold, ø 28 mm, height 9 mm; bezel set with
26 diamonds; sapphire crystal
Band: white gold, folding clasp
Remarks: dial made of red mother-of-pearl with paved
diamond markers
Price: $22,400
Variations: in yellow gold with brown mother-of-pearl dial

Polo

Reference number: GOA 28050
Movement: quartz, Piaget Caliber 690P
Functions: hours, minutes
Case: white gold, ø 28 mm, height 9 mm; sapphire crystal
Band: white gold, folding clasp
Remarks: meteorite dial
Price: $22,400

Tonneau Joaillerie

Reference number: GOA 27063
Movement: quartz, Piaget Caliber 59P
Functions: hours, minutes
Case: white gold, 18 x 33.6 mm, height 8 mm; case sides
completely paved with diamonds; sapphire crystal
Band: satin, folding clasp with diamonds
Remarks: genuine mother-of-pearl dial
Price: $19,000
Variations: in white gold, with mother-of-pearl dial,
with reptile skin strap

Tonneau Joaillerie

Reference number: GOA 29067
Movement: quartz, Piaget Caliber 59P
Functions: hours, minutes
Case: yellow gold, 18 x 33.6 mm, height 8 mm; case,
bracelet and dial completely paved with 659 diamonds;
sapphire crystal
Band: yellow gold, folding clasp
Price: $56,600
Variations: in white gold

Altiplano

Reference number: GOA 29107
Movement: quartz, Piaget Caliber 690P
Functions: hours, minutes
Case: yellow gold, 33 x 33 mm, height 8 mm; bezel set with
48 diamonds; sapphire crystal
Band: satin, buckle
Remarks: dial with paved diamond markers
Price: $12,500
Variations: in white gold; diverse dial variations (also pavé)

Caliber 9P2

Mechanical with manual winding, power reserve 36 hours
Functions: hours, minutes
Diameter: 20.8 mm
Height: 2.15 mm
Jewels: 18
Balance: with smooth wheel, three-legged
Frequency: 19,800 vph
Balance spring: flat hairspring with fine adjustment via micrometer screw
Shock protection: Incabloc
Remarks: base plate with perlage, beveled bridges with côtes de Genève

Caliber 551P

Mechanical with automatic winding, stop-seconds, power reserve 40 hours
Functions: hours, minutes, subsidiary seconds; power reserve display
Diameter: 20.5 mm
Height: 3.9 mm
Jewels: 27
Balance: glucydur
Frequency: 21,600 vph
Balance spring: flat hairspring with fine adjustment via index
Shock protection: Incabloc
Remarks: modular winding mechanism

Caliber 441P

Base caliber: 430P
Mechanical with manual winding, stop-seconds, power reserve 40 hours
Functions: hours, minutes, subsidiary seconds; date, power reserve display
Diameter: 20.5 mm; **Height:** 3.6 mm; **Jewels:** 20
Balance: glucydur; **Frequency:** 21,600 vph
Balance spring: flat hairspring with fine adjustment via index
Shock protection: Incabloc
Related calibers: 430P (hours, minutes); 420P (430P with date window); 410P (430P with sweep seconds/stop-seconds); 400P (430P with date window and sweep seconds/stop-seconds)

Caliber 500P

Mechanical with automatic winding, stop-seconds, power reserve 40 hours
Functions: hours, minutes, sweep seconds; date
Diameter: 20.5 mm
Height: 3.4 mm
Jewels: 26
Balance: glucydur
Frequency: 21,600 vph
Balance spring: flat hairspring with fine adjustment via index
Shock protection: Incabloc
Remarks: modular winding mechanism
Related Calibers: 510P (with sweep seconds only); 520P (with date window only); 530P (hours and minutes only)

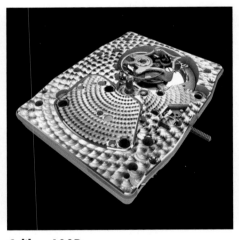

Caliber 600P

Mechanical with manual winding, one-minute tourbillon, power reserve 40 hours
Functions: hours, minutes, subsidiary seconds (on tourbillon cage); power reserve display
Dimensions: 22.4 x 28.7 mm
Height: 3.5 mm (without tourbillon cage)
Jewels: 24
Balance: glucydur, diameter 7.5 mm
Frequency: 21,600 vph
Remarks: flying tourbillon with cage made of titanium

Paul Picot

A clear sense of aesthetics and perfection, the mastery of watchmaking technology, and schooled eyes and hands: These are some of the secrets that unite to create Paul Picot's brand of watches.

The founding of Société des Montres Paul Picot in 1976 included a large portion of pioneering spirit. In the middle of the toughest crisis the Swiss watch industry ever had to face, when many historic names went under, one of the newest companies in *haute horlogerie* was created. This firm was born of the will to save the rich tra-

dition of the Swiss watch industry and let its true values once again come to light. The conventional customs of watchmaking were threatening to fall into disrepair; qualified masters of the craft were disappearing from the workplace, and the once-fascinating atmosphere of watchmakers' workshops had given way to the industrial hustle and bustle of anonymous trade names.

For company founder and president Mario Boiocchi, the only chance for the survival of European watch culture was to rediscover quality and precision. While Japanese and American competitors forced the Swiss

watch industry to make compromises in order to meet the demands of mass consumption, Paul Picot chose to walk a different path.

Although the market was calling for futuristic design and electronic technology, Paul Picot entered it with fine gold cases and mechanical watch movements. In the years to follow, it was sporty, refined collections that opened the market for the brand. Diver's watches and chronographs sealed the deal, and the elegant collections with their shaped cases have already begun to write chapters of watch history all their own. The diver's watch Le Plongeur has developed into an evergreen for Paul Picot. Featuring a unidirectionally rotating bezel outfitted with polished, angular numerals in relief on a granular background and an additional gripping edge, this powerful watch is just as elegant as it is practical, and just as attractive as it is robust — not every functional diver's watch needs to look like an iron lung. The middle ring made of hardened plastic that had originally served to reduce friction between the bezel and the case now serves an aesthetic purpose with its yellow signal coloring. In this way the Plongeur C-Type has evolved into a yacht club cult classic.

A real cult watch has also developed out of Paul Picot's newest creation. The Technograph features a three-dimensional, highly unconventional dial visual for a chronograph. In the middle, above everything else, sits the hour and minute display as a king on a throne. Underneath this raised main dial, the hands for the permanent subsidiary seconds and the chronograph's minute counter circulate. The ends of the hands are of differing lengths, thus sweeping two semicircle scales. Because, however, the hand arbors and the "unemployed" halves of the hands disappear under the main dial, the observer is left with the impression of two retrograde displays. The entire thing was conceived based upon a reliable Valjoux caliber whose dial train only had to be slightly modified.

Technograph

Reference number: 0334SG
Movement: automatic, ETA Valjoux Caliber 7750; ø 30 mm, height 7.9 mm; 25 jewels; 28,800 vph; dial train modification
Functions: hours, minutes, subsidiary seconds; chronograph; date
Case: stainless steel, ø 44 mm, height 15 mm; sapphire crystal; exhibition window case back; screwed-in crown; water-resistant to 100 m
Band: leather, folding clasp
Price: $7,500
Variations: with stainless steel bracelet ($8,400); in rose gold ($20,700); in white gold ($21,800)

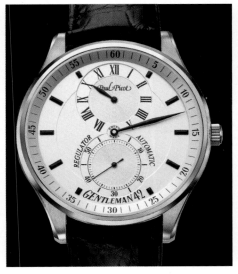

Gentleman Regulator

Reference number: 4114
Movement: automatic, PP Caliber 1000 (base ETA 2892 with module 3305); ø 25.6 mm, height 3.6 mm; 21 jewels (base movement); 28,800 vph
Functions: hours, (off-center) minutes, subsidiary seconds
Case: stainless steel, ø 42 mm, height 9.7 mm; sapphire crystal; water-resistant to 50 m
Band: reptile skin, buckle
Price: $4,100
Variations: with stainless steel bracelet ($4,500)

Gentleman Chrono GMT

Reference number: 20315
Movement: automatic, PP Caliber 8104 (base ETA 7750); ø 30 mm, height 7.9 mm; 25 jewels; 28,800 vph; with Tricompax dial train modification
Functions: hours, minutes, subsidiary seconds; chronograph; date; 24-hour display (second time zone)
Case: stainless steel, ø 42 mm, height 14.65 mm; sapphire crystal; screwed-in crown; water-resistant to 50 m
Band: reptile skin, buckle
Price: $5,250
Variations: with stainless steel bracelet ($5,600); in rose gold

Firshire Tonneau 3000 Retrograde

Reference number: 0773
Movement: automatic, PP Caliber 1300 (base ETA 2892-A2); ø 25.6 mm, height 3.6 mm (base movement); 34 jewels; 28,800 vph; officially certified chronometer (C.O.S.C.)
Functions: hours, minutes, subsidiary seconds (retrograde, 30 seconds)
Case: stainless steel, 49 x 37 mm, height 13 mm; sapphire crystal
Band: reptile skin, buckle
Price: $6,150
Variations: with stainless steel bracelet

Firshire Tonneau 3000 Regulateur

Reference number: 0740
Movement: automatic, PP Caliber 1100 (base ETA 2892-A2); ø 25.6 mm, height 3.6 mm (base movement); 30 jewels; 28,800 vph; officially certified chronometer (C.O.S.C.)
Functions: hours, (off-center) minutes, subsidiary seconds; date; power reserve display
Case: stainless steel, 49 x 37 mm, height 13 mm; sapphire crystal
Band: reptile skin, buckle
Price: $7,150
Variations: with stainless steel bracelet

Firshire 3000 Regulateur Limited Edition

Reference number: 0740LE
Movement: automatic, PP Caliber 1100 (base ETA 2892-A2); ø 25.6 mm, height 3.6 mm (base movement); 30 jewels; 28,800 vph; officially certified chronometer (C.O.S.C.)
Functions: hours, (off-center) minutes, subsidiary seconds; date; power reserve display
Case: stainless steel, 49 x 37 mm, height 13 mm; sapphire crystal
Band: reptile skin, buckle
Remarks: limited to 100 pieces
Price: $7,700
Variations: other color combinations also limited to 100 pcs.

Le Plongeur C-Type Chronograph
Reference number: 4116GR
Movement: automatic, ETA Caliber 7753; ø 30 mm, height 7.9 mm; 25 jewels; 28,800 vph; COSC chronometer
Functions: hours, minutes, subsidiary seconds; chronograph; date
Case: stainless steel, ø 43 mm, height 16.3 mm; unidirectionally rotating bezel with 60-minute divisions; sapphire crystal; screwed-in crown and buttons; water-resistant to 300 m
Band: rubber, folding clasp with extension
Remarks: limited to 500 pieces
Price: $6,600
Variations: with stainless steel bracelet

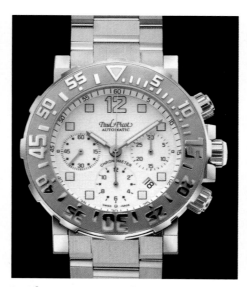

Le Plongeur C-Type Chronograph
Reference number: 4116BL
Movement: automatic, ETA Caliber 7753; ø 30 mm, height 7.9 mm; 25 jewels; 28,800 vph; COSC chronometer
Functions: hours, minutes, subsidiary seconds; chronograph; date
Case: stainless steel, ø 43 mm, height 16.3 mm; unidirectionally rotating bezel with 60-minute divisions; sapphire crystal; screwed-in crown and buttons; water-resistant to 300 m
Band: stainless steel, folding clasp with extension
Remarks: limited to 500 pieces
Price: $7,500
Variations: with rubber strap

Le Plongeur C-Type Date
Reference number: 4117
Movement: automatic, ETA Caliber 2824-2; ø 25.6 mm, height 4.6 mm; 25 jewels; 28,800 vph; officially certified chronometer (C.O.S.C.)
Functions: hours, minutes, sweep seconds; date
Case: stainless steel, ø 43 mm, height 13.3 mm; unidirectionally rotating bezel with 60-minute divisions; sapphire crystal; screwed-in crown; water-resistant to 300 m
Band: rubber, folding clasp with extension
Price: $3,850
Variations: with stainless steel bracelet ($4,800)

Majestic Chrono Rattrapante
Reference number: 0521 R
Movement: automatic, PP Caliber 1290 (base Jaquet 8932); ø 30 mm, height 7.9 mm; 25 jewels; 28,800 vph; officially certified chronometer (C.O.S.C.); solid gold rotor
Functions: hours, minutes, subsidiary seconds; split-seconds chronograph
Case: rose gold, 50.5 x 44.5 mm, height 15.5 mm; sapphire crystal; exhibition window case back; water-resistant to 50 m
Band: reptile skin, buckle
Price: $32,450
Variations: in yellow gold; in white gold; in stainless steel ($16,950)

Majestic Chronograph
Reference number: 0533 Y
Movement: automatic, ETA Caliber 7751; ø 30 mm, height 7.9 mm; 25 jewels; 28,800 vph; officially certified chronometer (C.O.S.C.); solid gold rotor
Functions: hours, minutes, subsidiary seconds; chronograph; date, day of the week, month, moon phase; 24-hour display
Case: yellow gold, 50.5 x 44.5 mm, height 15 mm; sapphire crystal; exhibition window case back; water-resistant to 50 m
Band: reptile skin, buckle
Price: $10,450
Variations: in rose gold; in white gold; in stainless steel

Atelier Technicum
Reference number: 102
Movement: automatic, PP Caliber 8888 (base ETA 7750); ø 30 mm, height 8.4 mm; 28 jewels; 28,800 vph; officially certified chronometer (C.O.S.C.); solid gold rotor
Functions: hours, minutes, subsidiary seconds; split-seconds chronograph; date, day of the week; power reserve display
Case: rose gold, ø 40 mm, height 15 mm; sapphire crystal; exhibition window case back; screwed-in crown; water-resistant to 50 m
Band: reptile skin, buckle
Price: $17,400
Variations: in yellow gold; in stainless steel

Navigating the World of Watches on the Web

by Rob Spayne

The "www" prefix in Internet addresses is an acronym for "World Wide Web." However, it might just as easily mean "Wide World of Watches." Or, perhaps, "Wild West of Watches." The microcosmic universe of watches on the web is diverse, dynamic, and rapidly evolving: There are opportunities of all kinds, thousands of places to visit, and dangers for the unwary. The online world is about information more than anything else, and this also holds true for horology. Watch websites present a wealth of information, organized into several categories. The main categories of horologically related websites can be broken down as follows:

Watch manufacturers maintain websites that serve as virtual catalogues, with the content and quality of the information ranging from primitive to outstanding. An example of excellence is www.omega.ch, which offers detailed information on the brand's current models, a museum area with images of historic models, and even fun, interactive demonstrations, such as that of the Speedmaster Split-Seconds Chronograph.

Other prime examples are *www.iwc.ch*, and *www.glashuette-original.com*, offering private areas with discussion forums, special collectors' auctions on historic models, and breaking news about new watches. Most brands also extend the opportunity of ordering a printed catalogue online as well.

Watch forums are sites reserved for virtual discussions. Participants post questions, digital images, watch reviews, and used timepieces for sale, among other subjects. Forums can be of general interest, specific to a watch brand, category-specific (i.e., vintage watches), and may have an international or local audience. Some of the more informative and lively forums can be found at:
www.timezone.com
www.ThePuristS.com
www.paneristi.com
www.pmwf.com ("Poor Man's Watch Forum").

Personal websites are created by individual aficionados wanting to share their watch collections or their knowledge about a certain brand or model. These sites are all about passion and offer the opportunity to learn about a watch brand in great detail. Some examples of these are:
www.oysterworld.de
www.watchesarefun.com
www.chrono-metrie.com, a site that also features a fun guide to watch brand pronunciation.

Watch dealers abound on the Internet, selling everything from brand-new and modern pre-owned watches to vintage timepieces. A very welcome recent trend is the appearance of authorized watch dealers online. Depending on a watch brand's policy, some dealers provide for online sales while others extend only virtual showcases without sales. One of the better sites along these lines is *www.watchbuys.com*, offering the latest German watch brands for sale from a trusted and reputable retailer. For vintage collectors, online or otherwise, *www.joseph-watches.com* is one of the most important dealers in the world, its business being based on the reputable German auction house's twenty-two-year-old legacy. There are hundreds of websites offering watches for sale, and, while the majority comprises honest businesses, fraudulent sites also exist. Before considering the purchase of a watch online, it is critical to determine if the dealer is a legitimate business or proprietor with an established history of honest sales.

A new site, *www.net2watches.com*, offers vintage and pre-owned goods from "exhibitors" in a gallery-style of setting. *Watch portals* are websites that serve as guides to the world of watches online and can help to make navigating this diverse universe of information more efficient and rewarding. The leading watch portals are:
www.watchfinder.net
www.chronophage.com.

One location that deserves special mention in a category all its own is *www.fhs.ch*, the website of the Federation of the Swiss Watch Industry FH. This site provides an excellent overview of the industry, replete with export statistics and business performance analyses of the top watch manufacturers.

Historically, the Internet has been a controversial subject in the watch industry, with only watch collectors and dealers braving the online landscape until recently. The increasing participation of watch brands and authorized watch dealers will greatly improve the diversity and safety of the online watch world, finally taking some of the "wild" out of the Wild West of Watches.

ROB SPAYNE HAS BEEN WORKING ON THE INTERNET FOR SEVEN YEARS, FOUNDING *WWW.WATCHFINDER.NET* IN 2000. HE IS ALSO AN EXPERIENCED WATCH ENTHUSIAST WHO HAS SUCCESSFULLY CREATED A PROFESSION FROM HIS TWO PASSIONS. HIS WEBSITE IS AN AUTHORITATIVE AND WELL-VISITED PORTAL FOR THE HOROLOGICALLY-MINDED.

Porsche Design

A clean and sober instrument-like look runs through Porsche Design's 2005 models. It is very obvious that this brand obligated to the sports car company based in Stuttgart has redesigned a number of its dials. The instruments found in Porsche's sports cars stood model for the dials' typography as the inclusion of numerous Arabic numerals instead of baton markers and wedges will attest. Thus it stands to reason that the new line was christened Dashboard. And something that will especially please fans of the brand is the fact that Porsche Design now once again offers completely black chronographs in the line, reminiscent of the first black chronographs that Professor Ferdinand Alexander Porsche created back in 1972.

And another piece of good news for fans: The Indicator is now ready for serial production. The world's first mechanical chronograph displaying the hours and minutes of stopped time digitally — but in a purely mechanical manner, of course — was first introduced at Baselworld 2004 as a prototype. First-class legibility was the primary goal of the chronograph's design, as Eterna's managing director and the project's initiator, Ernst F. Seyr, explains: "The most important demand on the Indicator was to give people as little room as possible to misinterpret." The project as a whole leaves absolutely no room for misinterpretation: The Indicator is proof of horological skill of a special kind, simultaneously waking the brands Porsche Design and Eterna, which are both produced under one roof in the Swiss watch town Grenchen, out of their Sleeping Beauty-like sleep.

The Porsche Design brand has always had its finger on the pulse of time regarding design, for it is Professor Porsche himself who is responsible for it. "The greatest thing that can happen to a designer is to have complete control of the production of his idea, from the beginning sketch to the finished product," the master of German product design is on record as saying. "But it can quickly turn into a nightmare."

To have complete responsibility for material, production quality, marketing, distribution, and after-sales service does require a few virtues foreign to most designers, and actually even goes against the grain in most cases. It entails compromising at the right time and the right place, not only accepting the hated red pencil but even using it oneself, exercising a measure of discipline and objectivity unheard-of in artistic circles, and the ability to let the head of production or distribution have a say. With this in mind, it is easy to see that Porsche Design AG's takeover of the established watch company Eterna was a very professional move. Its close economic ties to Porsche Lizenz GmbH also lend the sports watch brand additional advantages in distribution and image. The good reputation of the sports car definitely rubs off on the timepieces. And the quality of the products manufactured under the Porsche Design label also speaks a lucid language. First-class and excellently worked materials, classic yet modern cases, and clean design completely resisting superficial decoration constitute the characteristics of watches by Porsche Design. These are products that homogeneously fit into the line of other items created by F. A. Porsche's design studio. The company's style includes material combinations that may seem unusual at first glance, but are actually quite harmonious when the product is looked at more closely.

P'6612 PAC

Reference number: 6612.17.86
Movement: automatic, ETA Caliber 2894-2; ø 28.6 mm, height 6.1 mm; 37 jewels; 28,800 vph
Functions: hours, minutes, chronograph, subsidiary seconds, date
Case: aluminium, PVD-coated black, ø 42 mm, height 14.85 mm; bezel in rubber-coated titanium; sapphire crystal; exhibition window case back; screwed-in crown; water-resistant to 100 m
Band: titanium, folding clasp
Price: $5,400
Variations: with rubber or crocodile skin strap ($5,100)

P'6612 PTC

Reference number: 6612.15.44
Movement: automatic, ETA Caliber 2894-2; ø 28.6 mm, height 6.1 mm; 37 jewels; 28,800 vph
Functions: hours, minutes, subsidiary seconds; date
Case: titanium , ø 42 mm, height 14.85 mm; sapphire crystal; exhibition window case back; screwed-in crown; water-resistant to 100 m
Band: titanium, folding clasp
Price: $5,400
Variations: with rubber strap ($5,100), with black dial

P'6612 PGC

Reference number: 6612.70.51
Movement: automatic, ETA Caliber 2894-2; ø 28.6 mm, height 6.1 mm; 37 jewels; 28,800 vph
Functions: hours, minutes, sweep seconds; date
Case: white gold (18 karat), ø 42 mm, height 14.85 mm; bezel in white gold with diamonds; sapphire crystal; exhibition window case back; screwed-in crown; water-resistant to 100 m
Band: reptile skin, folding clasp
Price: $22,500
Variations: with rubber strap; in rose gold ($24,500)

P'6613 PGR

Reference number: 6613.69.50
Movement: automatic, ETA Caliber 7750 AR2; ø 30 mm, height 7.9 mm; 25 jewels; 28,800 vph
Functions: hours, minutes, subsidiary seconds; split-seconds chronograph; date
Case: rose gold, ø 42 mm, height 14.85 mm; sapphire crystal; exhibition window case back; screwed-in crown; water-resistant to 100 m
Band: reptile skin, folding clasp
Price: $17,000
Variations: with rubber strap; with grey dial

P'6612 PTC 911 Limited Edition

Reference number: 6612.11.20
Movement: automatic, ETA Caliber 2894-2; ø 28.6 mm, height 6.1 mm; 37 jewels; 28,800 vph
Functions: hours, minutes, subsidiary seconds; chronograph; date
Case: titanium, ø 42 mm, height 14.85 mm; sapphire crystal; exhibition window case back; screwed-in crown; water-resistant to 100 m
Band: rubber, folding clasp
Remarks: limited to 911 pieces per dial color, here in the Porsche color speed yellow
Price: $5,400

P'6510 P011

Reference number: 6625.41.42
Movement: automatic, ETA Caliber 7750; ø 30 mm, height 7.9 mm; 25 jewels; 28,800 vph
Functions: hours, minutes, subsidiary seconds; chronograph; date and day of the week
Case: stainless steel, ø 40.5 mm, height 14.2 mm; sapphire crystal; screwed-in crown; water-resistant to 120 m
Band: stainless steel, folding clasp
Price: $3,300
Variations: with rubber strap ($3,150), with grey dial; in titanium with titanium bracelet

Rado

The history of this brand began in the year 1957 when the first watches bearing the name Rado were produced — a relatively young brand compared with other Swiss marques. The cornerstone for its international success story was laid, however, in 1962. At that time, this company surprised the world with a revolutionary invention: the oval DiaStar, the first truly scratch-resistant watch ever, sporting a case made of scratchproof heavy metal. In 1985 its parent company, the Swatch Group, decided to utilize Rado's know-how and its extensive experience in developing materials. From then on the brand intensified its research activities at its home in Lengnau, Switzerland, and continued to produce only watches with extremely hard cases.

Within the Swatch Group, Rado was the most successful individual brand in the upper price segment for a long time, with consistent growth and appreciable turnover at a time that most brands would term "difficult." New creations kept the brand talked about and secured it a certain advantage over the competition. Nevertheless, numerous new model families in varying price categories allowed the "face" of this brand to lose its distinct image, and the splits Rado was performing between jeweled watches and high-tech icons threatened to tear the company apart. This was not lost on the brand's makers who reached back to the beginning of the brand's history to the "Swinging Sixties," a generation that was so important for music, fashion, and lifestyle, reissuing the first "real" Rado under the working title "The Original." The first customer reactions garnered at Baselworld 2005 were euphoric, and the term "Original" quickly became the catchword for the successful remake of 1962's DiaStar.

Although the DiaStar case was manufactured by mixing pure tungsten or titanium carbide powder with a binding agent, subjecting it to pressure equal to 1,000 bar, and sintering it at 1,450°C, the cases of the modern Rado "Original" models are made of injected materials closely related to high-tech ceramic. Today, as back then, Rado uses the general term "heavy metal" to describe it and equally as unchanged is the distinctive oval bezel shining in its secretive — and permanent — polish.

The rest of the Rado collection has undergone the usual face-lifts and innovation cycles, but the pioneering spirit of the ceramic researchers has remained unbroken. The company already holds more than thirty patents arising from the research and production of new case developments. Various powders, already mixed together with binding agents and additives to later create the desired color, are pressed into molds to make the cases, which are then fired and finally polished with diamond powder. In the meantime, Rado has broken all of the records for hard cases that it originally set itself. For the first time, a serial watch featuring a diamond surface was presented, created in close cooperation with the Amsterdam diamond house Gassan: This wristwatch bears a formula name rich in associations: V10k (for 10 kiloVickers, or 10,000 Vickers).

While Rado was still working with high temperatures and great amounts of pressure on the study prototypes Concept 1 and Vision 1, V10k was coated with a layer of synthetic diamond using the so-called CVD process (chemical vapor deposition). The problem with this was that the diamond coating only developed the highly polished surface so desired at a certain thickness. The case back and buckle of the V10k, harder than any other material at 10,000 Vickers (stainless steel only has 200 Vickers, for example), are made of skin-friendly titanium. The watch is set with the aid of a magnetic stylus and therefore needs no crown. With their unmistakable design, Rado watches have conquered a special place in the watch scene and can also be seen at important events. For this reason, Rado has sponsored tennis tournaments for the last twenty years and has also been active at the French Open, one of the most important tennis tournaments in the world, for the last ten years.

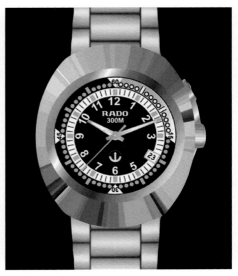

Original

Reference number: R 12 637 11 3
Movement: automatic, ETA Caliber 2824-2; ø 25.6 mm, height 4.6 mm; 25 jewels; 28,800 vph
Functions: hours, minutes, sweep seconds; date
Case: stainless steel, 30.6 x 46.2 mm, bezel in heavy metal; sapphire crystal, faceted; screwed-in crown; water-resistant to 100 m
Band: stainless steel, double folding clasp
Remarks: movable anchor symbol on the dial
Price: $995
Variations: with various dials

Original Chronograph

Reference number: R 12 638 15 3
Movement: quartz, ETA Caliber 256.262
Functions: hours, minutes, subsidiary seconds; split-seconds chronograph; date
Case: stainless steel, 30.6 x 46.2 mm, bezel in heavy metal; sapphire crystal; screwed-in crown; water-resistant to 100 m
Band: stainless steel, double folding clasp
Price: $1,290
Variations: with various dials

Original Diver

Reference number: R 12 639 01 3
Movement: automatic, ETA Caliber 2824-2; ø 25.6 mm, height 4.6 mm; 25 jewels; 28,800 vph
Functions: hours, minutes, sweep seconds; date
Case: stainless steel, 38.6 x 46.2 mm, bezel in heavy metal; unidirectionally rotating bezel with 60-minute divisions under crystal; sapphire crystal; screwed-in crown; water-resistant to 300 m
Band: stainless steel, double folding clasp
Price: $1,350

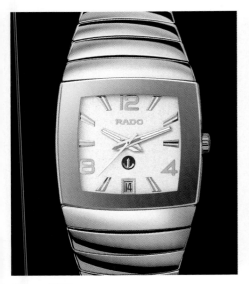

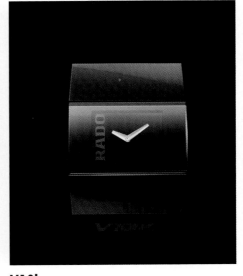

Sintra XXL

Reference number: R 13 598 10 2
Movement: automatic, ETA Caliber 2892-A2; ø 25.6 mm, height 3.6 mm; 21 jewels; 28,800 vph
Functions: hours, minutes, sweep seconds; date
Case: ceramic, 44.2 x 34.6 mm, height 11.4 mm; sapphire crystal
Band: ceramic, double folding clasp
Price: $2,600
Variations: various dial versions; with black rubber strap; also with black ceramic case

Ceramica

Reference number: R 21 347 20 2
Movement: quartz, ETA Caliber 256.111
Functions: hours, minutes; date
Case: ceramic, 32 x 27 mm, height 7.5 mm; sapphire crystal
Band: ceramic, double folding clasp
Price: upon request
Variations: in three sizes; various dial versions

V10k

Reference number: R 96 548 15 5
Movement: quartz, ETA Caliber 280.702
Functions: hours, minutes
Case: synthetic diamond, 38.5 x 19.5 mm, height 8 mm; sapphire crystal
Band: rubber, double folding clasp
Price: $4,900
Variations: with colorful straps; dial with diamonds

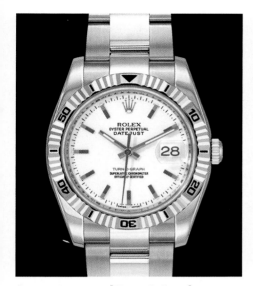

Oyster Perpetual Turn-O-Graph

Reference number: 116264
Movement: automatic, Rolex Caliber 3135; ø 28.5 mm, height 6 mm; 31 jewels; Breguet balance spring, glucydur balance with microstella regulating screws; COSC chronometer
Functions: hours, minutes, sweep seconds; date
Case: stainless steel, ø 36 mm, height 11.7 mm; bidirectionally rotating bezel in white gold, four ball bearings, faceted, with five-minute divisions; sapphire crystal with magnifying lens above the date; screwed-in crown; water-resistant to 100 m
Band: Oyster stainless steel, folding clasp with extension
Price: $5,700
Variations: with Jubilé link bracelet; various dial versions

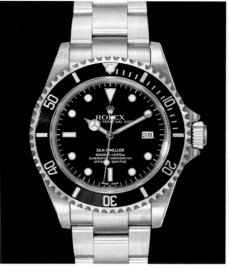

Oyster Perpetual Sea-Dweller 4000

Reference number: 16600
Movement: automatic, Rolex Caliber 3135; ø 28.5 mm, height 6 mm; 31 jewels; Breguet balance spring, glucydur balance with microstella regulating screws; COSC chronometer
Functions: hours, minutes, sweep seconds; date
Case: stainless steel, ø 40 mm, height 14.6 mm; unidirectionally rotating bezel with 60-minute divisions; sapphire crystal; Triplock screwed-in crown; water-resistant to 1220 m
Band: Oyster Fliplock stainless steel, folding clasp with security buckle und extension link
Remarks: helium valve on side of case
Price: $4,700

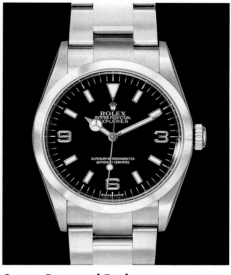

Oyster Perpetual Explorer

Reference number: 114270
Movement: automatic, Rolex Caliber 3185 (base Rolex 3135); ø 28.5 mm, height 6.4 mm; 31 jewels; Breguet balance spring, glucydur balance with microstella regulating screws; officially certified chronometer (C.O.S.C.)
Functions: hours, minutes, sweep seconds; date; 24-hour hand (second time zone)
Case: stainless steel, ø 36 mm, height 11.2 mm; sapphire crystal; screwed-in crown; water-resistant to 100 m
Band: Oysterlock steel, folding clasp with security buckle
Price: $3,750
Variations: with black dial

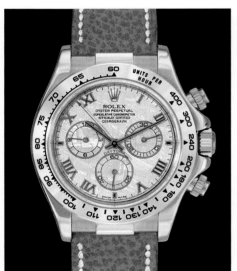

Oyster Perpetual Cosmograph Daytona

Reference number: 116519
Movement: automatic, Rolex Caliber 4130; ø 30.5 mm, height 6.5 mm; 44 jewels; Breguet balance spring, glucydur balance with microstella regulating screws; power reserve appx. 72 hours; officially certified chronometer (C.O.S.C.)
Functions: hours, minutes, subsidiary seconds; chronograph
Case: white gold, ø 40 mm, height 12.8 mm; bezel engraved with tachymeter scale; sapphire crystal; screwed-in crown and buttons; water-resistant to 100 m
Band: leather, folding clasp
Price: $21,400
Variations: various dial versions

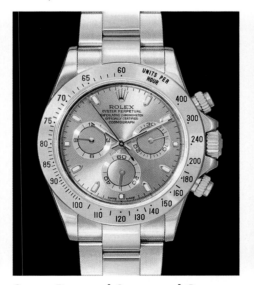

Oyster Perpetual Cosmograph Daytona

Reference number: 116523
Movement: automatic, Rolex Caliber 4130; ø 30.5 mm, height 6.5 mm; 44 jewels; Breguet balance spring, glucydur balance with microstella regulating screws; power reserve appx. 72 hours; officially certified chronometer (C.O.S.C.)
Functions: hours, minutes, subsidiary seconds; chronograph
Case: stainless steel, ø 40 mm, height 12.8 mm; bezel engraved with tachymeter scale; sapphire crystal; screwed-in crown and buttons; water-resistant to 100 m
Band: Oysterlock steel, folding clasp with security buckle
Price: $11,275
Variations: various dial versions

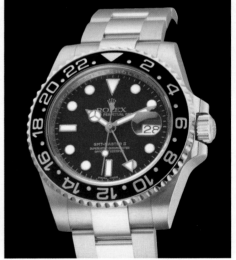

Oyster Perpetual GMT-Master II

Reference number: 116718 LN
Movement: automatic, Rolex Caliber 3185 (base Rolex 3135); ø 28.5 mm, height 6.4 mm; 31 jewels; Breguet balance spring, glucydur balance with microstella regulating screws; officially certified chronometer (C.O.S.C.)
Functions: hours, minutes, sweep seconds; date; 24-hour hand (second time zone)
Case: yellow gold, ø 40 mm, height 12.1 mm; bidirectionally rotating bezel with 24-hour scale; sapphire crystal with magnifying lens above the date; Triplock screwed-in crown
Band: Oysterlock yellow gold, folding clasp with security buckle
Price: $21,350

Daniel Roth

There are products whose shapes are just so strikingly obvious at first glance that they don't even need a logo on them. Their silhouettes are enough for the consumer to be able to associate them directly with the brand.

In the world of luxury watches there is a man who has also achieved this distinction of having his products directly recognized by their shape: Daniel Roth. The name was already well known in insider circles when this shy master watchmaker brought his first watch onto the market in 1990. Ever since, the Daniel Roth company has been one of the greats to grace the luxury industry. Master watchmakers had been constructing complicated watches long before Roth decided to make his own timepieces. However, industry insiders were quickly impressed not only by the fact that Roth's watches contained movements of excellent quality with original complications and extra displays created especially by the master, but also by the fact that all cases emanating from his production — both for women's and men's models — bore an interesting standard shape, a shape with no equal up to that point, a true innovation, the creation of which took about two years. The effort was worth the trouble, for the Daniel Roth brand now plays an important role in the high-end watch industry.

Because a portion of the movements used by Daniel Roth bear the sought-after Seal of Geneva, something only extended to watches that are manufactured in the Swiss city itself, the production of these movements takes place there. Alongside management and after-sales service, a small production area is located in the sober office building on the edge of the city. The heart of the brand beats, however, in the Vallée de Joux's Le Sentier.

Five years ago the Bulgari group bought the small *manufacture* and has since invested a great deal of money in the technical aspects and personnel of the brand. Today at Daniel Roth, it is possible to make completely proprietary watch movements. Two modern CNC machines utilizing forty-eight different tools produce the base plates, bridges, and cocks developed by two specialists in the company's design office. The necessary production software for the manufacture of the individual components is also developed in the old building located in Le Sentier. This know-how and these technical devices naturally benefit sister brands Gérald Genta and Bvlgari as well — as their fast-growing collections filled with horological specialties can attest.

Company founder and namesake Daniel Roth has completely withdrawn from the day-to-day business for personal reasons. However, the brand that bears his name still embodies the spirit of this world-famous watchmaker. And that is surely not only due to the unique silhouette of the watches, but also to very clever developments such as a new minute repeater that is simultaneously wound and activated by pushing a button found at nine o'clock. A small window at 12 o'clock shows the symbol of a bell when the striking mechanism is active so that the button is not pushed again by mistake. Furthermore, this is one of the only movements in the world containing a striking mechanism that is water-resistant to 30 meters.

The newly reworked perpetual calendar also shows the master's signature: The dial's numerals are dynamically embossed onto it, and the moon phase is embellished by an exact replica of the earth's satellite including craters and mountains. And everything is wrapped up neatly in Daniel Roth's characteristic case, the Ellipsocurvex.

Tourbillon 200 Hours Power Reserve

Reference number: 197.X.40.161.CN.BA
Movement: manually wound, Daniel Roth Caliber DR 720; 34.5 x 31.5 mm, height 6.3 mm; 25 jewels; 21,600 vph; one-minute tourbillon; power reserve 200 hours
Functions: hours and minutes (off-center), subsidiary seconds (tourbillon cage); date & power reserve display on back
Case: rose gold, 40.35 x 43.35 mm, height 12.9 mm; sapphire crystal; case back with hinged lid
Band: reptile skin, buckle
Remarks: numbered with individual master seal; possible to personalize the hinged lid
Price: $128,050

Tourbillon Perpetual Calendar Retro Date

Reference number: 199.Y.40.165.CN.BD
Movement: automatic, Daniel Roth Caliber DR 740/M 070; 26.5 x 29.5, height 7.9 mm; 43 jewels, 21,600 vph; one-minute tourbillon; movement beveled and decorated by hand, *côtes de Genève*
Functions: hours, minutes, subsidiary seconds; perpetual calendar with date (retrograde); day, month, year (retrograde)
Case: rose gold, 41 x 44 mm, height 14.9 mm; sapphire crystal; exhibition window case back
Band: reptile skin, folding clasp
Price: $140,850
Variations: in white gold; in platinum ($156,750); diamonds

Grande Sonnerie

Reference number: 607.X.60.166.CN.BD
Movement: automatic, Daniel Roth Caliber DR 760 (base GG 31000); ø 31.5 mm, height 8.75 mm; 82 jewels; 21,600 vph; one-minute tourbillon; movement beveled and decorated by hand, *côtes de Genève*
Functions: hours, minutes; minute repeater (large and small strike train, four hammers for Westminster gong); two power reserve displays for movement and repeater mechanism
Case: white gold, 40 x 43 mm, height 13 mm; sapphire crystal
Band: reptile skin, folding clasp
Remarks: limited edition of seven pieces
Price: upon request

Perpetual Calendar Moon Phases

Reference number: 118.X.60.154.CN.BA
Movement: automatic, Daniel Roth Caliber DR 114; 27 x 30 mm, height 5.28 mm; 27 jewels, 28,800 vph; movement decorated by hand, *côtes de Genève*
Functions: hours, minutes; perpetual calendar with date, day of the week, month, moon phase, leap year
Case: white gold, 38 x 41 mm, height 9.8 mm; sapphire crystal; exhibition window case back
Band: reptile skin, buckle
Price: $61,850
Variations: with gold bracelet ($73,500); in rose gold; with diamonds (from $71,350); in platinum ($73,500)

Perpetual Calendar Time Equation

Reference number: 121.Y.60.168.CN.BD
Movement: automatic, Daniel Roth Caliber DR 114; 26.5 x 29.5 mm, height 5.98 mm; 27 jewels, 28,800 vph; movement decorated by hand, *côtes de Genève*
Functions: hours, minutes; perpetual calendar with date, day of the week, month, moon phase, leap year; display for length of month and equation of time
Case: white gold, 41 x 44 mm, height 13 mm; sapphire crystal; exhibition window case back
Band: reptile skin, folding clasp
Price: $87,900
Variations: in rose gold; in platinum ($103,800)

Instantaneous Perpetual Calendar

Reference number: 119.X.40.161.CN.BA
Movement: automatic, Daniel Roth Caliber DR 114; 27 x 30 mm, height 5.28 mm; 27 jewels, 28,800 vph; movement partially skeletonized; instantaneous and spontaneous change of all calendar displays at midnight
Functions: hours, minutes, perpetual calendar with date, day of the week, month, moon phase, leap year
Case: rose gold, 38 x 41 mm, height 9.8 mm; sapphire crystal; exhibition window case back
Band: reptile skin, buckle
Price: $72,300
Variations: in white gold; in platinum ($84,000)

Ellipsocurvex Minute Repeater

Reference number: 308.Y.60.152.CN.BD
Movement: manually wound, Daniel Roth Caliber DR 750; ø 29.5 mm, height 4.1 mm; 37 jewels; 21,600 vph; movement decorated by hand, côtes de Genève
Functions: hours, minutes, subsidiary seconds; minute repeater; power reserve display
Case: white gold, 41 x 44 mm, height 11.9 mm; sapphire crystal; exhibition window case back
Band: reptile skin, folding clasp
Price: $211,900
Variations: in red gold; with diamonds ($222,500)

Ellipsocurvex Moon Phases

Reference number: 368.X.60.161.CN.BA
Movement: manually wound, Daniel Roth Caliber DR 904; 17.5 x 25 mm, height 3.85 mm; 19 jewels; 21,600 vph; movement decorated by hand, côtes de Genève
Functions: hours, minutes, subsidiary seconds; date; moon phase; power reserve display
Case: rose gold, 38 x 41 mm, height 9.45 mm; sapphire crystal; exhibition window case back
Band: reptile skin, buckle
Price: $25,100
Variations: with gold bracelet ($36,750); in white gold; with diamonds (from $34,600); in platinum ($36,750)

Ellipsocurvex Papillon

Reference number: 318.Y.70.351.CM.BD
Movement: automatic, Daniel Roth Caliber DR 115; ø 25.6 mm, height 5.28 mm; 31 jewels; 28,800 vph; movement decorated by hand, côtes de Genève
Functions: hours (jump); minutes (2 hands at the side, but not retrograde), subsidiary seconds (center)
Case: platinum, 41 x 44 mm, height 13.55 mm; sapphire crystal; exhibition window case back
Band: reptile skin, folding clasp
Remarks: limited edition of 500 pieces
Price: $44,500
Variations: in red or white gold ($32,850)

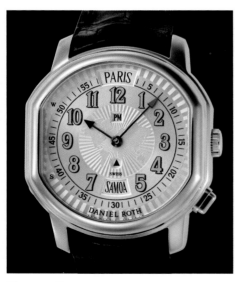

Metropolitan

Reference number: 857.X.10.160.CN.BD
Movement: automatic, Daniel Roth Caliber DR 700/21; 31.4 x 34.8 mm, height 6.35 mm; 26 jewels; 28,800 vph
Functions: hours, minutes; world time (second time zone) with day/night indication
Case: stainless steel, 38 x 41 mm, height 11.4 mm; sapphire crystal; exhibition window case back
Band: reptile skin, folding clasp
Price: $10,250
Variations: with stainless steel bracelet ($11,550); in rose or white gold (from $22,350)

Chronomax

Reference number: 347.Y.60.170.CN.BD
Movement: automatic, Daniel Roth Caliber DR 210 (base FP 4085); ø 25.6 mm, height 6.6 mm; 38 jewels; 21,600 vph; movement decorated by hand, côtes de Genève
Functions: hours, minutes, subsidiary seconds; chronograph; date; power reserve display Optimax
Case: white gold, 41 x 44 mm, height 14.9 mm; sapphire crystal; exhibition window case back
Band: reptile skin, folding clasp
Price: $27,450
Variations: in rose gold; with diamonds (from $38,050); in platinum ($39,100)

Athys

Reference number: 108.Z.50.300.CN.BD
Movement: manually wound, Daniel Roth Caliber DR 651 (base IWC 952); ø 37.8 mm, height 3.2 mm; 17 jewels; 18,000 vph
Functions: hours, minutes, subsidiary seconds (three-armed hand)
Case: red gold, 43 x 46 mm, height 9.5 mm; sapphire crystal; exhibition window case back
Band: reptile skin, folding clasp
Remarks: limited edition of 35 pieces
Price: $42,400
Variations: in white gold; in platinum ($54,050)

A sophisticated, contemporary design survey of fifty of the world's newest and most stylish bars and clubs, from Paris's funky Andy Wahloo to New York's state-of-the-art Quo.

By Bethan Ryder
150 color photographs, 50 architectural plans
192 pages · 10¼ × 10¼ in. · Cloth
ISBN 0-7892-0845-8 · $65.00

Scalfaro

Scalfaro, the result of the creative co-operation between two brothers who let their Mediterranean feel for life and their ideas of luxury flow into a distinct form, calls itself "contemporary luxury." Alexander and Dominik Kuhnle needed several years until they were finally able to formulate the dream of their own watch collection and translate it into wearable three-dimensionality.

Growing up in a family that can look back on a long tradition in the production and international distribution of precious jewelry, the brothers learned the meaning of creativity and the art of the craft early and developed a great amount of respect for these elements.

In order to distribute their exclusive creations, they traveled the world early on and forged close ties to the best jewelers. "Travel feeds all creativity," seems to be the apothegm of these brothers, and their watches represent the essence of design styles and lifestyles influenced by varying peoples around the globe.

The new interpretation of luxury stands for quality without compromise, passionate design, and high demands on composition and production. Scalfaro outfits its exclusive timekeepers, which are assembled in the workshops of experienced master watchmakers, wholly with highly refined Swiss automatic movements that have been decorated by

hand. Every element of a Scalfaro is created with great attention to detail and bears the signature of the brand's two founders. Building on a solidly dimensioned case, two different bezel shapes and dial cutaways determine the character of the two model families. Cap Ferrat presents itself with playful and elegant, baroquely curving contours despite the imposing stature of the watches. The Cap Ferrat Grand Tour only differs in a rotating bezel located underneath the crystal, which is set by an additional crown found at 10 o'clock. The Porto Cervo model, whose striking feature is an individualistic, flowing hexagon formed by the bezel and dial, comes across as a bit sportier.

The quality of the case, dial, and bands' workmanship is obvious. Both of the large model families are available on link bracelets or leather straps. The striking center link element that extends from the upper and lower parts of the watch case is continued all the way around the bracelet, while at that point on the leather strap there is a slim, padded track running the length of the material.

Great care was taken in the proportioning of the hands, the profile of the crown, and the design of the subsidiary seconds scale. The red 12, whether represented by a numeral or double marker, the solid crown protection, the screwed-in crown, and the screwed-on strap lugs are all wonderful details — but it is the screws that stand out most especially. These are special screws that were developed just for Scalfaro. The heads of these ScalfaScrews are reminiscent of Torx screws, but feature only five points. With their clear, harmoniously structured, and well-outfitted Scalfaro collection, the Kuhnle brothers have a good chance of breaking into the luxury watch markets currently dominated by men's watches, most especially since the brand's price level has been chosen so that demanding interested parties will have a hard time finding much comparison.

Cap Ferrat Grand Tour Chrono TriCompax
Reference number: A02A.04.06.2.12.Q16.20
Movement: automatic, ADK Caliber 150 (base ETA 7750); ø 30 mm, height 8.4 mm; 28 jewels; 28,800 vph; côtes de Genève, perlage, blued screws
Functions: hours, minutes, subsidiary seconds; chronograph; date
Case: stainless steel, ø 43 mm, height 14.9 mm; bidirectionally rotating bezel with 60-minute divisions under crystal; sapphire crystal; exhibition window case back; screwed-in crown; water-resistant to 100 m
Band: reptile skin, folding clasp
Price: $5,950

Cap Ferrat Grand Tour Chronograph Large Date Flyback
Reference number: A02A.05.01.2.12.Q01.20
Movement: automatic, ADK Caliber 151 (base ETA 7750); ø 30 mm, height 8.85 mm; 28 jewels; 28,800 vph; côtes de Genève, perlage, blued screws
Functions: hours, minutes, subsidiary seconds; chronograph with flyback function; large date
Case: stainless steel, ø 43 mm, height 15.9 mm; bidirectionally rotating bezel with 60-minute divisions under crystal; sapphire crystal; exhibition window case back; screwed-in crown
Band: reptile skin, folding clasp
Price: $7,250

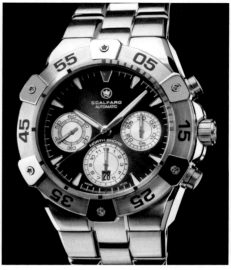

North Shore Chronograph TriCompax
Reference number: A04A.04.61.1.12.A00.31
Movement: automatic, ADK Caliber 150 (base ETA 7750); ø 30 mm, height 8.4 mm; 28 jewels; 28,800 vph; côtes de Genève, perlage, blued screws
Functions: hours, minutes, subsidiary seconds; chronograph; date
Case: stainless steel, ø 43.5 mm, height 16.9 mm; unidirectionally rotating bezel with applied claws; sapphire crystal; exhibition window case back; screwed-in crown; water-resistant to 100 m
Band: stainless steel, double folding clasp
Price: $6,950

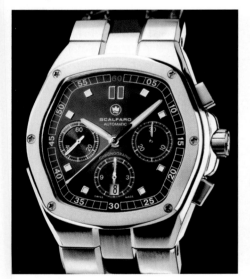

Porto Cervo Chronograph TriCompax
Reference number: A03A.04.01.1.12.Q01.20
Movement: automatic, ADK Caliber 150 (base ETA 7750); ø 30 mm, height 8.4 mm; 28 jewels; 28,800 vph; côtes de Genève, perlage, blued screws
Functions: hours, minutes, subsidiary seconds; chronograph; date
Case: stainless steel, ø 42 mm, height 14.8 mm; sapphire crystal; exhibition window case back; screwed-in crown; water-resistant to 100 m
Band: reptile skin, folding clasp
Price: $6,100
Variations: diverse dial versions; with steel bracelet

Porto Cervo Chronograph Large Date Flyback
Reference number: A03A.05.06.1.12.Q16.20
Movement: automatic, ADK Caliber 151 (base ETA 7750); ø 30 mm, height 8.85 mm; 28 jewels; 28,800 vph; côtes de Genève, perlage, blued screws
Functions: hours, minutes, subsidiary seconds; chronograph with flyback function; large date
Case: stainless steel, ø 42 mm, height 15.7 mm; sapphire crystal; exhibition window case back; screwed-in crown; water-resistant to 100 m
Band: reptile skin, folding clasp
Price: $7,450

North Shore Second Time Zone
Reference number: A04A.02.01.1.12.L01.10
Movement: automatic, ADK Caliber 148 (base ETA 2892-2); ø 25.6 mm, height 4.1 mm; 21 jewels; 28,800 vph; côtes de Genève, perlage, blued screws
Functions: hours, minutes, sweep seconds; date; 24-hour display (second time zone)
Case: stainless steel, ø 43.5 mm, height 15.6 mm; unidirectionally rotating with applied claws; sapphire crystal; exhibition window case back; screwed-in crown; water-resistant to 300 m
Band: leather, buckle
Price: $4,450

Jörg Schauer

We owe all progress to those who do not conform." Jörg Schauer's ad campaign rotates around this slogan. And Schauer is also someone who does not conform — at least in the design of his watches, he pretty much goes against the grain. Additionally, Schauer calls himself a "watch builder," quite an unusual term in this industry. Schauer doesn't care: The watches that bear his name are not put together by just anyone. Every one of the 800 watches that leave his workshop each year lands on Schauer's own bench before it goes. And this year there could be even more watches, for Schauer has a great deal of attractive new models on hand. For example, his most successful model has been given some new declinations: The Kleine Schauer is now available in two new variations. The predicate Phantom stands for the idea of showing the movement, but not all the way. The observer only sees the oscillating balance and the crown and ratchet wheels. The rest of its manually wound Durowe 7420, a vintage Pforzheim movement, disappears underneath a cover. And Schauer's creation Sportstop also deviates from mainstream design. It measures sports timings not with the usual chronograph movement, but with a very specialized case design: Synchronization of the hour and minute hands by two rotating bezels mark the starting time of an event and make a relatively precise reading of the amount of time passed possible in the end. Here the watch builder from Pforzheim was thinking a tick further than the rest. Schauer also makes customers' wishes outside of the current collection come true. Someone who purchases a GMT Individual, for example, also outfitted with a Durowe movement, can have exactly those cities printed onto the dial that are important for him or her personally, and the font of the names can even be individually chosen. Schauer offers similar individualization for a surcharge for each of his watches. The customer just needs to be a bit patient when waiting for his or her dream watch, though, for each serial model is worked and scheduled individually, causing Schauer's small team to run permanently at capacity. Although the cases received from the supplier are of the best quality, each one is polished yet again in Schauer's workshop. "My standards are just too high," he says with a grin. "I touch up absolutely everything!" When looking at these unconventional timepieces more closely, a quality of workmanship is discovered that deserves anyone's respect.

The design of Schauer's watches is not exactly of mass consumer taste: Relinquishing obvious decoration, the sheer weight of the case and the working of the cases' matte, unpolished surfaces lead one to believe that a "typical" watchmaker (if there is such a thing) is not at work here. Schauer has a different take on watches. For him, design, material, surface, and working of the details are most important. This is the goldsmith in him coming out. He creates functional, edgy cases with a visibly screwed-on bezel, and sober dials in simple black or white characterize the strict design. There will never be models that follow fashion trends in Schauer's workshop, for he only makes watches that he himself likes.

Kleine Schauer

Reference number: KLSCH/WAL
Movement: automatic, ETA Caliber 2824; ø 26 mm, height 4.6 mm; 25 jewels; 28,800 vph; autonomous Schauer rotor, blued screws
Functions: hours, minutes, sweep seconds
Case: stainless steel, ø 37 mm, height 9.2 mm; bezel secured with 12 screws; sapphire crystal; exhibition window case back; water-resistant to 50 m
Band: leather, buckle
Price: $1,695
Variations: with stainless steel milanaise bracelet ($1,895); dials in various colors; with date display

Automatic Day-Date

Reference number: Auto 2836-42WGL
Movement: automatic, ETA Caliber 2836; ø 26 mm, height 5.3 mm; 25 jewels; 28,800 vph; autonomous Schauer rotor, blued screws
Functions: hours, minutes, sweep seconds; date and day
Case: stainless steel, ø 42 mm, height 11 mm; bezel secured with 12 screws; sapphire crystal; exhibition window case back; water-resistant to 50 m
Band: rubber, folding clasp
Price: $2,095
Variations: with stainless steel Artus bracelet ($2,495); dials in black or white; case in 41 mm diameter

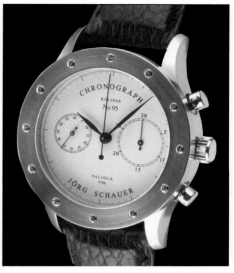

Chronograph Kulisse

Reference number: Edition 10
Movement: automatic, ETA Caliber 7750; ø 30 mm, height 7.9 mm; 28 jewels; 28,800 vph; decorated and with blued screws, exclusive Schauer rotor with engraving
Functions: hours, minutes, subsidiary seconds; chronograph
Case: stainless steel, ø 42 mm, height 15 mm; bezel secured with 12 screws; sapphire crystal; exhibition window case back; water-resistant to 50 m
Band: buffalo leather, buckle
Price: $3,250
Variations: with stainless steel Artus bracelet ($3,650); dials in black or white

Chronograph Kulisse

Reference number: Edition 12
Movement: automatic, ETA Caliber 7753 (base ETA 7750 Valjoux); ø 30 mm, height 7.9 mm; 28 jewels; 28,800 vph; decorated and with blued screws, exclusive Schauer rotor with engraving
Functions: hours, minutes, subsidiary seconds; chronograph
Case: stainless steel, ø 41 mm, height 15 mm; bezel secured with 12 screws; sapphire crystal; exhibition window case back; water-resistant to 50 m
Band: crocodile skin, buckle
Price: $3,395
Variations: with stainless steel Artus bracelet ($3,795)

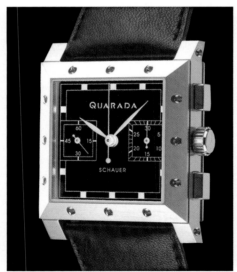

Quarada

Reference number: Quarada WL
Movement: automatic, ETA Caliber 7750; ø 30 mm, height 7.9 mm; 28 jewels; 28,800 vph; decorated and with blued screws, exclusive Schauer rotor with engraving
Functions: hours, minutes, subsidiary seconds; chronograph
Case: stainless steel, 35 x 35 mm, height 14 mm; bezel secured with 12 screws; sapphire crystal; exhibition window case back
Band: leather, buckle
Price: $5,395
Variations: with reptile skin strap

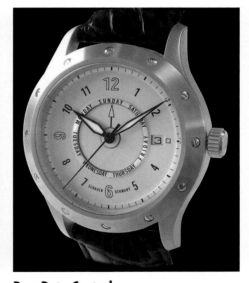

Day-Date Central

Reference number: Auto 2836-ZWL
Movement: automatic, ETA Caliber 2836; ø 26 mm, height 4.6 mm; 25 jewels; 28,800 vph; autonomous Schauer rotor, blued screws
Functions: hours, minutes, sweep seconds; date and day of the week
Case: stainless steel, ø 41 mm, height 12.9 mm; sapphire crystal; solid case back; water-resistant to 200 m
Band: crocodile skin, buckle
Price: $2,295
Variations: with stainless steel Artus bracelet ($2,695)

Alain Silberstein

This year I am not introducing any new watches." With this sentence, Alain Silberstein welcomed customers and interested parties to his booth at Baselworld last year. In answer to the incredulous astonishment this statement aroused, he continued with a mischievous grin, "I am putting on a parade." And, to be honest, this term really does fit the character of his unusual collection far better than another might.

Silberstein's watch models are divided into little families of up to sixteen models within the collection. They are divided thematically and are represented by matching colors.

"Life is not black and white, either," he says. And neither is the time, so why should timekeepers be?

Last year he introduced an absolute gaggle of tourbillons because in Silberstein's eyes, they display the highest concentration of movement mechanics possible. "And they are so superfluous that they once again become indispensable." Silberstein's play with fashion juggles up to seven different tones in one and the same watch. While others struggle with the fine tuning of watch movements, this architect and designer celebrates the fine adjustment of color. And any means of achieving this is all

right by him: enamel, galvanization, oxidation, PVD, paint, oil under crystal. Sometimes he completely does without the dial or sets fine, organically shimmering mother-of-pearl as a contrast to sandblasted or machined perlage surfaces.

Last year's tourbillon collection represented only the penultimate consequence of Silberstein's watch design theory. The colorful, graphically shaped hands of his watches have become true trademarks. The designer's mischievous humor jumps out at the casual observer from every detail of the dial, from every hand, and from every triangular crown, making a sober discussion about beauty, value, and wearability completely impossible. Silberstein, a designer — actually an architect — who lives and works in Besançon, France, often has his fun at the cost of functionality, but never at the cost of a function. The official chronometer certificate is just as important to him as the careful finishing of the movement, even if the latter is carried out according to Silberstein's own unorthodox standard. This year, the collection was presented under the motto "Colors of Time" and surprises the observer with cases aglow with lavish cloisonné painting in a rainbow of unusual color combinations. The observer certainly finds it hard to suppress a small grin at the sight of the *cloisons* in the same shapes as the camouflage found on a military truck, but Silberstein displays them in unusual palettes.

"I have no problem with being laughed at, but those who don't have the sense of humor to see beyond the facade are not the people I'm interested in," says the designer in his self-assured manner, then turns serious. "They have to realize that the humorous visual aspect conceals traditional challenges. Skeleton work on the watch movements, the use of enamel as a weatherproof way of adding color, and cases set with diamonds have always been part of the tradition of watchmaking. All I have done is to change the final result, but not the quality of what is actually flawless craftsmanship."

Sometimes it's difficult to know whether one should take him seriously or not. Silberstein just loves to play the part of the *enfant terrible* of the watchmaking scene, and he does it well. Reveling in the confused faces of those across from him, he sends his new collection out for another march in the parade.

LES COULEURS DU TEMPS
Alain Silberstein
ARCHITECTE HORLOGER

Krono Bauhaus 2 Seaweed

Reference number: KT0505
Movement: automatic, ETA Caliber 7751; ø 30 mm, height 7.9 mm; 25 jewels; 28,800 vph
Functions: hours, minutes, subsidiary seconds; chronograph; date, day of the week (Smileday), month, moon phase; 24-hour display
Case: stainless steel, painted in cloisonné, ø 39.8 mm, height 14.2 mm; sapphire crystal; exhibition window case back; water-resistant to 100 m
Band: rubber, folding clasp
Remarks: limited to 999 pieces, numbered
Price: 6,700 euros

Krono Bauhaus 2 Lichen

Reference number: KT0506
Movement: automatic, ETA Caliber 7751; ø 30 mm, height 7.9 mm; 25 jewels; 28,800 vph
Functions: hours, minutes, subsidiary seconds; chronograph; date, day of the week (Smileday), month, moon phase; 24-hour display
Case: stainless steel, painted in cloisonné, ø 39.8 mm, height 14.2 mm; sapphire crystal; exhibition window case back; water-resistant to 100 m
Band: rubber, folding clasp
Remarks: limited to 999 pieces, numbered
Price: 6,700 euros

Krono Bauhaus 2 Woodland

Reference number: KT0508
Movement: automatic, ETA Caliber 7751; ø 30 mm, height 7.9 mm; 25 jewels; 28,800 vph
Functions: hours, minutes, subsidiary seconds; chronograph; date, day of the week (Smileday), month, moon phase; 24-hour display
Case: stainless steel, painted in cloisonné, ø 39.8 mm, height 14.2 mm; sapphire crystal; exhibition window case back; water-resistant to 100 m
Band: rubber, folding clasp
Remarks: limited to 999 pieces, numbered
Price: 6,700 euros

Krono Bauhaus 2 Meadow

Reference number: KT0509
Movement: automatic, ETA Caliber 7751; ø 30 mm, height 7.9 mm; 25 jewels; 28,800 vph
Functions: hours, minutes, subsidiary seconds; chronograph; date, day of the week (Smileday), month, moon phase; 24-hour display
Case: stainless steel, painted in cloisonné, ø 39.8 mm, height 14.2 mm; sapphire crystal; exhibition window case back; water-resistant to 100 m
Band: rubber, folding clasp
Remarks: limited to 999 pieces, numbered
Price: 6,700 euros

Krono Bauhaus 2 Lilac

Reference number: KT0510
Movement: automatic, ETA Caliber 7751; ø 30 mm, height 7.9 mm; 25 jewels; 28,800 vph
Functions: hours, minutes, subsidiary seconds; chronograph; date, day of the week (Smileday), month, moon phase; 24-hour display
Case: stainless steel, painted in cloisonné, ø 39.8 mm, height 14.2 mm; sapphire crystal; exhibition window case back; water-resistant to 100 m
Band: rubber, folding clasp
Remarks: limited to 999 pieces, numbered
Price: 6,700 euros

Krono Bauhaus 2 Black Storm

Reference number: KT0511
Movement: automatic, ETA Caliber 7751; ø 30 mm, height 7.9 mm; 25 jewels; 28,800 vph
Functions: hours, minutes, subsidiary seconds; chronograph; date, day of the week (Smileday), month, moon phase; 24-hour display
Case: stainless steel, painted in cloisonné, ø 39.8 mm, height 14.2 mm; sapphire crystal; exhibition window case back; water-resistant to 100 m
Band: rubber, folding clasp
Remarks: limited to 999 pieces, numbered
Price: 6,700 euros

Tourbillon Seaweed

Reference number: TS0505
Movement: manually wound, ASC Caliber 1.3; ø 32 mm, height 5.5 mm; 25 jewels; 28,800 vph; flying one-minute tourbillon
Functions: hours, minutes; date
Case: stainless steel, painted in cloisonné, ø 38.8 mm, height 11.75 mm; sapphire crystal; exhibition window case back; water-resistant to 100 m
Band: reptile skin, folding clasp; comes with additional rubber strap
Remarks: limited to 500 pieces, numbered
Price: 50,000 euros

Tourbillon Lichen

Reference number: TS0506
Movement: manually wound, ASC Caliber 1.3; ø 32 mm, height 5.5 mm; 25 jewels; 28,800 vph; flying one-minute tourbillon
Functions: hours, minutes; date
Case: stainless steel, painted in cloisonné, ø 38.8 mm, height 11.75 mm; sapphire crystal; exhibition window case back; water-resistant to 100 m
Band: reptile skin, folding clasp; comes with additional rubber strap
Remarks: limited to 500 pieces, numbered
Price: 50,000 euros

Tourbillon Ice Cream

Reference number: TS0507
Movement: manually wound, ASC Caliber 1.3; ø 32 mm, height 5.5 mm; 25 jewels; 28,800 vph; flying one-minute tourbillon
Functions: hours, minutes; date
Case: stainless steel, painted in cloisonné, ø 38.8 mm, height 11.75 mm; sapphire crystal; exhibition window case back; water-resistant to 100 m
Band: reptile skin, folding clasp; comes with additional rubber strap
Remarks: limited to 500 pieces, numbered
Price: 50,000 euros

Tourbillon Black Storm

Reference number: TS05011
Movement: manually wound, ASC Caliber 1.3; ø 32 mm, height 5.5 mm; 25 jewels; 28,800 vph; flying one-minute tourbillon
Functions: hours, minutes; date
Case: stainless steel, painted in cloisonné, ø 38.8 mm, height 11.75 mm; sapphire crystal; exhibition window case back; water-resistant to 100 m
Band: reptile skin, folding clasp; comes with additional rubber strap
Remarks: limited to 500 pieces, numbered
Price: 50,000 euros

Tourbillon Wild Safari

Reference number: TS0601
Movement: manually wound, ASC Caliber 1.3; ø 32 mm, height 5.5 mm; 25 jewels; 28,800 vph; flying one-minute tourbillon
Functions: hours, minutes; date
Case: stainless steel, completely covered with alligator skin leather, ø 41 mm, height 12.5 mm; sapphire crystal; exhibition window case back
Band: reptile skin, buckle
Remarks: dial with cloisonné painting; limited to 500 pieces, numbered
Price: 50,000 euros

Tourbillon African Summer

Reference number: TMT2-002
Movement: manually wound, ASC Caliber 1.1; ø 31 mm, height 5.4 mm; 26 jewels; 28,800 vph; flying one-minute tourbillon; PVD-bronze movement finish
Functions: hours, minutes; date
Case: titanium, PVD-bronze, ø 40 mm, height 11 mm; sapphire crystal; exhibition window case back; water-resistant to 100 m
Band: reptile skin, folding clasp; comes with additional rubber strap
Remarks: limited to 500 pieces, numbered
Price: 44,000 euros

Rondo Krono Steel

Reference number: OK 11
Movement: automatic, Frédéric Piguet Caliber 1185;
ø 25.6 mm, height 5.4 mm; 37 jewels; 21,600 vph;
reworked by Alain Silberstein
Functions: hours, minutes, subsidiary seconds;
chronograph; date
Case: stainless steel, ø 42 mm, height 11.8 mm; sapphire
crystal; exhibition window case back; recessed crown and
buttons; water-resistant to 100 m
Band: rubber, folding clasp; with additional steel bracelet
Remarks: limited to 500 pieces, numbered
Price: 9,200 euros

Rondo Krono Steel

Reference number: OK 12
Movement: automatic, Frédéric Piguet Caliber 1185;
ø 25.6 mm, height 5.4 mm; 37 jewels; 21,600 vph;
reworked by Alain Silberstein
Functions: hours, minutes, subsidiary seconds;
chronograph; date
Case: stainless steel, ø 42 mm, height 11.8 mm; sapphire
crystal; exhibition window case back; recessed crown and
buttons; water-resistant to 100 m
Band: rubber, folding clasp; with additional steel bracelet
Remarks: limited to 500 pieces, numbered
Price: 9,200 euros

Bolido Krono Carbon Fiber

Reference number: BK 84
Movement: automatic, Frédéric Piguet Caliber 1185;
ø 25.6 mm, height 5.4 mm; 37 jewels; 21,600 vph;
reworked by Alain Silberstein
Functions: hours, minutes, subsidiary seconds;
chronograph; date
Case: stainless steel, 48 x 36 mm, height 13.5 mm; movable
cylindrical lugs made of carbon fiber; sapphire crystal;
exhibition window case back
Band: rubber, folding clasp; with additional steel bracelet
Remarks: limited to 250 pieces, numbered
Price: 10,000 euros

Pavé Krono

Reference number: VK 12
Movement: automatic, Frédéric Piguet Caliber 1185;
ø 25.6 mm, height 5.4 mm; 37 jewels; 21,600 vph;
reworked by Alain Silberstein
Functions: hours, minutes, subsidiary seconds;
chronograph; date
Case: stainless steel, 37.6 x 37.4 mm, height 11.5 mm;
sapphire crystal; exhibition window case back
Band: rubber, folding clasp; comes with additional stainless
steel bracelet
Remarks: limited to 500 pieces, numbered
Price: 9,200 euros

Pavé Krono

Reference number: VK 11
Movement: automatic, Frédéric Piguet Caliber 1185;
ø 25.6 mm, height 5.4 mm; 37 jewels; 21,600 vph;
reworked by Alain Silberstein
Functions: hours, minutes, subsidiary seconds;
chronograph; date
Case: stainless steel, 37.6 x 37.4 mm, height 11.5 mm;
sapphire crystal; exhibition window case back
Band: rubber, folding clasp; comes with additional stainless
steel bracelet
Remarks: limited to 500 pieces, numbered
Price: 9,200 euros

Pavé Smileday Alligator

Reference number: VS 21A
Movement: automatic, ETA Caliber 2836-2; ø 25.6 mm,
height 5.05 mm; 25 jewels; 28,800 vph
Functions: hours, minutes, sweep seconds; date; Smileday
Case: stainless steel, 37.6 x 37.4 mm, height 11.5 mm;
sapphire crystal; exhibition window case back
Band: rubber, folding clasp; comes with additional stainless
steel bracelet
Remarks: limited to 250 pieces, numbered
Price: 4,600 euros

Sinn

The introduction of submarine steel, the genuine material of which the hulls of submarines in current production are made, has presented this maker of "specialist watches" with another practical and effective hit. Different from other stainless steel alloys, this inconspicuous material is not just hard and thus brittle, but rather tough and more deformable. It's logical, actually: Hundreds of meters below sea level the protective hull of a submarine must not split or tear upon contact with a foreign object. Additionally, its characteristic resistance to corrosion in combination with its above-mentioned ductility makes it ideally fit the demands of professional diver's watches. For mechanical engineer Lothar Schmidt, owner and mentor of the brand Sinn, the decision was extremely clear: That which is good for large diving instruments must also be good for small ones as well.

The quality of the "instruments" that Schmidt gives professionals in his watches is a top priority in his company's philosophy. "We don't care how the professional uses his instrument. It is important to us, however, to offer him a good tool." he says. And because active pilots — an important and large target audience of the brand — are not sure themselves how to use a pilot's rotating bezel "properly," Sinn offers pilot's watches in three versions: with a rotating bezel that has a 60-minute scale going either to the left or the right or without any bezel at all.

The Duochronograph 756 Diapal is a great example of how much room for optimization simple products like a watch can offer. The case of this chronograph already contains a great deal of horological high tech. Here Schmidt presents the hardest steel watch case available on the market today, created with what Sinn has dubbed the Tegiment technology. Tegiment is a specialized process of treating steel developed for surgical instruments so that the surface is protectively coated (Latin *tegimentum*

means covering) and reaches a hardness of 1,200 Vickers. That is five to six times harder than the conventional steel used for watch cases. In addition, the watch is outfitted with a special gasket system for crown and pushers, protection against magnetic fields up to 80,000 A/m, and a dehumidifying capsule filled with copper sulphate. A patent pending for Schmidt's Diapal technology, also included in Model 756, documents that Sinn is not only on the technological cutting edge where case construction is concerned. Diapal literally stands for "**dia**mond **pal**lets" and describes an escapement system that does completely without lubrication. The pallet and escapement wheel materials were chosen so that they hardly produce friction, thus functioning better than those of a classic, freshly lubricated Swiss pallet escapement.

The backbone of the Sinn collection is still formed by exceptionally technical pilot's chronographs as well as military-styled diver's and sports watches. The high-tech substance titanium also plays a large part in the product philosophy as the case material, chiefly attracting technically oriented customers or those in demanding positions such as pilots, race car drivers, and extreme athletes.

In addition, an opening in the direction of elegant sporty can be noticed of late in the model palette, embodied above all by the watches of the Frankfurt series and featuring glossy, high-polished cases: Finance Watch, Time Zone Watch, and Finance Alarm. Important for the appearance of this line are the galvanically blackened, shiny dials with their polished applied elements. The otherwise unchanged, simple Sinn cases are now almost impossible to recognize.

Sinn customers are price-conscious watch lovers, who demand a lot of watch for their money. They are helped along by the Frankfurt company through its distribution system, for only one example. In Europe, the direct sale of the watches from the showroom in Germany's financial metropolis or from so-called depots helps Sinn to calculate its prices more precisely than if they were to adhere to conventional methods of sales through dealers. The central service station in Frankfurt also helps to save time and money. This concept is continued in Sinn's distribution in the United States, which uses the Internet as its chief sales channel.

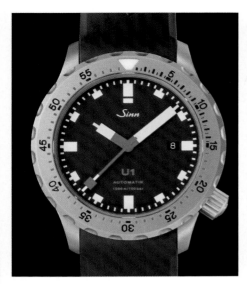

U1

Reference number: U1
Movement: automatic, ETA Caliber 2824-2; ø 25.6 mm, height 4.6 mm; 25 jewels; 28,800 vph
Functions: hours, minutes, sweep seconds; date
Case: submarine stainless steel, pearl-polished, ø 44 mm, height 14.35 mm; unidirectionally rotating bezel with 60-minute divisions; sapphire crystal, extra-hard anti-reflective coating; screwed-in crown; water-resistant to 1000 m
Band: rubber, folding clasp with wetsuit extension
Remarks: unlosable diver's rotating bezel
Price: $1,395

U2

Reference number: U2/EZM5
Movement: automatic, ETA Caliber 2893-2; ø 25.6 mm, height 4.1 mm; 21 jewels; 28,800 vph
Functions: hours, minutes, sweep seconds; 24-hour display (second time zone); date
Case: submarine stainless steel, pearl-polished, ø 44 mm, height 15.45 mm; unidirectionally rotating bezel with 60-minute divisions; sapphire crystal, extra-hard anti-reflective coating; screwed-in crown; water-resistant to 2000 m
Band: rubber, folding clasp with wetsuit extension
Remarks: unlosable diver's rotating bezel
Price: $2,595

EZM 2 (Official GSG9 Diver's Watch)

Reference number: EZM 2
Movement: quartz, ETA Caliber 955.612; case completely filled with oil making it pressure-proof to any reachable diving depth and legible under water from every angle
Functions: hours, minutes, sweep seconds; date
Case: stainless steel, pearl-polished, ø 41 mm, height 11.4 mm; unidirectionally rotating bezel with 60-minute divisions; sapphire crystal; screwed-in crown; infinitely water-resistant
Band: rubber, buckle
Price: $1,150
Variations: with leather strap; with stainless steel bracelet ($1,295)

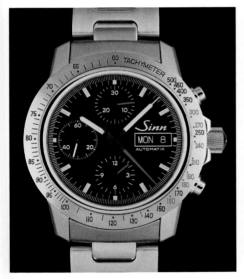

The Automobile Driver's Chronograph

Reference number: 303
Movement: automatic, ETA Caliber 7750; ø 30 mm, height 7.9 mm; 25 jewels; 28,800 vph; shockproof and amagnetic according to DIN
Functions: hours, minutes, subsidiary seconds; chronograph; date, day of the week
Case: polished stainless steel, ø 41 mm, height 16.5 mm; bezel engraved with tachymeter scale; sapphire crystal; embossed with highest tire speeds; screwed-in crown; water-resistant to 200 m
Band: stainless steel, folding clasp with overall extension
Price: $1,650

The Automatic Navigational Chronograph

Reference number: 903 St
Movement: automatic, ETA Caliber 7750 modified; ø 30 mm, height 7.9 mm; 25 jewels; 28,800 vph; finely finished with blued screws; shockproof and amagnetic according to DIN
Functions: hours, minutes, subsidiary seconds; chronograph; date
Case: polished stainless steel/satin-finished, ø 41 mm, height 14.5 mm; bidirectionally rotating bezel via crown with logarithmic scale; sapphire crystal; exhibition window case back; screwed-in crown; water-resistant to 100 m
Band: stainless steel, folding clasp with overall extension
Price: $2,750

The Rallye Chronograph

Reference number: 956 KLASSIK
Movement: automatic, ETA Caliber 7750; ø 30 mm, height 7.9 mm; 25 jewels; 28,800 vph; finely finished with blued screws; shockproof and amagnetic according to DIN
Functions: hours, minutes, subsidiary seconds; chronograph; date; power reserve display
Case: polished stainless steel, ø 41.5 mm, height 15 mm; sapphire crystal; exhibition window case back; screwed-in crown; water-resistant to 100 m
Band: leather, buckle
Remarks: 2 tachymeter scales
Price: $3,095

The Multifunctional Chronograph

Reference number: 900

Movement: automatic, ETA Valjoux Caliber 7750 modified; ø 30 mm, height 7.9 mm; 26 jewels; 28,800 vph; magnetic field protection to 80,000 A/m

Functions: hours, minutes, subsidiary seconds; chronograph; date; 24-hour display (second time zone)

Case: stainless steel, tegimented (1200 HV), ø 44 mm, height 15.5 mm; bidirectionally rotating bezel with 24-hour scale under crystal; sapphire crystal; embossed with calculation tables; screwed-in crown; water-resistant to 200 m

Band: calf skin, buckle

Price: $3,250

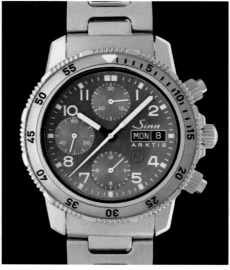

The Diver's Chronograph ARKTIS

Reference number: 203 ARKTIS

Movement: automatic, ETA Valjoux Caliber 7750; ø 30 mm, height 7.9 mm; 25 jewels; 28,800 vph; shockproof and amagnetic according to DIN; special oil

Functions: hours, minutes, subsidiary seconds; chronograph; date, day of the week

Case: polished stainless steel, ø 41 mm, height 16 mm; unidirectionally rotating bezel with 60-minute divisions; sapphire crystal; screwed-in crown and buttons; water-resistant to 300 m

Band: stainless steel, folding clasp with wetsuit extension

Remarks: case with inert gas and dehumidifying capsule

Price: $2,395

The Classic Pilot's Chronograph

Reference number: 103 St Sa

Movement: automatic, ETA Valjoux Caliber 7750 ; ø 30 mm, height 7.9 mm; 25 jewels; 28,800 vph; shockproof and amagnetic according to DIN

Functions: hours, minutes, subsidiary seconds; chronograph; date; day of the week

Case: polished stainless steel, ø 41 mm, height 16.5 mm; bidirectionally rotating bezel with 60-minute divisions; sapphire crystal; exhibition window case back; screwed-in crown and buttons; water-resistant to 200 m

Band: leather, buckle

Price: $1,750

The Frankfurt Finance Watch

Reference number: 6000

Movement: automatic, ETA Valjoux Caliber 7750 modified; ø 30 mm, height 8.4 mm; 25 jewels; 28,800 vph; finely finished with blued screws and engraved rotor; shockproof and amagnetic according to DIN

Functions: hours, minutes, subsidiary seconds; chronograph; date; additional 12-hour hand (second time zone)

Case: stainless steel, ø 38.5 mm, height 16.5 mm; bidirectionally rotating bezel with 24-hour scale and 12-hour scale on inner rotating ring (third time zone); sapphire crystal

Band: stainless steel, double folding clasp

Price: $3,895

The Frankfurt World Time Watch

Reference number: 6060

Movement: automatic, ETA Caliber 2893-2; ø 25.6 mm, height 4.1 mm; 21 jewels; 28,800 vph; finely finished with blued screws and engraved rotor; shockproof and amagnetic according to DIN

Functions: hours, minutes, sweep seconds; date; 24-hour display (second time zone)

Case: stainless steel, ø 38.5 mm, height 12 mm; bidirectionally rotating bezel with 24-hour scale and 12-hour scale on inner rotating ring (third time zone); sapphire crystal

Band: calf skin, buckle

Price: $2,650

The Frankfurt Finance Alarm

Reference number: 6066

Movement: automatic, AS Caliber 5008 (base AS Caliber 5008); ø 30.4 m, height 7.75 mm; 31 jewels; 28,800 vph; finely finished with blued screws and engraved rotor; shockproof and amagnetic according to DIN

Functions: hours, minutes, sweep seconds; date; 24-hour display (second time zone); alarm

Case: polished stainless steel, ø 38.5 mm, height 15 mm; bidirectionally rotating bezel with 24-hour scale and 12-hour scale on inner rotating ring (third time zone); sapphire crystal

Band: stainless steel, double folding clasp

Price: $4,695

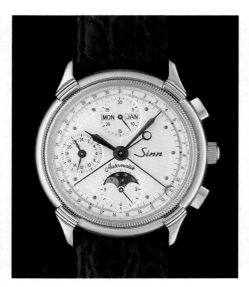

The Classically Elegant Chronograph

Reference number: 6015 St
Movement: automatic, ETA Valjoux Caliber 7751; ø 30 mm, height 7.9 mm; 25 jewels; 28,800 vph
Functions: hours, minutes, subsidiary seconds; chronograph; date, day of the week, month, moon phase; 24-hour display
Case: polished stainless steel/satin-finished, ø 37.5 mm, height 14 mm; acrylic crystal; water-resistant to 30 m
Band: leather, buckle
Price: $2,095
Variations: gold-plated version with leather strap

The Pilot's Chronograph

Reference number: 356 FLIEGER
Movement: automatic, ETA Caliber 7750; ø 30 mm, height 7.9 mm; 25 jewels; 28,800 vph; shockproof and amagnetic according to DIN
Functions: hours, minutes, subsidiary seconds; chronograph; date, day of the week
Case: stainless steel, pearl-polished, ø 38.5 mm, height 14 mm; acrylic crystal; screwed-in crown; water-resistant to 100 m
Band: leather, buckle
Price: $1,295
Variations: with stainless steel bracelet ($1,450); as UTC; with copper-colored dial, sapphire crystal for surcharge

The Pilot's Watch with Magnetic Field Protection

Reference number: 656
Movement: automatic, ETA Caliber 2824-2; ø 25.6 mm, height 4.6 mm; 25 jewels; 28,800 vph; magnetic field protection to 80,000 A/m
Functions: hours, minutes, sweep seconds; date
Case: stainless steel, pearl-polished, ø 38.5 mm, height 10.1 mm; sapphire crystal; screwed-in crown; water-resistant to 100 m
Band: leather, buckle
Price: $1,095
Variations: with stainless steel bracelet ($1,250)

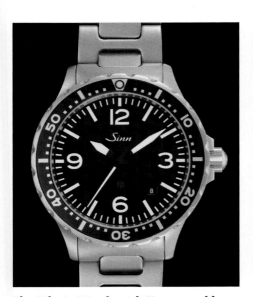

The Pilot's Watch with Unremovable Rotating Ring

Reference number: 657 Pilot
Movement: automatic, ETA Caliber 2824-2; ø 25.6 mm, height 4.6 mm; 25 jewels; 28,800 vph; magnetic field protection to 80,000 A/m
Functions: hours, minutes, sweep seconds; date
Case: stainless steel, pearl-polished, ø 41 mm, height 12 mm; bidirectionally rotating bezel with 60-minute divisions; sapphire crystal; screwed-in crown; water-resistant to 200 m
Band: stainless steel, folding clasp with overall extension
Remarks: unlosable diver's rotating bezel
Price: $1,450

The Pilot's Watch with Magnetic Field Protection and Second Time Zone

Reference number: 856 S
Movement: automatic, ETA Caliber 2893-2; ø 25.6 mm, height 4.1 mm; 21 jewels; 28,800 vph; shockproof and amagnetic according to DIN
Functions: hours, minutes, sweep seconds; date; 24-hour display (second time zone)
Case: stainless steel, hardened black (tegimented), ø 40 mm, height 10.7 mm; sapphire crystal; screwed-in crown; water-resistant to 200 m
Band: leather, buckle
Price: $1,550

The Duochronograph with Diapal Technology and Second Time Zone

Reference number: 756 DIAPAL
Movement: automatic, ETA Caliber 7750 modified; ø 30 mm, height 7.9 mm; 25 jewels; 28,800 vph; Diapal technology escapement; magnetic field protection to 80,000 A/m; shockproof and amagnetic according to DIN; dehumidifying capsule
Functions: hours, minutes, chronograph; date; additional 12-hour hand (second time zone)
Case: stainless steel, tegimented (1200 HV), ø 40 mm, height 13.7 mm; sapphire crystal; screwed-in crown
Band: Russian leather, buckle
Price: $2,595

Sothis

Sothis was the Egyptian goddess of the fixed star Sirius and master of the Nile's uncontrollable flooding (at least before the Aswan Dam was built), which left in its wake a fertile and therefore sought-after layer of silt along the river's course. This is what inspired Wolfgang Steinkrüger as he was looking around for a name for his watch brand in the mid-1990s.

While observing the night sky during walks with his dogs on cold, clear winter evenings, his attention had been attracted to the above-mentioned star located in the Canis Major constellation.

This designer hailing from Germany's Bielefeld, an enthusiastic collector of fascinating mechanical watches for more than twenty years, created his own watch for the first

time in 1996. He based it on a vintage Valjoux 88 caliber and had it put together by a goldsmith in Pforzheim.

The success of his debut as a watch manufacturer encouraged Steinkrüger to make a larger number of chronographs containing the trusty ETA Valjoux 7750 caliber. And at the Basel Watch Fair of 1997 he introduced this watch with three dial variations. In the same year, alongside some other models, he presented Spirit of the Moon.

This chronograph is based on the ETA Valjoux 7751, a variation of the above-mentioned 7750 caliber, containing displays for the day of the week and month, a date hand, and a moon phase using a traditional disk that revolves entirely in 59 days.

Sothis replaced this disk with a little hand that reminds one of a conductor's baton as it features a little circle at its tip. The little round frame alternately encircles different symbols that appear on a silver-colored, applied ring, and because it takes two lunar months for the hand to complete its revolution, there are two sets of them printed onto the ring in a slightly three-dimensional manner. While "full moon" and "first and last quarter" are displayed in the normal manner on the dial, the "new moon" phase, which could also be jokingly described as "the vanished moon," is symbolized by two stars. This has a certain logic to it, for even when the moon disappears for a while, the starry sky remains otherwise unchanged.

This unusual depiction of the moon phase featuring a circulating hand is as unique to the two new models as the date ring on the dial's flange: The chronograph models Ikarus and Osiris illustrate Steinkrüger's unmistakable brand of classicism in this collection. Both models are powered by finely finished Valjoux 7751 chronograph calibers with a complete calendar, and both are limited to 500 pieces worldwide.

Ikarus

Reference number: 025001-S
Movement: automatic, ETA Caliber 7751 modified;
ø 30 mm, height 7.9 mm; 25 jewels; 28,800 vph; finely
finished with *côtes de Genève*
Functions: hours, minutes, subsidiary seconds; chronograph;
date, day of the week, month, moon phase
Case: stainless steel, ø 42.5 mm, height 13.9 mm; sapphire
crystal; exhibition window case back; water-resistant to 50 m
Band: reptile skin, double folding clasp
Price: $3,950
Variations: with stainless steel bracelet ($4,600)

Osiris

Reference number: 025002-B
Movement: automatic, ETA Caliber 7751 modified;
ø 30 mm, height 7.9 mm; 25 jewels; 28,800 vph; finely
finished with *côtes de Genève*
Functions: hours, minutes, subsidiary seconds; chronograph;
date, day of the week, month, moon phase
Case: stainless steel, ø 42.5 mm, height 13.9 mm; sapphire
crystal; exhibition window case back; water-resistant to 50 m
Band: leather, double folding clasp
Price: $3,550
Variations: with stainless steel bracelet ($4,200);
with white dial

Big Bridge II

Reference number: 024001-B
Movement: automatic, ETA Caliber 2892-A2 with
chronograph module 2025 by Dubois-Dépraz; ø 30 mm,
height 6.9 mm; 57 jewels; 28,800 vph; finely finished with
côtes de Genève
Functions: hours, minutes, subsidiary seconds;
chronograph; date
Case: stainless steel, 50 x 37 mm, height 12.7 mm; sapphire
crystal; exhibition window case back; water-resistant to 50 m
Band: leather, double folding clasp
Price: $5,250
Variations: diverse dial colors and bands

Janus

Reference number: 024003-W
Movement: automatic, ETA Caliber 7750; ø 30 mm,
height 7.9 mm; 25 jewels; 28,800 vph; finely finished with
côtes de Genève
Functions: hours, minutes, subsidiary seconds; chronograph;
date and day of the week
Case: stainless steel, ø 42.5 mm, height 13.9 mm; sapphire
crystal; exhibition window case back; water-resistant to 50 m
Band: leather, double folding clasp
Price: $3,400
Variations: with black dial; with stainless steel
bracelet ($4,050)

Classico

Reference number: 021001-W
Movement: automatic, ETA Caliber 7753; ø 30 mm,
height 7.9 mm; 25 jewels; 28,800 vph; finely finished
with *côtes de Genève*
Functions: hours, minutes, subsidiary seconds;
chronograph; date
Case: stainless steel, ø 42.5 mm, height 13.9 mm; sapphire
crystal; exhibition window case back; water-resistant to 50 m
Band: stainless steel, double folding clasp
Price: $4,200
Variations: with black dial; with leather strap

Libra

Reference number: 024004-B
Movement: automatic, ETA Caliber 7753; ø 30 mm,
height 7.9 mm; 25 jewels; 28,800 vph; finely finished
with *côtes de Genève*
Functions: hours, minutes, subsidiary seconds;
chronograph; date
Case: stainless steel, ø 42.5 mm, height 13.9 mm; sapphire
crystal; exhibition window case back; water-resistant to 50 m
Band: leather, double folding clasp
Price: $3,550
Variations: with white dial; with stainless steel
bracelet ($4,200)

Stowa

Tradition meets the modern: The old German watch brand Stowa now functions according to this principle. With his new introductions, the brand's owner, Jörg Schauer, solely reinterprets successful vintage Stowa models. A current example is the striking diver's watch Seatime, which was originally manufactured in the 1960s. Tradition here means using the original plate from 1963 for the printing of this model's dial. Modern is the rotating bezel, which upon request can be delivered with aluminum PVD inlays in various colors. Modern is also the way these watches are distributed in an online shop at www.stowa.de. Watch fans with shallower pockets will find mechanical watches of good quality here.

Stowa was founded in 1927 in Hornberg, Germany, by Walter Storz. In the 1930s and '40s, the company situated in the Black Forest produced especially high-quality, reliable watches. The degree of excellence achieved by their watches brought Stowa a good reputation, and their pilot's and observation watches were of special note. Alongside IWC, A. Lange & Söhne, Wempe, and Laco, this brand was also one of the German air force's official suppliers. These watches had to be completely precise and trustworthy, as they were used in ways that demanded 100-percent accuracy. The pilot in his cockpit had to be just as sure as the officer on the deck of his ship that his watch was correct. These and other historic Stowa models can be admired in the Stowa watch museum maintained by Schauer in Engelsbrand, Germany. In 1996 he purchased the rights from the Storz family, thus ensuring that Stowa is now able to look back on seventy-eight years of uninterrupted watch manufacturing.

"Stowa — the German Quality Watch." This is how the traditional Pforzheim brand advertised during its heyday. This elementary concept is being carried on in the current day and age: The watches are as striking in their visuals as they are in their absolute functionality. In this way the old pilot's watches, their designs unfailingly adapted, have today become luxury wristwatches, and their technical straightforwardness and uncomplicated clarity have also been maintained. Alongside the pilot's series, a new marine series — also historical in nature — is being produced. In keeping with the motto, "Characteristically original — the details of a Stowa," all Stowa watches are striking in their attention to detail. Nearly every piece of every serial watch undergoes its own individual revision and examination. That the watches are "made in Germany" and thus labeled is enough reason for the new owners of the name to deliver the highest-quality products.

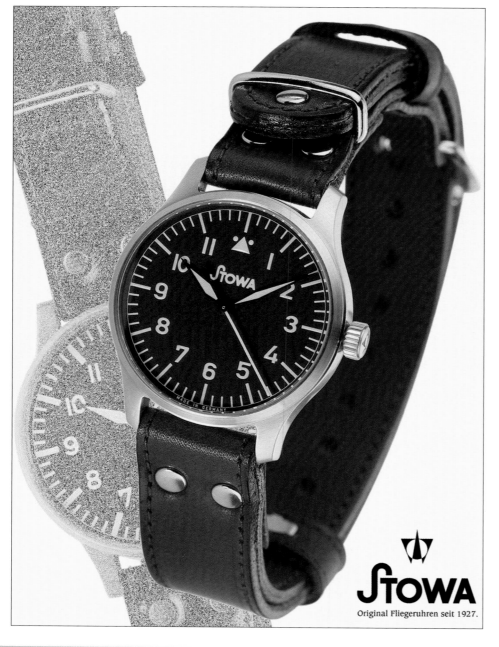

STOWA

Original Fliegeruhren seit 1927.

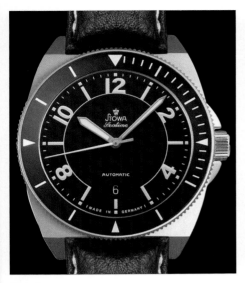

Seatime

Reference number: Seatime SZiSZDLuS
Movement: automatic, ETA Caliber 2824; ø 25.6 mm, height 4.6 mm; 25 jewels; 28,800 vph; exclusive STOWA rotor
Functions: hours, minutes, sweep seconds; date
Case: stainless steel, ø 42 mm, height 13 mm; unidirectionally rotating bezel with 60-minute divisions; sapphire crystal; water-resistant to 300 m
Band: leather, buckle
Price: 590 euros
Variations: with rubber or stainless steel bracelet (688 euros); various dial and bezel colors

Antea

Reference number: Antea weiss 12ZDLE
Movement: automatic, ETA Caliber 2824; ø 25.6 mm, height 4.6 mm; 25 jewels; 28,800 vph; exclusive STOWA rotor
Functions: hours, minutes, sweep seconds; date
Case: stainless steel, ø 39 mm, height 9.5 mm; sapphire crystal; exhibition window case back; water-resistant to 50 m
Band: leather, buckle
Price: 350 euros
Variations: with stainless steel milanaise bracelet (470 euros)

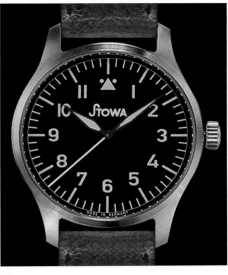

Airman

Reference number: Flieger F40LB
Movement: automatic, ETA Caliber 2824; ø 25.6 mm, height 4.6 mm; 25 jewels; 28,800 vph; exclusive STOWA rotor
Functions: hours, minutes, sweep seconds
Case: stainless steel, ø 40 mm, height 10.5 mm; sapphire crystal; exhibition window case back; water-resistant to 50 m
Band: camel leather, buckle
Price: 470 euros
Variations: with stainless steel milanaise bracelet (590 euros)

Marine

Reference number: Marine M40LB
Movement: automatic, ETA Caliber 2824; ø 25.6 mm, height 4.6 mm; 25 jewels; 28,800 vph; exclusive STOWA rotor
Functions: hours, minutes, sweep seconds; date
Case: stainless steel, ø 40 mm, height 10.5 mm; sapphire crystal; exhibition window case back; water-resistant to 50 m
Band: camel leather, buckle
Price: 450 euros
Variations: with stainless steel milanaise bracelet (570 euros)

Antea

Reference number: Kleine Sekunde
Movement: manually wound, ETA Caliber 7001 Peseux; ø 23.3 mm, height 4.5 mm; 17 jewels; 21,600 vph; decorated, blued screws
Functions: hours, minutes, subsidiary seconds
Case: stainless steel, ø 35.5 mm, height 6.9 mm; sapphire crystal; exhibition window case back; water-resistant to 30 m
Band: deer leather, buckle
Price: 390 euros
Variations: with stainless steel milanaise bracelet (510 euros)

Exima Chronometer

Reference number: Exima Chronometer
Movement: automatic, ETA Caliber 2824; ø 25.6 mm, height 4.6 mm; 25 jewels; 28,800 vph; côtes de Genève, blued screws; officially certified chronometer (C.O.S.C.)
Functions: hours, minutes, sweep seconds; date
Case: stainless steel, ø 37 mm, height 9.5 mm; sapphire crystal; exhibition window case back; water-resistant to 50 m
Band: leather, buckle
Remarks: distribution exclusively via mail-order catalogue "Manufactum"
Price: 690 euros
Variations: with stainless steel bracelet (810 euros)

Swiss Army

Swiss traditions are well cared for, and not only in the world of watches are 100-year and longer anniversaries celebrated. In 1884, Karl Elsener founded his knife cutlery in Ibach, near Schwyz, which is close to Lake Lucerne and the street that will take you to the infamous Gotthard Tunnel. He was soon the official supplier to the Swiss army.

At the beginning, he mainly manufactured simple and robust soldier's pocketknives, but in 1897, he patented his vision of a variable pocketknife containing several blades and tools. From then on, Elsener supplied the Swiss military with this "officer's knife" that has today become a national symbol.

In 1909, he created the brand name Victoria for his inventions, in honor of his mother, and after rustproof steel (called Inox, derived from inoxidable) was invented, the family business was renamed Victorinox in 1921.

Today, Carl Elsener senior and his son Carl junior employ about 1,000 people who manufacture 25 million knives annually. In 1989, father and son Elsener decided to strategically extend the product palette with a collection of sporty and robust wristwatches, which were at first mainly sold in the U.S. — and that with incredible success — under the brand name Swiss Army. Right from the beginning, the Swiss cross in the

brand's emblem didn't stand for Victorinox or the officer's knife, but for "Swiss made" and legendary Swiss quality.

Now the Swiss Army brand has moved into its next phase, and the red-and-white cross can be found on leisure clothing and outdoor accessories. And, something even more important for the watch fan, the watch collection is being clearly moved upmarket.

While the Swiss Army watch collections were mainly characterized by sporty quartz watches with a touch of military about them, including different additional functions and in varying case materials, the brand is now definitely going for a slightly different customer. Above all, it is the Professional collection that has become the big winner.

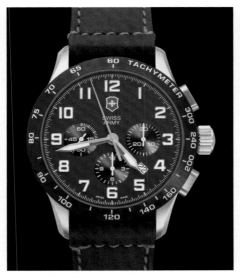

AirBoss Mach 4

Reference number: V.24044
Movement: manually wound, ETA Caliber 6498-2; ø 37.2 mm, height 4.5 mm; 17 jewels; 21,600 vph
Functions: hours, minutes, subsidiary seconds
Case: stainless steel, ø 45 mm, height 12.1 mm; bidirectionally rotating bezel under crystal with 60-minute scale settable via crown; sapphire crystal; exhibition window case back
Band: leather, buckle
Price: $650
Variations: with stainless steel bracelet

AirBoss Mach 6

Reference number: V.24785
Movement: automatic, ETA Valjoux Caliber 7753; ø 30.40 mm, height 7.90 mm; 27 jewels; 28,800 vph
Functions: hours, minutes, subsidiary seconds; chronograph; date
Case: stainless steel, ø 44 mm, height 14.90 mm; sapphire crystal; exhibition window case back
Band: leather, folding clasp
Price: $1,195
Variations: with black, red, or silver dial

Ambassador XL

Reference number: V.24151
Movement: manually wound, ETA Caliber 6498-1; ø 37.20 mm, height 4.5 mm; 17 jewels; 18,000 vph
Functions: hours, minutes, subsidiary seconds
Case: stainless steel, ø 45 mm, height 11.75 mm; sapphire crystal; exhibition window case back
Band: leather, buckle
Price: $550
Variations: with silver dial on black leather strap

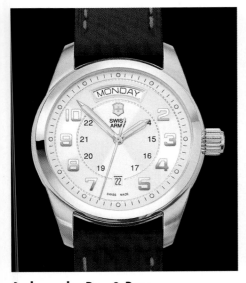

Ambassador Day & Date

Reference number: V.25149
Movement: automatic, ETA Caliber 2834-2; ø 29.6 mm, height 5.05 mm; 25 jewels; 28,800 vph
Functions: hours, minutes, sweep seconds; date, day
Case: stainless steel, ø 41 mm, height 11.15 mm; sapphire crystal; exhibition window case back
Band: leather, buckle
Price: $550
Variations: with black dial on brown leather strap; silver or black dial on stainless steel bracelet

Ground Force

Reference number: V.24791
Movement: automatic, ETA Caliber 2824-2; ø 26 mm, height 4.60 mm; 25 jewels; 28,800 vph
Functions: hours, minutes, sweep seconds; date
Case: stainless steel/titanium, ø 41 mm, height 12 mm; sapphire crystal; exhibition window case back; screwed-in crown
Band: stainless steel/titanium, double folding clasp with diver's extension
Price: $595
Variations: with silver or black dial on black strap; silver dial on stainless steel bracelet

ChronoPro

Reference number: V.24162
Movement: automatic, ETA Valjoux Caliber 7750; ø 30 mm, height 7.9 mm; 25 jewels; 28,800 vph
Functions: hours, minutes, subsidiary seconds; chronograph; date
Case: stainless steel, ø 42 mm, height 15.2 mm; sapphire crystal; exhibition window case back; screwed-in crown and buttons
Band: stainless steel, folding clasp with security button
Price: $1,195
Variations: on leather strap

TAG Heuer

Right from the beginning, TAG Heuer has been involved with sports — and especially sports timing. Whether horseback riding, track and field, or automobile and ski racing, measuring sports' best performances has been one central area of knowledge mastered by this Swiss watch manufacturer of chronographs and sports and prestigious watches since its founding in 1860. Charles-Auguste Heuer, son of the company's founder, developed the first mechanical timekeeping instrument capable of measuring hundredths of a second in 1916, a fact that helped the

Heuer brand become the Olympic Games official timekeeper in 1920, 1924, and 1928. The hand-held stopwatch Mikrograph, whose balance beat at a frequency of 360,000 oscillations per hour, was in its day a technical sensation and even from a modern point of view remains an outstanding achievement.

This is a tradition that the company tapped into when it presented the world's first mechanical wrist chronograph that could stop a hundredth of a second at Baselworld 2005. The Caliber 360 Concept Chronograph is outfitted with two watch

movements that are of course coupled to each other, but which function independently of each other. The time is shown by an automatic movement as precise as a chronometer that ticks at a frequency of 28,800 vibrations per hour, while the stop timing is made possible by a stopwatch movement that ticks at the same frequency as its forebear the Mikrotimer, but which is clearly smaller. The chronograph movement can be used to stop up to 100 minutes, after which it needs to be wound again by hand. A clever technical detail is the fact that both movements are wound by just one crown.

And just one year previously, TAG Heuer had already illustrated its brilliance in a true technical innovation. The presentation of a watch movement design breaking all the accepted laws of watchmaking surprised the watch world at Baselworld 2004. Energy transmission in the winding mechanism, for example, is not done as usual via toothed wheels in this movement, but rather by use of thirteen miniature toothed belts. The lion's share of the usual synthetic rubies used in a normal movement to reduce friction were exchanged for micro ball bearings. The oscillating weight, which generally rotates around its own axis in order to wind the mainspring, was exchanged for a linear weight that bounces back and forth. This new linear oscillating weight, a bar of platinum, winds the contents of four spring barrels placed in a v-shaped pair of rows, strongly reminiscent of the cylinders found in an automobile's motor. This spring barrel design was combined with the most attractive (TAG) Heuer timepiece of all time to give the concept watch its name: Monaco V4.

Both of these technical highlights are however still in concept stages and won't hit the markets until 2006 at the earliest. In exchange, TAG Heuer naturally offers its customers a large portfolio of conventional watches and chronographs available immediately. Especially in Europe, the mechanical classics Monza, Carrera, Monaco, and Autavia are proving extremely popular. Brand new is also the quartz-driven golfing watch that TAG Heuer has dedicated to its celebrity ambassador Tiger Woods. Since this watch only weighs 55 grams and, according to the company, can survive shocks up to 5,000 times that of gravity, this is one timepiece that does more than just look pretty on the wrist at tee time.

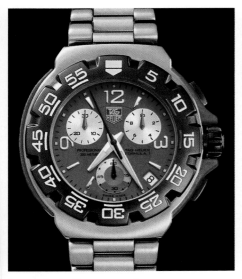

Formula 1 Chronograph

Reference number: CAC1112.BA0850
Movement: quartz, ETA Caliber G10.711
Functions: hours, minutes, sweep seconds; date
Case: stainless steel with plastic inlays, ø 40 mm, height 11.6 mm; unidirectionally rotating bezel with 60-minute divisions; sapphire crystal; screwed-in crown; water-resistant to 200 m
Band: stainless steel, security folding clasp
Price: $895
Variations: various dial colors (black, white), with rubber strap

Formula 1 Chronotimer

Reference number: CAC111D.BA0850
Movement: quartz, ETA Caliber 988.432; multifunctional electronic module with LCD display integrated into dial
Functions: hours, minutes; chronograph; perpetual calendar with date, second time zone, alarm, countdown in LCD display
Case: stainless steel with plastic inlays, ø 40 mm, height 11.6 mm; unidirectionally rotating bezel with 60-minute divisions; sapphire crystal; screwed-in crown; water-resistant to 200 m
Band: stainless steel, security folding clasp
Price: $995
Variations: with rubber strap

Formula 1 Lady Diamomds

Reference number: WAC1214.BC0839
Movement: quartz, ETA Caliber F05.111
Functions: hours, minutes, sweep seconds; date
Case: stainless steel , ø 37 mm, height 9.8 mm; unidirectionally rotating bezel set with 120 diamonds (0.79 ct); sapphire crystal; screwed-in crown; water-resistant to 200 m
Band: satin, buckle
Price: $1,895
Variations: with white and pink satin straps; various dial colors (white, pink)

Aquaracer

Reference number: WAF1110.FT0809
Movement: quartz, ETA Caliber F03.111
Functions: hours, minutes, sweep seconds; date
Case: stainless steel , ø 38.4 mm, unidirectionally rotating bezel with 60-minute divisions; sapphire crystal; screwed-in crown; water-resistant to 300 m
Band: rubber, buckle
Price: $1,095
Variations: with steel bracelet; various dial colors (silver, blue)

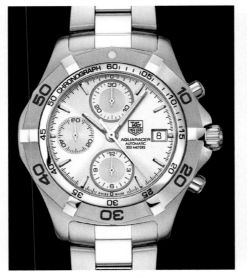

Aquaracer Automatic Chronograph

Reference number: CAF2111.BA0809
Movement: automatic, TAG Heuer Caliber 16 (base ETA 7750); ø 30 mm, height 7.9 mm; 25 jewels; 28,800 vph
Functions: hours, minutes, subsidiary seconds; chronograph; date
Case: stainless steel , ø 41 mm, unidirectionally rotating bezel with 60-minute divisions; sapphire crystal; screwed-in crown; water-resistant to 300 m
Band: stainless steel, security folding clasp with integrated extension
Price: $1,895
Variations: various dial colors (silver, blue)

Aquaracer Calibre S Chronograph

Reference number: CAF7110.BA0803
Movement: quartz, TAG Heuer Caliber Calibre S (base TAG Heuer Calibre S); with regatta countdown function, simplified legibility of the chronograph function
Functions: hours, minutes, sweep seconds; chronograph; regatta countdown
Case: stainless steel , ø 41 mm, bezel in aluminum with regatta countdown scale; sapphire crystal; screwed-in crown; water-resistant to 300 m
Band: stainless steel, security folding clasp with integrated extension
Price: $1,750

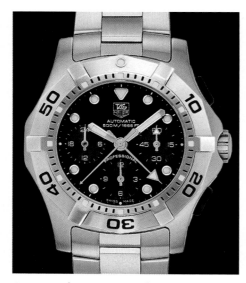

Aquagraph Automatic Chronograph

Reference number: CN211A.BA0353
Movement: automatic, TAG Heuer Caliber 60 (base Dubois-Dépraz 2073); ø 25.6 mm, height 7.4 mm; 46 jewels; 28,800 vph; automatic helium valve
Functions: hours, minutes, subsidiary seconds; chronograph; date
Case: stainless steel , ø 43 mm, height 14 mm; unidirectionally rotating bezel with 60-minute divisions and protection against accidental turning; sapphire crystal; screwed-in crown; buttons functional to 500 m depth; water-resistant to 500 m
Band: stainless steel, security folding clasp with extension
Price: $2,800

Professional Golf Watch

Reference number: WAE1110.FT6004
Movement: quartz, ETA Caliber 255.411; exceptionally high shockproofing to 5000 G
Functions: hours, minutes, sweep seconds; date
Case: stainless steel/titanium , 37.5 x 36.7 mm; sapphire crystal; screwed-in crown positioned at 9 o'clock; water-resistant to 50 m
Band: silicon rubber, clasp is opened by two buttons on case
Remarks: first timepiece to take ergonomic needs of golf players into account, developed in cooperaton with Tiger Woods; limited to 8,000 pieces; total weight 55g
Price: $1,295

Microtimer

Reference number: CS111C.FT6003
Movement: quartz, TAG Heuer Caliber HR 03 (base Valtronic HR03); multifunctional movement developed by TAG Heuer
Functions: hours, minutes, date; chronograph to 1/1000 second; alarm; second time zone; perpetual calendar; F1 timing with lap memory (80 laps) and best lap mode; dial illumination; stand-by
Case: stainless steel, 38 x 42.7 mm, height 12 mm; sapphire crystal; water-resistant to 100 m
Band: rubber, security folding clasp
Price: $1,995

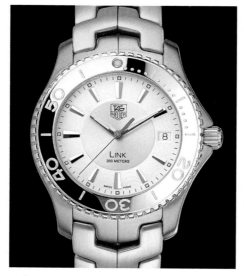

Link Quarz

Reference number: WJ1111.BA0570
Movement: quartz, ETA Caliber 905.112
Functions: hours, minutes, sweep seconds; date
Case: stainless steel, ø 39 mm, height 11 mm; unidirectionally rotating bezel with 60-minute divisions; sapphire crystal; screwed-in crown; water-resistant to 200 m
Band: stainless steel, security folding clasp
Price: $1,695
Variations: various dial colors

Link Automatic Chronograph

Reference number: CJF2110.BA0576
Movement: automatic, TAG Heuer Caliber 16 (base ETA 7750); ø 30 mm, height 7.9 mm; 25 jewels; 28,800 vph
Functions: hours, minutes, subsidiary seconds; chronograph; date
Case: stainless steel, ø 41 mm, height 16 mm; sapphire crystal; screwed-in crown; water-resistant to 200 m
Band: stainless steel, security folding clasp
Price: $2,695
Variations: various dial colors

Link Chronometer Chronograph Calibre 36

Reference number: CT511A.BA0564
Movement: automatic, TAG Heuer Caliber 36 (base Zenith El Primero 400); ø 30 mm, height 6.5 mm; 31 jewels; 36.600 vph; officially certified chronometer (C.O.S.C.)
Functions: hours, minutes, subsidiary seconds; chronograph; date
Case: stainless steel, ø 42 mm, height 14.5 mm; sapphire crystal; exhibition window case back; screwed-in crown; water-resistant to 200 m
Band: stainless steel, security folding clasp
Price: $5,495

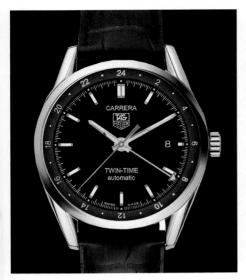

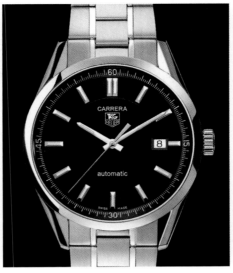

Carrera Automatic Twin-Time

Reference number: WV2115.FC6180
Movement: automatic, TAG Heuer Caliber 7 (base ETA 2893-2 GMT); ø 25.6 mm, height 4.6 mm; 25 jewels; 28,800 vph
Functions: hours, minutes, sweep seconds; date; 24-hour display (second time zone)
Case: stainless steel, ø 39 mm, height 12 mm; sapphire crystal; water-resistant to 50 m
Band: reptile skin, security folding clasp
Price: $1,795
Variations: with silver-colored dial; with calfskin leather strap with holes; with brown crocodile skin strap

Carrera Automatic

Reference number: WV211B.BA0787
Movement: automatic, TAG Heuer Caliber 5 (base ETA 2824); ø 25.6 mm, height 4.6 mm; 25 jewels; 28,800 vph
Functions: hours, minutes, sweep seconds; date
Case: stainless steel, ø 39 mm, height 12 mm; sapphire crystal; exhibition window case back; water-resistant to 50 m
Band: stainless steel, security folding clasp
Price: $1,495
Variations: with silver-colored dial

Carrera Chronograph Racing

Reference number: CV2113.FC6182
Movement: automatic, TAG Heuer Caliber 17 (base ETA 2894-2); ø 28.6 mm, height 6.1 mm; 37 jewels; 28,800 vph
Functions: hours, minutes, subsidiary seconds; chronograph; date
Case: stainless steel, ø 39 mm, height 14 mm; sapphire crystal; water-resistant to 50 m
Band: leather, security folding clasp
Price: $2,450
Variations: with silver-colored and black dial

Carrera Chronograph

Reference number: CV2010.BA0786
Movement: automatic, TAG Heuer Caliber 16 (base ETA 7750); ø 30 mm, height 7.9 mm; 25 jewels; 28,800 vph
Functions: hours, minutes, subsidiary seconds; chronograph; date
Case: stainless steel, ø 41 mm, height 16 mm; bezel in aluminum with tachymeter scale; sapphire crystal; exhibition window case back; water-resistant to 50 m
Band: stainless steel, security folding clasp
Price: $2,295
Variations: with calfskin leather strap with holes; silver dial with anthracite-colored totalizers

Monaco Chronograph Python

Reference number: CW2114.EB0017
Movement: automatic, TAG Heuer Caliber 17 (base ETA 2894-2); ø 28.6 mm, height 6.1 mm; 37 jewels; 28,800 vph
Functions: hours, minutes, subsidiary seconds; chronograph; date
Case: stainless steel, 40 x 40 mm, height 13.5 mm; Plexiglas; water-resistant to 50 m
Band: python skin, security folding clasp
Remarks: comes with chocolate brown crocodile skin leather strap in set
Price: $3,095

Monaco Chronograph Absolute White

Reference number: CW2117.FC6198
Movement: automatic, TAG Heuer Caliber 17 (base ETA 2894-2); ø 28.6 mm, height 6.1 mm; 37 jewels; 28,800 vph
Functions: hours, minutes, subsidiary seconds; chronograph; date
Case: stainless steel, 40 x 40 mm, height 13.5 mm; Plexiglas; water-resistant to 50 m
Band: leather, security folding clasp
Price: $2,995

Monaco Automatic

Reference number: WW2110.FT6005
Movement: automatic, TAG Heuer Caliber 6 (base ETA 2895-1); ø 25.6 mm, height 4.35 mm; 30 jewels; 28,800 vph
Functions: hours, minutes, subsidiary seconds; date
Case: stainless steel, 37 x 37 mm, height 12 mm; sapphire crystal; water-resistant to 50 m
Band: rubber, security folding clasp
Remarks: available from December 2005
Price: $1,995
Variations: with black crocodile skin strap; with blue dial and blue crocodile skin strap

Monaco Chronograph Steve McQueen

Reference number: CW2113.BA0780
Movement: automatic, TAG Heuer Caliber 17 (base ETA 2894-2); ø 28.6 mm, height 6.1 mm; 37 jewels; 28,800 vph
Functions: hours, minutes, subsidiary seconds; chronograph; date
Case: stainless steel, 40 x 40 mm, height 13.5 mm; Plexiglas; water-resistant to 50 m
Band: stainless steel, security folding clasp
Price: $2,995
Variations: with blue crocodile skin strap

Monaco Sixty-Nine

Reference number: CW9110.FC6177
Movement: manually wound, TAG Heuer Caliber 2 (base ETA 7001); additional TAG Heuer Caliber HR 03 (quartz)
Functions: hours, minutes, subsidiary seconds (front); chronograph to 1/1000 seconds; alarm; second time zone; perpetual calendar; F1 timer with lap time memory (80 laps) and best lap mode; dial illumination; stand-by (back)
Case: stainless steel, 40 x 41 mm, height 18 mm; sapphire crystal; water-resistant to 50 m
Band: reptile skin, security folding clasp
Remarks: patented rotating mechanism: case rotatable 180°
Price: $6,900

Autavia Chronograph

Reference number: CY2111.BA0775
Movement: automatic, TAG Heuer Caliber 11 (base Dubois-Dépraz 2022); ø 30 mm, height mm; 55 jewels; 28,800 vph
Functions: hours, minutes, subsidiary seconds; chronograph; date
Case: stainless steel, ø 42 mm, height 14 mm; bezel with tachymeter scale; sapphire crystal; water-resistant to 50 m
Band: stainless steel, security folding clasp
Price: $3,295
Variations: with calfskin leather strap; with silver dial and black totalizers

Monza Chronograph

Reference number: CR2113.FC6165
Movement: automatic, TAG Heuer Caliber 17 (base ETA 2894-2); ø 28.6 mm, height 6.1 mm; 37 jewels; 28,800 vph
Functions: hours, minutes, subsidiary seconds; chronograph; date
Case: stainless steel, ø 39.5 mm, height 13.5 mm; sapphire crystal; water-resistant to 50 m
Band: reptile skin, security folding clasp
Price: $2,950
Variations: with silver-colored dial; with black crocodile skin strap

Monza Chronometer Chronograph Calibre 36

Reference number: CR5111.FC6175
Movement: automatic, TAG Heuer Caliber 36 (base Zenith El Primero 400); ø 30 mm, height 6.5 mm; 31 jewels; 36,000 vph; officially certified chronometer (C.O.S.C.)
Functions: hours, minutes, subsidiary seconds; chronograph; date
Case: stainless steel, ø 39.5 mm, height 14 mm; sapphire crystal; exhibition window case back; water-resistant to 50 m
Band: reptile skin, security folding clasp
Price: $4,495
Variations: with black dial; with brown crocodile skin strap

Now Available at a Popular Price!

"Essential reading for anyone fascinated by today's markets and their rich history. Beautiful to look at and fun to read." —Michael Bloomberg

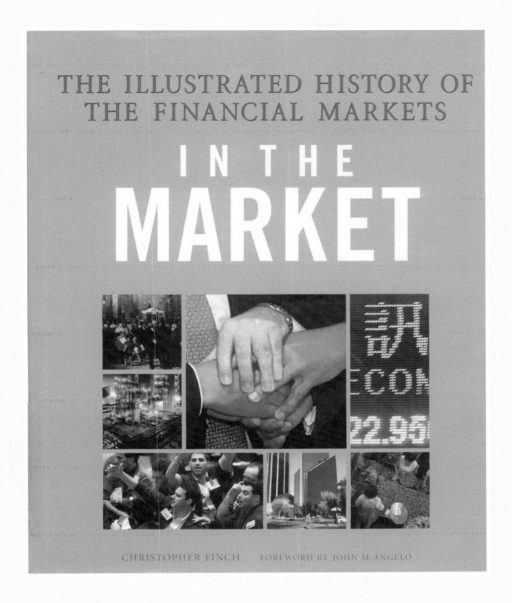

In the Market: The Illustrated History of the Financial Markets

This richly illustrated volume, which explores how capital markets have evolved since antiquity and explains their profound impact on every aspect of life today, is the perfect gift for finance and business professionals.

"Finch has produced a sumptuous book with a narrative that guides the reader from century to century, accompanied by lavish illustrations and a timeline of historic events . . . a beautifully designed and written book that will appeal to any business reader."
—*Library Journal*

By Christopher Finch
Preface by John M. Angelo
570 illustrations, 250 in full color
352 pages • 10 × 12 in. • Cloth
ISBN 0-7892-0014-7
Previously $75.00, **NOW $35.00**

Temption

This brand's name already shows what company founder Klaus Ulbrich is all about: Temption is a word that he invented, combining **tem**pus and func**tion**, thus intended to mean functional timekeeping. It is Ulbrich's demand upon himself to use the ideals typical of design aesthetics such as those of the Moderns and Wabi Sabi. Components including the overall simplicity of shapes come from the Bauhaus movement; the attention to materials and simple warmth, from Wabi Sabi. From both philosophical schools comes the idea of reducing to only that which is necessary — as well as the conclusion that less is often more. The focal point of Temption's design character is a paradigm that Ulbrich likes to call the "information pyramid." At the top of this pyramid are located the central hour and minute indicators; other functions follow underneath in order to give these main functions visual priority. For this reason, the most contrast within the dial visuals can be found between the dial and hands. The date window is the same color as the dial and not framed (so the dial remains calm); the totalizers and stop functions are not encircled, and the stop hands are not outfitted with arbors for the same reason. At the low end of this information pyramid is situated the brand's logo, most unimportant to reading the time, and for this reason it is printed in shiny black on a matte black background, where it may only be seen — and then quite clearly — when light shines on it from the side.

At a time when most smaller German watch manufacturers — including Temption — are producing relatively large watches, Temption has introduced a chronograph with a surprisingly small case diameter of 29.2 mm (and 9.6 mm height), striking in its delicateness. The Cora model may even be the smallest automatic wrist chronograph in current production.

In a certain way, the design of Cora's case has paved the road for the second generation of Temption watches. The Formula chronograph embodies this new concept in an especially attractive manner with lines that are clearer than ever, a technical transparence, and a distinct functional clarity. The use of color is not contrary here, for above all things it distinguishes the functions and displays from each other and everything else. That an attractive look and sporty elegance result from this is something that even the most sober of designers can fully take into account.

Chronograph Formula

Movement: automatic, Temption Caliber T17.1 (base ETA Valjoux 7750); ø 30 mm, height 7.8 mm; 25 jewels; 28,800 vph; rhodium-plated, perlage, blued screws

Functions: hours, minutes, subsidiary seconds; chronograph; date and day of the week

Case: stainless steel, ø 43 mm, height 14.5 mm; bezel engraved with tachymeter scale; sapphire crystal; exhibition window case back; screwed-in crown and buttons; water-resistant to 100 m

Band: leather, folding clasp

Price: $2,850

Chronograph with Complication

Reference number: CGK204W

Movement: automatic, Temption Caliber T18.1 (base ETA Valjoux 7751); ø 30 mm, height 7.8 mm; 25 jewels; 28,800 vph; rhodium-plated, perlage, blued screws

Functions: hours, minutes, subsidiary seconds; chronograph; date, day of the week, month, moon phase; 24-hour display

Case: stainless steel, ø 43 mm, height 14.5 mm; bezel engraved with tachymeter scale; sapphire crystal; exhibition window case back; screwed-in crown and buttons; water-resistant to 100 m

Band: leather, folding clasp

Price: $3,350

Chronograph with Complication

Reference number: CGK204B

Movement: automatic, Temption Caliber T18.1 (base ETA Valjoux 7751); ø 30 mm, height 7.8 mm; 25 jewels; 28,800 vph; rhodium-plated, perlage, blued screws

Functions: hours, minutes, subsidiary seconds; chronograph; date, day of the week, month, moon phase; 24-hour display

Case: stainless steel, ø 43 mm, height 14.5 mm; bezel engraved with tachymeter scale; sapphire crystal; exhibition window case back; screwed-in crown and buttons; water-resistant to 100 m

Band: leather, folding clasp

Price: $3,350

Automatic with Second Time Zone

Reference number: CM03

Movement: automatic, Temption Caliber T16.1 (base ETA 2893-2); ø 25.6 mm, height 4.1 mm; 21 jewels; 28,800 vph; rhodium-plated, perlage, blued screws

Functions: hours, minutes, sweep seconds; date; 24-hour hand (second time zone)

Case: stainless steel, ø 42 mm, height 10.7 mm; unidirectionally rotating bezel with 60-minute divisions; sapphire crystal; exhibition window case back; screwed-in crown; water-resistant to 100 m

Band: stainless steel, double folding clasp

Price: $1,790

Chronograph Rattrapante

Reference number: Cherubin-R

Movement: automatic, Temption Caliber T19.1 (base ETA Valjoux 7750); ø 30 mm, height 8.3 mm; 28 jewels; 28,800 vph; rhodium-plated, perlage, blued screws

Functions: hours, minutes, subsidiary seconds; split-seconds chronograph; date

Case: stainless steel, ø 42 mm, height 15.3 mm; sapphire crystal; exhibition window case back; screwed-in crown and buttons; water-resistant to 100 m

Band: leather, folding clasp

Price: $6,480

Chronograph Cora

Reference number:

Movement: automatic, Temption Caliber T22.1 (base ETA 2094); ø 23.9 mm, height 5.5 mm; 33 jewels; 28,800 vph; rhodium-plated, perlage, blued screws

Functions: hours, minutes, subsidiary seconds; chronograph; date

Case: stainless steel, ø 29.2 mm, height 9.6 mm; bezel and lugs set with brilliant-cut diamonds; sapphire crystal; exhibition window case back

Band: leather, folding clasp

Remarks: mother-of-pearl dial; smallest mechanical chrono

Price: $3,730 (without diamonds)

Tissot

Times change, but there is hardly another watch brand that has literally contributed to the worldwide fame of the Swiss watch industry as Tissot has. Along with entrepreneurial vision and good fortune in business dealings, one of the strongest characteristics of company presidents bearing the name Tissot for many generations was a propensity for travel.

The wild and woolly adventures experienced by Charles-Emile Tissot as he journeyed by sled and troika across Russia at the end of the nineteenth century are legend. Russia and North America then became the markets in which Tissot expanded and prospered.

Back home in Switzerland, the respective managers also knew what they were doing. A liaison with the Brandt company, which owned the Omega brand, led to the foundation of the Société Suisse pour l'Industrie Horlogère S.A. (S.S.I.H.), a forerunner of the SMH, today's Swatch Group, under whose umbrella Tissot still operates. Even then the areas of responsibility were very clearly defined and assigned: Omega was to handle the lower end of the luxury segment, and Tissot was to focus on the mid-priced watch category. One of the

results of this was that Tissot began to use a sophisticated modular system at a very early stage, so that with just five cases, for example, a total of forty different models were created.

Another effect of this division was that Tissot was also responsible for promoting innovation and technical development. As early as the beginning of the 1930s, Tissot produced the first antimagnetic watch; in 1960 the idea of a standard caliber was developed, a concept later adopted by the entire watchmaking industry; and in 1971 Tissot launched a new watch with a plastic mechanical movement. With the manufacture of these plastic watch movements, it was Tissot which actually cleared the path for injected plastic in watch production, a process that just a mere decade later would

make the greatest success in the history of the watchmaking industry possible: Swatch. Additionally, both the first autoquartz caliber and T-Touch technology, featuring sensors in the crystal that respond to touch, debuted in Tissot watches.

Tissot's recently chosen tag line, "Innovators by Tradition," sums it up nicely: For more than 150 years, Tissot has stood for innovation, unusual ideas, and an inventive spirit.

Another burst of popularity is being experienced by the brand since it has been especially active in sports timekeeping. The dynamic sports the company sponsors include cycling and motorcycling (track, street, and classic) and also team sports such as ice hockey and fencing, where Tissot functions as the official timekeeper.

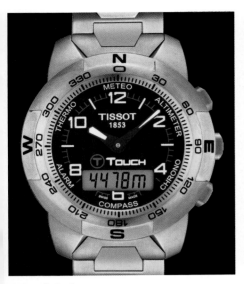

T-Touch Tech

Reference number: T33.7.788.51
Movement: quartz, ETA Caliber E40.305; multifunctional electronic module with LCD display integrated into dial
Functions: hours, minutes; chronograph, altimeter, thermometer, barometer, alarm and compass in LCD display, activated by sensors in crystal
Case: titanium, ø 41.5 mm, height 12 mm; bezel engraved with 360°-degree scale and directions; sapphire crystal with sensors
Band: titanium, folding clasp
Price: upon request
Variations: with rubber strap

PRS 516 Chrono Valjoux

Reference number: T91.1.487.81
Movement: automatic, ETA Caliber 7750 Valjoux; ø 30 mm, height 7.9 mm; 25 jewels; 28,800 vph
Functions: hours, minutes, subsidiary seconds; chronograph; date and day of the week
Case: stainless steel, ø 42 mm, height 14.75 mm; bezel with tachymeter scale; sapphire crystal; exhibition window case back
Band: stainless steel, folding clasp
Price: $1,050
Variations: with leather strap

Le Locle

Reference number: T41.1.423.71
Movement: automatic, ETA Caliber 2824-2; ø 25.6 mm, height 4.6 mm; 25 jewels; 28,800 vph; movement finely decorated
Functions: hours, minutes, sweep seconds; date
Case: stainless steel, ø 39.3 mm, height 9.2 mm; sapphire crystal; exhibition window case back
Band: leather, folding clasp
Price: $350
Variations: with PVD-coated case

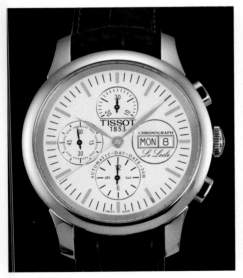

Le Locle Automatic Chronograph

Reference number: T41.1.317.31
Movement: automatic, ETA Caliber 7750; ø 30 mm, height 7.9 mm; 25 jewels; 28,800 vph; movement finely decorated
Functions: hours, minutes, subsidiary seconds; chronograph; date and day of the week
Case: stainless steel, ø 42.3 mm, height 13 mm; sapphire crystal; exhibition window case back
Band: leather, double folding clasp
Price: $850
Variations: with stainless steel bracelet and black dial

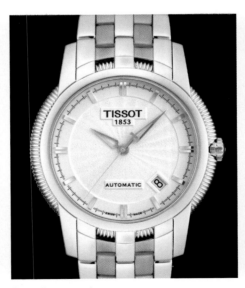

Ring Automatic

Reference number: T97.1.483.31
Movement: automatic, ETA Caliber 2824-2; ø 25.6 mm, height 4.6 mm; 25 jewels; 28,800 vph
Functions: hours, minutes, sweep seconds; date
Case: stainless steel, ø 39.5 mm, height 9.7 mm; sapphire crystal; exhibition window case back
Band: stainless steel, double folding clasp
Price: $450
Variations: various dial versions

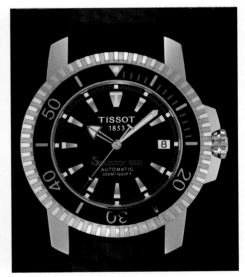

Diver Seastar 1000 Automatic

Reference number: T19.1.593.51
Movement: automatic, ETA Caliber 2824-2; ø 25.6 mm, height 4.6 mm; 25 jewels; 28,800 vph; finely decorated
Functions: hours, minutes, sweep seconds; date
Case: stainless steel, ø 44 mm, height 15.4 mm; unidirectionally rotating bezel with 60-minute divisions; sapphire crystal; exhibition window case back; screwed-in crown; water-resistant to 300 m
Band: rubber, folding clasp with overall extension
Price: $515
Variations: with stainless steel bracelet and various dial versions

Tutima

As far as the eye can see there is only water, and in the sky maybe only the contrails from a jet. The task: 3,600 sea miles as quickly as possible across the Atlantic — against wind, weather, and meter-high waves. It was a fantastic race against time, with the finish line in the harbor of Cuxhaven, Germany, securely in sight. Two years ago, Thomas Ebert sailed this stretch during the DaimlerChrysler North Atlantic Challenge: From Newport, Rhode Island, all the way across the Atlantic to Cuxhaven and then farther on to Hamburg.

On the side of his yacht in large letters was the Tutima logo. The name of this watch company is one that is usually associated with pilot's watches, even though the instrument maker is also committed to international sailing. Tutima was not only the timekeeper at 2005's Kiel Week, but also the host of the Tutima Montana Sailing Championships in Helena, Montana, a regatta of international importance.

Similar to Formula 1 racing, international regattas have basically become a battle of material today. Only with the most modern equipment and technically ripened materials do the participants have a chance at one of the top spots. Tutima and its team take on the challenge and have developed a new racing yacht for this season.

Thus, the company hailing from Ganderkesee, near Bremen, Germany, has come a long way. During World War II no one was certain that the company, back then part of Glashütte's *ébauche* factory UROFA, would even make it to the end of the war. UROFA's top finished products were distributed to jewelers under the name Tutima. UROFA's managing director, Dr. Ernst Kurtz, left Glashütte just before the end of the war and in the same year founded a new watch production in southern West Germany. In the year 1951 he moved Watch Factory Kurtz to a very northern region of Germany, the Lower Saxon province so to speak, the small town of Ganderkesee. Here he created Nurofa, Norddeutsche Uhren-Rohwerke-Fabrik, for the production of *ébauches* and next to it the company sales and marketing offices of Tutima-Uhren. Up to the end of the 1950s the company produced 70,000 *ébauches* per year, after which lack of profitability forced it to stop production of watch movements.

The fortunes of the Tutima brand then passed to a young businessman and former associate of Kurtz, Dieter Delecate. The tiny watch factory on Germany's northern coast somehow managed to survive the great plague that was killing off watch brands at the time of the quartz shock and became popular again during the renaissance of the mechanical watch in the late '80s with high-quality instrument watches that were manufactured exclusively in Germany with movements from Switzerland.

Today Tutima mainly manufactures functional pilot's watches, for among others the German armed forces. The collection also comprises various versions of the Tutima pilot's chronograph 1941. The newest model possesses a very obvious red dial with light red chronograph totalizers. It is easy to see that functionality has moved over to allow aesthetics a place right by its side as can be seen in the FX Bigdate whose case now shines in a modest rose gold.

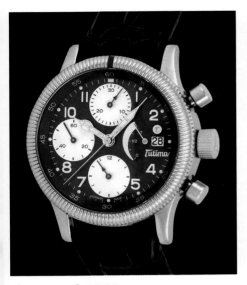

Chronograph F2 PR
Reference number: 780-83
Movement: automatic, modified ETA Valjoux Caliber 7750;
ø 30 mm, height 7.9 mm; 25 jewels; 28,800 vph
Functions: hours, minutes, subsidiary seconds; chronograph;
date; power reserve display
Case: stainless steel, ø 38.7 mm, height 15.8 mm;
bidirectionally rotating bezel with reference marker; sapphire
crystal; exhibition window case back; screwed-in crown;
water-resistant to 100 m
Band: reptile skin, folding clasp
Price: $4,000

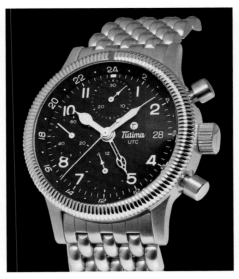

Flieger Chronograph F2 UTC
Reference number: 780-52
Movement: automatic, modified ETA Valjoux Caliber 7750;
ø 30 mm, height 7.9 mm; 25 jewels; 28,800 vph
Functions: hours, minutes, subsidiary seconds; chronograph;
date; 24-hour display (second time zone)
Case: stainless steel, ø 38.7 mm, height 15.8 mm;
bidirectionally rotating bezel with reference marker; sapphire
crystal; screwed-in crown; water-resistant to 100 m
Band: stainless steel, folding clasp
Price: $3,800

Flieger Chronograph F2 G
Reference number: 754-02
Movement: automatic, ETA Caliber 7750; ø 30 mm,
height 7.9 mm; 25 jewels; 28,800 vph
Functions: hours, minutes, subsidiary seconds;
chronograph; date
Case: yellow gold, ø 38.2 mm, height 15.7 mm;
bidirectionally rotating bezel with reference marker; sapphire
crystal; exhibition window case back; screwed-in crown;
water-resistant to 100 m
Band: yellow gold, folding clasp
Price: appx. $19,000

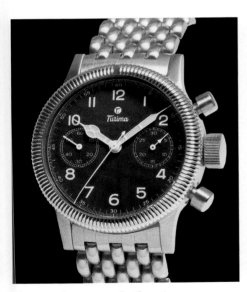

Flieger Chronograph Classic
Reference number: 783-02
Movement: manually wound, modified ETA Valjoux Caliber
7760; ø 30 mm, height 7 mm; 21 jewels; 28,800 vph
Functions: hours, minutes, subsidiary seconds; chronograph
Case: stainless steel, ø 38.7 mm, height 14.7 mm;
bidirectionally rotating bezel with reference marker; sapphire
crystal; water-resistant to 100 m
Band: stainless steel, folding clasp
Price: $3,300

FX Big Date
Reference number: 640-02
Movement: automatic, modified ETA Caliber 2892-A2;
ø 25 mm, height 5.1 mm; 28 jewels; 28,800 vph
Functions: hours, minutes, sweep seconds; large date;
power reserve display
Case: red gold, ø 38.5 mm, height 14.1 mm; sapphire
crystal; exhibition window case back; screwed-in crown;
water-resistant to 100 m
Band: reptile skin, folding clasp in red gold
Price: $8,900

Chronograph FX
Reference number: 788-31
Movement: automatic, ETA Caliber 7750; ø 30 mm,
height 7.9 mm; 25 jewels; 28,800 vph
Functions: hours, minutes, subsidiary seconds;
chronograph; date
Case: stainless steel, ø 38.5 mm, height 15.5 mm; sapphire
crystal; exhibition window case back; screwed-in crown;
water-resistant to 100 m
Band: leather, buckle
Price: $2,300

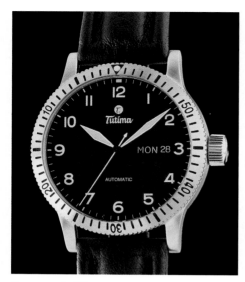

Automatic FX

Reference number: 631-31
Movement: automatic, ETA Caliber 2836-2; ø 26 mm, height 5.05 mm; 25 jewels; 28,800 vph
Functions: hours, minutes, sweep seconds; date and day of the week
Case: stainless steel, ø 38.5 mm, height 12.4 mm; bidirectionally rotating bezel with 60-minute divisions; sapphire crystal; exhibition window case back; screwed-in crown; water-resistant to 100 m
Band: leather, buckle
Price: $1,200

Automatic FX UTC

Reference number: 632-24
Movement: automatic, ETA Caliber 2893-2; ø 26 mm, height 4.1 mm; 21 jewels; 28,800 vph
Functions: hours, minutes, sweep seconds; date; 24-hour display (second time zone)
Case: stainless steel, ø 38.5 mm, height 11.7 mm; sapphire crystal; exhibition window case back; screwed-in crown; water-resistant to 100 m
Band: stainless steel, folding clasp
Price: $1,700

Military Flieger Chronograph TL

Reference number: 750-02
Movement: automatic, Nouvelle Lémania Caliber 5100; ø 31 mm, height 8.25 mm; 17 jewels; 28,800 vph
Functions: hours, minutes, subsidiary seconds; chronograph; date and day of the week; 24-hour display
Case: titanium, ø 43 mm, height 14.6 mm; bidirectionally rotating bezel with 60-minute divisions; sapphire crystal; screwed-in crown; water-resistant to 200 m
Band: titanium, folding clasp with overall extension
Price: $3,700

Military Flieger Chronograph TLG

Reference number: 738-02
Movement: automatic, Nouvelle Lémania Caliber 5100; ø 31 mm, height 8.25 mm; 17 jewels; 28,800 vph
Functions: hours, minutes, subsidiary seconds; chronograph; date and day of the week; 24-hour display
Case: titanium, ø 43 mm, height 14.6 mm; bidirectionally rotating bezel in yellow gold with 60-minute divisions; sapphire crystal; screwed-in crown; water-resistant to 200 m
Band: titanium/gold, folding clasp with overall extension
Price: $9,300

Commando II

Reference number: 760-42
Movement: automatic, Nouvelle Lémania Caliber 5100; ø 31 mm, height 8.25 mm; 17 jewels; 28,800 vph
Functions: hours, minutes; chronograph; date
Case: titanium, ø 43.2 mm, height 14.5 mm; sapphire crystal; screwed-in crown; water-resistant to 200 m
Band: titanium, folding clasp with overall extension
Price: $3,500

DI 300

Reference number: 629-12
Movement: automatic, ETA Caliber 2836-2; ø 26 mm, height 5.05 mm; 25 jewels; 28,800 vph
Functions: hours, minutes, sweep seconds; date and day of the week
Case: titanium, ø 43.8 mm, height 12.5 mm; unidirectionally rotating bezel with 60-minute divisions; sapphire crystal; screwed-in crown; water-resistant to 300 m
Band: titanium, folding clasp with overall extension
Price: $1,400

"witty, brilliant, authoritative"
—Robert M. Parker, Jr., *The Wine Advocate*

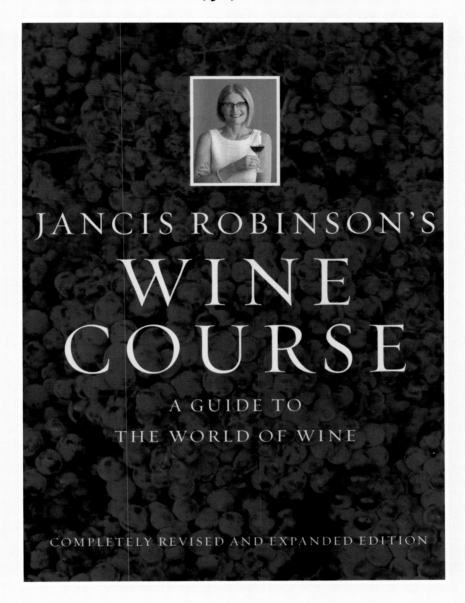

JANCIS ROBINSON'S

WINE COURSE

A GUIDE TO
THE WORLD OF WINE

COMPLETELY REVISED AND EXPANDED EDITION

Dedicated to ensuring that you get the most out of every glass, this volume explains how to taste and store wine, what to serve on special occasions at home, and how to pick the best value from a restaurant's wine list.

"She has an encyclopedic grasp of her subject and doesn't put a foot wrong . . . a splendid introduction to the world of wine."
—Stephen Brook, *Decanter Magazine*

By Jancis Robinson
170 full-color illustrations
352 pages · 8 × 11 in. · Cloth
ISBN 0-7892-0791-5 · $35.00

Vacheron Constantin

The oldest watch company in the world to have manufactured uninterruptedly celebrated its 250th anniversary in 2005 with a great deal of pomp — and with the launch of a small jubilee collection of remarkable watches. The range extends from the simple calendar watch Jubilé 1775, outfitted with a new automatic movement (Caliber 2475) and produced in a limited edition of 1,755 pieces, to an edition dedicated to the Métiers d'Art (artistic professions) of twelve times four watches featuring artfully enameled dials and two absolutely technical and aesthetic treasures. With such exquisite collector's pieces, Vacheron Constantin is underscoring its own technical know-how as a *manufacture*.

That Jean-Marc Vacheron was allowed to even learn the profession of watchmaker in Geneva, a city rich in guilds, not to mention open his own watch workshop, is something for which this weaver's son can thank the surprising loosening of the guild laws in 1745. He himself was born in Geneva, but his father originally came from the outskirts, and the guild laws had until then only allowed "real" citizens of the city access to such honorable artesian professions. The young man grabbed at his chance and at

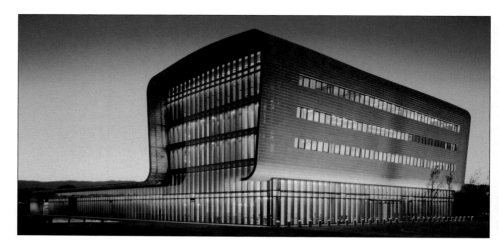

twenty-four years of age became one of the youngest *cabinotiers*, as the independent master craftsmen were called — after their cabinets located in the light-filled attics of their buildings. That was in 1755, one quarter of a millennium ago.

There is still a sort of guild law in the Swiss watch industry today, and it states that a watch brand may only call itself a *manufacture* if its movements (or at least important parts of them) are made in-house.

The fact that Vacheron Constantin was one of the forerunners of the industrialization to which the Swiss watch industry owed its world-renown in the twentieth century,

putting its money on division of labor, almost became the fine Genevan watch brand's undoing. The traditional art of fine watchmaking countered "soulless" quartz technology in the 1960s with nothing more than archaic production methods, and the purely technical quality of mechanical watches moved over to become mere authenticity. Vacheron Constantin has strongly invested in its own production capacity in the last few years and is now able to manufacture almost every little component it needs to produce its own movements. Thus, the Genevan brand has finally become one of the few genuine watch *manufactures* and, as a special honor in this anniversary year, may now even apply the Seal of Geneva visibly to its watches' dials.

In 1998 Vacheron Constantin purchased HDG in the Vallée de Joux's Le Sentier, a company that designs and produces high-quality watch movements for a handful of select clients using the most modern technology. In Le Sentier, therefore, the development of new movements and the production of *ébauches* of Vacheron Constantin's own design take place. The first completely autonomous production of the "new era" to be created here was manually wound Caliber 1400, introduced in April 2001. Now automatic Caliber 2475 follows in honor of the company's 250th anniversary, manufactured partially at HDG and partially at the factory in Geneva.

The personnel, space, and technical conditions at Vacheron Constantin today seem optimal: The new Plan-les-Ouates factory inaugurated in 2004 offers the best in working conditions for engineers and watchmakers with its individual, imaginative architecture. Some of the factory rooms are at the moment empty, but this can of course change again quickly.

Tour de l'Île

Reference number: 80250/000R-9145
Movement: manually wound, Vacheron Constantin Caliber 2750; ø 35.4 mm; flying one-minute tourbillon; 834 parts
Functions: hours, minutes; quarter-hour repeater; 24-hour display; moon phase; power reserve display; strike movement torque display. On the back: perpetual calendar with date, day, month, equation of time with times of sunrise and sunset, night sky with celestial chart
Case: white gold, ø 47 mm, height 17.8 mm; sapphire crystal
Band: reptile skin, buckle in white gold
Remarks: limited to 7 pcs. for company's 250th anniversary
Price: $1,600,000

Saint Gervais

Reference number: X80P7665
Movement: manually wound, Vacheron Constantin Caliber 2250; one-minute tourbillon; four spring barrels, power reserve 250 hours
Functions: hours, minutes; perpetual calendar with date, day of the week, month; double power reserve display
Case: platinum, ø 44 mm, height 13.5 mm; sapphire crystal; exhibition window case back
Band: reptile skin, folding clasp in white gold
Remarks: limited to 55 pieces on the occasion of the company's 250th anniversary
Price: $380,000

Métiers d'Art (Winter)

Reference number: X86P7668
Movement: automatic, Vacheron Constantin Caliber 2460
Functions: hours (jump), minutes, date and day as disk display
Case: platinum, ø 40 mm, height 12.10 mm; sapphire crystal; exhibition window case back
Band: reptile skin, buckle
Remarks: limited to 12 sets of 4 watches in three golds and platinum with enameled and relief miniatures of the four seasons; for the company's 250th anniversary
Price: $95,000
Variations: in white gold (spring); in yellow gold (summer); in rose gold (fall)

Jubilé 1755

Reference number: X85R7643
Movement: automatic, Vacheron Constantin Caliber 2475; ø 26.2 mm, height 5.5 mm; 27 jewels; 28,800 vph; finely finished with *côtes de Genève*
Functions: hours, minutes, sweep seconds; date and day of the week; power reserve display
Case: red gold, ø 40 mm, height 12.10 mm; sapphire crystal; exhibition window case back
Band: reptile skin, folding clasp
Remarks: limited to 500 pieces, for 250th anniversary
Price: upon request
Variations: yellow or white gold, platinum, ltd. to 250 pcs each

Les Complications Power Reserve

Reference number: X47J5351
Movement: automatic, Vacheron Constantin Caliber 1127; ø 26 mm, height 4.85 mm; 45 jewels; 28,800 vph; finely finished with *côtes de Genève*
Functions: hours, minutes, subsidiary seconds; date; power reserve display
Case: yellow gold, ø 36 mm, height 9.26 mm; sapphire crystal; exhibition window case back
Band: reptile skin, buckle
Price: upon request
Variations: in white gold

Toledo 1952

Reference number: X47G5709
Movement: automatic, Vacheron Constantin Caliber 1125; ø 26 mm, height 5.53 mm; 36 jewels; 28,800 vph; finely finished with *côtes de Genève*
Functions: hours, minutes, subsidiary seconds; date, day of the week, month, moon phase
Case: white gold, 35.7 x 41 mm, height 12.7 mm; sapphire crystal
Band: reptile skin, buckle
Price: $65,000
Variations: in yellow gold

Royal Eagle

Reference number: X42G5718
Movement: automatic, Vacheron Constantin Caliber 1206; ø 25.6 mm, height 4.92 mm; 31 jewels; 28,800 vph; finely finished with *côtes de Genève*
Functions: hours, minutes, subsidiary seconds; date, day of the week
Case: white gold, 35.6 x 48.5 mm, height 12 mm; sapphire crystal
Band: reptile skin, buckle
Price: $19,900
Variations: with diamonds; in yellow gold

Royal Eagle Dual Time

Reference number: X47G6962
Movement: automatic, Vacheron Constantin Caliber 1222H393; finely finished with *côtes de Genève*
Functions: hours, minutes; second time zone, day/night indication; date; power reserve display
Case: white gold, ø 36 mm, mm, height 11.21 mm; sapphire crystal; exhibition window case back
Band: reptile skin, folding clasp
Price: $24,900
Variations: in rose gold ($22,500)

Royal Eagle Chronograph

Reference number: X49R5715
Movement: automatic, Vacheron Constantin Caliber 1137; ø 25.6 mm, height 6.6 mm; 37 jewels; 21,600 vph; finely finished with *côtes de Genève*
Functions: hours, minutes, subsidiary seconds; chronograph; large date
Case: rose gold, 36.8 x 50.2 mm, height 14 mm; sapphire crystal; water-resistant to 50 m
Band: reptile skin, folding clasp
Price: $26,500
Variations: in stainless steel

Patrimony Small Seconds Rosé

Reference number: X81R6964
Movement: manually wound, Vacheron Constantin Caliber 1400; ø 20.35 mm, height 2.6 mm; 20 jewels; 28,800 vph; finely finished with Seal of Geneva
Functions: hours, minutes, subsidiary seconds
Case: rose gold, ø 35 mm, height 6.5 mm; sapphire crystal; exhibition window case back
Band: reptile skin, buckle
Price: $9,900
Variations: in yellow gold; in white gold

Patrimony 40 mm

Reference number: X81J6986
Movement: manually wound, Vacheron Constantin Caliber 1400; ø 20.35 mm, height 2.6 mm; 20 jewels; 28,800 vph; finely finished with Seal of Geneva
Functions: hours, minutes
Case: yellow gold, ø 40 mm, height 6.7 mm; sapphire crystal
Band: reptile skin, buckle
Price: $11,200
Variations: in white gold

Patrimony SM

Reference number: X25R7723
Movement: quartz, Vacheron Constantin Caliber 1202; finely finished with *côtes de Genève*
Functions: hours, minutes
Case: rose gold, ø 29 mm, height 6.30 mm; sapphire crystal
Band: reptile skin, buckle
Price: upon request
Variations: in white gold

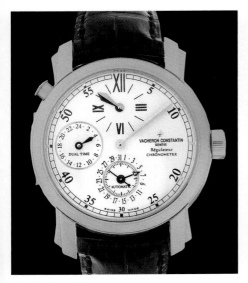

Malte Dual Time

Reference number: X42R5725
Movement: automatic, Vacheron Constantin Caliber 1206 RDT; ø 25.6 mm, height 4.92 mm; 31 jewels; 28,800 vph; finely finished with *côtes de Genève*; officially certified chronometer (C.O.S.C.)
Functions: hours (off-center), minutes, subsidiary seconds; date; 24-hour display (second time zone)
Case: rose gold, ø 38.5 mm, height 11 mm; sapphire crystal; exhibition window case back and hinged lid
Band: reptile skin, buckle
Price: $21,500
Variations: in yellow gold; in white gold

Malte Chronograph

Reference number: X47R6957
Movement: manually wound, Vacheron Constantin Caliber 1141; ø 27 mm, height 5.57 mm; 21 jewels; 18,000 vph; swan-neck fine adjustment, finely finished with *côtes de Genève*
Functions: hours, minutes, subsidiary seconds; chronograph
Case: rose gold, ø 41.5 mm, height 10.9 mm; sapphire crystal; exhibition window case back
Band: reptile skin, buckle
Price: $27,500
Variations: in white gold

Malte Perpetual Calendar Retrograde

Reference number: X47P5214
Movement: automatic, Vacheron Constantin Caliber 1126 QPR; ø 26 mm, height 5.05 mm; 36 jewels; 28,800 vph; finely finished with *côtes de Genève*
Functions: hours, minutes; perpetual calendar with date (retrograde), day of the week, month, year, leap year
Case: platinum, ø 38.5 mm, height 11.3 mm; sapphire crystal; exhibition window case back and hinged lid
Band: reptile skin, buckle
Price: $65,000
Variations: in rose gold

Malte Chronograph Perpetual Calendar

Reference number: X47J4954
Movement: manually wound, Vacheron Constantin Caliber 1141 QP; ø 27 mm, height 7.37 mm; 21 jewels; 18,000 vph; finely finished with *côtes de Genève*
Functions: hours, minutes, subsidiary seconds; chronograph; perpetual calendar with date, day of the week, month, moon phase, leap year
Case: yellow gold, ø 39 mm, height 13.75 mm; sapphire crystal; exhibition window case back and hinged lid
Band: reptile skin, buckle
Price: $77,000
Variations: in platinum

1972

Reference number: X25J6982
Movement: quartz, Vacheron Constantin Caliber 1202; finely finished
Functions: hours, minutes
Case: yellow gold, 23.4 x 34 mm, height 6,62 mm; bezel set with 46 brilliant-cut diamonds ; sapphire crystal
Band: reptile skin, buckle
Remarks: mother-of-pearl dial
Price: $12,100
Variations: in various variations

1972 Grand Modèle Cambré

Reference number: X25R6990
Movement: quartz, Vacheron Constantin Caliber 1202; finely finished
Functions: hours, minutes
Case: rose gold, 22.8 x 45 mm, height 7.25 mm; sapphire crystal
Band: reptile skin, buckle
Price: $10,900
Variations: with pink dial

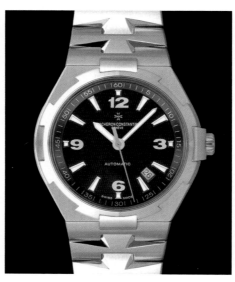

Overseas Ladies
Reference number: X25A7033
Movement: quartz, Vacheron Constantin Caliber 1207; finely finished
Functions: hours, minutes; date
Case: stainless steel, ø 34 mm, height 7.66 mm; sapphire crystal; water-resistant to 50 m
Band: stainless steel, folding clasp
Price: $6,600
Variations: various variations in stainless steel, also with brilliant-cut diamonds

Overseas
Reference number: X47A6953
Movement: automatic, Vacheron Constantin Caliber 1126; ø 26 mm, height 3.25 mm; 36 jewels; 28,800 vph; finely finished with *côtes de Genève*
Functions: hours, minutes, seconds; date
Case: stainless steel, ø 42 mm, height 9.7 mm; sapphire crystal; water-resistant to 150 m
Band: stainless steel, folding clasp
Price: $9,900
Variations: with white dial

Overseas Chronograph
Reference number: X47A6954
Movement: automatic, Vacheron Constantin Caliber 1137; ø 25.6 mm, height 6.6 mm; 37 jewels; 21,600 vph; finely finished with *côtes de Genève*
Functions: hours, minutes, subsidiary seconds; chronograph; date
Case: stainless steel, ø 42 mm, height 12.45 mm; sapphire crystal; water-resistant to 150 m
Band: stainless steel, folding clasp
Price: $14,000
Variations: with black dial

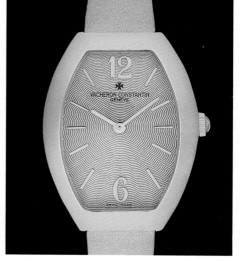

Égérie
Reference number: X25G5697
Movement: quartz, Vacheron Constantin Caliber 1202; finely finished
Functions: hours, minutes
Case: white gold, 27.5 x 39 mm, height 9.53 mm; bezel set with 48 brilliant-cut diamonds; sapphire crystal
Band: satin, buckle
Price: $15,900
Variations: in yellow gold

Égérie
Reference number: X25G5704
Movement: quartz, Vacheron Constantin Caliber 1202; finely finished
Functions: hours, minutes
Case: white gold, 27.5 x 39 mm, height 9.53 mm; case completely paved with 312 brilliant-cut diamonds; sapphire crystal
Band: satin, buckle set with 21 brilliant-cut diamonds
Price: $21,200
Variations: in yellow gold

Égérie
Reference number: X25J5698
Movement: quartz, Vacheron Constantin Caliber 1202; finely finished
Functions: hours, minutes
Case: yellow gold, 27.5 x 39 mm, height 9.53 mm; sapphire crystal
Band: satin, buckle
Price: $8,000
Variations: in various sizes, movement and case variations

Caliber 1400

Mechanical with manual winding, power reserve appx.
40 hours
Functions: hours, minutes, subsidiary seconds
Diameter: 20.3 mm (9''')
Height: 2.6 mm
Jewels: 20
Balance: glucydur
Frequency: 28,800 vph
Balance spring: flat hairspring with fine adjustment via index
Shock protection: Kif
Remarks: base plate with perlage, edges beveled, bridges with *côtes de Genève*; polished steel parts; Seal of Geneva

Caliber 1410

Mechanical with manual winding, power reserve appx.
40 hours
Functions: hours, minutes; moon phase; power reserve display
Diameter: 20.35 mm (9''')
Height: 4.2 mm
Jewels: 20
Balance: glucydur
Frequency: 28,800 vph
Balance spring: flat hairspring with fine adjustment via index
Shock protection: Kif
Remarks: base plate with perlage, edges beveled, bridges with *côtes de Genève*; polished steel parts; Seal of Geneva

Caliber 1003

Mechanical with manual winding, power reserve appx.
35 hours
Functions: hours, minutes
Diameter: 20.8 mm (9''')
Height: 1.64 mm
Jewels: 18
Balance: glucydur
Frequency: 18,000 vph
Balance spring: flat hairspring with fine adjustment via index
Shock protection: Kif
Remarks: base plate with perlage, edges beveled, bridges with *côtes de Genève*; Seal of Geneva

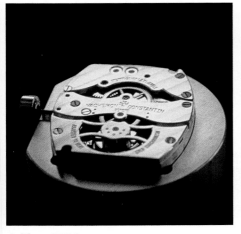

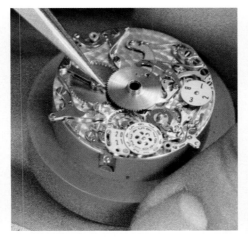

Caliber 1790

Mechanical with manual winding, one-minute tourbillon; power reserve appx. 40 hours
Functions: hours, minutes, subsidiary seconds (on tourbillon cage); date; power reserve display
Dimensions: 28.5 x 26.9 mm
Height: 6.1 mm
Jewels: 27
Balance: screw balance in tourbillon cage
Frequency: 18,000 vph
Remarks: base plate with perlage, edges beveled, bridges with *côtes de Genève*; polished steel parts; Seal of Geneva

Caliber 1126 QPR

Mechanical with automatic winding, power reserve appx.
38 hours
Base movement: Jaeger-LeCoultre
Functions: hours, minutes; perpetual calendar with date (retrograde); day, month, leap year indication
Diameter: 26 mm
Height: 5.05 mm
Jewels: 36
Balance: glucydur
Frequency: 28,800 vph
Remarks: base plate with perlage, edges beveled, bridges with *côtes de Genève*; polished steel parts; Seal of Geneva

Caliber 2475

Mechanical with automatic winding, power reserve appx.
55 hours
Functions: hours, minutes, sweep seconds; date, day, power reserve indication
Diameter: 26.2 mm
Height: 5.5 mm
Jewels: 27
Balance: glucydur
Frequency: 28,800 vph
Remarks: base plate with perlage, edges beveled, bridges with *côtes de Genève*; polished steel parts

Ventura

When competing with numerous world-famous brands that can claim a long tradition — or at least pretend they can — as a young, barely fourteen-year-old company we are able to allow ourselves the somewhat ironic remark that Ventura has no past, only a future." Company founder Pierre Nobs can barely keep a grin under control when uttering these words.

The ever-present omission of a past also has advantages: Ventura watches do not need to keep up the pretense of a pseudo-tradition, and so they can dare to include the completely unheard-of. The line at which style would become short-lived, "trendy" fashion is innately sensed by the likes of Hannes Wettstein, who is in charge of design at Ventura, and a close co-operation with leading figures of Swiss design and architecture guarantees a unique understanding of shapes, forms, and identity. Also when designing new dials, professional font developers such as Adrian Frutiger are sometimes asked to come on

board. In order to be able to forge such strategic alliances, Ventura needed to establish an uncompromising attitude toward quality. That is quite an extensive mandate, for not only are individual series subjected to the stringent testing of the C.O.S.C. to become certified chronometers, so is the company's entire range of mechanical watches.

"At Ventura, design is never created empirically. It is always the result of extensive research in the areas of functionality and ergonomics," says Nobs. The numerous international design prizes and awards are proof positive of this statement. So that this remains the case in the future, Ventura recently announced a new management and owner structure led by a group of Swiss individuals and investors. Founder Pierre Nobs remains on the board, along with longtime designer Hannes Wettstein. In the coming years, this company will specialize in digital watches with an emphasis on design and the development of their "manufacture" movements.

Ventura has always consistently invested in technical innovation. Cases and bracelets made of Titanox, the scratchproof, hardened version of pure titanium, and Durinox, the same in stainless steel, lend these products a unique longevity. With the development of the world's first — and still only — batteryless LCD watch (the models SPARC fx and px utilize auto-quartz technology) as well as the patented EasySkroll operating system of the v-tec Alpha, Ventura has become a leader in digital watch technology: These high-quality products come from the company's own electronic *manufacture*. Unfortunately for fans of mechanical watches, Ventura will discontinue its limited number of mechanical chronometers after May 2006. But, as was already mentioned above: The past isn't everything. It's just as important to have an eye on the future.

v-tec Alpha

Reference number: W155
Movement: quartz, Ventura Caliber VEN_03; multifunctional quartz movement with scroll wheel for menu (EasySkroll)
Functions: hours, minutes, seconds; chronograph; perpetual calendar with date, day, month, year; second time zone; alarm and countdown
Case: stainless steel (Durinox), 33.5 x 39 mm, height 8.5 mm; sapphire crystal
Band: stainless steel (Durinox), folding clasp
Price: $1,490
Variations: with leather strap ($1,290)

v-tec Delta

Reference number: W21.015
Movement: quartz, Ventura Caliber VEN_04; multifunctional quartz movement with scroll wheel for menu (EasySkroll)
Functions: hours, minutes, seconds; chronograph; perpetual calendar with date, day, month, year; second time zone; alarm and countdown
Case: stainless steel (Durinox), 35 x 40.6 mm, height 8.5 mm; sapphire crystal
Band: stainless steel (Durinox), black, folding clasp
Price: $1,390
Variations: with leather strap ($1,190)

SPARC fx

Reference number: W10 R
Movement: quartz, Ventura Caliber 99; autonomous energy supply via rotor and microgenerator; turns off automatically
Functions: hours, minutes; date, month
Case: Titanox, ø 35 mm, height 10.9mm; sapphire crystal; exhibition case back
Band: rubber, double folding clasp
Price: $2,200
Variations: with Titanox bracelet ($2,600)

SPARC px

Reference number: W11S
Movement: quartz, Ventura Caliber 99; autonomous energy supply via rotor and microgenerator; turns off automatically
Functions: hours, minutes; date, month
Case: stainless steel, 42.4 x 32.5 mm, height 8.4/11.7 mm; sapphire crystal; exhibition case back
Band: stainless steel, double folding clasp
Price: $1,900
Variations: with leather strap ($1,700); with white diamonds and strap ($8,600); with black diamonds and strap ($11,000)

EGO Chrono Square

Reference number: VM25.06.L
Movement: automatic, ETA Caliber 2894-2; ø 28.6 mm, height 6.1 mm; 37 jewels; 28,800 vph
Functions: hours, minutes, subsidiary seconds; chronograph; date
Case: stainless steel (Durinox), 37 x 37 mm, height 13.5 mm; sapphire crystal; exhibition case back
Band: stainless steel (Durinox), double folding clasp
Price: $4,300

v-matic LOGA

Reference number: VM6.11 T
Movement: automatic, ETA Valjoux Caliber 7750; ø 30 mm, height 7.9 mm; 25 jewels; 28,800 vph; officially certified chronometer (C.O.S.C.)
Functions: hours, minutes, subsidiary seconds; chronograph; date
Case: Titanox, ø 40.25 mm, height 14.7 mm; rotating flange with 60-minute scale under crystal; sapphire crystal; exhibition case back; screwed-in crown; water-resistant to 100 m
Band: leather, folding clasp
Price: $4,000
Variations: with Titanox bracelet ($4,400)

Vollmer

Hansjörg Vollmer, a third-generation manufacturer of metal bracelets for wristwatches, and his family have been in the watchmaking industry since 1922 when Ernst Vollmer, Hansjörg's grandfather, founded his first factory on August 15 of that year. In 1998, with the mechanical renaissance well underway, Hansjörg Vollmer bought the brand Aristo from its original founding family. This was a make originally founded in 1907 whose Pforzheim factory had produced up to 3,000 wristwatches daily, manufacturing a total of several million pieces until 1990. Vollmer bought a lot more than a name when he purchased the remains of this brand. He also acquired original ideas and archives to rummage around in from early eras, even though his main goal in manufacturing wristwatches was quite different

from that of the brand's first owners. His concept is to make his new watches into distinctly branded articles. He knows that this can only be achieved with quality, not quantity, thus turning the brand's founding concept 180 degrees.

This is completely different from the original roots when watchmaker Julius Epple had produced only a few different modest models. For three entire generations the Epple clan built the brand within the family fold. It was only Epple's grandson, Helmut, who trustingly placed the brand into Hansjörg Vollmer's hands. Since 1998 Vollmer has faithfully followed his own concept, bringing the make new renown as a name brand in Europe.

But before doing that, Vollmer's watches have made a quick detour through the demanding markets of Japan and the U.S.

In those countries the brand, known simply as Vollmer, celebrated the new millennium with successful automatic wristwatches modeled after observation watches of the German air force.

All the while, Hansjörg Vollmer has continued to poke around in his brand's historical records: While researching in the company's archives, he discovered dial sketches of old marine and railroad service watches, which he has resuscitated today and outfitted with modern automatic movements.

Vollmer chiefly uses the ETA caliber 2824-2, which is known as the general standard for reliable mechanics. Both now and then, the face of this brand is and was determined by simple, unadorned wristwatches with a strong military character.

It is exactly these interpretations of vintage models with which Vollmer re-creates that era for watch lovers of all ages, an era in which Julius Epple wrote the first chapter of this brand's history. Vollmer certainly finds more than enough inspiration in the well-kept company archives.

Another model line also thanks the archives for its creation, these being wristwatches "with a history." Among them is the Oversized Winged Midnight model with its sandblasted 44 mm stainless steel case, topped by an eminently grippable 10 mm *oignon*-style crown and sapphire crystal. This model and its variations follow the style of classic observation watches. Their finely adjusted movements are outfitted with an Incabloc shock protection and stop-seconds - a tribute to the modern in classic garb. And new for the fall is an officially certified chronometer version, certainly interesting for collectors.

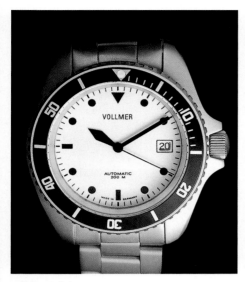

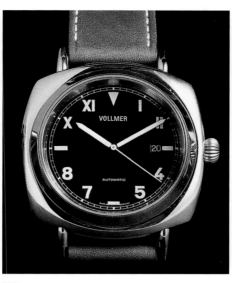

Nacht Schwimmer

Reference number: W522
Movement: automatic, ETA Caliber 2824-2; ø 25.6 mm, height 4.6 mm; 25 jewels; 28,800 vph; power reserve 36-42 hours
Functions: hours, minutes, sweep seconds; date
Case: stainless steel, ø 42 mm, height 11 mm; unidirectionally rotating bezel; anti-reflective sapphire crystal; screwed-down case back; screwed-in crown; water-resistant to 200 m
Band: stainless steel, double folding clasp
Price: $995

U5

Reference number: W521
Movement: automatic, ETA Caliber 2824-2; ø 25.6 mm, height 4.6 mm; 25 jewels; 28,800 vph; power reserve 36-42 hours
Functions: hours, minutes, sweep seconds; date
Case: stainless steel, ø 45 mm, height 13.5 mm; anti-reflective hardened mineral crystal; screwed-down exhibition case back; water-resistant to 50 m
Band: leather, buckle
Price: $995

Oversize Winged Midnight

Reference number: W216
Movement: automatic, ETA Caliber 2824-2; ø 25.6 mm, height 4.6 mm; 25 jewels; 28,800 vph; power reserve 36-42 hours
Functions: hours, minutes, sweep seconds; date
Case: stainless steel, ø 44 mm, height 11.5 mm; rotating bezel; anti-reflective sapphire crystal; screwed-down exhibition case back; water-resistant to 50 m
Band: leather, buckle
Price: $995
Variations: on steel milanaise bracelet

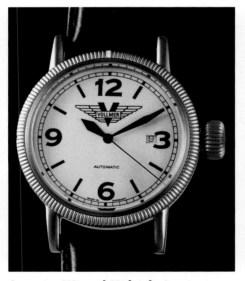

THE

Reference number: W536
Movement: automatic, ETA Caliber 2824-2; ø 25.6 mm, height 4.6 mm; 25 jewels; 28,800 vph; power reserve 36-42 hours
Functions: hours, minutes, sweep seconds; date
Case: stainless steel, ø 40 mm, height 10 mm; anti-reflective sapphire crystal; screwed-down exhibition case back; water-resistant to 50 m
Band: leather, buckle
Price: $995
Variations: on steel bracelet

Oversize Winged Midnight Luminous

Reference number: W217
Movement: automatic, ETA Caliber 2824-2; ø 25.6 mm, height 4.6 mm; 25 jewels; 28,800 vph; power reserve 36-42 hours
Functions: hours, minutes, sweep seconds; date
Case: stainless steel, ø 44 mm, height 11.5 mm; anti-reflective sapphire crystal; screwed-down exhibition case back; water-resistant to 50 m
Band: leather, buckle
Price: $995
Variations: on steel milanaise bracelet

Titanium Flieger Chronograph

Reference number: W404
Movement: automatic, ETA Valjoux Caliber 7750; ø 30 mm, height 7.9 mm; 25 jewels; 28,800 vph; power reserve 36-42 hours
Functions: hours, minutes, sweep seconds; chronograph; date, day
Case: titanium, ø 38 mm, height 11.5 mm; anti-reflective sapphire crystal; screwed-down case back; water-resistant to 50 m
Band: leather, buckle
Price: $2,750

George J. von Burg

With a cleanly structured collection of classic chronographs, George J von Burg is competing for the attention of America's watch-loving audience.

Even though one might assume this is a new brand, in all reality it isn't: As the son of a watchmaker, George Josef von Burg (1914-1986) had already learned about the manufacture of watches at a rather young age, acquiring all the necessary knowledge and skills. When he was barely twenty years old, he had already manufactured and sold his first timekeepers under the registered name of Geo Automatic. In the 1950s, von Burg immigrated with his family to the United States, where he founded a company for watch accessories. During this time, he purchased a watch factory in Switzerland, which he directed under the name Semag after returning from the U.S. His company expanded, and von Burg opened another branch of the factory in Claro (in the Swiss canton Tessin) where he

— one of the first of his guild to do this — manufactured mechanical watch movements for reputable watch brands on modern production machines. Claro Watch SA was founded in 1961 for the production of mechanical pallet escapement movements.

Semag and Claro developed into two of the largest manufacturers of mechanical movements and wristwatches, which were sold under various brand names all over the world. These companies are still owned by the von Burg family today and are managed by George J. von Burg II and George J. von Burg III.

The individual components of the chronographs come from various suppliers. They are, however, of the best quality, from the carefully polished cases and valuable leather straps to the finely finished Valjoux chronograph movements and cleanly structured dials. At first glance, the sweep chronograph hands inlaid with a luminous substance seem a bit surprising, but they

are an important style element that is incorporated into all three model families. The current collection of George J. von Burg comprises three product lines: Collectors Series, Chronograph Series, and Prestige Series. The Collectors Series is based on pure, undecorated shapes and communicates in fine details. Alongside a GMT chronograph with flyback function and a split-seconds chronograph called The Roman Rattrapante, the highlight of the company is also found in this series: The Perpetual Calendar Chronograph, limited to twenty pieces each in yellow, white, and rose gold. Conspicuous on the side of the case is the exceptionally fine relief engraving inspired by a medieval shield with a zigzag pattern. As a decorative element, it also appears in the center of the dial and on the deployant clasp. The blue stop hand in the form of a sword is inspired by the knight theme and builds a bridge back to the family's surname (Burg is German for castle). The von Burg family crest is embossed on the case back. And even the large, easily grippable crown bears the George J. von Burg hallmark.

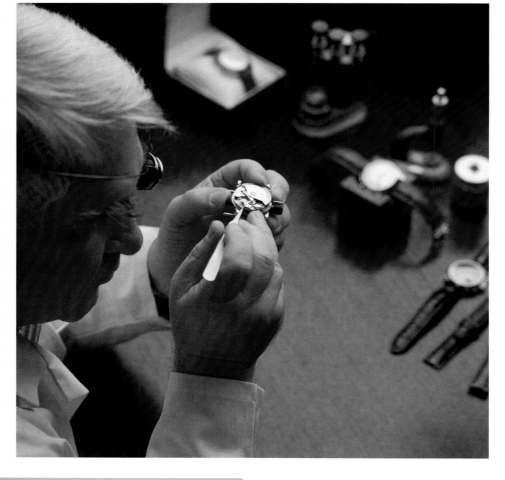

Roman Rattrapante

Reference number: 70021 C

Movement: automatic, GJVB Caliber 8721 (base ETA Valjoux 7750); ø 30 mm, height 7.9 mm; 27 jewels; 28,800 vph; finely finished with *côtes de Genève*

Functions: hours, minutes, subsidiary seconds; split-seconds chronograph; date

Case: stainless steel, ø 42 mm, height 16 mm; sapphire crystal; exhibition window case back; screwed-in crown

Band: reptile skin, buckle

Remarks: limited to 50 pieces

Price: $13,600

Variations: in yellow, rose or white gold, each limited to 50

GMT Flyback

Reference number: 80021 C

Movement: automatic, GJVB Caliber 8107 (base ETA Valjoux 7750); ø 30 mm, height 7.9 mm; 27 jewels; 28,800 vph; finely finished with *côtes de Genève*

Functions: hours, minutes, subsidiary seconds; chronograph with flyback function; date; 24-hour display (second time zone)

Case: stainless steel, ø 42 mm, height 16 mm; sapphire crystal; exhibition window case back; screwed-in crown; water-resistant to 50 m

Band: reptile skin, buckle

Remarks: limited to 50 pieces

Price: $8,200

Perpetual Calendar

Reference number: 71011 C

Movement: automatic, Dubois-Dépraz Caliber 2110 (base ETA 2892-A2); ø 30.5 mm, height 7.9 mm; 38 jewels; 28,800 vph; finely finished with *côtes de Genève*

Functions: hours, minutes, subsidiary seconds, chronograph; perpetual calendar with date, day of the week, month, moon phase and leap year

Case: rose gold, ø 42.3 mm, height 15.3 mm; sapphire crystal; exhibition window case back; screwed-in crown

Band: reptile skin, double folding clasp

Remarks: limited to 20 pieces

Price: $32,000

Classic Collection

Reference number: 20012 C

Movement: automatic, ETA Valjoux Caliber 7750; ø 30 mm, height 7.9 mm; 27 jewels; 28,800 vph

Functions: hours, minutes, subsidiary seconds; chronograph; date and day of the week

Case: stainless steel, gold-plated, ø 40 mm, height 15 mm; sapphire crystal; screwed-in crown; water-resistant to 100 m

Band: reptile skin, buckle

Price: $3,200

Variations: with gold-plated stainless steel bracelet; in polished stainless steel

Sport Collection

Reference number: 30021 C

Movement: automatic, ETA Caliber 7750; ø 30 mm, height 7.9 mm; 27 jewels; 28,800 vph

Functions: hours, minutes, subsidiary seconds; chronograph; date and day of the week

Case: stainless steel, ø 40 mm, height 15 mm; sapphire crystal; screwed-in crown; water-resistant to 100 m

Band: reptile skin, buckle

Price: $2,600

Variations: with stainless steel bracelet; in gold-plated stainless steel

Modern Collection

Reference number: 10021 B

Movement: automatic, ETA Caliber 7750; ø 30 mm, height 7.9 mm; 27 jewels; 28,800 vph

Functions: hours, minutes, subsidiary seconds; chronograph; date and day of the week

Case: stainless steel, ø 40 mm, height 15 mm; sapphire crystal; screwed-in crown; water-resistant to 100 m

Band: stainless steel, folding clasp

Price: $2,800

Variations: with reptile skin strap; in gold-plated stainless steel

Harry Winston

Although as a jeweler this company enjoys a worldwide reputation as a producer of costly timepieces set extravagantly with diamonds, its management is continually and increasingly stressing the brand's technical competence. In following this strategy, the company has called a wonderful new tradition to life. Harry Winston initiates collaborations with exceptional, independent watchmakers, always very well regarded in the field for their special talents. These artists exclusively design one or more new watches that are realized together with Harry Winston Rare Timepieces (HWRT) and — completely in line with the predicate "rare" in the brand's name — are introduced to the market in strictly limited editions called Opus.

Both for HWRT, the Genevan "branch" of the famed jeweler Harry Winston at home on New York's Fifth Avenue, as for the master watchmakers taking part does this cooperation bring a great deal of advantages with it. These horological artists take part in an important cooperative effort with an internationally renowned watch brand and receive a welcome opportunity to become more widely recognized for their work. Additionally, the relationship with Harry Winston allows them to make watches that their own independent master watchmakers' budgets would not normally be able to accommodate in terms of pre-financing materials and labor.

On the other hand, for Harry Winston it was important to free itself from the stigma of being a "jeweled watch brand" — something they could do with the recognized know-how of these independents. After Opus One by François-Paul Journe in 2001, Opus Two by Antoine Preziuso the following year, Opus 3 by Vianney Halter in 2003, and Opus 4 designed by Christophe Claret in 2004, Baselworld 2005 heralded more than just the arrival of spring. This year — and unfortunately for the final time, as managing director Max Büsser has confirmed — a new timepiece in the cycle of Opus masterpieces was presented.

Opus 5 is a creation of the young watchmaker Felix Baumgartner, and this masterpiece certainly belonged to the circle of the fair's most exceptional pieces in 2005. In an ingenious way it unites highly complicated mechanics with the advantages of a digital display (12-hour) and a classic analogue watch (minutes).

Since it is well known that a 12-hour display cannot provide any information about which half of the day the time shown is in, the Opus 5 was also outfitted with a clear yet attractive day/night indicator whose hands wander back and forth between a sun symbol and two illustrations of a waning moon as it appears in the northern hemisphere.

The power reserve display in the same size balances out the upper half of the dial. With markers that become increasingly dainty toward the lower end of the scale, this indication makes clear how much power the mainspring still contains. This timepiece has 122 hours of power reserve, or five full days, when fully wound.

Harry Winston Rare Timepieces sells about 4,000 watches each year in thirty-two countries. In 1999, 95 percent of these were jeweled pieces for women. But today the men's share has increased to a full 40 percent.

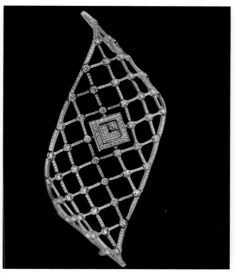

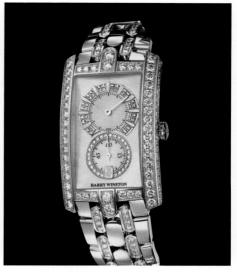

Avenue Black Rhodium

Reference number: 310/LQKLA11
Movement: quartz, ETA Caliber 901.001
Functions: hours, minutes
Case: white gold, 21 x 36 mm, height 6.24 mm; bezel and case sides set with 25 white diamonds und 49 pink sapphires; sapphire crystal
Band: satin, buckle in white gold
Price: $23,900
Variations: in yellow gold

Signature Lace

Reference number: 122/LQ14WW.D/D3
Movement: quartz, ETA Caliber 201.001
Functions: hours, minutes
Case: white gold, 18 x 18 mm, height 6.63 mm; bezel set with 48 diamonds; sapphire crystal
Band: white gold set with 939 diamonds,
Remarks: dial with 48 diamonds
Price: $184,100

Avenue C Midsize

Reference number: 330/UMWW.MD/D3.1
Movement: manually wound, HW Caliber 316; 21 x 27 mm, height 8.35 mm; 20 jewels; 21,600 vph
Functions: hours, minutes (off-center), subsidiary seconds
Case: white gold, 26 x 46 mm, height 10.85 mm; bezel and case sides set with diamonds; sapphire crystal; exhibition window case back
Band: white gold set with diamonds, folding clasp
Remarks: mother-of-pearl dial with diamonds
Price: $47,300
Variations: with leather strap

Excenter Biretro

Reference number: 200/UABI134WLMD/00
Movement: automatic, GP Caliber 3106 with module HW 2837; ø 25.6 mm, height 4.2 mm; 33 jewels; 28,800 vph
Functions: hours, minutes (off-center), subsidiary seconds (retrograde); date, day of the week (retrograde)
Case: white gold, ø 34 mm, bezel and lugs set with diamonds; sapphire crystal; exhibition window case back
Band: reptile skin, folding clasp
Remarks: mother-of-pearl dial with diamonds
Price: $39,200

Excenter Chrono

Reference number: 200MCRA39RL
Movement: automatic, FP Caliber 1185 with module HW 2831; ø 32 mm, height 7.2 mm; 49 jewels; 28,800 vph
Functions: hours, minutes (off-center), subsidiary seconds (retrograde); chronograph with 30-minute and 12-hour counter (both retrograde)
Case: rose gold, ø 39 mm, height 12 mm; sapphire crystal; exhibition window case back
Band: reptile skin, folding clasp
Price: $25,400
Variations: in yellow gold; in white gold

Excenter Tourbillon

Reference number: 20/MMT40PL.T
Movement: manually wound, HW Caliber 400A; ø 31.9 mm, height 7.45 mm; 43 jewels; 28,800 vph; one-minute tourbillon; developed in cooperation with Peter Speake-Marin
Functions: hours, minutes
Case: platinum, ø 44 mm, height 12.65 mm; sapphire crystal; exhibition window case back
Band: reptile skin, folding clasp
Price: $102,400
Variations: in rose gold

Xemex

Ruedi Külling had a dream: He dreamed of developing a completely new brand where he could determine everything himself, from the name of the product to its publicity. Not an easy task even if Külling is one of the most renowned and successful graphic designers in Switzerland. As a man of action, it was clear to him right from the beginning that the product would need to be a watch brand — after all, he had earned his first paycheck with an exclusive timepiece.

The months of conception, thinking about a name, and designing were well worth it, as he finally introduced a small series of watches at Baselworld in 1996: Xemex was the name of the brand, and Offroad was its first model.

Time has passed, and Külling's brand is now nine years old and looks good as never before. After the Offroad line paved a way into the industry, Külling increased his collection with three other model lines: Avenue, Speedway, and Piccadilly. Külling has achieved giving each of his series a different aura: The Offroad is a solid, round model without compromise — his philosophy of a watch that can be worn through thick and thin. The square version is the Avenue. Just as striking, but in an edged case, it is something for the finer streets of this world. The Speedway, however, stands for velocity. Streamlined and solid is the way he designed the case of this series. Another highlight is formed by Piccadilly as a distinguished, soft version of the Offroad. If the first model was a Land Rover, then the Piccadilly is definitely the SUV of the Xemex watches. It's a watch in which the Offroad genes are recognizable, but one that can also be worn with a suit. Xemex watches all have movable strap lugs. They are all of high-quality manufacture. And the harmonious proportions of the

dials allow anyone to recognize the graphic designer's schooled eye. The Avenue Petit Seconde model with the cutaway for the subsidiary seconds especially ennobles Külling's consistency in the design of his watches. This one is the steel proof of his design motto "simplify, objectify, clarify." The newest product issuing from the house of Xemex is the Piccadilly Calendario, which impressively shows how elegantly practical functions can be added to a watch: Business people will certainly be overjoyed about the large calendar week display near 12 o'clock. The date and day of the week are located at 3 and 9 o'clock respectively. A power reserve display shows how long the automatic movement and its Soprod module still have to tick if the watch were set down.

And just recently a little color was added to the collection. At first Külling only used black and white, but the new, yellow dial of the Offroad gives the watch a completely new charisma.

Külling goes all the way. "If I had to change the movement for design reasons, I would not hesitate to do it." It will be exciting to see what comes next from Xemex, especially considering that the brand's tenth birthday takes place in 2006.

Piccadilly Calendario Reserve 2005

Reference number: 8500.01
Movement: automatic, Soprod Caliber 9075 (base ETA 2892-A2); ø 25.6 mm, height 5.1 mm; 21 jewels; 28,800 vph
Functions: hours, minutes, sweep seconds; date, day of the week, 52 calendar weeks; power reserve display
Case: stainless steel, movable lugs, ø 40 mm, height 11.5 mm; sapphire crystal; exhibition window case back; screwed-in crown; water-resistant to 50 m
Band: leather, buckle
Price: upon request

Piccadilly Big Date

Reference number: 811.01
Movement: automatic, ETA Caliber 2896; ø 25.6 mm, height 4.85 mm; 22 jewels; 28,800 vph
Functions: hours, minutes, sweep seconds; large date
Case: stainless steel, movable lugs, ø 40 mm, height 10.8 mm; sapphire crystal; exhibition window case back; screwed-in crown; water-resistant to 50 m
Band: leather, buckle
Price: $2,895
Variations: with black dial

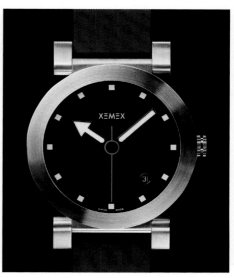

Offroad

Reference number: 215.03
Movement: automatic, ETA Caliber 2824-2; ø 25.6 mm, height 4.6 mm; 25 jewels; 28,800 vph
Functions: hours, minutes, sweep seconds; date
Case: stainless steel, movable lugs, ø 38 mm, height 10.5 mm; sapphire crystal; exhibition window case back; screwed-in crown; water-resistant to 50 m
Band: rubber, buckle
Price: $1,395
Variations: with leather strap; with stainless steel bracelet

Avenue

Reference number: 2805.01
Movement: automatic, ETA Caliber 2824-2; ø 25.6 mm, height 4.6 mm; 25 jewels; 28,800 vph
Functions: hours, minutes, sweep seconds; date
Case: stainless steel, movable lugs, 33 x 37.3 mm, height 10.3 mm; sapphire crystal; exhibition window case back; screwed-in crown; water-resistant to 50 m
Band: leather, folding clasp
Price: $2,595

XE 5000

Reference number: 5500.03
Movement: automatic, ETA Valjoux Caliber 7750; ø 30 mm, height 7.9 mm; 25 jewels; 28,800 vph
Functions: hours, minutes, subsidiary seconds; chronograph; date
Case: stainless steel, movable lugs, ø 44 mm, height 15.2 mm; sapphire crystal; exhibition window case back; recessed crown; water-resistant to 50 m
Band: rubber, double folding clasp
Price: $3,950
Variations: dial in black or signal yellow

Avenue Chronograph

Reference number: 2350.04
Movement: automatic, ETA Caliber 2894-2; ø 28.6 mm, height 6.1 mm; 37 jewels; 28,800 vph
Functions: hours, minutes, subsidiary seconds, chronograph; date
Case: stainless steel, movable lugs, 33 x 37.3 mm, height 12.1 mm; sapphire crystal; exhibition window case back; screwed-in crown; water-resistant to 50 m
Band: leather, folding clasp
Price: $4,950
Variations: with stainless steel bracelet

Dino Zei

The man actually behind Panerai's meteoric rise to the forefront of the watch world is not an employee of the Richemont group. Nor is he Swiss. In fact, Dino Zei, a native Italian with a background in naval engineering, is about as far removed from that as they come.

Zei spent many years in the service of his country's navy. However, in 1972 when Giuseppe Panerai passed away, Zei finally left his governmental employer to manage Guido Panerai e Figlio, a company that was involved in important and delicate work for the navy's special units.

Zei literally shaped the face of the Panerai watch brand, kicking off the massive oversized trend that has since gone down in watch history and thereby shaping the face of modern Florentine watchmaking. Difficulties in Panerai's other division caused the sale of the watch brand and trademark to Cartier in 1997. But it wasn't long before the rest was also sold, at which point Zei retired. That was in 1999.

This was a retirement that was not to last, and Zei is back once again at the occupation he loves so much. Teaming with Anonimo's Federico Massacesi, Zei is

embarking upon a very special — and familial — collaboration. Anonimo's very Florentine watch style was instantly recognized as such by the former Panerai executive, and it seemed a natural for him to turn to this "anonymous" brand upon expressing the desire to return to the horological arena. He now applies his considerable skills in research and development, as well as in an advisory role.

"Anonimo has a special way of manufacturing," says Zei in his typically understated manner. "I am very proud to be associated with it."

The collaboration has thus far produced four collection timepieces and a limited-edition set of two which Scott Moskovitz, U.S. distributor and part owner of Anonimo, terms "a merging of the two brands' styles." He continues, "These models are true to Panerai form, but with original cases, different from Anonimo's, and certainly pre-Panerai in style."

Like Anonimo, the timepieces in Dino Zei's line are housed in special cases that were milled from one entire piece of metal to avoid changing their molecular structure. The Dino Zei models also employ Kodiak straps, the process under patent at Anonimo giving calfskin the ability to be immersed in any type of water for extended periods of time without damage. And it goes without saying that the black stainless steel models were treated with Ox-Pro, another process under patent at Anonimo.

Narvalo

Reference number: 11004
Movement: automatic, Dubois-Dépraz Caliber (base ETA 2892-2, modified); ø 25.6 mm, 28,800 vph; with additional module for subsidiary seconds and large date disks; movement finished *luxe perlée*, *soigné* finished rotor
Functions: hours, minutes, subsidiary seconds; large date
Case: stainless steel, ø 43.5 mm, screw-locked bezel and case back; sapphire crystal; case back with off-center window; water-resistant to 120 m
Band: Kodiak calf skin, buckle
Price: $4,200

Marea

Reference number: 11003
Movement: automatic, Jaquet Caliber 8112, modified (base ETA Valjoux 7750); ø 30 mm; 28,800 vph, power reserve 40 hours; additional Tricompax module, movement and rotor with *soigné* finish
Functions: hours, minutes, subsidiary seconds; flyback chronograph, 24-hours display
Case: stainless steel, ø 43.5 mm, screw-locked bezel and case back; sapphire crystal; case back with off-center window; water-resistant to 120 m
Band: Kodiak calf skin, buckle
Price: $7,200

Nemo

Reference number: 11001
Movement: automatic, ETA Valjoux Caliber 7750, modified; ø 30 mm, 25 jewels; 28,800 vph, power reserve 40 hours
Functions: hours, minutes, subsidiary seconds; chronograph; date, day
Case: stainless steel, ø 43.5 mm, screw-locked bezel and case back; sapphire crystal; case back with off-center window; screwed-in crown; water-resistant to 120 m
Band: Kodiak calf skin, buckle
Price: $4,800

Jalea

Reference number: 11002
Movement: automatic, ETA Caliber 28362-2, modified with Candino module; ø 25.6 mm; 28,800 vph, power reserve 36 hours
Functions: hours, minutes, subsidiary seconds; date
Case: stainless steel, ø 43.5 mm, screw-locked bezel and case back; sapphire crystal; case back with off-center window; screwed-in crown; water-resistant to 120 m
Band: Kodiak calf skin, buckle
Price: $4,400

Cronografo Nemo Limited Edition

Movement: manually wound, ETA Valjoux Caliber 7760, modified; ø 30 mm, 25 jewels; 28,800 vph, power reserve 40 hours; adjusted in 4 positions
Functions: hours, minutes, chronograph; date, day
Case: stainless steel, ø 43.5 mm, screw-locked bezel and case back; sapphire crystal; case back with off-center window; screwed-in crown; water-resistant to 120 m
Band: Kodiak calf skin, buckle
Remarks: limited edition of 50 sets
Price: $8,800 only as a set

Cronografo Nemo Limited Edition

Movement: manually wound, ETA Valjoux Caliber 7760, modified; ø 30 mm, 25 jewels; 28,800 vph, power reserve 40 hours; adjusted in 4 positions
Functions: hours, minutes, chronograph; date, day
Case: stainless steel, Ox-Pro blackened, ø 43.5 mm, screw-locked bezel and case back; sapphire crystal; case back with off-center window; screwed-in crown; water-resistant to 120 m
Band: Kodiak calf skin, buckle
Remarks: limited edition of 50 sets
Price: $8,800 only as a set

Zenith

Zenith president Thierry Nataf has invested millions in the renovations of his watch *manufacture*: The entire research and development department has received a complete face-lift. Additionally, Nataf has hired specialists from outside the industry, such as vector graphic experts, and put them at a desk with watch movement designers — in order to optimize the products technically. "From the very first moment, I understood what type of potential this brand has. And it hurt my soul to see how others have adorned themselves with this *manufacture's* values. Zenith is something very special and deserves much more respect," Nataf says of his reasons for transferring from Paris to the Swiss Jura in the name of Louis Vuitton, Moet & Hennessy (LVMH).

The modernization of the outdated machines at Zenith was a top priority for the engineer. He saw the *manufacture* as a Sleeping Beauty that needed to be brought back to life after years of vegetating. And because Nataf is convinced that "modern watchmaking is a mixture of craft and futuristic music" he sees the company "once again looking at the beginning of a little revolution."

The extensive reworking of the El Primero caliber family bears witness not only to new caliber numbers, but also to a thoroughly improved finish on all components.

Nataf's second priority was to "get back to the Zenith style." That the *manufacture's* products were sold at ruinously undervalued prices in comparison to those of the competition was only one side of the coin. A larger handicap was the missing glamour and shine according to Nataf. "But it is so easy to combine technology and glamour in such a fascinating product as the mechanical wristwatch."

And the Zenith boss thoroughly put his ideas into reality: Not only did he polish up the brand name of Zenith with lavish television commercials, he also set off a fireworks display of technical highlights beginning with the world's first tourbillon to beat at 36,000 vibrations per hour. And as if that were not enough, the automatic chronograph's little tourbillon cage additionally received a date ring running counter-clockwise around it. The new Open chronograph seems like a snap to make with its unimpeded view of the balance through the dial. But it's a snap with a system, for recently the Chronomaster Open Retrograde has had power reserve and retrograde date displays added to the central hand stem.

In addition, it's become obvious that the reduction of the case diameter on the small Open could be announcing a return to classic case sizes — directly after Zenith had just finished propagating the XXL case of the last few years.

And the ladies can also be happy that they no longer have to wear men's models: The Baby Star line developed especially for women has a comfortable case diameter of 32 mm and can be sporty or elegant depending on the strap and dial color chosen — but always feminine and definitely glamorous.

Grande ChronoMaster XXT Tourbillon

Reference number: 18.1260.4005/01.C505
Movement: automatic, Zenith Caliber 4005 El Primero; ø 35 mm, height 7.55 mm; 35 jewels; 36,000 vph; one-minute tourbillon; contrarotating date ring between bridge and cage
Functions: hours, minutes; chronograph; date
Case: rose gold, ø 45 mm, height 14.1 mm; sapphire crystal; exhibition window case back
Band: crocodile skin, threefold folding clasp
Price: $115,000
Variations: in white gold; in platinum with and without 60 diamonds (6.2 ct)

ChronoMaster Open Retrograde XXT

Reference number: 40.1260.4023/01.C505
Movement: automatic, Zenith Caliber 4023 El Primero; ø 30 mm, height 7.75 mm; 39 jewels; 36,000 vph; movement partially skeletonized under cutaway in dial
Functions: hours, minutes, subsidiary seconds; chronograph; date; power reserve display
Case: platinum, ø 45 mm, height 14.5 mm; sapphire crystal; exhibition window case back
Band: crocodile skin, threefold folding clasp
Price: $43,000
Variations: in 40 mm case diameter

ChronoMaster Open XXT

Reference number: 18.1260.4021/01.C505
Movement: automatic, Zenith Caliber 4021 El Primero; ø 30 mm, height 7.75 mm; 39 jewels; 36,000 vph; movement partially skeletonized under cutaway in dial
Functions: hours, minutes, subsidiary seconds; chronograph; power reserve display
Case: rose gold, ø 45 mm, height 14.1 mm; sapphire crystal; exhibition window case back
Band: crocodile skin, threefold folding clasp
Price: $19,000
Variations: stainless steel on steel bracelet ($8,300), crocodile skin, or rubber strap ($7,500); various dials

ChronoMaster Open

Reference number: 03.1260.4021/73.C505
Movement: automatic, Zenith Caliber 4021 El Primero; ø 30 mm, height 7.75 mm; 39 jewels; 36,000 vph; movement partially skeletonized under cutaway in dial
Functions: hours, minutes, subsidiary seconds; chronograph; power reserve display
Case: stainless steel, ø 45 mm, height 14.1 mm; sapphire crystal; exhibition window case back
Band: crocodile skin, threefold folding clasp
Price: $6,800
Variations: on steel ($7,500) or rubber strap ($6,800); 40 mm case diameter; in rose gold ($14,900); various dials

Port Royal Open Concept

Reference number: 95.0550.4021/77.C550
Movement: automatic, Zenith Caliber 4021C El Primero; ø 30 mm, height 7.75 mm; 39 jewels; 36,000 vph; movement partially skeletonized under cutaway in dial; transparent dial made of TR90, COSC chronometer
Functions: hours, minutes, subsidiary seconds; chronograph; power reserve display
Case: titanium, 36 x 51 mm, height 14.3 mm; sapphire crystal; exhibition window case back
Band: carbon fiber/leather, threefold folding clasp
Price: $14,500
Variations: in 34 x 48 mm case size

Port Royal Open

Reference number: 03.0550.4021/01.R512
Movement: automatic, Zenith Caliber 4021B El Primero; ø 30 mm, height 7.75 mm; 39 jewels; 36,000 vph; movement partially skeletonized under cutaway in dial
Functions: hours, minutes, subsidiary seconds; chronograph; power reserve display
Case: stainless steel, 36 x 51 mm, height 14.1 mm; sapphire crystal; exhibition window case back
Band: rubber, threefold folding clasp
Price: $7,500
Variations: with leather strap; with anthracite-colored dial and black rubber or leather strap; in 34 x 48 mm case size

Grande ChronoMaster GT

Reference number: 1403.1240.4001/01.C495
Movement: automatic, Zenith Caliber 4001 El Primero;
ø 30 mm, height 7.55 mm; 31 jewels; 36,000 vph; officially
certified chronometer (C.O.S.C.)
Functions: hours, minutes, subsidiary seconds; chronograph;
date, day of the week, month, moon phase
Case: stainless steel, ø 42 mm, height 12.9 mm; sapphire
crystal; exhibition window case back
Band: crocodile skin, threefold folding clasp
Price: $10,200
Variations: in rose or white gold ($22,100); in yellow
gold ($21,000)

Grande Class Rattrapante Grande Date

Reference number: 65.0520.4026/21.C492
Movement: automatic, Zenith Caliber 4026 El Primero;
ø 30 mm, height 9.35 mm; 32 jewels; 36,000 vph; officially
certified chronometer (C.O.S.C.)
Functions: hours, minutes, subsidiary seconds; split-seconds
chronograph; large date
Case: white gold, ø 44 mm, height 14.3 mm; sapphire
crystal; exhibition window case back
Band: crocodile skin, threefold folding clasp
Price: $36,000

Grande Class Grande Date

Reference number: 03.0520.4010/21.R511
Movement: automatic, Zenith Caliber 4010 El Primero;
ø 30 mm, height 7.65 mm; 31 jewels; 36,000 vph; officially
certified chronometer (C.O.S.C.)
Functions: hours, minutes, subsidiary seconds;
chronograph; large date
Case: stainless steel, ø 44 mm, height 14 mm; sapphire
crystal; exhibition window case back
Band: rubber, threefold folding clasp
Price: upon request
Variations: with reptile skin strap

Class El Primero

Reference number: 03.510.4002/21.C492
Movement: automatic, Zenith Caliber 4002 El Primero; ø 30
mm, height 6.5 mm; 31 jewels; 36,000 vph; COSC chronometer
Functions: hours, minutes, subsidiary seconds;
chronograph; date
Case: stainless steel, ø 40 mm, height 13.9 mm; sapphire
crystal; exhibition window case back
Band: crocodile skin, threefold folding clasp
Price: $5,500
Variations: on stainless steel bracelet ($6,200); with silver-
colored dial; in 44 mm case diameter; in rose gold; in white
gold; with various dial and strap variations

Grande Class Power Reserve Dual Time

Reference number: 18.0520.683/01.C492
Movement: automatic, Zenith Caliber Elite 683; ø 25.6 mm,
height 4.95 mm; 36 jewels; 28,800 vph
Functions: hours, minutes, subsidiary seconds; date; power
reserve display; 24-hour display (second time zone)
Case: rose gold, ø 44 mm, height 11 mm; sapphire crystal;
exhibition window case back
Band: crocodile skin, threefold folding clasp
Price: $8,500
Variations: in stainless steel ($4,300), yellow gold
($8,000), white gold ($8,500); with link bracelet

Class Dual Time

Reference number: 03.1125.682/02.C490
Movement: automatic, Zenith Caliber Elite 682; ø 25.6 mm,
height 3.75 mm; 26 jewels; 28,800 vph
Functions: hours, minutes, subsidiary seconds; 24-hour
display (second time zone); date
Case: stainless steel, ø 39 mm, height 9.4 mm; sapphire
crystal; exhibition window case back
Band: crocodile skin, threefold folding clasp
Price: $4,700
Variations: in rose or white gold ($8,600); in yellow gold
($8,200); with grey dial

Grande Port Royal Elite Power Reserve

Reference number: 03.550.685/01.C507
Movement: automatic, Zenith Caliber Elite 685; ø 25.6 mm, height 4.48 mm; 38 jewels; 28,800 vph
Functions: hours, minutes, subsidiary seconds; date; power reserve display
Case: stainless steel, 36 x 51 mm, height 10.2 mm; sapphire crystal; exhibition window case back
Band: crocodile skin, threefold folding clasp
Price: $5,500
Variations: with a stainless steel bracelet ($6,100) or a rubber strap

Port Royal Rectangle Elite

Reference number: 01.0251.684/02.C504
Movement: automatic, Zenith Caliber Elite 684; ø 25.6 mm, height 3.28 mm; 26 jewels; 28,800 vph
Functions: hours, minutes, subsidiary seconds; date
Case: stainless steel, 31 x 44 mm, height 12 mm; sapphire crystal
Band: crocodile skin, threefold folding clasp
Price: $3,600
Variations: black dial; on stainless steel bracelet

Star Open

Reference number: 18.1230.4021/01.C588
Movement: automatic, Zenith Caliber 4021 El Primero; ø 30 mm, height 7.75 mm; 39 jewels; 36,000 vph; movement partially skeletonized under heart-shaped dial cutaway
Functions: hours, minutes, subsidiary seconds; chronograph; power reserve display
Case: rose gold, ø 37.5 mm, height 13 mm; sapphire crystal; exhibition window case back
Band: crocodile skin, threefold folding clasp
Price: $5,800
Variations: with diamond-set bezel; in yellow gold; in stainless steel with colorful dials, with and without diamonds

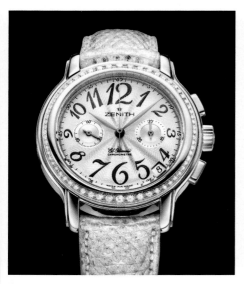

Star

Reference number: 18.1230.4021/01.C588
Movement: automatic, Zenith Caliber 4002 El Primero; ø 30 mm, height 6.5 mm; 31 jewels; 36,000 vph; officially certified chronometer (C.O.S.C.)
Functions: hours, minutes, subsidiary seconds; chronograph; date
Case: stainless steel, ø 37.5 mm, height 13 mm; bezel set with diamonds; sapphire crystal; exhibition window case back
Band: crocodile skin, threefold folding clasp
Price: upon request
Variations: in yellow gold; in stainless steel with colorful dials, with and without diamonds

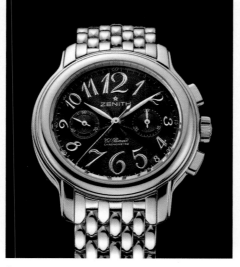

Star

Reference number: 03.1230.4002./21.M1230
Movement: automatic, Zenith Caliber 4002 El Primero; ø 30 mm, height 6.5 mm; 31 jewels; 36,000 vph; officially certified chronometer (C.O.S.C.)
Functions: hours, minutes, subsidiary seconds; chronograph; date
Case: stainless steel, ø 37.5 mm, height 13 mm; sapphire crystal; exhibition window case back
Band: stainless steel, threefold folding clasp
Price: $5,000
Variations: with colorful dials and matching leather or rubber straps; with stainless steel bracelet

Baby Star

Reference number: 03.1220.67/21.C531
Movement: automatic, Zenith Caliber Elite 67; ø 25.6 mm, height 3.81 mm; 27 jewels; 28,800 vph
Functions: hours, minutes, sweep seconds
Case: stainless steel, ø 32 mm, height 11 mm; sapphire crystal; exhibition window case back
Band: lizard skin, buckle
Price: $8,300
Variations: on mink strap; with colorful dials and matching leather straps; in stainless steel and in rose gold; in yellow gold

El Primero 4001

Base caliber: El Primero 410
Mechanical with automatic winding, power reserve more than 50 hours, ball-bearing rotor; column-wheel control of chronograph functions
Functions: hours, minutes, subsidiary seconds; complete calendar (date, day, month, moon phase); chronograph with flyback function
Diameter: 30 mm (13'''); **Height:** 7.55 mm; **Jewels:** 31
Balance: glucydur
Frequency: 36,000 vph
Balance spring: self-compensating flat hairspring with fine adjustment
Shock protection: Kif
Remarks: 355 components; quick-set date and moon phase

El Primero 4002

Base caliber: El Primero 400
Mechanical with automatic winding, power reserve more than 50 hours, ball-bearing rotor; column-wheel control of chronograph functions
Functions: hours, minutes, subsidiary seconds; date; chronograph
Diameter: 30 mm (13'''); **Height:** 6.5 mm
Jewels: 31
Balance: glucydur
Frequency: 36,000 vph
Balance spring: self-compensating flat hairspring with fine adjustment
Shock protection: Kif
Remarks: 266 components; quick-set date

El Primero 4003

Base caliber: El Primero 410
Mechanical with automatic winding, power reserve more than 50 hours, ball-bearing rotor; column-wheel control of chronograph functions
Functions: hours, minutes, subsidiary seconds; perpetual calendar (date, day, month, moon phase); chronograph with flyback function
Diameter: 30 mm (13'''); **Height:** 8.1 mm; **Jewels:** 31
Balance: glucydur; **Frequency:** 36,000 vph
Balance spring: self-compensating flat hairspring with fine adjustment
Shock protection: Kif
Remarks: moon phase with disk display; quick-set date and moon phase

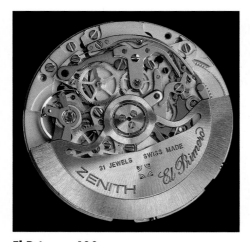

El Primero 400

Mechanical with automatic winding, power reserve more than 50 hours, ball-bearing rotor; column-wheel control of chronograph functions
Functions: hours, minutes, subsidiary seconds; date; chronograph
Diameter: 30 mm (13'''); **Height:** 6.5 mm; **Jewels:** 31
Balance: glucydur
Frequency: 36,000 vph
Balance spring: self-compensating flat hairspring with fine adjustment
Shock protection: Kif
Remarks: 280 components; quick-set date
Related calibers: 410 (additional indicators: day, month, moon phase), 354 components

Caliber 4021 (Open)

Mechanical with automatic winding, power reserve more than 50 hours; ball-bearing rotor; column-wheel control of chronograph functions
Functions: hours, minutes, subsidiary seconds; chronograph; power reserve display
Diameter: 30 mm (13'''); **Height:** 6.5 mm; **Jewels:** 39
Balance: glucydur
Frequency: 36,000 vph
Balance spring: self-compensating flat hairspring with fine adjustment
Shock protection: Kif
Remarks: base plate in the area of the escapement is open and the flat parts are skeletonized

Elite 685

Mechanical with automatic winding, power reserve more than 50 hours, ball-bearing rotor, unidirectionally winding; stop-seconds
Functions: hours, minutes, subsidiary seconds; date; power reserve indicator
Diameter: 26.2 mm (11 1/2'''); **Height:** 4.28 mm
Jewels: 38
Frequency: 28,800 vph
Balance spring: self-compensating flat hairspring with fine adjustment via micrometer screw
Shock protection: Kif
Options: without date/seconds (661), date/sweep seconds (670), date/sweep seconds/24h (672), date/subsidiary seconds (680), date/subsidiary seconds/24h (682)

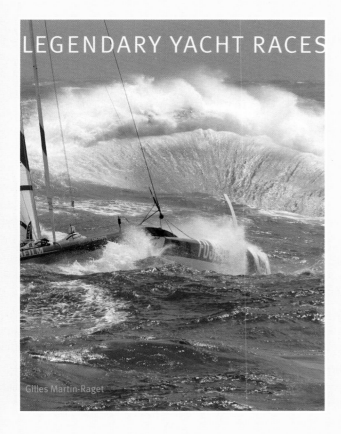

Gilles Martin-Raget

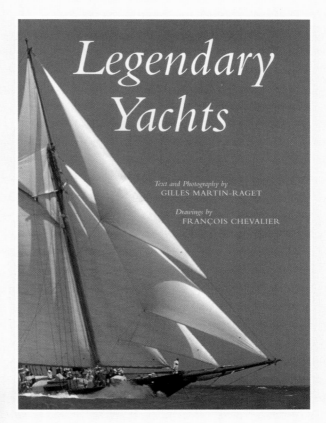

Legendary Yacht Races

A thrilling, firsthand photographic portrayal of the world's most storied and prestigious yachting regattas and events, including the America's Cup, The Race, the Vendée, and the Rum Route.

Text and photography by
Gilles Martin-Raget
200 full-color illustrations
184 pages • 10¼ × 13¼ in. • Cloth
ISBN 0-7892-0800-8 • $55.00

Legendary Yachts

A vibrantly illustrated tribute to the great racing yachts of yesteryear and the current yachting renaissance, providing an insider's perspective on five top regattas and on classic boats like *Pen Duick* and *Shenandoah*.

Text and photography by
Gilles Martin-Raget
Drawings by François Chevalier
300 full-color illustrations, 90 black-and-white drawings
200 pages • 9 × 12¼ in. • Cloth
ISBN 0-7892-0637-4 • $55.00

Zeno

One of the most important towns on Switzerland's watchmaking map has always been La-Chaux-de-Fonds, where in 1868 Jules Godat founded a small pocket watch manufacturing company called Godat & Co., producing fine pocket watches with solid silver cases and women's pendant watches in small quantities. The small factory he built was taken over by the company of A. Eigeldinger & Fils in 1920.

The Eigeldinger family business specialized in military wristwatches, producing pieces encased in stainless steel, silver, gold, and platinum that featured mechanical movements with diameters of up to 43 mm. The owner's son, André-Charles Eigeldinger, introduced the Zeno brand, the name of which is derived from the Greek word *zenodopolus*, meaning "gift of Zeus" or "divine offering."

The first watches carrying the Zeno brand name were manufactured in 1922, and in 1949 Zeno watches were first exhibited at the Basel Watch Fair. In the '60s, watches were also produced under the name of FHB (Felix Huber Basel) and Aida.

Felix W. Huber bought the rights to the Zeno name in 1963. The brand attracted international attention with 1969's futuristic Spaceman model, made of the then absolutely novel material fiberglass; the vacuum-compressed, hermetically sealed diver's watch Compressor, manufactured from 1970 until 1973; and the acquisition of other Swiss watch factories such as Josmar, Jupiter, Corona, Dalil, Fleuron, Penelope, Le Clip, Helveco, Imhof, and Jean Roulet.

Today Zeno, a Swiss company that has managed to remain independent, is now called Zeno Watch Basel, honoring the city it has called home since 1963, and is still headed up by Huber. Further workshops are to be found in the Jura near Neuchâtel and in the Italian-language Swiss canton of Tessin.

The company prides itself on offering the most quality and design innovation available for a reasonable price. In recent years Zeno has made a name for itself in the growing arena of oversized watches. Although the company's expanding palette (featuring more than 1,500 models, including variations) comprises both men's and women's watches in almost every variation imaginable (mechanical and quartz, pocket watches, military watches, diver's watches, and sports watches) in every combination of materials, it is the extra-large format of the Pilot family that has given Zeno its characteristic look. These leading models are based on Zeno pilot's watches that were produced in 1965, at that time measuring 37 mm in diameter. In comparison, the contemporary Pilot Oversized measures 47.5 mm in diameter, surely one of the largest wristwatches made today, and is available as an automatic or manually wound model and with chronograph and GMT complications as well as C.O.S.C. certification.

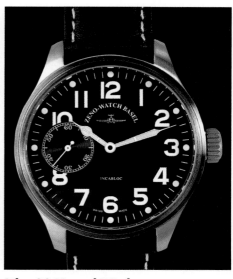

Pilot OS Chronograph

Reference number: 855J TVDD B-SV

Movement: automatic, ETA Valjoux Caliber 7750; ø 30 mm, height 7.9 mm; 25 jewels; 28,800 vph

Functions: hours, minutes, subsidiary seconds; chronograph; date and day of the week

Case: stainless steel, ø 47.5 mm, height 17 mm; mineral crystal; exhibition window case back

Band: leather, buckle

Price: $1,490

Variations: with sapphire crystal; with stainless steel bracelet; various dial versions

Pilot OS Pointer

Reference number: 8554 Z D-SV

Movement: automatic, ETA Caliber 2824-2; ø 25.6 mm, height 4.6 mm; 25 jewels; 28,800 vph

Functions: hours, minutes, sweep seconds; date

Case: stainless steel, ø 47.5 mm, height 15 mm; mineral crystal; exhibition window case back

Band: leather, buckle

Price: $675

Variations: with sapphire crystal; with stainless steel bracelet; various dial versions

Pilot OS Manual Wind

Reference number: 8558/9 B-SV

Movement: manually wound, ETA Unitas Caliber 6497; ø 36.6 mm, height 4.5 mm; 17 jewels; 21,600 vph

Functions: hours, minutes, subsidiary seconds

Case: stainless steel, ø 47.5 mm, height 15 mm; mineral crystal; exhibition window case back

Band: leather, buckle

Price: $650

Variations: subsidiary seconds at 6 o'clock; with stainless steel bracelet

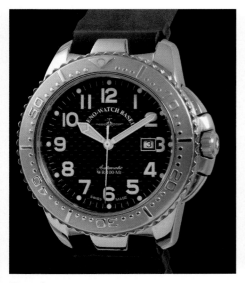

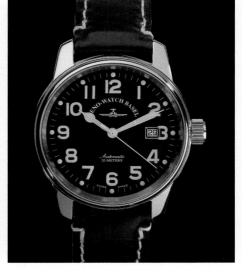

Hercules

Reference number: 4554 S1

Movement: automatic, ETA Caliber 2824-2; ø 25.6 mm, height 4.6 mm; 25 jewels; 28,800 vph

Functions: hours, minutes, sweep seconds; date

Case: stainless steel, ø 44 mm, height 12 mm; unidirectionally rotating bezel with 60-minute divisions; mineral crystal; exhibition window case back

Band: rubber, buckle

Remarks: carbon fiber dial

Price: $810

Variations: also as GMT model with second time zone or as chronograph

Goda 2

Reference number: 7751 WH

Movement: automatic, ETA Valjoux Caliber 7751; ø 30 mm, height 7.9 mm; 25 jewels; 28,800 vph; finely finished with côtes de Genève

Functions: hours, minutes, subsidiary seconds; chronograph; date, day of the week, month, moon phase

Case: stainless steel, ø 42 mm, height 13 mm; sapphire crystal; exhibition window case back

Band: leather, buckle

Price: $1,855

Variations: with sapphire crystal; with stainless steel bracelet; various dial versions

Pilot Classic

Reference number: 6554 SW

Movement: automatic, ETA Caliber 2824-2; ø 25.6 mm, height 4.6 mm; 25 jewels; 28,800 vph

Functions: hours, minutes, sweep seconds; date

Case: stainless steel, ø 40.5 mm, height 12.5 mm; mineral crystal; exhibition window case back

Band: leather, buckle

Price: $470

Variations: with silver dial; with sapphire crystal; with stainless steel bracelet

ETA

This Swatch Group movement manufacturer produces more than five million movements a year. And after the withdrawal of Richemont's Jaeger-LeCoultre as well as Swatch Group sisters Nouvelle Lémania and Frédéric Piguet from the business of selling movements on the free market, most watch brands can hardly help but beat down the door of this full service manufacturer. ETA offers a broad spectrum of automatic movements in various dimensions with different functions, chronograph movements in varying configurations, as well as pocket watch classics (Calibers 6497 and 98) and manually wound calibers of days gone by (Calibers 1727 and 7001) — this company offers everything that a manufacturer's heart could desire. That's not to mention the sheer variety of quartz technology: from inexpensive three-hand mechanisms to highly complicated multi-functional movements and futuristic Etaquartz featuring autonomous energy creation using a rotor and generator.

The almost stereotypical accusation of ETA being "mass goods," however, might just sound like praise in the ears of new ETA director Thomas Meier: He knows only too well how difficult it is to consistently manufacture high-quality filigreed micromechanical technology. This is certainly one of the reasons why there are no (longer) any other movement factories today in Europe that can compete with ETA, or that would want to. Since the success of Swatch — a pure ETA product — millions of Swiss francs have been invested in new development and manufacturing technologies. ETA today owns more than twenty production locales in Switzerland, France, Germany, Malaysia, and Thailand. ETA, which was created from an amalgamation of several independent ébauche manufacturers called Ebauches SA, still delivers some of its movements as half-done "kits" to be reassembled, rebuilt, and/or decorated. These go to specialized workshops such as Soprod, Sellita, La Joux-Perret (Jaquet), and Dubois-Dépraz as Swiss watch tradition has dictated for decades. This practice is supposed to come to an end soon: The Swatch Group's concern management is no longer interested in leaving the lion's share of movement upscaling to others, but will only deliver complete movements in the future, ready for encasing, with personalization and individualization already done as the client wishes.

Caliber 2660

Mechanical with manual winding, power reserve 42 hours
Functions: hours, minutes, sweep seconds
Diameter: 17.2 mm (7 3/4''')
Height: 3.5 mm
Jewels: 17
Frequency: 28,800 vph
Fine adjustment system:
ETACHRON

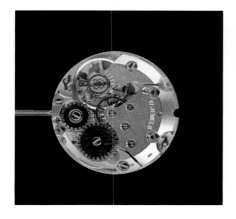

Caliber 1727

Mechanical with manual winding, power reserve 50 hours
Functions: hours, minutes, subsidiary seconds at 6 o'clock
Diameter: 19.4 mm (8 3/4''')
Height: 3.5 mm
Jewels: 19
Frequency: 21,600 vph
Fine adjustment system:
ETACHRON
Remark: Movement based on
prototype AS 1727

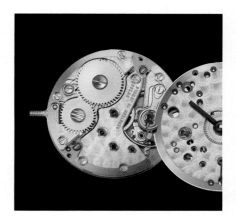

Caliber 7001

Mechanical with manual winding, ultraflat, power reserve 42 hours
Functions: hours, minutes, subsidiary seconds at 6 o'clock
Diameter: 23.3 mm (10 1/2''')
Height: 2.5 mm
Jewels: 17
Frequency: 21,600 vph
Fine adjustment system:
ETACHRON

Caliber 2801-2

Mechanical with manual winding, power reserve 42 hours
Functions: hours, minutes, sweep seconds
Diameter: 25.6 mm (11 1/2''')
Height: 3.35 mm
Jewels: 17
Frequency: 28,800 vph
Fine adjustment system:
ETACHRON
Related caliber: 2804-2
(with date window and quick-set)

Caliber 7765

Mechanical with manual winding, stop-seconds, power reserve 42 hours
Functions: hours, minutes, subsidiary seconds at 9 o'clock; chronograph
(30-minute counter at 12 o'clock, sweep stop second hand);
date window with quick-set at 3 o'clock
Diameter: 30 mm (13 1/4''')
Height: 6.35 mm
Jewels: 17
Frequency: 28,800 vph
Fine adjustment system:
ETACHRON with index
Related calibers: 7760 (with
additional 12-hour counter at
6 o'clock and day window at
3 o'clock; height 7 mm); 7750 and
7751 (automatic versions)

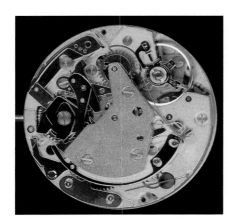

Caliber 6497/6498

Only a few watch fans know that ETA still manufactures two pure pocket watch movements. Caliber 6497 (a so-called Lépine movement, subsidiary seconds located on the lengthened winding stem) and 6498 (a so-called hunter, subsidiary seconds in a right angle to the winding stem) are available in two qualities: as 6497-1 and 6498-1 (rather sober, undecorated version); 6497-2 and 6498-2 (with off-center stripe decoration on bridges and cocks as well as beveled and striped crown and ratchet wheels). The photograph shows Lépine Caliber 6497-2.
Functions: hours, minutes, subsidiary seconds
Diameter: 36.6 mm (16 1/2 ''')
Height: 4.5 mm
Jewels: 17
Frequency: 21,600 vph
Fine adjustment system:
ETACHRON with index

Caliber 2671

Mechanical with automatic winding, ball-bearing rotor, stop-seconds, power reserve 38 hours

Functions: hours, minutes, sweep seconds; date window with quick-set at 3 o'clock

Diameter: 17.2 mm (7 3/4''')

Height: 4.8 mm

Jewels: 25

Frequency: 28,800 vph

Fine adjustment system: ETACHRON with index

Related calibers: 2678 (additional day window at 3 o'clock, height 5.35 mm)

Caliber 2681

Mechanical with automatic winding, ball-bearing rotor, stop-seconds, power reserve 38 hours

Functions: hours, minutes, sweep seconds; day/date window with quick-set at 3 o'clock

Diameter: 19.4 mm (8 3/4''')

Height: 4.8 mm

Jewels: 25

Frequency: 28,800 vph

Fine adjustment system: ETACHRON with index

Related calibers: 2685 (sweep date hand and moon phase at 6 o'clock)

Caliber 2000

Mechanical with automatic winding, ball-bearing rotor, stop-seconds, power reserve 40 hours

Functions: hours, minutes, sweep seconds; date window with quick-set at 3 o'clock

Diameter: 19.4 mm (8 3/4''')

Height: 3.6 mm

Jewels: 20

Frequency: 28,800 vph

Fine adjustment system: ETACHRON with index

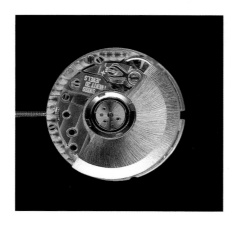

Caliber 2004

Mechanical with automatic winding, ball-bearing rotor, stop-seconds, power reserve 40 hours

Functions: hours, minutes, sweep seconds; date window with quick-set at 3 o'clock

Diameter: 23.3 mm (10 1/2''')

Height: 3.6 mm

Jewels: 20

Frequency: 28,800 vph

Fine adjustment system: ETACHRON with index

Caliber 2824-2

Mechanical with automatic winding, ball-bearing rotor, stop-seconds, power reserve 38 hours

Functions: hours, minutes, sweep seconds; date window with quick-set at 3 o'clock

Diameter: 25.6 mm (11 1/2''')

Height: 4.6 mm

Jewels: 25

Frequency: 28,800 vph

Fine adjustment system: ETACHRON with index

Related Calibers: 2836-2 (additional day window at 3 o'clock, height 5.05 mm)

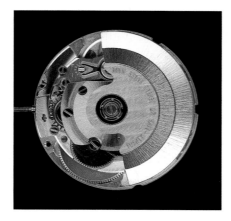

Caliber 2834-2

Mechanical with automatic winding, ball-bearing rotor, stop-seconds, power reserve 38 hours

Functions: hours, minutes, sweep seconds; date window with quick-set at 3 o'clock and day display with quick-set at 12 o'clock

Diameter: 29 mm (13''')

Height: 5.05 mm

Jewels: 25

Frequency: 28,800 vph

Fine adjustment system: ETACHRON with index

De Grisogono, Inc.
21 East 63rd Street, 5th Floor
New York, NY 10021
Tel.: 212-821-0280, Fax: 212-821-0281
www.degrisogono.com

DeLaneau North America Inc.
431 Post Road East, Suite 14
Westport, CT 06880
Tel.: 203-227-9082, Fax: 203-227-9182
www.delaneau.com

DeWitt
Wings of Time
530 Lincoln Road, Suite 200
Miami Beach, FL 33139
Tel: 305-531-2600, Fax: 305-531-6002
www.dewitt.ch

Doxa Watches USA
Houston, Texas
Tel.: 713-344-1266
sales@doxawatches.com
www.doxawatches.com

Dubey & Schaldenbrand
PK Time Group LLC
30 West 57th Street, 2nd Floor
New York, NY 10019
Tel.: 888-919-TIME, Fax: 212-397-0960
info@pktime.com
www.pktime.com

Roger Dubuis
Helvetia Time Co., Inc.
100 N. Wilkes-Barre Boulevard, Suite 303
Wilkes-Barre, PA 18702
Tel.: 717-822-1900, Fax: 717-822-4699

Alfred Dunhill Americas LLC
645 Fifth Avenue, 5th Floor
New York, NY 10022
Tel.: 800-541-0738, Fax: 212-750-8841
www.dunhill.com

Ebel U.S.A. Inc.
750 Lexington Avenue
New York, NY 10022
Tel.: 212-888-3235, Fax: 212-888-6719
www.ebel.ch

Eberhard
DOMUSHora
1784 West Avenue Bay 3
Miami Beach, FL 33139
Tel.: 305-538-9300, Fax: 305-534-1952
info@domushora.com
www.eberhard-co-watches.ch

Epos
GNT Incorporated
P.O. Box 6724
Providence, RI 02940
Tel.: 1-800-689-2225
www.gntwatches.com

Louis Erard
Wolf Designs
22761 Pacific Coast Highway, Suite 107
Malibu, CA 90265
Tel.: 310-456-7072, Fax: 310-456-8393
www.louiserard.ch

terna SA
Schützengasse 46
2540 Grenchen, Switzerland
Tel.: (011-41) 32-654 72 11, Fax: 654 72 12
www.eterna.ch

Jacques Etoile
DECHUSA Watches
1210 N. Cherokee Avenue 225
Los Angeles, CA 90038
Tel.: 323-461-7230
jetoile-usa@comcast.net
www.jacquesetoile.com

Fabergé
Mohr Time GmbH
Simmlerstr. 13-14
75172 Pforzheim, Germany
Tel.: (011-49) 7231-918 70, Fax: 332 15
info@mohr-time.de

Formex
Chronotime, Inc.
87 Main Street
Peapack, NJ 07977
Tel.: 908-781-0600, Fax: 908-781-9877
www.formexwatch.com

Fortis
LWR Time Ltd.
15 South Franklin Street, Suite 214
Wilkes-Barre, PA 18711
Tel.: 570-408-1640, Fax: 570-408-1657
www.fortis-watch.com

Gérald Genta
730 Fifth Avenue
New York, NY 10019
Tel.: 1-866-DrandGG

Gevril
23 Dover Terrace
Monsey, NY 10952
Tel.: 866-425-9882, Fax: 845-425-9897
info@gevril.net
www.gevril.net

Girard-Perregaux
Tradema of America, Inc.
201 Route 17 North
Rutherford, NJ 07070
Tel.: 1-877-846-3447, Fax: 201-507-1553
gpwebmaster@girard-perregaux-usa.com
www.girard-perregaux-usa.com

Glashütte Original
The Swatch Group (U.S.), Inc.
1200 Harbor Boulevard
Weehawken, NJ 07087
Tel.: 201-271-1400, Fax: 201-271-4633
www.glashuette-original.com

Glycine, LLC
444 Madison Avenue, Suite 601
New York, NY 10022
Tel.: 212-688-4500, Fax: 212-888-5025
www.glycine-watch.ch

Graham
British Masters, LLC
444 Madison Avenue, Suite 601
New York, NY 10022
Tel.: 212-688-4500, Fax: 212-888-5025
www.thebritishmasters.biz

Hanhart
Eric Armin, Inc.
Fine Watch Division
118 Bauer Drive, P.O. Box 7046
Oakland, NJ 07436-7046
Tel.: 800-272-0272
www.hanhartusa.com

Harwood
LWR Time Ltd.
15 South Franklin Street, Suite 214
Wilkes-Barre, PA 18711
Tel.: 570-408-1640, Fax: 570-408-1657
www.harwood-watch.com

Hautlence
6, Place des Halles
2000 Neuchâtel, Switzerland
Tel.: (011-41) 32-722 65 50, Fax: 722 65 59
www.hautlence.biz

Hermès of Paris, Inc.
55 East 59th Street
New York, NY 10022
Tel.: 800-441-4488, Fax: 212-835-6460
www.hermes.com

Hublot
MDM of America, Inc.
500 Cypress Creek Road West, Suite 430
Fort Lauderdale, FL 33309
Tel.: 800-536-0636, Fax: 954-568-6337
www.hublot.ch

IWC North America
645 Fifth Avenue, 6th Floor
New York, NY 10022
Tel.: 1-800-432-9330, Fax: 212-872-1312
www.iwc.ch

Jacob & Co. Watches, Inc.
1196 Avenue of the Americas
New York, NY 10039
Tel.: 866-522-6210, Fax: 212-719-0074
contact@jacobandco.com
www.jacobandco.com

Jacques Lemans
Swiss Watch International
101 South State Road 7, Suite 201
Hollywood, FL 33023
Tel: 866-SHOP-SWI, Fax: 954-985-1828
www.theswigroup.com

Jaeger-LeCoultre
645 Fifth Avenue
New York, NY 10022
Tel.: 800-JLC-TIME
www.jaeger-lecoultre.com

Montres Jaquet Droz SA
Rue Jaquet Droz 5
2300 La Chaux-de-Fonds, Switzerland
Tel.: (011-41) 32-911 28 88, Fax: 911 28 85
jd@jaquet-droz.com
www.jaquet-droz.com

Jean-Mairet & Gillman
Vision of Time, Inc.
9559 Collins Avenue, Suite 706
Surfside, FL 33154
Tel.: 305-868-1168, Fax: 305-402-2333
www.jean-mairetgillman.com

JeanRichard
Tradema of America, Inc.
201 Route 17 North, 8th Floor
Rutherford, NJ 07070
Tel.: 1-877-357-8463, Fax: 201-507-1553
webmaster@djr-usa.com
www.djr-usa.com

Cédric Johner
Chemin de la Montagne 13
1224 Chêne-Bougerie, Switzerland
Tel.: (011-41) 22-348 44 80, Fax: 349 90 80
cedric.johner@span.ch
www.cedric-johner.ch

F.P. Journe – Invenit et Fecit
Wings of Time
530 Lincoln Road, Suite 200
Miami Beach, FL 33139
Tel: 305-531-2600, Fax: 305-531-6002
www.fpjourne.com

Urban Jürgensen & Sønner
Glück-Auf-Str. 1
50127 Bergheim, Germany
Tel.:(011-49) 2271-911 12, Fax: 974 23
j.schmidt@juergensen-watch.de
www.juergensen-watch.de

Kobold Instruments Inc.
1801 Parkway View Drive
Pittsburgh, PA 15205
Tel.: 412-788-2830, Fax: 412-788-4890
info@koboldusa.com
www.koboldusa.com

Maurice Lacroix USA
17835 Ventura Boulevard, Suite 301
Encino, CA 91316-3629
Tel.: 1-800-794-7736, Fax: 818-609-7079
www.mauricelacroixusa.com

Lange Uhren GmbH
Altenberger Str. 15
01768 Glashütte, Germany
Tel.: (011-49) 35053-44 0, Fax: 44 100
info@lange-soehne.com
www.lange-soehne.com

Limes
DECHUSA Watches
1210 N. Cherokee Avenue 225
Los Angeles, CA 90038
Tel.: 323-461-7230
www.limeswatches-us.com
limes-us@comcast.net

Longines
The Swatch Group (U.S.), Inc.
1200 Harbor Boulevard
Weehawken, NJ 07087
Tel.: 201-271-1400, Fax: 201-271-4633
www.longines.com

Giuliano Mazzuoli
Fifth Avenue Luxury Group
306 West Somerdale Road
Vorhees, NJ 08043
Tel.: 800-988-3254, Fax: 859-673-5979

Meistersinger
WatchBuys
Tel.: 888-333-4895
www.watchbuys.com

Richard Mille USA
9595 Wilshire Boulevard, Suite 511
Beverly Hills, CA 90212
Tel.: 310-205-5555, Fax: 310-279-1000
www.richardmilleusa.com

Milus International SA
Route de Reuchenette 19
2502 Biel, Switzerland
Tel.:(011-41) 32-344 39 39, Fax: 344 39 38
info@milus.com
www.milus.com

H. Moser & Cie.
Moser Schaffhausen AG
Rundbuckstr. 10
8212 Neuhausen am Rheinfall, Switzerland
Tel.: (011-41) 52-670 15 59, Fax: 670 15 67
info@h-moser.com
www.h-moser.com

Les Ateliers Louis Moinet SA
Épancheurs 24
2012 Auvernier, Switzerland
info@louismoinet.com
www.louismoinet.com

Montblanc International
26 Main Street
Chatham, NJ 07928
Tel.: 908-508-2301
www.montblanc.com

Movado Group, Inc.
650 From Road
Paramus, NJ 07652
Tel.: 201-267-8115, Fax: 201-267-8020
www.movado.com

Nautische Instrumente Mühle GmbH
Müglitztalstr. 7
01768 Glashuette, Germany
sales@muehle-glashutte.info
www.muehle-uhren.com

Montres Franck Muller USA, Inc.
207 W. 25th Street, 8th Floor
New York, NY 10001
Tel.: 212-463-8898, Fax: 212-463-7082
www.franckmullerusa.com

Ulysse Nardin Inc.
6001 Broken Sound Parkway, Suite 504
Boca Raton, FL 33487
Tel.: 561-988-6400, Fax: 561-988-0123
usa@ulysse-nardin.com
www.ulysse-nardin.com

NBY
1717 West 6th St., Suite 212
Austin, TX 78703
Tel.: 512-499-0123, Fax: 512-499-8112
info@time-central.com
www.martinbraunusa.com

Armand Nicolet
Fifth Avenue Luxury Group
306 West Somerdale Road
Vorhees, NJ 08043
Tel.: 800-988-3254, Fax: 859-673-5979
www.armandnicolet.com

Nivrel
WatchBuys
Tel.: 888-333-4895
www.watchbuys.com

Nomos USA
AMEICO
1 Church Street
New Milford, CT 06776
Tel.: 860-354-8765, Fax: 860-354-8620
info@ameico.com
www.glashuette.com

Officina del Tempo
DOMUSHora
1784 West Avenue Bay 3
Miami Beach, FL 33139
Tel.: 305-538-9300, Fax: 305-534-1952
info@domushora.com

Officine Panerai
645 Fifth Avenue
New York, NY 10022
Tel.: 1-877-PANERAI
Fax: 212-891-2315
www.panerai.com

Omega
The Swatch Group (U.S.), Inc.
1200 Harbor Boulevard
Weehawken, NJ 07087
Tel.: 201-271-1400, Fax: 201-271-4633
www.omegawatches.com

Oris USA, Inc.
2 Skyline Drive
Hawthorne, NY 10532
Tel.: 914-347-6747, Fax: 914-347-4782
sales@orisusa.com
www.oris-watch.com

Orbita Corporation
1205 Culbreth Drive
Wilmington, NC 28405
Tel.: 910-256-5300, Fax: 910-256-5356
info@orbita.net
www.orbita.net

Parmigiani Fleurier USA
33552 Valle Road
San Juan Capistrano, CA 92675
Tel.: 949-489-2885, Fax: 949-488-0116
www.parmigiani.ch

Patek Philippe
1 Rockefeller Plaza, #930
New York, NY 10020
Tel.: 212-581-0870, Fax: 212-956-6399
info@patek.com
www.patek.com

Piaget
663 Fifth Avenue, 7th Floor
New York, NY 10022
Tel.: 212-355-6444, Fax: 212-909-4332

Paul Picot
International Time Group
7700 Congress Avenue, Suite 1115
Boca Raton, FL 33487
Tel.: 561-241-3509, Fax: 561-241-3574
www.paulpicot.ch

Porsche Design
540 Madison Avenue, 34th Floor
New York, NY 10022
Tel.: 212 904-0408, Fax: 212 904-0409
www.porsche-design.com

Rado
The Swatch Group (U.S.), Inc.
1200 Harbor Boulevard
Weehawken, NJ 07087
Tel.: 201-271-1400, Fax: 201-271-4633
www.rado.com

Auguste Reymond USA
Tel.: 214-686-4883, Fax: 972-380-2288
info@augustereymond.com
www.augustereymond.ch

RGM Watch Company
801 West Main Street
Mount Joy, PA 17552
Tel.: 717-653-9799, Fax: 717-653-9770
rgmwatches@aol.com

Rolex Watch U.S.A., Inc.
Rolex Building, 665 Fifth Avenue
New York, NY 10022-5358
Tel.: 212-758-7700, Fax: 212-826-8617
www.rolex.com

Daniel Roth
730 Fifth Avenue
New York, NY 10019
Tel.: 1-866-DrandGG

Scalfaro International
Schönblickstraße 22
75242 Neuhausen, Germany
Tel.: (011-49) 7234-94 99 620, Fax: 54 73
www.scalfaro.ch

Scatola del Tempo
Fifth Avenue Luxury Group
306 West Somerdale Road
Vorhees, NJ 08043
Tel.: 800-988-3254, Fax: 859-673-5979

Jörg Schauer
WatchBuys
Tel.: 888-333-4895
www.watchbuys.com

Galerie Alain Silberstein
200 Boulevard Saint-Germain
75007 Paris, France
Tel.: (011-33) 1-45 44 10 10, Fax: 45 44 53 53
www.a-silberstein.fr

Sinn
WatchBuys
Tel.: 888-333-4895
www.watchbuys.com

Sothis Fine Watches
WatchBuys
Tel.: 888-333-4895
www.watchbuys.com

Stowa
Salmbacher Weg 52
75331 Engelsbrand, Germany
Tel.: (011-49) 7082-930 60, Fax.: 930 62
info1@stowa.de
www.stowa.de

SWI
Swiss Watch International
101 South State Road 7, Suite 201
Hollywood, FL 33023
Tel: 866-SHOP-SWI, Fax: 954-985-1828
www.theswigroup.com

Swiss Army Brands, Inc.
One Research Drive, P.O. Box 874
Shelton, CT 06484-0874
Tel.: 203-929-6391, Fax: 203-944-2105
www.swissarmy.com

TAG Heuer
LVMH Watch & Jewelry USA
960 S. Springfield Avenue
Springfield, NJ 07081
Tel.: 973-467-1890
www.tagheuer.com

Temption GmbH
Raistinger Str. 53
71083 Herrenberg, Germany
Tel.: (011-49) 7032-97 79 54, Fax: 97 79 55
ftemption@aol.com
www.temption-watches.de

Tissot
The Swatch Group (U.S.), Inc.
1200 Harbor Boulevard
Weehawken, NJ 07087
Tel.: 201-271-1400, Fax: 201-271-4633

www.tissot.ch
Tutima USA, Inc.
20710 Manhattan Place
Torrance, CA 90501
Tel.: 1-TUTIMA-USA-1, Fax: 310-381-2930
www.tutima.com

Vacheron Constantin
Richemont North America
Fifth Avenue and 52nd Street
New York, NY 10022
Tel.: 212-753-0111, Fax: 212-753-7250
www.vacheron-constantin.com

Ventura USA, Inc.
Geissbüelstr. 15
8604 Volketswil, Switzerland
Tel.: (011-41) 1-908 55 92, Fax: 908 55 22
info@ventura.ch
www.ventura.ch

Vollmer
GNT Incorporated
P.O. Box 6724
Providence, RI 02940
Tel.: 1-800-689-2225
www.gntwatches.com

George J von Burg
c/o Ernst Benz USA
555 South Old Woodward Avenue
Birmingham, MI 48009
Tel.: 248-203-2323, Fax: 248-203-6633
www.gjvb.com

Harry Winston, Inc.
718 Fifth Avenue
New York, NY 10019
Tel.: 1-800-848-3948, Fax: 212-582-4605
www.hwtimepieces.com

Xemex
Universal Watch Co., Inc.
5016 Schuster Street
Las Vegas, NV 89118
Tel.: 1-800-360-2568
info@silverprince.com
www.xemex.com

Zenith
LVMH Watch & Jewelry USA
960 S. Springfield Avenue
Springfield, NJ 07081
Tel.: 973-467-1890, Fax: 973-467-5495
www.zenith-watches.com

Zeno USA, LLC
12900 Preston Road, Suite 1035
Dallas, TX 75230
Tel.: 972-404-ZENO, Fax: 972-404-4660
sales@zenowatchbasel.com
www.zenowatchbasel.com

Copyright © 2005 HEEL Verlag GmbH, Königswinter, Germany

English-language translation copyright © 2005 Abbeville Press,
137 Varick Street, New York, NY 10013.

Editor-in-Chief: Peter Braun
Senior Editor: Elizabeth Doerr
Production and Layout: Collibri Prepress GmbH
Printed by: Druckhaus Kaufmann GmbH

For more information about editorial content and advertising,
please contact:
Elizabeth Doerr
Wehlauer Str. 25a, 76139 Karlsruhe, Germany,
Fax: +49 / 721 / 680 29 72, DoerrElizabeth@aol.com

For more information about book sales, please contact:
Abbeville Press, 137 Varick Street, New York, NY 10013, 1-800-ARTBOOK,
www.abbeville.com

ISBN 0-7892-0862-8

Eighth Edition

2 4 6 8 10 9 7 5 3 1

Library of Congress Cataloging-in-Publication Data available upon request.

For bulk and premium sales and for text adoption procedures, write to Customer Service Manager,
Abbeville Press, 137 Varick Street, New York, NY 10013 or call 1-800-ARTBOOK

For further information about this title please contact Abbeville Press.

ISBN 0-7892-0862-8   U.S. $35.00

EAN

9 780789 208620   53500